Histories of two hundred and fifty-one divisions of the German army which participated in the war (1914-1918)

Unknown

Alpha Editions

This edition published in 2019

ISBN : 9789353860899

Design and Setting By
Alpha Editions
email - alphaedis@gmail.com

HISTORIES

OF

TWO HUNDRED AND FIFTY-ONE DIVISIONS OF THE GERMAN ARMY WHICH PARTICIPATED IN THE WAR (1914–1918)

92

COMPILED FROM RECORDS OF INTELLIGENCE
SECTION OF THE GENERAL STAFF, AMERICAN
EXPEDITIONARY FORCES, AT GENERAL HEAD-
QUARTERS : : CHAUMONT, FRANCE : : 1919

WASHINGTON
GOVERNMENT PRINTING OFFICE
1920

A498671

WAR DEPARTMENT

Document No. 905

Office of The Adjutant General

ADDITIONAL COPIES

OF THIS PUBLICATION MAY BE PROCURED FROM
THE SUPERINTENDENT OF DOCUMENTS
GOVERNMENT PRINTING OFFICE
WASHINGTON, D. C.

AT

60 CENTS PER COPY

CONTENTS.

4 CONTENTS.

CONTENTS.

5

INTRODUCTION.

The following pages contain the record of the organization and service of the 251 divisions of the German Army during the years 1914, 1915, 1916, 1917, and 1918, or during as many of these years as they existed—for a number of them were created after the war had started. The record of each has been known as a "divisional history."

The history of an enemy division is a summary of all the information obtained from all sources. It includes the latest composition—that is, the regiments and other units that make up the division; a record of its past engagements; its recruitment and racial features; commanders; present strength; and morale. On a basis of these factors the division's fighting quality is rated on a standard of classes adopted by General Headquarters and noted in the history. The data is collected and filed daily at various troop headquarters and eventually in the Enemy Order of Battle subsection of the General Staff, Intelligence Section at the General Headquarters. The information comes chiefly from the front-line troops, resulting from their observation, reconnaissance, and the interrogation of the prisoners they take. This evidence is often fragmentary and inconclusive, being gathered as more or less disassociated items, here and there along the whole front. But when it is consolidated and collated it becomes of great value and warrants deductions which may be depended upon.

Prisoners' statements and captured documents are the source of almost all the information contained in a divisional history. The outline of the past engagements of a division is known from the Battle-Order records. Prisoners add to this specific account of successes, citations, failures, internal disturbance, etc. The divisional composition is established by prisoners, and in the case of the smaller divisional units from addresses on captured letters. The effective strength is deduced from prisoners' stories of recent losses incurred and drafts of new men arriving. In estimating the quality of a division the Intelligence Section considers principally the conditions under which the enemy command has used it in previous military operations.

All this information is kept posted up to date so that a history of present value can be written without delay and dispatched to our front-line troops opposite whom a new or additional enemy unit has appeared or is about to appear.

The use to our troops of these histories is obvious. Much of the information contained is of direct value to our commanders. The strength, morale, and fighting qualities of the opposing divisions are, of course, an important factor in our plans and operations. Other items, such as the names of the enemy commanders, assist the examining officer in checking the veracity and accuracy of prisoners' statements. It has been often observed that the more the intelligence officer knows or appears to know of the prisoner's organization the better results he obtains from his questions. The uses to which information of the enemy may be put have proved so various and unexpected that the principle is established that no fact about the enemy is too unimportant to be recorded.

In preparing this set of Histories of German Divisions the histories published by French General Headquarters have been used for the years prior to 1918. For the last year of the war the histories were written by the Second Section of the General Staff, General Headquarters, A. E. F., from the American records. These included all information from American sources and also that which was received from Allied armies.

Alpine Corps.
COMPOSITION.

	1915 Brigade	1915 Regiment	1916 Brigade	1916 Regiment	1917 Brigade	1917 Regiment	1918 Brigade	1918 Regiment
Infantry	1 Bav. Jag. 2 Jag.	1 Bav. Jag. Body Inf. 2 Jag. 3 Jag.	1 Bav. Jag. 2 Jag.	Body Inf. 1 Bav. Jag. 2 Jag. 3 Jag.	1 Bav. Jag.	Body Inf. 1 Bav. Jag. 2 Jag.	1 Bav. Jag.	Body Inf. 1 Bav. Jag. 2 Jag.
Cavalry								3 Sqn. 4 Bav. Light Cav. Rgt.
Artillery	203 F. A. Rgt.		2 Mountain F. A. Abt. Detch. of the 187, 203, and 204 F. A. Rgts.		Art. Command: 203 F. A. Rgt. (1 Abt.) 6 Mountain A. Abt.		7 Art. Command: 204 F. A. Rgt. 1 Abt. 1 Bav. Res. Ft. A. Rgt. 6th Mountain Art. Abt. (Staff and 1, 2, and 17 Btries.). 1401 Light Am. Col. 1402 Light Am. Col. 1403 Light Am. Col.	
Engineers and Liaisons.			102 Pion. Co. 105 Pion. Co. 106 Pion. Co. 175 Mountain T. M. Co.		Pion. Btn.: 102 Pion. Co. 283 Pion. Co. 175 T. M. Co. 204 Bav. T. M. Co. 102 Bav. Searchlight Section. 622 Tel. Detch. 88 Div. Wireless Detch.		9 Bav. Pion. Btn.: 102 Pion. Co. 283 Pion. Co. 175 Mountain T. M. Co. 102 Searchlight Section. 622 Signal Command: 622 Tel. Detch. 133 Bav. Wireless Detcb.	
Medical and Veterinary.					201 Ambulance Co. 239 Ambulance Co. 202 Field Hospital. 203 Field Hospital. 18 Bav. Field Hospital. Vet. Hospital.		201 Ambulance Co. 239 Ambulance Co. 201 Field Hospital. 44 Bav. Field Hospital. 18 Bav. Field Hospital.	

			695 Bav. M. T. Col.
Transport........		444 M. T. Col. 695 M. T. Col. 790 M. T. Col.	
Odd units......	201 Mountain M. G. Detch. 202 Mountain M. G. Detch. 205 Mountain M. G. Detch. 209 Mountain M. G. Detch.	201 Mountain M. G. Detch. 202 Mountain M. G. Detch. 205 Mountain M. G. Detch. 209 Mountain M. G. Detch.	
Attached......		Cyclist Btn. (dissolved in June).	

HISTORY.

1915.

The Alpine Corps was formed in May, 1915.

ITALY.

1. At the end of May, 1915, it was sent by way of Innsbruck to the Trentino, where it remained until October 16 (vicinity of Campitello). It took part in several smaller actions (particularly on Sept. 24).

FRANCE.

2. On October 17 it left Bozen and went to France by way of Innsbruck, Neu-Ulm, Stuttgart, Deux-Ponts, and detrained at Laonnois on the Mezieres-Rethel line on October 19.

3. It remained in this area until October 25. At that time it was transferred to Serbia by way of Mezieres, Germershein, Augsburg, Munich, Vienna, Budapest, Temesvar. It detrained at Weisskirchen on October 29.

SERBIA.

4. The Alpine Corps advanced in Serbia by way of Kragujevac and Kraljevo as far as Novipasar (near the Montenegrin frontier); from that place to Mitrovica. Elements of the Alpine Corps remained south of Uskub until the end of March, 1916.

1916.

FRANCE.

1. On March 21, 1916, the Alpine Corps was taken to Hungary by way of Belgrade, and then to France. Itinerary: Budapest, Breslau, Dresden, Leipzig, Cologne, Aix-la-Chapelle, Liege, Charleville.

2. It went into line on the front east of Rheims (the Leib Regiment at Cernay) on April 1.

VERDUN.

3. Relieved at the beginning of May, it went to rest in the vicinity of Charleville. About May 30 it went to the Spincourt area by way of Sedan. At the beginning of June it went into action at Verdun north of the Vaux Fort, northeast of Fleury, and took part in the attacks launched in this sector during the month of June (attack of June 23 upon Thiaumont).

4. After reorganization, at the end of June or the beginning of July, the Alpine Corps came back into line near Fleury on July 11.

ARGONNE.

5. After having lost 71 per cent of its Infantry in the various attacks at Verdun, the Alpine Corps was withdrawn on August 12 and took over the sector Fontaine-aux-Charmes-Vauquois, in the Argonne. The 3d Jaeger Regiment was taken from it and entered into the composition of the 200th Division (Carpathian Corps).

6. In the first half of September the Alpine Corps left the Argonne and entrained for Roumania.

ROUMANIA.

7. At the end of September it went into action in the vicinity of Hermannstadt, then in the vicinity of Brasso. On December 10 it reached Ploesci; it was at Rimnicu-Sarat on the 24th. Upon the stablization of the Roumanian front it occupied the front of Panciu-Focsani. During the active period in Roumania the Leib Regiment lost heavily.

1917.

1. Relieved northwest of Focsani on April 6, 1917, the Alpine Corps was sent to Hungary, in the vicinity of Karlsburg. After a rest of three weeks it was transferred to the western front. Itinerary: Karlsburg (May 10), Szegdin, Budapest, Vienna, Salzburg, Rosenheim, Munich, Strassburg, Colmar, Neu-Breisach.

UPPER ALSACE.

2. On June 15 it went into line on the Alsatian front (Rhone-Rhine Canal, Aspach).

3. On July 20 it was withdrawn from the front and sent to rest.

ROUMANIA.

4. At the beginning of August it was again sent to Roumania. It took over its old sector near Focsani and received the Russo-Roumanian attacks launched between Briala and Panciu.

ITALY.

5. In September it was sent to the Italian front.

IZONZO.

6. On October 24 it attacked on both sides of the Tolmino and took possession of Mont Cucco on the 25th. It rested in November.

MONTE TOMBA.

7. On November 25 it was engaged at Monte Tomba, and on December 12 on the slopes of Monfenera, with the exception of the 1st Jaeger Regiment, which was in reserve.

8. Relieved between December 15 and December 20, it remained behind the lines until the middle of January, 1918.

RECRUITING.

The Leib Regiment and the 1st Regiment of Jaegers are Bavarian, recruited principally from upper Bavaria. The 2d Regiment of Jaegers is purely Prussian.

VALUE—1917 ESTIMATE.

The discipline and firmness of the commanding officers make the Alpine Corps an elite body, of a genuine combat value.

1918.

LORRAINE.

1. In January the Alpine Corps entrained for Alsace (itinerary Salzburg, Munich, Ulm, Friburg, Saverne); then went to rest in the region of Sarreburg.

2. It remained here undergoing training until the 10th of April.

3. It was sent to Flanders, via Metz, Sedan, Namur, and detrained near Lille on the 12th.

BATTLE OF THE LYS.

4. The division was engaged northeast of Bailleul from the 14th to the 18th. It then rested east of Lille until the 23d. It reentered the line on the Kemmel–Locre front, where it remained until about the 10th of May, when it was withdrawn, after having suffered heavy losses.

5. It moved then to the Ghent region, where it rested until the end of July. It then rested near Tourcoing until the 8th of August. It entrained at Tourcoing and Tournai on the 8th and went to St. Quentin via Ham.

BATTLE OF PICARDY.

6. The division entered line in the Hallu–Fransart–Hattencourt sector north of Roye on the 11th. On the 27th it fell back along the Somme Canal near Bethencourt. It was withdrawn from line the beginning of September.

7. It came back to line almost immediately north of Peronne in the Moislain sector; on the 7th it was thrown back upon Longavesnes–Epehy–Villers–Guislain, where it was withdrawn on the 23d, after losing heavily (861 prisoners).

8. Elements of the Alpine Corps were identified at Walincourt in rear of the front on October 10.

BALKANS.

9. Sent to the eastern front, the Alpine Corps reinforced the troops in the Balkans near Nish in October.

VALUE—1918 ESTIMATE.

The Alpine Corps was considered one of the best German units. It showed its worth by retaking the village of Hallu on the 11th of August, and while counter-attacking at Moislains on the 2d of September. Nevertheless, the morale was lowered. The Alpine Corps comprised about 3,500 Infantry combatants early in August. It lost about 700 prisoners in August and September.

Bavarian Cavalry Division.

COMPOSITION.

	1918	
	Brigade.	Regiment.
Cavalry	1 Bav. Cav. 4 Bav. Cav. 5 Bav. Cav.	1 Heavy Reiter. 1 Bav. Ulan. 2 Bav. Ulan. 1 Bav. Light Cav. 6 Bav. Light Cav.
Artillery	5 Bav. Horse Art. Abt.	
Engineers and Liaisons	Pion. Detch. 1 Bav. M. G. Btry. 300 Bav. T. M. Co.	
Attached	Glatz Landst. Inf. Btn. (VI/9).	

HISTORY.

1918.

1. The units of this division were used on police duty in the Ukraine and in Roumania in the spring of 1918. A part of the division was serving in the Crimea in the early summer. It continued in that general area through the year.

VALUE.

The division was rated as fourth class.

Bavarian Ersatz Division.

COMPOSITION.

	1914 Brigade.	1914 Regiment.	1915 Brigade.	1915 Regiment.	1916 Brigade.	1916 Regiment.	1917 Brigade.	1917 Regiment.	1918 Brigade.	1918 Regiment.
Infantry	3 Bav. Res. 59 Ldw.	4 Bav. Res. 15 Bav. Res. 28 Ers. 120 Ldw.	3 Bav. Res. 59 Ldw.	4 Bav. Res. 15 Bav. Res. 28 Ers. 120 Ldw.	3 Bav. Res. 59 Ldw.	4 Bav. Res. 15 Bav. Res. 28 Ers. 81 Ldw.	3 Bav. Res.	4 Bav. Res. 15 Bav. Res. 28 Ers.	3 Bav. Res.	18 Bav. Res. 4 Bav. Res. 15 Bav. Res.
Cavalry					Ers. Cav. Detch. (1 Bav. C. Dist.).	(1 Bav. C.	1 Sqn. 6 Bav. Res. Cav. Rgt. 1 Bav. C. Dist. Ers. Cav. Aht.	Res. Schutz.	1 Sqn. 6 Bav. Res. Cav. Schützen Rgt.	
Artillery			1 Ers. Abt. F. A. (1 Bav. C. D.). 2 Ers. Btry. 8 Bav. F. A. Rgt.				Art. Command: Bav. Ers. F. A. Rgt.		19 Bav. Art. Command: Bav. Ers. F. A. Rgt.	
Engineers and Liaisons.					2 Ldw. Pion. Co. (2 Bav. C. D.). 3 Ldw. Pion. Co. (3 Bav. C. D.). 1 Bav. Mining Co. 1 Bav. Heavy T. M. Detch.		Pion. Btn.: 4 Bav. Ldw. Pion. Co. 6 Bav. Ldw. Pion. Co. 1 Bav. Mining Co. 100 Bav. T. M. Co. 5 Bav. Res. Searchlight Section. 551 Tel. Detch.		13 Bav. Pion. Btn. 4 Bav. Ldw. Pion. Co. 6 Bav. Ldw. Pion. Co. 5 Bav. Res. Searchlight Section. 100 Bav. T. M. Co. 551 Bav. Tel. Detch.	
Medical and Veterinary.							9 Bav. Ambulance Co. 40 Bav. Field Hospital. 41 Bav. Field Hospital. 33 Bav. Vet. Hospital.		9 Bav. Ambulance Co. 40 Bav. Field Hospital. 41 Bav. Field Hospital. 33 Bav. Vet. Hospital.	
Transport.							767 M. T. Col.		767 M. T. Col.	

¹ Composition at the time of dissolution.

HISTORY.

(Bavaria.)

1914.

The Bavarian Ersatz Division consisted, at the outbreak of the war, of the three mixed Bavarian Ersatz brigades, Nos. 1, 5, 9 (12 battalions), which detrained on August 17 and 18 in the region of Schelestadt. But afterwards this designation indicated a composite division (Benzino Division) formed from the 3d Bavarian Reserve Brigade and the 59th Landwehr Brigade (28th Ersatz, Baden) and the 120th Landwehr Regiment (Wurttemberg).

VOSGES.

1. The Benzino Division was first engaged in the Vosges (St. Marie Ridge, St. Die, Laveline) until September.

HAYE.

2. After a rest in the Valley of the Bruche, it entrained at the end of September for Mars-la-Tour and reinforced the 3d Bavarian Corps in the St. Mihiel area.

1915.

WOEVRE.

1. The Benzino Division occupied the area east of St. Mihiel (Spada to Apremont) during the entire year 1915. In November it took the name of Bavarian Ersatz Division.

2. The division rested in Lorraine from December, 1915, to the end of February, 1916.

1916.

At the beginning of February, 1916, the 120th Landwehr Regiment was repla ;ed by a Prussian Regiment, the 81st Landwehr.

WOEVRE.

1. On February 28, 1916, the Bavarian Ersatz Division took over the sector of Fresnes-en-Woëvre-Ronvaux. It remained there until the end of October, 1916. On October 17, the 4th Bavarian Reserve Regiment left the division temporarily to go to Galicia, to the 199th Division, and came back in November.

SOMME.

2. From October 25 to November 15 the Bavarian Ersatz Division took part in the battle of the Somme east of Gueudecourt, with the exception of the 81st Landwehr, which was definitely detached from the division.

3. Transferred to the Aisne, it went into line in the vicinity of Craonne at the end of November.

1917.

AISNE.

1. On the Aisne front, east of Craonne, the Bavarian Ersatz Division received the French offensive of April, and its conduct gained the order "Pour le Mérite" for its general.

2. Relieved at the end of April, it occupied a sector in the Apremont Wood from the middle of May to the end of August.

YPRES.

3. On September 1 it was in Belgium, where it was engaged on both sides of the Ypres-Menin road until September 25. The 3d Battalion of the 4th Bavarian Reserve Regiment was almost destroyed on September 20.

GALICIA.

4. At the beginning of October the division was transferred to the eastern front and sent into line southeast of Tarnopol in December.

5. At the end of autumn 1917, the 28th Ersatz Regiment (Baden) was withdrawn from the division and replaced by the 18th Bavarian Reserve. The division was then entirely Bavarian.

RECRUITING.

The Bavarian Ersatz Division is recruited from the 1st and 2d Bavarian Corps districts.

VALUE—1917 ESTIMATE.

The Bavarian Ersatz Division is a very mediocre division.

1918.

VERDUN.

1. The division held the quiet Verdun sector until July 12, when it was relieved by the 231st Division.

VESLE.

2. It was moved to the Vesle front and on July 25 relieved the 40th Division near Oulchy-lê-Chateau. It remained in this sector until August 12, when it was withdrawn and sent to rest in the vicinity of Meubeuge.

CHAMPAGNE.

3. On September 1 it proceeded to Mauchault and during the first days of September relieved the 88th Division in line near Perthes. It was in the fighting between September 23 and October 3 in Champagne, losing about 2,000 men in that engagement.

4. The division was so reduced in strength that it was dissolved shortly after its retirement from line in October. The 18th Bavarian Reserve Regiment was dissolved and the men drafted to the 15th Bavarian Division. The 15th Bavarian Reserve Regiment was also dissolved.

VALUE—1918 ESTIMATE.

The division was rated as third class. It was used only in defensive sectors during 1918.

Jaeger Division.
COMPOSITION.

	1917 Brigade.	1917 Regiment.	1918 Brigade.	1918 Regiment.	1919 Brigade.	1919 Regiment.
Infantry		11 Jag. 12 Jag. 13 Jag.			5 Ers.	11 Jag. 12 Jag. 13 Jag.
Cavalry					1 Sqn. 10 Drag. Rgt. Staff, 2 Ulan Rgt. Staff, 8 Bav. Light Cav. Rgt.	
Artillery	203 F. A. Rgt. (Würt.).		24 F. A. Rgt.		224 Art. Command: 24 F. A. Rgt. 3 Abt. 24 Res. Ft. A. Rgt. 780 Light Am. Col. 793 Light Am. Col. 1,050 Light Am. Col.	
Engineers and Liaisons					422 Pion. Btn.: Gd. Pion. Detch. (Casuals). 5 Pion. Detch. (Casuals). 9 Pion. Detch. (Casuals). 174 T. M. Co. 215 Searchlight Section. 901 Signal Command: 805 Tel. Detch. 901 Tel. Detch. 48 Wireless Detch.	
Medical and Veterinary	524 Ambulance Co.				241 Ambulance Co. 34 Field Hospital. 46 Res. Field Hospital. 143 Vet. Hospital.	
Transport					670 M. T. Col.	

HISTORY.

1917.

The Jaeger Division appears to have been formed about November, 1917.

In November and December the Division was engaged on the Italian front at Monte-Tomba. Relieved at the beginning of January, 1918, it was sent to rest.

VALUE—1917 ESTIMATE.

The Jaeger Division is a very good Division.

1918.

1. The division again entrained March 20 and was transported to the area northeast of St. Quentin by way of Strasbourg, Treves, Cologne, Liege, Namur, Charleroi, Maubeuge, Bohain. From there it marched to the region south of Chaulnes and rested three weeks.

SOMME.

2. It was in line in the Villers-Bretonneux sector from April 27 to May 19–20. After its withdrawal from line it rested southwest of Guise (Bernot, Hauteville) from 25th to 30th. The division marched toward the front by Ham (May 30) and arrived in the neighborhood of Lassigny on June 7–8.

OISE.

3. The division was engaged near Lassigny (Le Plessier) on June 9 and advanced as far as Elincourt. It was relieved about mid-June.

4. It rested between St. Quentin and Guise for a time, and was then railed to Alsace (near Mulhausen), where it rested during four weeks. It entrained at Mulhausen about July 24–27 and was moved to Liesse (northeast of Laon) on July 30. From there it marched toward the front north of Soissons.

SECOND BATTLE OF THE MARNE.

5. The division was engaged at Soissons and Pommiers, then at Bieuxy-Juvigny, from August 2 to 28. It rested for two weeks and returned to line at Gouzaucourt on September 12. Between September 27–30 it was forced to fall back on La Vacquerie and Gonnelieu. It was relieved at the end of the month after suffering very heavy losses.

CAMBRESIS.

6. On October 6–7 the division was reengaged south of Cambrai (Walincourt). It fell back on Briastre by Caudry and on the 15th retired from the front. It rested from October 15 to 22. On the 12th the division is known to have received a reinforcement of 600 men.

7. It was engaged southwest of Le Quesnoy from October 22 to November 1, losing numerous prisoners on the 24th. After a short rest it was again in line at Etreux and south of Le Quesnoy on November 4–5. It retreated by Pont-sux-Sambre on November 6.

VALUE—1918 ESTIMATE.

The division was rated as second class. It was used as an attack division in the Matz offensive, but in general the division was used to replace assault divisions and hold an important sector.

125651°—20——2

1st Guard Division.
COMPOSITION.

	1914 Brigade.	1914 Regiment.	1915 Brigade.	1915 Regiment.	1916 Brigade.	1916 Regiment.	1917 Brigade.	1917 Regiment.	1918 Brigade.	1918 Regiment.
Infantry	1 Gd. / 2 Gd.	1 Ft. Gd. / 3 Ft. Gd. / 2 Ft. Gd. / 4 Ft. Gd.	1 Gd. / 2 Gd.	1 Ft. Gd. / 3 Ft. Gd. / 2 Ft. Gd. / 4 Ft. Gd.	1 Gd. (2 Gd.)	1 Ft. Gd. / 2 Ft. Gd. / 4 Ft. Gd.	1 Gd.	1 Ft. Gd. / 2 Ft. Gd. / 4 Ft. Gd.	1 Gd.	1 Ft. / 2 Ft. / 4 Ft.
Cavalry					Gd. Regt. (Massow): 1st, 2d, 3d, 4th Sqns, Body Gd. Hus. Regt. 2d Sqn. 6th Drag. Regt.		1st Sqn. Body Gd. Hussar Regt. 3d Sqn. Body Gd. Hussar Regt. 2d Sqn. 6th Dragoon Regt.			3 Sqn. Body Gd. Hus. Rgt.
Artillery	1st Gd. Brig.; 1st Gd. Rgt. 3d Gd. Rgt.		1st Gd. Brig.; 1st Gd. Rgt. 3d Gd. Rgt.		1st Gd. Brig.; 1st Gd. Rgt. 3d Gd. Rgt.		1st Gd. Art. Command: 1st. Gd. Rgt.		1 Gd. Art. Command: 1 Gd. F. A. Rgt. (less 4 and 5 Abt.). 1 Abt., L. Gd. Ft. A. Rgt. (1, 2, and 4 Btries.). 870 Light Am. Col. 1099 Light Am. Col. 1128 Light Am. Col.	
Engineers and Liaisons.			1st Gd. Eng. Btn.: Field Co. Gd. Pions. 1st Gd. Pontoon Engs. 4th Gd. Tel. Detch.		1st Gd. Eng. Btn.: 1st Gd. Pion. Co. 1st Gd. T. M. Co. 1st Gd. Pontoon Engs. 1st Gd. Tel. Detch.		1st Gd. Eng. Btn.: 5th Gd. Pion. Co. 1st Gd. T. M. Co. 1st Gd. Pontoon Ens. 1st Gd. Tel. Detch.		Gd. Pion. Btn.: 1 Co. Gd. Pions. 5 Co. Gd. Pions. 23 Searchlight Section. 1 Gd. Signal Command: 1 Gd. Tel. Detch. 45 Wireless Detch.	
Medical and Veterinary.							Field Hospital. 1st Ambulance Co. Vet. Hospital.		1 Ambulance Co. 4 Field Hospital. 6 Field Hospital. 1 Gd. Vet. Hospital.	
Transport.							M. T. Col.			
Attached.							35 M. G. Btn. Sharpshooter Co.			

HISTORY.

1914.
BELGIUM.

1. Detrained on the 11th and 12th of August in "Prussian Wallonia," at Weismes and neighboring stations. Entered Belgium August 13, via Stavelot; crossed the Meuse at Huy on the 18th. The 23d it fought at Fosse and St. Gerard, after having crossed the Sambre at Jemmapes. Fought at Fournaux on the 24th. Was engaged, August 29, between Guise and Vervins (le Sourd, Leme).

MARNE.

2. It fought next on the Marne (St. Gond marsh).

3. It was in Artois near Hebuterne the end of September.

FLANDERS.

4. In November the 1st Bde. was in Flanders (Gheluvelt); the 2d Bde. remained at Hebuterne. From the beginning of the campaign until January 19, 1915, the 3d Ft. Gd. Regt. suffered casualties of 49 officers and 2,707 men.

1915.
CHAMPAGNE.

1. The beginning of January the 1st Bde. went from Gheluvelt to Champagne.

2. The beginning of February the 2d Bde. rejoined the 1st.

3. In March the division went to Alsace, where the whole Guard Corps was brought together again.

RUSSIA.

4. In April the division went to Russia (Galicia), detraining at Bochnia the 22d.

5. It fought at Tarnow and Krasnoslaw, skirted Brest-Litowsk, and pushed on to Krobin. The losses of the 3d Ft. Gd. Regt. in Russia (May 15–Aug. 31) were 17 officers and 2,116 men. The 1st Ft. Gd. Regt. lost 53 officers and 3,005 men.

FRANCE.

6. Brought back by stages to Warsaw; entrained about the 15th of September for the western front. Itinerary: Thorn, Posen, Frankfort-on-the-Oder, Berlin, Cassel, Giessen, Coblentz, Treves, Luxemburg, Namur, Charleroi.

ARTOIS.

7. Reassembled at Charleroi, the division was alerted September 25, and engaged on the Artois front (Folie). Losses of the 1st Ft. Gd. Regt. in the fighting of the end of September amounted to 1,522.

8. Relieved October 20, it took over the Lassigny-Beuvraignes sector.

1916.

1. The division remained in the calm Lassigny sector until July 20, 1916.

2. After some days rest in the neighborhood of Nesles, the division went by stages to the Peronne region, where it was put in reserve.

SOMME.

3. August 15 it relieved, in the course of the battle of the Somme, what was left of the 1st Bavarian Reserve Division.

4. The division lost heavily (5,000 men, only 300 of whom were prisoners) during the attacks of the 19th and 20th of August and at the time of the costly defense of Clery (Sept. 3), and therefore it was relieved.

5. Reassembled in the Catelet region, and having received reenforcements, it went back into line south of the Somme, in the Biaches-Barleux sector. Its losses there were considerably less.

1917.

1. The division was withdrawn from the Biaches-Barleux sector the end of January.

2. It reformed, went through a course of training, and then proceeded to the Guiscard region. During February, 1917, it received 500 reenforcements (1917 class, recuperated men). In March its depot was empty (all the men having been sent to the division).

3. The beginning of April the division reassembled in the Sissonne region.

CHEMIN DE DAMES.

4. As early as April 12, before the French attack on the Aisne front, it was alerted. April 17 it was engaged in the Ailles-Hurtebise sector. There it went through the attack of May 5. (Losses, 2,500 to 3,000 men for the whole division, only 141 prisoners.)

5. Relieved a few days later, it took over a sector in the Argonne (Grand Courte-Chaussee), where it remained the month of June.

RUSSIA.

6. On July 4 it left for Russia. (Itinerary: Namur, Liège, Aix-la-Chapelle, Duesseldorf, Minden, Hanover, Berlin, Frankfort-on-the-Oder, Posen, Lodz, Brest-Litowsk, Kovel, Lemberg, Ozidow; it detrained July 9.)

7. The division participated in the counterattack against the Russians, and later in the attack of Riga.

FRANCE.

It was brought back to France in the middle of October. (Entrained at Riga Oct. 16. Itinerary: Koenigsberg, Posen, Halle, Cassel, Coblentz, Sedan, Novion-Porcien; detrained near Rethel, Oct. 21.)

9. The division took over the Marquise sector in Champagne the end of October.

VALUE—1917 ESTIMATE.

The 1st Guard Division may be considered one of the very best German divisions. Excellent conduct under fire.

It displayed on the Aisne as well as on the Somme energy and determination while on the defensive.

Among its heavy losses there was an exceedingly small number of prisoners.

Again on the Aisne (April–May, 1917), it displayed remarkable military qualities.

It received important reenforcements of the younger classes (15–16–17), 30 per cent from the class of 1917.

Its normal value was reduced temporarily on account of the arrival of elements which had never been under fire (June, 1917).

Prisoners taken in the Argonne (June, 1917) seemed less keen for fighting.

1918.

FRANCE.

1. The division remained in line until the 21st of January.

It was withdrawn at that date and put through a course of training in open warfare until March 1, when it entered line east of Reims (relieving 203d Division), remaining in until the 15th in order to become familiar with the terrain.

SOMME.

3. It remained in close support north of Montdidier, and finally entered line March 28 near Hangest-en-Santerre, fighting until April 5, and giving a good account of itself.

CHIMAY.

4. The division went through another course of training in the Chimay area until May 27.

AISNE.

5. The division entered line in the Grivesnes sector. It fought very well in this the Aisne offensive, immediately after which its commander, Prince Eitel Friedrich, was promoted from colonel to major general, but suffered exceedingly heavy losses. It was withdrawn June 7, going to rest in the Charleroi region, where it remained until July 16.

MARNE.

6. It entered line on that date east of Dormans, and despite stubborn resistance by the French succeeded in making some headway. July 22-23 it moved slightly to the west, relieving the 6th Bavarian Reserve Division near Passy-sur-Marne. It moved back, giving ground to the Allied counter offensive, and was finally withdrawn from line north of Fere-en-Tardenois August 5.

CRECY-AU-MONT.

7. The division rested then until August 25 in the vicinity of Rethel, and then came into line near Crecy-au-Mont and fought until September 6.

ARGONNE.

8. September 20 the division moved eastward and relieved the 53d Reserve Division in the Varennes sector, where it was when (Sept. 26) it was swamped by the opening of the American Meuse-Argonne offensive. It did not resist as strongly as it might have, and so the 5th Guard Division moved to its support. Withdrawn on the 29th, it, in turn, returned October 3 to support the 5th Guard. It was finally withdrawn on the 8th after it had most of its battalions reduced to one company. It left 1,788 prisoners in our hands; its total losses probably being about 4,000.

CHAMPAGNE.

The division was identified in line farther to the west October 14 at Olizy, and near Chestres on the 21st. It remained in line in this region contesting the French advance until the Armistice.

VALUE—1918 ESTIMATE.

Throughout the war the division was rated as one of the very best German shock divisions. During the last year it fought a great deal and, until the last stages, very well. It suffered severe losses, and finally, due to the lack of effectives, it was found impossible to refill its depleted ranks; its morale deteriorated and it did not fight well.

1st Guard Reserve Division.
COMPOSITION.

	1914 Brigade.	1914 Regiment.	1915 Brigade.	1915 Regiment.	1916 Brigade.	1916 Regiment.	1917 Brigade.	1917 Regiment.	1918 Brigade.	1918 Regiment.
Infantry......	1 Gd. Res., 15 Res., Gd. Res. Snipers Btn.	1 Gd. Res., 2 Gd. Res., 64 Res., 93 Res.	1 Gd. Res., 15 Res., Gd. Res. Snipers Btn.	1 Gd. Res., 2 Gd. Res., 64 Res., 93 Res.	1 Gd. Res.	1 Gd. Res., 2 Gd. Res., 64 Res.	1 Gd. Res.	1 Gd. Res., 2 Gd. Res., 64 Res.	1 Gd. Res.	1 Gd. Res., 2 Gd. Res., 64 Res.
Cavalry......	Gd. Res. Dragoons (3 Sqns.).		Gd. Res. Drag. Rgt.		Gd. Res. Dragoon Rgt. (2 Sqns.).		Gd. Res. Drag. Rgt. (1st Sqn.).		1 Sqn. Gd. Res. Drag. Rgt.	
Artillery......	1 Gd. Res. F. A. Rgt. 3 Gd. Res. F. A. Rgt.		1 Gd. Res. F. A. Rgt. 3 Gd. Res. F. A. Rgt.		1 Gd. Res. F. A. Rgt. 3 Gd. Res. F. A. Rgt.		7 Gd. Art. Command. 1 Gd. Res. F. A. Rgt. (9 Batteries).		8 Gd. Art. Command: 1 Gd. Res. F. A. Rgt. 2 Abt. 1 Ft. A. Rgt. (Staff, 7, 8, and 13 Baties.). 701 Light Am. Col. 1269 Light Am. Col. 1328 Light Am. Col.	
Engineers and Liaisons.			2d and 3d Field Cos. (1 Eng. Btn. 28). 1 Gd. Res. Pontoon Engrs. 1 Gd. Res. Tel. Detch.		2d and 3d Field Cos. (1 Eng. Btn. 28). 1 Gd. Res. Pontoon Engs. 1 Gd. Res. Tel. Detch. 5 Gd. T. M. Co.		(2) Eng. Btn.: 2d and 3d Cos. 28 Pion. 5 Gd. T. M. Co. 401 (Gd.) Tel. Detch.		28 Pion. Btn.: 2 Co. 28 Pions. 3 Co. 28 Pions. 61 Searchlight Section. 401 Gd. Signals Command: 401 Gd. Tel. Detch. 17 Wireless Detch.	
Medical and Veterinary.							268 Ambulance Co. 395 Field Hospital. Vet. Hospital.		266 Ambulance Co. 389 Field Hospital. 395 Field Hospital. 401 Vet. Hospital.	
Transport......							M. T. Col.		701 M. T. Col.	

HISTORY.

1914.

BELGIUM.

1. At the beginning of the war the 1st Guard Reserve Division forming, together with the 3d Guard Division, the Guard Reserve Corps swept into Belgium—as part of the 2d Army under von Buelow—the 16th of August, crossed the Meuse at Ardenne (massacres) the 20th, and pushed on as far as Namur. On the 29th the two divisions (Guard Reserve Corps) were brought back to Aix-la-Chapelle, and left for east Prussia September 1.

POLAND.

2. The beginning of October the Guard Reserve Corps, attached to the Southern Army Group, took part in the invasion of the southern part of Poland, fought at Opatow (Oct. 4), and suffered severe losses at Lodz while retreating from the Russian armies.

3. During the winter of 1914–15 it fought on the Bzura.

1915.

POLAND.

1. In February, 1915, the Guard Reserve Corps was split up. The 1st Guard Reserve Division was sent to the north of the Vistula, in the Mlawa-Prasnysz region. By the 6th of March the 1st Guard Reserve Infantry Regiment had already had its thirty-ninth engagement there (letter).

2. In March the 93d Reserve Regiment was attached to the 4th Guard Division (new). During the summer of 1915 the 1st Guard Reserve Division was engaged in the operations to the north of the Vistula (von Gallwitz's army).

SMOGORNI.

3. The pursuit of the Russians brought the division as far as the neighborhood of Smogorni-Vishnev, where it took part in violent fighting and where it was relieved the middle of September.

FRANCE.

4. During the early days of October it entrained at Grodno for the western front. (Itinerary: Warsaw, Posen, Berlin, Hanover, Aix-la-Chapelle, Liège, Cambrai.)

CAMBRAI.

5. It went into rest cantonments on the banks of the Scheldt between Marcoing and Bouchain (November–December).

1916.

1. The 1st Guard Reserve Division and the 4th Guard Division then formed the reconstituted Guard Reserve Corps.

2. During January and February, 1916, the division was employed on defensive works in the Wytschaete-Messines sector; it also held a sector in that region. At the same time it underwent a course of training in the neighborhood of Cambrai.

ARTOIS.

3. The beginning of May the division took over the sector south of Neuville-St. Vaast.

SOMME.

4. At the end of July it was engaged on the Somme (Belloy-Barleux).

5. After August 19 it spent some days at rest near Cambrai, and came back into line until September 8 between the Mouquet Farm and Martinpuich. It suffered local attacks, in which it was constantly pushed back with heavy losses.

FLANDERS.

6. After a rest in the neighborhood of Cambrai it was sent to a calm sector to the north of Ypres, near the Ypres-Pilkem road.

SOMME.

7. November 5 the division returned to the Somme (Warlencourt) where it spent the winter of 1916–17.

1917.

SOMME.

1. In March, 1917, the 1st Guard Reserve Division commenced the withdrawal movement on the Hindenburg Line, leaving prisoners in rear-guard actions (Pys-Grevillers region). It was withdrawn from the front about March 20 to go to rest near Tournai.

2. The 1st Guard Reserve Division and the 4th Guard Division then became independent divisions.

ARTOIS.

3. April 25 the division took over the Oppy-Gavrelle sector and fought off the British attacks.

4. Relieved the beginning of May, it was sent to rest at Templeuve, and was later employed in the construction of defensive works near Cambrai (May).

FLANDERS.

5. The 1st of June it was carried to Tourcoing, and from there to Warneton, June 8 it went into line to the east of Messines, where it relieved the 3d Bavarian Division, very much worn out the day before. It was itself withdrawn as early as the 12th.

ARTOIS.

6. The division then went back to Artois and held the Moeuvres-Pronville front (June 21–22 to Aug. 16) taking part in no important action.

LENS.

7. After some days rest at Douai, it became reengaged August 21, on the Lens front, in a series of very heavy conflicts following the attack of August 15. The 64th Reserve Infantry Regiment was particularly exhausted. Gas attacks caused it to suffer equally heavy losses in September and December.

8. The division remained in this sector until the end of 1917. In November it sent some elements to reinforce the Cambrai front against the British attack.

VALUE—1917 ESTIMATE.

The division was recruited in all provinces of Prussia, like the rest of the Guard. Despite their numbers, the 64th and 93d Reserve Infantry Regiments do not come (to any considerable extent) from the 3d and 4th Corps Districts. The 93d Reserve Infantry Regiments came from what was, before its dissolution, a "guard landwehr battalion (Magdeburg)" (seal of pay book).

The 1st Guard Reserve Division is not above the average German division in value. The Alsatians in its ranks were withdrawn and sent to Russia in 1916, but there are still numerous Poles, who do not constitute an element of strength. It seems much less to be feared than most of the Prussian organizations that do not have the "Litze" (braiding), less, too, than the Wurttemburgers of the 13th Corps District and the better Bavarian troops. (British document, February, 1918.)

1918.

LENS.

1. The 1st Guard Reserve Division was relieved in the Lens sector by the 220th Division the first of the year and was withdrawn, remaining at rest in this region until it relieved the 220th Division, February 4.

CARVIN.

2. The division was relieved by the 220th Division February 20 and went to the Carvin area, where it went through a course of training in open warfare so as to become the assault division of the Souchez Group.

SOMME.

3. The opening day of the March 21 offensive the division was identified at Lagnicourt (northeast of Bapaume). It was very probably "leap-frogged" by some other division the next day, but it reappeared the 27th near Bucquoy, in a straight line with the advance taken as a whole. It suffered exceedingly heavy losses, finally having to utilize its pioneers as Infantry.

LA BASSÉE.

4. April 20 the division was withdrawn from the Somme front and marched to Givenchy (just north of the La Bassée Canal) the next day, where it relieved the 4th Ersatz Division. It fought there until about May 21, giving a good account of itself, considering its weakened condition, and as a result its brigade commander was promoted a lieutenant general, and the division commander received Pour le Mérite.

GRAMMONT.

5. The division moved to the Grammont area, where it underwent a course of training with artillery and aeroplanes in preparation for a coming offensive.

LA BASSÉE.

6. It relieved the 38th Division at Festubert, north of the La Bassée Canal July 5; it was relieved July 14 by the 18th Reserve Division.

7. The division rested in the Fauquissart area, and then relieved the 12th Reserve Division north of Hinges the night of August 2-3. It was relieved about August 26 by extension of front of the neighboring divisions.

CAMBRAI.

8. The 2d of September the division reinforced the front north of the Arras-Cambrai Road. About the 10th it side-slipped south, for it was identified southwest of Moeuvres. It remained here, suffering heavy casualties (450 prisoners), and was relieved by the 7th Cavalry Division during the night of September 22–23.

9. It remained in this region, however, and was thrown back into line in attempt to stem the British advance, being identified at Bourlon September 28; withdrawn about October 5.

10. The division returned October 16–17, relieving the 30th Division east of Neuvilly, and was withdrawn about the 20th.

11. November 4 it was identified north of Landrecies. It took part in the general retirement, being identified south of Berlaimont November 5, and east of Maubeuge on the 9th.

VALUE—1918 ESTIMATE.

The 1st Guard Reserve Division was rated as in the first of four classes. During 1918 it did not fight brilliantly, but it was always to be depended upon. It was called upon to fight much in heavy engagements, and suffered very severe losses.

Guard Ersatz Division.
COMPOSITION.

	1914–15 Brigade	1914–15 Regiment	1916 Brigade	1916 Regiment	1917 Brigade	1917 Regiment	1918 Brigade	1918 Regiment
Infantry	1 Gd. Mixed Ers. 5 Gd. Mixed Ers.	1 Gd. Ers. (1, 2, and 6 Gd. Bde. Ers. Btns.). 2 Gd. Ers. (3, 4, and 5 Gd. Bde. Ers. Btns.). 357 (5 Ers. Btn. 2d C. Dist. and 5 Ers. Btn. 1 C. Dist.). 358 (6, 7, and 8 Ers. Btns. 2d C. Dist.).	1 Gd. Mixed Ers. 5 Gd. Mixed Ers.	6 Gd. (former 1 Gd. Ers.). 7 Gd. (former 2 Gd. Ers.). 357. 358.	Gd. Ers.	6 Gd. 7 Gd. 399.	Gd. Ers.	6 Gd. 7 Gd. 399.
Cavalry	Gd. Ers. Cav. Detach.		1st Sqn. Gd. Cav. Rgt.		5th Sqn. 2d Gd. Uhlan Rgt.		5 Sqn. 2 Gd. Uhlan Rgt.	
Artillery	1st Ers. Abt. (1st and 2d Gd. F. A. Rgt.). 38th F. A. Rgt.		7th Gd. F. A. Rgt.		6th Gd. Art. Command: 7 Gd. F. A. Rgt.		6 Gd. Art. Command: 7 Gd. F. A. Rgt. 89 Ft. A. Btn. 759 Light Am. Col. 814 Light Am. Col. 886 Light Am. Col.	
Engineers and Liaisons.	1 Co. Gd. Ers. Pion. Btn. 1 Ers. Co. 2 Pion. Btn.		301 (Gd.) Pion. Co. 302 Pion. Co. 7 Gd. T. M. Co.		Eng. Btn.: 301 (Gd.) Pion. Co. 302 Pion. Co. 7 Gd. T. M. Co. 292 Searchlight Section. 551 Gd. Tel. Detch.		501 Pion. Btn.: 301 Gd. Pion. Co. 302 Pion. Co. 49 Searchlight Section. 551 Gd. Tel. Detch. 86 Wireless Detch.	
Medical and Veterinary.					62 Ambulance Co. 133 Field Hospital. 134 Field Hospital. 209 Vet. Hospital.		63 Ambulance Co. 133 Field Hospital. 134 Field Hospital. 209 Vet. Hospital.	
Transport					M. T. Col.		761 M. T. Col.	
Attached	32 Ldw. Btn. 2d C. Dist. (1915).		81 Labor Btn.					

HISTORY.

1914-15.

Formed in August, 1914, by grouping the Guard Ersatz Battalions and the Ersatz Battalions of the 2d Corps District, the division detrained at Saverne August 19. In reserve during the battle on the 20th, it crossed the frontier on the 23d with the 6th Army, fought southeast of Lunéville the first days of September, and toward the end of the same month it went to Haye (Woevre).

HAYE.

1. There it formed part of the Ersatz Corps and held various sectors of the region until March, 1916 (St. Baussant, Flirey, Bois de Mort-Mare, etc.).

1916.

1. In March, 1916, the 1st Guard Ersatz Mixed Bde. (6th and 7th Guard Regiments) left the Apremont region to go to the north of Combres and to the south of Fresnes-en-Woevre.

VERDUN.

2. After a rest of 10 days at St. Marie aux Chenes (Apr. 24–May 3) it went to the front north of Verdun.   May 11–12 it entered line in the Bois-Nawé (west of Douaumont), where it took part in several attacks (notably that of May 25).   It rested in June, and fought again, beginning July 1, to the southeast of the Thiaumont works.

3. The 5th Guard Ersatz Mixed Bde. which had remained in the Montsec region, entrained at Vigneulles-St. Benoît (July 23–26), detrained at Spincourt, and during the night of August 3–4 entered line to the east of Fleury. Together with the 1st Bde., it took part in the attack of August 5, and both suffered heavy losses.

4. The Guard Ersatz Division was withdrawn from line the end of August, after having lost 50 per cent of its infantry before Verdun.

FLIREY-EN-HAYE.

5. After a rest in the region west of Spincourt it went back into line to the north of Flirey en Haye; it remained there until about the 5th of November.

In September the 357th and the 358th Infantry Regiments were attached to the Bavarian Ersatz Division and the 214th Division, respectively.   The Guard Ersatz Division received in exchange a regiment newly formed from companies taken from the 6th and 7th Guard and the 357th Infantry Regiments.

COTE DU POIVRE.

6. The division rested in November, leaving December 18 to go to the region north of Côte du Poivre, following the French attack of December 15.

1917.

1. About January 15, 1917, the Guard Ersatz Division was withdrawn from the Verdun front and sent to Champagne (St. Hilaire sector).

2. Relieved toward the end of March, the division was sent to reserve in the Chateau-Porcien region, which it quitted April 12.

AISNE.

3. April 16 and the days following elements of the division counterattacked toward Berméricourt; then relieving (Apr. 18) the remnants of the 21st Division, the Guard Ersatz Division went through the French attack of May 4.   It left this front soon after.

4. May; rest in rear of the Champagne front.

RUSSIA.

5. After a stay in a sector in Haye to the north of Flirey (from the beginning of June to the middle of July), the division was carried to the eastern front (July 23–27)). (Itinerary: Sarrebrucken, Kreuznach, Frankfort, Leipsic, Cottbus, Glogau, Warsaw, Grodno, Vilna.)

6. The Kaiser reviewed the division July 29.   From the 1st to the 17th of August it was trained in open warfare near Vilna.

RIGA.

7. Taken to Chavli (Aug. 28), then to the Gross-Ekkau region, the division entered line in the Uxkuell region and participated in the Riga offensive, entering Riga September 3–4.

FRANCE.

8. September 8 the division entrained for the western front. (Itinerary: Chavli, Kovno, Eydtkuhnen, Insterberg, Posen, Cottbus, Leipsic, Frankfort, Thionville, Briey.) It encamped near Spincourt, and then, about October 10, entered line to the north of Bezonvaux.

VALUE—1917 ESTIMATE.

The Guard Ersatz Division was recruited all over Prussia just as all the other Guard divisions.

Good division. The 6th and 7th Guard Regiments are not to be considered as tried troops. The 399th Infantry Regiment seems to have but a slight combative value.

The men are said to have shown dissatisfaction when they left Russia for the western front. Desertions are said to have taken place en route. (Inter. pris. Dec. 15–17.)

1918.

VERDUN.

1. The division remained north of Verdun until February 20, when it was relieved and went to Damvillers, entrained, and went to the Arlon area and was trained until March 15.

SOMME.

2. It entrained at Arlon on that date and traveled via Charleroi to Mons, where it arrived the following day. By night marches the division passed through Maubeuge-Bavai-Englefontaine-Fontaine au Bois-Bazuel-Le Cateau-Busigny-Bohain-Fresnoy-Péronne, without taking part in any fighting. It came into line March 25–26, and was heavily engaged at Proyart the 27th.

HANGARD.

3. The division was withdrawn about April 6, after having large casualties, and reinforced the front near Hangard the night of April 9–10, not being relieved until about May 4. Flanking divisions extended their fronts.

MONS.

4. It rested northwest of Mons until the end of June.

CHAMPAGNE.

5. It then went to reserve in Champagne, and entered line west of Auberive July 15. It was withdrawn on the 21st.

OULCHY LE CHATEAU.

6. The division was identified in line north of Oulchy le Chateau July 29, where it fought until withdrawn, about August 9.

ALSACE.

7. It went into rest cantonments at Helfrantzkirch (northeast of Basle), and remained there until September 25.

YPRES.

8. Prisoners of the division were captured southwest of Roulers, and they stated that it entered line October 5–6. The division remained in line fighting stubbornly, but to no purpose, until withdrawn, November 7.

VALUE—1918 ESTIMATE.

Reliable information is to the effect that the Guard Ersatz, the Guard Cavalry, and the Jaeger Divisions bore the title "Oberste Heeresleitungs Angriffsdivisionen," and that they were held under the direct control of the Supreme Command. Nevertheless, the Guard Ersatz has always been considered as being in the second of four classes.

Guard Cavalry Division.
COMPOSITION.

	1918	
	Brigade.	Regiment.
Infantry..	5 Ldw. Inf........	
Cavalry..	11 Cav............	1 Cuirassier. 8 Drag.
	14 Cav............	5 Uhlan. 8 Hus. 11 Hus.
	38 Cav............	2 Mounted Jag. 6 Mounted Jag. 4 Cuirassier. Gd. Cuirassier (1 Sqn. of 4 Mounted Jag.).

Artillery...	132 Art. Command:
	  3 Gd. F. A. Rgt.
	  226 F. A. Rgt.	

Engineers and Liaisons............................	412 Pion. Btn.:
	  307 Pion. Co.
	  2 Ers. Pion. Co.
	  183 Wireless Detch.
	  286 and 385 T. M. Cos.	

Medical and Veterinary............................	257 Ambulance Co. 302 Field Hospital. 315 Field Hospital. 286 Vet. Hospital.	
Attached	Balloon Sqn. No. 33. 290 Reconnaissance Flight.	

HISTORY.
1918.

1. The division left the eastern theater in the middle of March. It was reconstituted in the camp at Zossen (south of Berlin), and was then moved to the Maubeuge area, where it underwent six weeks' training for open warfare. It now consisted of 9 dismounted regiments, grouped in 3 brigades, 2 companies of pioneers, and a trench mortar company.

CHAMPAGNE.

2. About May 28 the division relieved the 23d Division east of the Suippe. It was relieved about July 2, and on the 15th returned to strengthen the battle front near Souain. It was relieved about July 20.

SOISSONS.

3. The division was moved to the Soissons area, and on August 22 relieved the Jaeger Division east of Soissons. It retired from the front about September 5.

CHAMPAGNE.

4. On September 23–24 it relieved the 15th Bavarian Division north of Prosnes, and was thereafter constantly in line in Champagne. The direction of its final retreat lay through Herpy (Nov. 1), St. Ferguex (5th), Rethel (6th), and Rocquigny (7th).

VALUE.

The division was rated as second class. It was reported to be one of the General Headquarters attack divisions held under direct control of the Supreme Command. After the failure of the July offensive east of Reims the division was constantly on the defensive.

1st Division.
COMPOSITION.

	1914		1915		1916		1917		1918	
	Brigade.	Regiment.	Brigade.	Regiment.	Brigade.	Regiment.	Brigade.	Regiment.	Brigade.	Regiment.
Infantry.......	1. 2.	1 Gren. 41. 3 Gren. 43.	1. 2.	1 Gren. 41. 3 Gren. 43.	1. 2.	1 Gren. 41. 3 Gren. 43.	1.	1 Gren. 3 Gren. 43.	1.	1 Gren. 3 Gren. 43.
Cavalry.......	8 Uhlan. Regt.		(?)		(?)		3d Sqn. 8 Uhlan. Regt.		3 Sqn. 8 Uhlan. Regt.	
Artillery......	1 Brig.: 16 F. A. Rgt. 52 F. A. Rgt.		1 Brig.: 16 F. A. Rgt. 52 F. A. Rgt.		1 Brig.: 16 F. A. Rgt. 52 F. A. Rgt.		(z) Art. Command: 16 F. A. Rgt. 52 F. A. Rgt.		1 Art. Command: 16 F. A. Rgt. 1 Abt. 10 Ft. A. Rgt. (Staff, 1, 3, and 4 Btries.) 1083 Light Am. Col. 1095 Light Am. Col. 1096 Light Am. Col.	
Engineers and Liaisons.			1 Eng. Btn. (1 C. Dist.): Field Co. 1 Pion. 1 Pontoon Engs. 1 Tel. Detch.		1 Eng. Btn. (1 C. Dist.): 271 Pion. Co. (Oct., 1917). 1 Pontoon Engs. 1 Tel. Detch. 1 T. M. Co. 3d Co. 1 Pions.		112 Eng. Btn.: 3d Co. 1 Pions. (2). 271 Pion. Co. 1 T. M. Co. 1 Tel. Detch. 305, 311, 312, and 392 Searchlight Sections.		110 Pion. Btn.: 3 Co. 1 Pions. 1 T. M. Co. 108 Searchlight Section. 1 Signal Command: 1 Tel. Detch. 43 Wireless Detch.	
Medical and Veterinary.							4 Ambulance Co. Field Hospital. 1 Vet. Hospital.		4 Ambulance Co. 13 Field Hospital. 16 Field Hospital. 1 Vet. Hospital.	
Transport....							M. T. Col.		534 M. T. Col.	
Attached......					100 Labor Btn.		66 M. G. S. S. Detch. 54, 55, 56, and 57 Light M. G. Sections.			

HISTORY.

1914–15.

Along with the 2d Division, the 1st Division forms the 1st Army Corps (Koenigsberg).

RUSSIA.

1. The 1st Army Corps was engaged on the Russian front at the very beginning of the war.

2. Up until November the 1st Division participated in the operations of East Prussia, and notably in the battle of Tannenberg (Aug. 27–29).

3. In December the two division of the 1st Corps separated. The 2d Division remained in the north; the 1st Division went to the 9th Army, from December, 1914, to January, 1915 (Bzura-Rawka), then to the Army of the South, operating in the Carpathians and on the Dniester, from February, 1915, to February, 1916.

1916.

FRANCE.

1. The division went to France in March, 1916. The 41st Infantry Regiment detrained March 13 near Metz; the 48th Infantry Regiment at Hagondange March 5.

VERDUN.

2. The division was put in line near Vaux April 20, fought in the bois de la Caillette in May, in the bois de Vaux Chapitre, and the bois Fumin in June and July. It suffered enormous losses there. In the 1st Company of the 41st Infantry Regiment, the numbers on the pay books passed from 1,359 (Apr. 10) to 1,674 (July 19), indicating the arrival of at least 316 reinforcements. From the beginning of the war until July, 1916, the regiment had received an average of 1,360 men per company.

RUSSIA.

3. At the end of July, 1916, the 1st Division, leaving behind the 41st Infantry Regiment, which fought before Verdun in August, was once more taken to the eastern front, where it formed part of the Carpathian Corps.

1917.

BUKOWINA.

1. In July, 1917, the division was in the Kirlibaba-Dorna-Vatra region. Beginning July 27, it followed up the retreating Russians, halting, early in August, in the Sereth region.

FRANCE.

2. The division entrained, the beginning of December, near Czernowitz, and was carried to the French front. (Itinerary: Kolomea, Stanislau, Lemberg, Tarnow, Oppeln, Breslau, Dresden, Leipsic, Halle, Cassel, Coblentz, Treves.) Ordered to Lorraine, it was sent to the region east of Etain, relieving the 13th Reserve Division and occupying the sector in front of Moulainville (Dec. 27; still there Jan. 23, 1918).

VALUE—1917 ESTIMATE.

Theoretically, the regiments of the 1st Division are recruited in East Prussia, but since the 1st Corps District, sparsely populated and of restricted size, could not keep it up alone, the elements coming from outside this district are numerous. During the stay on the eastern front Alsace-Lorrainers were used in considerable number. While in France the division's ranks were filled up with the aid of the abundant resources of Brandenburg and Silesia (3rd and 4th Corps Districts); consequently, the division does not display to any degree the local character like the majority of the German divisions.

The 1st Division was on the Russian front from August, 1914, until December, 1917, with the exception of the period April–July, 1916, during which it was engaged before Verdun.

The troops of the division fraternized with the Russians for about three weeks in April, but this came to an end early in May with the arrival opposite them of new Russian troops, who received their advances with bullets.   (Inter. pris., Jan. 24, 1918.)

1918.

WOEVRE.

1.. The division remained in line in the Verdun sector until relieved by the 11th Bavarian division about February 15.

2. It moved to the Conflans area, where it went through a course of training in open warfare in order to fit itself to become an assault division.   At this time, too, it exchanged its Alsatians for Prussians of the 78th Reserve Division.

SOMME.

3. March 27 the division reinforced the front at Bray, north of the Somme.   It fought until the 30th, and lost to such an extent that its companies, which had been filled up while in the Conflans area, were reduced to an average strength of 40 men.

4. It was withdrawn March 30, and rested immediately in rear of the position it had held in line until about April 19.

5. The following day the division went back into line just south of the Somme, and immediately suffered heavily.   It was relieved May 2 by the 24th Reserve Division.

6. The division went to rest in the Peruwelz area, and then had some more training in the same region.

CHAMPAGNE.

7. Early in July the division was identified in reserve near Hirson.

8. July 16 it entered line near St. Hilaire, and was withdrawn the 20th.

RHEIMS.

9. It was immediately thrown into line in the Bois de Vrigny, where it fought in an attempt to prevent the Allies from annihilating the German troops in the Soissons-Chateau Thierry–Rheims pocket.

LAON.

10. About August 10 the division was withdrawn and went to rest in the region of Laon.

LAFFAUX.

September 3 it relieved the 27th Division near Laffaux, and, being surprised by a French attack, lost heavily (2,300 prisoners).

12. September 16 it was relieved by the 29th Division.

RHEIMS.

13. The division came back into line near Betheny (northeast of Rheims) on October 2 and was withdrawn about the 8th.

ST. FERGEUX.

14. It reentered line in the St. Fergeux region October 14, and was again withdrawn the 29th.

LIART.

15. November 7 the division was identified near Liart (south of Rocroi), and remained in line until the armistice.

VALUE—1918 ESTIMATE.

The division was rated as third class.

1st Reserve Division.
COMPOSITION.

	1914 Brigade	1914 Regiment	1915 Brigade	1915 Regiment	1916 Brigade	1916 Regiment	1917 Brigade	1917 Regiment	1918 Brigade	1918 Regiment
Infantry	1 Res. 72 Res. 1 Res.	1 Res. 3 Res. 18 Res. 59 Res. Jag. Btn.	1 Res. 72 Res. 1 Res.	1 Res. 3 Res. 18 Res. 59 Res. Jag. Btn.	1 Res. 72 Res. 1 Res.	1 Res. 3 Res. 18 Res. 59 Res. Jag. Btn.	1 Res. 1 Res.	1 Res. 3 Res. 59 Res. Jag. Btn.	1 Res.	1 Res. 3 Res. 59 Res.
Cavalry		1 Res. Uhl. Rgt. (3 Sqns.). 1 Res. Ers. Cav. Rgt. (3 Sqns.).	1 Res. Uhl. Rgt. 1 Res. Ers. Cav. Regt.		1 Res. Uhl. Rgt.		1 Res. Uhl. Rgt. (. Sqns.).		4 Sqn. 2 Gd. Uhlan Rgt.	
Artillery	1 Res. F. A. Rgt. (6 Btries.).		1 Res. F. A. Rgt.		1 Res. F. A. Rgt.		1 Res. F. A. Rgt. (9 Btries.).		1 Res. F. A. Rgt. 2 Abt. 1 Res. Ft. A. Rgt. 1363 Light Am. Col. 1390 Light Am. Col. 1393 Light Am. Col.	
Engineers and Liaisons.			2 Eng. Btn. No. 1: Res. Co. 1 Pion. Btn. 1 Res. Pontoon Engs. 1 Res. Tel. Detch.		4 Field Co. 2d Pion. Btn. 201 T. M. Co. 1 Res. Pontoon Engs. 1 Res. Tel. Detch.		301 Eng. Btn. ( ): 4 Co. Pion. Btn. 1 Co. Pion. Btn. 201 T. M. Co. 348 Searchlight Section. Tel. Detch.		301 Pion. Btn.: 4 Co. 2 Pions. 1 Co. 34 Res. Pions. 201 T. M. Co. 31 Searchlight Section. 401 Signals Command: 401 Tel. Detch. 158 Wireless Detch.	
Medical and veterinary.							501 Ambulance Co. 399 Field Hospital. 9 Res. Field Hospital. Vet. Hospital.		501 Ambulance Co. 399 Field Hospital. 9 Res. Field Hospital. 137 Vet. Hospital.	
Transport.							M. T. Col.			

HISTORY.

1914–15.

RUSSIA.

1. The 1st Reserve Division was on the Russian front from August, 1914, until November 1, 1917, at which time it entrained for France.

EAST PRUSSIA—POLAND.

2. In 1914 it and the 36th Reserve Division formed the 1st Reserve Corps (Gen. Otto von Buelow). It took part in the operations of East Prussia (Hindenburg's Army), in the Lodz maneuver (Von Mackensen's Army), and in the combats on the Bzura.

3. In February, 1915, the division was in the Prasnysz region, northeast of the Bohr-Narew line.

COURLAND.

4. In May, as part of Eichhorn's Army, it took part in the raid on Courland.

1916.

GALICIA.

1. It was on the Dvina in the Friedrichstadt region until July.

2. In August it was identified in Galicia, in Bothmer's Army, opposed to the Broussiloff offensive. Here it had heavy losses. (The 11th Company of the 3d Infantry Regiment, in particular, was reduced to 30 men.) During September the division was reinforced. The depot at Friedrichstadt, near Warsaw, was completely emptied to make good its losses.

COURLAND.

3. Toward the end of September elements of the division were in line near Friedrichstadt, along the Dvina, in a calm sector. The 18th Reserve Infantry Regiment was attached to the newly formed 225th Division.

1917.

1. January 5, 1917, the division was taken to the Mitau region, where it helped stop the Russian attack. Losses in this sector were light, but there was considerable discontent due to the cold.

2. The division was relieved about the 15th of March and sent to the neighborhood of Gross-Eckau, near Mitau, where it rested two months.

RIGA.

3. The middle of May it was put back into line before Riga. It took part in the offensive against that city in September, stayed there from the 3d to the 7th of September, and then took up again its march toward the east. It organized its positions about 70 kilometers from Riga, near Hintzenberg (or Hildersberg?) (near Wenden) and established itself there.

FRANCE.

4. Relieved the end of October, it entrained near Wenden for the western front (Itinerary: Riga, Mitau, Kovno, Eidtkuhnen, Insterburg, Thorn, Posen, Lissa, Breslau, Cottbus, Leipsic, Erfuhrt, Frankfort-on-the-Main, Sarrebruecken, Thionville, Sedan, Vouziers.) It detrained November 6 at Semide (southeast of Vouziers).

CHAMPAGNE.

5. After a rest of two days, the division went into line in the St. Hilaire sector (east of Vaudesincourt-Auherive).

VALUE—1917 ESTIMATE.

The division was recruited in East Prussia and, as a result of insufficient local resources, from divers other localities—a great many Alsace-Lorrainers during the sojourn on the Russian front.

The 1st Reserve Division has taken part in all the important attacks which have taken place on the eastern front since the beginning of the war. It seems, however, from interrogation of deserters (in Champagne, November, 1917), that the cadres and men were little prepared for war as it was waged on the western front.

1918.
CHAMPAGNE.

1. The division remained in line east of Auberive until relieved by the 23d Division April 30.

MONTDIDIER.

2. May 13–14 it relieved the 76th Reserve Division in the Givesnes sector.

3. It was relieved August 4, but came back into line on the 10th a little farther to the north, in the region of Hangest-en-Santerre. It was withdrawn a few days later and rested several days in the neighborhood.

4. August 19 it relieved the 75th Reserve Division near Beuvraignes. It fought until relieved September 2.

ST. QUENTIN.

5. After 10 days' rest it relieved the 21st Division near Le Verguier, northwest of St. Quentin. It was withdrawn on the 20th.

RIBEMONT.

6. October 1 the division relieved the 208th Division near Ribemont. Withdrawn October 31.

DOMPIERRE.

7. It came back into line November 7 and remained until the armistice.

VALUE—1918 ESTIMATE.

The division has suffered very heavily, notwithstanding the fact that, until about the 10th of August, it had taken no part in any really important actions this year. On the 18th of September the 1st Reserve Regiment was almost wiped out, its three battalion officers being captured with their staffs. It had also suffered a great many casualties the 9th and 10th of August. It is difficult to estimate the strength of its companies, owing to the fact that it is still in an active sector, but it is probably not over 50 rifles.

In the main the recruitment is East Prussian. There have been many Alsace-Lorrainers in its ranks, but since many of these have deserted there are probably not a great many of them left. For the most part the men are between 25 and 35 years old, but there are many older men and something less than 10 per cent of the division is made up by recruits of the 1919 class. It is again to be noted that the division was not employed in any of the German offensives this year.

Its conduct was remarkable in no way during the division's participation in the heavy fighting around Hangest, Beuvraignes, and to the north of St. Quentin. During the early part of the year, when the division was in line in Champagne, there were a great many desertions, especially among the Alsace-Lorraine element. There have also been many cases of mutiny, especially in the 59th Reserve, the worst of the three regiments. About the middle of August a batch of some 500 recruits started out from the interior for the division. To sustain the morale of the men, these recruits were told they were going to simply support the artillery. Notwithstanding this, less than 250 men remained when the draft reached its true destination—the front lines. The men are very tired of the war, but on the whole seem resigned to the necessity of doing their duty.

The 1st Reserve is rated as a third-class division.

1st Landwehr Division.
COMPOSITION.

	1914		1915		1916		1917		1918	
	Brigade.	Regiment.	Brigade.	Regiment.	Brigade.	Regiment.	Brigade.	Regiment.	Brigade.	Regiment.
Infantry	6 Mixed Ldw. 34 Mixed Ldw.	34 Ldw. 49 Ldw. 31 Ldw. 84 Ldw.	6 Ldw. 34 Mixed Ldw.	34 Ldw. 49 Ldw. 31 Ldw. 33 Ldw. 84 Ldw.	34 Ldw.	31 Ldw. 37 Ldw. 84 Ldw.	34 Ldw.	31 Ldw. 33 Ldw. 84 Ldw.	34 Ldw.	31 Ldw. 33 Ldw. 84 Ldw.
Cavalry			90 Ldw. Cav. Rgt. 2d Sqn. 10 Drag. Rgt.	34 Ldw. Cav. Rgt. 2d Sqn. 10 Drag. Rgt.	2d Sqn. 10 Drag. Rgt.		2d Sqn. 12 Horse Jag.		3 Sqn. 12 Horse Jag. Rgt.	
Artillery			96 F. A. Rgt. 219 F. A. Rgt.		128 Art. Command: 96 F. A. Rgt.				96 F. A. Rgt. 782 Light Am. Col. 1036 Light Am. Col. 1047 Light Am. Col.	
Engineers and Liaisons.			1 Co. 23 Pion. Btn. 2 Co. 23 Ers. Pion. Btn.		(401) Eng. Btn.: 1 Co. 1 Ers. Pion. Btn. 3 Co. 26 Ers. Pion. Btn. 304 T. M. Co. 279 Searchlight Section. 501 Tel. Detch.				401 Pion. Btn.: 1 Ers. Co. 1 Pions. 2 Ldw. Co. 2 C. Dist. Pions. 301 T. M. Co. 142 Searchlight Section. 501 Signal Command: 501 Tel. Detch. 190 Wireless Detch.	
Medical and Veterinary.					215 Ambulance Co. 2 Ldw. Field Hospital. 9 Ldw. Field Hospital. 201 Vet. Hospital.				215 Ambulance Co. 146 Field Hospital. 279 Field Hospital. 201 Vet. Hospital.	
Transport.					M. T. Col.					
Odd Units.										

HISTORY.

1914–15.

Called Jacobi's Division at the beginning of the war, and a part of the 1st Landwehr Corps, the 1st Landwehr Division fought under this corps on the eastern front. It was first called the 10th Landwehr Division, taking the name of 1st Landwehr Division in July, 1915. It comprised the 6th Mixed Landwehr Brigade (34th and 49th Landwehr Regiments) and the 34th Mixed Landwehr Brigade (31st and 84th Landwehr Regiments).

EAST PRUSSIA, POLAND.

1. First engaged in East Prussia (Angerburg, Gumbinnen, August, 1914, to January, 1915), Jacobi's Division took part in the operations between Mariampol and Suwalki. Early in March, 1915, it was before Lomza; then in the Ossowiec region on the Bobr. It was at this time that the division became known as the 1st Landwehr Division, and the 33d Landwehr Regiment was attached to it.

2. At the beginning of August the division was in the Kalvariia region, Suwalki. It took part in the summer offensive, but remained in support, never doing any actual fighting.

COURLAND.

3. After a rest on the Little Berezina, it went to Courland, going into line in the Uxkuell region (October).

1916.

1. The division remained to the south of Riga until the end of July, 1916.

VOLHYNIA.

2. In August it went to Volhynia, where it took over the Borovno sector (on the Stokhod) and held it for more than a year, until about November, 1917. The 6th Landwehr Brigade was taken away and remained in the Mitau region (April, 1916). Since then the division has been composed of only three regiments.

1917.

VOLHYNIA.

1. Relieved in the Borovno sector toward the end of 1917, went to rest in the vicinity of Kovel. In January, 1918, the division received reinforcements from the 9th Landwehr Regiment (dissolved) and also from the 20th Landsturm Regiment. It had already had men of the 1919 class since November, 1917. Still more arrived in February, 1918, when the division was on the point of departing for Belgium.

VALUE—1917 ESTIMATE.

In theory, the 31st and 84th Landwehr Regiments were recruited in the 9th Corps District; the 33d Landwehr Regiment in the 1st Corps District. Latterly, however, widely diversified elements have been introduced—men of the 20th Landsturm Regiment (18th Corps District); from the 9th Landsturm Regiment (2d Corps District); also men from the 3d, 7th, and 17th Districts (class 1919). There is, too, a considerable number of Alsace-Lorrainers (33d Landwehr Regiment).

The 1st Landwehr is a mediocre division, composed of old men and of others that have little military value. (March, 1918.)

1918.

BELGIUM.

1. The division was then taken to the western front, and after some time spent in reserve (it was probably trained in the methods of warfare employed on the western front, although there is no evidence to establish it) it relieved the 35th Division

near Merckem, March 20.   It was relieved about April 19 by elements of the 83d Division.

2. April 26 it was identified in the St. Julien-Hooge sector, replacing part of the 236th Division, which side slipped to the south.   In an unsuccessful attack during this time it suffered exceedingly heavy losses.

ALSACE.

3. The division was relieved by the 6th Cavalry Division during the night of July 27–28 and went to rest in the Vosges.

4. About October 3 the division relieved the 30th Bavarian Reserve Division near Aspach le Bas.

WOEVRE.

5. It was withdrawn from this sector soon afterwards to be thrown in to meet the American advance east of the Meuse, being identified west of Flabas October 16. They lost heavily, staying in until the armistice.

VALUE—1918 ESTIMATE.

The 1st Landwehr is rated as a third-class division.   Still, although many of its younger men were sent to other divisions just before it came to the western front, it did rather well, its commanding officer having been promoted after its participation in the battle of the Lys, and the division as a whole having been lauded several times in the official communiques.

1st Bavarian Division.

COMPOSITION.

	1914		1915		1916		1917		1918	
	Brigade.	Regiment.	Brigade.	Regiment.	Brigade.	Regiment.	Brigade.	Regiment.	Brigade.	Regiment.
Infantry	1 Bav. 2 Bav.	Body Inf. 1 Bav. 2 Bav. 16 Bav.	1 Bav. 2 Bav.	1 Bav. 2 Bav. 24 Bav.	2 Bav.	2 Bav. 1 Bav. 24 Bav.	1 Bav.	2 Bav. 1 Bav. 24 Bav.	1 Bav.	1 Bav. 2 Bav. 24 Bav.
Cavalry	8 Bav. Light Cav.					8 Bav. Light Cav. (3 Sqns).	8 Bav. Light Cav. (2d and 3d Sqns).			2 Sqn. 8 Bav. Light Cav. Rgt.
Artillery	1 Bav. Brig.: 1 Bav. F. A. Rgt. 7 Bav. F. A. Rgt.		1 Bav. Brig.: 1 Bav. F. A. Rgt. 7 Bav. F. A. Rgt.		1 Bav. Brig.: 1 Bav. F. A. Rgt. 7 Bav. F. A. Rgt.		1 Bav. Art. Command:	1 Bav. F. A. Rgt.	1 Bav. Art. Command: 1 Bav. F. A. Rgt. 9 Bav. Ft. A. Btn. 123 Bav. Light Am. Col. 146 Bav. Light Am. Col. 158 Bav. Light Am. Col	
Engineers and Liaisons.	1 Bav. Eng. Btn. (1st and 3d Field Cos.).		1 Bav. Eng. Btn. (1 and 3 Field Cos.); 1 Bav. Pontoon Engs. 1 Bav. Tel. Detch.		1 Bav. Eng. Btn. (1 and 3 Field Cos.); 1 Bav. T. M. Co. 1 Bav. Pontoon Engs. 1 Bav. Tel. Detch.		1 and 3 Bav. Pion. Cos. 1 Bav. T. M. Co. 1 Bav. Searchlight Section. 1 Bav. Tel. Detch. 1 Bav. Pontoon Engs.		1 Bav. Pion. Btn.: 1 Bav. Pion. Co. 3 Bav. Pion. Co. 1 Bav. T. M. Co. 1 Bav. Searchlight Section. 1 Bav. Signal Command: 1 Bav. Tel. Detch. 40 Wireless Detch.	
Medical and Veterinary.							1 Bav. Ambulance Co. Field Hospital. Vet. Hospital.		1 Bav. Ambulance Co. 3 Bav. Field Hospital. 4 Bav. Field Hospital.	
Transport.							M. T. Col.			

HISTORY.

1914.

LORRAINE.

1. At the beginning of the war the 1st Bavarian Division, forming, with the 2d Bavarian Division, the 1st Bavarian Corps, was part of the 6th Army (Bavarian Crown Prince). It detrained at Sarrebruecken (Aug. 8–9), crossed the frontier, sacked Badonviller the 12th, and withdrew to the north of Sarrebruecken the 17th. It fought at Sarrebruecken the 20th. In liaison on the left with the Badeners of the 14th Corps, it crossed the frontier and advanced to Nossoncourt and Xaffévillers (Sept. 6) via Baccarat. September 12 the division, having been withdrawn, was reassembled at Peltre (near Metz). It then entrained at Metz the 14th and 15th, and detrained near Namur, reaching Péronne the 24th.

SOMME.

2. In the last days of September, 1914, at the time of the "race to the sea," the two divisions of the 1st Bavarian Corps were in the 2d Army (Von Buelow), which operated on the Somme in the Péronne region. They became heavily engaged notably at Combles (Oct. 24) and at Maricourt (Dec. 17). By November 4 the 1st Bavarian Regiment had had casualties of 63 officers and 2,090 men since the beginning of the war. (Casualty list.)

1915.

ARTOIS.

1. The 1st Bavarian Division was kept in line on the Somme (Dompierre-Maricourt) until October, 1915. Its composition was changed—the Body Infantry Regiment went to the Alpine Corps, the 16th Infantry to the 10th Bavarian Division. In return, the 24th Infantry (a new formation) was received.

2. The division was taken to the region north of Arras (Neuville-Souchez sector), where it remained almost seven months (October, 1915–May, 1916).

1916.

VERDUN.

1. About May, 1916, the division was relieved to the west of Vimy and sent to the Verdun front, where it took part in the battles near Douaumont (May 23), and in those of June 1 and 8.

2. Re-formed in the Romagne-sous-les-Côtes area, it reentered line about June 22 for new attacks. During this offensive the division suffered severely. It was relieved at the beginning of July.

3. After a short rest behind the Verdun front the division reoccupied the Apremont-St. Mihiel sector, remaining there until October 11, when it was reconstituted, receiving large reinforcements (recuperates and men of the 1916 class).

SOMME.

4. Taken to the Caudry sector (near Cambrai), it was engaged on the Somme (Sailly-Saillisel, Morval) October 13 to end of November, where its losses were once again exceedingly heavy.

5. The division reappeared in the region of St. Mihiel (Bois d'Ailly-Forêt d'Apremont sector) the beginning of December, and remained there until the early days of May, 1917.

1917.

PLATEAU DE CALIFORNIE.

1. Entrained about May 7 at Vigneulles, it proceeded to the Laon region, where it was in reserve (May 8–12). The following day it took over the sector west of Hurtebise, where it participated in several attacks (May 20–June 17), losing heavily therein.

2. The division was relieved June 21 and went to rest south of Mézières (La Francheville, etc.), where it was reconstituted.

CHAMPAGNE.

3. July 25 it went back into line on the Champagne front (sector south of Ste. Marie-a-Py); it did not take part in any important engagements there.

4. The division was withdrawn December 27.

VALUE—1917 ESTIMATE.

The division was recruited in the southern part of Bavaria. The presence of contingents from the Bavarian Alps was responsible for the withdrawal of the Body Regiment to form the Alpine Corps.

Despite the losses it suffered during May and June in the Hurtebise sector, the 1st Bavarian Division may still be considered a good division. It has had time to reconstitute itself during the long calm period spent in Champagne (July 25-Dec. 27, 1917).

1918.

ARGONNE.

1. Withdrawn from line, the division was put through a course of training. It relieved the 80th Reserve Division north of Vauquois February 17.

2. It was relieved by the 80th Reserve Division about the 1st of March.

ST. QUENTIN.

3. The opening day of the March offensive the division reinforced the front south of St. Quentin. It was withdrawn the next day.

4. March 23 it came back into line north of Chauny. It was withdrawn about the 30th.

LASSIGNY.

5. April 6 it relieved the 3d Bavarian Division west of Lassigny. It was in turn relieved by the 3d Bavarian Division on the 12th.

CHAMPAGNE.

6. Having suffered a great deal in the fighting on the Somme, the division was taken to a quiet sector in Champagne, relieving the 52d Reserve Division May 1 north of Souain. About June 30 it was relieved by the 30th Division.

7. It reinforced the front near Souain July 15. It was withdrawn about the 31st.

SOISSONS.

8. The division entered line northeast of Soissons August 11.

NOYON.

9. It was relieved by the Jaeger Division about August 19, and moved to the west, taking over the Cuts sector, southeast of Noyon, August 20, and was withdrawn the 22d.

COUCY-LE-CHATEAU.

10. August 31 the division was identified at Folembray, northwest of Coucy-le-Chateau; withdrawn about September 12.

CHAMPAGNE.

11. About September 27 it took over the Manre sector, southeast of Vouziers, where it remained, fighting, until the signing of the armistice.

VALUE—1918 ESTIMATE.

The 1st Bavarian is rated as a first-class assault division; it was utilized as such throughout 1918. It fought well; its losses were severe.

1st Bavarian Reserve Division.

COMPOSITION.

	1914		1915		1916		1917		1918	
	Brigade.	Regiment.	Brigade.	Regiment.	Brigade.	Regiment.	Brigade.	Regiment.	Brigade.	Regiment.
Infantry	1 Bav. Res. 2 Bav. Res.	1 Bav. Res. 2 Bav. Res. 3 Bav. Res. 12 Bav. Res.	1 Bav. Res. 2 Bav. Res.	1 Bav. Res. 2 Bav. Res. 3 Bav. Res. 12 Bav. Res.	1 Bav. Res.	1 Bav. Res. 2 Bav. Res. 3 Bav. Res.	1 Bav. Res.	1 Bav. Res. 2 Bav. Res. 3 Bav. Res.	1 Bav. Res.	1 Bav. Res. 2 Bav. Res. 3 Bav. Res.
Cavalry	1 Bav. Res. Cav. Rgt.		1 Bav. Res. Cav. Rgt.		1 Bav. Res. Cav. Rgt.		3 Bav. Light Cav. Rgt. (3d Sqn.).	3 Bav. Light Cav. Rgt. (3d Sqn.).	3 Sqn. 3 Bav. Light Cav. Rgt.	
Artillery	1 Bav. Res. F. A. Rgt.		1 Bav. Res. F. A. Rgt.		1 Bav. Res. F. A. Rgt.		13 Bav. Art. Command:	1 Bav. Res. F. A. Rgt.	13 Bav. Art. Command: 1 Bav. Res. F. A. Rgt. 1 Abt. 1 Bav. Ft. A. Rgt. (Staff, 1, 2, and 4 Btries.) 101 Bav. Light Am. Col. 145 Bav. Light Am. Col. 147 Bav. Light Am. Col.	
Engineers and Liaisons.			1 Bav. Res. Eng. Btn. 1 Bav. Res. Pont. Eng. 1 Bav. Res. Tel. Detch.		2d and 4th Bav. Res. Pion. Cos. 201 Bav. T. M. Co. 1 Bav. Res. Pont. Engs. 1 Bav. Res. Tel. Detch.		17 Bav. Eng. Btn.: 1 Bav. Res. Pion. Co. 3 Bav. Res. Pion. Co. 17 Bav. Res. Pion. Co. 201 T. M. Co. 1 Bav.Res. Searchlight Section. 401 Bav. Tel. Detch.		17 Bav. Pion. Btn.: 1 Bav. Res. Pion. Co. 17 Bav. Res. Pion Co. 201 Bav. Res. Pion Co. 18 Bav. Searchlight Section. 401 Bav. Signals Command: 401 Bav. Tel. Detch. 106 Bav. Wireless Detch.	
Medical and Veterinary.							15 Bav. Ambulance Co. 45 Bav. Field Hospital. 48 Bav. Field Hospital. 49 Bav. Field Hospital. Vet. Hospital.		15 Bav. Ambulance Co. 45 Bav. Field Hospital. 48 Bav. Field Hospital.	
Transport.							750 M. T. Col.		750 M. T. Col.	

HISTORY.

1914.

LORRAINE.

1. The Bavarian Reserve Division (1st Bavarian Reserve Corps, with the 5th Bavarian Reserve Division) was at the beginning of the war part of the 6th Army (Prince Rupprecht of Bavaria), and detrained in Lorraine August 13–14. After having helped to check the French offensive in Lorraine, participated in the battle of August 20, entered Luneville, and after having fought at Einville, early in September, it went to rest in the vicinity of the Paris-Avricourt railroad, and later march to Metz by stages.

ARRAS.

2. September 27–28 the division entrained at Metz and was carried to Cambrai. Entering line between Douai and Arras, it fought at Izel, Gavrelle, Rouvroy (Oct. 2–3). On the 5th its right wing was at Souchez, the whole 1st Bavarian Reserve Corps being then in line north of Arras. October 23 the two divisions of the corps attacked violently along the Carency-Roclincourt front; they remained in line until June, 1915, the 1st Bavarian Division being between Roclincourt and Écurie.

1915.

NEUVILLE–ST. VAAST.

1. In May, 1915, the 1st Bavarian Reserve Division was engaged at Neuville-St. Vaast, when it was reinforced by two battalions of the 99th Reserve Infantry Regiment. The 2d Bavarian Reserve Regiment suffered casualties of 14 officers and 1,413 men (casualty list).

LE LABYRINTHE.

2. In June the division fought at the Labyrinth.

3. It continued to hold the sector north of the Scarpe, but moved toward the south in December, the front of the 1st Bavarian Reserve Corps extending as far as Blaireville.

1916.

1. The division remained in line east of Arras, straddling the Scarpe until August, 1916. From May to August, it comprised the 12th Bavarian Reserve Regiment, instead of the 3d Bavarian Reserve Regiment, loaned temporarily by the 5th Bavarian Reserve Division.

SOMME.

2. Withdrawn August 8, it went to the Somme. It was engaged the 12th in the Clery sector, and was relieved as early as the 15th by the 1st Guard Division after having suffered heavily.

3. The second fortnight in August the division was at rest near Cambrai. The end of that month and early in September, some elements of the division were engaged near Clery and Martinpuich in order to facilitate reliefs.

AISNE.

4. About the middle of September the 1st Bavarian Reserve Corps was withdrawn from the region of the Somme and sent to the Aisne, where the 1st Bavarian Reserve Division occupied a sector to the west of Craonne until the beginning of December.

5. Brought back north of the Somme, it sent some elements into line in the Beaumont-Hamel sector (north of the Ancre, December–January).

1917.

ARTOIS.

1. After sometime at rest, the division went back into line February 27 to the north of Arras (Roclincourt-Neuville-St. Vaast). April 9 it received the full shock of the British attack—lost the villages of Thelus and Bailleul and 1,500 prisoners.

LA BASSÉE.

2. Relieved about the 15th of April, the division rested, and then entered line north of the La Bassée Canal (east of Festubert). It remained here five months, taking no part in any important engagements but suffering losses as a result of gas attacks.

FLANDERS.

3. It left for Belgium October 6–7, and took over the Zandvoorde sector (southeast of Ypres) on the 8th.

VALUE—1917 ESTIMATE.

The 1st Bavarian Reserve Division is a good division, but its combatant value can not be compared to that of the active Bavarian divisions.

1918.

1. Here it remained in line until February 11, when it was relieved by the 239th Division and withdrawn to rest in the Menin area, before it had suffered many casualties.

DIXMUDE.

2. March 9 it relieved the 54th Reserve Division in the Dixmude sector. It was relieved on the 22d by the extension of the fronts of the neighboring divisions.

3. It marched to Zedelghem the same day, and reached Seclin on the 23d. The 28th it came into reserve near Douai. It was undoubtedly intended to reinforce the German attack on the Arras front on the 28th, but as this was a complete failure, it returned to the Carvin area.

LYS.

4. April 9 the division reinforced the front near Richebourg-St. Vaast, and took part in the initial attack on the Lys battle front the same day. It advanced through Lacouture, Vieille-Chapelle, and had reached Zelobes April 10. After the first day's fighting it met with a strong resistance and suffered heavily. It was relieved near Robecq by the 239th Division, April 18.

LOOS.

5. April 27 the division relieved elements of the 207th Division east of Loos (south of the La Bassée Canal).

YPRES.

6. It was relieved by the 16th Division about September 27, marched to Carvin, which it left September 29, and entrained at Seclin for Heule, whence it marched into line via Moorseele. It was identified near Roulers October 4. It was relieved by the 6th Cavalry Division October 16.

7. After a rest of only a few days the division came back into line on the 23d to the south of Deynze, whence it was withdrawn about October 31. It did not return to line.

VALUE—1918 ESTIMATE.

The 1st Bavarian Reserve Division took part in no real fighting with the exception of the Lys offensive, in which it did nothing to distinguish itself. It would seem that the division does not deserve to be rated higher than third in a scale of four classes.

1st Bavarian Landwehr Division.
COMPOSITION.

	1914 Brigade	1914 Regiment	1915 Brigade	1915 Regiment	1916 Brigade	1916 Regiment	1917 Brigade	1917 Regiment	1918 Brigade	1918 Regiment
Infantry	13 Bav. Ldw.; 14 Bav. Ldw.; 60 Mixed Ldw.	8 Bav. Ldw., 10 Bav. Ldw.; 15 Bav. Ldw., 122 Ldw.; 60 Ldw., 71 Ldw.	5 Bav. Ldw.; 14 Bav. Ldw.; 13 Bav. Ldw.	4 Bav. Ldw., 5 Bav. Ldw.; 15 Bav. Ldw., 122 Ldw.; 8 Bav. Ldw., 10 Bav. Ldw.	5 Bav. Ldw.; 9 Bav. Mixed Ldw.; 13 Bav. Ldw.	4 Bav. Ldw., 5 Bav. Ldw.; 6 Bav. Ldw., 7 Bav. Ldw; 8 Bav. Ldw., 10 Bav. Ldw., 60 Res.	9 Bav. Ers.	4 Bav. Ldw., 6 Bav. Ldw., 7 Bav. Ldw.	5 Bav. Ldw.	4 Bav. Ldw., 6 Bav. Ldw., 7 Bav. Ldw.
Cavalry	......		1st Sqn. 2d Bav. Corps Dist. Ldw. Rgt.		1st Sqn. 2d Bav. Corps Dist. Ldw. Rgt.		1st Sqn. 8 Bav. Light Cav. Rgt.		1 Sqn. 8 Bav. Light Cav. Rgt.	
Artillery	2 Ldst. F. A. Abtl.		2 Ldst. F. A. Abtl.		1 Bav. Ldw. F. A. Rgt.		Art. Command: 1 Bav. Ldw. F. A. Rgt.		1 Bav. Ldw. F. A. Rgt.	
Engineers and Liaisons.	......		1 Ldw. Pion. Co. (2d Bav. Corps Dist.).		18 Bav. Res. Pion. Co., 3 Bav. Ldw. Pion. Co., 301 Bav. T. M. Co.		(24 Bav.) Eng. Btn., 18 Bav. Res. Pion. Co., 1 Bav. Ldw. Pion. Co., 301 Bav. T. M. Co., 501 Bav. Tel.-Detch.		24 Bav. Pion. Btn.: 18 Bav. Res. Pion. Co., 1 Bav. Ldw. Pion. Co., 24 Bav. Searchlight Section, 4 Bav. Res. Searchlight Section. 501 Bav. Signals Command: 501 Bav. Tel. Detch., 191 Bav. Wireless Detch.	
Medical and Veterinary.							21 Bav. Ambulance Co., 62 Bav. Field Hospital. Vet. Hospital.		21 Bav. Ambulance Co., 61 Bav. Field Hospital, 62 Bav. Field Hospital.	
Transport					38 Railway Const. Co. Ldst. Inf. Btn., Rosenheim (3d Btn. 1 Bav. Corps Dist.), Ldst. Inf. Btn., 2d Augsburg (10th Btn. 1 Bav. Corps Dist.).		325 M. T. Col.			
Attached							154 Labor Btn., 168 Labor Btn.			

HISTORY.

LORRAINE. 1914.

1. The origin of the 1st Bavarian Landwehr Division dates from the stabilization of the Lorraine front after the check of the Germans before Grand-Couronne in September, 1914.

2. At the beginning of the war the different elements which were to enter into the composition of the division were employed in Lorraine in rear of the combatant troops. The 71st Landwehr Regiment came from the war garrison of Strasburg.

3. These elements grouped in three brigades forming the 1st Bavarian Landwehr Division, were brought up to the front early in September and put into line in the Chateau-Salins sector (from Jallaucourt to the Rhine-Marne Canal).

LORRAINE. 1915.

1. From that time on the division occupied the same front in Lorraine, on each side of the Rhine-Marne Canal, broadening or narrowing its front according to the number of troops in line in the region.

2. During the summer of 1915 its limit was carried to the southeast gradually as far as the Luneville-Avricourt railway, next to the region south of Leintrey; to the northeast as far as the western ledge of the Foret de Bezange.

3. In May, 1915, the 60th Landwehr Bde. was detached from the division, and replaced by the 5th Bavarian Landwehr Bde. (4th and 5th Bavarian Landwehr Regiments) coming from the 10th Ersatz Division.

LORRAINE. 1916.

1. South of Leintrey—western edge of the Foret de Bezange. In January, 1916, the 14th Bavarian Landwehr Bde. was detached from the 1st Bavarian Landwehr Division; the 122d Landwehr Regiment (Wurttemburg) passed to the 2d Landwehr Division; the 15th Bavarian Landwehr Regiment to the 39th Bavarian Landwehr Division. The brigade was replaced by the 9th Bavarian Landwehr Bde. (6th and 7th Bavarian Landwehr Regiments). The division thus became entirely Bavarian; it was increased, shortly after, by the addition of the 60th Reserve Regiment, which was later (September) attached to the 221st Division.

2. In July, 1916, the 13th Bavarian Landwehr Bde. was withdrawn from the division and replaced by battalions of Landsturm.

LORRAINE. 1917.

1. In January, 1917, the division's sector was shortened—it was limited on the southeast by the western edge of the Foret de Paroy. In March it ended northwest of Juvrecourt. In June it extended itself once more to the southeast, fixing itself finally in July between Juvrecourt and the eastern edge of the Foret de Paroy; the limits have not varied since then.

2. About the first of the year the 5th Bavarian Landwehr Regiment passed to the 2d Bavarian Landwehr Division (new formation—Russian front).

VALUE—1917 ESTIMATE.

The 1st Bavarian Landwehr Division established itself on the Lorraine front in September, 1914, after the hard fighting in that region had ceased. It executed some important raids with its assault company, notably in June, 1917 (Foret de Paroy), and November (Arracourt region). In general, however, it remained exclusively on the defensive. It is made up of men whose physical value is often diminished; who have, consequently, waged only position warfare, and that upon a defensive front.

LORRAINE. 1918.

1. The division remained in the Parroy sector in Lorraine throughout 1918, and, with the exception of a very few raids executed by the divisional Stosstrupp, did nothing.

VALUE—1918 ESTIMATE.

Losses and reinforcements have been few. The strength of the companies appears to be about 80 men, of an average age of 35–40 years. The 1st Bavarian Landwehr is rated as a fourth-class division.

1st Cavalry Division.

COMPOSITION.

	1918	
	Brigade.	Regiment.
Cavalry	1 Cav. (1 C. Dist.). 2 Cav (1 C. Dist.). 43 Cav. (1 C. Dist..	3 Cuirassier. 1 Drag. 12 Uhlan. 9 Horse Jag. 8 Uhlan (3 and 5 Sqns. detached). 10 Horse Jag.(2 and 3 Sqns. detached)
Artillery	35 Horse Art. Abt.	
Engineers and Liaisons	(?) Dion. Detchs. 347 Searchlight Section.	
Medical and Veterinary	65 Vet. Hospital. 142 Vet. Hospital. 70 Ambulance Co.	
Odd units	152 Cyclist Co. 153 Cyclist Co. 159 Cyclist Co.	
Attached	3 Hus. Rgt. (1, 3, 4, and 6 Sqn.).	

HISTORY.

1918.

1. Throughout 1918 the separate elements of this division were used in police duty in the Ukraine, in Lithuania, and along the Danube.

VALUE—1918 ESTIMATE.

As the division did not operate as a division in 1918, no estimate can be given of its fighting value.

1st Naval Division.
COMPOSITION.

	1914 Brigade	1914 Regiment	1915 Brigade	1915 Regiment	1916 Brigade	1916 Regiment	1917 Brigade	1917 Regiment	1918 Brigade	1918 Regiment
Infantry	1 Nav. 2 Nav.		1 Nav. 2 Nav.		1 Nav. 2 Nav.		1 Nav.		1 Mar.	1 Mat. 2 Mat. 6 Mat.
	The 1, 2, 3, 4, 5, and 6th Marine Fus. Rgts. and the 4th Marine Inf. Rgt. alternated between the 1st and 2d Naval Division.									
Cavalry	1 Ldw. Sqn. (10 C. Dist.).						4 Sqn. 6 Cuirassier Rgt.			
Artillery	1 and 2 Ldw. F. A. Detch. (10 C. Dist.).		Nav. Brig.: 1 Nav. F. A. Rgt. 2 Nav. F. A. Rgt. Torpedo-Matrosen Art. Rgt.		1 Nav. F. A. Rgt. 2 Nav. F. A. Rgt. 3 Nav. F. A. Rgt. Torpedo-Matrosen Art. Rgt.		288 Ldw. F. A. Rgt. Torpedo-Matrosen Art. Rgt.		Mar. F. A. Rgt. 1 Mat. A. Rgt. Marine Corps 1st Ft. A. M. Col. 2 Light A. Col. of the Mar. F. A. Rgt.	
Engineers and Liaisons.					1 Nav. Pion. Co. 2 Nav. Pion. Co. 165 T. M. Co.		1 Nav. Pion. Btn.: 1 Nav. Pion. Co. 2 Nav. Pion. Co. 337 Pion. Co. 165 Nav. T. M. Co. Tel. Detch.		1 Mar. Pion. Btn.: 1 Mar. Pion. Co. 4 Mar. Pion. Co. 2 Entrenching Co. 291 Mar. Signal Command: 291 Mar. Tel. Detch. 291 Wireless Detch.	
Medical and Veterinary.							Ambulance Co. 1 Nav. Field Hospital. Vet. Hospital.		1 Mar. Ambulance Co. 1 Mar. Field Hospital. Vet. Hospital (Ostend).	
Transports.							M. T. Col.			
Odd units.									1 Sect. Flanders Reconnaissance Flight. 2 Sect. Flanders Reconnaissance Flight.	
Attached.					124 Labor Btn.		41 Cyclist Co.			

HISTORY.

1914-1917.

1. BELGIUM. At the beginning of the war the Field Army contained only one naval division. This division entered Belgium on September 4, 1914, detrained at Brussels, and on September 6 took up its position to the left of the corps which was besieging Antwerp. After the taking of the city on October 10 the division marched along the coast, arrived at a point between Ostend and Bruges on October 23, and on November 2 relieved the 4th Ersatz Division on the front of Nieuport-St. Georges.

2. On November 24, 1914, the Naval Corps was formed by adding a 2d Naval Division to the 1st.

3. After this time the Naval Corps occupied the sea front and the sector of the coast in occupied Flanders. The staffs of the 1st and 2d Naval Divisions were permanently in command of this sector—the sea front (from Raversyde to the frontier of Zeeland as far as Maldegem was assigned to the 1st Naval Division; the front on land from the North Sea to Schoorbakke, 4 kilometers southeast Nieuport, to the 2d Naval Division). The six regiments of Marine Fusileers alternated between the two sectors, and consequently changed from one division to the other.

4. In April, 1917, the three naval infantry regiments were withdrawn from the 1st and 2d Naval Divisions to organize a new Division, the 3d Naval Division. These regiments had already formed a provisional division, from the end of September, 1916, to January, 1917, when they were engaged on the Somme. After fighting east of Ypres (August to November, 1917), the 3d Naval Division came into line at Nieuport (Lombartzyde) to the right of the 2d Naval Division in December.

VALUE—1917 ESTIMATE.

The Marine or Sailor Fusileers, recruited at the beginning of the war from among the seamen or the population of the ports, had only a mediocre combat value at the time.

Since 1917, in consequence of reinforcements taken from the land army, and also in consequence of reducing the age of the effectives, the regiments of Naval Fusileers seem to be of better quality.

From a recruiting standpoint, they may be compared with the active divisions of the German Army.

1918.

1. The division was out of line in 1918 until May 1. From that date until November 4 it held the extreme right of the German line.

VALUE—1918 ESTIMATE.

The division was rated as fourth class. Until the last month of the war its front was quiet.

125651°—20——4

2d Guard Division.
COMPOSITION.

	1914 Brigade.	1914 Regiment.	1915 Brigade.	1915 Regiment.	1916 Brigade.	1916 Regiment.	1917 Brigade.	1917 Regiment.	1918 Brigade.	1918 Regiment.
Infantry	3 Gd 4 Gd. 5 Gd.	1 Gren. 3 Gren. 4 Gren. 5 Gren. 5 Ft.	3 Gd. 4 Gd.	1 Gren. 3 Gren. 2 Gren. 4 Gren.	3 Gd. 4 Gd.	1 Gren. 3 Gren. 2 Gren. 4 Gren.	3 Gd.	1 Gren. 2 Gren. 4 Gren.	3 Gd.	1 Gren. 2 Gren. 4 Gren.
Cavalry			4 Gd. Brig.: Body Guard Hus. Rgt. 2 Gd. Uhlan Rgt.		Cav. Rgt. Schlotheim. 2 and 5 Sqns. 2 Gd. Uhlan Rgt. 1 Sqn. 6 Drag. Rgt. Ers. Sqn. 2 Uhlan Rgt. Ers. Sqn. 1 Horse Jag. Rgt.		1 Sqn. 6 Drag. Rgt.		1 Sqn. Body Gd. Hus. Rgt.	
Artillery	2 Gd. Brig.: 2 Gd. F. A. Rgt. 4 Gd. F. A. Rgt.		2 Gd. Brig.: 2 Gd. F. A. Rgt. 4 Gd. F. A. Rgt.		2 Gd. Brig.: 2 Gd. F. A. Rgt. 4 Gd. F. A. Rgt.		2 Gd. Art. Command.: 2 Gd. F. A. Rgt.		2 Gd. F. A. Rgt. 3 Abt. 3 Ft. A. Rgt. (Staff, 10, 11, and 12 Btries.). 535 Ft. A. Btry. 965 Light Am. Col. 1385 Light Am. Col. 1386 Light Am. Col.	
Engineers and liaisons.			1 Gd. Eng. Btn.: Field Co. Gd. Pion. Btn. 2 Gd. Pont. Engrs. 2 Gd. Tel. Detch.		1 Gd. Eng. Btn.: 2 Co. Gd. Pion. Btn. 1 Co. 28 Pion. Btn. 281 Pion. Co. 2 Gd. Pont. Engs. 2 Gd. Tel. Detch. 2 Gd. T. M. Co.		102 Eng. Btn.: 2 Co. Gd. Pion. Btn. 3 Co. Gd. Pion. Btn. 2 Gd. T. M. Co. 278, 281, and 298 Search- light Sections. 2 Gd. Tel. Detch.		102 Pion. Btn.: 2 Co. Gd. Pions. 3 Co. Gd. Pions. 211 Searchlight Section 2 Gd. Signals Command.: 2 Gd. Tel. Detch. 78 Wireless Detch.	
Medical and Veterinary.							2 Ambulance Co. 2 Field Hospital. 3 Field Hospital. 2 Gd. Vet. Hospital.		2 Ambulance Co. 2 Field Hospital. 3 Field Hospital. 2 Gd. Vet. Hospital.	

Attached.....

2 M. G. S. S. Detch.
1 Abtl. 43 Res. F. A. Rgt.
3 Abtl. 43 Res. F. A. Rgt.
1 Abtl. 16 Ft. A. Rgt.
2 Abtl. 11 Res. Ft. A. Rgt.
  with transport.
10 Btry. 13 Res. Ft. A. Rgt.
190 Ft. Btry.
9 Btry. 12 Res. Ft. A. Rgt.
  with transport.
1 Btry. 57 Ldw. Ft. A. Rgt.
3 Co. 87 Labor Btn.
1 Co. 8 Ammunition Train.
1133 Wireless Detch. (from 27
  Div.).
289 Pigeon Loft.
3 Balloon Section.
327 Ammunition Train.
191 M. T. Col.
216 M. T. Col.
853 M. T. Col.
865 M. T. Col.
188 Depot Supply Train.

HISTORY.

1914.

FRANCE.

1. Entrained August 9 to 11 (notebooks). Detrained at Beutgenbach (12 kilos east of Malmedy). Entered Belgium August 14. Crossed the Meuse at Huy August 18. Crossed the Sambre at Auvelais (Aug. 22) on the right of the 1st Guard Division. Fought at Falisolle and Aisemont the 23d; at Mettet the 24th. Fought on the 29th at Haution and Vallee-aux-Bleds; on the 30th at St. Pierre (west of Vervins), on the left of the 1st Guard Division.

2. From there via Lugny, Boncourt, La Malmaison, Ville-aux-Bois, Sarcy, Epernay, Avize, Vertus; fought after September 6 at Ecury-le-Repos and Normee.

3. Retreated on the 9th at Vertus; 10th at Tauxieres; 11th at Thuizy. Was before Reims until September 30.

4. In Artois in October (Bucquoy, Monchy-aux-Bois, Adinfer), near the 1st Guard Division. Split up in November like the latter; sent one of its brigades, the 4th, in the region of Ypres (Gheluvelt), and remained there until the end of December.

1915.

RUSSIA.

1. In January the division was again assembled. At rest at Douai from the end of January till the middle of February. On the Monchy-aux-Bois-Puisieux front till the end of March. Entrained March 30 at Cambrai for Schelestadt (Alsace), where it was placed at rest.

2. In April transferred to Galicia (Neu-Samdek, Apr. 26–30).

3. Beginning on May 2 it took part in Mackensen's offensive—Battle of Gorlitz, May 2–3; at Jaroslav, May 16; battle of Krasnostav, July 17; crossed the Bug August 24. At Zegrje, on the Narew, September 14.

4. On September 16 it returned to Novo-Georgievsk and entrained for the western front. Detrained at Nivelles September 20.

FRANCE–LORETTE.

5. The division was at rest for one month in Belgium.

6. On October 25 entrained for Orchies and reached Henin-Lietard by stages and fought at Lorette on November 5 for 6 days. It suffered casualties again there.

7. The division went into line in the region between Noyon and Roye.

1916.

FRANCE–SOMME.

1. The 2d Guard Division remained in the sector of the region Noyon-Roye until August, 1916.

2. On August 15 it was sent to the Somme region (Chilly), where it suffered heavy losses both to the north and to the south of Peronne.

3. From October 1 to the end of December, 1916, it fought for a second time south of Peronne.

1917.

1. At the end of January the division was sent to rest near Guise. To the east of Clery-sur-Somme, end of February.

2. Then it held the Siegfried line, near Roisel and St. Quentin, for five or six days (beginning of March).

3. Entrained for Vervins and sent back to rest (Mar. 16 to Apr. 12).

CHEMIN DES DAMES.

4. About April 12 the division was sent to Sissonne. Went into line between Hurtebise and Craonne (Apr. 20 to 22), supporting or relieving the units of the 5th Guard Division. It remained for three weeks in the region of Craonne and Amifontaine. It suffered new losses and still heavier ones on Californie Plateau.

5. On May 11 the division went to the Argonne by road (La Harazee, May 17) and was reorganized, receiving replacements from the 613th, 614th, and 615th Regiments, which were dissolved.

RUSSIA.

6. Withdrawn from the line at the beginning of July and entrained for the eastern front (from July 4 to 10), via Charleville, Givet, Namur, Liege, Herbestal, Hanover, Berlin, Posen, Skalmiercyze, Ozidof.

7. Took part in the attack on the Sereth (July 19); relieved August 1 and sent to rest.

RIGA.

8. On August 9 entrained at Horlodylow and took part in the attack on Uxkull (Sept. 1). On the 4th it entered Riga.

FRANCE.

9. From September 7 to 9 the division entrained for France, via Zanke, Mitaul Vilna, Kovno, Posen, Berlin, Hanover, Dusseldorf, Aix-la-Chapelle, Liege, Namur, Givet, Charleville.

LA MALMAISON.

Beginning September 21 it was sent to Laon. About the 28th it went into line in the Malmaison sector. On October 23 the French attack commenced and caused them very heavy losses (1,860 prisoners, of whom 50 officers, and many wounded). Relieved on the 25th and its regiments, much reduced in strength, were sent to the region of Vervins.

11. In the middle of November it held the sector of St. Mihiel, Forests of Apremont. The regiment received replacements from the interior and from the Russian front taken from the 226th Division.

VALUE—1917 ESTIMATE.

The 2d Guard Division had the reputation of being a good division. It suffered heavy losses in the Aisne sector in May, 1917. However, even after this attack the morale of the men on the whole seemed quite high. At the Malmaison attack, October 3, the troops of the division, after three days, were completely defeated.

During the last battles the division showed only moderate fighting value.

1918.

1. The 2d Guard Division was relieved by the 201st Division January 11 and went to rest at Metz.

2. Here the division underwent a 10 weeks' course of training. March 18 it entrained at Metz and traveled via Thionville to St. Amand, where it detrained on the evening of March 19. It went then via Marchiennes (Mar. 20–21), Montigny (Mar. 21–22), to Lambres, where it arrived the evening of March 22. After 5 days' rest here the division moved up to the line at Vitry-en-Artois (Mar. 27) to reinforce the front for the attack north of the Scarpe on the 28th. Except for one battalion of the 1st Guard Grenadier Regiment, the division took part in the fighting, as the attack was unsuccessful.

OREUIL.

3. The following day it marched via Arleux-Morchies-Beaumetz-Haplincourt-Le Transloy-Les Boeufs-Maricourt, crossing the Somme at Suzanne-Proyart-Framerville-Aix-Mézières. It went into reserve east of Mailly-Raineval, where it remained until April 5, when it came into line north of Rouvrel. It was relieved by the 6th Reserve Division May 2.

AISNE.

4. The division reinforced the Aisne battle front about May 26 to the west of Vailly. It was relieved, June 17, by the 40th Division.

MARNE.

5. After a rest in the Marle region the division reinforced the front near Chatillon-sur-Marne July 15.   It was withdrawn on the 22d.

SOMME.

6. August 27 the division reinforced the front south of the Somme near Dompierre. It was relieved, September 3, by the Alpine Corps, after suffering heavy losses, and losing 1,450 prisoners.

LE CATELET.

7. During the night of September 11–12 it reinforced the front near Ronssoy (west of Le Catelet).   It was withdrawn October 9.

YPRES.

8. After resting a fortnight the division relieved the 52d Reserve Division at Machelen, October 24.   It was relieved by the 6th Cavalry Division November 4, and did not return to line.

VALUE—1918 ESTIMATE.

The 2d Guard Division is rated as a first-class assault division.   It participated in a great deal of heavy fighting during 1918 and always acquitted itself very well. It was mentioned in the official communiqués on several occasions.   Between the end of August and October 9 it had lost 2,800 in prisoners alone.   Indeed, its losses must have been very heavy, since there is positive evidence at hand to show that it received 4,000 replacements between August 10 and October 10.

2d Guard Reserve Division.

COMPOSITION.

	1914 Brigade	1914 Regiment	1915 Brigade	1915 Regiment	1916 Brigade	1916 Regiment	1917 Brigade	1917 Regiment	1918 Brigade	1918 Regiment
Infantry	26 Res. 38 Res. 10 Res. Jag. Btn.	15 Res. 55 Res. 77 Res. 91 Res.	26 Res. 38 Res. 10 Res. Jag. Btn.	15 Res. 55 Res. 77 Res. 91 Res.	26 Res. 38 Res.	15 Res. 55 Res. 77 Res. 91 Res.	38 Res.	15 Res. 77 Res. 91 Res.	38 Res.	15 Res. 77 Res. 91 Res.
Cavalry		2 Res. Uhlan Rgt. (3 Sqns.).						2d Sqn. 2 Res. Uhlan Regt.	4 Cav. Sqn.	
Artillery	20 Res. F. A. Rgt. (6 Btries.).					20 Res. F. A. Rgt.	8 Gd. Art. Command: 20 Res. F. A. Rgt. (9 Btries.).		116 Art. Command: 20 Res. F. A. Rgt. 2 Abt. 23 Ft. A. Rgt. (4 and 6 Btries.). 714 Light Am. Col. 911 Light Am. Col. 1237 Light Am. Col.	
Engineers and Liaisons	4 Field Co. 2d Pion. Btn. No. 10.		4 Field Co. 2d Pion. Btn. No. 10.		4 and 6 Field Cos. 2 Pion. Btn. No. 10. 2 Gd. Res. Pontoon Engs. 2 Gd. Res. Tel. Detch.		4 and 6 Field Cos. Pion. Btn. No. 10. 6 Gd. T. M. Co. 260 Searchlight section. 402 Tel. Detch. (Gd.).		302 Pion. Btn.: 6 Co. 10 Pions. 6 Gd. T. M. Co. 212 Searchlight section. 402 Gd. Signals Commands: 402 Tel. Detch. 21 Wireless Detch.	
Medical and Veterinary							268 Ambulance Co. 339, 390, 17, and 45 Res. Field Hospitals. Vet. Hospital.		268 Ambulance Co. 45 Res. Field Hospital. 17 Res. Field Hospital. 204 Vet. Hospital.	
Transport							M. T. Col.		702 M. T. Col.	

HISTORY.

(15th Reserve: Eighth District—Westphalia. 77th and 91st Reserve: Tenth District—Hanover.)

1914.

BELGIUM.

1. At the beginning of the war the 2d Reserve Guard Division was grouped with the 19th Reserve Division in the 10th Reserve Corps. This corps formed a part of the Second German Army (Von Bülow).

The division entrained at Zulpich August 10, entered Belgium the 14th, passed the Meuse near Liege the 17th, surrounded Namur on the north, crossed the Sambre to the west of Charleroi on the 22d, fought at Marbaix the 23d, and the 29th and 30th at Ribemont and St. Quentin.

MARNE–CHAMPAGNE.

2. The 2d Reserve Guard Division was engaged in the battle of the Marne between Sezanne and Montmirail (Sept. 6–7). It retreated through Epernay and fought on the Rheims front. It held its position on this front (Courcy sector) up to the month of February, 1915.

1915.

ARTOIS.

1. Toward the middle of February, 1915, the two brigades of the 2d Reserve Guard Division were separated. The 26th Brigade went into the line between Thiescourt and the Oise and the 38th Brigade went to the forest of the Argonne.

2. Regrouped in Alsace in the vicinity of Schlestadt toward the end of April, the 2d Reserve Guard Division was transported about May 20 to the district of La Bassee. It was engaged in the Cuinchy-Givenchy sector (June–July).

3. About the 1st of August the division was sent to rest east of Cambrai.

4. In September it occupied the sector of Vingles-Hulluch to the south of the La Bassee Canal. September 25–26 it took part in the third battle of the Artois and suffered great losses. Portions of the 2d Reserve Guard Division participated in the attack near Loos October 8.

5. The division remained in the district of La Bassee up to April, 1916.

1916.

SOMME.

1. The 2d Reserve Guard Division was relieved about April 7 of the Cuichy-Canal sector of La Bassee. After a rest in Belgium in the vicinity of Tournai, the division was placed in the Gommecourt sector (Somme), end of May.

2. The Franco-British offensive found it in this sector July 1. It was severely engaged from July to November, 1916, sometimes in the vicinity of Pozieres, Thiepval, Bazentin-le-Petit (from July to September), sometimes farther north, and suffered serious losses (51 per cent of its personnel).

3. The 2d Reserve Guard Division was maintained in the Gommecourt-Hebuterne sector during the entire winter of 1916–17. At the end of 1916 it ceded the 55th Reserve Infantry to the 220th Division (organization).

. 1917.

HINDENBURG LINE.

1. The middle of March, 1917, the 2d Reserve Guard Division participated in the retreat of the German Army; it went back through Bucquoy, Lagnicourt, Beaumetzles-Cambrai toward the Hindenburg line. It established itself on this line between Queant and Boursies until the end of May.

FLANDERS.

2. At the beginning of June the division remained at rest several days in the vicinity of Cambrai, and was then transported to the Thielt (Pitthem-Eeghem) district (end of June). At the beginning of July it approached the front toward Staden.

3. On July 31, certain elements of the division, being surprised and later reassembled on the western border of the Houthulst forest, counter attacked in the direction of Bixschoote and suffered rather heavy losses.

4. The 2d Reserve Guard Division remained in this sector eight days. It was relieved August 8–9 and sent to rest in the district of Gand (Lakeren-Ostnieuwecerke) till the beginning of September.

5. About the 10th of September it was sent into the line on the front west of Passchendaele (southeast of St. Julien). It was withdrawn from this position toward the end of the month in order to go in again, almost immediately, to the southeast of Armentieres.

6. It remained there until the end of November, after which it reappeared on the front west and north of Passchendaele in December.

7. It was relieved February 1, 1918, and went into the district of Roulers.

VALUE—1917 ESTIMATE.

The 2d Reserve Guard Division was always considered as being an excellent division because it had always fought well, though it showed only mediocre fighting qualities to the north of Ypres in 1917.

The 31st of July it counterattacked without energy and without success in the direction of Bixschoote. During the approach, a great number of men remained in the rear.

Following this, its attitude was passive.

1918.

FLANDERS.

1. The division remained in the Passchendaele sector until withdrawn about January 9.

2. It came back into line, relieving the 199th Division, during the night of January 23–24, north of Passchendaele. It was relieved by the 239th Division February 1.

3. February 7 it relieved the 239th Division; relieved by 41st Division March 3. It then was trained for a fortnight.

CAMBRAI.

4. March 21 the division reinforced the Cambrai front near St. Léger, fighting, with heavy losses, until the 26th.

ARRAS.

5. It came back into line west of Neuville-Vitasse about April 3, relieving the 236th Division. April 29 the division was relieved by the extension of the fronts of the neighboring divisions.

6. It went to the Douai area and rested there until coming into line in the Gavrelle sector during the night of June 7–8; it relieved the 187th Division. It was relieved by the 187th Division June 20 and went to be reconstituted in the Tournai area, receiving a draft from the 427th Infantry Regiment and another of over 500 men from Germany.

7. The division relieved the 5th Bavarian Reserve Division, near Bucquoy, August 7. During the heavy fighting that followed it lost 2,400 in prisoners alone. It was withdrawn August 25.

8. September 2 it reinforced the front near the Arras-Cambrai road, whence it was withdrawn about the middle of the month.

LA BASSÉE.

9. It then relieved the 9th Reserve Division near Neuve-Chapelle September 26.

FLANDERS.

10. October 5 prisoners belonging to the division were identified near Ledeghem
It remained there, being identified by prisoners November 11.

VALUE—1918 ESTIMATE.

The general commanding the 2d Guard Reserve Division was decorated in February
and again in May. The last decoration was Pour le Mérite, and was accompanied
by promotion. August 15 Gen. Petersdorff reprimanded the division because, as he
said, "within 14 days, 1 noncommissioned officer and 10 other ranks have been missing
from the division * * *." It is considered as a second-class division.

2d Division.

COMPOSITION.

	1914 Brigade.	1914 Regiment.	1915 Brigade.	1915 Regiment.	1916 Brigade.	1916 Regiment.	1917 Brigade.	1917 Regiment.	1918 Brigade.	1918 Regiment.
Infantry	3. 4.	4 Gren. 44. 33 Fus. 45.	3. 4.	4 Gren. 44. 33 Fus. 45.	3.	4 Gren. 33 Fus. 44. 3 Landst.	3.	4 Gren. 33 Fus. 44.	3.	4 Gren. 33 Fus. 44.
Cavalry		10 Horse Jag. Rgt.					10 Horse Jag. Rgt. (2d Sqn.).		10 Horse Jag. Rgt. (2 Sqn.).	
Artillery	2 Brig.; 1 F. A. Rgt. 37 F. A. Rgt.		2 Brig.; 1 F. A. Rgt. 37 F. A. Rgt.		2 Brig.; 1 F. A. Rgt. 37 F. A. Rgt.		2 Art. Command: 1 F. A. Rgt.		2 Art. Command: 1 F. A. Rgt. 4 Abt. 6 Res. Ft. A. Rgt. 872 Light Am. Col. 1,364 Light Am. Col. 1,392 Light Am. Col.	
Engineers and liaisons.			1 Pion. Btn. No. 1: Field Co. 1 Pion. Btn. 2 Pontoon, Engrs. 2 Tel. Detch.		1 Pion. Btn. No. 1: 2 Co. 1 Pion. Btn. 2 T. M. Co. 2 Pontoon, Engrs. 2 Tel. Detch.		1 Pion. Btn. No. 1: 2 Co. 1 Pion. 4 Co. 1 Pion. 2 T. M. Co. 2 Searchlight Section. 2 Tel. Detch.		1 Pion. Btn.: 2 Co. 1 Pion. 4 Co. 1 Pion. 2 Searchlight Section. 2 Signals Command. 2 Tel. Detch. 159 Wireless Detch.	
Medical and veterinary.							Ambulance Co. 11 Field Hospital. 12 Field Hospital. 195 Vet. Hospital.		5 Ambulance Co. 11 Field Hospital. 12 Field Hospital. 195 Vet. Hospital.	
Transport							535 M. T. Col.		535 M. T. Col.	
Attached							150 Bav. Anti-Aircraft Section. Cyclist Detch. 2 Landst. Btn.			

HISTORY.

(First District—Oriental Prussia.)

1914.

The first and second divisions formed the 1st Army Corps.

RUSSIA.

1. At the beginning of the war the 2d Division was sent to the Russian front. Up to the month of November it participated in the operations in Oriental Prussia (Tannenberg, Aug. 27–29).

2. In November, 1914, the 2d Division, minus one brigade, which continued to hold its old sector, was withdrawn and included in the group which attacked in the direction of Lodz and operated between the Vistula and the Warta; continuing its activities, it attempted to cross the Bzura-Rawka opposite Warsaw in the district of Lowicz.

1915.

1. At the beginning of February, 1915, it reappeared in Oriental Prussia and participated in the offensive which ejected the Russians from this Province. It was engaged in its entirety in the district of Lyck and marched upon Augustowo and Grodno.

2. The Russian counter attack launched in the vicinity of Prasnysz toward the end of March drew the 2d Division to this sector.

3. In July during the development of the Hindenburg offensive, it emerged from the Ostrolenka-Pultusk line and proceeded in a northerly direction.

4. Upon the stabilization of the front the 2d Division held a sector between Illukst and Lake Drisviaty (Dwinsk District).

1916.

1. At the end of July, 1916, portions of the 2d Division were assigned to duty in Galicia to oppose the Russian advance.

1917.

1. The reconstituted 2d Division was engaged in the Mitau sector up to the end of January, 1917; all its units were identified in the vicinity of Kalnzen.

2. On February 8 it entrained at Mitau for the western front. (Itinerary: Chavli, Kovno, Insterburg, Königsberg, Stettin, Hamburg, Münster, Aix-la-Chapelle, Liège, Louvain, Bruxelles, Audenarde.)

BELGIUM.

3. Detrained February 13 and remained at rest up to the end of March. It received reinforcements of various classes of men (wounded, convalescents, class 1917 reservists).

4. The division occupied the Wytschaete sector from the 25th of March to the beginning of June. (On April 15 and May 10 and 15 it received the first reinforcements from the class of 1918, the last having had only three months' instruction; in all, 4,460 men between January 1 and June 1.) On June 7 it left 2,825 men in the hands of British troops.

5. On June 10 the 2d Division retired from the Belgian front. It was placed at rest in the district of Audenarde in June and then entrained for the eastern front (end of June).

RUSSIA.

6. It arrived in Russia at the beginning of July and was put at rest in the district of Vilna. On July 14 it was identified in the Illukst District.

FRANCE.

7. It returned to France on the 25th of November. It entrained on this date at Kovno and was transported over the following itinerary: Insterburg, Thorn, Posen, Frankfort-sur-Oder, Berlin, Paderborn, Crefeld, Aix-la-Chapelle, Liège, Namur, Vouziers (Nov. 30).

8. On December 27 it relieved the 1st Bavarian Division in the Souain-Somme-Py sector.

VALUE—1917 ESTIMATE.

Except during the period March-June, 1917, when the 2d Division was fighting in Belgium, it continuously occupied the Russian front from the beginning of the war till December, 1917.

1918.

CHAMPAGNE.

1. The 2d Division remained in line in the Souaine-Somme-Py region until relieved by the 87th Division about April 2. It went back to the Army depot at Semide, where it stayed about a week drilling and maneuvering. April 10 it entrained at Machault, and went via Rethel, Liart, Marle, and detrained at La Ferté-Chevresis, encamping in the vicinity. It traveled by St. Simon (Apr. 11), Ham, Solente (5 km. east of Roye), and Laboissiére, where it stayed until April 30.

MONTDIDIER.

2. May 1 the division relieved the 51st Reserve Division at Monchel, south of Montdidier; relieved August 31.

ST. QUENTIN.

3. The division was identified in line near Essigny-le-Grand, south of St. Quentin, September 5; it was relieved about the 15th by the extension of the fronts of the neighboring divisions.

4. During the night of September 20-21 it went back into line north of St. Quentin, in the Bellenglise sector. It was withdrawn about the 10th.

5. The division rested for a fortnight in the Avesnes area, then came into line October 24, relieving the 19th Reserve Division east of Ribemont (southeast of St. Quentin). It was withdrawn from line early in November and did not return.

VALUE—1918 ESTIMATE.

The 2d is rated as a third-class division. It was used in a great deal of heavy fighting and suffered severe losses (July 23 it lost 54 officers and 1,800 men in prisoners alone west of the Avre; the 9th and 10th of August it lost 443 prisoners; in its engagements between August 8 and October 1 it lost over 1,500 prisoners). Nevertheless, it was never used as an attacking division, but confined itself to holding the sectors allotted it; on account of its weakened condition and lowered morale (there are several cases of insubordination on record), it did not acquit itself any too well.

2d Landwehr Division.

COMPOSITION.

	1914		1915		1916		1917		1918	
	Brigade.	Regiment.	Brigade.	Regiment.	Brigade.	Regiment.	Brigade.	Regiment.	Brigade.	Regiment.
Infantry	53 Mixed Ldw. 9 Bav. Mixed Ldw.	124 Ldw. 125 Ldw. 6 Bav. Ldw. 7 Bav. Ldw.	53 Mixed Ldw. 9 Bav. Mixed Ldw.	124 Ldw. 125 Ldw. 6 Bav. Ldw. 7 Bav. Ldw.	53 Mixed Ldw. (-)	124 Ldw. 125 Ldw. 120 Ldw. 122 Ldw. 6 Res. Jäg. Btn.	54 Ldw.	120 Ldw. 122 Ldw. 125 Ldw.	54 Ldw.	120 Ldw. 122 Ldw. 125 Ldw.
Cavalry	3 Ldw. Sqn. (13 C. Dist.).		3 Ldw. Sqn. (13 C. Dist.).		3 Ldw. Sqn. (13 C. Dist.). 3 Landst. Sqn. (13 C. Dist.).		3 Ldw. Sqn. (13 C. Dist.). 4 Sqn. 20 Uhlan Rgt.		4 Sqn. 20 Uhlan Rgt.	
Artillery	1 Ldw. Btry. Landst. Btn. (13 C. Dist.).		1 Ldw. Btry. Landst. Btn. (13 C. Dist.).		2 Ldw. Rgt.		142 Art. Command: 2 Ldw. Rgt.		2 Ldw. F. A. Rgt.	
Engineers and Liaisons.					6 Co. 13 Pion. 3 Co. 13 Pion. 302 T. M. Co.		(402) Eng. Btn.: 1 Ldw. Co. 13 Pion. 5 Ldw. Co. 13 Pion. 302 T. M. Co. 299 Searchlight Section. 502 Tel. Detach.		402 Pion. Btn.: 1 Ldw. Co. 13 C. Dist. Pions. 5 Ldw. Co. 13 C. Dist. Pions. 302 T. M. Co. 224 Searchlight Section. 502 Signals Command. 502 Tel. Detach. 176 Wireless Detach.	
Medical and Veterinary.							572 Ambulance Co. Ldw. Field Hosp. Vet. Hospital.		572 Ambulance Co. 254 Field Hospital. 25 Ldw. Field Hospital. 502 Vet. Hospital.	
Transport.							722 M. T. Col.		772 M. T. Col.	

HISTORY.

(Thirteenth District—Wurttemberg.)

1914.

ʀGONNE.

1. The 2d Landsturm Division (Franke Division) forms a part of the Argonne ɔup and has continuously occupied sectors of this district since September, 1914. ɪ the beginning of the campaign it comprised a Wurttemberg and a Bavarian bri- de. Engaged at Etain August 24, 1914, it crossed the Meuse at Stenay on the 31st. 2. Beginning with September it occupied the line in the woods of Cheppy and ılancourt.

1915.

ʀGONNE.

1. Vauquois-bois de Malancourt sector.
2. At the end of September, 1915, portions of the division (one battalion of the ı and one of the 7th Bavarian Landsturm) were assigned to service in the district Massiges; they rejoined the Vauquois sector at the end of October.

1916.

ʀGONNE.

1. Vauquois-bois d'Avocourt and Malancourt sector.
2. At the beginning of 1916 the 2d Landsturm Division was reconstituted with clusively Wurttemberg elements, including the 120th Landsturm, withdrawn ɪm the Bavarian Ersatz Division, and the 122d Landsturm, proceeding from the 1st ɪvarian Landsturm Division. The 9th Bavarian brigade went over to the 1st ɪvarian Landsturm Division.

1917.

ʀGONNE.

1. In the Cheppy-bois d'Avocourt wood sector.
2. At the end of August, 1917, the 2d Landsturm Division changed places with ə 2d Bavarian Division and took the Nord Four sector of Paris-Bolante-Courte- ɪausse.

VALUE—1917 ESTIMATE.

3ector division. Did not leave Argonne from the beginning of the war. On ʋeral occasions it furnished young men to active and reserve Wurttemberg regi- ɪnts, replacing them by older Landsturm men.

1918.

ʀGONNE.

Γhe division remained in line in the Apremont sector, engaging in but little activity til the American attack of September 26. From that time on until it was with- ɪwn, October 25, it fought a great deal.

VALUE—1918 ESTIMATE.

Vlost of the young men of the division were taken from it to be sent to other organi- ɪons early in the year. October 12 the corps commander telegraphed the King of ɪrttemberg (the 2d Landwehr Division comes from Wurttemberg): "The 2d Land- hr Division * * * has particularly distinguished itself by its bravery and in- pidity during the last combats in the Argonne and has thus contributed toward the lure of the enemy's attempt to break through." It was badly used on the opening y of the American attack, but it fought hard. It loaned companies to various other ʁisions, including the 1st and 5th Guard Divisions, and for days at a time these ɪndwehr troops were making the greatest resistance in the Aire Valley. While ə division lost only 795 prisoners during the offensive, its total losses undoubtedly ɪ above 5,000, there being evidence to show that many companies did not have ʁe than 25 men, there being only three companies per battalion, and—in at least ə case—only two battalions in the regiment. It is rated as a fourth-class division.

2d Bavarian Division.

COMPOSITION.

	1914 Brigade	1914 Regiment	1915 Brigade	1915 Regiment	1916 Brigade	1916 Regiment	1917 Brigade	1917 Regiment	1918 Brigade	1918 Regiment
Infantry	3 Bav. 4 Bav.	3 Bav. 20 Bav. 12 Bav. 15 Bav.	3 Bav. 4 Bav.	3 Bav. 20 Bav. 12 Bav. 15 Bav.	4 Bav.	12 Bav. 15 Bav. 20 Bav.	4 Bav.	12 Bav. 15 Bav. 20 Bav.	4 Bav.	12 Bav. 15 Bav. 20 Bav.
Cavalry		4 Bav. Light Cav. Rgt.				3 Sqns. 4 Bav. Light Cav. Rgt.		2 and 3 Sqns. 8 Bav. Light Cav. Rgt.		3 Sqns. 8 Bav. Light Cav. Rgt.
Artillery	2 Bav. Brig.:	4 Bav. F. A. Rgt. 9 Bav. F. A. Rgt.	2 Bav. Brig.:	4 Bav. F. A. Rgt. 9 Bav. F. A. Rgt.	2 Bav. Brig.: 2 Bav. F. A. Rgt. 9 Bav. F. A. Rgt.		2 Bav. Art. Command: 9 Bav. F. A. Rgt.		2 Bav. Art. Command: 9 Nav. F. A. Rgt. 1 Abt. 3 Bav. Res. Ft. A. Rgt.	151 Bav. Light Am. Col. 153 Bav. Light Am. Col. 160 Bav. Light Am. Col.
Engineers and Liaisons.	2 Field Co. 1 Bav. Pion. Btn.		2 Field Co. 1 Bav. Pion. Btn. 2 Bav. Pont. Engs. 2 Bav. Tel. Detch.		2 and 4 Field Cos. 1 Bav. Pion. Btn. 2 Res. Co. 19 Pions. 2 Bav. T. M. Co. 2 Bav. Pont. Engs. 2 Bav. Tel. Detch.		2 and 4 Bav. Pion. Cos. 2 Bav. T. M. Co. 2 Bav. Tel. Detch.		7 Bav. Pion. Btn. 2 Bav. Pion. Co. 4 Bav. Pion. Co. 2 Bav. T. M. Co. 2 Bav. Signals Command: 2 Bav. Tel. Detch. 107 Wireless Detch.	
Medical and Veterinary.							2 Bav. Ambulance Co. Field Hospital. Vet. Hospital.		2 Bav. Ambulance Co. 6 Bav. Field Hospital. 8 Bav. Field Hospital.	
Transport.							M. T. Col.		682 M. T. Col.	

HISTORY.

(First Bavarian District—Southwest of Bavaria, Bavarian Swabia.)

1914.

LORRAINE.

1. At the beginning of August the 2d Bavarian Division which, with the 1st Bavarian Division, formed the 1st Bavarian Corps, was a part of the army of the Crown Prince of Bavaria (6th Army). The 3d Brigade, covering troops, detrained at Reding near Saarburg, the 3d of August. On the 9th the division was at its full strength. It proceeded to the frontier, reached Badonviller, and retired as far as Gosselming (west of Saarburg) the 17th of August, gave battle there on the 20th, and recrossed the frontier. It advanced as far as Xaffevillers (Sept. 7), whence it retired to Morhange (Sept. 10). On September 15 the division entrained at Metz. It detrained near Namur, gained Peronne by stages, and was engaged at Foucaucourt the 24th.

SOMME.

2. Together with the 1st Bavarian Corps it was attached to the 2d Army (Von Bülow), operating on the Somme in the district of Peronne. It took part in the fiercely contested battles which took place there but a short time after the stabilization of the front and suffered serious losses. At the beginning of the campaign, October 30, the 12th Infantry had 50 officers and 1,910 men who were unable to take part in action (lists of losses).

3. The division was maintained in this district up to the month of October, 1915, first to the south of the Somme, later, at the beginning of November, 1914, between Dompierre and Maricourt.

1915.

ARTOIS.

1. In April, 1915, the division was reduced to three regiments through the cession of the 3d Infantry to the 11th Bavarian Division. Between the 10th and 15th of October, 1915, the 2d Bavarian Division was placed on the Artois front in the Neuville-Souchez sector.

2. About the 20th of December it was in the line at Bailleul-Sire-Berthoult between the western part of the Lille road and the Arras road.

3. It remained there until the beginning of May, 1916.

1916.

VERDUN.

1. At this date it was relieved and transported to Verdun. It participated in the violent battles which took place there in May and June in the vicinity of Douaumont and suffered serious losses (50 per cent of its personnel). It was reconstituted in June in the district of Merke-Romagne-sur-les-Cotes (reinforcement of from 50 to 100 men per company), and went back to the line near Thiaumont. It suffered serious losses in the attack of June 23 (the companies of the 12th Bavarian Regiment were reduced to about 40 men).

LORRAINE.

2. The 2d Bavarian Division was withdrawn from this zone of combat about the 15th of July and was sent to the Apremont-St. Mihiel sector, where it was reconstituted. It received numerous reinforcements (convalescents and class 16 men). During this period, which extends up to October 15, it did not take part in any serious operation.

SOMME.

3. At the end of October it was transported to the Somme (Sailly-Saillisel sector), where it was again put to a severe test.

4. After staying a month in the Somme district it reoccupied the lines in the St. Mihiel sector at the beginning of December.

1917.

CALIFORNIE PLATEAU.

. 1. The 2d Bavarian Division was withdrawn from the St. Mihiel sector between the 2d and 5th of May, 1917, and entrained at Mars-la-Tour on the 6th, whence it was transported via Conflans to Montcornet, where, during the night of the 8th, it gained the sector situated to the east of Hurtebise.

2. From the 9th on the 2d Bavarian Division engaged some of its elements on the salient northeast of Californie Plateau (May 9 and 10).

3. The division occupied this sector up to the end of May and participated in serious engagements notably those of the 13th and 22d of May to the northwest of the plateau. It was put to a very severe test. (The 9th Company of the 20th Battalion was reduced to 45 men.)

ARGONNE.

4. The 2d Bavarian Division was relieved at the beginning of June and sent to rest for 15 days at Camp Sissonne; later it was transported to the Argonne, where it occupied the Grande Courte-Chausse sector. During this rest it received two reinforcements—700 to 800 men June 28 and 300 men in July.

5. At the end of August it changed sectors and went into the line toward Bois d'Avocourt (Bois de Cheppy).

MEUSE.

6. The division was withdrawn from this sector at the end of October and remained in repose in the vicinity of Stenay up to the middle of November, whence it was directed to the sector west of the Bois-le-Chaume. The 12th Bavarian Regiment, which had been sent in reserve to the southeast of Altkirch about the 10th of November to ward off an expected French attack in Alsace, rejoined the division December 6.

7. The 2d Bavarian Division remained in this sector (southeast of Beaumont) up to January, 1918, and then went to rest in the district of Longwy.

VALUE—1917 ESTIMATE.

The 2d Bavarian Division participated on the 9th and 10th of May, 1917, in violent but unsuccessful counterattacks on the salient northeast of the Californie Plateau. It appears that the Bavarians were always placed in the most dangerous positions and that they were sacrificed by the Prussians.

In spite of this condition the 2d Bavarian Division still showed itself as a good division (July, 1917).

1918.

MEUSE.

1. The division remained in line north of the Bois des Fosses until relieved by the 19th Reserve Division, January 14. It went then to the Longwy region, where it was put through a stiff course of training in open warfare.

AMIENS.

2. March 23 it entrained at Audun-le-Roman, and traveled via Longwy-Sedan-Charleville-Hirson-Anor-Avesnes-Le Cateau-Bertry-Caudry to Cambrai, where it detrained March 24–25. At first the division marched in the direction of Bapaumes, but was diverted in a southerly direction on the way and passed through Le Transloy-Sailly-Saillisel-Péronne-Villers-Carbonnel-Estrées-Foucaucourt and billeted at Beaucourt-en-Santerre on the night of March 30–31. April 2 it attacked at Morisel, and two days later to the southwest of Morisel. It fought then until the 15th, when it side-slipped to the north, relieving the 54th Division, its place being taken by the 15th Division. It was relieved about May 4 by the 21st Division.

3. It moved to the area southeast of Ghent, and there was reconstituted and trained. June 2, it relieved the 14th Bavarian Division in the Morisel sector. It was relieved the middle of the month by the extension of fronts of the neighboring divisions.

CHAMPAGNE.

4. It rested in rear of the front in Champagne for about a month and then entered line in the Navarin sector (north of Souain), being identified by prisoners, July 15. It was withdrawn on the 20th.

VESLE.

5. August 4 the division relieved the 22d Division at Jonchery (on the Vesle, east of Fismes). It remained in line, taking part in the general retirement, until the armistice.

VALUE—1918 ESTIMATE.

The 2d Bavarian is one of the very best German shock divisions. It was called upon to do a great deal of heavy fighting, and always acquitted itself well. It suffered severe losses in consequence, but these were made good as long as the German High Command had replacements at its disposal.

2d Bavarian Landwehr Division.

COMPOSITION.

	1917		1918	
	Brigade.	Regiment.	Brigade.	Regiment.
Infantry...............	9 Bav. Ldw.	2 Bav. Ldw. 5 Bav. Ldw. 10 Bav. Ldw.	9 Bav. Ldw.	2 Bav. Ldw. 5 Bav. Ldw. 10 Bav. Ldw.
Cavalry...............	5th Sqn. 4th Bav. Light Cav.		3 Sqn. 1 Bav. Res. Cav. Rgt.	
Artillery...............	Art. command: 2 Bav. Ldw. F. A. Rgt. 811 and 905 F. A. Btries.		2 Bav. Ldw. F. A. Rgt.	
Engineers and Liaisons.	(25 Bav.) Eng. Btn.: 2 Bav. Ldw. Pion. Co. 3 Bav. Ldw. Pion. Co. 302 Bav. T. M. Co. 502 Tel. Detch.		25 Bav. Pion. Btn.: 2 Bav. Ldw. Pion. Co. 3 Bav. Ldw. Pion. Co. 12 Bav. Searchlight Section. 502 Signals Command: 502 Tel. Detch.	
Medical and Veterinary.	24 Bav. Ambulance Co. 17 Bav. Field Hospital. 63 Bav. Field Hospital. 32 Vet. Hospital.		24 Bav. Ambulance Co. 63 Bav. Field Hospital. 17 Bav. Field Hospital.	
Transports............	M. T. Col.			
Attached...............	156 Labor Btn.			

HISTORY.

(Bavaria.)

1917.

The 2d Bavarian Landwehr Division was formed in Lorraine at the end of December, 1916, and the beginning of January, 1917. Two of its regiments, the 5th Bavarian Landwehr and the 10th Bavarian Landwehr, were assigned respectively to the 1st Bavarian Landwehr Division and the 33d Reserve Division, at that time on the Lorraine front. The 2d Bavarian Landwehr was ceded by the 6th Bavarian Landwehr Division, which held a Vosges sector.

RUSSIA.

1. As soon as it was constituted the 2d Bavarian Landwehr Division was transported to the Eastern front via Frankfort and Leipzig.

COURLANDE.

2. Directed to Courlande and attached to the 8th Army it entered the line in the vicinity of Friedrichstadt (middle of January, 1917) and remained in this district up till February, 1918. In September it participated in the operations against Riga. In December a number of men were detached in order to reinforce the 10th Bavarian Division.

VALUE—1917 ESTIMATE.

It remained on the Russian front from the time of its formation (January, 1917). It held the calm sector of Courlande in 1917; it occupied Livonia in 1918 (May). Men under 35 years of age were withdrawn from the 5th Bavarian Landwehr in December, 1917 (letter). It is rated as a 4th class division.

2d Cavalry Division.

COMPOSITION.

	1918	
	Brigade.	Regiment.
Cavalry	22 Cav. (11 C. D.).	5 Drag. Rgt.
		14 Hus. Rgt.
	25 Cav. (18 C. Dist.).	23 Gd. Drag. Rgt. (1 Sqn. Detch.).
		24 Gd. Drag. Rgt. (3 Sqn. detached).
	7 Bav. Cav. (Sieben-burgische).	4 Bav. Light Cav. Rgt. (3 Sqn. detached).
		5 Bav. Light Cav. Rgt. (3 Sqn. detached).
Artillery	15 Horse Art. Abt.	
Engineers and Liaisons	2 Vac. Pion. Detch.	
	7 Cav. Pion. Detch..	
	200 Bav. T. M. Co.	
Medical and Veterinary	21 Ambulance Co.	
Odd units	2 M. G. Btry.	
	3 M. G. Btry.	
Attached	4 Jag. Btn.	
	1 Cyclist Co. 3 Jag. Btn.	
	2 Cyclist Co. 3 Jag. Btn.	

HISTORY.

1918.

1. The division was in the Stochod sector until February 28, when it advanced through Kiev and Kharhov to Rostov, where it was on August 4. At this date the division occupied the area between Kharkov and Rostov. The troops were frequently attacked by armed bands or by mobs. In this way they suffered some heavy losses. The German cruiser *Goeben*, which had been supporting them, was damaged by fire and had to put into Constantinople.

Nothing was known of the division's movements after August, 1918.

VALUE—1918 ESTIMATE.

The division was considered as 4th class.

2d Naval Division.

COMPOSITION.

	1915 Brigade	1915 Regiment	1916 Brigade	1916 Regiment	1917 Brigade	1917 Regiment	1918 Brigade	1918 Regiment
Infantry	3 Nav. 4 Nav.	The 1, 2, 3, 4, 5, and 6th Marine Fus. Rgts. and the 4th Marine Inf. Rgt. alternated between the 1st and 2d Naval Divisions.	3 Nav. 4 Nav.		3 Nav. 4 Nav.		3 Mar.	3 Mat. 4 Mat. 5 Mat.
Cavalry							4 Sqn. 10 Hus. Rgt.	
Artillery			Marine E. A. Abt.		1 Mar. F. A. Rgt. 2 Mar. F. A. Rgt. 3 Mar. F. A. Rgt.		3 Mar. Art. Rgt.	
Engineers and liaisons			3 Nav. Pion. Co.		2 Nav. Pion. Btn.; 3 Nav. Pion. Co. 4 Nav. Pion. Co. 377 Pion. Co. Tel. Detch.		2 Mar. Pion. Btn.; 2 Mar. Pion. Co. 3 Mar. Pion. Co. 3 Entrenching Co. 4 Entrenching Co. 292 Signal Command: 292 Tel. Detch.	
Medical and Veterinary					Ambulance Co. Field Hospital. Vet. Hospital.		2 Mar. Ambulance Co. 3 Mar. Field Hospital. 4 Mar. Field Hospital.	
Transports					M. T. Col.			
Attached			27 Labor Btn.		Coast Defense Btn.			

HISTORY.

1915.

BELGIUM.

1. The 2d Naval Division, formed November 24, 1914, was a part of the Naval Corps at this time.

Since its formation the 6th Naval Fusileer Regiments of the Corps alternate in Flanders between the coast sector (2d Naval Division) and the sea front (1st Naval Division).

1916.

2. In September, 1916, the 3d Naval Infantry Regiment was transferred to the Naval Division, which later became the 3d Naval Division, engaged on the Somme.

1917.

FLANDERS.

Sector of the coast and sea front.   The staff of the 2d Naval Division remained in charge of the coast sector.

1918.

1. In early March the division was relieved in its sector southeast of Nieuport and took over the coast sector from the 3d Naval Division.   Elements of the division reinforced the German attacking forces north of Bixschoote on April 17.

2. After October 15, the division retreated toward Ostend and Maldeghem.   It was last identified at Wachtebeke on November 2.   On the day of the armistice it was considered to be in reserve of the 4th Army.

VALUE—1918 ESTIMATE.

The division was rated as fourth class.

3d Guard Division.[1]
COMPOSITION.

	1914 Brigade	1914 Regiment	1915 Brigade	1915 Regiment	1916 Brigade	1916 Regiment	1917 Brigade	1917 Regiment	1918 Brigade	1918 Regiment
Infantry	5 Gd. 6 Gd. (Instruction.)	5 Ft. 5 Gren. Gd. Fus. Lehr Rgt.	5 Gd. 6 Gd.	5 Ft. 5 Gren. Gd. Fus. Lehr Rgt.	6 Gd.	Gd. Fus. Lehr Rgt. 9 Gren.	6 Gd.	Gd. Fus. Lehr Rgt. 9 Gren.	6 Gd.	Lehr Rgt. Fus. Rgt. 9 Gren.
Cavalry		Gd. Res. Uhlan Rgt.				Gd. Res. Uhlan Rgt. (?Sqns.).		3d Sqn. Gd. Res. Uhlan Rgt. 1st Sqn. 2 Gd. Drag. Rgt.	1 Sqn. 2 Gd. Drag. Rgt.	
Artillery	5 Gd. F. A. Rgt. 6 Gd. F. A. Rgt. (Formed of the Juterbog Instruction Rgt.)		3 Brig.: 5 Gd. F. A. Rgt. 6 Gd. F. A. Rgt.		3 Brig.: 5 Gd. F. A. Rgt. 6 Gd. F. A. Rgt.		(*) Art. Command: 5 Gd. F. A. Rgt.		5 Gd. F. A. Rgt. 1 Abt. 2 Gd. Ft. A. Rgt. (Staff, 1 and 3 Btries.). 936 Light Am. Col. 936 Light Am. Col. 1347 Light Am. Col.	
Engineers and Liaisons.			(?) Pion. Co. 3 Gd. Pont. Engs. 3 Gd. Tel. Detch.		(?) Pion. Co. 3 Gd. T. M. Co. 3 Gd. Pont. Engs. 3 Gd. Tel. Detch.		(104) Pion. Btn. 1 Co. 28 Pions. 274 Pion. Co. 3 Gd. T. M. Co. 290 Searchlight Section. 3 Gd. Tel. Detch. 55 Tel. Detch.		104 Pion. Btn.: 1 Co. 28 Pions. 274 Pion. Co. 198 Searchlight Section. 3 Gd. Signals Command: 3 Gd. Tel. Detch. 90 Wireless Detch.	
Medical and Veterinary.							7 Ambulance Co. 265 Ambulaboe Co. 393 Ambulance Co. Field Hospital. Vet. Hospital.		265 Ambulance Co. 393 Field Hospital. 35 Field Hospital. 3 Gd. Vet. Hospital.	
Transport							M. T. Col.		532 M. T. Col.	
Attached					75 Anti-Aircraft Section.		75 Anti-Aircraft Section.			

[1] Organized in August, 1914; elements taken from 1st and 2d Guard Divisions.

HISTORY.

1914.

FRANCE.

1. In August, 1914, the 3d Guard Division was first directed to the Western Front. It fought below Namur.

RUSSIA.

2. The 27th of August the division was transported to Silesia via Oriental Prussia. It took part in the invasion of southern Poland.

3. The group of armies of which it formed a part was turned back and was obliged to retire to Lodz.

4. During the winter of 1914–15 it took part in the severe engagements on the Bzura.

1915.

1. At the beginning of 1915 the 3d Guard Division was dismembered; the 5th Brigade was sent to Oriental Prussia; the 6th Brigade, to the south of the Carpathians, was engaged in the Uzsok defile district.

2. In March, 1915, the 6th Brigade alone formed the 3d Guard Division, with the addition of the 9th Grenadier Regiment to its own two regiments. Thus formed, the 3d Guard Division took part in the campaign of the summer of 1915. (Carpathians Oriental Galicia. Linsingen's army.)

3. The division took up its position before Tarnopol and passed the winter of 1915–16 there. (Bothmer's army.)

1916.

FRANCE.

1. In April, 1916, the 3d Guard Division was transported to the Western Front. It occupied a sector in Champagne and took part in no serious engagements.

2. It was sent to rest at Valenciennes the 1st of June.

SOMME.

3. The 1st of July (beginning of the Franco-British offensive) the 3d Guard Division went into the line on the Somme. It was put to a severe test there, particularly in the Thiepval district (57.5 per cent loss).

4. After the Somme it was sent to the Dixmude front.

GALICIA.

5. It was transported to Galicia (beginning of September) by the following itinerary: Liège, Cologne, Leipzig, Dresden, Cracow, Przemysl.

6. At Halicz the 3d Guard Division took part in the German counteroffensive, and again suffered great losses.

FRANCE.

7. It was sent back to the Western Front on the 24th of November by the following itinerary: Lemberg, Jaroslaw, Gorlitz, Dresden, Chemnitz, Nurnberg, Heilbronn, Strasbourg, Mulhouse, Rheinweiler, and having arrived there the 20th of November, was sent to rest for a month.

1917.

LORRAINE.

1. Beginning with January and up to April 6, 1917, the division occupied the sector of the forest of Parroy.

2. The 8th of April it entrained at Metz, and arrived at Cambrai via Montmedy, Sedan, and Charleville

ARTOIS.

3. Engaged in action before Arras in order to repulse the English offensive from April 15 on, it participated in severe battles (May).

4. On the 18th of May the division was relieved and sent into the Cambrai district. After a short period of repose it occupied the Pronville-Inchy-en-Artois sector (June 1–22).

5. It was sent in reserve to the Bruges sector (June 22).

6. It was transported to Thourout the 9th of July and remained there at rest until July 29.

YPRES.

7. On the 31st of July, the date of the great British attack, the 3d Guard Division suffered very heavy losses (1,000 prisoners) in relieving the 23d Reserve Division in the Pilken sector.

ALSACE.

8. It was relieved the 5th and 6th of August and transported to Alsace, where it was placed at rest. At the beginning of September it occupied the Altkirch sector.

FLANDERS.

9. About the 7th of October the division was again sent to Flanders to the northeast of Zonnebecke.

10. The 3d Guard Division left the Ypres front (Zonnebecke) at the beginning of November, 1917.

CAMBRAI.

11. After remaining in the vicinity of Ghent it went into action before Cambrai near the Bourlon wood (Nov. 22).

12. It was relieved the 10th of December and went to rest in the Vendegies District (south of Valenciennes—division maneuvers).

1918.

CAMBRAI.

1. The division returned to the line in the sector, southwest of Cambrai on January 10, relieving the 21st Reserve Division. It remained in line until the 119th Division relieved it on February 12.

2. The division retired to Hem-Lenglet (north of Cambrai) where it rested and underwent instruction.

BATTLE OF PICARDY.

3. The division entered the line on March 19, between Inchy-en-Artois and Pronville. Engaged in the advance between the 21st and 24th. It suffered heavy losses on the 22d in the fighting north of Beaumetz, passing to the second line on the 24th. The division came back and participated in the fighting about Bucquoy and Hebuterne, March 26–April 3.

4. Returning from the Somme front about April 4, the division was at rest until April 18.

BATTLE OF THE LYS.

5. The division was engaged on the Lys, northeast of Estaires, after April 18, then north of Kemmel from April 30 to May 5. Heavy losses featured the fighting.

6. After resting at Halluin for seven days the division was moved by rail to Lorraine by the route Namur, Treves, Saarbruck, Sarreguemines.

LORRAINE.

7. On May 18 the division relieved the 202d Division in the Chateau Salins sector. While in this quiet sector the division received reinforcements. When it left the line on June 24, the division was comparatively fresh and an available reinforcement for a battle front.

HAMPAGNE.

8. On leaving Lorraine the division moved to Rozay-sur-Lene, July 1, and later uthward to Hannogne.

9. In the offensive of July 15, the division fought east of Rheims in the region of es Monts. Between the 15th and 31st heavy losses were suffered. It is known to ave received a draft of 300 men in July.

10. While at rest behind the Champagne front further drafts of men from Russia and umania were received.

11. The division held the line in Champagne north of St. Hilaire-le-Grand from ugust 15 to September 18.

12. Upon relief the division was first sent to Laon, but was hastily entrained and urried to Machault, where it entered the line immediately.

ATTLE OF ARGONNE.

13. From September 27 to October 5 the division was engaged between Somme-Py nd Manre; then it fought near Orfeuil where 900 prisoners were lost. Acting as a ear guard, the division covered the retreat from Machault to Voziers. Extremely eavy losses were reported in this period.

14. Withdrawn on the 8th, the division was moved by truck to Romagne. After wo days in reserve it entered the line on the 12th, now opposing the first American rmy. In this sector it fought vigorously, making perhaps the stiffest resistance ncountered in the offensive.

15. The division went out on October 17 and rested until the 26th.

16. Reengaged northeast of Attigny (Rilly-aux-Dies) on the 26th, the division ontinued in line until the armistice. The last identification was southeast of Mezieres n November 7. Five hundred prisoners were lost by the division during their last eriod in line.

VALUE—1918 ESTIMATE.

The 3d Guard Division was rated as one of the best German divisions. It was ompletely exhausted in the offensive of March and April and suffered from a low norale in July and August. The Argonne Battle losses were very severe for the ivision. The regiments were reduced to 200 and 300 effectives.

3d Division.
COMPOSITION.

	1914 Brigade	1914 Regiment	1915 Brigade	1915 Regiment	1916 Brigade	1916 Regiment	1917 Brigade	1917 Regiment	1918 Brigade	1918 Regiment
Infantry	5. 6.	2 Gren. 9 Gren. 34 Fus. 42.	5. 6.	2 Gren. 9 Gren. 34 Fus. 42.	6.	34 Fus. 42. 4 Ldw. (1, 2, and 4 Btns.).	6.	426. 428. 4 Ldw. (1, 2, and 4 Btns.).	6.	381. (?) 428.
Cavalry		3 Horse Gren. Rgt.					3 Horse Gren. Rgt. (3d Sqn.).		3 Sqn. 3 Horse Gren. Rgt.	
Artillery	3 Brig.: 2 F. A. Rgt. 38 F. A. Rgt.		3 Brig.: 2 F. A. Rgt. 38 F. A. Rgt.		3 Brig.: 2 F. A. Rgt. 38 F. A. Rgt.		3 Art. Command: 38 F. A. Rgt.		(?).	
Engineers and Liaisons.			1 Pion. Btn. No. 2: Field Co. 2 Pions. 3 Pont. Engs. 3 Tel. Detch.		1 Pion. Btn. No. 2: 1 Co. 2 Pions. 3 Pont. Engs. 3 Tel. Detch. 3 T. M. Co.		1 Pion. Btn. No. 2: 1 Co. 2 Pions. 3 Tel. Detch. 3 Co. 32 Pions. 3 T. M. Co. 283 and 301 Searchlight Sections.		108 Pion. Btn.: 1 Co. 6 Ldw. Pions. 2 Ldw. Co. 4 C. Dist. Pion. 110 Searchlight Section. 3 Signals Command: 3 Tel. Detch.	
Medical and Veterinary.							7 Ambulance Co. 18 Field Hospital. 24 Field Hospital. Vet. Hospital.		7 Ambulance Co. 23 Field Hospital. 24 Field Hospital. 189 Vet. Hospital.	
Transports.							6 Truck train. 7 Truck train. 436 M. T. Col.			

HISTORY.

THIRD DIVISION.

(Second District—Pomerania).

1914.

1. The 3d and 4th Division together composed the 2d Army Corps (Stettin).

2. At the beginning of the war it gave up one of its five regiments, the 54th Infantry, or the formation of the 36th Reserve Division, which operated against Russia.

BELGIUM.

3. In August, 1914, the 3d Division formed a part of the 1st Army (Von Kluck). It invaded Belgium the 13th and 14th of August, passing through Vise (Aug. 14), Hasselt (Aug. 17), Aerschot (Aug. 19), Laeken (Aug. 21) and entered France on the 24th.

MARNE.

4. It was at Cambrai on the 26th and on the Somme the 28th. It took part in the Battle of the Marne at Vareddes on the 7th of September (district northeast of Meaux).

5. Was situated to the north of Soissons after the retreat. The 2d of October it was in the district south of Roye; on the 4th it fought near Beauvraignes.

6. At the beginning of November it was transported to Flanders (Wytschaete-Messines District) where it remained till the end of the month.

RUSSIA.

7. It then entrained for Russia (end of November). On its arrival it was divided. The 5th Brigade was attached to the 8th Army in Oriental Prussia, the 6th Brigade to the 10th Army to the east of Lodz.

1915.

1. During the first months of 1915 the two brigades remained separated and changed position with their respective armies. The 5th Brigade went into the government of Souvalki near the frontier of Oriental Prussia; the 6th into Poland near Prasnysz and the Narew.

2. In May, at the time of the formation of new divisions, the 5th Brigade was broken up. The 2d Grenadiers, then in Courland, went over to the Homeyer Brigade which then became the 109th Division; the 9th Grenadiers went as the third Regiment to the 3d Guard Division which abandoned one of its brigades (the 4th Guard) for the formation of a 4th Guard Division.

3. The 3d Division, reduced to the 6th Brigade, completed itself by the addition of the 4th Landwehr Regiment (1st, 2d, and 4th Battalions). The progress of the Russian offensive conducted it into the Vidzy District, where it firmly established itself.

1916.

1. Its composition varied still more in the course of the year 1916 and it lost the two active regiments which it still had. The 42d Infantry left it in September to go to the Kovel District and from there to Macedonia; in December the 34th Fusiliers left it definitely in order to go to Courland. In exchange it received two regiments formed in the autumn, the 426th and the 428th Infantry.

1917.

1. There was no change of composition or position during 1917.

1918.

The division remained in the east throughout the year. Its movements were obscure. The division was rated fourth class.

3d Landwehr Division.

COMPOSITION.

	1914		1915		1916		1917		1918	
	Brigade.	Regiment.	Brigade.	Regiment.	Brigade.	Regiment.	Brigade.	Regiment.	Brigade.	Regiment.
Infantry	18 Ldw. 19 Ldw.	6 Ldw. 7 Ldw. 37 Ldw. 46 Ldw.	18 Ldw. 19 Ldw.	6 Ldw. 7 Ldw. 37 Ldw. 46 Ldw.	18 Ldw. 19 Ldw.	6 Ldw. 7 Ldw. 37 Ldw. 46 Ldw.	17 Ldw.	6 Ldw. 4 Ldw. 46 Ldw. 327 Ldw.	17 Ldw.	6 Ldw. 7 Ldw. 46 Ldw.
Cavalry		1 Ldw. Cav. Rgt. (3 Sqns.).		1 Ldw. Cav. Rgt.		1 Ldw. Cav. Rgt.		(?)		3 Sqn. 4 Drag. Rgt.
Artillery		3 Ldw. F. A. Rgt. (Ers. Abtls. of 20, 41, and 56, F. A. Rgts.		3 Ldw. F. A. Rgt.		3 Ldw. F. A. Rgt.		Art. Command: 3 Ldw. F. A. Rgt. (9 Btries.), 913 Batry.		3 Ldw. F. A. Rgt.
Engineers and Liaisons.						1 Ldw. Survey Sect, 2 Ldw. Survey Sect, 1 Ers. Co. 5 Pions. 303 T. M. Co.		(403) Pion. Btn.; 1 Ers. Co. 5 Pions. 4 Co. 17 Pions. 344 Pion. Co. 303 T. M. Co 246 Searchlight Section. 503 Tel. Ditch.		418 Pion. Btn. 1 Ers. Co. 5 Pions. 139 Searchlight Section. 503 Signal Command: 503 Tel. Detch.
Medical and Veterinary.								230 Ambulance Co. 21 Ldw. Field Hospital. Vet. Hospital.		230 Ambulance Co. 322 Field Hospital. 22 Ldw. Field Hospital. 503 Vet. Hospital.
Transports								537 M. T. Col.		773 M. T. Col.
Attached		17 Mixed Ers. Brig. (17, 18, 19, 20, and 77 Brig. Ers. Btns.).						2 Neisse Landst. Inf. Btn. (8 C. Dist. Btn. No. 22.).		

HISTORY.

(Fifth District—Posen.)

1914.

RUSSIA.

At the beginning of the war the 3d Landwehr Division formed a part of the 2d Landwehr Corps (old 6th Landwehr Corps) and always occupied the eastern front.

POLAND.

1. Up to the German offensive of the summer of 1915 the 3d Landwehr Division, along with the 2d Landwehr Corps, participated in the Polish campaign. At the end of October, 1914, it was identified before Warsaw (Rawa-Vistula); in the middle of November it was in retreat to the south and east of Czenstochow; in December it was to the west of Kielce.

1915.

POLAND.

1. In January, 1915, the 2d Landwehr Corps was still in the Kielce District.

2. Toward the middle of February a brigade (19th Landwehr Brigade) was detached to the northeast of Warsaw (Plock-Mlawa). Reassembled to the west of Kielce in April, the 3d Landwehr Division remained between the Vistula and the Pilica until July.

BARANOVITCHI.

3. The division took part in the offensive against the Russians (July-August); it was before Ivangorod July 20 and arrived in the vicinity of Baranovitchi toward the end of August.

4. In October it was in the line near Goroditche. In November it took the Liakhovitchi sector (south of Baranovitchi).

1916.

1. The 3d Landwehr Division remained to the southeast of Baranovitchi (Liakhovitchi) for more than two years (November, 1915–January, 1918). The 37th Landwehr became independent in July, 1916, and received various successive additions. About the same date the 3d Landwehr Division furnished a part of the elements necessary to the formation of the 420th Infantry. In return the 327th Landwehr was assigned to it, and it kept this regiment until June, 1917, ceding it at that time to the 4th Landwehr Division.

1917.

1. Liakhovitchi sector. In November the 3d Landwehr Division sent an important reinforcement to the 9th Division (particularly to the 7th Grenadiers); two months later a smaller reinforcement was sent to the 43d Reserve Division, which was preparing to leave the eastern front.

1918.

The division remained in the eastern theatre throughout the year.

VALUE—1918 ESTIMATE.

The division remained on the Russian front from the beginning of the war. Fighting value mediocre. It was rated as fourth class.

3d Bavarian Division.

COMPOSITION.

	1914 Brigade	1914 Regiment	1915 Brigade	1915 Regiment	1916 Brigade	1916 Regiment	1917 Brigade	1917 Regiment	1918 Brigade	1918 Regiment
Infantry	5 Bav. 6 Bav.	22 Bav. 23 Bav. 17 Bav. 18 Bav.	5 Bav. 6 Bav.	22 Bav. 23 Bav. 17 Bav. 18 Bav.	6 Bav.	17 Bav. 23 Bav. 18 Bav.	6 Bav.	17 Bav. 18 Bav. 23 Bav.	6 Bav.	17 Bav. 18 Bav. 23 Bav.
Cavalry		3 Bav. Light Cav. Rgt.				3 Bav. Light Cav. Rgt. (3 Sqns.).		4th Sqn. 3 Bav. Light Cav. Rgt.		4 Sqn. 3 Bav. Light Cav. Rgt.
Artillery	3 Bav. Brig.:	5 Bav. F. A. Rgt. 12 Bav. F. A. Rgt.	3 Bav. Brig.:	5 Bav. F. A. Rgt. 12 Bav. F. A. Rgt.	3 Bav. Brig.;	5 Bav. F. A. Rgt. 12 Bav. F. A. Rgt.		3 Bav. Art. Command: 12 Bav. F. A. Rgt.?		3 Bav. Art. Command: 12 Bav. F. A. Rgt. 1 Abt. 2 Bav. Ft. A. Rgt. 149 Bav. Light Am. Col. 150 Bav. Light Am. Col. 162 Bav. Light Am. Col.
Engineers and Liaisons.		1 and 3 Field Cos. 2 Bav. Pion. Btn.		1 and 3 Field Cos. 2 Bav. Pion. Btn. 3 Bav. Pont. Engs. 3 Bav. Tel. Detch.		1 and 3 Field Cos. 2 Bav. Pion. Btn. 18 Bav. Res. Pion. Co. 3 Bav. T. M. Co. 3 Bav. Pont. Engs. 3 Bav. Tel. Detch		5 and 7 Bav. Pion. Cos. 3 Bav. T. M. Co. 2 Bav. Searchlight Section. 3 Bav. Tel. Detch.		2 Bav. Pion. Btn.: 5 Bav. Pion. Co. 7 Bav. Pion. Co. 3 Bav. Searchlight Section 3 Bav. Signals Command: 3 Bav. Tel. Detch. 77 Wireless Detch
Medical and Veterinary.								4 Bav. Ambulance Co. 9 Bav. Field Hospital. Vet. Hospital.		4 Bav. Ambulance Co. 9 Bav. Field Hospital 16 Bav. Field Hospital.
Transports.								683 Bav. M. T. Col.		683 Bav. M. T. Col.
Attached.						Inf. Pion. Co. of the 3 Bav. Div.				

HISTORY.

(Second Bavarian District—Bavaria, Bavarian Palatinate.)

1914.

LORRAINE.

1. At the time of the declaration of war the 3d Bavarian Division and the 4th Bavarian Division constituted the 2d Bavarian Army Corps. At the beginning of August, 1914, the 2d Bavarian Army Corps formed a part of the 6th Army (Crown Prince of Bavaria). It detrained at Faulquemont (Lorraine) on August 8, and the 3d Bavarian Division was to the north of Château-Salins on the 10th. It took part in the Battle of Morhange on the 20th, passed the frontier, pillaged Gerbeviller on its way, and advanced as far as the left bank of the Mortagne. Forced to turn back, it moved near Metz the 15th of September and entrained the 19th.

SOMME-FLANDERS.

2. Similar to the 1st Bavarian Army Corps, the 2d Bavarian Army Corps was attached to the 2d Army and fought in the Peronne District (end of September); then it was transported to Flanders, where it rejoined the 6th Army.

3. From November, 1914, to October, 1915, the 2d Bavarian Army Corps occupied the front from the Ypres-Comines Canal as far as Douve. During this period it generally remained on the defensive.

1915.

1. In April, 1915, the 3d Bavarian Division ceded the 22d Infantry to the 11th Bavarian Division, formed at this time.

In June, 1915, the 3d Bavarian Division was sent as a reinforcement for a short time to the Arras sector.

ARTOIS.

2. In the month of October the 2d Bavarian Army Corps (3d and 4th Bavarian Divisions) was transported to the Auchy-Loos sector and kept there until August, 1916.

1916.

1. In the Loos sector the 2d Bavarian Army Corps showed itself very active. It undertook mine works and executed them with great rapidity. At the end of April it attempted a gas attack; this latter had no success, however.

SOMME.

2. The 3d Bavarian Division left the Loos sector with its Army Corps about August 25 and went into the Somme District. It occupied the Martinpuich-Bazentin-le-Petit sector up to the 15th of September and fought with characteristic stubbornness. Its total losses during this period reached 4,976 men (55 per cent).

3. The Division retired from the Somme September 27 and was sent to the Douve sector (from this river to the Armentières-Lille railroad). It remained there till the end of March, 1917.

1917.

ARTOIS.

1. The 3d Bavarian Division was relieved from Armentieres March 20, 1917. It was transported to the Arras District, situated on the Scarpe front, on April 11. It suffered considerable loss in the two unfortunate counterattacks of Monchy-le-Preux and in the French counterattack of April 23.

2. The division was withdrawn from the front April 25 and sent to rest in the Roubaix zone until the beginning of June.

FLANDERS.

3. On June 5 the 3d Bavarian Division began to relieve the 40th Division in the Messines sector. The British attack took place on the 7th during this relief. The division lost the village and the summit of Messines. It suffered considerable loss and left 1,531 prisoners in the hands of the enemy. (The 17th Battalion was reduced to 800 men; the 23d suffered about equal losses; the 18th lost fewer men.)

LORRAINE.

4. The 3d Bavarian Division was withdrawn from the Messines sector June 8, 1917, and taken to the Conflans area. After a short period of repose, during which it

was partially reconstituted, it was put into the line in the sector of the Bezange forest (south of Château-Salins) July 18.

5. The 3d Bavarian Division received a reinforcement of 4,500 men—convalescents, exclusively—between June 8 and the end of August. (At the end of August the personnel averaged only 120 men who drew rations (80 combatants) per company in the 17th Battalion.) The losses sustained the 7th of June had not been made good by the 28th of August.

6. The division was sent into Lorraine for rest and reconstitution, remaining on the defensive, and pursuing the instruction of its detachments in the use of light minne-werfers and assault tactics.

AISNE.

7. It left Lorraine in the middle of October. On the 28th it occupied the Aisne front to the north of Braye-en-Laonnois (Trucy sector). The 17th Battalion was the only one to engage in the October battles which preceded the German retreat to the north of the Ailette.

VALUE—1917 ESTIMATE.

The 3d Bavarian Division is one of the best German units.

It always fought well, showing great energy in the offensive and preserving a great tenacity in the defensive.

Nevertheless, the fighting value of this division appears to have diminished during the course of the year 1917.

1918.

1. About January 1 the division was relieved and went into training in the region Fournes-Chimay, where it remained for four weeks.

ST. GOBAIN.

2. The division relieved the 47th Reserve Division near Septvaux about February 1, and occupied the line until March 28.

3. Retired from the front on the 28th; the division was sent toward Chauny-La Fere, where it constituted the reserve division of the 8th Reserve Corps.

NOYON.

4. In April the division alternated between short periods in line and brief rests. North of Plemont it relieved the 7th Reserve Division about April 2, was relieved by the 1st Bavarian Division a few days later, and returned to line about April 11, relieving the 1st Bavarian Division. About this time the division received a draft of 900 men of the 1919 class.

5. The division was withdrawn from the Lassigny front about May 25.

BATTLE OF THE OISE.

6. The division participated in the Oise fighting of June, although it did not take a direct part in the opening attack. It supported the effort of the 3d Bavarian Reserve Division, lending some battalions, from which prisoners were taken. About the middle of June the division passed to the second line, rested two weeks, and returned to the Montdidier-Noyon front about June 30.

LASSIGNY.

7. The division remained in line throughout July and encountered the Allied attack of middle August. About August 21 it was withdrawn.

8. Between August 21 and October 7 the division was not satisfactorily identified. Elements were reported near Terguier in September, near Ypres, and in the region of St. Etienne-Arnes.

WOEVRE.

9. The division entered the Woevre line on October 7, near Manheulles, where it remained until the armistice.

VALUE—1918 ESTIMATE.

The division was used during 1918 as a sector-holding division. It took no prominent part in the offensives of the year.

3d RESERVE DIVISION.

COMPOSITION.

	1914 Brigade.	1914 Regiment.	1915 Brigade.	1915 Regiment.	1916 Brigade.	1916 Regiment.	1917 Brigade.	1917 Regiment.	1918 Brigade.	1918 Regiment.
Infantry	5 Res. 6 Res.	2 Res. 9 Res. 34 Res. 49 Res.	5 Res. 6 Res.	2 Res. 9 Res. 34 Res. 49 Res.	5 Res. 6 Res.	2 Res. 9 Res. 20 Landst. 49 Res.	5 Res.	2 Res. 49 Res. 34 Fus.	5 Res.	2. 34 Fus. 49 Res.
Cavalry		5 Res. Dragoon Rgt. (3 Sqns.).	5 Res. Dragoon Rgt.						1 Sqn. 22 Drag. Rgt.	
Artillery		3 Res. F. A. Rgt. (6 Btries.).	3 Res. F. A. Rgt.		3 Res. F. A. Rgt.		73 Art. Command: 3 Res. F. A. Rgt. (9 Btries.).		73 Art. Command; 3 Res. F. A. Rgt. 4 Abt. 14 Res. Ft. A. Rgt. 865 Light Am. Col. 1177 Light Am. Col. 1195 Light Am. Col.	
Engineers and Liaisons.			2d Pion. Btn. No. 2: Field Co. 2 Pions. 3 Res. Pont. Engs. 3 Res. Tel. Detch.		2d Pion. Btn. No. 2: 2 Res. Co. 2 Pions. 203 T. M. Co. 3 Res. Pont. Engs. 3 Res. Tel. Detch.		303 Pion. Btn. (?): 2 Res. Co. 2 Pions. 2 Co. 34 Res. Pions. 203 M. T. Co. 403 Tel. Detch. 3 Res. Pont. Engs.		303 Pion. Btn.: 2 Res. Co. 2 Pions. 203 T. M. Co. 196 Searchlight Section. 403 Signals Command: 403 Tel. Detch. 33 Wireless Detch.	
Medical and Veterinary.							502 Ambulance Co. 14 Field Hospital. 15 Field Hospital. 16 Field Hospital. 163 Vet. Hospital.		502 Ambulance Co. 14 Res. Field Hospital. 15 Res. Field Hospital. 163 Vet. Hospital.	
Transport.							704 M. T. Col.		704 M. T. Col.	
Attached.							154 Cyclist Co.			

HISTORY.

(2d District—Pomerania.)

1914.

EAST PRUSSIA–RUSSIA.

1. At the beginning of the war the 3d Reserve Division, recruited in the 2d District (Pomerania), formed a part of the 8th German Army (Hindenburg). It fought with this army in eastern Prussia; it was engaged in the battle of Tannenberg (Aug. 26–28), in the battles of Biallo, Lyck, Suwalki, and Augustowo (September–October).

1915.

1. In February, 1915, the 3d Reserve Division participated in the battle of the Mazurian Lakes, and in May in the battles on the Polish frontier.

2. During the great offensive of the summer of 1915 the division was engaged in the operations on the Bobr, which resulted in the taking of Ossovietz. In August it fought in the vicinity of Kovno. It participated in the siege of this city (Aug. 13–18) at the battle of Niemen (Aug. 19–Sept. 8). When the front was stabilized it took position to the north of Smorgoni (southeast of Vilna).

1916.

1. The 3d Reserve Division occupied this sector (north of Smorgoni) up to March, 1917. At this time it was placed in reserve in the Vilna sector.

BELGIUM.

2. At the beginning of May, 1917, it was sent to the western front. It entrained May 13 at Soly (east of Vilna), and was transported via Vilna, Wirballen, Gumbinnen, Berlin, Hanover, Aix-la-Chapelle, Liege, Louvain, and Brussels up to Bruges, where it detrained May 18. It was sent to rest in this district until June 4.

3. On this date the division was transported to the district north of St. Quentin and went into the line on the 8th in the Vendhuille-Bellicourt sector (west of Catelet), where it habituated itself to the western front.

1917.

YPRES.

4. The division was relieved the end of July. After having been in reserve for several days it engaged in the battle of Ypres on the Frezenberg front on August 4; here it was severely tried by artillery fire.

5. It was withdrawn from the front August 18 and sent to rest, first at Tournai and later in the Moorslede District.

6. On September 23 it was again sent into the line in the battle of Flanders to the south of Zonnebeke (Polygone wood), and again suffered serious losses on the 26th.

ALSACE.

7. The 3d Reserve Division was relieved September 28 and transported to Alsace (Mulhouse District), where it remained in repose up to the middle of October.

8. About the 10th or 15th of October it occupied the sector north of the canal from the Rhone to the Rhine, and remained there till the end of October.

9. At this time it was withdrawn from the front. It entrained for Metz November 10. In December it was in the vicinity of Sissone.

AISNE.

10. About December 13 it entered the line in the Craonne sector (Juvincourt area). At the beginning of January it took over the neighboring sector (Bouconville).

Very mediocre morale. The 49th Reserve Regiment was very severely tested by losses and desertions to such a point that it had to be returned to the rear after August 18, 1917. September 26 the 8th Company of the same regiment refused to take part in the attack. The relatively high proportion of men of the 2d Landsturm levy may be responsible for these facts, since they formed part of the regiments of the Second District.

According to prisoners captured in February, 1918, the 3d Reserve Division seemed to be of mediocre quality: "6,000 men lost in Flanders, poorly replaced by men 50 per cent of whom were old, many being above 40, and by 30 per cent Poles."

Nevertheless, despite the mediocrity of its personnel, it must be noted that the 49th Reserve was subjected to a special training for attack troops in November and December.

1918.

LAON.

1. The division held the line in the Craonne sector until about April 20, when it was relieved.

OISE.

2. It reappeared on May 1 near Hainvillers (southeast of Montdidier), where it remained until about June 20. The division was in the thick of the June fighting on the Oise and lost heavily.

3. About June 20 the division went to rest in the region of Guise.

MARNE.

4. The division participated in the fighting between the Marne and Soissons when the Allies delivered their attack on the Marne salient. It relieved the 115th Division at Longpont on July 18 and withstood the attack until July 31. The 49th Reserve Regiment was almost annihilated in the course of the fighting near Mery. The other regiments were reduced to 70–80 rifles per company.

5. Retired from the front on July 31, the division rested at La Capelle until September 1.

CAMBRAI.

6. The division came into line east of Chevisy on September 2. Its composition had been altered by the disbandment of the 2d Reserve Regiment and the addition of the 2d Grenadier Regiment from the 109th Division. The British attack on the Somme of September 12 engulfed the division, which lost 1,300 prisoners.

BELGIUM.

7. It was withdrawn about September 27 and transferred to Belgium, where it entered the line near Dixmude on September 29. It held the line in this sector until October 16, when it passed into the second line for a week's rest. Returning to line on the 23d, it remained in line until the armistice.

The division is rated as a third-class division. Its morale was on the whole bad. The Polish elements deserted freely. In July pillaging of supply trains was apparently prevalent in the divisional area. Elements of the division refused to fight in the Oise battle in June, and the German command appeared to have confidence in its fighting value.

3d Naval Division.

COMPOSITION.

	1917		1918	
	Brigade.	Regiment.	Brigade.	Regiment.
Infantry...............	4 Nav.	1 Mar. 2 Mar. 3 Mar.	Mar. Inf. Brig.	1 Mar. 2 Mar. 3 Mar.
Cavalry...............	....		3 Sqn. 7 Hus. Rgt.	
Artillery...............	9 F. A. Rgt.		2 Matr. F. A. Rgt. 925 Light Am. Col. 1234 Light Am. Col. 1292 Light Am. Col.	
Engineers and Liaisons	1 Co. Mar. Pion. Btn. 3 Co. Mar. Pion. Btn. 337 Pion. Co. 165 T. M. Co.		115 Pion. Btn. 1 Res. Co. 24 Pions. 293 Signal Command: 293 Tel. Detch. 68 Wireless Detch.	
Medical and Veterinary	....		610 Ambulance Co. 2 Mar. Field Hospital. 390 Field Hospital. 569 Vet. Hospital.	
Transports...............	....		679 M. T. Col.	
Attached...............	Coast Defense Btn.			

HISTORY.

1917.

1. The 3d Naval Division was organized in April, 1917. Its Regiments (1st, 2d, and 3d Naval Infantry) were detached from the Naval Corps, before the constitution of the division, to take part in the attacks upon Steenstraat on April 22, 1915, and on the Somme from September, 1916, to April, 1917. Since its formation the 3d Naval Division has scarcely left the coast.

FLANDERS.

2. In August, 1917, the 3d Naval Division occupied the sector of Lombartzyde.
3. In October it was in action on the Ypres front at Poelcappelle.
4. In December it again took over the sector of Lombartzyde.

RECRUITING.

The 3d Naval Division is recruited from the entire German Empire, the naval troops being imperial troops.

VALUE—1917 ESTIMATE.

Before the war the troops of the 3d Naval Division were landing and occupying troops for the German colonies. They are good units whose recruiting has been kept up to a high standard.

1918.

ALBERT.

1. The division was relieved north of St. Georges about the 1st of March and moved to Valenciennes, where it arrived about the 13th. From March 18 to 23 it moved up

to the front by stages via Haussy-Cattenieres-Lesdain.   On the 23d it followed up the advance, passing through Fins and Manancourt on the 24th-25th and coming into action at Contalmaison on the 25th.   It captured Albert on the 26th.   The division held a sector west of Albert until mid-April, and on April 24 returned to its former sector west of Anthuille.   It was relieved about the end of May by the 24th Division.

2.   On June 20 the division returned to relieve the 24th Division in the Aveluy sector.   In mid-July the company strength was low.   No drafts had been received recently and sickness was prevalent.   This, together with the August spell in line, had considerably reduced the morale of the division.   It was relieved on August 19 by the 83d Division.

SCARPE-SOMME.

3.   The division rested at Flers for five days, when it came into line west of Grevillers on the night of August 23-24 to reinforce the line.   It was withdrawn in a few days (Aug. 26) and rested at Cambrai.   Five hundred prisoners were taken from the division in this period.

4.   The division rested at Thourout during the first half of September.   On the 27th it was engaged west of Marcoing and fought in that area until the end of the month. The total prisoners captured from the division was 700.

5.   After two weeks' rest in the Cambrai area, the division returned to line at Molain on October 17.   It fought in the Molain-Catillon area until October 23, when it was relieved by the 19th Reserve Division.   On November 1 it was again in line, northwest of the Hattencourt Farm.   The last identification was at Any, on November 7.

VALUE—1918 ESTIMATE.

The division was rated as third class.   Its use in the Somme March offensive and as an intervention division in the Scarpe-Somme battle suggest that the division was a second class division.

4th Guard Division.
COMPOSITION.

	1915		1916		1917		1918 [1]	
	Brigade.	Regiment.	Brigade.	Regiment.	Brigade.	Regiment.	Brigade.	Regiment.
Infantry		5 Ft. 5 Gren. 93 Res.	5 Gd.	5 Ft. 5 Gren. 93 Res.	5 Gd.	5 Ft. 5 Gren. 93 Res.	5 Gd.	6 Ft. 5 Gren. 93 Res.
Cavalry			3d Sqn. Gd. Res. Ulan Regt.		2d Sqn. Gd. Res. Drag. Rgt.		2d Sqn. Gd. Res. Drag. Rgt.	
Artillery			(z) 2d Gd. Res. F. A. Rgt. 6 Gd. F. A. Rgt.		4 Gd. Art. Command: 6 Gd. F. A. Rgt.		4 Gd. Art. Command: 6 Gd. F. A. Rgt. 3 Abt. 1 Gd. Ft. A. Rgt. (5, 6, and 10 Btries). 1208 Light Am. Col. 1285 Light Am. Col. 1359 Light Am. Col.	
Engineers and Liaisons.			(z) Co. 3 Gd. Pions. 261 Pion. Co. 4 Gd. T. M. Co. 4 Gd. Pont. Engrs. 4 Gd. Tel. Detch.		106 Pion. Btn.: 261 Pion. Co. 269 Pion. Co. 4 Gd. T. M. Co. 315 Searchlight Section. 4 Gd. Tel. Detch.		106 Pion. Btn. 261 Pion. Co. 269 Pion. Co. 4 Gd. T. M. Co. 4 Gd. Signals Command: 4 Gd. Tel. Detch. 61 Wireless Detch.	
Medical and Veterinary.					267 Ambulance Co. 392 Field Hospital. 397 Field Hospital. Vet. Hospital.		267 Ambulance Co. 392 Field Hospital. 397 Field Hospital. 4 Gd. Vet. Hospital.	
Transports					13 Gd. Truck Train. 533 M. T. Col.		533 M. T. Col.	
Attached					32 M. G. S. S. Detch. 70 Anti-Aircraft Section.		44 Observation Group. 72 Sound Ranging Section. 244 Reconnaissance Flight. 20 Balloon Sqn.	

1 According to a document of Aug. 21, 1918.

HISTORY.

1915.

The 4th Guard Division was formed on the Russian front in March, 1915.

RUSSIA.

1. From March 14 to July 12 the 4th Guard Division was in line near Przasnysz. It belonged to Gallwitz's army, which was operating north of the Vistula.

2. From July 13 to September 28 the division took part in many fights, notably on the Narew, and took part in the pursuit as far as the region of the marshes of Lithuania.

3. Withdrawn from the front and reached Kovno on foot, where it entrained for the Western Front on October 10 via Koenigsberg, Luebeck, Hamburg, Aix-la-Chapelle, Namur. Detrained at Douai and sent to rest

FRANCE.

4. From November 14 to 26 it occupied a sector near Arras, then went to rest near Cambrai.

5. From December 15, 1915, to January 4, 1916, it built entrenchments in the region of Wytschaete-Messines.

1916.

1. During January and February, 1916, the 4th Guard Division continued its entrenching work in the sector Wytschaete-Messines and held the sector at the same time.

2. Until the end of April, 1917, the 4th Guard Division, together with the 1st Reserve Guard Division, formed the reserve corps of the guard. Both these divisions were put through a course of training with a view to active operations.

3. From May 9 to July 23 the division remained in line northeast of Neuville-St. Vaast.

SOMME.

4. Engaged in the battle of the Somme July 25 (Estres sector), suffered heavy losses and was withdrawn August 19. Engaged again after a few days of rest and fought some severe local battles until September 10 (Thiepval sector).

5. After seven days of rest behind the Flanders front it held a quiet sector north of Ypres from September 17 to October 25.

6. From November 6 to 25 it was again sent to the Somme, where it was subjected to several heavy local attacks (Warlencourt sector).

1917.

1. Remained in the Warlencourt sector until March 17, 1917. It was relieved immediately after it had retired to the Hindenburg line.

LENS.

2. After three weeks' rest in the region of Tournai it was sent by stages to the south of Lens, where it went back in the lines. It suffered considerable losses there. Withdrawn from the front July 11.

3. At rest in the region of Pont-a-Vendin and Meurchin. On August 15 the division was hurried up to the north of Lens. It attacked to regain the lost ground but in vain. Its losses were extremely heavy.

4. The division stayed in line until September 15.

FLANDERS.

5. At rest for a week behind the front. Entrained September 23 and 24 at Carvin for Flanders.

6. It was at first in the reserve of the army, but went into line September 27 east of Zonnebeke. After one of its regiments had attacked and was stopped by the British artillery fire (Oct. 22), the division obtained replacements and on October 4 renewed

its attempt to retake the heights lost on September 26. Warned by a British attack, they became demoralized and fled in disorder toward Becelaere. The losses of the 4th Guard Division were so heavy that it had to be relieved on October 5 to 7.

7. Entrained for Guise and arrived there October 10. Went into line on the 14th in the sector of Itancourt, southeast of St. Quentin, and was still holding it in December. Its forces were much reduced by the attacks in Flanders and were reinforced by neighboring units (13th Landwehr Division).

VALUE—1917 ESTIMATE.

Formerly an excellent combat unit, having that traditional esprit de corps which animated the regiments of the Prussian Guards. At the present time (November, 1917) it has lost a good part of its fighting value. It seems to have been much weakened by the battle of Ypres (October, 1917).

1918.

GUISE.

1. The division rested during January near d'Origny Ste. Benoite (west of Guise).

SOMME.

2. On February 4 the division came into line northwest of Bellenglise. It was relieved about the middle of February.

3. Upon relief, it marched via Bohain to St. Souplet, near Le Cateau. Here the division underwent a course of training in this area until March 18, when it marched via Bohain-Brancourt-Montbrehain-Ramicourt back to its old sector at Bellenglise, arriving in line March 20.

BATTLE OF PICARDY.

4. The division attacked in the first line and advanced by Hesbecourt March 21–26. Passing into support for eight days it was reengaged April 3–8 near Bouzencourt and le Hamel, suffering very heavy losses. Between the 8th and the 24th the division rested. It was in line again near Marcelcave from the 22d to the end of April, participating in the attack at Villers-Bretoneaux on the 24th. Heavy losses were again sustained.

5. Again the division went to rest at St. Souplet, near le Cateau. The 2d Battalion of the 427th Regiment, dissolved, arrived as a reinforcement for the division on May 27. The division was moved by rail to Flavy le Martel on night of June 1. It marched by nights to Canny sur Matz (by Golancourt, Guiscard, and Candor) and entered the line on the night of June 8–9.

BATTLE OF THE OISE.

6. The division attacked on the 9th between Roye sur Matz and Canny sur Matz. It penetrated by Marquelise to Antheuil. The French counterattack threw it back north of Antheuil on the 11th. The division stayed in line until the 19th.

LORRAINE.

7. After resting at Bohain until June 29 the division was moved to Lorraine by Valenciennes-Brussels-Namur-Saarburg. Here it was rested and reconstituted.

8. The division returned by rail to Athies sur Laon on July 22. From there it marched to Moussy sur Aisne by stages and then in trucks to Mareuil en Dole on July 25.

BATTLE OF THE MARNE, VESLE, AISNE.

9. The division was engaged July 27 southeast of Fere en Tardenois. It fell back toward Fismes on August 1–2, from where it was shifted into the Courlandon-Breuil sector, which it held from August 14 to the beginning of September. On the 5th it moved to the south of Glennes, remaining there until the 30th, when it fell back across the canal. The division was relieved on October 2, but turned back to line on the 5th to cover the retreat near Benu au Bac. On the 7th it went to rest for a week.

ARDENNES.

10. Reengaged west of Chateau Porcien from October 14 to November 5. The 93d Regiment was mentioned in the German communique of November 2 as fighting especially well. In the retreat the division passed through Renneville and Rubigny, where it was last identified on November 11.

VALUE—1918 ESTIMATE.

The division was always regarded as a first-class fighting division, although the losses on the Somme in March and the setback on the Oise in June lowered its value. Constant fighting impaired the morale and kept the effectives low, but the division was always to be included in the first-class divisions.

4th Division.
COMPOSITION.

	1914 Brigade	1914 Regiment	1915 Brigade	1915 Regiment	1916 Brigade	1916 Regiment	1917 Brigade	1917 Regiment	1918 Brigade	1918 Regiment
Infantry	7. 8.	14. 149. 49. 140.	7. 8.	14. 149. 49. 140.	7. 8.	14. 149. 49. 140.	8.	14. 49. 140.	8.	14. 49. 140.
Cavalry	12 Drag. Rgt. (v. Arnim).		12 Drag. Regt.				3d Sqn. Horse Gren. Rgt.		2 Sqn. 3 Horse Gren. Rgt.	
Artillery	4 Brig.:	17 F. A. Rgt. 53 F. A. Rgt.	4 Brig.:	17 F. A. Rgt. 53 F. A. Rgt.	4 Brig.:	17 F. A. Rgt. 53 F. A. Rgt.	4 Art. Command:	53 F. A. Rgt.	4 Art. Command: 53 F. A. Rgt. 48 Ft. A. Btn. 939 Light Am. Col. 945 Light Am. Col. 1319 Light Am. Col.	
Engineers and Liaisons.			1 Pion. Btn. No. 2: Field Co. 1 Pion. Btn. No. 2. 4 Pont. Engs. 4 Tel. Detch.		1 Pion. Btn. No. 2: 2 Co. 2 Pions. 4 T. M. Co. 4 Pont. Engs. 4 Tel. Detch.		114 Pion. Btn.: 2 Co. 2 Pions. 5 Co. 2 Pions. 2 Co. 114 Pions. 4 T. M. Co. 7 Searchlight Section. 4 Tel. Detch. 4 Pont. Engs.		114 Pion. Btn.: 2 Co. 2 Pions. 5 Co. 2 Pions. 4 T. M. Co. 55 Searchlight Section. 4 Signals Command: 4 Tel. Detch. 72 Wireless Detch.	
Medical and Veterinary.							6 Ambulance Co. 17 Field Hospital. Vet. Hospital.		6 Ambulance Co. 17 Field Hospital. 19 Field Hospital. 131 Vet. Hospital.	
Transport							8 Truck Train. 9 Truck Train. 537 M. T. Col.		537 M. T. Col.	
Attached							Construction Co.			

HISTORY.

(Second District—Pomerania.)

1914.

FRANCE.

1. At the beginning of the campaign the 4th Division fought on the Western Front until November, 1914. It detrained at Rheydt on August 9 and 10, and entered Belgium on the 14th and France on the 25th. Fought at Sailly-Saillisel on the 28th; reached Grand-Morin September 5 and fought at Acy en Multien on the 6th. After retreating to the north of Soissons it remained south of Roye from the end of September to the end of October, and was near Ypres in November.

RUSSIA.

2. Sent to Russia and took part in the second offensive on Warsaw.

1915.

1. In January it took part in the battles of Bolimow. In February it went to the Carpathians (Army of the South under Linsingen). Took part in the offensive on Lemburg.

2. About September 27, 1915, it was relieved in the region south of. Baranovitchi and entrained at Kobryn for the Western Front.

FRANCE.

3. It arrived in the vicinity of Sedan at the beginning of October. After a few days' rest it marched to the north of Tahure.

4. On October 30 the division took part in the attack of Butte De Tahure and suffered severe losses.

5. At the beginning of November it left Champagne for. the region of Reims where its units went into the trenches on November 8. Until the beginning of April, 1916, it held the sector northwest of Prunay.

1916.

1. At the beginning of April the division was sent to rest in the vicinity of Rethel. During this period (Nov. 15 to Apr. 16) its losses were light.

VERDUN.

2. At the beginning of May the division was sent to the region of Verdun. On May 4 it took part on the attack on Hill 304, where it suffered heavy losses.

3. Relieved May 15 and sent to rest in the region of Mouzon-Carignan, from where it went to the region of Damvillers.

4. At the beginning of July it was sent to hold the sector of Thiaumont at the moment when the French recommenced their offensive in that region. Its losses were very heavy.

5. On August 3 it left Thiaumont for the region of Cumieres, on the left bank of the Meuse (Aug. 5).

6. At the end of September it held the sector Malancourt-Avocourt.

7. Relieved at the end of October and trained at Dun. After a short rest it went into line in December northeast of Vaux.

1917.

1. The division remained in the Vaux sector until April 17.

2. It relieved the 10th Reserve Division in the region of Satigneul (night of Apr. 15–16) a few hours before the beginning of our attack. It remained in this sector until May 5 and was subjected to French attacks of April 16 and May 4.

3. Beginning May 5, it was relieved and went into camp in the region of Caurel.

CHAMPAGNE.

4. On May 7 and the following days it went into the sector of Grille Mont Haut and held this until June 19.

5. The division was put in reserve on this date in the region Epove-Warmeriville.

6. Went into line in the sector Moronvilliers (July 19 and days following) until the end of October.

BELGIUM.

7. At the end of October it entrained at Juniville and went to Belgium, where it held the sector Poelcapelle until November 24.

8. It went into line again east of Armentieres on November 30 and was still in that sector on January 11, 1918.

RECRUITING.

In spite of heavy losses suffered several times, it would seem that they wished to keep up the Pomeranian character of the 4th Division, although it received in September, 1915, some men of the 1915 class from Hesse-Nassau, and later on a number of Brandenburgers and Silesians, as the third and sixth districts often furnished their ratio to the districts temporarily out of men.   A great majority of men, however, came from Pomerania, and as the resources of this Province in men are limited it was necessary, to keep up the provincial composition of this division, to draw from the Landwehr depots and the battalions of Pomeranian Landsturm.   Since it was impossible to maintain the quality of the division, it seems that they were anxious to maintain its nationality.

VALUE.

The 4th Division was always a very good division and gave proof of very fine military qualities in all the battles in which it took part, especially in the sector of Sapigneul during the offensives of April 16 and May 4, 1917.   It would seem that the nature of the replacements they received, especially the most recent ones, has considerably altered the value of this division.

1918.

1. The division was relieved from the front of Armentieres on January 23, and went to rest and instruction in the Oisene area (southwest of Deyuze).   After four weeks the division entrained at Roubaix on March 16 and detrained at Douai on the following day.   Hence it marched by stages to Neuville St. Remy, a suburb of Cambrai.   The division was concentrated south of Inchy on the night of March 20–21.

BATTLE OF PICARDY.

2. Engaged on March 21, the division advanced by Doignies and Herrnies.   It passed to rest on the 24th and was reengaged from March 26 to April 6 at Miraumont, Hebuterne, and Colincamps.   The division suffered very heavy losses in the engagement.

3. Relieved from the Hebuterne front on April 6, the division rested two weeks in the Bapaune-Cambrai area.   The division moved north to the Lys front via Douai-Lille.

BATTLE OF THE LYS.

4. The division was in line west of Merville from April 23 to May 14.

5. While at rest north of Tournai, the division was reconstituted and prepared for another heavy engagement.

6. The division entrained for Loos on June 30 and moved on to Sailly sur la Lys on July 18.

ıE LYS WITHDRAWAL.

7. The division came into line near Merris on July 27.   It lost 500 prisoners south of eteren on August 18.   On the 30th the division fell back on Bailleul and later to ıc St. Maur and Fleurbaix.   It was relieved at Fleurbaix on October 11.

8. The division rested from the 11th to the 21st near Denain.

9. Again the division was engaged to the east and northeast of Solesmes and near ɘ Quesnoy, retreating to Beaurain, Ghissignies, and Ruesnes.   It passed in the second ıe on November 1, but came back to the line south of Le Quesnoy about November

It retreated by Locquignol toward Mauberge, where it was last identified on ovember 9.

VALUE—1918 ESTIMATE.

The 4th Division was a very good division.   In 1918 its morale was mediocre, due ı the young recruits.

4th Ersatz Division.
COMPOSITION.

	1914		1915		1916		1917		1918	
	Brigade.	Regiment.	Brigade.	Regiment.	Brigade.	Regiment.	Brigade.	Regiment.	Brigade.	Regiment.
Infantry	9 Ers. 13 Ers. 33 Ers.	9, 10, 11, and 12, Brig. Ers. Btns. 13, 14, 15, and 16, Brig. Ers. Btns. 33, 34, 35, 36, and 81, Brig. Ers. Btns.	9 Ers. 13 Ers. 33 Ers.	9, 10, 11, and 12, Brig. Ers. Btns. 13, 14, 15, and 16, Brig. Ers. Btns. 33, 34, 35, and 81, Brig. Ers. Btns.	9 Mixed Ers. 13 Mixed Ers.	359, 360. 361, 362.	13 Ers.	360, 361, 362.	13 Ers.	214 Res, 360, 362.
Cavalry	Ers. Detchs. of the 9, 13, and 33 Ers. Brigs.		Ers. Detchs. of the 9, 13, and 33 Ers. Brigs.		4 Ers. Cav. Sqn.		Ers. Cav. Detch. (3d C. Dist.)		3 Sqn. 10 Hus. Rgt.	
Artillery	1 Ers. Abt. of the 18 and 39 F. A. Rgt. 1 Ers. Abts. of the 40 and 75 F. A. Rgt. 1 Ers. Abts. of the 45 and 60 F. A. Rgt.		1 Ers. Abts. of the 18 and 39 F. A. Rgt. 1 Ers. Abts. of the 40 and 75 F. A. Rgt. 1 Ers. Abts. of the 45 and 60 F. A. Rgt.		90 F. A. Rgt. 91 F. A. Rgt.		139 Art. Command: 90 F. A. Rgt.		139 Art. Command: 90 F. A. Rgt. 119 Ft. A. Btn. 1052 Light Am. Col. 1059 Light Am. Col. 1323 Light Am. Col.	
Engineers and Liaisons.	1 Ers. Co., 3 Pions. 1 Ers. Co., 4 Pions. 1 Ers. Co., 9 Pions.		1 Ers. Co., 3 Pions. 1 Ers. Co., 4 Pions. 1 Ers. Co., 9 Pions.		303 Pion. Co. 304 Pion. Co. 305 Pion. Co. 161 T. M. Co.		504 Pion. Btn.: 304 Pion. Co. 305 Pion. Co. 161 T. M. Co. 251 Searchlight Section. 554 Tel. Detch.		504 Pion. Btn.: 304 Pion. Co. 305 Pion. Co. 161 T. M. Co. 59 Searchlight Section. 554 Signal Command: 554 Tel. Detch. 123 Wireless Detch.	
Medical and Veterinary.							64 Ambulance Co. 135 Field Hospital. 136 Field Hospital. Vet. Hospital.		64 Ambulance Co. 135 Field Hospital. 136 Field Hospital. 136 Vet. Hospital.	
Transports									762 M. T. Col.	
Attached			1 Res. Co., 25 Pions.		103 Antiaircraft Section. 2 Res. Co., 25 Pions.					

HISTORY.

(360th and 361st: Fourth District—Prussian Saxony.   362d: Ninth District—Schleswig–Holstein.)

1914.

The 4th Ersatz Division was organized in August, 1914, by grouping together brigade Ersatz Battalions coming from the Third, Fourth, and Ninth districts (Brandenburg Prussian-Saxony, Mecklenburg, Schleswig-Holstein, and Hansa towns).

LORRAINE.

1. Detrained August 18 at Teterchen (Lorraine) and at the battle of the 20th the division was in the rear of the 2d Bavarian Corps. It fought on the 22d along the Marne-Rhine Canal between Einville and Dombasle, retreated on the 23d, suffered heavy losses on the 25th at Mazerulles, and engaged only a few units of its 9th Brigade in the attack on Nancy in September.

2. On September 15 the division went to rest west of Delme. On the 23d it entrained at Rening (Sarralbee-Benestroff line), passed through Metz, Luxembürg, Arlon, Marche, Liége, Louvain and detrained September 25, 1915, at Brussels.

BELGIUM.

3. From there it went to Bruges (Oct. 14), then Ostend (Oct. 16). On the 17th by the road along the coast it marched from Ostend to Nieuport (Oct. 30).   It then went into the line in front of the Belgians on the right bank of the Yser (November).

1915.

DIXMUDE.

1. Remained in the sector north of Dixmude during the whole of 1915.

2. At the end of July, 1915, the brigade Ersatz Battalions of the division were grouped into regiments. The 4th Ersatz Division was made up of the 359th, 360th, 361st and 362d Infantry. With the 37th Landwehr Brigade and the 2d Reserve Ersatz Brigade (Basedow Division) it constituted the Werder Corps (December).

1916.

1. The division was kept in the region of Dixmude until April, 1916.

2. After April a part of the division was sent east of Ypres between the Ypres-Roulers Railway and the Comines Canal. Some of the units of the division remained in line near Dixmude. .

SOMME.

3. About September 27 the division left Belgium for the Somme, where it was engaged during the first two weeks of October near Le Sars.

4. On October 15 it returned to Belgium and went back to the sector east of Ypres in November.

5. Sent to rest about November 30 and sent back to the Somme south of Bapaume, about the middle of December.

1917.

1. Remained south of Bapaume (Le Transloy-Gueudecourt) until the end of February, 1917.

2. About the middle of March it relieved the 14th Bavarian Division in the same sector at the beginning of the retirement of the German troops, withdrew to the east of Bertincourt, via Neuville-Bourjonval, Metz en Courtuere, and fought on the Trescault-Havricourt line (April).

ARTOIS.

3. Relieved about April 26 or 28 and sent north of the Scarpe about May 10. Engaged near Roeux until about May 18 and suffered heavy losses (more than 800 prisoners).

4. At the end of May it was sent to the Eastern Front. The 361st Infantry entrained May 26 at Vitry en Artois, via Paderborn-Halle-Leipzig-Dresden-Breslau-Lemburg.

GALICIA.

5. Until July the division remained in reserve in Galicia with the Bothmer army.

6. In July it held the sector south of Brzezany. Took part in the offensive against the Russians, and in September was near Radautz, where it remained until December. Due to some of its forces being transferred to other organizations more than to its losses, the companies of the 362d Infantry from August to October, had fallen from 120 men to 70 (examinations of Russians).

FRANCE.

7. Relieved December 4 and entrained the 16th for the Western Front, via Lemberg-Cracow-Breslau-Berlin-Hanover-Aix la Chapelle-Brussels-Courtrai-Tournai. Detrained the 26th.

RECRUITING.

360th Infantry: Brandenburg and Prussia Saxony. 361st and 362d Infantry: Prussia Saxony, Hanover, Schleswig-Holstein and Hansa towns.

VALUE.

A fairly good division.

1918.

LA BASSEE.

1. The first entry into line of the division was on January 18 in the sector south of the La Bassee Canal, relieving the 6th Bavarian Division.

BATTLE OF THE LYS.

2. On the 5th of April the division crossed north of the canal and attacked in the Gorre-Givenchy-Festubert region. Seven hundred prisoners were lost on April 9, besides heavy casualties. The division was relieved on April 20–21.

WOEVRE.

3. The division was moved to the region south of Metz for a rest. About May 18 it took up a sector south of Les Esparges, which it held until about June 13.

4. After resting near Conflans until June 25, it entrained in the Woevre and moved by Sedan-Charleville to the region east of Laon, arriving on June 28. It preceeded to the line by the road through Fismes.

AISNES-MARNE.

5. The division was engaged at Bussiares, Torcy, and Hautevisnes between June 30 and July 18. It met the attack of July 18 and was thrown back toward Oulchy le Chateau. On the 24th it was relieved.

6. The division rested at Perthes for a week and then moved to Novy. It entrained at Amagne on August 12 and traveled to Ostrecourt, where it remained for two weeks. On August 28 it occupied the Dricourt-Queant line astride the Arras-Cambria road.

SECOND BATTLE OF PICARDY.

7. Engaged on the 29th, the division came in for some heavy fighting. It was thrown back on Dury (Sept. 2) and after losing 1,650 prisoners was relieved on September 5.

8. The division rested until the middle of September. The 214th Reserve Regiment coming from the dissolved 46th Reserve Division, replaced the 361st Regiment.

9. The division was engaged near the La Bassee Canal from September 16 to October 1. It rested until the 16th, when it was reengaged southwest of Lille. In the retreat it fell back by Wavrin, Seclin, Cysoing, Ere, Mons and Blaugies. The last identification was at Boussu on November 9.

VALUE—1918 ESTIMATE.

The division was rated as a third-class division. At no time in 1918 did it distinguish itself, especially not in the Lys battle. Before the July 18 attack, the infantry effectives of the division numbered about 3,200. In October the battalions were reduced to three companies.

4th Landwehr Division.
COMPOSITION.

	1914 Brigade	1914 Regiment	1915 Brigade	1915 Regiment	1916 Brigade	1916 Regiment	1917 Brigade	1917 Regiment	1918 Brigade	1918 Regiment[1]
Infantry	22 Ldw. 23 Ldw.	11 Ldw. 51 Ldw. 22 Ldw. 23 Ldw.	22 Ldw. 23 Ldw.	11 Ldw. 51 Ldw. 22 Ldw. 23 Ldw.	22 Ldw. 23 Ldw.	11 Ldw. 51 Ldw. 22 Ldw. 23 Ldw.	22 Ldw.	11 Ldw. 23 Ldw. 51 Ldw. 404.	22 Ldw.	23 Ldw. (?) 51 Ldw.
Cavalry		Ers. Cav. Rgt. of the 4 Ldw. Div. (4 Sqns.). 2 Ldw. Cav. Rgt. (3 Sqns.).	Ers. Cav. Rgt. of the 4 Ldw. Div.		Ers. Cav. Rgt. of the 4 Ldw. Div.		3 Sqn. 4 Drag. Rgt.			
Artillery	4 Ldw. F. A. Rgt. (Ers. Abtls. 6, 42, and 56 F. A. Rgt.).		4 Ldw. F. A. Rgt.		4 Ldw. F. A. Rgt.		Art. Command: 4 Ldw. F. A. Rgt. (9 Btries.).		4 Ldw. F. A. Rgt. (Staff, 2 Abt. Staff and 5 and 6 Btries.).	
Engineers and Liaisons.	1 Ers. Co. 6 Pions.		1 Ers. Co. 6 Pions.		1 Ers. Co. 6 Pions. 2 Ers. Co. 6 Pions. 304 T. M. Co.		(404) Pion. Btn.; 1 Ers. Co. 6 Pions. 2 Ers. Co. 6 Pions. 304 T. M. Co. 25 Light Fortress Searchlight Section. 323 and 332 Searchlight Sections. Tel. Detch.		2 Ers. Co. 6 Pions. 304 Signals Command: 504 Tel. Detch.	
Medical and Veterinary.							236 Ambulance Co. 19 Ldw. Field Hospital. 20 Ldw. Field Hospital. Vet. Hospital.		236 Ambulance Co. 19 Ldw. Field Hospital. 504 Vet. Hospital.	
Transport							785 T. M. Co.			
Attached	21 Mixed Ers. Brig. (21, 22, 23, 24, and 78, Brig. Ers. Btsn.) Dis. in Sept.						7th Munster Landst. Inf. Btn. (7 C. Dist. Batn. No. 69) arrived from 3 Ldw. Div.			

[1] The elements below are those grouped in the 4th Landwehr Division Postal Zone. Other elements belonging to the 4th Landwehr Division but operating in other sectors (Nov. 13) are listed as attached to the divisions they are operating under.

HISTORY.

(Sixth District—Silesia.)

1914.

At the beginning of the war the 4th Landwehr Division, with the 3d Landwehr Division, formed the 2d Landwehr Corps (former 7th Landwehr Corps), which was engaged on the Eastern Front.

POLAND.

1. The 4th Landwehr Division at the beginning of September, 1914, took part in the battle of Tarnowka with the 3d Landwehr Division, then in the operations before Warsaw and the retreat following the enveloping movement of the Russians at Lodz. In December it was located between the Vistula and Pilica (at Czenstochow, Dec. 1; near Kielee, Dec. 28).

1915.

1. Until July, 1915, the division remained on the Polish front (left bank of the Vistula) between Radom and Gravowiec.

BARANOVITCHI.

2. Took part in the offensive against the Russians, which carried it through the region of Baranovitchi in July to August.

1916.

1. Held the front northeast of Baranovitchi from September, 1915, until the beginning of 1918. In 1916 it contributed drafts to the 420th Infantry.

1917.

1. Sector of Baranovitchi. The division had many of its forces transferred to the Western Front: In November, 1917, for the 52d Division; in February, 1918, for the 5th Reserve Division, but during 1917 it was reinforced by the 404th Infantry, coming from the 18th Landwehr Division.

VALUE—1917 ESTIMATE.

Mediocre.

1918.

UKRAINE.

1. At the beginning of April, 1918, the 4th Landwehr Division marched into Russia. On the 14th of April, the 11th Landwehr Regiment was near Minsk; and at the beginning of May it was east of Kiev, along with the 404th Regiment.

On June 15 the 23d and 51st Landwehr Regiments were identified near Ochra.

3. A man of the 51st Landwehr Regiment wrote on October 23: "The latest news is that the 4th Landwehr Division is going into France." The division was still in Russia on October 28 and was never identified on the Western Front.

4th Bavarian Division.

COMPOSITION.

	1914 Brigade	1914 Regiment	1915 Brigade	1915 Regiment	1916 Brigade	1916 Regiment	1917 Brigade	1917 Regiment	1918 Brigade	1918 Regiment
Infantry	7 Bav. 5 Bav. Res.	5 Bav. 9 Bav. 5 Bav. Res. 8 Bav. Res.	7 Bav. 5 Bav. Res.	5 Bav. 9 Bav. 5 Bav. Res. 8 Bav. Res.	7 Bav.	5 Bav. 5 Bav. Res. 9 Bav.	7 Bav.	5 Bav. 5 Bav. Res. 9 Bav.	7 Bav.	4 Bav. 5 Bav. 9 Bav.
Cavalry	5 Bav. Light Cav.				5 Bav. Light Cav. (3 Sqns.).		3 Bav. Light Cav. (5th Sqn.).		5 Sqn. 3 Bav. Light Cav. Rgt.	
Artillery	4 Bav. Brig.: 2 Bav. F. A. Rgt. 11 Bav. F. A. Rgt.		4 Bav. Brig.: 2 Bav. F. A. Rgt. 11 Bav. F. A. Rgt.		4 Bav. Brig.: 2 Bav. F. A. Rgt. 11 Bav. F. A. Rgt.		4 Bav. Art. Command: 2 Bav. F. A. Rgt. 11 Bav. F. A. Rgt. (?)		4 Bav. Art. Command: 2 Abt. 4 Bav. F. A. Rgt. 122 Bav. Light Am. Col. 134 Bav. Light Am. Col. 135 Bav. Light Am. Col.	
Engineers and Liaisons.	2d Field Co. 2 Bav. Pion. Btn.		2d Field Co. 2 Bav. Pion. Btn. 4 Bav. Pont. Engs. 4 Bav. Tel. Detch.		2d and 5th Field Cos. 2 Bav. Pion. Btn. 4 Bav. T. M. Co. 4 Bav. Pont. Engs. 4 Bav. Tel. Detch.		6 Bav. Pion. Co. 9 Bav. Pion. Co. 4 Bav. T. M. Co. 4 Bav. Tel. Detch.		8 Bav. Pion. Btn.: 6 Bav. Pion. Co. 9 Bav. Pion. Co. 14 Bav. T. M. Co. 4 Bav. Searchlight Section. 4 Bav. Signal Command: 4 Bav. Tel. Detch. 108 Bav. Wireless Detch.	
Medical and Veterinary.							5 Bav. Ambulance Co. 11 Bav. Field Hospital. Vet. Hospital.		5 Bav. Ambulance Co. 11 Bav. Field Hospital. 12 Bav. Field Hospital.	
Transports							M. T. Col.		684 Bav. M. T. Col.	
Attached					35 Labor Btn.					

HISTORY.

(Second Bavarian District—Bavaria and Lower Franconia.)

1914.

1. At mobilization the 4th Bavarian Division, with the 3d Bavarian Division, formed the 2d Bavarian Army Corps. It transferred its 8th Brigade (Metz Garrison) to the 33d Reserve Division and replaced it by the 5th Bavarian Reserve Brigade, organized in the Palatinate. The other brigade, the 7th, detrained, commencing August 3, between Morhange and Remilly. The reserve brigade detrained August 10 at St. Avold. Assembled the 18th in the rear of the Metz-Strasbourg Railroad and with the 2d Bavarian Army Corps constituted the 6th Army (Crown Prince Ruprecht of Bavaria).

LORRAINE.

2. On August 20 it fought west of Morhange. Then it captured the fort of Manon-viller (with the 22d Bavarian of the 3d Bavarian Division) and advanced to Mortagne, south of Luniville. September 11 it was withdrawn to the rear.

SOMME.

3. September 18 the division entrained at Metz for Namur, from where it went to the north of Peronne (Sept. 25). It then became part of the 2d Army and fought from September 26 to the middle of October in the region north of the Somme (Fricout, Mametz, Montauban).

FLANDERS.

4. During the third and fourth weeks of October (beginning the 23d) it went to Flanders (6th Army) south of Ypres. It held the sector of Wytschaete from November 14 to October 15 and was on the defensive. November 9 the 5th Infantry was reduced to less than 800 men (notebooks).

1915.

In March, 1915, the 8th Reserve Infantry was transferred from this division to the 10th Bavarian Division.

ARTOIS.

1. September 26, 1915, some of its units fought on the Loos-Hulluch front at the time of the British attack. In the counter attack, during which these troops retook ditch No. 8, they suffered severe losses.

In November the whole division was in the region of Loos south of Hulluch, where it stayed until August 16. In this sector it carried on mine warfare. About the end of April, 1916, it lost 1,100 men while attempting a gas attack.

1916.

SOMME.

1. Toward the end of August, 1916, the division was sent to the Somme.

2. It was engaged between Martinpuich and Longueval, where it fought violent battles for the Bois Haut (Aug. 25–28 to Sept. 15). Its total losses were 5,361 men, or 60 per cent of its effectives.

FLANDERS.

3. Again sent to Flanders and held the sector northeast of Armentieres (east of the Bois de Ploegsteert) from October 16 to June 17.

1917.

1. In June, 1917, while still in line in front of Bois de Ploegsteert, it was in part subjected to the British attack against Messines ridge, and suffered especially from the artillery preparations. It lost 200 prisoners.

2. Relieved from the Belgian front about June 16 and sent to rest in the region of Audenarde until July 7.

3. Beginning July 9, it was engaged southeast of Armentieres (between the Lys nd Wez-Macquart) July and August.

4. Withdrawn from the Armentieres sector in the middle of September and went nto line northeast of Ypres, between Zonnebeke and Passchendaele, from September 26 to October 27. Suffered heavy losses (30 per cent of its forces).

LORRAINE.

5. October 11 entrained at Pitthem and went to Conflans the 13th from where it rent into line in the region of Thiaucourt (Limey sector). It was there still in February, 1918.

RECRUITING.

Lower Franconia and Bavarian Palatinate.

VALUE—1917 ESTIMATE.

The 4th Bavarian Division went through some very severe offensive and defensive ights and came through them with honors.

The prisoners examined gave proof of vigor and tenacity if not of intelligence. As soon as it is filled up again this division shall again take its place on the most ffective fronts (December, 1917).

It is to be noted that February, 1918, it is not yet completely filled up and does not seem to be in shape for an offensive.

1918.

1. The division remained in the quiet Thiaucourt sector until late March when t was relieved by the 40th Division. On April 14 it entrained at Nancieulles and raveled via Audun le Romain-Longuyon-Sedan-Charleville-Hirson-Avesnes-Denain-Orchies to Rouchin. It marched to Armentieres, arriving on April 16, and proceeded o reserve near Bailleul on the following day.

KEMMEL.

2. On the 23d of April the division came into line northeast of Dranoutre, suffered heavy losses about here, and was relieved about May 1.

3. The division rested until June 11 in the north of France. During this time it vas reviewed by the King of Bavaria and Prince Franz. The division commander vas decorated.

FLANDERS.

4. It returned to line near Merris about June 11. It continued in line, suffering heavy losses until July 10.

5. The division rested out of line until August 17.

6. It was reengaged on August 17 east of Bucquoy, coming from Lille via Cambria Velu Beuguy. It was withdrawn from the battle north of Bapaume on August 25, after losing 1,600 prisoners.

7. The division rested near Tourcoing until late in September.

8. On September 29 the division was identified in line in Champagne, north of Maure. Its composition had been changed by the disbandment of the 5th Bavarian Reserve Regiment and the substitution of the 4th Bavarian Regiment from the dissolved 14th Bavarian Division. The division continued on this front, with short periods in the second line, until November 4. It was identified north of Marvaux October 4), near Monthois (October 11), between Namdy and Falaise (October .9). The division was considered in reserve 3d Army between November 4 and the armistice.

VALUE—1918 ESTIMATE.

The division was of the first quality. It saw heavy fighting and showed itself very aggressive in attack and tenacious in defense. The extensive replacements vhich have been necessary did not improve the morale, but due to the high quality and spirit of the organization, it was always to be considered as a first-class division.

4th Cavalry Division (Dismounted).

COMPOSITION.

	1918	
	Brigade.	Regiment.
	39 Cav............	38 Ldw. Inf. Rgt. 40 Ldw. Inf. Rgt. 9 Res. Schutzen Uhlan Rgt. 89 Schutzen Rgt. 87 Schutzen Rgt.
Engineers and Liaisons................................	2 Ldw. Pion. Co., 14 C. Dist. Pions.	
Medical and Veterinary................................	99 Ambulance Co.	
Attached..	Landst. Inf. Btns. VII–54 Munster. XIV–14 Bruchsae. IV–15 Jorgan. XVI–7 2d Saarlouis XIV5 1st Offenburg	

HISTORY.

1918.

1. The 4th Cavalry Division entrained in the Riga region on the 1st of April, 1918, for the Western Front. It detrained at Molsheim in Alsace on April 7, and went into line near the Ban de Sapt (Vosges). The division had recently been reorganized. During April a report was received stating that Lieut Gen. von Krame, commander of the 39th Cavalry Brigade, had been decorated. The division continued to hold the Alsace sector until the armistice.

VALUE—1918 ESTIMATE.

The division was rated as fourth class.

5th Guard Division.

COMPOSITION.

	1917		1918	
	Brigade.	Regiment.	Brigade.	Regiment.
Infantry...............	2 Gd.	3 Ft. 3 Gren. 20.	2 Gd.	3 Ft. 3 Gren. 20.
Cavalry...............	1 Sqn. 2 Gd. Uhlan Rgt.		1 Sqn. 2 Gd. Uhlan Rgt.	
Artillery...............	5 Gd. Art. Command: 4 Gd. F. A. Rgt.		5 Gd. Art. Command: 4 Gd. F. A. Rgt. 1 Abt. 1 Gd. Res. Ft. A. Rgt. 1180 Light Am. Col. 1181 Light Am. Col. 1203 Light Am. Col.	
Engineers and Liaisons.	100 Pion. Btn.: 4 Gd. Pions. 1 Gd. Res. Pion. Co. 9 Gd. T. M. Co. (?) 28 Searchlight Section. 5 Gd. Tel. Detch.		100 Pion. Btn.: 4 Gd. Pion. Co. 1 Gd. Res. Pion. Co. 9 Gd. T. M. Co. 195 Searchlight Section. 5 Gd. Signal Command: 5 Gd. Tel. Detch. 149 Wireless Detch.	
Medical and Veterinary.	3 Ambulance Co. 8 Field Hospital. 9 Field Hospital. Vet. Hospital.		3 Ambulance Co. 8 Field Hospital. 9 Field Hospital. 5 Gd. Vet. Hospital.	
Transports............	M. T. Col. 680 Divisional M. T. Col.		680 M. T. Col.	
Odd units.............	Field Recruit Depot No. 815.			
Attached.............	3 Abt. 43 Res. F. A. Rgt. 2 Abt. 3 Bav. Ft. A. Rgt. 2 Abt. 11 Res. Ft. A. Rgt. 2 Abt. 21 Ft. A. Rgt. 3 Btry. 57 Ldw. Ft. A. Rgt. 5 Btry. 57 Ldw. Ft. A. Rgt. 6 Btry. 57 Ldw. Ft. A. Rgt. 10 Btry. 13 Res. Ft. A. Rgt. 11 Btry. 13 Res. Ft. A. Rgt. 6 Btry. 17 Bav. Ft. A. Rgt. 464 Ft. A. Btry. 4 Co. 8 T. M. Btn. 3 Co. 8 T. M. Btn. 1 Co. 5 Road. Const. Btn. No. 72. 3 Co. 166 Labor Btn. 43 Res. Pion. Co. 199 Signal Btn. 307 Signal Btn. 2 Field Signal Co. 60 Balloon Section. 114 Supply Train. 21 Munition Train. 181 Munition Train. 190 Munition Train. 374 Munition Train. 517 Munition Train. 560 Supply Train. 50 Supply Train. 1 Field Bakery.			

HISTORY.

1917.

Organized in February, 1917, from regiments transferred from already existing units (3d Foot Guards, transferred from the 1st Guard Division; 3d Grenadier Guards, transferred from the 2d Guard Division; 20th Infantry, from the 212th Division, previously belonging to the 6th).

CRAONNE.

1. It appeared for the first time in line about March 20 between Craonne and Hurtebise, where it suffered heavy losses, April 16 to 18.

2. Relieved May 4 and went to a calm sector in the region of Preqmontreq.

3. About June 5-6 it was sent to rest in the region north and northwest of Laon. June 20 it was located in the region of Sissonne, where it remained until July 7.

CALIFORNIE PLATEAU.

4. On the night of July 7-8 it arrived in this sector. It executed a violent attack on July 19 and again suffered heavy losses. Relieved July 27.

5. Reinforced by drafts from depots in Brandenburg and rested in the region of Mauregny en Haye and Barenton sur Cerre, and then went through a methodical and intensive training at the camp at Chivy les Etouvelles.

CHEMIN DES DAMES.

6. About August 20 it relieved the 43d Reserve Division on the Chemin des Dames between Pantheon and La Royere; suffered considerable losses during the French offensive of October 23.

7. In the region of Vervins at the beginning of November, with its battalions greatly reduced.

8. Went into line near Hargicourt at the end of November.

RECRUITING.

The 20th Infantry (3d Brandenburg) was a regiment from the Province of Brandenburg.

The 3d Foot Guards and the 3d Grenadier Guards were drawn not only from Brandenburg, but generally from the Kingdom of Prussia.

VALUE—1917 ESTIMATE.

The 5th Guard Division must be considered one of the best divisions of the German Army. Its regiments are extremely good.

The Division had been brought to the Aisne to retake the Californie Plateau, and it showed wonderful energy in this work (July 19, 1917). October 23, 1917, at the Chemin des Dames, in spite of its great losses and of the fact that the 1918 class formed about 20 per cent of its effectives, the division showed great resistance, and left only a comparatively small number of prisoners in our hands (about 300).

1918.

1. The division arrived at Fourmies on January 10 for training and maneuvers. About February 14 it marched to Avesnes, where it rested until March 5. It then marched to St. Quentin by night marches, passing through Hornblieres, Dallow, Happencourt, Tugny, and crossed the Crozat Canal between Ham and St. Simon on March 23.

BATTLE OF PICARDY.

2. On the night of the 23d it relieved the 45th Reserve Division in front of Golancourt, where it met a lively resistance. From the 24th to the 27th it was in army reserve resting in the region Golancourt le Plesses Patte d'Oie. On the 28th it moved

>y Flavy le Meldux, Ecuvilly, Catigny, Candor, and entered line west of Lassigny on he 29th, relieving the 1st Bavarian Division. On the 30th it attacked west of the Roye sur Matz railroad but was stopped by our counterattacks. Until April 10 the division was in line at Beuvraignes and at Roye sur Matz. On the 8th it received 400 men, mostly of the 1919 class, in reinforcements.

3. Withdrawn from line on April 4, the division moved by degrees to the northeast of Laon on April 24, where it was reorganized, reinforced, and rested near Rozay sur Serre. By night marches it moved to the Aisne front and entered line on May 26, between Corbeny and the Californie Plateau.

BATTLE OF AISNE.

4. It fought in the offensive from May 27 to 30, advancing by Guyencourt, Fismes, } guy, Cierges, and Vincelles. Between May 31 and June 7 it was in reserve at Cououges, Sergy, Beuvardes, Grisolles, and Sommelous. The division was reengaged northwest of Chateau Thierry on June 7 against the American 2d Division.

CHATEAU THIERRY.

5. In the three weeks the division was in the Torcy-Hautevesnes sector it lost most heavily. Several companies of the 20th Regiment were annihilated on June 8-9; the others were reduced to 30–40 rifles. The division lost about one-half its effectives in this period.

6. It was withdrawn about June 30 and reconstituted in reserve of the Torcy sector near Coincy from July 1 to 17.

BATTLE OF THE MARNE.

7. The division came back on the 18th and engaged in rear-guard fighting near Monthiers and Grisolles. It was engaged on defensive works near Blanzy les Fismes from July 29 to August 8.

8. It rested in the region of Bruyeres from August 2–8, when it was transported to Belgium by Marle-Hirson to rest. On the 31st it was alerted and entrained, the regiments following with a day's interval by Mauberg-St. Quentin, detraining at Laon and Crepy en Laonnois. From that point it moved by foot to Vauxaillon front.

AISNE–AILETTE.

9. On September 3 the division relieved the 238th Division east of Louilly. In the succeeding days it suffered very heavily. It was relieved on September 16.

10. The division left the Laon area on September 16 and detrained that night at St. Juvin, where it rested until September 24. The heavy losses of the division were made good while there.

ARGONNE.

11. It entered the line opposite the American 1st Army on September 27 in the region of Montblainville. After heavy losses, which caused a partial disintegration of the division, it withdrew on October 8. The 3d Guard Grenadier Regiment was practically destroyed in this fighting.

WOEVRE.

12. It was transported to the Woevre and on October 19 was engaged east of Verdun at Chatillon sous les Cotes. Here it remained until the armistice.

VALUE—1918 ESTIMATE.

The division was rated as a first-class division, but after its rough handling in the Hautevesnes-Torcy sector it lost much of its value as an attack division.

Both on the Aisne in September and in the Argonne the division's losses were extremely heavy. Battalions were reduced to three companies in October. By the 0th of October the remnants of the companies were combined to make one.

5th Division.
COMPOSITION.

	1914 Brigade	1914 Regiment	1915 Brigade	1915 Regiment	1916 Brigade	1916 Regiment	1917 Brigade	1917 Regiment	1918 Brigade	1918 Regiment
Infantry	9. 10.	8 Body Gren. 48. 12 Gren. 52.	9. 10.	8 Body Gren. 48. 12 Gren. 52.	10.	8 Body Gren. 12 Gren. 52.	10.	8 Body Gren. 12 Gren. 52.	10.	8 Body Gren. 12 Gren. 52.
Cavalry	3 Hus. Rgt. (3 Sqns.)......			(?)	3 Hus. Rgt. (3 Sqns.).		3 Hus. Rgt. (?).		3 Sqn. 3 Hus. Rgt.	
Artillery	5 Brig.: 18 F. A. Rgt. 54 F. A. Rgt.		5 Brig.: 18 F. A. Rgt. 54 F. A. Rgt.		5 Brig.: 18 F. A. Rgt. 54 F. A. Rgt.		5 Art. Command: 18 F. A. Rgt.		142 Art. Command: 18 F. A. Rgt. 67 F. A. Btn. (Staff and 1, 2, and 3 Btries). 848 Light Am. Col. 879 Light Am. Col. 792 Light Am. Col	
Engineers and Liasions			1 Pion. Btn. No. 3: Field Co. 3 Pions. 5 Pont. Engs. 5 Tel. Detch.		1 Pion. Btn. No. 3: 1 Co. 3 Pions. 5 Pont. Engs. 5 Tel. Detch. 5 T. M. Co.		116 Pion. Btn. (formerly 1 Pion. Btn. No. 3): 1 Co. 3 Pions. 2 Co. 3 Pions. 5 T. M. Co. 319 Searchlight Section. 5 Tel. Detch. 99 Searchlight Section.		116 Pion. Btn.: 1 Co. 3 Pions. 2 Co. 3 Pions. 14 Bav. Pion. Co. 5 T. M. Co. 35 Searchlight Section. 5 Signal Command: 5 Tel. Detch. 29 Wireless Detch.	
Medical and Veterinary.							9 Ambulance Co. Field Hospital. Vet. Hospital.		9 Ambulance Co. 27 Field Hospital. 26 Field Hospital. 5 Vet. Hospital.	
Transports							11 Supply Train.		538 M. T. Col.	
Attached					Field M. G. Co. of the 10 Brig.		M. T. Col. M. G. S. S. Detch. No. 5. 68 Anti-Aircraft Sect.			

HISTORY.

(Third District—Brandenburg.)

1914.

FRANCE.

1. The 5th Division with the 6th Division formed the 3d Army Corps. At the beginning of the campaign it was part of the 1st Army, (Von Kluck). It detrained near Aix la Chapelle August 9 and 10, entered Belgium the 14th, and passed through Louvain the 19th. Took part in the battle of Charleroi and the battle of the Marne (at Sancy and Cerneux, Sept. 6), then in the battles between the Aisne and the Marne in September, and was finally stabilized between the Aisne and the Oise, in the region Vailly and Soissons.

1915.

1. Battle of Soissons (Jan. 13).

2. About June 10 the 5th Division was no longer a part of the 1st Army. July 1 it was sent to Douai, and about July 14 held the sector before Arras.

3. September 25, 1915, took part in the attacks in Champagne.

BELGIUM.

4. Went to Belgium in December. About December 25 was at rest in the region Hirson-Avesnes.

1916.

VERDUN.

1. At the beginning of February, 1916, it was in the region of Spincourt.

2. At the end of February at Verdun. It fought near Herbebois February 23. It attacked Douaumont February 26 and suffered severe losses. It was again engaged from March 8 to 15 and from April 22 to the end of the May.

SOMME.

3. July at the Somme (Longueval, Bois Delville). Suffered heavy losses.

4. Middle of August in Champagne (Auberive) until October 12.

VERDUN.

5. December, 1916, it went again to Verdun (region of Vaux, Dec. 7). Units of the 5th Division were engaged as reinforcements during the French attack of December 15. The division was withdrawn from the Verdun front about December 25 and sent to the region of Mulhouse.

1917.

ALSACE.

1. Stayed in Upper Alsace (region of Mulhouse and Ferrette) until April 20, 1917. It held temporarily a calm sector in the Vosges region, but during this period it is used particularly for entrenching works on the French front and the Swiss frontier.

CHAMPAGNE.

2. It was alarmed. It entrained in the region of Mulhouse and was sent through Montmedy and Sedan to Champagne, where it went into line on April 23 in the Mont-Haut sector, where it suffered very heavy losses.

3. Left Champagne front at the beginning of May.

4. Toward the end of June it was in the Woevre in the region between Conflans and Briey.

5. At the beginning of July it was again in the Champagne (Téton sector).

RUSSIA.

6. Sent to the Eastern Front in July and relieved at the beginning of September by the 6th Reserve Division in the region of Zbrucz.

ITALY.

7. About October sent from Galicia to Italy.

FRANCE.

8. Sent from Italy to France at the beginning of January, 1918, and at rest behind the front in Champagne. January 20, 1918, it went into line near Butte du Mesnil.

Essentially from Brandenburg (Regiments of the Mark, as the communiques sometimes call it), and its provincial character has been carefully maintained.

VALUE—1917 ESTIMATE.

Although not as good as at the beginning of the war, the morale of the 5th Division seemed good and its fighting value worthy of consideration (July 17).

1918.

1. After its return from Italy the division rested and trained at Chenois, near Charleville, from January 1 to March 1, when it moved to Anderlues-Resbaix (west of Charleroi) from March 1 to 14. On that date it moved to the front by night marches by Maubeuge, Landrecies, Wassigny, and Etaves.

BATTLE OF PICARDY.

2. It took its place in line between Lesdins and Remancourt (north of St. Quentin) on the night of March 20–21. The next day it was engaged in support of the 25th Division, advancing via Morcourt and Fayet. It took part in the attack on Holnon Wood and reached Attilly that night. It continued to advance on the 22d via Beauvois-Lanchy-Uguy-Quivieres-Croix-Moleguaux to a point east of Falvy. On the 24th it forced the crossing of the Somme at Falvy and Pargny and reached Morchain that night. It was at Omilcourt on the 25th and captured Chaulnes on the 26th; from there it advanced to Fouquescourt and Rouvroy on the 27th, crossed the Avre, and when the line stabilized near Aubvillers the division withdrew, March 28. Its losses in the fighting were extremely heavy. In crossing the Somme it especially distinguished itself.

3. The division rested until April 3, when it was reengaged between Sauvillers and Grivesnes from April 3–12. It again lost heavily, especially the 52d Regiment, during the attack of April 4 near the Bois de Arrachies.

4. It rested and trained from April 13 to May 23 at Iron et Vadencourt, near Guise. It is known to have received 1,000 men from Beverloo on April 14. From May 23 to 26 it marched toward the Aisne front by night, through Parpeville, Monceau le Neuf, Aisis sur Serre, Couvron, Laniscourt, Foucancourt.

BATTLE OF THE AISNE.

5. On the night of June 26 it entered line southeast of Lizy. In the offensive the division advanced by Chavignon, Malmaison, Ureguy, region of Pommiers, Mercin, Pernant, east of Ambleny. It was partially relieved on June 7 and the last elements withdrawn by June 13.

6. The division rested between Guise and Le Nouvion (Mannappes Lechelle) from the middle of June to July 18. During this period the Spanish sickness ravished the troops. Reinforcements reconstituted the division during this period. On July 19 the division was transported to Anezy le Chateau by way of Wassigny, Guise, Mesbricourt. By marches it moved by steps to south of Soissons.

BATTLE OF THE MARNE.

7. On July 21 the division was engaged near Buzancy. It fell back to the Vesle by Acy on August 1–2. It remained in the sector south of Vailly (Ciry–Salsogne, Sermoise) until September 5, when it retired to the line Vailly-Celle sur Aisne. After losing more than 1,000 prisoners it was relieved on September 18.

ARDENNES.

8. The division was reengaged in the region of Jonchery on September 28. It retired north of the Aisne (Sept. 30) toward Berry au Bac. Again retreated October 0 by Prouvais, La Malmaison, to Nizy le Comte. It was in line there until October 7, when it retired to the second line for a week. It was reengaged in the same region rom October 25 to November 5, when it retreated by Rozoy and Brunehamel with xtremely heavy losses.

VALUE—1918 ESTIMATE.

Before the summer of 1918 the 5th Division was an excellent assault division, requently mentioned in German communiques. But after August, 1918, it became a sector-holding division. It was almost constantly in line after July 21 with consequent lowering of morale and discipline. In November it had but two battalions per regiment and three companies per battalion.

5th Reserve Division.
COMPOSITION.

	1914 Brigade.	1914 Regiment.	1915 Brigade.	1915 Regiment.	1916 Brigade.	1916 Regiment.	1917 Brigade.	1917 Regiment.	1918 Brigade.	1918 Regiment.
Infantry	9 Res. 10 Res. 3 Res. Jag. Btn.	8 Res. 48 Res. 12 Res. 52 Res.	9 Res. 10 Res. 3 Res. Jag. Btn.	8 Res. 48 Res. 12 Res. 52 Res.	10 Res.	8 Res. 12 Res. 48 Res.	10 Res.	8 Res. 12 Res. 48 Res.	9 Res.	8 Res. 12 Res. 48 Res.
Cavalry	2 Res. Dragoon Rgt. (3 Sqns.).				2 Res. Drag. Rgt.		2 Res. Drag. Rgt. (?) (1 Sqn.).		5 Sqn. 4 Drag. Rgt.	
Artillery	5 Res. F. A. Rgt. (6 Btries.).		5 Res. F. A. Rgt.		5 Res. F. A. Rgt.		90 Art. Command: 5 Res. F. A. Rgt..........		90 Art. Command: 5 Res. F. A. Rgt. 4 Abt. 17 Res. Ft. A. Rgt. 1086 Light Am. Col. 1176 Light Am. Col. 1202 Light Am. Col.	
Engineers and liaisons.	4 Field Co. and 2 Res. Co. of the 2 Pion. Btn. No. 3.		4 Field Co. and 2 Res. Co. of the 2 Pion. Btn. No. 3. 205 T. M. Co. 5 Res. Pont. Engs. 5 Res. Tel. Detch.		4 Field Co. and 2 Res. Co. of the 2 Pion. Btn. No. 3. 205 T. M. Co. 5 Res. Pont. Engs. 5 Res. Tel. Detch.		(305) Pion. Btn.: 4 Co. 3 Pions. 2 Res. Co. 3 Pions. 205 T. M. Co. Tel. Detch.		505 Pion. Btn.: 4 Co. 3 Pions. 2 Res. Co. 3 Pions. 205 T. M. Co. 69 Searchlight Section. 405 Signal Command: 405 Tel. Detch. 44 Wireless Detch.	
Medical and Veterinary.							503 Ambulance Co. 64 Res. Field Hospital. 65 Res. Field Hospital. Vet. Hospital.		503 Ambulance Co. 64 Res. Field Hospital. 65 Res. Field Hospital. 135 Res. Vet. Hospital.	
Transports.							M. T. Col.		705 M. T. Col.	

HISTORY.

(Third District—Brandenburg.)

1914.

The 5th Reserve Division is organically a part of the 3d Reserve Corps, with the h Reserve Division.

ELGIUM.

1. At the beginning of the war the division belonged to the 1st Army (Von Kluck). etrained at Crefeld from August 10 to 12; entered Belgium the 18th. The 3d Reserve rps was sent to France. The division was at Malines on August 22, at Vilvorde the th, and fought against the Belgians on that day. The 3d Reserve Corps then turned ward Antwerp, which it besieged. After the city was taken the corps advanced ward the sea through Ghent, Bruges, October 13 to 16. The 19th the 5th Reserve ivision attacked in the direction of Nieuport. At the beginning of November it ught in the vicinity of Bixschoote, in the forest of Houthulst; then until the end of ovember it held the Dixmude-Langmarck front.

USSIA.

2. About December 2 the division entrained for the eastern front. On arriving in ussia it became part of Mackensen's army (9th Army). It was sent to the Bzura.

1915.

1. In February, 1915, the division was attached to the 10th Army and took part in e battle of Prasnysz.

2. In May one of its brigades remained before Kovno with the 10th Army (Gen. n Eichhorn). The other brigade joined the 3d Reserve Corps of the 9th Army en. von Fabeck) and fought on the Bzura. The 52d Reserve Infantry was trans- red to the 107th Division.

3. In July the division was reorganized. It was attached to the 9th Army before arsaw and fought between the Bzura and the Pilica.

4. In November, after crossing the Vistula and the Bug it arrived before Barano- tchi. It remained in this region until March, 1917.

1916.

1. On January 1, 1916, it held the eastern sector of Novo-Grudok, north of Bara- vitchi.

2. At the beginning of April the division was placed in reserve behind this sector.

3. During the first two weeks of July it was engaged between Gorodivche and ranovitchi to oppose the Russian offensive started on this part of the front. On ly 8 it suffered heavy losses. (The 8th Reserve had 1,200 men out of action.)

1917.

ANCE.

1. It was relieved in this area about the middle of April and sent to the Western ont.

2. Entrained between the 17th and 18th of April at Molczacz (Baranovitchi sector) d went to France, via Brest–Litovsk–Warsaw–Oppeln–Breslau–Goerlitz–Dresden– ipzig–Sondershausen–Frankfort on Main–Sarrebrucken–Metz. It detrained at urs la Tour.

JEVRE.

3. It was then sent to St. Maurice sous les Cotes, where it rested for a few days d then went to the Cotes de Meuse, east of the Combres Heights. It went into sector before Combres (Calonne trench) on May 15 or 16, and there became accus- ned to the Western Front.

CALIFORNIE PLATEAU.

4. Relieved May 27, it was sent behind the Aisne front; spent about three weeks in the Sissonne region, and about June 19 went into line on Californie Plateau near Chaevreux. On June 24, July 3 and 22, the division executed some violent attacks on Californie Plateau, and some of its units lost half their men.

5. Partially relieved about July 23, the units of the division were sent to rest successively at St. Erme, Ramecourt, and La Selve. Before August 10 it was back on Californie Plateau (region of Craonne south of Corbeny).

6. The division took part on the same position in the general retreat of November 1 which brought the German lines back to the north of the Ailette following the French attack of La Malmaison. The division remained on these new lines (south and west of Corbeny) until January 22, 1918.

7. Relieved on this date and put through a course of training in the region of Chimay. On February 18 it marched to the sector of Juvincourt.

RECRUITING.

Brandenburg.

VALUE—1917 ESTIMATE.

The division is considered by the Germans as a very good division. Its original elements came from the best corps, the Brandenburg corps, but it contains a large proportion of Poles. The division needs rest and replacements. When reconstituted it will probably again be a good unit. (Dec. 29, 1917.)

1918.

LAON.

1. On February 21 the division relieved the 113th Division at Juvincourt, which sector it held until March 26.

PICARDY.

2. It was withdrawn to reinforce the battle front at Chauny, where it appeared on April 2. About April 11, it retired to second line, from which it returned to the battle front on April 25, relieving the 242d Division at Couchy le Pots. The division continued to hold this sector until early June.

NOYON.

3. Between June 1 and 10 it was moved from the Couchy le Pots sector to reinforce the Montdidier-Noyon battle front, where it was identified on June 12 near Courcelles. It was withdrawn on June 17.

4. During July the division rested in rear of the Amiens front.

SOMME.

5. It came into line on August 8 at Trace le Mont. In the opening week of the offensive it lost many prisoners and retired from the line about August 20 to rest near St. Gobain. On the 29th it returned to line near Arblencourt-Champs. It withdrew early in September but returned to support the 80th Reserve Division in a counterattack executed in the region Sancy-Vauxillon September 16–18.

6. Following this the division was rested near Laon. On October 7 it was entrained and moved to the region of Tupigny-Mennevret.

7. It was engaged on October 9 to the east of Bohain before the extreme right of the 4th British Army. It was relieved in this sector on October 23 by the 200th Division. At this time the division was very low in effectives; two regiments had three battalions of three companies and one regiment had but two battalions. The average company strength was about 50 men.

8. Retired to rest for 15 days, the division returned to line on November 5, near Wiege Faty. It was last identified at Trelon on November 11.

VALUE—1918 ESTIMATE.

The division was rated as a second-class division. In the earlier years it was a very good division, but through losses and lack of reinforcements during 1918 considerably reduced its value.

COMPOSITION.

	1916		1917		1918		1918	
	Brigade.	Regiment.	Brigade.	Regiment.	Brigade.	Regiment.	Brigade.	Regiment.
Infantry......	37 Mixed Ldw. 2 Res. Ers.	73 Ldw. 74 Ldw. 4 Res. Ers. 3 Res. Ers.	37 Ldw.	3 Res. Ers. 73 Ldw. 74 Ldw.	37 Ldw.	73 Ldw. 74 Ldw. 8 Landst.	37 Ldw.	73 Ldw. 74 Ldw. (?)
Cavalry......		8 Cuirassier Rgt. (Ers. Sqn.).	8 Cuirassier Rgt. (Ers. Sqn.). 88 Cav. Rgt. (3 Sqn.).				1 Sqn. 16 Drag. Rgt.	
Artillery......	102 F. A. Abtl. (1 Ers. Abt. 26 F. A. Rgt).		102 F. A. Regt.				250 Ldw. F. A. Rgt.	
Engineers and liaisons.	161 T. M. Co.		Pion. Btn.: (?) 2 Landst. Co. 9 C. Dist. Pions. 405 T. M. Co. 303 Searchlight Section. 555 Tel. Detch.				2 Landst. Co. 9 C. Dist Pions. 111 Searchlight Section. 555 Signal Command. 555 Tel. Detch.	
Medical and veterinary.			269 Ambulance Co. (?) (11 Ldw.) Field Hospital. 505 Vet. Hospital.				269 Ambulance Co. 500 Field Hospital. 11 Ldw. Field Hospital. 505 Vet. Hospital.	
Transports......	763 M. T. Col.		763 M. T. Col.				763 M. T. Col.	
Attached......			2 Insterburg Landst. Inf. Btn. (1 C. Dist. Btn. No. 6).					

HISTORY.

(73d Landwehr and 74th Landwehr: Tenth District—Hanover. 8th Landsturm:
Eighth District—Rhine Province.)

1916.

The 5th Ersatz Division was organized in the fall of 1915 with the name of Basedow Division. It comprised the 37th Landwehr Brigade (73d and 74th Landwehr); until then attached to the 26th Reserve Corps, and the 2d Reserve Ersatz Brigade (3d Ersatz Reserve and 4th Reserve Brigade), situated in the Dixmude sector. With the 4th Ersatz Division, the Basedow Division, which became the 5th Ersatz Division in 1916, constituted at the end of 1915 the Werde Corps.

BELGIUM.

1. From January to October, 1916 the division remained in Belgium (region of Yser, then southeast of Ypres). However, the 4th Ersatz Reserve was transferred to the 206th Division at the beginning of September.

SOMME.

2. Withdrawn from the Ypres front at the beginning of October, the division was sent to the Somme and engaged north of Courcelette from October 19 to 30.

3. In November it was sent to rest behind the Champagne front.

RUSSIA.

4. At the beginning of December it was sent to Russia (the 73d Landwehr entrained December 11 northeast of Reims, via Dusseldorf-Hamburg-Koenigsburg-Tilsit-Pone-viej. Detrained at Elovka the 16th).

1917.

COURLAND.

Sent into line in the Illukst sector (region of Dvinsk) at the beginning of January 1917 and remained in this country during the whole year (Illukst, Lake Stenten, Kchtchava). Its losses were very small—17 killed and 20 wounded in the 3d Ersatz Reserve from the end of December, 1916, to the end of August, 1917. Because the sector was so quiet the division had only small forces during the last months of 1917. The 73d Landwehr at the end of November had only 60 to 65 men per company (examination of Russians).

VALUE—1917 ESTIMATE.

The division remained for a long time in the quiet sectors of the Russian front and seems to have had only moderate fighting value.

1918.

COURLAND.

1. The 5th Ersatz Division was still in the vicinity of Dvinsk in February. In March it exchanged the 3d Ersatz Regiment for the 8th Landsturm Regiment of the 87th Division, the latter being on the point of leaving for France.

LIVONIA.

2. The division advanced into Livonia (in March) and remained in the Pskov-Ostrov region as late as June 27th. The 74th Landwehr Regiment was identified here on August 6, but the rest of the division was identified near Mitau during July.

3. Toward the end of October, it was reported that the division, having been refitted, had come to the Western Front via Trier and Rethel however, the division was never actually identified on the Western Front.

VALUE—1918 ESTIMATE.

The division was rated as 4th class.

COMPOSITION.

	1914 Brigade	1914 Regiment	1915 Brigade	1915 Regiment	1916 Brigade	1916 Regiment	1917 Brigade	1917 Regiment	1918 Brigade	1918 Regiment
Infantry	14 Ldw. 30 Ldw.	36 Ldw. 66 Ldw. 17 Ldw. 25 Ldw. 65 Ldw.	14 Ldw. 30 Ldw.	36 Ldw. 66 Ldw. 25 Ldw. 65 Ldw.	14 Ldw. 30 Ldw.	36 Ldw. 66 Ldw. 25 Ldw. 65 Ldw.	30 Ldw.	25 Ldw. 36 Ldw. 65 Ldw.	30 Ldw.	25 Ldw. 36 Ldw. 65 Ldw.
Cavalry						4 Sqn. 1 Uhlan Rgt.	2 Sqn. 16 Uhlan Rgt.		2 Sqn. 16 Uhlan Rgt.	
Artillery					1 and 2 Landst. 4 C. Dist. Batteries. F. A. 256 Ldw. F. A. Rgt. (left in July).		Art. Command: 256 Ldw. F. A. Rgt.		256 Ldw. F. A. Rgt. 1,415 Light Am. Col.	
Engineers and Liaisons.	1 Ldw. 11 C. Dist. Pion. Co.				1 Ldw. 11 C. Dist. Pion. Co. 1 Ldw. 16 C. Dist. Pion. Co. 305 T. M. Co.		(405) Pion. Btn.: 1 Ldw. 11 C. Dist. Pion. Co. 1 Ldw. 16 C. Dist. Pion. Co. 305 T. M. Co. 321 Searchlight Section. Tel. Detch.		405 Pion. Btn.: 1 Ldw. Co. 11 C. Dist. Pions. 1 Ldw. Co. 16 C. Dist. Pions. 305 T. M. Co. 217 Searchlight Section. 505 Signal Command: 505 Tel. Detch. 92 Wireless Detch.	
Medical and Veterinary.							Ambulance Co. 151 Field Hospital. Vet. Hospital.		12 Ambulance Co. 67 Field Hospital. 79 Field Hospital.	
Transports							M. T. Col.		775 M. T. Col.	
Attached			93 Ldw. Inf. Regt. (June to Sept.)							

HISTORY.

(25th Landwehr and 65th Landwehr: Eighth District—Rhine Province.   36th Landwehr: Fourth District—Prussian Saxony.)

1914.

The 5th Landwehr Division is composed of two Landwehr brigades meant to be the war garrison of Metz, where they detrained August 9 and 10, 1914: 14th Landwehr Brigade from the Fourth District (36th Landwehr and 66th Landwehr); 30th Landwehr Brigade from the Eighth District (25th Landwehr and 65th Landwehr). The 17th Landwehr was under the 14th Brigade.

WOEVRE.

1. During the first days of September the 14th Landwehr Brigade was engaged at Fresnes and Marcheville (in Woevre), near the 33d Reserve Division. It fought on the Cotes de Meuse, near Champlon and Les Eparges, at the beginning of October and suffered heavy losses there.

2. In December the two brigades (14th Landwehr Brigade and 30th Landwehr Brigade) were united in the Woevre (Warcq, Hennemont, Marcheville, Champlon, Saulx). The division at that time was part of the Von Strantz detachment.

1915.

1. The division remained in the sector between Warcq and Saulx en Woevre during the whole of 1915. In January the 17th Landwehr, from which many men had deserted, was sent to Russia, where it assisted in the formation of the 85th Landwehr Division.

1916.

COTES DE MEUSE.

1. At the time of the Verdun offensive the division was present during the attacks on the Cotes de Meuse, near Braquis, Ronvaux, Manhuelles, at the end of February to March, 1916.

2. Toward the end of March the 14th Landwehr Brigade took the place of the First Guard Ersatz Brigade (Guard Ersatz Division) in the Apremont sector.

3. The 30th Landwehr Brigade was kept before the Cotes de Meuse (region of Fresnes en Woevre) until July. It then rejoined the other brigade east of St. Mihiel.

1917.

FOREST OF APREMONT.

1. The division from this time on did not leave the Forest of Apremont sector. In April, 1917, the 66th Landwehr was transferred to the 23d Landwehr Division, newly organized, and soon sent to Russia.

VALUE—1917 ESTIMATE.

A sector unit.

1918.

1. On April 12 the division undertook a local operation in the Apremont sector in an effort to divert troops and artillery from the Somme front. About 800 men of the Storm Battalion were engaged. Forty-seven prisoners were lost in the attack. Aside from this the sector continued very quiet until September 12.

BATTLE OF ST. MIHIEL.

2. The division was engaged in the attack in the St. Mihiel salient. It lost heavily in prisoners, among whom were the entire staff of the 3d Battalion, 65th Landwehr Regiment, which was taken on September 12 in the Bois de Thiaucourt. The division retreated with orders to take up positions between the first and second positions of

Hindenburg line.   Here it had orders to hold the Mihiel Zone under all circum-
nces.

. The division continued in line until the armistice.

VALUE—1918 ESTIMATE.

The 5th Landwehr Division was rated as a fourth-class division.   In 1918 it held
Apremont sector continuously, showing no initiative or capacity for offensive
eration, but due to the small losses and heavy effectives it offered as much resistance
our attack in September as did the other German divisions in the salient.

5th Bavarian Division.

COMPOSITION.

	1914 Brigade.	1914 Regiment.	1915 Brigade.	1915 Regiment.	1916 Brigade.	1916 Regiment.	1917 Brigade.	1917 Regiment.	1918 Brigade.	1918 Regiment.
Infantry	9 Bav. 10 Bav. 2 Bav. Res. Jag. Btn.	14 Bav. 21 Bav. 7 Bav. 19 Bav. Jag. Btn.	9 Bav. 10 Bav. 2 Bav. Res. Jag. Btn.	14 Bav. 21 Bav. 7 Bav. 19 Bav. Jag. Btn.	9 Bav. 10 Bav.	14 Bav. 21 Bav. 7 Bav. 19 Bav.	10 Bav.	7 Bav. 19 Bav. 21 Bav.	10 Bav.	7 Bav. 19 Bav. 21 Bav.
Cavalry	7 Bav. Light Cav. Rgt.		7 Bav. Light Cav. Rgt.		7 Bav. Light Cav. Rgt. (2 Sqns.).		2 Bav. Light Cav. Rgt. (4 Sqns.).		4 Sqns. 2 Bav. Light Cav. Rgt.	
Artillery	5 Bav. Brig.; 6 Bav. F. A. rgt. 10 Bav. F. A. Rgt.		5 Bav. Brig.; 6 Bav. F. A. Rgt. 10 Bav. F. A. Rgt.		5 Bav. Brig.; 6 Bav. F. A. Rgt. 10 Bav. F. A. Rgt.		5 Bav. Art. Command.; 6 Bav. F.A.Rgt.(6 Btries.).		5 Bav. Art. Command. 10 Bav. F. A. Rgt. 3 Abt. 1 Bav. F. A. Rgt. (Staff, and 9, 10, and 11 Btries.). 103 Bav. Light Am. Col. 109 Bav. Light Am. Col. 166 Bav. Light Am. Col.	
Engineers and Liaisons.	1 and 4 Field Cos. 3 Bav. Pion. Btn.		1 and 4 Field Cos. 3 Bav. Pion. Btn. 5 Bav. Pont. Engs. 5 Bav. Tel. Detch.		1 and 4 Field Cos. 3 Bav. Pion. Btn. 5 Bav. T. M. Co. 5 Bav. Pont. Engs. 5 Bav. Tel. Detch.		(3) 5 Bav. Pion. Btn. 10 Bav. Pion. Co. 13 Bav. Pion. Co. 5 Bav. T. M. Co. 5 Bav. Tel. Detch.		3 Bav. Pion. Btn.: 10 Bav. Pion. Co. 13 Bav. Pion. Co. 5 Bav. Searchlight Section. 5 Bav. Signal Command: 5 Bav. Tel. Detch. 100 Bav. Wireless Detch.	
Medical and Veterinary.							3 Bav. Ambulance Co. 6 Bav. Ambulance Co. Field Hospital. Vet. Hospital.		6 Bav. Ambulance Co. 21 Bav. Field Hospital. 25 Field Hospital.	
Transport							114 M. T. Col.		685 M. T. Col.	
Attached					84 Labor Btn. Anti-Aircraft. Section 1 Bav. Balloon Sqn.					

HISTORY.

(Upper and Middle Franconia—Bavaria.)

1914.

LORRAINE.

1. At the beginning of the war the division was a part of the 3d Bavarian Army Corps, with the 6th Bavarian Division, and was part of the 6th Army (Crown Prince Ruprecht of Bavaria). Detrained between Boulay and Courcelles from August 9 to 11, t fought August 20 on the right of the 2d Bavarian Corps at Oron, Lusy, Fremery. Crossed the frontier on the 22d and advanced to Sanon, fighting on the 25th at Serres nd Hoéville, and on September 2 at Einville Wood. During the days following it ormed the left of the troops attacking Nancy by way of Champenoux.

VOEVRE.

2. After its failure the division was assembled at Metz on September 13 and 14. The 19th it was at Mars-la-Tour. From there going through La Haye it reached the Jotes de Meuse. The 7th Infantry took Nonsard the 20th and Heudicourt the 21st. Marching on the left of the 6th Bavarian Division, which went up the hill, the 5th Bavarian Division, walking along the summit, established itself in the forest of Apremont at the beginning of September 25 and held it during the whole of 1915, and, except for the months of October and November, 1915, during the summer of 1916. Its losses were quite high during the first two months of the campaign. On October 4 the 1st Company of the 14th Infantry had only 1 officer and 41 men (notebooks).

1915.

CHAMPAGNE.

1. October 6, 1915, the division was sent to Champagne, via Audun le Roman-Longuyon-Sedan, to relieve the 16th Reserve Division which had been crushed by the French attack of September 25. It was engaged south of Tahure (La Courtine) beginning October 13.

VOEVRE.

2. At the beginning of December it returned to its old sector east of St. Mihiel.

1916.

ARTOIS.

1. In July, 1916, the division was withdrawn from the St. Mihiel salient and sent o Artois. It held the Lens-Vimy sector until the end of August, 1916.

SOMME.

2. September 7 to 8 it was engaged in the Somme (Delville Wood-Ginchy). It uffered heavy losses in the fights around Ginchy and during the British attack of September 15 (Flers, Gueudecourt).

ARTOIS.

3. Relieved September 20, it went back into line after a few days of rest in the ector Neuve-Chapelle, south of the Armentieres road.

1917.

ARTOIS.

1. The division remained on the front south of Armentieres during the whole winter 916 to 1917. In February it was reduced to three regiments on the transfer of the 4th Infantry to the 16th Bavarian Division, newly organized.

2. It left the lines at the end of April, but at the beginning of May went to the sector orth of Arras, where it fought heavily at Fresnoy on May 7 and southeast of Gavrelle n June 28.

BELGIUM.

3. Withdrawn from the Oppy-Gavrelle front July 1 and sent to rest near the Belgian-Dutch front. It went through a period of training at the Brasschaet camp in July.

FLANDERS.

4. About August 6 it entrained and went to Gits, via Lokeren, Ghent, Thielt, and Pitthen. From there it went to Roulers. On August 10 held the sector south of St. Julien, east of Ypres, where it suffered heavy losses in the fighting of August 15 and days following. Relieved August 24.

5. After a period of rest the division went back into line September 8, in the quiet sector of Deulemont (south of the Lys) and held it until the end of February, 1918.

RECRUITING.

Upper and Middle Franconia (3d Bavarian District).

VALUE—1917 ESTIMATE.

Although not among the best Bavarian divisions, it was a good combat unit. In 1917 it did well at Arras and on the Ypres front where it suffered heavy losses (information from the British, February, 1918).

1918.

1. About February 13 the division was relieved, moved to Tourcoing (Feb. 14), and trained in that area until March 17, when it marched to Roubaix. It entrained and moved to Fressies (5 miles north of Cambrai), rested until the 19th, and moved to the front.

BATTLE OF PICARDY.

2. It was engaged east of Cambrai (Vaux-Vrancourt) on March 22. Retiring to second line about April 4, it rested near Sapignies until about April 11, when it was identified southeast of Boyelles. It was relieved by the 111th Division on May 6.

3. The division trained in the Somain area until May 22, when it was moved by trucks via Cantin and Palluel to Ecourt. A day later it marched to Bullecourt and relieved the 221st Division on night of May 24–25. Lieut. Gen. v. Endres, the division commander, was promoted to the command of the 1st Bavarian Corps about this time The division was relieved in the Boyelles sector on July 15 by the 21st Reserve Division.

BATTLE OF THE SOMME.

4. After resting behind the Arras Front the division entered the line near Lihons on August 10. After suffering heavy losses it withdrew from the battle front south of Peronne on September 24 and retired to the Le Cateau region.

5. It rested for a week and returned to the battle at Rumilly on the night of September 30–October 1. About October 12, after heavy losses, it was withdrawn and rested near Valenciennes.

6. On October 25 it was again put in line at Rameguies-Chin. It was last identified at Mourcourt on November 9.

VALUE—1918 ESTIMATE.

The 5th Bavarian Division was a first-class division. In 1918, it was almost constantly engaged in the most active sectors on the British front.

5th Bavarian Reserve Division.
COMPOSITION.

	1914 Brigade.	1914 Regiment.	1915 Brigade.	1915 Regiment.	1916 Brigade.	1916 Regiment.	1917 Brigade.	1917 Regiment.	1918 Brigade.	1918 Regiment.
Infantry	9 Bav. Res. 11 Bav. Res. 1 Bav. Res. Jag. Btn.	6 Bav. Res. 7 Bav. Res. 10 Bav. Res. 13 Bav. Res.	9 Bav. Res. 11 Bav. Res. 1 Bav. Res. Jag. Btn.	6 Bav. Res. 7 Bav. Res. 10 Bav. Res. 13 Bav. Res. 39 Ldw.	9 Bav. Res. 1 Bav. Res. Jag. Btn.	10 Bav. Res. 7 Bav. Res. 3 Bav. Res. 12 Bav. Res. Jag. Btn.	11 Bav. Res.	10 Bav. Res. 7 Bav. Res. 12 Bav. Res.	11 Bav. Res.	7 Bav. Res. 10 Bav. Res. 12 Bav. Res.
Cavalry	5 Bav. Res. Cav. Rgt. (3 Sqns.).		5 Bav. Res. Cav. Rgt.		(?)			(?)	2 Sqn. 3 Bav. Light Cav. Rgt.	
Artillery	5 Bav. Res. F. A. Rgt. (6 Btries.).		5 Bav. Res. F. A. Rgt.		5 Bav. Res. F. A. Rgt. (9 Btries.).		17 Bav. Art. Command: 5 Bav. Res. F. A. Rgt. (9 Btries.).		17 Bav. Art. Command: 5 Bav. Res. Ft. A. Rgt. 17 Bav. Ft. A. Btn. 102 Bav. Light Am. Col. 104 Bav. Light Am. Col. 119 Bav. Light Am. Col.	
Engineers and Liaisons.	4 Field Co. and 1 Res. Co. 2 Bav. Res. Pion. Btn.		4 Field Co. and 1 Res. Co. 2 Bav. Res. Pion. Btn. 5 Res. Pont. Engs. 5 Res. Tel. Detch.		4 Field Co. and 1 Res. Co. 2 Bav. Res. Pion. Btn. 205 Bav. T. M. Co. 5 Bav. Res. Cable Pont. Engs. 5 Bav. Res. Tel. Detch.		(18) Bav. Pion. Btn. 2 Bav. Res. Pion. Co. 19 Bav. Res. Pion. Co 205 Bav. T. M. Co. 405 Bav. Tel. Detch.		18 Bav. Pion. Btn.: 2 Bav. Res. Pion. Co. 19 Bav. Res. Pion. Co. 205 Bav. T. M. Co. 8 Bav. Searchlight Section. 405 Bav. Signal Command: 405 Tel. Detch. 103 Wireless Detch.	
Medical and Veterinary.							16 Bav. Ambulance Co. 46 Bav. Field Hospital. 56 Bav. Field Hospital. Vet. Hospital.		16 Bav. Ambulance Co. 46 Bav. Field Hospital. 50 Bav. Field Hospital.	
Transports							M. T. Col.		751 Bav. M. T. Col.	
Odd units										
Attached										

HISTORY.

(Third Bavarian District—Upper Palatinate, Upper and Middle Franconia.)

1914.

LORRAINE.

1. The division constituted, with the 5th Bavarian Reserve Division, the 1st Bavarian Reserve Corps, and at the beginning of the war was part of the army of Crown Prince Ruprecht of Bavaria (6th Army). It detrained from August 11 to 13 between Sarreguemines and Sarralbe. It fought August 20 on the left of the 21st Corps at Loudrefeing, was engaged the 26th at Maixe, September 2 at Deuxville, northwest of Luniville, and remained a few days longer behind Luniville.

2. On September 13 it was in line on the Seille and the Paris-Avricourt Railroad and remained there until the last days of the month.

ARTOIS.

3. September 28 and 29 the division entrained at Metz. Detrained the 30th and October 1 at Valenciennes. Engaged north of Arras (Roclincourt-Carency) in October and November and took position in the sector.

1915.

In January, 1915, the division was increased by the 39th Landwehr Infantry (Westphalian), coming from Brussels and sent as punishment to the Artois front. In March and April two of its regiments were transferred, the 6th Reserve to the 10th Bavarian Division, and the 13th to the 11th Bavarian Division.

ARTOIS.

1. May 9, 1915, the division suffered very heavy losses during the French offensive of Carency-Souchez. (The 10th Reserve Infantry lost 35 officers and 1,711 men, the 1st Reserve Bavarian Battalion of Chasseurs lost 13 officers and 750 men.)

2. In the middle of June the division was moved south of the Scarpe in front of Arras (Blangy sector).

1916.

In January, 1916, the 39th Landwehr Infantry went to Russia.

1. The division remained in Artois until August, 1916, and was increased by a regiment from the 1st Bavarian Division (3d Reserve Infantry later replaced by the 12th Reserve Infantry).

SOMME.

2. Relieved about August 7, the division was sent to the Somme and was engaged near Maurepas from the middle of August to September. Heavy losses. August 19 the 2d Battalion of the 10th Reserve Infantry was reduced to 150 men (letter). September 1 the 3d Battalion of the 7th Reserve Infantry borrowed 200 men from the 5th Bavarian Ersatz (letter).

AISNE.

3. In the middle of September the division was sent to the Aisne, where it held a quiet sector east of Craonne until the end of November.

SOMME.

4. About December 9 the division returned to the Somme (south of Saillisel.)

1917.

1. The division was withdrawn from the Somme front at the end of January, 1917, and sent to rest in the vicinity of Cambrai until April.

AISNE.

2. At the beginning of April it was sent east of Laon to the region of St. Erme, and reinforced the front south of Juvincourt between the Miette and the Aisne about

April 12 in anticipation of the French offensive. It was subjected to the attack of the 16th and suffered heavy losses (2,000 prisoners).

ST. MIHIEL.

3. Withdrawn from the Aisne front about April 20, the division was reconstituted north of Laon (?), and on May 1 held the St. Mihiel sector (Chauvoncourt-Spada).

4. October 7 it left the region of St. Mihiel.

FLANDERS.

5. Sent to Flanders and sent into line October 12 near the Ypres-Roulers Railroad (Zonnebeke). In November it was left of Artois, where it held, after intervals of relief, a sector north of the Scarpe (from Gavrelle to Acheville). It was still there at the end of February, 1918.

RECRUITING.

3d Bavarian Division (Upper Palatinate, Upper and Middle Franconia).

VALUE—1917 ESTIMATE.

Good division, which has always fought well (October, 1917). April 16, 1917, it fought with great tenacity.

1918.

1. Early in January the division was relieved in its sector north of the Scarpe and went to rest north of Douai.

SCARPE.

2. It was reengaged southeast of Gavrelle on February 21, when it was in line during the attack. It took no prominent part in the offensive and was withdrawn about the 1st of April.

SOMME.

3. On April 7-8 it came in line south of Hebuterne, where it was engaged until April 16. After eight days' rest it came into line south of the Ayette, relieving the 195th Division on April 24. It was not withdrawn until July 24.

ALSACE.

4. The division moved to Muelhausen, via Belgium and Germany, a trip of 10 days. While at rest there it was frequently alerted in anticipation of an expected Allied attack in that region. On September 4 it returned through Germany and Belgium to Douai, where the British were attacking.

5. It left Douai on September 22, detraining at Dun sur Meuse on September 23. From there the division marched to the front.

MEUSE-ARGONNE.

6. On September 27 it was engaged at Daunevoux. It was engaged throughout the entire Meuse-Argonne battle on the American front. At Montfaucon it was forced back with heavy losses. The division affected relief by regiments, which were sent to close support to be reconstituted by drafts. Five hundred replacements were received early in October. The initial company combat strength averaged 60 men. On November 4 this had been reduced to 20. During the retreat of November 1-2 the division crossed the Meuse and took up a position on the east bank.

VALUE—1918 ESTIMATE.

The 5th Bavarian Reserve Division was rated as a second-class division. Apart from the Meuse-Argonne offensive, it did not see much heavy fighting during the year. Its effectives had been almost completely used up by the time of the armistice.

5th Cavalry Division.

COMPOSITION.[1]

	1918	
	Brigade.	Regiment.
Cavalry	9 Cav	4 Drag. 10 Uhlan.
	11 Cav	1 Cuirassier. 8 Drag.
	12 Cav	4 Hus. 6 Hus.
Artillery	5 Horse Art. Abt. (5.7 cm.).	
Medical and Veterinary	643 Ambulance Co.	
Odd units	1 M. G. Btry. 5 Cav. Pion. Detch.	
Attached	52 Ldw. Inf. Rgt.	

[1] At the time of its dissolution, July, 1918.

HISTORY.

1918.

There were repeated rumors of the division being on the Western Front in 1918, but no satisfactory identification was ever received.

According to a deserter of the 8th Dragoon Regiment, who left his regiment in Jeumont, south of Binche, on May 20, the entire 5th Cavalry Division entrained in Russia about March 6 and detrained at Zossen, south of Berlin, where it was re-formed and trained. On the 26th of April the division moved to St. Amand, from where it moved two weeks later to the Jeumont and Marpent area.

Evidence points to the dissolution of the division on the Western Front about July, 1918.

VALUE—1918 ESTIMATE.

The division was rated as a fourth-class division.

6th Division.
COMPOSITION.

	1914		1915		1916		1917		1918	
	Brigade.	Regiment.	Brigade.	Regiment.	Brigade.	Regiment.	Brigade.	Regiment.	Brigade.	Regiment.
Infantry	11. 12. 3 Jäg. Btn.	20. 35 Fus. 24. 64.	11. 12.	20. 35 Fus. 24. 64.	12.	20. 24. 64.	12.	24. 64. 396.	12.	24. 64. 396.
Cavalry		3 Hus. Rgt. (3 Sqns.).				3 Hus. Regt. (3 Sqns.).		3 Hus. Regt. (5 Sqns.).		5 Sqn. 3 Hus. Rgt.
Artillery	6 Brig.: 3 F. A. Rgt. 39 F. A. Rgt.		6 Brig.: 3 F. A. Rgt. 39 F. A. Rgt.		6 Brig.: 3 F. A. Rgt. 39 F. A. Rgt.		6 Art. Command: 3 F. A. Rgt.		64 Art. Command: 1 Abt. 3 Ft. A. Rgt. (Staff and 2 and 4 Btries). 1087 Light Am. Col. 1168 Light Am. Col. 1205 Light Am. Col.	3 F. A. Rgt.
Engineers and Liaisons.			1 Pion. Btn. No. 3: Field Co. 3 Pions. 6 Pont. Engs. 6 Tel. Detch.		1 Pion. Btn. No. 3: 2 Co. 3 Pions. 6 T. M. Co. 6 Pont. Engs. 6 Tel. Detch.		1 Pion. Btn. No. 3: (now 116 Pion. Btn.): 3 Co. 3 pions. 5 Co. 3 pions. 6 T. M. Co. 6 Tel. Detch.		3 Pion. Btn.: 3 Co. 3 Pions. 5 Co. 3 Pions. 6 T. M. Co. 64 Searchlight Section. 6 Signal Command: 6 Tel. Detch. 2 Wireless Detch.	
Medical and Veterinary.							Ambulance Co. Field Hospital. Vet. Hospital.		8 Ambulance Co. 29 Field Hospital. 31 Field Hospital. 233 Vet. Hospital.	
Transport.							M. T. Col.		539 M. T. Col.	
Attached.					M. G. Co. to the 12 Brig.		242, 244, 245, and 246 Mountain M. G. Detch., Naumburg Landst. Inf. Btn. (IV C. Dist. No. 11).			

HISTORY.

(Third District—Brandenburg.)

1914.

At mobilization the 6th Division formed, together with the 5th Division, the 3d Army Corps (Berlin).

CHARLEROI–MARNE.

1. At the beginning of the war the 3d Army Corps belonged to the 1st Army (Von Kluck). Entered Belgium August 4 and the 11th Brigade made part of the unit which attacked Liège. Its reservists rejoined it there. The 12th Brigade crossed the Belgian frontier August 15; then the division, completely filled up, marched via Tongres, Louvain, and Hal. It fought the 24th at Mons and Frameries. Going via Villers-Cotterets (Sept. 1), La Ferté-Milon, it arrived at Petit-Morin September 4. Engaged the 6th between Montceaux and Courgivaux on the left of the 5th Division. Obliged to retreat, it established itself on the right bank of the Aisne in the region of Soissons. It remained there until the end of June, 1915.

AISNE.

2. From October 30 to November 30, 1914, the division, reinforced by units of neighboring organizations, directed a successful offensive against the French troops in the region Chavonne-Soupir and threw them back on the left bank of the Aisne November 17 to 19, 1914.

1915.

1. From the end of January to July, 1915, the Aisne front was held by the division and remained quiet, the division suffering no losses. At the end of March the 35th Fusilier Regiment was transferred to 56th Division (new division).

ARTOIS.

2. Relieved from the region of Soissons toward the end of June and sent to Artois. On July 14 it took the place of the Bavarians before Arras. Withdrawn from the front toward the beginning of August and sent to rest between Valenciennes and Cambrai.

SERBIA.

3. September 23 it entrained for the Eastern Front. With the 25th Reserve Division it constituted, on the Serbo-Hungarian frontier, a new 3d Army Corps belonging to the Gallwitz Army. October 9 it crossed the Danube and remained in Serbia until the capture of Kragujewatz. During this October campaign the division suffered greatly.

FRANCE.

4. Returned to the Western Front at the beginning of December. Sent to rest and reorganized in the region Hirson-Avesnes.

1916.

1. At the end of January and the beginning of February, 1916, it was sent to the front north of Verdun (Romagne-Mangiennes area).

VERDUN.

2. February 22 it was engaged with the 5th Division in the zone between the western limits of Herbebois and the eastern slopes of the Cotes de Meuse. The two divisions did not go beyond Fort Douaumont, captured by the 24th Infantry. Their violent attacks on the village February 26 to 28 were repulsed. March 2 the regiments were withdrawn from the front and filled up.

3. On March 8 new and unsuccessful attacks against the village of Douaumont and the Hardaumont defenses.

l. About March 15 the 3d Army Corps was withdrawn from the front. The 6th vision went to the region of Mulhouse to be reorganized. On April 25 the division s again engaged (south of Douaumont-Caillette Wood) and again suffered heavily. is probable that each of its regiments were completely reorganized after each attack Douaumont (more than 60 per cent losses).

5. At the end of May the division was relieved and sent to rest in the region of Ville Montois.

AMPAGNE.

7. In the middle of June it was sent to Champagne and occupied quiet sectors rtheast of Prunay, then east of Auberive. It remained there till the end of September. It exchanged its 20th Infantry Regiment for the 396th Infantry Regiment, anized September 26. (See illustration.)

MME.

3. At the beginning of October sent to the Somme and was engaged in the region Gueudecourt and again suffered heavily, October 8 to 29.

tGONNE.

9. Withdrawn from the Somme front at the end of October; went to the Argonne the sector Fille-Morte-Boureuilles, November 30 to beginning of April, 1917.

1917.

1. At the beginning of April, 1917, the division was sent to Alsace. It stayed out two weeks in the region of Mulhouse.

IAMPAGNE.

2. About April 20 sent to Champagne and took over a sector south of Moronbilliers here it was subjected to the French attack of April 30. It had to be relieved a few ys after, as it suffered great losses at Mont-Haut (50 to 75 men per company).

3. The division returned to Alsace and was reorganized behind the front in the gion of Mulhouse.

USSIA.

4. About July 1 sent to the Eastern Front in Galicia, where it held a sector in the alat region.

RANCE.

Withdrawn from this front at the beginning of October it entrained for France, ginning the 7th, southeast of Tarnopol, and traveled via Lemberg-Cracow-Dresden-ssel-Coblentz-Treves-Thionville-Montmedy-Charleville-Vouziers.

ISNE.

5. After staying a few days around Vouziers and Marle the division was sent on ctober 23, the date of the French offensive, precipitately near Laon. October 24 d 25 it took over a sector on the Ailette in the region of Lizy (Urcel sector) and was ill holding it January 24, 1918, after a period of rest in Laon in November.

RECRUITING.

Same remarks as for the 5th Division.

VALUE—1917 ESTIMATE.

The 3d Army Corps was always considered as one of the star corps of the Prussian my. The 6th Division was among the best in Germany.

The military qualities seem to have been considerably lessened after the losses ffered, notably before Verdun and in the Mont Haut sector. It must be noted, wever, that, according to the examination of a deserter on November 2, 1917, the 6th Regiment is still considered as an excellent unit whose morale is intact.

Losses before Verdun (February to May, 1916): 20th Infantry, 2,904 men (633 killed); 24th Infantry, 2,691 (584 killed); 64th Infantry, 2,819 (603 killed); 3d Battalion of Chasseurs, 1,422 (219 killed).   Total, 9,831 men (2,039 killed).

1918.

AISNE.

1. The division was relieved by the 6th Bavarian Reserve Division January 12. It, in turn, relieved the 6th Bavarian Reserve Division the 24th.   February 22 it was again relieved by the 6th Bavarian Reserve Division.   It rested then in the Maubeuge area, where it underwent a thorough course of training.   The division then marched via Catillon, Bohain, Fresnoy le Grand, Le Verguier, Berthaucourt, Vermand, Marteville, Trefcon, Monchy Lagache.

PERONNE.

2. It came into line S. E. of that city near Meharicourt, March 24, relieving the 113th Division.

AISNE.

3. It was withdrawn from line about the 10th of April, and went to the Guise area, where, with the 5th Division, it was put through another course of training.   It reinforced the battle front near Juvigny, May 27.   It was withdrawn from line August 4.

It moved via Anizy le Chateau, southwest of Laon, Guise, Grougis, Bohain, Bertry, Neuvilly, Solesmes, Valenciennes, Ghent, to Turkyen (northwest of Roulers).   The division remained here until September 7, when it entrained at Roulers and traveled via Lille and Denain to Iwuy, remaining in reserve in the Sancourt-Proville area until the 14th, when it was moved up into support near Ribecourt.

CAMBRAI.

4. During the night of September 17–18 it reentered the line and counterattacked against Havrincourt (southwest of Cambrai).   It was withdrawn October 1, after suffering heavy losses.

5. The division came back into line near Escadoeuvres (northeast of Cambrai), October 7.   It was withdrawn on the 17th.

VALENCIENNES.

6. October 23 the division entered line near Escautpont (north of Valenciennes).

7. It was withdrawn a few days later, and reappeared in line south of Valenciennes on the 29th.   The night of November 7–8 it was relieved by the 185th Division.

VALUE—1918 ESTIMATE.

According to an article by Prof. Wegener in the Koelnische Zeitung, March 30, the 6th Division "particularly distinguished itself" in the Somme offensive.   It did very well, too, in the Aisne attack and also in the German attempts to prevent the Allied advance beginning July 18.   It suffered very heavy losses—e. g., 1,550 prisoners in its two engagements on the Cambrai front during September and early October; nevertheless, it is still to be considered as one of the best German shock divisions.

COMPOSITION.[1]

	1914 Brigade	1914 Regiment	1915 Brigade	1915 Regiment	1916 Brigade	1916 Regiment	1917 Brigade	1917 Regiment	1918 Brigade	1918 Regiment
Infantry	11 Res. 12 Res.	20 Res. 24 Res. 26 Res. 35 Res.	11 Res. 12 Res.	20 Res. 24 Res. 26 Res. 35 Res.	11 Res. 12 Res.	20 Res. 35 Res. 24 Res. 19 Landst.	12 Res.	20 Res. 24 Res. 35 Res.	12 Res.	20 Res. 24 Res. 35 Res.
Cavalry		3 Res. Uhlan Rgt. (3 Sqns.).			3 Res. Uhlan Rgt.			3 Res. Uhlan Rgt.? (1 Sqn.).		
Artillery	6 Res. F. A. Rgt. (6 Btries.).		6 Res. F. A. Rgt.		6 Res. F. A. Rgt.		94 Art. Command: 6 Res. F. A. Rgt. (9 Btries.).		94 Art. Command: 6 Res. F. A. Rgt.	
Engineers and Liaisons.	1 Res. Co. 2 Pion. Btn. No. 3.		1 Res. Co. 2 Pion. Btn. No. 3. 6 Res. Pont. Engs. 6 Res. Tel. Detch.		1 Res. Co. 3 Pion. Btn. No. 3. 3 Co. 34 Res. Pions. 206 T. M. Co. 6 Res. Pont. Engs. 6 Res. Tel. Detch.		(306) Pion. Btn.: 5 Co. 1 Pions. 1 Res. Co. 3 Pions. 205 T. M. Co. 274 Searchlight Section. 405 Tel. Detch.		1 Res. Co. (2 Pion. Btn. No. 3). 3 Co. 34 Res. Pion. Btn. 274 Searchlight Section. 206 T. M. Co. 406th Tel. Detch.	
Medical and Veterinary.							516 Ambulance Co. 19 Res. Field Hospital. 20 Res. Field Hospital. Vet. Hospital.		516 Ambulance Co. 18 Res. Field Hospital. 19 Res. Field Hospital. 20 Res. Field Hospital. 144 Vet. Hospital.	
Transports							M. T. Col.		706 M. T. Col.	
Attached					151 Cyclist Co. 102 Labor Btn.		151 Cyclist Co.			

[1] At time of dissolution, Aug. 23, 1918.

HISTORY.

(Third District—Brandenburg.)

1914.

The 6th Reserve Division belonged organically to the 3d Reserve Corps, like the 5th Reserve Division.

BELGIUM.

1. At the beginning of the war the 3d Reserve Corps belonged to the 1st German Army (Gen. von Kluck). The 6th Reserve Division detrained August 10 in the region of Crefeld, entered Belgium the 17th, passed through Belgian Limburg at the beginning of September, moved on Malines to oppose the Belgian offensive. September 9 the division attacked the Belgian troops in the region of Louvain and then took part in the siege of Antwerp.

YSER.

2. After the fall of Antwerp it moved toward the sea from October 13 to 16, through Ghent, Bruges, and Ostend. It concentrated near Thourout October 19 and fought along the Yser Canal. It fought violently in the region of Nieuport-Dixmude at the end of October and the beginning of November.

RUSSIA.

3. At the beginning of December the 3d Reserve Corps went to Russia, the 6th Reserve Division being withdrawn from the Belgian front about the middle of November.

1915.

POLAND.

1. On arriving on the Eastern Front the division was engaged on the Bzura and before Warsaw (9th Army, under Mackensen).

2. In July, 1915, it became a part of Von Buelow's army, which marched on the left wing (north) of the German forces during the offensive against Russia (summer and fall of 1915).

DVINA.

3. In November the division still belonged to Von Buelow's army, called the Niemen army, and was engaged on the Dvina.

1916.

COURLAND.

1. In February, 1916, the division (8th Army under Von **Buelow**) held a sector in the region of Riga-Friedrichstadt.

2. During its stay in Russia the division did not have very heavy losses except in July, 1916, when it opposed violent Russian attacks near Kekkau.

1917.

COURLAND.

1. Relieved from the Kekkau sector in May, 1917, and was sent to the Western Front.

FRANCE.

2. Entrained about May 6 at Mitau and sent via Cottbus, Cassel, Coblentz, Treves, Thionville to Dun, where it detrained May 13.

MORT HOMME—HILL 304.

3. At the end of May the division went into line on the left bank of the Meuse in the sector Mort Homme—Hill 304. On June 29 some of the units of the division supported an attack attempted by the 10th Reserve Division against Hill 304 and suffered heavy losses. August 20 the French offensive struck them. Its losses were enormous. Two of its regiments, the 24th Reserve and 20th Reserve, were nearly

wiped out.   The 35th Reserve was not weakened quite so much, yet was seriously diminished.   The division lost 2,800 prisoners.

RUSSIA.

4. Withdrawn from the front, the division was sent to Galicia at the end of September.   It was still there January 31 on the old Austro-Russian frontier after furnishing reinforcements to the Western Front.

RECRUITING.

Brandenburg.

VALUE—1917 ESTIMATE.

The 6th Reserve Division, a short time after its return from the Eastern Front, was considered about as follows: "Its value is mediocre.   In spite of its units from Brandenburg and the recent creation of shock troops, its long stay in Russia has greatly depreciated its fighting value" (July 11, 1917).

This judgment was completely verified August 20, 1917: "The 6th Reserve Division on the whole opposed no resistance to the French attack of August 20 at any point. * * *   The conduct of a good number of its officers seems not to have been edifying. A good many seized the pretext of intoxication or gave unsatisfactory reasons for withdrawing to the rear" (October, 1917).

The German command thought best to send this division back to the Eastern Front (September, 1917).

1918.

FRANCE.

The 6th Reserve Division entrained at Zborow the evening of March 8, and traveled via Sokal–Brest Litovsk–Varsovia–Kaliscz–Lissa–Gorlitz–Bautzen–Dresden–Leipsic–Weimar – Erfurth – Eisenach – Bebra – Fulda – Hanau – Frankfort – Mainz – Kreuznach – Thionville–Sedan to Balhain (northeast of Asfeld), where it arrived March 15.

The division rested at Villers (near Asfeld) until the 25th of March, when it reentrained and traveled to Crécy sur Serre.   From there it marched via Mesbrecourt–Pouilly sur Serre–La Fère–Liez–Commonchon to the area northeast of Noyon, and remained in reserve for some days.   Elements of the division came into line west of Chauny at the end of March, but were soon withdrawn.   About the 1st of April the whole division marched to Roye and remained there until the 15th, when it continued its march via Erches and Arvillers to Plessier, relieving the 2d Guard Division southwest of Moreuil May 1.

The beginning of August it was relieved by the 24th Division and shortly after it was dissolved and the men composing it were sent as drafts to the 5th and 6th Divisions.

VALUE—1918 ESTIMATE.

The only aggressive action of the division on the Western Front during 1918 was a raid carried out by a battalion against the French lines in the La Gaune woods (southwest of Moreuil) early in May; it was not a success, and it is estimated that practically the whole attacking force was wiped out. The 6th Reserve is rated as a third-class division.

6th Bavarian Division.
COMPOSITION.

	1914 Brigade	1914 Regiment	1915 Brigade	1915 Regiment	1916 Brigade	1916 Regiment	1917 Brigade	1917 Regiment	1918 Brigade	1918 Regiment
Infantry	11 Bav. 12 Bav.	10 Bav. 13 Bav. 6 Bav. 11 Bav.	11 Bav. 12 Bav.	10 Bav. 13 Bav. 6 Bav. 11 Bav.	11 Bav. 12 Bav.	10 Bav. 13 Bav. 6 Bav. 11 Bav.	11 Bav.	10 Bav. 6 Bav. 13 Bav.	11 Bav.	6 Bav. 10 Bav. 13 Bav.
Cavalry	2 Bav. Light Cav. Rgt.		2 Bav. Light Cav. Rgt.		2 Bav. Light Cav. Rgt. (2 Sqns.)		2 Bav. Light Cav. Rgt. (3d Sqn.)		3 Sqn. 2 Bav. Light Cav. Rgt.	
Artillery	6 Bav. Brig.: 3 Bav. F. A. Rgt. 8 Bav. F. A. Rgt.		6 Bav. Brig.: 3 Bav. F. A. Rgt. 8 Bav. F. A. Rgt.		6 Bav. Brig.: 3 Bav. F. A. Rgt. 8 Bav. F. A. Rgt.		6 Bav. Art. Command: 8 Bav. F. A. Rgt.		6 Bav. Art. Command: 3 Bav. F. A. Rgt. 2 Abt. 1 Bav. Res. Ft. A. Rgt. 115 Bav. Light Am. Col. 142 Bav. Light Am. Col. 169 Bav. Light Am. Col.	
Engineers and Liaisons.	2 and 3 Field Cos. 3 Bav. Pion. Btn.		2 and 3 Field Cos. 3 Bav. Pion. Btn. 6 Bav. Pont. Engs. 6 Bav. Tel. Detch.		2 Field Co. 3 Bav. Pion. Btn. 6 Bav. T. M. Co. 6 Bav. Pont. Engs. 6 Bav. Tel. Detch.		(?) Bav. Pion. Btn.: 11 Bav. Pion. Co. 12 Bav. Pion. Co. 6 Bav. T. M. Co. z (42) Searchlight Section. 6 Bav. Tel. Detch.		6 Bav. Pion. Btn.: 11 Bav. Pion. Co. 12 Bav. Pion. Co. 6 Bav. T. M. Co. 6 Bav. Searchlight Section. 6 Bav. Signal Command: 6 Bav. Tel. Detch. 101 Bav. Wireless Detch.	
Medical and Veterinary.							7 Bav. Ambulance Co. Field Hospital. 6 Bav. Vet. Hospital.		7 Bav. Ambulance Co. 20 Bav. Field Hospital. 24 Bav. Field Hospital. 6 Bav. Vet. Hospital.	
Transports							M. T. Col.		686 M. T. Col.	
Attached					46 Bav. Anti-Aircraft Section.					

HISTORY.

(Upper Palatinate and part of Lower Bavaria.)

1914.

LORRAINE.

1. In August, 1914, the 6th Bavarian Division with the 5th Bavarian Division contituted the 3d Bavarian Corps and was part of the 6th Bavarian Army (Crown Prince Rupprecht of Bavaria). One of its brigades, the 11th, detrained, beginning August 4, at Remilly as a covering force. August 20 the division fought on the right of the 5th Bavarian Division at Prevecourt and Delme. They crossed the French frontier with this division on the 22d and were engaged the 25th at Maixe on the Sanon and north of Luneville during the first days of September. Also with the 5th Bavarian Division, it was near Champenoux September 8, at the time of the attack against Nancy until the 11th, and then retreated.

COTES DE MEUSE.

2. Assembled at Metz from the 14th to the 17th, the division went on the 18th to the west of the Moselle. It reached and climbed the Cotes de Meuse the 21st and attacked the fort of the Camp des Romains and St. Mihiel the 27th.

ST. MIHIEL.

3. Following these attacks which continued during October and ended in the capture of the fort and of St. Mihiel, the division established itself from Chauvoncourt to Spada in November to December.

1915.

ST. MIHIEL.

1. The division remained in the sector of the St. Mihiel salient (Chauvoncourt-Spada–Lamorville) during the whole of 1915 and until June, 1916.

1916.

VERDUN.

1. About June 20, 1916, the 11th Bavarian Brigade was relieved from the St. Mihiel sector and sent to Longuyon and from there to the Verdun front. It participated in opposing the French attack of June 23 (with the Alpine Corps) on Thiaumont and suffered heavy losses.

2. Sent to rest July 4.

3. The 12th Brigade withdrew from the St. Mihiel front July 13 and 16 and went into line before Fleury, beginning July 17 to 18 (11th Regiment). Its losses were such that on July 26 the replacement depot of the 11th Infantry at Ratisbonne was ordered by telegraph to furnish immediately 500 replacements (letter).

4. On August 2 and 3 the whole division was fighting in this sector and lost heavily.

SOMME.

5. The division left the Verdun front about August 5. After a short stay in the Argonne it was sent to the Somme at the beginning of September, fought between Sars and Gueudecourt September 15 to 27 and again suffered serious losses.

ARTOIS.

6. On August 1 the division took over the sector of Neuve Chapelle–Festubert, and remained there until May 10, 1917.

1917.

1. At the end of January, 1917, the 11th Infantry and the 3d Field Artillery were transferred to the 6th Bavarian Division (new).

ARTOIS.

2. The division was relieved from the Neuve Chapelle sector May 10 and went into line northeast of Arras (Oppy, Fresnoy, Acheville), in the middle of May. They suffered some loss from gas attacks.

FLANDERS.

3. The division left Artois September 10 and went to Flanders (sector northeast of Langemarck) September 29. The British attack of October 4 caused it heavy losses and it lost Poelcappelle to the British.

4. Relieved October 8, sent to rest, and reorganized.

ARTOIS.

5. On October 18 it appeared south of the La Bassee Canal, where it suffered again from gas attacks.

RECRUITING.

Upper Palatinate and part of Lower Bavaria (Third Bavarian district).

VALUE—1917 ESTIMATE.

The morale of the division was good. On the Fresnoy front in 1917 it showed activity and enterprise. It always reacted quickly against attacks, but it seems that it could easily be persuaded to adopt a more passive attitude if circumstances were such as to permit it (information of the British, February, 1918).

1918.

1. The 6th Bavarian Division was relieved south of the La Bassee Canal by the 4th Ersatz Division, January 18, and went to rest in the area south of Tournai.

LILLE.

2. About the middle of February it relieved the 187th Division south of the Bois Grenier (west of Lille). About the 24th it was relieved by the 10th Ersatz Division, and went back nearer Lille, where it probably received training in open warfare, although this fact has never been definitely established.

CAMBRAI.

3. For the Somme offensive, the division was sent to the Cambrai front, entering the line March 20, near Bullecourt, and attacking the following day. Little progress was made by the Germans on this part of the front, and the division lost heavily in many attacks. It was withdrawn about March 26.

DIXMUDE.

4. April 4 it relieved the 214th Division south of Dixmude. A very elaborate attack against the Belgians was planned to take place here April 17, and it was to be made by the 6th Bavarian Division and some elements of adjoining units. It was presumed that the German successes at Mount Kemel had shaken the line to the north and that the whole Ypres salient could be captured. Preparations were made, and the attack attempted, but it failed completely, and the Belgians not only threw the enemy back but took a great many prisoners. It was withdrawn about the 19th and went to rest for a week near Ruddervoorde (south of Bruges), although some of its elements held part of the sector of the 1st Landwehr Division east of Merckem for a day or two.

VERDUN.

5. The division was sent to the Verdun region via Brussels–Namur–Sedan–Montmedy, and went into camp in the vicinity of Chauvency (west of Montmedy), where it remained 10 days.

MEUSE.

6. May 24 it relieved the 22d Division near Beaumont (north of Verdun).

ROYE.

7. It was relieved about August 7, and after resting a few days moved up to the Roye region. It was identified in the Bois des Loges August 16; it had relieved the 206th Division. The division remained in line retiring in the face of the Allied advance, but fighting stubbornly, especially near Campagne, Montigny, and Essigny le Grand; at the last-named place it counterattacked violently, but in vain, September 29. It was still in line when the armistice was signed.

VALUE—1918 ESTIMATE.

The 6th Bavarian is rated as one of the 45 best enemy divisions. It suffered extremely heavy losses, but since it always fought well—though not brilliantly, during 1918—the German High Command sent it as many replacements as it could. The morale has always been good, but quite anti-Prussian.

6th Bavarian Reserve Division.
COMPOSITION.

	1914 Brigade.	1914 Regiment.	1915 Brigade.	1915 Regiment.	1916 Brigade.	1916 Regiment.	1917 Brigade.	1917 Regiment.	1918 Brigade.	1918 Regiment.
Infantry	12 Bav. Res. 14 Bav. Res.	16 Bav. Res. 17 Bav. Res. 20 Bav. Res. 21 Bav. Res.	12 Bav. Res. 14 Bav. Res.	16 Bav. Res. 17 Bav. Res. 20 Bav. Res. 21 Bav. Res.	12 Bav. Res. 14 Bav. Res.	16 Bav. Res. 17 Bav. Res. 20 Bav. Res. 21 Bav. Res.	12 Bav. Res.	16 Bav. Res. 17 Bav. Res. 20 Bav. Res.	12 Bav. Res.	25 Bav. Res. 16 Bav. Res. 20 Bav. Res.
Cavalry	6 Bav. Res. Cav. Rgt.		6 Bav. Res. Cav. Rgt.		6 Bav. Res. Cav. Rgt.		6 Bav. Res. Cav. Rgt. (? Sqns.)		3 Sqn. 5 Bav. Light Cav. Rgt.	
Artillery	6 Bav. Res. F. A. Rgt. (9 Btries.).		6 Bav. Res. F. A. Rgt.		6 Bav. Res. F. A. Rgt.		18 Bav. Art. Command:	6 Bav. Res. F. A. Regt.	18 Bav. Art. Command: 19 Bav. F. A. Rgt. 12 Bav. Ft. A. Btn. 143 Bav. Light Am. Col. 110 Bav. Light Am. Col. 107 Bav. Light Am. Col.	
Engineers and Liaisons.	6 Bav. Res. Pion. Co.		6 Bav. Res. Pion. Co.		6 Bav. Res. Pion. Co. 10 Bav. Res. Pion. Co. 206 Bav. T. M. Co. 6 Bav. Res. Pont. Engrs. 6 Bav. Res. Tel. Detch.		(19 Bav.) Pion. Btn.: 6 Bav. Res. Pion. Co. 7 Bav. Res. Pion. Co. 206 Bav. T. M. Co. 2 Bav. Res. Searchlight Section. 406 Bav. Res. Tel. Detch.		19 Bav. Pion. Btn.: 6 Bav. Res. Pion. Co. 7 Bav. Res. Pion. Co. 206 Bav. T. M. Co. 19 Bav. Searchlight Section. 406 Signal Command: 406 Tel. Detch. 144 Wireless Detch.	
Medical and Veterinary.							17 Bav. Ambulance Co. 53 Bav. Field Hospital. Vet. Hospital.		17 Bav. Ambulance Co. 53 Bav. Field Hospital. 54 Bav. Field Hospital.	
Transports							M. T. Col.		752 M. T. Col.	

HISTORY.

16th Bavarian Reserve Regiment: First Bavarian District.   17th Bavarian Reserve Regiment: Second Bavarian District.   20th Bavarian Reserve Regiment: (?).)

1914.

FLANDERS.

1. This division was organized in Bavaria in September, 1914, and sent to Belgium about October 21.   Assembled in the vicinity of Lille and was sent toward Dadizeele the 27th and was near Gheluvelt October 29, but does not seem to have been in the fight.

2. November 1 it was sent south of Ypres between Hollebeke and Messines.   It attacked in the direction of Wytschaete November 2 and suffered heavy losses: 11th Company, 4 officers and 181 men (16th Reserve Regiment); 6th company of the 17th Reserve Regiment, 5 officers and 228 men (casualty lists).   November 6 the 3d company of the 21st Reserve Regiment was reduced to 3 provisional officers and 63 men (notebook).

1915.

FLANDERS.

1. The division remained in the Messines-Wytschaete sector until the beginning of March, 1915.

2. Relieved between March 6 and 8 and sent the 11th as reinforcements to the 7th Corps at Neuve Chapelle.   Then sent to rest in the region of Roubaix in March.

LILLE.

3. Beginning of April it went into line southwest of Lille between Grenier Wood and Aubers and held this sector until the end of September, 1916.

1916.

1. July 19, 1916, the division suffered heavy losses in opposing the British attack southeast of Laventie.

SOMME.

2. Relieved from the Lille front about September 27 and engaged in the Somme district near Eaucourt l'Abbaye and Gueudecourt until October 13.   Again suffered heavily.

ARTOIS.

3. October 25 it took over the Vimy-Lievin sector, south of Lens.

1917.

1. The division held the front south of Lens during all the winter of 1916 to 1917 and executed many raids.

2. February 12 sent to rest near Douai and reorganized in February and March. One of its regiments, the 21st Reserve, was transferred to the 16th Bavarian Division, newly organized.

3. March 14 it went into line north of the La Bassee Canal.

4. Withdrawn from this sector at the end of April and was engaged May 8 northeast of Arras, at Oppy Gavrelle, until May 11.   In the middle of June it returned to this sector for a few days and does not seem to have suffered heavy losses.

YPRES.

5. After a rest near Douai until the end of June the division was sent to Flanders. Was first placed in reserve south of Thielt during the first few weeks of July and engaged the 18th southeast of Ypres in the Ledeghem sector.   Lost heavily from the artillery preparation and was relieved July 30 before the British attack.

ALSACE.

6. Sent to Alsace and held the Altkirch sector from the middle of August to beginning of October.

LAONNOIS.

7. About October 16 to 17 it was sent to the region of Lizy, southwest of Laon. It relieved on the Ailette, east of Anizy le Chateau, about October 25, the remains of the 14th and 52d Divisions, decimated by the French attack of the 23d.

8. The division was not heavily engaged in the sector of Lizy. It continued to hold it in November and December 1917 and January 1918. During this period it was sent to Vervins for rest and training.

VALUE—1917 ESTIMATE.

The division was organized as an attack unit. From January 24 to February 19, 1918, it went through a training for the offensive in the vicinity of Vervins including breaking-through maneuvers, Feb. 1 with a Prussian division at Vallee aux Bleds; another divisional maneuver February 11 before the German Crown Prince and Gen, Ludendorff; third divisional maneuver February 18 (examination of prisoners, Feb. 28, 1918). It is to be noted that in Flanders, where the division had the only important fight it had in 1917 it suffered heavily. Its morale was so weakened that it had to be withdrawn before the British attack.

1918.

VERVINS.

1. The 6th Bavarian Reserve Division was relieved in the Anizy le Chateau region by the 6th Division, January 24 and went to the vicinity of Vervins where it was put through a course of training in open warfare, in which artillery and aeroplanes participated. These exercises were supervised by the Crown Prince and Ludendorff.

2. February 22 it relieved the 6th Division in its former section. About the end of the month the division was relieved by elements of the 13th Landwehr Division, and by the extension of the flanks of the neighboring divisions, going to rest in the Chauny region.

SOMME.

3. Toward the middle of April the division relieved the 206th Division near Mesnil St. Georges (southwest of Montdidier). It was relieved by the 25th Reserve Division April 21.

AILETTE.

4. There is some doubt as to where the division went; it was reported northeast of Ghent, northeast of Laon, and in Lorraine. There is some evidence to show that it relieved the 222d Division near Anizy le Chateau during the night of May 2–3. This front was very quiet until the German offensive of May 27, in which attack the 6th Bavarian Reserve Division did not attack in the front line—being "leap-frogged" by the 5th and 6th Divisions acting as shock units—but followed up the advance coming into line between these two divisions during the night of the 27th-28th. It was at this time definitely identified. In the attack on Terny (May 28), the division met with strong resistance and suffered heavily. June 1 it captured Le Port, but lost it again to the French on June 7, with severe losses. It was relieved about the 15th by the 53d Reserve Division.

MARNE.

5. July 17 it was identified near Passy sur Marne (west of Dormans). It was withdrawn August 6 and spent a fortnight refitting.

BAPAUME.

6. August 23 it reinforced the front near Ervillers (northwest of Bapaume) having traveled via Cambrai, Bourlon, and Beugnâtre. The division was withdrawn early in September.

YPRES.

7. It relieved the 8th Division southwest of Messines during the night of September 17–18.   Just before coming into line the 17th Bavarian Reserve Infantry Regiment was dissolved and its men drafted to the other two regiments of the division.   It was replaced by the 25th Bavarian Infantry Regiment from the 14th Bavarian Division which was dissolved at this time.   Likewise, the 6th Bavarian Reserve Field Artillery Regiment was dissolved and replaced by the 19th Bavarian Field Artillery Regiment from the 10th Bavarian Division disbanded in July.   The division remained in line until the armistice was signed, withdrawing through Wytschaete–Houthem-Comines Marcke-Ooteghem and Krinstraat.

VALUE—1918 ESTIMATE.

The 6th Bavarian Reserve is rated as a second-class division, which seems justified not only from opinions concerning its ability as a fighting unit coming from Allied sources, but also from the fact that, although it had a course of training in "breaking through" in February, it was never so used by the German High Command, serving rather as a "follow up" division.   (Cf. May 27 offensive.)   The division suffered heavy losses during its 1918 engagements; indeed, some prisoners captured the middle of September said that it was to be broken up.   They were mistaken, but one of the infantry regiments and the artillery regiment were disbanded.

6th Bavarian Landwehr Division.
COMPOSITION.

	1914 Brigade	1914 Regiment	1915 Brigade	1915 Regiment	1916 Brigade	1916 Regiment	1917 Brigade	1917 Regiment	1918 Brigade	1918 Regiment
Infantry	Von Frech. 1 Bav. Mixed Ldw. 2 Bav. Mixed Ldw.	121 Ldw. 123 Ldw. 1 Bav. Ldw. 2 Bav. Ldw. 3 Bav. Ldw. 12 Bav. Ldw.	1 Bav. Mixed Ldw. 2 Bav. Mixed Ldw.	1 Bav. Ldw. 2 Bav. Ldw. 3 Bav. Ldw. 12 Bav. Ldw.	1 Bav. Mixed Ldw. 2 Bav. Mixed Ldw.	1 Bav. Ldw. 2 Bav. Ldw. 3 Bav. Ldw. 12 Bav. Ldw.	2 Bav. Ldw.	1 Bav. Ldw. 2 Bav. Ldw. 12 Bav. Ldw.	2 Bav. Ldw.	1 Bav. Ldw. 3 Bav. Ldw. 12 Bav. Ldw.
Cavalry			1 Ldw. Sqn. of the 1 Bav. C. Dist.		1 Ldw. Sqn. and 2 Ldw. Sqn. of 1 Bav. C. Dist.		2d Sqn. 2 Bav. Light Cav. Rgt. 2d Sqn. 2 Bav. Light Cav. Rgt.		2 Sqn. 2 Bav. Light Cav. Rgt.	
Artillery					6 Bav. Ldw. F. A. Rgt. 2 Bav. Ldw. F. A. Abt. 10 Bav. Mountain Art. Btry.		23 Bav. Art. Command: 6 Bav. Ldw. F. A. Rgt.		6 Bav. Ldw. F. A. Rgt. (3 Abt., Staff, and 8 Btry).	
Engineers and Liaisons.					16 Bav. Res. Pion. Co. 250 Pion Co. 14 C. Dist. 1 Ldw. Pion. Co. 1 Bav. C. Dist. 1 Landst. Pion. Co. 1 Bav. C. Dist. 2 Landst. Pion. Co.		26 Bav. Pion. Btln. 16 Bav. Res. Pion. Co. 306 Bav. T. M. Co. 10 Bav. Res. Searchlight Section. 506 Bav. Tel. Detch.		26 Bav. Pion Btn.: 16 Bav. Res. Pion. Co. 26 Bav. Searchlight Section. 506 Bav. Signal Command: 506 Bav. Tel.-Detch. 192 Bav. Wireless Detch.	
Medical and Veterinary.							560 Ambulance Co. 19 Bav. Field Hospital. 59 Bav. Field Hospital. 36 Vet. Hospital.		19 Bav. Ambulance Co. 60 Bav. Field Hospital. 59 Bav. Field Hospital.	
Transports.							47 Bav. M. T. Col. 49 Bav. M. T. Col.		794 Bav. M. T. Col.	
Attached.	Landshut Inf. Btn. (1 Bav. C. Dist. Btn. Landst. No. 7). Nuremberg Inf. Btn. (3 Bav. C. Dist. Landst. Btn. No. 1).				3 and 5 Cos. (Wurtt) Ski Btns. Fribourg Landst. Inf. Btn. (14 C. Dist. 1 Btn. No. 2). 1 Cologne 2 Landst. Inf. Btn. (8 C. Dist. Btn. No. 14). 65 Labor Btn.		Neustadt Landst. Inf. Btn. (2 Bav. C. Dist. Btn. No. 4). Bomberg Landst. Inf. Btn. (2 Bav C. Dist. Btn. No. 10). Ansbach Landst. Inf. Btn. (3 Bav. C. Dist. Btn. No. 2). 1 Cologne 2 Landst. Inf. Btn. (8 C. Dist. Btn. No. 14).			

HISTORY.

(First Bavarian District.)

1914.

ALSACE.

1. The division was sent into the Vosges at the beginning of the campaign (3 brigades, of which one was from Wurtemberg). It fought in the valley of the Fecht in August, 1914. Beginning with October it occupied the region Ste. Marie aux Mines-Col du Bonhomme. October 2 the 1st Bavarian Brigade entrained at Colmar for Belgium and garrisoned Antwerp until December.

2. At the beginning of November the 3d Bavarian Landwehr Division took part in the attacks on the Violu.

1915.

1. From February to April, 1915, the units which at that time made up this division were again separated. The 1st Bavarian Landwehr (mixed) Brigade came back from Belgium in the middle of December and went to Champagne (Souain-Somme-Py) to reinforce the 15th Division; the 2d Mixed Brigade continued to hold the Orbey la Poutroye sector south of Bonhomme (valley of the Weiss). The Wurtemberg Brigade (von Frech) was transferred in April to the 7th Landwehr Division (Wurtemberg) in upper Alsace.

2. In April, 1915, the remaining two brigades were assembled on the Vosges front (Orbey, Valley of the Weiss) and from that time on held this sector without much change.

3. In July some units of the division fought in the region of the Linge.

1916.

1. Vosges sector (valley of the Weiss, Col du Bonhomme). At the end of December, 1916, the 2d Bavarian Landwehr was transferred to the 2d Bavarian Landwehr Division (new).

1917.

1. In 1917 the division extended its sector from the region of Col du Bonhomme to the valley of the Fecht (Munster).

VALUE—1917 ESTIMATE.

The division was in line in the region of Orbey (south of Col du Bonhomme) from 1915 on. It is a mediocre division made up of elderly men. The companies have no shock troops. All the important operations are executed by the assault company of the division.

1918.

ALSACE.

1. The 6th Bavarian Landwehr Division occupied the sector extending from south of Le Bonhomme to just west of Muenster, all through the year, being still in line when the armistice was signed.

VALUE—1918 ESTIMATE.

The division is a fourth-class one, being used only to hold one of the calmest sectors on the western front. All the young men were taken away from the division (except those in machine-gun and assault companies) and exchanged for older ones. In October the father of six children was captured. Morale was low, discipline poor. Several prisoners stated that the men did not hesitate to say, even in front of their officers, that the war had been lost by Germany and that they were thoroughly sick of it.

6th Cavalry Division (Dismounted).

COMPOSITION.

	1918	
	Brigade.	Regiment.
Cavalry	5 Cav	2 Drag. 3 Uhlan. 7 Cuirassier.
	45 Cav	7 Res. Drag. 13 Hus. 13 Horse Jag.
	3 Cav	2 Cuirassier. 9 Uhlan. 12 Hus.
Artillery	133 Art. command.	
Engineers and Liaisons	21 Pion. Btn. 319 T. M. Co. 674 Wireless Detcb.	
Medical and Veterinary	256 Ambulance Co. 106 Field Hospital. 261 Vet. Hospital.	
Attached	70 Ldw. Inf. Brig.	

HISTORY.

1918.

ALSACE.

1. The division held the Badonviller sector until the last of April, when it was relieved by the 21st Landwehr Division. It rested at Mulhausen until July. At this time it was reorganized as a division of nine dismounted cavalry regiments.

YPRES.

2. On July 1 it entrained at Sierenz and traveled via Saarburg-Eupen-Liege-Brussels-Courtrai to Ingelmunster, where it detrained on July 3. The division then went into rest billets in the Iseghem-Winkel St. Eloi and Lendelede area, and on the night of July 27–28 it relieved the 1st Landwehr Division east of Ypres.

CAMBRAI.

3. It was relieved in Flanders and railed via Cambrai to Fins, where it detrained August 31. On September 4 it was in line at Manancourt and Nurlun. It was engaged in heavy fighting until September 25, when it was withdrawn from the battle front southwest of Cambrai after losing 400 prisoners.

BELGIUM.

4. It reinforced the Ypres battle front at Ledeghem on October 1 and fought there for about one week. It rested out of line a week and returned on October 15 to line east of Gulleghem. Two weeks later it was withdrawn in the Waereghem area.

5. On November 3 the division was again in line at Hermelgem. It was withdrawn within a few days and on the day of the armistice it was considered to be in reserve of the 4th German Army.

VALUE—1918 ESTIMATE.

The division was rated as fourth class. Its use in the active Ypres and Cambrai fronts indicates that it should have been rated higher after its reorganization in the summer.

7th Division.
COMPOSITION.

	1914		1915		1916		1917		1918	
	Brigade.	Regiment.	Brigade.	Regiment.	Brigade.	Regiment.	Brigade.	Regiment.	Brigade.	Regiment.
Infantry	13. 14.	26. 66. 27. 165.	13. 14.	26. 66. 27. 165.	14.	26. 27. 165.	14.	26. 165. 393.	14.	26. 165. 393.
Cavalry	10 Hus. Rgt. (3 Sqns.).		10 Hus. Rgt. (3 Sqns.).		10 Hus. Rgt. (3 Sqns.).		2 Sqn. 10 Hus. Rgt.		2 Sqn. 10 Hus. Rgt.	
Artillery	7 Brig.; 4 F. A. Rgt. 40 F. A. Rgt.		7 Brig.; 4 F. A. Rgt. 40 F. A. Rgt.		7 Brig.; 4 F. A. Rgt. 40 F. A. Rgt.		7 Brig.; 40 F. A. Rgt.		7 Art. Command: 40 F. A. Rgt. 4 Abt. 24 Res. Ft. A. Rgt. 124 Light Am. Col. 1298 Light Am. Col. 1301 Light Am. Col.	
Engineers and Liaisons.			1 Pion. Btn. No. 4. Field Co. 4 Pions. 7 Pont. Engrs. 7 Tel. Detch.		1 Pion. Btn. No. 4: 1 Co. 4 Pions. 7 T. M. Co. 7 Pont. Engrs. 7 Tel. Detch.		118 Pion. Btn. (formerly 1 Pion. Btn. No. 4: 1 Co. 4 Pions. 3 Co. 4 Pions. 7 T. M. Co. 7 Tel. Detch. 7 Pont. Engs.		4 Pion. Btn.: 1 Co. 4 Pions. 3 Co. 4 Pions. 43 Searchlight Section. 7 Signal Command: 7 Tel. Detch. 122 Bav., Wireless Detch.	
Medical and Veterinary.							10 Ambulance Co. Field Hospital. Vet. Hospital.		10 Ambulance Co. 37 Field Hospital. 41 Field Hospital. 7 Vet. Hospital.	
Transports							M. T. Col.		540 M. T. Col.	
Attached							88 Labor Btn. (5th Co.).			

HISTORY.

(Fourth District—Prussian Saxony.)

1914.

The Seventh Division was recruited in the Province of Prussian Saxony and, with the 8th Division, belonged to the 4th Army Corps (Magdeburg).

MARNE.

1. The 14th Brigade, which had already obtained reservists July 30, entrained on the evening of August 2 and was one of the six brigades ordered to take Liege. The whole division moved into the region of Liege August 15. It belonged to the 1st Army (Von Kluck), and passed through Louvain August 18 and through Brussels the 20th. On the 23d it was on the Haine, west of St. Ghislain. On the 24th between Quiévrain and Audregnies it threatened to envelop the Allied left. Going through Le Cateau and Peronne on August 28, the division passed through Grand Morin and arrived at Choisy, southeast of Coulommiers, from where it was sent in all haste to the aid of the right wing of the 1st Army (Etavigny, etc.).

BELGIUM.

2. After the retreat it went to the north of the Aisne below Soissons until the last days of September (fights at Cuisy en Almont, Morsain, Nouvron, Fontenoy).

3. At the end of September it was attached to the 6th Army (Crown Prince of Bavaria) and sent to Artois.

ARTOIS.

4. At the beginning of October it fought south of Arras (Monchy aux Bois, Ransart, Wailly). It established itself south of the Scarpe.

5. It held the sector until the end of May, 1915. During this period it limited itself to organizing defensively.

1915.

1. In March the division was reduced to three regiments by the transfer of the 66th Infantry to the 52d Division (new).

2. In May, 1915, at the time of the French offensive in Artois some units of the division were sent as reinforcements to the region of Neuville–St. Vaast. It left some prisoners and suffered heavy losses on May 12 to 13.

ARTOIS.

3. June 12 the division left the sector south of the Scarpe and went into line the 13th between Lorette and Angres (from the Souchez–Aix Noulette Road to the Blanc work). The French offensive struck it June 13 and the days following north of the road from Souchez to Aix Noulette. It was forced to give ground and lost many prisoners (250 men, among them 6 officers from the 26th Infantry north of Bois Carre; the 2d Battalion of the 26th Infantry lost 12 officers and 597 men out of action, according to the Prussian casualty lists).

4. At the beginning of July the division established itself south of the railroad from Grenay to Lens, north of Souchez. September 25 it fought in the third battle of Artois, north of Bois en Hache, before Angres and Lievin. It showed considerable energy, but again had many of its men captured.

5. The division remained in this sector southwest of Loos (south of the Lens–Bethune Road; Lens–Grenay Railroad) until July, 1916.

1916.

1. Until the beginning of July, 1916, the division had no serious battles.

2. About July 3 the division was relieved from the Loos front. On the 13th it was at Cambrai.

SOMME.

3. July 14 and 15 it began to be engaged in the battle of the Somme between Pozieres and Bazentin le Petit. It suffered terrible losses. Relieved May 28.

ARTOIS.

4. After a rest in the region of Valenciennes it went into line east of Arras August 9 and stayed there until September 17. At this time it transferred its 27th Infantry to the 211th Division and took in exchange the 393d Infantry, composed of levies from the regiments of the 7th, 8th, and 12th Divisions, 50th Reserve Division and 38th Landwehr Brigade.

SOMME.

5. About September 18 it again took part in the battle of the Somme in the sector of Courcelette. It fought bravely and again suffered heavily.

ARTOIS.

6. Withdrawn from the Somme about October 2 and went into the sector southeast of Loos October 5. Again withdrawn from this sector November 10 it went almost immediately into the line south of the La Bassee Canal and stayed there until May 28, 1917.

1917.

ARTOIS.

1. During the winter of 1916–17 the division had no big battles, but suffered from raids executed by the British troops.

FLANDERS.

2. May 28 it was withdrawn from the La Bassee front and sent to the region of Ypres (sector of Hollebeke-Wytschaete) June 8 to 19.

ALSACE.

3. At the beginning of July it was sent to Alsace to the vicinity of Mulhouse where it rested.

4. July 27 to 28 it entrained again for Artois via Mulhouse–Strassbourg–Sarreguemines–Metz–Thionville–Sedan–Hirson–Valenciennes–St. Amand.

ARTOIS.

5. After a few days' rest in the region of St. Amand and Orchies July 28 to August 3, it went into the lines north of Lens (Loos sector) where it lost heavily from August 9 to the beginning of September.

BELGIUM.

6. Relieved then and sent to rest at Pont a Marcq, it went back into the line between the La Bassee Canal and Hulluch September 21. Withdrawn from this sector during October and sent to the region of Ypres where it held a front on October 29 between Becelaere and Gheluvelt. It was still identified there January 29, 1918.

RECRUITING.

Province of Magdeburg (Prussian Saxony) and part of Thuringia. The 393d Infantry gets replacements from the depot of the 153d Infantry (Altenburg). Its resources from these replacements are as a rule sufficient and the Fourth District has even furnished recruits to the regiments of the Fourteenth. In exchange when it has relatively few replacements it has been helped out by Polish drafts from Silesia (Sixth District).

1918.

1. The division was relieved on February 4 and rested in the Eecloo area, participating in a large-scale maneuver.

2. It returned to line in the Becelaere sector on March 3, relieving the 8th Bavarian Reserve Division. It was withdrawn March 26.

BATTLE OF THE LYS.

3. It fought near Hollebeke, Messines, Wytschaete, between April 9 and May 1. It took part in the attack on the Ypres-Comines Canal on April 25.

4. During May it was at rest in Belgium near Deyuze (Cruyhautern). It entrained for Nesle about June 8, moving through Audenarde, Coutrai, Lille, Douai, Cambrai, and Ham. It marched to the front, southeast of Montdidier by Roye and Tilloloy June 9–11.

5. It was in line near Ressons-Marqueglise from June 14 to 24.

6. The division rested south of St. Quentin June 26 to 29, then at Origny June 30 to July 4. It entrained at Origny on July 4 and moved to Sedan by Guise, Hirson, Liart, and Charleville. It was north of Grandpre from July 5 to 10. On the 10th it was sent toward the Champagne front by Grandpre, Monthois, and Maure.

BATTLE OF RHEIMS.

7. The division was engaged at Repon, east of Tahure, on July 15. Heavy losses were incurred during the attack of July 15. It was taken out on August 15.

AILETTE.

8. It was moved by railroad to Chauny (by Laon) and detrained about August 20. About this time a dozen men per company were received.

9. On August 26–27 it entered line south of Juvigny (north of Soissons). In the fighting that followed the division was withdrawn to Leuilly on the night of August 31–Sept 1. It was relieved on the 3d after losing 605 prisoners. The German communique of August 30 credited the 165th Regiment with the destruction of 20 tanks in one attack.

BATTLE OF THE ARGONNE.

10. The division rested near Attigny until September 24, when it reinforced the Somme-Py front. It was engaged until October 22 with very heavy losses. It returned from the second line two days later to assist in covering the retreat between La Neuville en Tourne a Fuy and Juniville. From there it fell back on the Aisne (Ambly) and was retired on October 14.

VALUE—1918 ESTIMATE.

The division was rated as first class.

7th Reserve Division.

COMPOSITION.

	1914 Brigade.	1914 Regiment.	1915 Brigade.	1915 Regiment.	1916 Brigade.	1916 Regiment.	1917 Brigade.	1917 Regiment.	1918 Brigade.	1918 Regiment.
Infantry	13 Res. 14 Res. 4 Res. Jäg. Btn.	27 Res. 36 Res. 66 Res. 72 Res.	13 Res. 14 Res. 4 Res. Jäg. Btn.	27 Res. 36 Res. 66 Res. 72 Res.	14 Res. 4 Res. Jäg. Btn.	36 Res. 66 Res. 72 Res.	14 Res.	36 Res. 66 Res. 72 Res.	14 Res.	36 Res. 66 Res. 72 Res.
Cavalry	1 Res. Heavy Cav. Rgt. (3 Sqns.).				1 Res. Heavy Cav. Rgt.		1 Res. Heavy Cav. Rgt. (1 Sqn.).		3 Sqn. 9 Drag. Rgt.	
Artillery	7 Res. F. A. Rgt. (6 Btries.).		7 Res. F. A. Rgt.		7 Res. F. A. Rgt. (9 Btries.).		95 Art. Command: 7 Res. F. A. Rgt. (9 Btries.).		95 Art. Command: 7 Res. F. A. Rgt. 52 Ft. A. Btn. 889 Light Am. Col. 1106 Light Am. Col. 1126 Light Am. Col.	
Engineers and Liaisons.	4 Field Co. 2 Pion. Btn No. 4.		4 Field Co. 2 Pion. Btn. No. 4: 7 Res. Pont.-Engs. 7 Res. Tel—Detch.		4 Field Co. 2 Pion. Btn. No. 4: 248 Pion. Co. 207 T. M. Co. 7 Res. Pont.–Engs. 7 Res. Tel.–Detch.		307 Pion. Btn.: 4 Co. 4 Pions. 248 Pion. Co. 207 T. M. Co. 407 Tel.–Detch.		307 Pion. Btn.: 4 Co. 4 Pions. 248 Pion. Co. 207 T. M. Co. 130 Searchlight Section. 407 Signal Command: 407 Tel. Detch. 42 Wireless Detch.	
Medical and Veterinary.							504 Ambulance Co. 22 Res. Field Hospital. 49 Res. Field Hospital. Vet. Hospital.		504 Ambulance Co. 22 Res. Field Hospital. 24 Res. Field Hospital. 407 Vet. Hospital.	
Transports.							M. T. Col.		707 M. T. Col.	

HISTORY.

(Fourth District—Prussian Saxony.)

1914.

1. At the beginning of the war the 7th Reserve Division was part of the 4th Reserve Corps.

BELGIUM.

2. It detrained August 10 to 12, 1914, near Dusseldorf, and was part of the 1st Army (Von Kluck). Reached Brussels via Tongres (Aug. 19) and Louvain, and advanced toward Paris through Enghien, Ath, Conde, Amiens (Aug. 30–31), Clermont, Creil, and Senlis (Sept. 4).

MARNE.

3. At the battle of the Marne it was engaged northwest of Crouy sur Ourcq (Puisieux, Neufmoutiers, Monthyon) and suffered heavy losses, September 6 and 7.

4. From September 8 to 11 it withdrew through Villers Cotterets, Coeuvres, Port Fontenoy. It fought for a long time in the region of Nouvron.

AISNE.

5. After the front was stabilized it held the lines between the Soissons–Laon Road to southwest of Nouvron.

6. November 12 it had considerable losses at the attack of the Plateau of Nouvron.

1915.

1. The division held the Nouvron sector until September, 1915.

2. In January, 1915, some of the units of the division were engaged in the fights around Soissons, January 12 and 13.

3. In June several battalions were sent toward Quennevieres as reinforcements at the beginning of the French attack.

CHAMPAGNE.

4. Relieved about September 22 to 25, the division was sent to Champagne at the beginning of October. Suffered heavy losses in the region of Tahure October 30.

1916.

1. Withdrawn at the end of January, 1916, from the sector of Tahure. It was sent to rest north of Rethel. It went back into line only for a short time toward the end of February north of Prosnes (the 36th Reserve Regiment alone appeared in this sector).

2. About May 10 the division was sent to the camp of Sissonne.

VERDUN.

3. It was sent to the Verdun front and took part in the attack of June 1 on Thiaumont–Damploup in the sector of Bois de la Caillette. Suffered very heavy losses June 2 and 3 and at the attack of Bois de Vaux Chapitre on June 21. Total of losses before Verdun, 8,200 men. On June 16 the companies of the 36th Reserve were reduced to an average of 30 men (prisoners' statements). From June 1 to 5 the 10th Company of the 72d Reserves received no less than 138 replacements.

ARGONNE.

4. The division was withdrawn from the Verdun front about July 1. Sent to the Argonne and occupied the sector north of Ville sur Tourbe (between Main de Massiges and the Aisne) until the end of August. It was reorganized in this region.

SOMME.

5. After a rest in the vicinity of Longwy it was sent to the Somme and fought in the region of Gueudecourt September 23 to October 11.

ARGONNE.

6. About October 14 the division took over its old sector north of Ville sur Tourbe, south of Cernay en Dormois.

1917.

MEUSE.

1. Withdrawn from the Argonne front about January 8, 1917, and sent, February 5, before Verdun (region of Louvemont, north of Chambrettes), where it was kept until the beginning of April.

2. The division next held the sector of Cernay les Reims at the end of April to May 25.

CHAMPAGNE.

3. About May 30 and 31 it was sent into line before Teton (region of Moronvilliers) until the middle of August.

4. After a rest in the vicinity of Aussonce the division went into line at the beginning of September in the region of Nauroy, sector of Mont Haut-Cornillet. Relieved January, 1918, and sent to rest north of Rethel.

RECRUITING.

Prussian Saxony and part of Thuringia.

VALUE—1917 ESTIMATE.

At Tahure in October, 1915, and at Verdun the division obtained only mediocre results in spite of heavy losses. "This division seems to be rather a sector division than a shock unit."

1918.

RETHEL.

1. On January 14 the division was relieved by the 14th Bavarian Division and sent to Wassigny (north of Rethel) to rest and train. On March 14 it started by night marches toward St. Quentin, bivouacking in the woods by day and avoiding all villages. The itinerary followed was Dezy le Gros–Bucy les Pierrepont–Marlerigny et Mesnil–St. Laurent, where it arrived March 21.

BATTLE OF PICARDY.

2. From the 22d to the 28th the division was in army reserve. It followed the general advance through Itancourt, Essigny, Grand Serancourt, St. Simon, Golancourt, Muirancourt, and Candor. On March 29 it relieved the 1st Bavarian Division east of Lassigny, where it attacked on the day following. It suffered such heavy losses that it was hastily relieved on the night of March 31–April 1.

AISNE.

3. It came into line near Reims on April 26 relieving the 25th Reserve Division between the Miettl and the Aisne. It took part in the offensive of May 27. About June 1 the division was relieved in the sector east of Ville en Tardenois.

CHAMPAGNE.

4. The division moved to Champagne and relieved the Guard Cavalry Division on July 6. It passed into the second line on July 14 to permit a fresh division to pass through for the attack. It returned to line on the 20th, relieving the 1st Division near St. Hilaire. During July the 66th Reserve Regiment is known to have received drafts, raising the company strength to 100.

SOISSONS.

5. Between August 4 and 20 the exact date is not known, the division was moved from line in Champagne to the front west of Chavigny, where it was engaged on August It took part in heavy fighting in that region until its relief about August 31.

6. The division arrived at Fourmies from Laon on September 8, where it rested and trained until September 17. It entrained at Trelon and moved to Grandpre, from where it marched to the front by way of St. Juvin and Brieulles.

MEUSE-ARGONNE.

7. The division was in line on the day of the American attack September 26, holding the sector immediately west of the Meuse. It was swamped on the opening attack without offering any considerable resistance. It was withdrawn on the 28th, but on October 9 elements were returned to fill a gap in the former sector of the 1st A. H. division. The last elements were finally withdrawn about October 25. The losses of the division in the Argonne are estimated at 3,500, including 2,260 prisoners.

VALUE—1918 ESTIMATE.

The division was rated as a second-class division. Its efforts in 1918 were generally unsuccessful in spite of heavy losses. By the time of the armistice it had been almost annihilated.

7th Landwehr Division.
COMPOSITION.

	1914 Brigade	1914 Regiment	1915 Brigade	1915 Regiment	1916 Brigade	1916 Regiment	1917 Brigade	1917 Regiment	1918 Brigade	1918 Regiment
Infantry	Mathy (55). 52.	119 Ldw. 40 Ldw. 123 Ldw. 121 Ldw.	52 Ldw.	119 Ldw. 121 Ldw. 123 Ldw.	51 Ldw. 52 Ldw.	119 Ldw. 123 Ldw. 121 Ldw. 126 Ldw.	52 Ldw.	122 Res. 121 Ldw. 126 Ldw.	52 Ldw.	122 Res. 121 Ldw. 126 Ldw.
Cavalry				2 Ldw. Sqn. (13 C. Dist.).		2 Ldw. Sqn. (13 C. Dist.).		2 Ldw. Sqn. (13 C. Dist.). 1 Sqn. 20 Uhlan Rgt.		
Artillery			1 Ldw. F. A. Rgt.		1 Ldw. F. A. Rgt.		Art. Command: 1 Ldw. F. A. Rgt.		1 Ldw. F. A. Rgt. (except the 3d Abt. Staff and 7 and 9 Btrles). 1025 Light Am. Col.	
Engineers and Liaisons.						2 Ldw. Co. 13 C. Dist. Pions. 4 Ldw. Co. 13 C. Dist. Pions. 6 Ldw. Co. 13 C. Dist. Pions. 307 T. M. Co.		(407) Pion. Btn.: 2 Ldw. Co. 13 Pions. 3 Ldw. Co. 13 Pions. 307 T. M. Co. 334 Searchlight Section. 507 Tel. Detch.	407 Pion. Btn.; 2 Ldw. Co. 13 C. Dist. Pions. 141 Searchlight Section. 507 Signal Command: 507 Tel. Detch.	
Medical and Veterinary.								571 Ambulance Co. 258 Field Hospital. 33 Ldw. Field Hospital. Vet. Hospital.	571 Ambulance Co. 258 Field Hospital. 33 Ldw. Field Hospital. 47 Vet. Hospital.	
Transports								M. T. Col.	776 M. T. Col.	
Odd units						1 Cyclist Co.		1 Cyclist Co.		
Attached						13 Balloon Sqn. 59 Labor Btn.				

HISTORY.

(Thirteenth District—Wurtemberg.)

1914.

ALSACE.

1. The 7th Landwehr Division did not leave Alsace from its organization in 1915 until February, 1917. Its first units appeared there beginning August 9, 1914, the date of the detraining of the 121st Landwehr at Neuf Brisach. The 119th Landwehr fought south of Mulhouse beginning August 19, and the 40th Landwehr at Dornach near Mulhouse on the same day.

2. In October, 1917, the 52d and 55th Brigades, which were to compose in 1915 the 7th Landwehr Division, were part of the Gaede Army Group and occupied the region of Munster, Guebwiller, Cernay.

3. In December the 123d Landwehr took part in the attacks on Hartmannswiller-kopf.

1915.

ALSACE.

1. In March, 1915, the 52d Brigade was in line in the valleys of the Fecht and the Lauch. The 119th Landwehr was south of Cernay. In April the 40th Landwehr (Baden) left the division and was transferred for some time to the 6th Landwehr Division (Bavarian).

2. The 7th Landwehr Division then contained the 119th, 121st and 123d Landwehr, to which a fourth regiment was joined, the 126th Landwehr, formed by drafts from the three others. The division, from then on exclusively Wurtemberger, from that time held the sector Wattwiller-Rhone-Rhine Canal (Cernay–Altkirch).

1916.

ALSACE.

1. Cernay–Altkirch sector.

1917.

ALSACE-LORRAINE.

1. The division remained on the Mulhouse front (Cernay–Altkirch) until February 20, 1917. Relieved on that date and sent to Lorraine (Leintrey–Badonviller sector), where it replaced the 33d Reserve Division. It was at this time that the division was decreased to three regiments; its 119th Landwehr and 123d Landwehr were transferred to the 26th Landwehr Division and it obtained the 122d Reserves from the 54th Reserve Division.

RUSSIA–VOLHYNIA.

2. The division left the Lorraine front in the middle of May. Entrained beginning May 14 at Sarrebourg and sent to the Eastern Front via Nurnberg -Warsaw–Lublin–Kovel–Vladimir Volynski. It took over the Kisselin sector (Volhynia).

RECRUITING.

From April, 1915 on, the division was entirely composed from men from Wurtemberg.

VALUE—1917 ESTIMATE.

A mediocre division, much reduced by transferring its most energetic units to active regiments and Wurtemberg reserve regiments and receiving in exchange older men.

1918.

UKRAINE.

1. In February, 1918, the 7th Landwehr Division left the Kisselin region and advanced into the Ukraine. "We are going into Russia to succor the Ukrainians," wrote a man of the 122d Reserve Regiment from the Rovno region on February 26.

)n April 1, the 126th Landwehr Regiment was identified between Kiev and Odessa; long with the 122d Reserve Regiment it was identified near Odessa on the 9th.

2. On May 11 the division was identified south of Ekaterinoslav and on the 4th of uly at Rostov on the Don.

3. The division was reported to have been sent to the Danube front about the middle f October, but it was never actually identified there.

VALUE—1918 ESTIMATE.

The division was rated as fourth class.

7th Cavalry Division (Dismounted).

COMPOSITION.

	1918	
	Brigade.	Regiment.
Cavalry...	28 Cav.	11 Uhlan. 15 Uhlan.
		4 Res. Uhlan.
	30 Cav.	9 Hus. 15 Drag. 25 Drag.,
	41 Cav	26 Drag. 5 Cuirassier. 4 Uhlan.
Engineers and Liaisons....................................	19 Pion. Btn. (1, 2, and 3 Cos.) : 6 Cav. Pion. Detch. 312 T. M. Co. 186 Wireless Detch.	
Medical and Veterinary..................................	606 Ambulance Co.	
Odd Units...	10 M. G. S. S. Detch. (1, 2, and 3 Cos.).	
Attached..	5 F. A. Rgt. (10 and 11 Btries.).	

HISTORY.

1918.

1. The division held the Guebwiller (Alsace) sector until the end of May. It rested in the Saarebourg area until mid-July, when it was railed to Belgium (Courtrai area).

2. After resting near Courtrai for two weeks, the division entrained at Lauwe on August 13 for Armentieres, where it remained until August 23. It went into line in the Kemmel area for three days. The division was then railed back to Tourcoing, from where it was transferred by trucks to Lagnicourt on August 26 and came into line on the following day at Ecoust.

ARRAS–CAMBRAI.

3. In two weeks the division was heavily engaged in the Arras battle. It was relieved on September 9, after losing more than 700 prisoners. The division rested in the Cambrai area until September 22, when it relieved the 1st Guard Reserve Division north of Moeuvres. It was withdrawn on September 30.

BELGIUM.

4. The division entrained at Solesmes on October 5 and detrained at Mouscron. It remained here until October 14, when it moved to Deerlyck, and on the 17th elements counterattacked between Courtrai and Harlebeke. It was engaged until its relief on October 29 by the 49th Reserve Division northwest of Anseghem. The division was considered to be in reserve of the 10th German Army at the time of the armistice.

VALUE—1918 ESTIMATE.

The division was rated as fourth class. Its use on the Cambrai and Belgium fronts in September and October indicate that it might have been considered a third-class division after its reorganization.

COMPOSITION.

	1914 Brigade.	1914 Regiment.	1915 Brigade.	1915 Regiment.	1916 Brigade.	1916 Regiment.	1917 Brigade.	1917 Regiment.	1918 Brigade.	1918 Regiment.
Infantry	15. 16.	36 Fus. 93. 72. 153.	15. 16.	36 Fus. 93. 72. 153.	16.	72. 93. 153.	16.	72. 93. 153.	16.	72. 93. 153.
Cavalry	10 Hus. Rgt. (3 Sqns.).		10 Hus. Rgt. (3 Sqns.).		10 Hus. Rgt. (3 Sqns.).		10 Hus. Rgt. (. Sqns.).		5 Sqns. 10 Hus. Rgt.	
Artillery	8 Brig.: 74 F. A. Rgt. 75 F. A. Rgt.		8 Brig.: 74 F. A. Rgt. 75 F. A. Rgt.		8 Brig. 74 F. A. Rgt. 75 F. A. Rgt.		8 Art. Command: 74 F. A. Rgt.		8 Art. Command: 74 F. A. Rgt. 1 Abt. 1 Res. Ft. A. Rgt. 815 Light Am. Col. 963 Light Am. Col. 1247 Light Am. Col.	
Engineers and Liaisons.			1 Pion. Btn. No. 4: Field Co. 4 Pions. 8 Pont. Engs. 8 Tel. Detch.		1 Pion. Btn. No. 4: 2 Co. 4 Pions. 8 T. M. Co. 8 Pont. Engs. 8 Tel. Detch.		118 Pion. Btn. or 1 Pion. Btn. No. 4: 2 Co. 4 Pions. 5 Co. 4 Pions. 8 T. M. Co. 8 Tel. Detch.		118 Pion. Btn.: 2 Co. 4 Pions. 5 Co. 4 Pions. 8 T. M. Co. 95 Searchlight Section. 8 Signal Command: 8 Tel. Detch. 95 Wireless Detch.	
Medical and Veterinary.							Ambulance Co. 31 Field Hospital. Vet. Hospital.		11 Ambulance Co. 36 Field Hospital. 39 Field Hospital. 8 Vet. Hospital.	
Transports.							M. T. Col.			
Attached.					72 Anti-Aircraft Section. 7 Balloon Sqn.		72 Anti-Aircraft Section.			

HISTORY.

(Fourth District—Prussian Saxony.)

1914.

FRANCE.

1. With the 7th Division, the 8th Division formed the 4th Army Corps. It detrained August 10 to 12 near Dusseldorf and, with that corps, was part of the 1st Army (Von Kluck). Entered Belgium the 15th, passed through Louvain the 19th, and through Brussels the 20th, and executed with the 7th Division an enveloping movement on the left of the Allies. Fought at Solesmes the 26th and arrived east of Coulommiers September 6, from where it was sent in a great hurry to the right of the 1st Army, with the 7th Division (Lizy sur Ourcq-Plessis, Placy, etc.). September 8 the 11th Company of the 93d Infantry was reduced to 96 men (notebook).

2. After the retreat, beginning the 15th, it was engaged against the left wing of the British north of Soissons (battle of the Aisne, Cuffies, Chavigny, Pasly, etc.).

3. At the end of September it went with the 4th Army Corps to Artois with the 6th Army.

4. At the beginning of October it took part in the attacks south of Arras and held the lines near Monchy aux Bois.

1915.

1. The division held the Monchy sector during the first few months of 1915. At the end of May it was relieved from this sector and put in the reserve of the army near Douai after transferring the 36th Fusiliers to the 113th Division, newly formed (March).

2. During the first two weeks of June it went into line in the Souchez sector and opposed the French attacks. Relieved at the beginning of September and became army reserve near Tourcoing and Roubaix.

LOOS.

3. At the battle of Loos during the counterattack the division suffered heavy losses in September and October.

1916.

1. In 1916 until the battle of the Somme the division did not take part in any serious engagements. It was established in the Loos sector. July 3 it left this front for the Somme.

SOMME.

2. In the middle of July it went into battle on the Pozieres-Longueval-Bois Delville front and suffered very heavy losses.

3. Toward the end of July it was relieved and sent to rest in the region of Valenciennes.

4. August 9 it took over a quiet sector before Arras and stayed there about five weeks.

5. About September 18 it again went into the battle of the Somme. It held the Thiepval-Courcelette sector, where it had some hard fighting, which caused it heavy losses.

ARTOIS.

6. October 1 it left this sector to again hold the trenches northeast of Loos.

1917.

1. During the winter of 1916–17 the division had no heavy fighting. However, in April, May, and June it had serious losses due to the many raids executed by the British.

2. Toward the end of July and the beginning of August the division suffered considerably from artillery fire. It was relieved before the attack of the British before Lens.

CHAMPAGNE.

3. August 5 it entrained for Rethel. Rested for some time in the region of Semide, then held the sector west of Butte du Mesnil from August 15 to September 15.

BELGIUM.

4. About September 18 it was sent in the region of Bouziers and October 4 went into line west of Becelaere (Belgium), and shortly afterwards, October 9, south of Hollebeke. It was still there January 20, 1918.

RECRUITING.

Province of Prussian Saxony, Duchy of Anhalt, and part of Thuringia. Same remarks as for the 7th Division. The fluctuations in the resources of the region are evidenced by the following facts: On November 4, 1917, a man came to the 5th Company of the 93d Infantry who was born in 1898 in the Eighth District, was a farmer, and had been called up September 3, having had just two months of training. He was sent by a depot in Cologne.

VALUE—1917 ESTIMATE.

Since the battles of 1914 the division remained entirely on the offensive. It always defended itself well in attacks and held its positions with tenacity.

During its stay on the Champagne it did not show any activity, but also it had no desertions. It may be said that its morale is good. (September, 1917).

1918.

1. The division was relieved by the 17th Reserve Division in the Hollebeke sector about January 31. It rested and trained near Coutrai during February and until March 7.

2. On March 7 it was engaged west of Zandvoorde, where it was in line until April 11.

BATTLE OF THE LYS.

3. The division came into the battle line west of Merville on April 11, which town it captured. About the 23d it passed to the second line.

4. The division rested for two weeks at Canteleu (a suburb of Lille). It returned to a rest camp north of Kemmel about May 12th.

YPRES.

5. It was engaged south of Ypres from May 15 until the 1st of July in the sector, with division headquarters at Halluin.

6. The division rested near Coutrai during July, from where it returned to its former sector south of Ypres on July 26 and was in line until the night of September 17–18.

LE CATELET.

7. It was moved south to relieve the Alpine Corps at Vendhuile, where it came in on September 23. In the fighting the division was driven back by Aubencheul-Villers Outreaux on Maretz–Clary early in October. After suffering heavy casualties and losing over 400 prisoners, it was withdrawn on October 14.

8. The division rested in the Guise area until October 22.

9. It was reengaged north of Le Cateau on October 22-23, but withdrew about November 1. On the 5th it was identified in line north of Maulde, where it remained until the end.

VALUE—1918 ESTIMATE.

The division was regarded as a first-class division. A majority of its men came from the younger classes. Its effectives were high and the morale good. Apart from the Armentieres offensive in April, the division was on the defensive during 1918.

8th Landwehr Division.
COMPOSITION.

	1915 Brigade.	1915 Regiment.	1916 Brigade.	1916 Regiment.	1917 Brigade.	1917 Regiment.	1918 Brigade.	1918 Regiment.
Infantry	56 Ldw.	108 Ldw. 110 Ldw. 109 Landst.	56 Ldw.	109 Ldw. 110 Ldw. 109 Landst.	56 Ldw.	109 Ldw. 110 Ldw. 111 Ldw.	56 Ldw.	109 Ldw. 110 Ldw. 111 Ldw.
Cavalry	2 Ldw. Sqn. 14 C. Dist.		2 Ldw. Sqn. 14 C. Dist. (dissolved late 1916). 3 Landst. Sqn. 14 C. Dist.		1 Sqn. 5 Horse Jag. Rgt. (?)			1 Sqn. 5 Horse Jag. Rgt.
Artillery	Landst. F. A. Abt. (14 C. Dist.).		8 Ldw. F. A. Regt.		Art. command: 8 Ldw. F. A. Rgt.		8 Ldw. F. A. Rgt. 803 Light Am. Col. 1416 Light Am. Col.	
Engineers and Liaisons.	4 Co. 14 Pions. 2 Res. Co. 14 Pions.		4 Co. 14 Pions. 2 Res. Co. 14 Pions. 308 T. M. Co.		408 Pion. Btn.: 1 Res. Co. 14 Pions. 2 Res. Co. 14 Pions. 308 T. M. Co. 305 Searchlight Section. 508 Tel. Detch.		408 Pion. Btn.: 1 Res. Co. 14 Pions. 2 Res. Co. 14 Pions. 308 T. M. Co. 216 Searchlight Section. 508 Signal Command: 508 Tel. Detch. 177 Wireless Detch.	
Medical and Veterinary.					559 Ambulance Co. 321 (?) Field Hospital. Vet. Hospital.		559 Ambulance Co. 321 Field Hospital. 7 Field Hospital. 563 Vet. Hospital.	
Transports			777 M. T. Col.		777 M. T. Col.		777 M. T. Col.	
Odd								
Attached	Fribourg Landst. Inf. Btn. (14 C. Dist. Btn. No. 7). 2 Heidelberg Landst. Inf. Btn. (14 C. Dist. Btn. No. 13).		68 Labor Btn. Pforzheim Landst. Inf. Btn. (14 C. Dist. Btn. No. 21).					

HISTORY.

(Fourteenth District—Grand Duchy of Baden.)

1915.

The 8th Landwehr Division was formed February, 1915, from Baden troops, which ntered Alsace at the beginning of the campaign (the 110th Landwehr detrained Aug. 11, 1914, at Neuenburg near Mullheim and the 109th Landwehr on the same late), and the 109th Landsturm organized at the beginning of 1915 from five Baden Landsturm battalions.

ALSACE.

The division held the same sector between Altkirch and the Swiss Frontier from ts formation until January, 1917.

1916.

1. In February, 1916, the 109th Landwehr and the 110th Landwehr, which had up to that time remained on the defensive, took part in the attacks between Seppois and Largitzen and against the Scoonholz, northwest of Altkirch. They executed many raids during 1916.

2. The 109th Landsturm, which was in line at one end of the front, was broken up in May, 1916, and replaced in the division by the 111th Landwehr, newly formed, consisting in reality of three Landsturm battalions already stationed in Alsace, of which two were part of the 109th Landsturm (XIV 23 and XIV 25).

COTES DE MEUSE.

About January 23, 1917, the division was withdrawn from the Alsace front and sent to the Cotes de Meuse, where it took over the sector west of Fresnes en Woevre. April 15 the division moved toward the north and held the lines to the Etain-Verdun road.

RECRUITING.

Entirely from Baden.

VALUE—1917 ESTIMATE.

The division was a defense division (May, 1918). Each company had one shocktroop squad per platoon (prisoners' statements Dec. 8, 1917).

Like the 2d and 7th Landwehr Divisions, but to a smaller degree, the 8th Landwehr Division had some of its men transferred to active units; thus, in November, 1917, it transferred some men to 121st Division, then near it.

1918.

The division continued in the Woevre sector during 1918. Through failure to identify it, it was considered as out of line September 21 and September 25.

VALUE—1918 ESTIMATE.

It was rated as a fourth-class division. Its losses apart from the St. Mihiel attack were negligible. In the attack it did fairly well, without heavy loss. The morale was fair.

125651°—20——11

8th Bavarian Reserve Division.

COMPOSITION.

	1915		1916		1917		1918	
	Brigade.	Regiment.	Brigade.	Regiment.	Brigade.	Regiment.	Brigade.	Regiment.
Infantry......	15 Bav. Res. 16 Bav. Res.	18 Bav. Res. 19 Bav. Res. 22 Bav. Res. 23 Bav. Res.	15 Bav. Res. 16 Bav. Res. Wurt. Mountain Btn.	18 Bav. Res. 19 Bav. Res. 22 Bav. Res. 23 Bav. Res.	15 Bav. Res. 16 Bav. Res.	18 Bav. Res. 19 Bav. Res. 22 Bav. Res. 23 Bav. Res.	15 Bav. Res.	19 Bav. Res. 22 Bav. Res. 23 Bav. Res.
Cavalry......	8 Bav. Res. Cav. Detch.		8 Bav. Res. Cav. Detch.		8 Bav. Res. Cav. Detch.		8 Bav. Res. Cav. Detch.	
Artillery......	8 Bav. Res. F. A. Rgt. 9 Bav. Res. F. A. Rgt.		8 Bav. Res. F. A. Rgt. 9 Bav. Res. F. A. Rgt.		8 Bav. Art. Command: 8 Bav. Res. F. A. Rgt. 9 Bav. Res. F. A. Rgt.		8 Bav. Art. Command: 9 Bav. Res. F. A. Rgt. 19 Bav. Ft. A. Btn. 105 Bav. Light Am. Col. 171 Bav. Light Am. Col. 172 Bav. Light Am. Col.	
Engineers and liaisons.	9 Bav. Res. Pion. Co.		8 Bav. Res. Pion. Co. 9 Bav. Res. Pion. Co. 208 Bav. T. M. Co. 8 Bav. Res. Pont. Engs. 8 Bav. Res. Tel. Detch.		(20 Bav.) Pion. Btn.: 5 Bav. Res. Pion. Co. 8 Bav. Res. Pion. Co. 9 Bav. Res. Pion. Co. 208 Bav. T. M. Co. 3 Bav. Res. Searchlight Section. 303 Tel. Detch.		20 Bav. Pion. Btn.: 8 Bav. Res. Pion. Co. 9 Bav. Res. Pion. Co. 20 Bav. Searchlight Section. 208 Bav. T. M. Col. 408 Bav. Signal Command: 408 Bav. Tel. Detch. 99 Wireless Detch.	
Medical and Veterinary.					18 Bav. Ambulance Co. 30 Bav. Ambulance Co. 55 Bav. Field Hospital. Vet. Hospital.		18 Bav. Ambulance Co. 65 Bav. Field Hospital. 57 Bav. Field Hospital.	
Transports......							753 M. T. Col.	

| Attached...... | 8 Bav. Res. Cyclist Co.
81 Anti-Aircraft Section.
6 Bav. Labor Btn.
64 Labor Btn.
69 Labor Btn. | 8 Bav. Res. Cyclist Co. | 1 Landst. Inf. Btn. 10 C. Dist.
1, 2, and 3 Abtls. 24 Res. F. A. Rgt.
69 Ldw. F. A. Btn.
14, 33, and 34 Mortar Btries.
52 Searchlight Section.
94 Pion. Btn.
66 Balloon Sqn.
115 Observation Section.
2 Sound Ranging Section.
286 Reconnaissance Flight.
Elements attached in October, 1918. |

HISTORY.

(19th Bavarian Reserve: First Bavarian District. 22d Bavarian Reserve: Second
Bavarian District. 23d Bavarian Reserve: Third Bavarian District.)

1915.

ALSACE.

1. The division was organized in January, 1915 (second series of new reserve
divisions) and was identified on the front for the first time at the beginning of February, 1915, in the valley of the Lauch and at Hartmannswillerkopf. It fought at
the end of February in the region of Munster-Metzeral-Sultzeren. On the 24th it
took part in the attack of Reichackerkopf and lost heavily.

2. Since that time and until May the division remained in the same sector of Alsace.

GALICIA.

3. Relieved at the end of May and sent to Galicia, where it became part of the 11th
Army and cooperated in the capture of Przemsl June 3.

ALSACE.

4. Returned to the Western Front at the beginning of July and went to rest in the
region of Schelestadt (Alsace); then went into line again about July 14 in the valley
of the Fecht (Reichackerkopf-Metzeral). It repulsed an attack of the French July
20 at Reichackerkopf.

1916.

ALSACE.

1. The division remained in Alsace, sector of Metzeral-Sondernach, for a year from
July, 1915, to July, 1916. During this period it did not take part in any action.

SOMME.

2. About July 10, 1916, it entrained at Mulhouse, Colmar, and Pfaffenheim, south
of Colmar, and went to the Somme, south of Péronne, and was in reserve until July 20.
July 21 and 22 it was engaged between Maurepas and Guillemont (the 23d Bavarian
Reserve was detached and went to the east of Estrées).

3. Relieved August 15 after suffering heavy losses during the attacks of July 30
and August 12. Reorganized in the region of St. Quentin, then went back into line
for a short time west of Roye at the beginning of September.

4. Withdrawn from the region of Roye in the middle of September and sent to
the Roumanian front October 13 to 23, via Mons-Maubeuge-Namur-Liége-Aixla
Chapelle-Cologne-Cassel-Halle-Leipzig-Prague-Brunn-Budapest-Arad.

1917.

ROUMANIA.

5. Took part in the operations on the frontier of Transylvania in the region of the
Oltu in October to November and in the valley of the Trotus in December.

GALICIA.

2. In July it left Roumania and went to Galicia. At the end of July it was in the
region of Nowitza. August 27 it fought at Bojan. In September it was at Czernowitz and went to rest near Radautz in Bukowina beginning September 6. After
being reviewed by the Emperor September 27 it was filled up again (men of the 1918
class with less than four months' training were sent to the 22d Reserve Infantry)
and sent to the Western Front.

BELGIUM.

3. It entrained October 15 at Kolomea. Itinerary: Stanislau-Lemberg-Cracow-
Leipzig-Northeim-Paderborn-Aix la Chapelle-Liege-Louvain-Malines-Brussels-
Bruges, and detrained at Thourout October 23.

4. October 26 the division took over the Aschhoop sector near Dixmude.

RECRUITING.

It seems to come from all over Bavaria.

VALUE—1917 ESTIMATE.

The division had no serious fighting from August, 1916, on. Its losses on the Eastern Front were few. It was trained especially for mountain warfare, and they carried on this sort of warfare for a long time in Alsace, Galicia, and Roumania.

1918.

1. On January 24 the division was relieved at Dixmude and sent to Ghent for rest. From there it was transferred to Courtrai.

BELGIUM.

2. It relieved the 7th Division in the Becelaere sector on February 4, a quiet part at that time, and remained until March 7, when it was in turn relieved by the 7th Division.

BATTLE OF THE LYS.

3. It rested at Ostend until the Lys battle began, when it returned to attack on April 9 in the Estaires sector, which was defended by Portuguese. It advanced toward Calonne sur Lys, where it was withdrawn about April 14. The losses were 50 per cent of the effectives in this fighting.

WOEVRE.

4. Upon relief the division entrained on April 20 at Rouhaix and moved to Conflans. On May 11 it relieved the 78th Reserve Division north of Seicheprey. It was in line in this sector until June 27. A draft of 300 men were received late in June.

CHAMPAGNE.

5. The division rested at Conflans until July 4. It was then moved to Wassigny (north of Rethel) on the 5th. It marched toward the front by Herpy and St. Remy July 8 to 14. It was in reserve on July 15 east of Reims, in support of the 15th Bavarian Division. The division was not actively engaged in this offensive.

6. Withdrawn from Champagne, the division marched toward the front south of the Vesle by Warnerville, Soivre, and Jonchery, Vendeuil.

VESLE.

7. It was engaged west of Reims (St. Euphraise, Vrigny) between July 22 and August 8.

8. About August 22 the division arrived in the area northeast of Ath from the Aisne front to refit and train.

ARDENNES.

9. It was engaged west of La Pompelle on September 20, retreating to the Suippe, south of Bazancourt, about October 1, then toward Chateau Porcien and Faizy. It was relieved about October 15.

10. It rested for 10 days at Son and St. Fergeux, receiving 150 to 200 men per regiment as drafts.

11. On the 25th the division returned to line in the Chateau Porcien sector. It retired in November by Son, Chappes, Dommely, and La Romagn, where it was last identified on November 7.

VALUE—1918 ESTIMATE.

The division was rated as a first-class division, though it was considered as a shade under the class of the best divisions. It fought hard on the Lys, losing but 1 prisoner. It was not used later as an attack division. The morale was good.

8th Cavalry Division.

COMPOSITION.[1]

	1918	
	Brigade.	Regiment.
Cavalry	39 Cav. 40 Cav. 38 Cav.	Guard Reiter. 17 Uhlan. Karabinier. 21 Uhlan. 2 Jager. 6 Jag.
Artillery	12 Horse Art. Det.	
Engineers and Liaisons	Pion. Detch. 8 M. G. Btry. 260 Searchlight Section.	
Medical and Veterinary	54 Field Hospital.	

Attached	44 Cav. Brig.:
	  11 Horse Jag. Rgt.
	  9 Res. Uhlan Schutzen Rgt.
	  87 Cav. Schutzen Rgt.
	  89 Cav. Schutzen Rgt.
	7 Landst. Inf. Rgt.	

[1] At the time of its dissolution, April, 1918.

HISTORY.

1918.

The division continued on the Eastern Front, employed in small police detachments, until about April 1, when it was dissolved.

VALUE—1918 ESTIMATE

The division was rated as a fourth-class division.

9th DIVISION.
COMPOSITION.

	1914 Brig.	1914 Regt.	1915 Brig.	1915 Regt.	1916 Brig.	1916 Regt.	1917 Brig.	1917 Regt.	1918 Brig.	1918 Regt.
Infantry	17. 18.	19. 58. 7 Gren. 154.	17. 18.	19. 58. 7 Gren. 154.	18.	7 Gren. 19. 154.	18.	7 Gren. 19. 154.	18.	7. 19. 154.
Cavalry	1 Uhlan Regt.				1 and 2 Sqns., 1 Uhlan Regt.		2 Sqn. 1 Horse Jag. Rgt.		2 Sqn. 1 Horse Jag. Rgt.	
Artillery	9 brig.; 5 F. A. Rgt. 41 F. A. Rgt.		9 brig.; 5 F. A. Rgt. 41 F. A. Rgt.		9 brig.; 5 F. A. Rgt. 41 F. A. Rgt.		9 Art. command: 5 F. A. Rgt.		9 Art. command: 5 F. A. Rgt. (except 4 Abt.) 2 Abt. 6 Res. Ft. A. Rgt. (5, 6, and 12 Btries.). 907 Light Am. Col. 1175 Light Am. Col. 1201 Light Am. Col.	
Engineers and Liaisons.			1 Pion. Btn. No. 55: Field Co. 5 Pioms. 9 Pont. Engs. 9 Tel. Detch.		1 Pion. Btn. No. 5: 1 Co. 5 Pioms. 9 Pont. Detch. 9 T. M. Co.		120 Pion. Btn.: 1 Co. 5 Pioms. 5 Co. 5 Pioms. 304 Searchlight Section. 9 Tel. Detch.		120 Pion. Btn.: 5 Co. 5 Pioms. 1 Co. 5 Pioms. 9 T. M. Co. 194 Searchlight Section. 9 Signal Command: 9 Tel. Detch. 53 Wireless Detch.	
Medical and Veterinary.							14 Ambulance Co. 45 Field Hospital. 48 Field Hospital. 52 Field Hospital. 9 Vet. Hospital.		14 Ambulance Co. 48 Field Hospital. 52 Field Hospital. 9 Vet. Hospital.	
Transports							M. T. Col.		542 M. T. Col.	
Attached					37 Searchlight Section.		37 Searchlight Section.			

HISTORY.

(Fifth District—Lower Silesia.)

1914.

COTES DE MEUSE.

1. The 9th Division with the 10th Division, formed the 5th Army Corps (Posen), and at the beginning of the war was part of the 5th Army (German Crown Prince). Detrained August 9 to 10 in annexed Lorraine, near Bouzonville, and fought August 22 at Virton. After a number of marches and countermarches in Woevre, it established itself during the first days of September with the 10th Division in a sector of Cotes de Meuse (Calonne trench). It remained there about two years from September, 1914, to September, 1916, with rest billets in the villages of the Woevre at the foot of the hills (Thillot, Woel, Hannonville, etc.).

1915.

LES EPARGES.

1. In the spring of 1915 it took part in the battles of Les Eparges where it suffered heavily. In March it transferred its 58th Infantry to the 119th Division, newly formed, which was operating in Galicia beginning with April.

1916.

VERDUN.

1. At the beginning of September, 1916, the division was withdrawn from the sector of Calonne trench and relieved the 14th Bavarian Division in the woods of Vaux Chapitre (Verdun). In this last sector it suffered huge losses. October 24, 1916, it lost 700 men captured.

2. Relieved at the beginning of November and reorganized with men of all ages from depots of the Fifth District.

3. November 4 it entrained behind Douaumont; was sent to the Aisne and put in the line November 8 in the sector of Nouvron, where it remained until the middle of February, 1917.

1917.

COTES DE MEUSE.

1. Entrained at Laon during the last two weeks of February, 1917, and sent to Vigneulles, via Charleville–Conflans–Chambley; and again went into the sector of Calonne trench between February 18 and the end of April.

CALIFORNIE PLATEAU.

2. Relieved at the end of April and sent from Mars la Tour–Vigneulles (via Conflans–Sedan–Liart) to the region of Rozoy sur Serre. After a few days' rest in the vicinity of Sissonne it was engaged beginning May 6 in the attacks on the plateaus of Vauclerc and Californie, where some of its regiments suffered heavy losses, especially on the Winterberg.

3. Beginning May 18 the division did not attack any more but merely held the sector (Californie–Chevreux les Courtines). However, our attack of May 22 to 24 caused it heavy losses.

4. At the end of May the 9th Division was replaced by the 41st Division. It received reinforcements. (The 19th Infantry received 200 men June 14. About May 25, 60 men of the 1918 class were sent to the 6th Company of this regiment.) From May 13 to June 13 the 10th Company of the 154th Infantry received 68 men at least, most of them of the 1918 class.

5. About June 17–18 the division appeared in the sector of Juvincourt, where it attacked on the night of August 4–5 without success. Relieved about September 8 without having losses in this last sector.

HEMINS DES DAMES.

6. During September it was sent to rest in the region of Pierrepont–Missy–Liesse. ngaged in the sector of Bovettes–Pargny–Filain from October 23 to 27 and with- :awn from this front at the beginning of November after some of its regiments had iffered heavy losses during the battle of October 23 to 25.

7. About the middle of November the division went to the sector of Chevregny, 'ter a rest of about two weeks in the region of Laon, during which it was filled up ;ain. It held this sector until the beginning of December. December 8 it was in ie vicinity of Laon. January 11, 1918, some of the units were at Liesse.

RECRUITING.

The division (Fifth District) was recruited in Lower Silesia, where the German opulation is much more numerous than the Polish population. Although it received ıen from the Second and Third Districts in 1913 and men from the Seventh District ı 1916, it could without great difficulty get all its men from its original territory. Its :placements come almost entirely from Lower Silesia, and in emergency from Silesia. : is more homogeneous than the 10th Division, where the Polish elements have to e balanced off by Germans.

VALUE—1917 ESTIMATE.

Among the various German units which were engaged in front of Verdun and at alifornie Plateau, the 9th Division was one of those which showed the least resistance.

1918.

1. The division was relieved on the Chemin des Dames front on December 29 and 'ent to rest and train in the Guise area until the middle of March, when it proceeded) the battle front.

IATTLE OF PICARDY.

2. It was at Marcy on March 20. On the 21st it followed up the attack without being ngaged through Happencourt, Artemps, Tugny, Dury, Pithon, Ham, and Nesle Mar. 25). It was engaged on the 26th near Roye and advanced by Montdidier to 'est of Mesnil–St. Georges March 27–28. Its attack of March 30 on Ayencourt- :oyancourt met with heavy losses.

[ONTDIDIER.

3. The division was withdrawn on April 1 for a short rest, during which it received draft of 400 men. It returned to line southwest of Montdidier and was in line from .pril 5 to 8.

4. Until the 18th it was in reserve near La Boissiere and later near Nesle until .pril 24.

5. It rested near Hirson and Vervins during May, again receiving drafts to the num- er of 300 men.

IATTLE OF THE AISNE.

6. On May 20 it marched by night stages to the Aisne front, passing through Froid- ıont, Verneuil sur Serre, and Bruyeres. On the opening day it advanced in reserve y Presles, Monampteuil, and Pargny Filain. It was engaged on the 28th at Sancy- 'regny and advanced in the first line south of Soissons, Venizel, Missy sur Aisne, 'ourmelles, Noyant, Chazelle, and Poisy (May 30). Its losses in front of Chazelle rere particularly heavy. It was relieved on June 8. An official German document ives the division losses between May 28 and June 2 as 96 officers and 2,830 men.

7. It rested in the vicinity of Rethel and Novion–Porcien (June 15 to July 7) and econstituted by drafts. It moved toward the Aisne front on July 10, going into eserve northeast of Rheims for a week. Alerted on the 17th it moved to Oulchy le 'hateau.

SECOND BATTLE OF THE MARNE.

8. The division was engaged near Hartennes and Varcy from July 20 to August 2. It was driven back on Fismes on that date and relieved the next day.

9. In August it rested and trained near Vailly and in the vicinity of Laon. After the 24th it was north of Rheims.

CHAMPAGNE.

10. The division was engaged east of La Pompelle from September 20 to the beginning of October. On the 3d it was forced back on Isles Bazancourt, and later to Nanteuil sur Aisne. On October 17 it was relieved.

11. Two days later it was entrained for Flanders, but at Mons directed toward Avesnes and La Capelle.

12. Its last engagement was north of Guise from October 21 to November 4; then near Novin and Avesnes. 1,800 prisoners were taken on November 4.

VALUE—1918 ESTIMATE.

The division was rated as a first-class division. Its performance in 1918 was not of the best, however. It was engaged in the Somme, Aisne, and Marne actions without winning special credit. Discipline was reported to be lax, and morale poor at the end.

COMPOSITION.

	1914 Brigade.	1914 Regiment.	1915 Brigade.	1915 Regiment.	1916 Brigade.	1916 Regiment.	1917 Brigade.	1917 Regiment.	1918 Brigade.	1918 Regiment.
Infantry......	17 Res.	6 Res. 7 Res. 19 Res. 5 Res. Jag. Btn.	17 Res.	19 Res. 7 Res. 6 Res. 5 Res. Jag. Btn.	17 Res.	6 Res. 19 Res. 102 (Ldw.). 5 Res. Jag. Btn. 98 Res. 395.	18 Res.	6 Res. 19 Res. 395.	18 Res.	6 Res. 19 Res. 395.
Cavalry......		3 Res. Dragoon Rgt. (3 Sqns.).			3 Res. Dragoon Rgt.		1 and 3 Sqns. 3 Res. Dragoon Rgt.		3 Sqn. 3 Res. Drag. Rgt.	
Artillery......	9 Res. F. A. Rgt. (6 Btries.).		9 Res. F. A. Rgt.		9 Res. F. A. Rgt.		97 Art. Command: 9 Res. F. A. Rgt. (9 Btries.).		97 Art. Command: 9 Res. F. A. Rgt. (Staff and 1 and 3 Btries.). 735 Light Am. Col. 1287 Light Am. Col. 1361 Light Am. Col.	
Engineers and Liaisons.	4 Field Co. 2 Pion. Btn. No. 5. 2 Res. Co. 2 Pion. Btn. No. 5.		4 Field Co. 2 Pion. Btn. No. 5. 2 Res. Co. 2 Pion. Btn. No. 5. 9 Res. Pont. Engs. 9 Res. Tel. Detch.		4 Co. 2 Pion. Btn. No. 5. 2090 T. M. Co. 9 Pont. Engs. 9 Tel. Detch.		309 Pion. Btn.: 4 Co. 55 Pions. 1 Res. Co. 18 Pions. 209 T. M. Co. 409 Tel. Detch.		309 Pion. Btn.: 4 Co. 5 Pions. 1 Res. Co. 18 Pions. 209 T. M. Co. 29 Searchlight Section. 409 Signal Command: 409 Tel. Detch. 28 Wireless Detch.	
Medical and Veterinary.							519 Ambulance Co. Field Hospital. Vet. Hospital.		519 Ambulance Co. 13 Res. Field Hospital 25 Res. Field Hospital 409 Vet. Hospital.	
Transports...							M. T. Col.		708 M. T. Col.	

HISTORY.

(Fifth District—Posen.)

1914.

The division was part of the 5th Reserve Corps with the 10th Reserve Division.

MEUSE–WOEVRE.

1. At the beginning of the war it belonged to the 5th German Army (Imperial Crown Prince). Concentrated in the region of Sarrebruck and crossed the southern part of Belgian Luxemburg; fought August 22 near Ville en Montois and September 1 in the region of Consenvoye–Flabas, and was kept east of the Meuse near Sivry September 2. Toward the end of September and the beginning of October the division sent a few units to the left bank of the Meuse (Forges–Malancourt–Chattancourt). The division established itself in Woevre during the last two weeks of October and at the beginning of November in the region Etraye–Wavrille–Romagne, where it did some fighting at Maucourt November 10.

FLANDERS.

2. About November 13 the division was sent from the region of Verdun to Flanders. Some units of the division fought near Poelcappelle and south of Bixschoote in support of the 3d Reserve Corps. It suffered very heavy losses.

3. Again sent to Woevre during the month of December.

1915.

WOEVRE.

1. In January, 1915, the division held the region Gincrey–Etrain–Warcq. It remained in this section during the whole of 1915 and until the end of February, 1916. In April it transferred its 7th Reserve Infantry to form the 121st Division.

1916.

VERDUN.

1. A few days before the Verdun offensive (end of February, 1916,) the regiments of the division were relieved. The 6th Reserve and the 19th Reserve organized with their best units one attack battalion each. These battalions took part with the 15th Army Corps in the violent action at the beginning and suffered heavy losses.

2. March 7 its units were reorganized behind the front and the division advanced through Maucourt–Ornes and established itself north of Vaux. March 9 and 10 the three regiments of the division attacked successfully the village and fort of Vaux. They were repulsed nearly everywhere with very heavy losses.

3. About March 12 the division was relieved from before Vaux and sent to rest in the region of Senon–Amel.

4. Went back into line about March 20 south of Damploup. It did not attack any more, but bombardments caused it heavy losses.

5. Relieved about the end of April and sent to rest in the vicinity of Saverne (Alsace) until June 12.

CHAMPAGNE.

6. About June 20 it went into line in Champagne (sector of Souain–Tahure) but did not take part in any important action.

SOMME.

7. Withdrawn from the front about September 20 or 25 and sent to the Somme. Engaged between the eastern limit of Bouchavesnes and the main Péronne road until October 18. It had a few losses.

8. After a period of rest, probably in the vicinity of Vouziers, it was again sent to the Somme, first behind the front southeast of Bapaume December 1, then about December 17 in line in the sector of Bouchavenes–Bois de St. Pierre–Vaast until February, 1917.

1917.

1. In February, 1917, the division held on the Somme the sector north of the Ancre—south of Achiet le Petit.

2. Withdrawn from the front about March 10 and sent to rest in the region of Cambrai, and was established on a new front about March 20 west of Catelet near Gouzeaucourt, Villers Guislain.

ARTOIS.

3. About April 15 it was relieved and went into line south of the Scarpe, northeast of Monchy le Preaux, from the beginning of May till the beginning of June.

FLANDERS.

4. It was again at the front east of Armentieres from the middle of June till about July 10, then after a rest in the vicinity of Ghent it was in line on the Ypres road at Menin, east of Klein–Zillebeke, from August 10 to September 25, and fought especially on the 20th, on which date it suffered heavily. The 11th Company of the 6th Reserve Infantry was reduced to 20 men, and the 12th to 27. The 19th Reserve Infantry had the same losses. The 3d Company of the 395th Infantry lost half of its men. (Summary of information Sept. 21 and Oct. 24, 1917.)

CAMBRAI.

5. Reorganized in the region of Cambrai and from that time on held various sectors of this front. It fought November 23 to 30 at Banteux, Masnières, and in December south of Marcoing. In January, 1918, it was at La Vacquerie and was relieved there February 21.

RECRUITING.

The Province of Posen, with a few units from other districts, for example the ninth, to reduce the proportion of Poles.

VALUE—1917 ESTIMATE.

The division fought well in many battles at the end of 1917, especially east of Ypres and before Cambrai.

1918.

BATTLE OF PICARDY.

1. The division reinforced the front southwest of Cambrai on March 22 and advanced by Montaubau–Maricourt to west of Albert. It was relieved about the 1st of April. After losing heavily in the offensive it was withdrawn.

LENS.

2. It came into line in the quiet sector near Lens about April 10, relieving the 2th Reserve Division. On the 23d it shifted its sector south to Avion. The 12th Reserve Division returned from the Lys front to relieve it on about April 29.

3. The division moved north and entered the battle line in the Festubert sector on April 29. It continued in this sector until September 27, effecting only local reliefs. It reentered at once at Marcoing on September 29. A month later it arrived at Ath from line and went into line on November 2 at Hermes. The last identification was at Ellezelle on November 10.

VALUE—1918 ESTIMATE.

The division was rated as a second-class division. During 1918 its length of stay on the British front was remarkable. Nothing is known of its morale or losses.

9th Landwehr Division.

COMPOSITION.

	1915 Brigade.	1915 Regiment.	1916 Brigade.	1916 Regiment.	1917 Brigade.	1917 Regiment.	1918 Brigade.	1918 Regiment.
Infantry	43 Ldw. 49 Mixed Ldw.	32 Ldw. 83 Ldw. 116 Ldw. 118 Ldw. 56 Ldw.	76 Ldw. 49 Ldw.	79 Ldw. 83 Ldw. 116 Ldw. 118 Ldw.	76 Ldw.	83 Ldw. 116 Ldw. 118 Ldw.	76 Ldw.	83 Ldw. 116 Ldw. 118 Ldw.
Cavalry	Ldw. Cav. Rgt. (18 C. Dist.).		Ldw. Cav. Rgt. (18 C. Dist.).		1 Sqn. 4 Res. Drag. Rgt.		1 Sqn. 4 Res. Drag. Rgt.	
Artillery	Ldw. F. A. Rgt.		Ldw. F. A. Rgt.		(?) Art. command: 9 Ldw. F. A. Rgt.		9 Ldw. F. A. Rgt.	
Engineers and Liaisons.	1 Ldw. Pion. Co. (18 C. Dist.).		2 Ldw. Pion. Co. (10 C. Dist.). 1 Ldw. Pion. Co. (18 C. Dist.). 309 T. M. Co.		(409) Pion. Btn.: 2 Ldw. Pion. Co. (10 C. Dist.). 1 Ldw. Pion. Co. (18 C. Dist.). 309 T. M. Co. 509 Tel. Detch.		409 Pion. Btn.: 2 Ldw. Co. 10 C. Dist. Pions. 1 Ldw. Co. 18 C. Dist. Pions. 309 T. M. Co. 183 Searchlight Section. 509 Signal Command: 509 Tel. Detch. 136 Wireless Detch.	
Medical and Veterinary.					566 Ambulance Co. 62 Field Hospital. 86 Field Hospital. 396 Field Hospital. Vet. Hospital.		566 Ambulance Co. 62 Field Hospital. 13 Ldw. Field Hospital. 509 Vet. Hospital.	
Transports					221 M. T. Col. 904 M. T. Col.			
Attached					151 Labor Btn. 171 Labor Btn.			

HISTORY.

(83d Landwehr: Eleventh District—Thuringia and Electoral Hesse. 116th Landwehr and 118th Landwehr: Eighteenth District—Grand Duchy of Hesse.)

1915.

ARGONNE.

1. This division was organized in the Argonne at the beginning of 1915 from infantry units in sector in that region and in Champagne. The 43d Landwehr Brigade detrained at Boulay (Lorraine) August 20, 1914, and fought in the Woevre the 24th. The 49th Landwehr Brigade was sent to Luxemburg August 20, followed the Eighteenth Reserve Corps, and took part with it in the battle of the Marne. In October the two brigades were in the Argonne.

2. From the time of its organization did not leave the Argonne. From the beginning of 1915 it held the sector at or near the Aisne (north of Ville sur Tourbe and north of Vienne le Chateau).

1916.

ARGONNE.

1. Sector north of Vienne le Chateau, from the region of Rouvroy to the ravine of Fontaine aux Charnes.

1917.

ARGONNE.

1. Sector north of Vienne le Chateau.

RECRUITING.

83d Landwehr: Electorate Hesse and Thuringia. 116th and 118th Landwehr: Grand Duchy of Hesse and Rhenish country. The document of July 11, 1917, calls the two regiments in question "Rhenish."

At the end of 1917 and during the first months of 1918 the division exchanged a large number of men with the divisions stationed near it, which modified its regional composition to a certain degree.

VALUE—1917 ESTIMATE.

Sector division. (1918.)

The division had one storm company in July, 1917, and each regiment had a 'Stosstrupp."

1918.

The division continued to hold the sector in the Argonne Woods until the American attack on September 26. It was engaged on the opening days and withdrew on the 8th. The shattered elements were re-formed and reentered at once on the extreme right flank of the 4th French Army in the vicinity of the Aisne. The last identification was at Villers sur le Mont on November 10.

VALUE—1918 ESTIMATE.

The division was rated as a fourth-class division. On the defensive it showed some fighting ability.

9th Bavarian Reserve Division.
COMPOSITION.

	1916		1917		1918[1]	
	Brigade.	Regiment.	Brigade.	Regiment.	Brigade.	Regiment.
Infantry	17 Bav. Res.	11 Bav. Res. 14 Bav. Res. 3 Bav. Ers.	17 Bav. Res.	11 Bav. Res. 14 Bav. Res. 3 Bav. Ers.	17 Bav. Res.	11 Bav. Res. 14 Bav. Res. 3 Bav. Ers.
Cavalry			1 Sqn. 1 Bav. Res. Cav. Rgt.		1 Sqn. 1 Bav. Res. Cav. Rgt.	
Artillery	11 Bav. Res. F. A. Rgt. (9 Btries.).		9 Bav. Art. Command: 11 Bav. Res. F. A. Rgt.		9 Bav. Art. Command: 11 Bav. Res. F. A. Rgt.	
Engineers and Liaisons			(21) Pion. Btn.: 8 Bav. Pion. Co. 12 Bav. Res. Pion. Co. 209 Bav. T. M. Co. 409 Tel. Detch.		8 Bav. Pion. Co. 12 Bav. Res. Pion. Co. 209 Tel. Detch. 409 Tel. Detch. 105 Bav. Wireless Detch.	
Medical and Veterinary			13 Bav. Ambulance Co. 30 Bav. Field Hospital. 58 Bav. Field Hospital. 29 Bav. Vet. Hospital. 30 Bav. Vet. Hospital.		13 Bav. Ambulance Co. 30th Bav. Field Hospital. 58th Bav. Field Hospital. 29 Bav. Vet. Hospital.	
Transports			M. T. Col.		M. T. Col.	

[1] Composition at time of dissolution, July 24.

HISTORY.

(Third Bavarian District—Upper Palatinate, Upper and Middle Franconia.)

1916.

1. This division was formed at the beginning of October, 1916, at Caudry and icinity, and was one of the series of divisions organized at that time from drafts of nits from already existing divisions.

ISNE.

2. Went into line at the beginning of October east of Craonne, in the sector of Ville u Bois.

3. At the beginning of December it was sent to rest between Cambrai and Le Cateau.

1917.

IOMME.

1. The division was sent to the Somme and sent in its regiments singly to reinforce he sectors of Saillisel and Transloy in January, 1917.

AISNE.

2. At the beginning of February the division was sent back to the region of Laon– a Malmaison. It returned to the sector of Ville au Bois, where it opposed the French iffensive of April 16 and lost 2,300 captured and many casualties; the 2d and 3d Battalions of the 14th Reserve Infantry were almost all taken prisoners.

LORRAINE.

3. Relieved April 20 and sent to Lorraine, where it occupied the sector of Moncel– Arracourt May 1 to the beginning of August.

FLANDERS.

4. August 1 it entrained at St. Avold for Flanders. Detrained at Roulers and was blaced in reserve in the region Staden–Zarren from August 9 to 16. It fought August 17 north of Ypres at Bixschoote–Langemarck, suffered heavy losses, and remained n line only three days.

WOEVRE.

5. August 24 it took over the sector of the Apremont forest near St. Mihiel until he end of October.

FLANDERS.

6. Returned to Flanders and sent to rest in the vicinity of Bruges and Ostend in October and November. About November 22 it went into line in the sector of Lombartzyde and left it at the beginning of December.

CAMBRAI.

7. It returned almost immediately to the front south of Cambrai (Gonnelieu– Villers–Guislain) in December, then to the sector of Hargicourt in January, 1918.

RECRUITING.

Almost entirely from the Third Bavarian District—Upper Palatinate, Upper and Lower Franconia.

VALUE—1917 ESTIMATE.

The division opposed a considerable resistance to the French attack of April 16, 1916, and gave proof of good qualities and defense.

1918.

1. The division was not engaged on March 21, being in reserve near Estrees from the 21st to the 24th. It was then used to clear up the ground near Bellenglise until March 27. It marched to the front by Mont St. Quentin, Vermandovillers, and Harvonnieres.

125651°—20——12

VILLERS BRETONNEUX.

2. From April 4 to 21 it was engaged near Villers Bretonneux. In the counter-attack of the opening day a battalion of the 11th Bavarian Reserve Regiment ran away. For a week the division was in reserve south of Bray sur Somme. On April 27 it returned to line northeast of Villers Bretonneux, remaining until May 6.

3. It rested west of St. Quentin from May 11 to 17.

BATTLE OF THE MATZ.

4. On the 19th the division entered the line on the Oise east of Noyon. After the 26th it was in front of Noyon. The division took part in the attack of June 6 on Suzay-Thiescourt-Passel. Relieved about the middle of June, the division was disbanded about June 27. Its regiments were turned into the 12th Bavarian Division.

VALUE—1918 ESTIMATE.

The division was rated as a second-class division. It was inferior to the other Bavarian units. Its morale was bad prior to its dissolution.

9th Cavalry Division.

COMPOSITION.[1]

	1918	
	Brigade.	Regiment.
Cavalry	13 Cav. 14 Cav.	4 Cuirassier. 8 Hus. 11 Hus. 5 Uhlan.
Artillery	10 Horse Art. Abt.	
Engineers and Liaisons	5 M. G. Btry. 7 M. G. Btry. 9 Cav. Pion. Detch. 415 T. M. Co.	
Medical and Veterinary	574 Ambulance Co.	
Attached	Saxon Res. Reiter Rgt. 3 Heavy Res. Cav. Schutzen Rgt.	

[1] At the time of its dissolution, June, 1918.

HISTORY.

1918.

The division was employed in police duty in the Ukraine until about July 1, when it was dissolved.

VALUE 1918—ESTIMATE.

The division was rated as fourth class.

10th Division.
COMPOSITION.

	1914 Brigade.	1914 Regiment.	1915 Brigade.	1915 Regiment.	1916 Brigade.	1916 Regiment.	1917 Brigade.	1917 Regiment.	1918 Brigade.	1918 Regiment.
Infantry.......	19. 20.	6 Gren. 46. 47. 50.	19. 20.	6 Gren. 46. 47. 50.	20.	6 Gren. 47. 50.	20.	6 Gren. 47. 398.	20.	6 Gren. 47. 398.
Cavalry......	1 Horse Jag. Rgt.		....		1 Horse Jag. Rgt. (3 Sqns.).		3 Sqn. 1 Horse Jag. Rgt.		3 Sqn. 1 Horse Jag. Rgt.	
Artillery......	10 Brig.: 20 F. A. Rgt. 56 F. A. Rgt.		10 Brig.: 20 F. A. Rgt. 56 F. A. Rgt.		10 Brig.: 20 F. A. Rgt. 56 F. A. Rgt.		10 Art. Command: 56 F. A. Rgt.		10 Art. Command: 56 F. A. Rgt. 2 Abt. 11 Ft. A. Rgt. (5, 6, and 7 Btries.). 890 Light Am. Col. 1171 Light Am. Col. 1194 Light Am. Col.	
Engineers and Liaisons.	2 Co. 5 Pions. 3 Co. 5 Pions.		1 Pion. Btn. No. 5: 2 Co. 5 Pions. 3 Co. 5 Pions. Field Co. 16 Pions. 10 Pont. Engs. 10 Tel. Detch.		1 Pion. Btn. No. 5: 2 Co. 5 Pions. 3 Co. 5 Pions. 1 Res. Co. 27 Pions. 10 T. M. Co. 10 Pont. Engs. 10 Tel. Detch.		1 Pion. Btn. No. 5: 2 Co. 5 Pions. 3 Co. 5 Pions. 10 T. M. Co. 46 Heavy Field Searchlight Section. 10 Tel. Detch. 308 and 309 Searchlight Sections.		5 Pion. Btn.: 2 Co. 5 Pions. 3 Co. 5 Pions. 10 T. M. Co. 70 Searchlight Section. 10 Signal Command: 10 Tel. Detch. 146 Wireless Detch.	
Medical and Veterinary.	....		....		....		13 Ambulance Co. 46 Field Hospital. 50 Field Hospital. Vet. Hospital.		13 Ambulance Co. 218 Ambulance Co. 46 Field Hospital. 50 Field Hospital. 164 Field Hospital. 10 Vet. Hospital.	
Transports.....	....		....		....		M. T. Col.		543 M. T. Col.	

HISTORY.

(Fifth district—Posen.)

1914.

The 10th Division at mobilization belonged to the 5th Army Corps (Posen). Detrained August 10 and 11 near Sarrelouis and belonged to the 5th Army (Prussian Crown Prince). Entered Luxemburg the 18th, passed through Arlon the 20th, and left it on the evening of the 21st.

1. Took part in the combat of August 22, 1914 at Ethe, near Virton, next to the 9th Division. August 28 it was north of Thionville, expecting to leave for Russia. August 30 it continued its march in the Woevre, reached the Cotes de Meuse, and attacked the fort of Troyon September 7.

LES EPARGES.

2. After the battle of the Marne it held the sector of the Cotes de Meuse east of Verdun (Les Eparges–Callone) which it held almost all the time until October 1916. Took part in the series of combats which took place in this sector between April and July, 1915.

1915

1. At the time of our offensive of September and October, 1915, in Champagne, the 10th Division sent some of its units there, but they returned to Woevre about December 10, 1915, after four weeks' rest in Lorraine.

WOEVRE.

2. After this and until the beginning of October, 1916, the Division held its sector of the Cotes de Meuse.

1916.

VERDUN.

1. In October 1916 the division was relieved and took over the sector of Douaumon in November. It suffered heavy losses December 15, when the French defeated it severely, and had to be withdrawn from the front.

1917.

COTES DE MEUSE.

1. Reorganized at the beginning of January, 1917, after a three weeks' rest in the region of Mars la Tour, and took over again its former sector of the Cotes de Meuse at the beginning of March, remaining there until the end of April.

AISNE.

2. Entrained May 1 at Mars la Tour and sent via Conflans–Montmedy–Sedan–Charleville–Hirson to the region north of the Aisne, where it took over a sector northwest of Braye en Laonnois. It made an attack there May 18 but did not lose very heavily.

3. On June 20 it was relieved and sent to rest near Crecy sur Serre. Left this region about July 25 and spent six days at Gizy and vicinity.

CHEMINS DE DAMES.

4. On July 30 it went into line in the sector from Ailles to Hurtebise. Its regiment suffered a great deal from our artillery fire. During the attack of August 31 to September 1 the division suffered heavy losses.

5. About September 15 the division was relieved. On the 20th it took over the sector of St. Gobain.

6. At the beginning of the French attack at the end of October an emergency call was sent the 23d for some of the units of the division which were at rest in the region of Crepy en Laonnois and during the night of the 23d–24th they went into line to cover the retreat of the divisions in line.

FOREST OF ST. GOBAIN.

The greater part of the division remained in line in the forest of St. Gobain during this attack. The division was relieved about the middle of December; and on December 15 it was behind the St. Quentin front. At the end of January 18 the division relieved the 211th division in the sector of Ailles.

RECRUITING.

The 10th Division differs from the 9th in that its normal recruiting district (Province of Posen) is composed mostly of Poles. There are, therefore, a large number of Poles in its ranks, but it is evident that they are trying to mix them with Prussians, who are less liable to desert. The 47th Infantry on December 15, 1916, before Verdun contained men from the ninth and tenth districts. The 398th Infantry, whose companies were taken from various divisions, for example the 9th, the 10th and the 103d, obtained from the 103d Division Hessian and Thuringian units. There is the same variety in the 6th Grenadiers, which contained at the end of 1912 besides the original drafts from the district, men from the ninth and tenth districts, as well as from the eighteenth district, the latter belonging to the trained Landsturm (2d Bav.).

VALUE.

Until the attack of Verdun, the 10th division always had the reputation of being a good division composed of good units. At the time of the attack of the French December 10, 1915, however, the division which was in the sector north of Verdun did not seem to defend itself as stubbornly as might be expected. It should, however, be noted that 15 per cent of the forces were at that time weakened by sickness. During the German attack of May 18, 1917, the 47th Infantry clearly gave the impression that it was quite inferior to the two other regiments of the division. (The presence of Poles in the 47th should be noted.) August 31, 1917 at the Chemin des Dames, the units of the 10th division resisted well and counterattacked with vigor September 1,

1918.

1. The division was relieved in the Ailles on February 20 and went to rest and train for a month. It was at Montcornet, later near Saint Richaumont, Voulpaix, and La Vallee-aux-Bleds. It marched toward the St. Quintin front on March 20, by Origny-St. Benoite and Itancourt.

BATTLE OF PICARDY.

2. It was in the second line on March 21 and 22, advancing through Urvillers and Essigny. It was engaged March 23 to 25, crossing the Crozat Canal to the west of Jussy, Cugny, and Guiscard. It rested on the 25th and 26th. The division was reengaged on March 27 to the 30th in the vicinity of Libermont, Ognolles, Beuvraignes (27th) Conchy les Pots (28th–31st). The losses were heavy on the 27th and 28th. The division passed into the second line on the 31st and then to reserve at Solente (east of Roye) until the 30th of April.

3. The division rested and trained from May 5 to 20 at Jeantes la Ville and Nampcelle la Cour (east of Vervins). It received a draft of 800 men on May 18.

4. The division marched toward the Aisne front through Montigny le Franc, Marchais, Montaigu, and Mauregny, May 25 and 26, by night.

BATTLE OF THE AISNE.

5. It attacked on the Chemin des Dames on May 27, near Ailles, its former sector. It was in the front line of the advance through Paissy, Oeuilly, Barbonval, Blanzy, Bazoches (27th), Mareuil en Dole, (28th), south of Fere en Tardenois, (29th), south of Beuvardes (30th), south of Boureschcs. It retired from the front about June 8.

BATTLE OF THE MARNE.

6. The division was at rest near Sissonne after the middle of June to July 7. It marched to the front via Eppes, Brenelle, Foret de Fere, July 7 to 11. It crossed the Marne on the morning of the 15th, by pontoons, having passed through the sector of the 10th Ldw. Div. The division's objective was a line 8 klms. south of the river, which was to have been reached by 11 a. m. The advance was completely checked by the American Division (3d) south of the Marne. The division lost 400 prisoners and many casualties.

7. The division was taken out within a few days and rested at Arcy-St. Restitute. It was engaged near Vierzy on the 26th and was thrown back on the Vesle by August 1, when it was relieved.

THE WOEVRE.

8. The division was taken to Athies-sous-Laon, where it entrained on August 5 for Mars-la-Tour. The itinerary included Hirson, Charleville, Sedan. It camped at Sponville until the night of August 18–19. It relieved the 277th Division in the sector Richecourt, Lahayville, St. Baussant. The division had absorbed the 255th Division, dissolved on August 7, and its losses in men and material had been made up. The division sustained the American attack of September 12 and was thrown back north of Thiaucourt on Jaulny, Rembercourt. The division lost heavily in casualties and prisoners. Practically the entire 3d Battalion of the 398th Regiment was captured on the first day. It was taken out on September 20.

MOSELLE.

9. The division was reassembled at Loringen, near Metz. From the dissolved 77th Reserve Division the 257th Reserve Regiment was turned into the 6th Gren. Regiment (10th Division), the 419th into the 398th Regiment, and the 332d into the 47th Regiment. Other drafts from Germany were received to reconstitute the division. On the 5th of October the division entered the sector east of the Moselle (Nomeny), where it remained until October 28.

MEUSE-ARGONNE.

10. The division returned to Metz and moved by rail for Pelte, via Metz-Longuyon-Montmedy. It went into position on November 3 northwest of Stenay. The last identification was on the Meuse on November 11.

VALUE.

The division was rated as a first-class division. It behaved creditably in the Somme and Aisne offensives. It was completely defeated on the Marne, from which it never recovered. The inferior qualities of the drafts received in August and September lowered the fighting value of the division.

10th Reserve Division.
COMPOSITION.

	1914		1915		1916		1917		1918	
	Brigade.	Regiment.	Brigade.	Regiment.	Brigade.	Regiment.	Brigade.	Regiment.	Brigade.	Regiment.
Infantry.	18 Res. 77.	37 Res. 46 Res. 37 Fus. 155.	19 Res. 77. (37 Res. Rgt. passed to 119 D. April, 1915.)	37 Res. 46 Res. 98 Res. 37 Fus. 155.	19 Res. 77.	37 Res. 98 Res. 37 Fus. 155.	77.	37 Res. 37 Fus. 155.	77.	37 Fus. 155. 37 Res.
Cavalry.	6 Res. Uhlan Rgt. (3 Sqns.)		6 Res. Uhlan Rgt.		6 Res. Uhlan Rgt.		(?) 6 Res. Uhlan Rgt.		1 Sqn. 3 Res. Drag. Rgt.	
Artillery.	10 Res. F. A. Rgt. (6 Btries.).		10 Res. F. A. Rgt.		10 Res. F. A. Rgt.		(?) Art. Command: Res. F. A. (139gt. Btries.).		61 Art. Command: 10 Res. F. A. Rgt. 10 Res. F. A. Rgt. 2 Abt. 66 F. A. Rgt. 1 Abt. 3 Res. Ft. A. Rgt. 736 Light Am. Col. 1107 Light Am. Col. 1123 Light Am. Col.	
Engineers and Liaisons.			Res. Co. 5 Pions. 10 Res. Pont. Engs. 10 Res. Tel. Detch.		1 Res. Co. 5 Pions. 210 T. M. Co. 10 Res. Pont. Engs. 10 Res. Tel. Detch.		(310) Pion. Btn.: 1 Res. Co. 5 Pions. 2 Res. Co. 5 Pions. 210 T. M. Co. Tel Detch.		310 Pion. Btn.: 1 Res. Co. 5 Pions. 2 Co. 5 Res. Pions. 210 T. M. Co. 192 Searchlight Section. 410 Signal Command: 410 Tel. Detch. 1 Wireless Detch.	
Medical and Veterinary.							505 Ambulance Co. 26 Res. Hospital Field. 28 Res. Field Hospital. 410 Vet. Hospital.		505 Ambulance Co. 26 Res. Field Hospital 28 Res. Field Hospital 410 Vet. Hospital.	
Transports.							M. T. Col.		709 M. T. Col.	
Attached.									10 M. G. S. S. Detch. 254 Mountain M. G. Detch. 254 Reconnaissance Flight. (Elements attached Sept. 22, 1918.)	

HISTORY.

(Fifth District—Posen.)

1914.

FRANCE.

1. At mobilization the division, with the 9th Reserve Division, formed the 5th Reserve Corps. It was part of the 5th Army (Crown Prince of Prussia) and took part in the offensive which went around Verdun from the north. It fought at Ville en Montois August 22, in the Region of Consenvoiye-Flabas September 1, and in the vicinity of Sivry sur Meuse September 2. It remained on the right bank of the Meuse until the end of September.

MEUSE.

2. About October 1 some of the units of the 10th Reserve Division were sent to :he left bank (Cuisy-Forges-Gercourt).

3. At the beginning of November the division was regrouped iu the region of Damvillers (right bank). Took part in the attacks toward Azannes November 10 und established itself in the sector of Consenvoye-Azannes (northeast of Orne-Bois les Caures in November and December).

1915.

1. The division held the region east of Consenvoye-Flabas-Bois des Caures-Azannes mtil the Verdun offensive February, 1916.

VOEVRE.

2. At the end of September, 1915, at the beginning of the French attack in Cham->agne, some units of the division (battalions of the 37th Reserves and 98th Reserves ºere sent as reinforcements to vicinity of Ville sur Tourbe and Massiges.)

1916.

'ERDUN.

1. About February 15, 1916, the division was relieved from the sector on the right ank of the Meuse and put in reserve. During the first days of the offensive it ngaged only a few attack battalions. Beginning March 12 it was in line before 'aux and Fort Vaux and had very heavy losses. April 3 the 8th of the 37th Fusiliers ιceived at least 64 replacements (recuperated men who entered the service the receding November and recovered wounded and sick).

2. The division was relieved at the end of April and sent to rest in the region of [ulhouse from the beginning of May to June 12.

HAMPAGNE.

3. Sent to Champagne and held the sector north of Tahure, south of Somme Py, ntil September 20.

OMME.

4. After a few days' rest it was sent to the Somme south of the St. Pierre Wood-Vaast om October 5 to 15. It suffered very heavy losses there.

5. At rest for 13 days, then entrained, and went to Dun via Hirson-Mézières-ιarleville-Sedan October 23.

ORT HOMME.

6. It held the sector of Mort Homme (left bank of the Meuse) from October 28 to ːbruary 8, 1917.

1917.

1. The division was at rest in the middle of February, 1917, in the region of Sedan, then of Dizy le Gros.

AISNE.

2. At the beginning of March it went into line in the region of Berry au Bac (from Hill 108 to Spigneul). It was relieved at the beginning of the French attack April 16. The French artillery preparation caused it heavy losses.

MORT HOMME—HILL 304.

3. From April 24 to May 15 it was in line in its old sector—Cumierès-Mort Homme—and from the middle of May till July 19 in the adjoining sector—Hill 304–Avocourt Wood. It attacked June 28 and 29 and opposed our counterattacks of July 12 to 17, suffering heavy losses.

4. Withdrawn from the front about July 19.

5. At rest near Sedan and reorganized (replacements from the Fifth District and Eighteenth District (Frankfort on Main).

CHAMPAGNE.

6. It then took over the sector Vitry-Cernay les Reims about August 8. Remained there until about October 27.

7. November 9 it went into line north of Craonne in the region of Chermizy-Bouconville (?). Some of the units of the division were not in this sector. After a rest in the camp of Sissonne and at Poilcourt, end of October to middle of December, they went into line in the sector Miette–Aisne about December 17. About that date the division was regrouped north of Berry au Bac, where it was still in February, 1918.

RECRUITING.

Province of Posen. The differences were made up by the Sixth District mostly.

VALUE—1917 ESTIMATE.

The division is considered as a "big attack" division. In April, 1917, in the region of Berry au Bac it executed a well-conducted attack on Satigneul. The offensive value of the division showed itself again during the attacks of June 28–29 of 1917 at Hill 304.

There is no lack of volunteers for dangerous missions, and the motto of the division is said to be: "Get after the enemy and beat 'em wherever you find 'em." The commanding general of the division and the colonel commanding the 155th consider that their men are able to endure hard battles (November, 1917).

1918.

BATTLE OF PICARDY.

1. The division was relieved about March 15 and sent to reenforce the Somme front. It was engaged near Beaulieu les Fontaines on March 25–26, where it remained until April 7. Heavy casualties were reported in this offensive.

BATTLE OF THE AISNE.

2. The division rested until May 27, when it took part in the offensive at Mont Notre Dame. About June 15 it was withdrawn to Athies (Laon), where it rested fallen until July 15.

SECOND BATTLE OF THE MARNE.

3. On July 15 the division was again engaged south of the Marne at Montvoisin and Oeuilly on the opening day. It retired from the Vesle front, to which it had fallen back, about August 5.

ᵀESLE.

4. After resting three weeks at Asfeld the division returned to the Vesle front on ᴸugust 28 near Chalon sur Vesle and was engaged until September 18.

5. On the 18th the division was directed by stages to Laon and entered the line outh of Laon at Ferme–Colombe on the 22d. The division appears to have been onstantly in action until November 1, and possibly until the armistice. It was uccessively identified at Chevrigny, Montceau le Waast (Oct. 14), southeast of ꟿoulle (Oct. 27), south of Banogne (Nov. 1). The last identification was at Maubert–ꟿontaine on November 10.

VALUE—1918 ESTIMATE.

The division was rated as a first-class division. It fought hard in most of the ꟾffensives of the year, and when on the defensive put up a hard, steady fight for ꟾwo months without relief.

10th Ersatz Division.
COMPOSITION.

	1914 Brigade.	1914 Regiment.	1915 Brigade.	1915 Regiment.	1916 Brigade.	1916 Regiment.	1917 Brigade.	1917 Regiment.	1918 Brigade.	1918 Regiment.
Infantry	37 Ers. 25 Ers. 43 Ers.	37, 38, 39, and 40 Brig. Ers. Btns. 25, 26, 27, 28, and 79 Brig. Ers. Btns. 43, 44, 76, and 83 Brig. Ers. Btns.	37 Ers. 25 Ers. 43 Ers.	37, 38, 39, and 40 Brig. Ers. Btns. 25, 26, 27, 28, and 79 Brig. Ers. Btns. 43, 44, 76, and 83 Brig. Ers. Btns.	25 Mixed Ers. 43 Mixed Ers.	369. 368. 370. 371.	43 Ers.	369. 370. 371.	43 Ers.	369. 370. 371.
Cavalry	Ers. Cav. Detch. of 25 Ers. Brig. Ers. Cav. Detch. of 43 Ers. Brig.		Ers. Cav. Detch. of 25 Ers. Brig. Ers. Cav. Detch. of 43 Ers. Brig.		10 Cav. Sqn. 2 Sqn. Horse Jag. Rgt.		1 Sqn. 1 Horse Jag. Rgt. Ers. Sqn. 2 Horse Jag. Rgt.		1 Sqn. 1 Horse Jag. Rgt.	
Artillery	1 Ers. Abt. (46 and 62 F. A. Rgts.), 1 Ers. Abt. (22 and 43 F. A. Rgts.), 1 Ers. Abt. (47 and 55 F. A. Rgts.),		1 Ers. Abt. (46 and 62 F. A. Rgts.), 1 Ers. Abt. (22 and 43 F. A. Rgts.), 1 Ers. Abt. (47 and 55 F. A. Rgts.),		94 F. A. Rgt. 95 F. A. Rgt.		95 F. A. Rgt.		95 F. A. Rgt. 156 Ft. A. Btn. 1058 Light Am. Col. 1060 Light Am. Col. 1065 Light Am. Col.	
Engineers and Liaisons.	1 Ers. Co. 10 Pions. 3 Ers. Co. 11 Pions.		1 Ers. Co. 10 Pions. 3 Ers. Co. 11 Pions. 2 Ldw. Pion. Co. (3 C. Dist.).	1 Ers. Co. 10 Pions. 3 Ers. Co. 11 Pions. 2 Ldw. Pion. Co. (3 C. Dist.).	2 Res. Co. 27 Pions. 2 Ldw. Pion. Co. (3 C. Dist.). 307 Pion. Co. 309 Pion. Co. 163 T. M. Co.		Pion. Btn.: 1 Ers. Co. 10 Pions. 307 Pion. Co. 308 Pion. Co. 163 T. M. Co. 261 Searchlight Section. 304 Tel. Detch.		510 Pion. Btn.: 246 Pion. Co. 308 Pion. Co. 57 Searchlight Section. 560 Signal Command: 560 Tel. Detch. 109 Wireless Detch.	
Medical and Veterinary.							66 Ambulance Co. 139 Field Hospital. 140 Field Hospital. Vet. Hospital.		66 Ambulance Co. 139 Field Hospital. 140 Field Hospital. 212 Vet. Hospital.	
Transports							M. T. Col.		765 M. T. Col.	
Attached					27 Balloon Sqn.					

HISTORY.

(369th and 370th: Seventh District—Westphalia. 371st: Eleventh District—
Thuringia.)

1914.

This division was organized as early as August, 1914. It comprised the 25th, 37th, and 43d Mixed Ersatz Brigades, themselves constituted by the Brigade Ersatz Battalions of the Tenth, Seventh, and Eleventh Districts (Hanover, Oldenburg, Brunswick, Westphalia, Electoral Hesse, and Thuringia).

LORRAINE.

1. Detrained August 17 and 18 near Sarrelouis and brought quickly to the rear of the 3d Bavarian Corps August 20, and crossed the frontier the 25th. September 7 it had heavy losses at the attack against Nancy (Champenoux). The 40th Brigade Ersatz Battalion lost half its forces (notebook). It continued, however, to take part in the operations in Lorraine in the region of Moncel until September 12, 1914, after which it went to rest near Chateau Salins.

HAYE.

2. September 28 it entrained for Novéant and went into line on the Haye front, where it held various sectors (Loupmont, Richecourt, Apremont).

1915.

HAYE.

1. During 1915 the division continued to hold the Lorraine front (Haye): Loupmont, Seicheprey, Lahayville, Mort Mare Wood.

2. At the end of July the division was reorganized. Its brigade Ersatz battalions were grouped into regiments and formed the 368th, 369th, 370th, and 371st Infantry. The companies were filled up again. The 9th company of the 370th Infantry received not less than 76 replacements in August (1915 class called up in May).

1916.

WOEVRE.

1. The division remained in the Flirey–Limey sector until the end of August, 1916. At that date it was relieved by the Guard Ersatz Division and sent to rest in the region of Thiaucourt.

SOMME.

2. By September 5, leaving the 368th Regiment, which was transferred to the 213th Division, it entrained at Montmédy and went to the south of the Somme via Laon, Tergnier, and St. Quentin. It fought south of Berny en Santerre from September 14 to 25 and suffered considerable losses.

CHAMPAGNE.

3. After a short rest in the region of St. Quentin the division was sent to Champagne. Until November 12 it held, without any particular incidents, the Ste. Marie à Py and Somme Py sector.

4. From the middle of November to the middle of December it was sent to rest in the region of Attigny.

MEUSE.

5. December 28 it took over the Ornes–Bezonvaux sector.

1917.

1. Held the Verdun front (Bezonvaux) until April 19, 1917.

CHAMPAGNE.

2. Between April 20 and 25 it returned to Champagne and took part in the attack south of Moronvilliers from the beginning of May to the beginning of June. From June 9 to beginning of August it was in line in the region of Regniéville–Remenauville (Haye).

FLANDERS.

4. After a rest behind the Lorraine front, the division entrained at Chambley August 21 for Belgium. About September 24 it was engaged before Ypres near Poelcappelle.

GALICIA.

5. Withdrawn from the Belgium front about October 7 and entrained the 10th for Galicia, where it was identified south of Skala, November 17.

RECRUITING.

Westphalia and Rhine Provinces: 369th and 370th Infantry. Thuringia: 371st Infantry.

VALUE—1917 ESTIMATE.

The division suffered heavy losses in Champagne in May, 1917, and at Ypres in September and October, 1917. The division has only moderate value.

1918.

BATTLE OF THE LYS.

1. The division remained in line until the attack on the Lys in April. It was engaged north of the La Bassee Canal (Givenchy, Festubert, southeast of Lacre), from April 9 to 24. The losses were heavy, including 700 prisoners. The 360th Regiment suffered the most in the fighting.

2. It was relieved on the 12th and rested in rear of the line until the 29th, when it returned to its former sector at Locre until May 3.

3. The division rested near Roubaix (Bondues, Wambrechies) until the beginning of July. According to reports, sickness was very general throughout the division at the time.

LA BASSEE CANAL.

4. On July 14 the division entered the line south of the La Bassee Canal, coming via Lille and Seclin. It remained in this sector until October 2.

5. It moved southward to reenforce the Cambrai–St. Quentin battle front on October 7, coming into line east of Tilloy. It fell back toward Valenciennes through Escaudoevres, Iwny (Oct. 11), Verchain (Oct. 21), Maing (Oct. 24–25), Famars (Oct. 27), north of Le Quesnoy (Oct. 27). It retired to the second line about November 1, but was reengaged southeast of Antoingt on November 9.

VALUE.

The 10th Ersatz Division was rated as a third-class division. Its service in 1918 was as a sector-holding division. It appears to have been a division of average value.

10th Landwehr Division.

COMPOSITION.

	1915 Brigade	1915 Regiment	1916 Brigade	1916 Regiment	1917 Brigade	1917 Regiment	1918 Brigade	1918 Regiment
Infantry	9 Ldw.	1 E. Konigsberg (377). 3 E. Konigsberg (378). 24 Ldw. 48 Ldw.	(?) 180.	372. 373. 377. 378.	180.	372. 377. 378.	180.	372. 377. 378.
Cavalry	91 Ldw. Cav. Rgt.		91 Ldw. Cav. Rgt.		5 Sqn. 7 Dragoon Rgt.		5 Sqn. 7 Drag. Rgt.	
Artillery	97 F. A. Rgt.		97 F. A. Rgt.		130 Art. command: 97 F. A. Rgt.		130 Art. command: 97 F. A. Rgt.	
Engineers and Liaisons			3 Co. 2 Pions. 310 T. M. Co.		410 Pion. Btn.: 3 Co. 2 Pions. 320 Searchlight Section. Tel. Detch.		3 Field Co. 1 Pion. Btn. No. 2. 1 Landst. Co. 5 C. Dist. Pions. 310 T. M. Co. 510 Tel. Detch.	
Medical and Veterinary					213 Ambulance Co. 147 Field Hospital. 148 Field Hospital. 210 Vet. Hospital.		213 Ambulance Co. 147 Field Hospital. 148 Field Hospital. — Vet. Hospital.	
Transports					— M. T. Col.		— M. T. Col.	
Attached			437 Inf. Rgt.		1 Landst. Pion. Btn. (4 C. Dist.).			

HISTORY.

(First District—Eastern Prussia.)

1915.

The present 10th Landwehr Division (the old 10th Landwehr Division took the name of the 1st Landwehr Division) was built around the 9th Landwehr Brigade (Brandenburg), which was brought to Koenigsburg as early as August 14, 1914, to constitute its war garrison. It found at Koenigsburg some of the mobile depot battalions of the regiments of the 1st Army Corps, from which came the three Koenigsburg Ersatz infantry regiments, which became, respectively, the 376th, 377th, and 378th Infantry. The present 372d Infantry is the former Ersatz infantry regiment of the 10th Landwehr Division.

POLAND.

1. These troops, at first fighting in eastern Prussia, took part in the campaign in Poland with the 1st Landwehr Corps, beginning with the first part of 1915.

2. About the end of July, 1915, the division took part in the offensive against the Russians, forced the passage of the Narew, and advanced east of Vilna to the region of Vileiki in September.

LAKE NAROTCH.

3. After the front was stabilized it established itself between Spiagla and Lake Svir, south of Lake Narotch.

1916.

1. The division remained in line near Lake Svir until July, 1916.

VOLHYNIA.

2. About July 27 the units of the division were relieved from the front of Lake Narotch and sent to Volhynia to the Von Linsingen Army. The 9th Landwehr Brigade became independent and did not follow the division, which was reduced to three regiments. These were engaged on the banks of the Stokhod at the end of July at Lokatchi and Kachovka and remained in line in the region of Kisselin and Sviniouki until the beginning of 1918

1917.

VOLHYNIA.

1. January to December, 1917, in the Kisselin-Sviniouki sector.

2. In November, 1917, the three regiments of the division furnished 60 men per company for the Western Front, picked from the strongest, and received in exchange older men. In October, 16 men per company had already been transferred to the 14th Division following the latter's losses on the Ainse.

RECRUITING.

The division is sufficiently homogeneous, the regiments as a rule coming from eastern Prussia. However, the necessity of filling up the ranks before being sent to France brought it a number of men from other Provinces.

VALUE—1917 ESTIMATE.

In spite of its drafts, which are good, and the large number of officers, many of whom are in the active army, the division remained on the Eastern Front until March, 1918. Up to the present time it has received no training with a view to warfare on the Western Front, and must be considered for the time being as of mediocre value (April, 1918). The men of more than 35 years of age were left in Russia as abruestungs kommando (cleaning up and salvage).

1918.

SECOND BATTLE OF THE MARNE.

1. On June 3 the division entrained in the Woevre and traveled via Conflans–Sedan–Mezieres–Laon to Malmaison, where it detrained on June 4. It marched to the front via Fismes, Fere en Tardenois, and Fresnes. It came into line on the Marne near Mont St. Pere about June 10. Here it was in line until July 15, when it dropped back to permit an attacking division to pass through. In the retreat the division again came into line a few days later and was heavily engaged on the defense until about August 1.

2. Heavy losses, including 300 prisoners on July 23, led to the dissolution of the division. Its effectives were turned into other fresh divisions. The 372d, 377th, and 378th went to the 37th Division, 36th Division, and 201st Division in the order named.

VALUE—1918 ESTIMATE.

The division was rated as a fourth-class division.

125651°—20——13

10th Bavarian Division.
COMPOSITION.

	1915 Brigade.	1915 Regiment.	1916 Brigade.	1916 Regiment.	1917 Brigade.	1917 Regiment.	1918 [1] Brigade.	1918 [1] Regiment.
Infantry	20 Bav.	16 Bav. 6 Bav. Res. 8 Bav. Res.	20 Bav.	16 Bav. 6 Bav. Res. 8 Bav. Res.	20 Bav.	16 Bav. 6 Bav. Res. 8 Bav. Res.	20 Bav.	16 Bav. 6 Bav. Res. 8 Bav. Res.
Cavalry		3 Sqn. 5 Bav. Light Cav. Rgt.	5 Bav. Light Cav. Rgt. (3 Sqns.).		3 Sqn. 5 Bav. Light Cav. Rgt.		3 Sqn. 5 Bav. Light Cav. Rgt.	
Artillery	10 Bav. Brig.: 19 Bav. F. A. Rgt. (6 Btries.). 20 Bav. F. A. Rgt. (6 Btries., of which 3 are How.).		10 Bav. Brig.: 19 Bav. F. A. Rgt. 20 Bav. F. A. Rgt.		10 Bav. Art. Command: 19 Bav. F. A. Rgt. 20 Bav. F. A. Rgt.		10 Bav. Art. Command: 20 Bav. F. A. Rgt.	
Engineers and Liaisons.	20 Bav. Pion. Co.		20 Bav. Pion. Co. 10 Bav. T. M. Co. 10 Bav. Pont. Engs. 10 Bav. Tel. Detch.		10 Bav. Pion. Btn.: 20 Bav. Pion. Co. 23 Bav. Pion. Co. 19 Searchlight Section. Tel. Detch.		10 Bav. Pion. Btn.: 20 Bav. Pion. Co. 23 Bav. Pion. Co. 19 Searchlight Section. 10 Bav. T. M. Co. 10 Bav. Tel. Detch. 97 Wireless Detch.	
Medical and Veterinary.					10 Bav. Ambulance Co. 31 Bav. Field Hospital. 34 Bav. Field Hospital. Vet. Hospital.		10 Bav. Ambulance Co. 31 Bav. Field Hospital. 34 Bav. Field Hospital. 10 Bav. Vet. Hospital.	
Transports					M. T. Col.		690 Bav. M. T. Col.	
Odd Units			10 Bav. Cyclist Co.		10 Bav. Cyclist Co.		10 Bav. Cyclist Co.	
Attached							19 Bav. F. A. Rgt.	

[1] Composition at time of dissolution, August, 1918.

HISTORY.

(16th Bavarian: First Bavarian District—Lower Bavaria. 6th Reserve Bavarian and 8th Reserve Bavarian: Second Bavarian District—Bavarian Palatinate.)

1915.

This division was organized in Belgium in March, 1915. Its three infantry regiments were drawn from already existing Bavarian divisions—the 16th Bavarian from the 1st Bavarian Division, the 6th Reserve Bavarian from the 5th Bavarian Reserve Division, and the 8th Bavarian Reserves from the 4th Bavarian Division.

1. In April ,1915, the division was in the region of Tournai.

SOMME.

2. In May it took over the sector of Lihons-Estrees road to Foucaucourt, which it occupied until the Franco-British offensive of 1916.

3. In October some units of the division were sent as reinforcements to Neuville-St. Vaast and to Champagne.

1916.

SOMME.

1. Remained in the Foucaucourt-Lihons sector until the middle of June, 1916.

2. At the end of June it was sent south of Bapaume and took part in the battle of the Somme near Contalmaison, Bazentin le Petit, and Longueval from July 1 to the end of July. The 6th Reserve Infantry suffered heavily. Its 2d Battalion lost 11 officers and 724 men (casualty lists).

GALICIA.

3. About the middle of August the division was sent to the Eastern Front (Stanislau) and the trip lasted from August 13 to 18.

BUKOVINA.

4. September and October: Bukovina (Dorna-Vatra, Kirlibaba, west of Mont Capoul). It fought against the right wing of the Roumanian Army.

TRANSYLVANIA.

5. From November, 1916, to the end of January, 1917, it held the sector of Tolgyes in Transylvania.

1917.

GALICIA.

1. At the beginning of February, 1917, the division left the Roumanian front and went to Galicia (sector of Zalosce) from February to May, being attached to the 2d Austro-Hungarian Army.

FRANCE.

2. In May the division returned to France, via Zloczow (May 19), Lemberg, Cracow, Breslau, Frankfort on Main, Treves.

ALSACE.

Detrained about May 25 in the region of Mulhouse; then was sent to rest and training in Upper Alsace at the beginning of June and sent to Belgium (June 12 to 14).

FLANDERS.

3. Fought south of the Ypres-Comines canal where it opposed the attack of July 31. It then went to the region of Catelet (sector of Gonnelieu) from August 12 to the end of September. It was near Becelaere in October.

RUSSIA.

4. At the end of October it was again sent to the Eastern Front. After a few weeks' rest at Brest Litovsk it returned to France without having fought. Entrained November 22 at Brest Litovsk and detrained in Lorraine the 27th. Itinerary: Warsaw-Posen Erfurt.

LORRAINE.

5. On November 29 to 30 it went into line in the forest of Bezange and was relieved in the middle of January, 1918.

The 16th Infantry: Lower Bavaria. The two other regiments: Bavarian Palantinate.

VALUE—1917 ESTIMATE.

The greater part of the division is composed of young men. It does not seem to have suffered any losses for a long time. However, its morale seems to have been shaken at times. When it was sent from St. Quentin to Ypres at the end of September, 1917, it is believed that the officers of the 16th Infantry had trouble in preventing a mutiny. (British Information Bulletin, Oct. 12, 1917.)

1918.

1. The division was relieved in the Vosges on May 13 and rested near Dieuze until May 30. It entrained and moved by Metz and Sedan, Charleville, Liart, and detrained near Laon on the 30th–31st. It moved to the front by Bruyeres, Braye en Laennois, Mont Notre-Dame, Neuilly-St. Front.

BATTLE OF THE AISNE AND MARNE.

2. It was reengaged southeast of Troesnes–Passy en Valois (on the Ourcq) from June 5 to July 18. It was thrown back on Rozet St. Albin (July 20) and then west of Armentieres (21st). About that date the division was relieved.

The division was dissolved in August and its units sent to the 6th Bavarian Reserve Division, 11th Bavarian Division, and 14th Bavarian Division.

VALUE—1918 ESTIMATE.

The division was rated as a second-class division. In 1918 it saw but six weeks of active fighting before it was dissolved.

11th Division.
COMPOSITION.

	1914 Brigade	1914 Regiment	1915 Brigade	1915 Regiment	1916 Brigade	1916 Regiment	1917 Brigade	1917 Regiment	1918 Brigade	1918 Regiment
Infantry	21. 22.	10 Gren. 38 Fus. 11 Gren. 51.	21. 22.	10 Gren. 38 Fus. 11 Gren. 51.	21. 22.	10 Gren. 38 Fus. 11 Gren. 51.	21.	10 Gren. 38 Fus. 51.	21.	10 Gren. 38 Fus. 51.
Cavalry	2 Uhlan Rgt.			1 and 4 Sqns, 2 Uhlan Rgt.		....		2 Sqn. 2 Uhlan Rgt.		2 Sqn. 2 Uhlan Rgt.
Artillery	11 Brig.: 6 F. A. Rgt. 42 F. A. Rgt.		11 Brig.: 6 F. A. Rgt. 42 F. A. Rgt.		11 Brig: 6 F. A. Rgt. (64.9 cm. gun Bries.). 42 F. A. Rgt.		11 Art. Command: 42 F. A. Rgt.		11 Art. Command: 42 F. A. Rgt. 131 (M) Ft. A. Btn. (Staff, and 1, 2, and 3 Btries.). 904 Light Am. Col. 1367 Light Am. Col. 1368 Light Am. Col.	
Engineers and Liaisons.			1 Pion. Btn. No. 6: Field Co. 6 Pions. 11 Pont. Engs. 11 Tel. Detch.		1 Pion. Btn. No. 6: 1 Co. 6 Pions. 5 Co. 6 Pions. 11 T. M. Co. 11 Pont. Engs. 11 Tel. Detch.		122 Pion. Btn.: 1 Co. 6 Pions. 5 Co. 6 Pions. 11 T. M. Co. 269 Searchlight Section. 11 Tel. Detch.		122 Pion. Btn. 1 Co. 6 Pions. 5 Co. 6 Pions. 11 T. M. Co. 187 Searchlight Section. 11 Signal Command: 11 Tel. Detch. 3 wireless Detch.	
Medical and Veterinary.							16 Ambulance Co. 55 Field Hospital. 59 Field Hospital. 61 Field Hospital. Vet. Hospital.		16 Ambulance Co. 59 Field Hospital. 61 Field Hospital. 11 Vet. Hospital.	
Transports							544 M. T. Col. 644 M. T. Col.		544 M. T. Col.	
Attached					Anti-aircraft Section. 38 Labor Btn.		Anti-aircraft Section.			

HISTORY.

(Sixth District—Silesia.)

1914.

FRANCE.

1. The 11th Division belonged to the 6th Army Corps and detrained at Merzig August 10 and 11, 1914, passed through Luxemburg the 17th, and entered Belgian Luxemburg the 18th.

2. It belonged to the 5th Army (Prussian Crown Prince) and took part in the battle of August 22 at Tintigny, St. Vincent, and Belle Fontaine. It crossed the Meuse the 29th below Stenay, passed through Varennes and Ste. Menehould. September 7, at the high point of the German advance, it was near Revigny.

RHEIMS.

3. After the battle of the Marne it established itself at the western edge of the Argonne (from Binarville to Cernay en Bormois).

ARGONNE.

4. October 4 it fought at Binarville. October 21 the 22d Brigade was at Beine, east of Rheims. The 21st Brigade remained in the Argonne.

1915.

1. At the end of January, 1915, the 21st Brigade returned to the Rheims sector.

CHAMPAGNE.

In February the 22d Brigade was attached temporarily in support of the 8th Reserve Corps on the Champagne front (east).

2. About the middle of June the division went to Artois to reinforce the 6th Army in preparation for the French offensive.

SOUCHEZ.

3. At the end of June it held the sector north of Souchez, east of Neuville St. Vaast. It executed many unsuccessful attacks on Souchez and the Chateau of Carleul. It suffered considerable losses during July. September 25 and 26 it had more losses before La Folie. Relieved at the end of September and sent to rest in the region of Cambrai. The casualty lists for the 10th Grenadiers show 432 killed, 1,023 wounded, 64 missing; total, 1,519 men. The losses were hastily made good from October 5 to 14 by replacements with less than three months' training (oldest class Landsturm 2d Band and 1915 class men who entered service in July). The 9th Company of the 10th Grenadiers received in this way at least 119 men and the 12th Company of the 38th Fusiliers about the same.

4. During the first two weeks of October the division went into line in the sector astride the Somme.

1916.

FRISE.

1. At the end of January, 1916, the division took part in the attack which ended in the taking of the village of Frise and suffered very heavy losses.

2. On May 25 it was relieved, and a short time afterwards took over the sector south of the Amiens–St. Quentin road. (At the end of June the first 1917-class soldiers arrived with older classes put back, taken from the mines and factories of Silesia.)

SOMME.

3. In this sector it opposed the French attack of July 1 and days following. It suffered heavily and lost a large number of prisoners to the French. (The 11th Grenadiers, whose battalions had fought in three different places, separated from the rest of the division, had to have at least 181 replacements to complete the 11th Company. They arrived from July 6 to 20.)

4. It was withdrawn from this sector about the end of July and sent to the region of St. Quentin to be reorganized.

5. On August 1 the division took over the trenches in the sector Andechy-Beuvraignes.

SOMME.

6. September 4 it again went in to the battle of the Somme between Deniecourt and Vermandovillers. During these two actions in the Somme it suffered 83 per cent losses.

7. Relieved October 10 and took over the sector of Prunay the 24th, which it held until December 12, then went to rest near St. Quentin. The 11th Grenadiers left the division in October and were transferred to the 101st Division in Macedonia.

1917.

1. On January 4, 1917, the division went into line in the sector of Lassigny, then on February 10 in the sector of Ablaincourt, south of the Somme.

2. About the middle of the month of March the division retreated, with the other German forces engaged in the Somme, to the Hindenburg line.

3. March 29 it was sent to the Arras front.

ARTOIS.

April 19 it opposed south of the Scarpe the first shock of the British attack. In spite of a desperate defense it was routed and lost 2,200 prisoners to the British. The 51st Infantry was reduced to 600 men (prisoners' statements) and its 12th Company to 6 men.

4. On April 11 the division was relieved and reorganized in the region of Bruges. It received replacements especially from the 623d Infantry, which was dissolved, organized, and trained at the camp at Neuhammer.

FLANDERS.

5. At the beginning of June it was in support of the Wytschaete-Messines front when the British attacked. It then held this sector until June 26 and suffered heavy losses again (June 8 and 9).

WOEVRE.

6. After a few days' rest it was sent to Metz and then put in line in the sector of Flirey (in Haye), end of July to September 15.

7. Relieved about the middle of September, and in October took over a sector on the Champagne front.

FLANDERS.

8. At the end of October it was sent to Flanders and went into line near Passchendeale. Withdrawn at the end of December and went to the rear of the front in the region of Maubeuge.

RECRUITING.

The division was recruited in the regions of Breslau, Glatz, and Schweidnitz from a German population. The Poles, therefore, coming from the Province of Silesia, are in the minority. The Sixth District is thickly populated and was able by itself to maintain the division even during the period of heavy losses.

VALUE—1917 ESTIMATE.

In spite of the heavy losses suffered at the Somme, Arras, and Wytschaete the division always fought well. Its value is diminished by the presence of a certain number of Poles who were generally ready to desert when they had a chance. Lieut. Col. Schwerck, commanding the 51st Infantry, received the order "Pour le Merite" after the battle of Arras. This reward, which has been given to only six other regimental commanders, seems to prove that the fighting value of the 11th Division at Arras in April, 1917, was greatly appreciated by the German High Command.

1918.

CHAMPAGNE.

1. The 11th Division rested first in the Maubeuge region, and later near Charleville and Laon for about two months. About March 1 it relieved the 51st Reserve Division in the Butte de Mesnil. Here nothing except minor trench raids was attempted. Most of the older men were exchanged for young ones. It was relieved by the 88th Division April 15.

LASSIGNY.

2. April 20 it relieved elements of the 34th and 37th Divisions south of Dives. (east of Lassigny). It was relieved by the 202d Division during the night of May 22–23. It rested then for about 10 days in the Guiscard region.

MONTDIDIER.

3. June 9 it reinforced the Montdidier-Noyon battle front south of Thiescourt (west of Noyon). It attacked the first day of the offensive as an attack division. It attacked on a front of 1,500 yards, with Compiegne as its final objective (its orders were captured), but did poorly, succeeding only in reaching Machemont—less than half way. In this engagement it suffered heavy losses. It was withdrawn the 16th and went to rest in the Guiscard region, where it received some 1,300 replacements.

4. The division relieved the 222d Division near Rubescourt (south of Montdidier) July 19. In the fighting which followed, the division lost heavily. The 10th Regiment received 300 replacements August 2; relieved about the 12th.

5. It reentered line near Varesnes the 22d and was withdrawn the 28th.

ST. QUENTIN.

6. September 8 it came back into line southwest of St. Quentin near Jussy. It was withdrawn about the 20th.

7. Four days later the division was identified north of St. Quentin in the Gricourt sector; withdrawn the 2d of October.

8. It came back into line about the 12th near Barisis (south of LaFere). The division took part in the general German retirement and was identified successively at Remies, Mesbrecourt, Léa Ferte-Chevresis, Monceau le Neuf, Le Herie la Vieville, St. Algis, and Champ Bouvier. It was still in line when the armistice was signed.

VALUE—1918 ESTIMATE.

The 11th is rated as a good second-class division. It did not do well in the battle of the Oise, but everywhere else its conduct under fire was characterized by considerable tenacity. Losses were very heavy. Numerous cases of desertion, especially to the interior; a large number of replacements—returned prisoners from Russia—are said to have mutinied at Breslau.

11th Reserve Division.

COMPOSITION.

	1914		1915		1916		1917		1918	
	Brigade.	Regiment.	Brigade.	Regiment.	Brigade.	Regiment.	Brigade.	Regiment.	Brigade.	Regiment.
Infantry......	21 Res. 23.	10 Res, 11 Res, 22, 156.	21 Res. 23.	10 Res, 11 Res, 22, 156.	23.	10 Res, 22, 156.	23.	10 Res, 22, 156.	23.	22, 156, 10 Res.
Cavalry......	3 Res. Hus. Rgt. (3 Sqns.).				4 Res. Hus. Rgt.		1 Sqn. 4 Res. Hus. Rgt.		1 Sqn. 4 Res. Cav. Rgt.	
Artillery......	11 Res. F. A. Rgt. (6 Btries.).		11 Res. F. A. Rgt.		11 Res. F. A. Rgt.		(9) Art. Command: 11 Res. F. A. Rgt. (9 Btries.).		11 Res. F. A. Rgt. 1 Abt. 5 Res. Ft. A. Rgt. 748 Light Am. Col. 1242 Light Am. Col. 1296 Light Am. Col.	
Engineers and Liaisons.	4 Field Co. 2 Pion. Btn. No. 6. 11 Res. Pont. Engs. 11 Res. Tel. Detch.		4 Field Co. 2 Pion. Btn. No. 6. 11 Res. Pont. Engs. 11 Res. Tel. Detch.		4 Field Co. 2 Pion. Btn. No. 6. 211 T. M. Co. 11 Res. Pont. Engs. 11 Res. Tel. Detch.		(311) Pion. Btn.: 4 Co. 6 Pions. 2 Res. Co. 25 Pion. Btn. 211 T. M. Co. 4 Heavy Field Searchlight Section. 411 Tel. Detch.		311 Pion. Btn.: 4 Co. 6 Pions. 2 Res. Co. 25 Pions 211 T. M. Co. 39 Searchlight Section. 411 Signal Command: 117 Wireless Detch. 411 Tel. Detch.	
Medical and Veterinary.							506 Ambulance Co. 29 Res. Field Hospital. 32 Res. Field Hospital. 411 Vet. Hospital.		506 Ambulance Co. 29 Res. Field Hospital. 32 Res. Field Hospital. 411 Vet. Hospital.	
Transports....							M. T. Col.			
Attached......					95 Anti-Aircraft Section.					

HISTORY.

(Sixth District—Silesia.).

1914.

FRANCE.

1. This division, with the 12th Reserve Division, formed the 6th Reserve Corps.

LORRAINE-MEUSE.

2. At the beginning of the war it belonged to the 5th Army (Prussian Crown Prince). Fought at Arrancy from August 22 to 25; crossed the Meuse the 21st of September. Fought in the region of Cierges September 2; advanced nearly to Triaucourt September 9 and retreated through the east of the Argonne near Montfaucon September 11 to 17.

3. At the end of September it established itself at the eastern edge of the Argonne (Varennes-Malancourt wood). It occupied this region until the Verdun offensive in February, 1916.

1915.

1. January to December, 1915, the division held the sector of Malancourt wood, south of Montfaucon, in Argonne. In April the 11th Reserve Infantry was transferred to form the 117th Division.

1916.

VERDUN.

1. In February, 1916, when the battle of Verdun commenced, the division was still in its sector on the left bank of the Meuse.

2. In March it fought near Bethencourt. It took this village April 9. Relieved about May 15 after suffering very heavy losses (68 per cent of its infantry).

3. Sent to rest and reorganized with replacements from the 1916 class.

SOMME.

4. It was at first army reserve in the region of Cambrai at the beginning of June. Then a hurry call was sent for the division June 27 and it went into the battle of the Somme.

5. July 2 to 3 it relieved some units of the 12th Division and 10th Bavarian Division on the front Hardecourt to the Somme and suffered enormous losses from July 2 to 9.

6. Received replacements July 10 and suffered again heavily between the 10th and 20th in the same region. It was withdrawn from the Somme front about July 24.

FLANDERS.

7. Reconstituted again with replacements from the depots of the 12th Army Corps and sent at the end of July and beginning of August to the east of Armentieres, south of the Lys, and held this sector until September 20 to 27.

SOMME.

8. At the end of September the division returned to the Somme, between the Somme and Barleux. It opposed the attack of the French October 18 to 19 in the sector of Biaches.

9. The division was relieved from the Somme area at the beginning of November.

ARTOIS.

10. Sent to Artois and went into line at the beginning of December in the sector of Lens, between Loos and Lievin.

1917.

1. About March 24 to 25, 1917, the division was withdrawn from the Artois front.

2. In line for six weeks between Cambrai and St. Quentin, in the sector Bellicourt-Bellenglise, from the end of March to May 10. Returned about May 14 to 15 to the region of Lens, where it stayed until August 20. (Attack of the Canadians on its right flank Aug. 15.)

ARTOIS–FLANDERS.

3. At rest in the vicinity of St. Amand (Artois) at the end of August and beginning of September. Held the front south of Lens (sector Frenoy-Acheville) September 9. In November it was sent to Flanders near Passchendaele, where it alternated with the 12th Reserve Division until January, 1918. At rest from the middle of January and went back into line February 24 south of the forest of Houthulst.

RECRUITING.

Silesia. Drafts from other districts—for example, the fourth—to counterbalance the Polish element.

VALUE—1917 ESTIMATE.

At the present time (February, 1918) it is difficult to form a precise opinion of the fighting qualities of this division, as it has not been seriously engaged since the battle of the Somme. In the sector of Lens and Frenoy the heavy losses which it suffered from gas have no doubt caused a certain weakening of the morale. (One company of the 156th Infantry was reduced to 24 men.)

In Flanders the division held a difficult sector, but arrived at a time when active operations were coming to an end. The nature of the ground has been the main cause of its losses. (Information from the British, Feb. 9, 1918.)

1918.

PASSCHENDAELE.

1. The division remained in line south of Passchendaele until January 16, when it was relieved by the 31st Division. It then moved to the Oostroosebeke area, where it underwent a course of training in open warfare.

YPRES.

2. February 24 the division relieved the 199th Division astride the Ypres-Staden railway (northeast of Ypres).

ARMENTIERES.

3. It was relieved about the 18th of March by the extension of front of the neighboring divisions, and one regiment was identified by prisoners as having reenforced the front south of Villers-Carbonnel (southwest of Peronne). This regiment was relieved March 26 and went to join the remainder of the division which was resting in the Turcoing area. April 9 the division reenforced the front in the Croix du Bac sector (north of the La Bassee Canal). It was withdrawn about the 16th, after losing heavily, and went to rest in the vicinity of Laventie.

4. April 28 it relieved the 81st Reserve Division southwest of Meteren. It was withdrawn about the 6th of May, going to be reconstituted in the area southeast of Bailleul.

5. It relieved the 12th Division southwest of Meteren during the night of May 18–19, remaining in line until June 7, when it was withdrawn to rest in the Courtrai area.

6. During the night of June 22–23 the division relieved the 216th Division in the Locre sector (west of Kemmel). Here it fought until a day or two before the armistice, when it seems to have been withdrawn.

VALUE—1918 ESTIMATE.

The 11th Reserve is rated as a second-class division. It has fought a great deal during 1918, especially since June, and has lost heavily. Its record has not been brilliant.

11th Landwehr Division.
COMPOSITION.

	1915		1916		1917		1918	
	Brigade.	Regiment.	Brigade.	Regiment.	Brigade.	Regiment.	Brigade.	Regiment.
Infantry	33 Ldw. 70 Mixed Ldw.	75 Ldw. 76 Ldw. 5 Ldw. 18 Ldw.	33 Ldw. 70 Mixed Ldw.	75 Ldw. 76 Ldw. 5 Ldw. 18 Ldw.	33 Ldw.	18 Ldw. 75 Ldw. 76 Ldw.	70 Ldw.	18 Ldw. 75 Ldw. 424.
Cavalry	92 Ldw. Cav. Rgt.		92 Ldw. Cav. Rgt.		1 Sqn. 11 Dragoon Rgt. (?).		1 Sqn. 11 Drag. Rgt.	
Artillery	98 F. A. Rgt.		98 F. A. Rgt. 910 Btry. F. A.		131 Art. Command: 98 F. A. Rgt. 910 Btry. F. A.		98 F. A. Rgt. 1018 Light Am. Col.	
Engineers and liaisons.			1 and 2 Ldw. Pion. Cos. (3 C. Dist.). 311 T. M. Co.		(411) Pion. Btn.: 1 Co. 1 Pions. 1 Ldw. Co. 3 Pions. 311 T. M. Co. 353 Searchlight Section. 279 Searchlight Section. 511 Tel. Detch.		4 Landst. Co. 3 C. Dist. Pions. 359 Searchlight Section. 79 Searchlight Section. 511 Signal Command. 511 Tel. Detch.	
Medical and Veterinary.					217 Sanitary Co. 10 Ldw. Field Hospital. 17 Ldw. Field Hospital.		217 Ambulance Co. 105 Field Hospital. 150 Field Hospital. 211 Vet. Hospital.	
Odd Units			11 Ldw. Div. Cyclist Co.		11 Ldw. Div. Cyclist Co.			
Attached					70 Ldw. Brig.: "1 (424 Inf. & Consbruch Rgts. "1 and 2 Allenstein.") (20 C. Dist. 1 and 2 Btns. Landst.). 1 Lotzen Landst. Btn. (20 C. Dist. Btn. No. 4). Neustadt Landst. Btn. (17 C. Dist. Landst. Btn. No. 9).			

HISTORY.

(18th Landwehr: Twentieth District—Eastern part of West Prussia. 75th Landwehr and 76th Landwehr: Ninth District—Schleswig-Holstein and Mecklemburg.)

1914.

EASTERN PRUSSIA–POLAND.

1. This division is the former Von Einem Division, which, with the Jacobi Division (former 10th Landwehr Division), formed the 1st Landwehr Corps on the Eastern Front in 1914–15. It took part in the battle of Tannenberg in August and fought near Lyck in October, 1914.

2. From November to December the 1st Landwehr Corps held the defiles of the Masurian Lakes, the 33d and 70th Landwehr Brigades being in the region of Angerburg and Loetzen.

1915.

1. In February, 1915, the 1st Landwehr Corps was identified between Mariampol and Suwalki.

2. From March to August the Von Einem Division, which became the 11th Landwehr Division, was in line before the fortress of Ossowiec.

VICHNEV.

3. The offensive against the Russians brought it to the railroad Molodetchno-Lida, near Vichnev, in September. It established its positions there and remained more than two years, from September, 1915, to the beginning of 1918.

1916.

1. Vichnev-Krevo sector.

2. Toward the end of 1916 the 424th Infantry was assigned to the 11th Landwehr Division, which had given its 5th Landwehr to the 218th Division in October.

1917.

1. Vichnev-Krevo sector.

VALUE—1917 ESTIMATE.

On the Russian front since the beginning of the war. Mediocre quality.

1918.

UKRAINE.

1. The 11th Landwehr Division, which was still in line south of Krevo in January, 1918, marched to the east in February. On April 30 it was identified in the Ukraine between Kiev and Koursk. About the middle of May it was in the Soumy region. A man of the 75th Landwehr Regiment wrote on the 16th of June: "I am still at Kiev, but I tell you one thing, it is much worse here than in the trenches, for there one has the enemy in front, while here it is just the opposite. The people are so badly disposed toward us they would eat us alive if they were able, but they can not."[2]

RUSSIA.

2. The middle of July the division was identified south of Moscow. During all this time men were taken from the division and sent as replacements to the Western Front.

3. Early in November elements of the division were identified along the Danube.

VALUE—1918 ESTIMATE.

The division was rated as fourth class.

11th Bavarian Division.

COMPOSITION.

	1915 Brigade.	1915 Regiment.	1916 Brigade.	1916 Regiment.	1917 Brigade.	1917 Regiment.	1918 Brigade.	1918 Regiment.
Infantry	21 Bav.	3 Bav. 22 Bav. 13 Bav. Res.	21 Bav.	3 Bav. 22 Bav. 13 Bav. Res.	21 Bav.	3 Bav. 22 Bav. 13 Bav. Res.	21 Bav.	16 Bav. 3 Bav. 22 Bav.
Cavalry			4 Sqn. 7 Bav. Light Cav. Rgt.		1 Sqn. 7 Bav. Light Cav. Rgt. 2 Sqn. 7 Bav. Light Cav. Rgt.		2 Sqn. 7 Light Cav. Rgt. (Bavarian).	
Artillery	21 Bav. F. A. Rgt.		21 Bav. F. A. Rgt.		11 Bav. Art. Command: 21 Bav. F. A. Rgt.		11 Bav. Art. Command: 21 Bav. F. A. Rgt. 11 Bav. Ft. A. Btn. 124 Bav. Light Am. Col. 125 Bav. Light Am. Col. 129 Bav. Light Am. Col.	
Engineers and Liaisons.	19 Bav. Pion. Co. 21 Bav. Pion. Co.		19 Bav. Pion. Co. 21 Bav. Pion. Co. 11 Bav. T. M. Co. 11 Bav. Pont. Engs. 11 Bav. Tel. Detch.		(11 Bav.) Pion. Btn.: 19 Bav. Pion. Co. 21 Bav. Pion. Co. 11 Bav. T. M. Co. 11 Bav. Tel. Detch.		11 Bav. Pion. Btn.: 19 Bav. Pion. Co. 21 Bav. Pion. Co. 11 Bav. T. M. Co. 11 Bav. Searchlight Section. 11 Bav. Signal Command: 11 Bav. Tel. Detch. 11 Bav. Wireless Detch. 179 Bav. Wireless Detch.	
Medical and Veterinary.					11 Bav. Ambulance Co. 35 Field Hospital. 37 Field Hospital. 11 Vet. Hospital.		11 Bav. Ambulance Co. 35 Bav. Field Hospital. 37 Bav. Field Hospital.	
Transports.					M. T. Col. 691 Divisional M. T. Col.		691 M. T. Col.	

	11 Bav. Cyclist Co.	11 Bav. Cyclist Co.
Odd Units......		
Attached......		M. G. S. Detch. No. 47. 308 Supply Train. 1107 Wireless Detch. 286 and 287 Field Signal Sections Pigeon Loft. 2 Co. 29 Pions. 3 Co. 29 Pions. 1 Co. 7 Pions. Pfungstadt Landst. Inf. Btn. 2 Munster Landst. Btn. 1 Co. 60 Labor Btn. 1 Co. 12 Labor Btn. (Bayr.).

HISTORY.

(3d Bavarian: First Bavarian District.)   (22d Bavarian: Second Bavarian District.)
(13th Reserve Bavarian: Third Bavarian District.)

1915.

Organized in April, 1915, in Galicia, in the Carpathians.

GALICIA.

1. This division belonged to Mackensen's army during the offensive in Galicia and took part in the capture of Przemysl May 31, 1915.

BUG.

2. Sent north, fought at Rava Ruska, and reached the Bug in the region of Cholm-Vlodava. Withdrew from the front at the end of August.

SERBIA.

3. In September and October the division took part in the campaign against Serbia with Mackensen's army. Crossed the Danube October 8 to 11; Valley of the Morawa; region of Monastir (November).

4. Left the front November 15 and went to rest in Hungary at Weisskirchen until the beginning of February, 1916.

1916.

FRANCE.

1. From February 9 to 10, 1916, the division entrained for the Western Front. Itinerary: Temesvar–Szegedin–Baja–Marburg–Graz–Salzburg–Munich–Ingolstadt–Wurzburg–Frankfort on Main–Coblentz–Cologne–Liège–Malines. Detrained at Antwerp February 15.

2. At rest in the region of Antwerp until March 1, and on that date it entrained for Vouziers.

VERDUN.

3. Sent to the Verdun front (sector of Avocourt wood, Mar. 8), attacked March 20 and 22 and April 11 and suffered considerable losses; 75 per cent of its infantry out of action.

4. Relieved at the beginning of June and sent to rest in the region of Thionville, then sent to Cambrai.

RUSSIA.

5. June 14 it returned to Russia. Itinerary: Solesme Busigny–Maubeuge–Liège–Aix la Chapelle–Hanover–Brest Litovsk–Kovel.

KOVEL.

6. Went into action immediately and counterattacked near the Kovel-Rovno Railroad and suffered heavy losses.

ROUMANIA.

7. In October it took part in the Roumanian campaign (Valley of the Jiul).

1917.

FRANCE.

1. Withdrawn from the Braila front at the beginning of January, 1917, and again entrained for France on the 10th. Itinerary: Bucarest–Budapest–Vienna–Salzburg–Munich. Detrained the 22d at Barr (Alsace).

ALSACE.

2. In April held the sector Burnhaupt–Rhone–Rhine canal.

AISNE.

3. Sent from Mulhouse to Marle April 26 to 28, then to the south of Laon and took over the sector of Cernay May 5 to 6, where its losses were due especially to artillery fire.

4. At rest in the region of Laon June 6 to August 3.

5. Coucy sector August 3 to September 15. The division did not have any hard action here, but suffered again from bombardment.

6. September 15, at rest in the vicinity of Sedan for one month.

FLANDERS.

7. Entrained at Sedan October 15 to 17; detrained at Courtrai October 18; went into line the 22d in the sector of Passchendaele, where it suffered heavily from the British attack of the 26th. Relieved immediately after this engagement and reorganized.

8. November 2 the division went back into line south of Passchendaele, but did not have any serious actions.

9. November 10, relieved and sent to rest.

COTES DE MEUSE.

10. From November 18 to January 12, 1918, the division held the sector Chauvoncourt–Seuzey north of St. Mihiel. It took part in no infantry actions.

RECRUITING.

The whole of the Bavarian country.

VALUE—1917 ESTIMATE.

This division may be considered good. It took part on the Eastern and Western Fronts in a large number of battles, "Przemysl, Verdun, Argesul, Filipesci" (speech of William II), and did well everywhere (January, 1918).

1918.

LOUVRE.

1. The 11th Bavarian Division remained in the Seuzey sector, resting and being reconstituted, until relieved by the 82d Reserve Division on January 12.

2. About the middle of February it relieved the 1st Division in the Etain sector. This, too, was a very quiet sector and the division was not identified by contact. It was relieved about March 27 by the 10th Landwehr Division, and remained in rear of the Verdun front for a fortnight. It is probable that it was trained during this period, but the fact has never been definitely established.

ARMENTIERES.

3. The division was then sent to the Armentieres front, where it relieved the 214th Division in the Neuve Eglise sector (northwest of Armentieres) April 13–14. Here it took part in very heavy fighting, especially south of Mount Kemmel, and suffered heavy losses as a result. It was withdrawn on the 26th of April, and proceeded to the area northeast of Ghent, detraining at Wachtebeke on the 29th. Here it was brought up to strength and reviewed by the King of Bavaria on May 20.

SOISSONS.

4. About June 3 the division left the Ghent region; it was identified in rear of the front in the region of Soissons on June 9. A few days later it reinforced the front near Coeuvres (southwest of Soissons). It was relieved by the 14th Division on June 21.

5. After resting immediately in rear of the front, it suffered severe losses from bombardment by gas shells during this period. The division came back into line in the Courmelles sector (south of Soissons) about July 15. July 18 it lost over 2,400 in prisoners alone. It was withdrawn about July 22.

YPRES.

6. The division rested for about a month. It was reconstituted, it being found necessary to dissolve one company in each battalion. August 26 the division relieved

the 49th Reserve Division east of Boesinghe (northwest of Ypres).   It fought, taking part in the general retirement, until withdrawn October 2, after losing more than 500 prisoners.

GHENT.

7. The division reinforced the front near Beveren (southwest of Ghent), and had not been withdrawn up to the time the armistice was signed.

VALUE—1918 ESTIMATE.

The 11th Bavarian is rated as being in the first of four classes of divisions. It fought well during 1918, but not brilliantly. Its losses were heavy, but not in comparison with other German divisions.

12th Division.
COMPOSITION.

	1914 Brigade	1914 Regiment	1915 Brigade	1915 Regiment	1916 Brigade	1916 Regiment	1917 Brigade	1917 Regiment	1918 Brigade	1918 Regiment
Infantry	34. 78.	23. 62. 63. 157.	24. 78.	23. 62. 63. 157.	24.	23. 62. 63.	24.	23. 62. 63.	24.	23. 62. 63.
Cavalry		11 Horse Jäg. Rgt.				6 Sqn. 10 Hus. Rgt.		4 Sqn. 2 Uhlan Rgt.		4 Sqn. 2 Uhlan Rgt.
Artillery	12 Brig.: 21 F. A. Rgt. 57 F. A. Rgt.		12 Brig.: 21 F. A. Rgt. 57 F. A. Rgt.		12 Brig.: 21 F. A. Rgt. 57 F. A. Rgt.		12 Art. Command: 21 F. A. Rgt.		12 Art. Command: 21 F. A. Rgt. 68 Ft. A. Btn. 851 Light Am. Col. 887 Light Am. Col. 937 Light Am. Col.	
Engineers and Liaisons.			1 Pion. Btn. No. 6: Field Co. 6 Pions. 12 Pont. Engs. 12 Tel. Detch.		1 Pion. Btn. No. 6: 2 Co. 6 Pions. 3 Co. 6 Pions. 12 T. M. Co. 12 Pont. Engs. 12 Tel. Detch.		1 Pion. Btn. No. 6: 3 Co. 6 Pions. 12 T. M. Co. 6 Searchlight Section. 10 Tel. Detch. 116, 117, and 118 Signal Detch.		6 Pion. Btn. 2 Co. 6 Pions. 3 Co. 6 Pions. 12 T. M. Co. 100 Searchlight Section. 12 Signal Command: 12 Tel. Detch. 182 Wireless Detch.	
Medical and Veterinary.							15 Ambulance Co. 51 Field Hospital. 57 Field Hospital. Vet. Hospital.		15 Ambulance Co. 57 Field Hospital. 60 Field Hospital. 12 Vet. Hospital.	
Transports							27 Supply Train. M. T. Col.		545 M. T. Col.	
Attached					17 Antiaircraft section		17 Antiaircraft section			

HISTORY.

(6th Corps District—Upper Silesia.)

1914.

FRANCE.

1. The 12th Division, forming with the 11th Division the 6th Army Corps (Breslau), formed a part of the 5th Army (German Crown Prince) at the beginning of the war, took part in the battle of August 22 at Rossignol les Bulles, entered France August 24, passed the Meuse above Mouzon on August 28, and took part in the battle on September 7 at Laheycourt and Villotte near Louppy.

CHAMPAGNE.

2. After the battle of the Marne it was engaged (Sept. 21) at Berru and at Nogent l'Abbesse (east of Rheims). It remained on the Rheims front until the middle of June, 1915.

1915.

ARTOIS.

1. In April the 12th Division gave the 157th Infantry Regiment to the 117th Division, a new formation.

2. Toward the middle of June, 1915, the 6th Army Corps was relieved on the Rheims front and transferred to Artois. The 12th Division then occupied a sector to the south of Souchez, from which it was relieved toward the end of September. In the Souchez sector it took part in some very heavy engagements (1st to the 16th of July).

3. After a rather short rest period in the region of Cambrai, the division took its position in the sector which crosses the Somme (during the first half of October).

1916.

SOMME.

1. On the 1st of July, 1916, the 12th Division received the entire weight of the English attack north of the Somme (sectors Contalmaison–Hardecourt) and suffered very heavily (losses 61.5 per cent).

2. It was relieved on July 12 and reorganized in the vicinity of Cambrai.

3. About the 20th of July the 12th Division again took part in the battle of the Somme (in the sector northeast of Pozières), where it suffered heavy losses.

4. About the 9th of August it was relieved, and on the 21st went into the calm sector of Monchy aux Bois (south of Arras), which it held until October 16.

ANCRE.

5. The 12th Division then held (Oct. 25 to Nov. 19) the sector north of the Ancre (Beaumont–Hamel) and suffered heavy losses (Nov. 14).

6. It was transferred to Champagne and took over the sector of Prunay on December 12.

RUSSIA.

7. At the end of December it was relieved from this quiet sector and entrained on December 28, at Warmeriville for the Russian front by the route Aix la Chapelle-Cologne-Hanover-Luneburg-Hamburg-Stettin-Königsberg-Tilsit-Chavli-Ponieviej It detrained southwest of Illuxt on January 2, 1917.

1917.

1. On the Russian front the 12th Division did not take part in any important battles. (Sector in the region of Dwinsk.)

FRANCE.

2. Relieved about the end of May, 1917, it returned to the Western Front. Itinerary Jelowka (May 27) –Insterburg–Posen–Leipzig–Weimar–Cologne–Saarbrucken. Detrained at Metz June 3 and reentrained on the 9th at Ars sur Moselle for Mouscron, by way of Metz–Luxemburg–Namur–Tournai, and detrained at Gheluwe.

1917.

3. It remained in reserve first on the Wytschaete–Messines front, and then (Aug. 1) relieved the 22d Reserve Division in the sector east of Klein-Zillebeke after the Franco-British attack. In this sector the division did not engage in battle but suffered greatly from artillery bombardments.

ITALY.

4. It was relieved on August 20 and transferred to Alsace for reorganization and rest. It remained in the region west of Bâle until the end of September. It was then sent to the Italian front, to the 14th German Army, where it was engaged in the Tolmino sector on October 25, and relieved on the Piave about the 8th of December.

FRANCE.

5. The 12th Division was brought back from Italy to the French front about December 25. At the beginning of January, 1918, it was in the neighborhood of Zabern.

RECRUITING.

The 12th Division is recruited from Upper Silesia, a great mining and industrial center, which suffices to insure its own full recruiting and even helps out other districts less populated or temporarily below strength. The sending of these men outside of the district has the advantage of reducing, in its own regiments, the Polish element, which dominates in Upper Silesia.

VALUE—1917 ESTIMATE.

The 12th Division fought well at the Somme.

It appears to have been reorganized during its stay at Zabern (January, 1918). It has always been considered a good division.

1918.

LORRAINE.

1. On January 24 the 12th division entered the Domevre sector, relieving the 233d Division. It was relieved on February 20 and went to rest and train in Alsace. On March 18 it entrained at Froeschweiler and moved to Ath, from where it marched to the Gory–Belloune area, south of Douai (a march of 40 miles).

BATTLE OF PICARDY.

2. On the 23d the division moved to Drury and up the Cambrai–Arras road to Vis en Artois, coming into line on the night of March 23–24. It attacked on the 24th, but was held up by the British artillery fire. It remained in line until April 1, making little progress in spite of heavy and costly fighting.

BATTLE OF THE LYS.

3. The division rested in the suburbs of Douai until mid-April. It was engaged northeast of Merris on the 17th. It appears to have received replacements in the interim. The division passed into the second line on May 18, after suffering especially heavy losses. In recognition of the service of the 12th Division, south of Arras and in the Lys battle, Gen. Lequis, the division commander, received the Order of Merit in May.

4. The division was at rest near Renaix (Belgium) from May 29 to July 12. It entrained at Audenarde on the 12th and moved to Perenchies (via Coutrai and Lille).

METEREN.

5. The division was engaged south of Meteren on the night of July 19–20; here it remained until August 28. In a local operation on August 18 the division lost 300 prisoners, otherwise the sector was quiet.

BATTLE OF CAMBRAI.

6. It entrained near Armentieres on August 28 and went to a point north of Douai (Le Forest). It was engaged southeast of Morchies on September 3, and in the days following was driven back on Inchy en Artois, Marquion (3d to 13th). By the end of September it had passed Bourlon, Epinoy, Aubencheul au Bac, and Fressies. The division was relieved about October 6. The division lost more than 1,100 prisoners.

7. It was reengaged on October 11 southeast of Armentieres. It retreated by Lille (Oct. 20) east of Tourcoing, and at Helchin. On the 25th it was relieved.

8. On November 3 it was again in line east of Joulain and remained until the armistice. In withdrawing the division passed Maresches, Jenlain, Autreppe, and Blangies.

VALUE—1918 ESTIMATE.

The division was rated as a second-class division. It was actively engaged in the spring offensives and did well. After the middle of July it was almost constantly engaged in hard defensive fighting.

12th Reserve Division.

COMPOSITION.

	1914		1915		1916		1917		1918	
	Brigade.	Regiment.	Brigade.	Regiment.	Brigade.	Regiment.	Brigade.	Regiment.	Brigade.	Regiment.
Infantry	22 Res. 23 Res. 6 Res.	38 Res. 51 Res. 22 Res. 23 Res. Jag. Btn.	22 Res. 23 Res. 6 Res.	38 Res. 51 Res. 22 Res. 23 Res. Jag. Btn.	22 Res. 6 Res.	23 Res. 38 Res. 51 Res. Jag. Btn.	22 Res.	23 Res. 38 Res. 51 Res.	22 Res.	23 Res. 38 Res. 51 Res.
Cavalry	4 Res. Uhlan Rgt. (3 Squs.).		4 Res. Uhlan Rgt.		4 Res. Uhlan Rgt.		(?)		2 Sqn. 4 Res. Hus. Rgt.	
Artillery	12 Res. F. A. Rgt. (6 Btries.).		12 Res. F. A. Rgt.		12 Res. F. A. Regt.		(?) Art. Command: 12 Res. F. A. Rgt. (9 Btries.).		99 Art. Command: 12 Res. F. A. Regt. 133 Ft. A. Btn. 830 Light Am. Col. 1243 Light Am. Col. 1297 Light Am. Col.	
Engineers and liaisons.	1 and 2 Res. Cos. 2 Pion. Btn. No. 6.		1 and 2 Res. Cos. 2 Pion. Btn. No. 6. 12 Res. Pont. Engs. 12 Res. Tel. Detch.		1 and 2 Res. Cos. 2 Pion. Btn. No. 6. 212 T. M. Co. 12 Res. Pont. Engs. 12 Res. Tel. Detch.		312 Pion Btn.: 1 Res. Co. 6 Pions. 2 Res. Co. 6 Pions. 212 T. M. Co. (23) (?) Searchlight Section. 412 Tel. Detch.		312 Pion Btn. 1 Res. Co. 6 Pions. 2 Res. Co. 6 Pions. 212 T. M. Co. 105 Searchlight Section. 412 Signal Command. 412 Tel. Detch. 114 Wireless Detch.	
Medical and veterinary.							Ambulance Co. 30 Res. Field Hospital. Vet. Hospital.		520 Ambulance Co. 30 Res. Field Hospital. 31 Res. Field Hospital. 412 Vet. Hospital.	
Transports							711 M. T. Col.		711 M. T. Col.	
Attached					7 and 132 Anti-Aircraft Sections. 8 Bav. Labor Btn.					

HISTORY.

12th Reserve Division: (6th Corps District—Silesia).

1914.

The 12th Reserve Division formed, with the 11th Reserve Division, the 6th Reserve Corps, formed in Silesia at the time of mobilization.

MEUSE-ARGONNE.

1. At the outbreak of the war, the division detrained at Sarrebruecken; fought in the neighborhood of Arrancy from the 22d to the 25th of August; remained at Mangiennes from the 27th to the 30th; crossed the Meuse on September 1; was beaten back with heavy losses on September 2 near Cierges; was at Rarécourt on the 7th and near Triaucourt on the 9th; spread out to the east of the Argonne upon Gercourt (11th to the 13th) and Montfaucon (Sept. 17).

2. At the end of September to the end of October took up its position east of Varennes in the district of Malancourt-Chattancourt and toward the end of October took its final position north of Bethencourt (southeast of Cuisy-Bois de Forges).

3. The division occupied this sector until the German offensive upon Verdun (end of February, 1916).

1915.

1. January to December, 1915, sector north of Bethencourt-Bois de Forges.

In April the 27th Infantry Regiment Reserve was transferred to the 117th Division, a new formation.

2. In September, 1915, elements of the 12th Reserve Division (battalion of the 23d Reserve Infantry Regiment) were detached in Champagne (Main de Massiges) to reinforce divisions engaged in fighting.

1916.

1. At the end of February, when the Verdun offensive began, the 12th Reserve Division still held the line in the region of Bois de Forges.

VERDUN.

2. On the 6th of March, 1916, the division went into action; it took the village of Forges and, on March 10, the Corbeaux wood. It vainly attacked the Mort Homme.

3. It was withdrawn from the Verdun front in the middle of May, after suffering heavy losses (71 per cent of its infantry). It was first at rest in the Thionville region, and then in reserve in the Cambrai region, at the beginning of June.

SOMME.

4. On July 2 it took part in the battle of the Somme (sector of Montauban-Hardecourt). It counterattacked near the Trônes wood and suffered very heavy losses. It was relieved about July 14, completely exhausted. (On the 10th of July not a single officer remained in the 2d Battalion of the 38th Reserve Infantry Regiment (letter). From the 17th of March to the 5th of July the 5th Company of the 23d Reserve Infantry Regiment received no less than 326 men as replacements).

5. On July 15 it was sent to rest in the Manancourt region. Elements of the division still remained in line, along the Somme near Guillemont, until August 1.

FLANDERS.

6. From the beginning of August until September 26–27, the 12th Reserve Division occupied a sector north of the Lys, near Armentières (Warneton-Messines), where it once more suffered losses.

SOMME.

7. At the end of September the division was once more on the Somme front (Barleux-Berny). It remained there until the beginning of November without suffering any great losses.

ARTOIS.

8. Transferred to Artois, it went into line on Vimy Ridge (sector Vimy–Roclincourt) at the beginning of December. It suffered fairly heavy losses. At the present time, 17 per cent of the prisoners from the 51st Reserve Infantry Regiment belong to the 1917 class.

1917.

1. The 12th Reserve Division remained on the Vimy front until February 27, 1917.

2. It was resting in the Avesnes region during the month of March.

3. From April 9–12 to May 24 it held the lines between Itancourt and the Oise.

ST. QUENTIN.

4. After a fortnight's rest in the Guise region, it occupied (from the beginning of June to Aug. 6–8), the St. Quentin sector (south of Fayet).

FLANDERS.

5. On August 7 the division entrained for Flanders, at Fresnoy le Grand. Disembarking near Courtrai, it was first in reserve near Passchendaele. A few of the elements of the division engaged in battle at Langemarck on the 17th of August. It was in line in the St. Julien sector (northeast of Ypres) on August 20, and relieved on August 24, after suffering heavy losses.

ST. QUENTIN.

6. In rest at Origny, from August 29 to September 9, the division then occupied the sector southwest of St. Quentin (Sept. 9 to Nov. 11–12).

It left at this latter date to occupy the front south of Passchendaele until the middle of February, 1918, being relieved several times in the interval.

RECRUITING.

Silesia, especially Upper Silesia. In 1916, following the losses suffered at Verdun, a great number of the replacement troops consisted of men from the 3d and 4th Corps Districts (Brandenburg and Prussian Saxony) and of the 1916 class, and of returned convalescents of the 9th and 10th Corps Districts (Schleswig–Holstein and Hanover). This measure was not only dictated by necessity, but contributed to counterbalance the original Polish element.

VALUE—1917 ESTIMATE.

At Ypres (August, 1917), a certain number of men of the 51st Reserve Infantry Regiment refused to go into the trenches; according to prisoners, desertions to the rear were frequent, especially among the younger men.

The combat morale of the 12th Reserve Division may, however, have been restored during its long stay in the relatively quiet sector of St. Quentin (September to November, 1917).

1918.

FLANDERS.

1. On February 4 the division relieved the 12th Reserve Division in the Moorslede sector which it held until February 14.

LENS.

2. It was relieved by the 31st Division and moved south to relieve the 17th Division on night of February 17–18. It held this front until about April 10, when it was relieved by the 9th Reserve Division.

BATTLE OF THE LYS.

3. The division reinforced the battle front at Neuve Eglise on April 13 and fought until about April 25, suffering heavy losses. One company of the 51st Reserve Regiment was reduced to 9 men.

4. Upon relief, the division returned to its former sector near Lens, where it was identified near Avion on April 27. It remained here until June 14, when it moved north and entered the line northeast of Hinges on June 17–18. About August 6, the division was relieved by the 1st Guard Reserve Division.

ARRAS.

5. It moved to Douai and rested until its return to line near Ecoust on night of August 20–31 to resist the British attack. Before its withdrawal on the 11th it had lost nearly 900 prisoners.

LENS.

6. The division rested at Cambrai during September and reentered the Lens sector on October 2. During October it was engaged at Noyelles (11th) Wattines (19th), and Rumignies (21st). It appears to have been out of line for a few days, returning on the night of November 3–4 west of Orsinval. It was at Wargnies le Petit (5th), St. Waast la Vallee (6th), Bavai (7th), northeast of Taisnieres (9th), and Villers St. Guislain (11th).

VALUE—1918 ESTIMATE.

The division was rated as second class. It appears to have been used principally as a sector-holding division on moderately active fronts.

12th Landwehr Division.
COMPOSITION.

	1915 Brigade	1915 Regiment	1916 Brigade	1916 Regiment	1917 Brigade	1917 Regiment	1918 Brigade	1918 Regiment
Infantry	55 Ldw. 82 Ldw.	87 Ldw. (1 and 4 Btns. 87 Ldw. and 5 Btn. 76 Ldw. Rgt.), 99 Ldw. (4 Btn.), 40 Ldw., 56 Ldw. Gd. Jag. Btn. Gd. Rifle Btn. 14 Jag. Btn.	55 Ldw. 82 Ldw.	87 Ldw. 99 Ldw. (4th Btn.) 40 Ldw. 56 Ldw. Gd. Jag. Btn. Gd. Rifle Btn. 9 Jag. Btn.	55 Ldw.	56 Ldw. 87 Ldw. 435 Ldw. (include 4th Btn. 99 Ldw. Rgt.).	....	87 Ldw.
Cavalry	....				2 Sqn. 7 Res. Dragoon Rgt.		1 Sqn. 9 Res. Hus. Rgt.	
Artillery	1 Ers. Abt. 14 F. A. Rgt. 1 Ers. Abt. 30 F. A. Rgt.		30 Res. F. A. Rgt. 1 Mountain A. Btry. 9 Mountain A. Btry. 11 Mountain A. Btry. 18 Mountain A. Btry.		Art. Command: 12 Ldw. F. A. Rgt.		252 Ldw. F. A. Rgt. 2 Bav. Ldw. Ft. A. Btn. (2d Btry.).	
Engineers and Liaisons	....		(?) 2 Ldw. Pion. Co. (14 C. Dist.). 312 T. M. Co.		412 Pion. Btn.: 1 Ldw. Co. 4 Pions. 2 Ldw. Co. 14 Pions. 2 Ldw. Co. 16 Pions. 312 T. M. Co. 268 Searchlight Section. 512 Tel. Detch.		415 Pion. Btn.: 1 Ldw. Co. 4 C. Dist. Pions. Landst. Ers. Co. 8 C. Dist. Pions. 75 Searchlight Section. 478 Signal Command: 478 Tel. Detch. 140 Wireless Detch.	
Medical and Veterinary	....				564 Ambulance Co. 568 Ambulance Co. 14 Ldw. Field Hospital. 15 Ldw. Field Hospital. Vet. Field Hospital.		564 Ambulance Co.	
Transports	....				M. T. Col.			
Attached	....				58 Art. Survey Section. 5 Labor Btn. 63 Labor Btn. 227, 228, and 251 Heavy M. G. Detch.			

HISTORY.

(56th Landwehr Regiment: 7th Corps District—Westphalia. 87th Landwehr Regiment: 18th Corps District—Hesse. 436th Landwehr Regiment: 15th Corps District—Alsace.)

1915.

ALSACE.

1. The 12th Landwehr Division was formed toward the end of April, 1915, with the elements of the Landwehr, which were distributed along the Alsatian front, between the Fecht and the district of Cernay, and which were assigned to the Fuchs Division at the time of the attacks upon Hartmannswillerkopf (March–April). The active brigade of the Fuchs Division having left the Vosges for Champagne, the 12th Landwehr Division grouped these elements of the Landwehr and occupied until May, 1917, the sectors included between the valley of Munster and Cernay. On the 21st of December, 1915, the 14th Jager Battalion, attached to the division, lost at Hartmannswillerkopf 840 killed, wounded, and missing (official list of casualties), and was withdrawn to be reorganized in Belgium.

1916.

ALSACE.

1. Sector Guebwiller-Cernay.

At the end of September, 1916, the 40th Landwehr Regiment left the 12th Landwehr Division to be assigned to the 33d Division. It was replaced by the 436th Landwehr Regiment, which had been formed in May of the preceding year.

In October the battalions of Jagers and of the riflemen of the guard and the 9th Battalion of Jagers, attached to the 12th Landwehr Division, were sent to Macedonia.

1917.

ALSACE.

1. January–May, 1917. Sector Munster–Cernay.

GALICIA.

2. Relieved on the Alsatian front about the middle of May, the 12th Landwehr Division was transferred to Galicia. Itinerary: Cernay-Strassborg-Karlsruhe-Ludwigsburg-Munich, Salzburg-Vienna-Lemberg-Zloczow.

3. It occupied the sector south of Brody and northwest of Zalosce until the beginning of 1918. It took part in the attacks of July, 1917.

In the course of the final months of 1917 the 12th Landwehr Division had numerous troops taken to fill up units on the Western Front or to be sent to the 227th Division, 197th Division, or the 33d Reserve Division.

VALUE—1917 ESTIMATE.

The 12th Landwehr Division, which was on the Alsatian front until May, 1917 and then in Galicia, appears to be of mediocre quality.

1918.

1. The history of the component elements of this division after their arrival on the Western Front is uncertain. Between March and June the 56th Landwehr Regiment was in the 6th Army, the 436th Landwehr Regiment was in the 2d Army, and the 87th Landwehr Regiment was in the 18th Army. The men of these units were assigned to various kinds of police work, guarding prisoners, etc. The staff of the division during this period was believed to be in Finland. About July 15 the division had been announced as dissolved by the French, British, and American general headquarters.

ALSACE.

2. On August 7 the 87th Landwehr Regiment and the 436th Landwehr Regiment were joined as infantry under the 21st Landwehr Brigade Staff, Gen. Hoffman, of the 14th Landwehr Division. The 56th Landwehr Regiment was also identified in this region and the division was regarded as reconstituted in October.

3. Later identifications disclosed that the regiments were not forming a division but were acting independently. The division was again classed as dissolved about the middle of October.

VALUE—1918 ESTIMATE.

The division was rated as a third-class division.

12th Bavarian Division.

COMPOSITION.

	1916		1917		1918	
	Brigade.	Regiment.	Brigade.	Regiment.	Brigade.	Regiment.
Infantry	22 Bav.	26 Bav. 27 Bav. 28 Bav.	22 Bav.	26 Bav. 27 Bav. 28 Bav.	22 Bav.	26 Bav. 27 Bav. 28 Bav.
Cavalry	4 Sqn. 7 Bav. Light Cav. Rgt.		4 Sqn. 7 Bav. Light Cav. Rgt.		1 Sqn. 7 Bav. Light Cav. Rgt.	
Artillery	22 Bav. F. A. Rgt.		22 Bav. F. A. Rgt.		12 Bav. Art. Command: 22 Bav. F. A. Rgt. 8 Bav. Ft. A. Btn. 136 Light Am. Col. 137 Light Am. Col. 138 Light Am. Col.	
Engineers and Liaisons	22 Bav. Pion. Co.		(12 Bav.) Pion. Btn.: 22 Bav. Pion. Co. 26 Bav. Pion. Co. 12 Bav. T. M. Co. 12 Bav. Tel. Detch.		12 Bav. Pion. Btn.: 22 Bav. Pion. Co. 26 Bav. Pion. Co. 12 Bav. T. M. Co. 16 Bav. Searchlight Section. 12 Bav. Signal Command: 12 Bav. Tel. Detch. 189 Wireless Detch.	
Medical and Veterinary			12 Bav. Ambulance Co. 38 Bav. Field Hospital. 39 Bav. Field Hospital. Vet. Hospital.		12 Bav. Ambulance Co. 38 Bav. Field Hospital. 39 Bav. Field Hospital. 16 Bav. Vet. Hospital.	
Transports			M. T. Col.		692 M. T. Col.	

HISTORY.

(Bavaria.)

1916.

It was formed about the middle of the summer of 1916. It was assembled in July, 1916, at Grafenwoehr Camp (Bavaria), and remained until the end of July in the Valley of the Fecht, and then entrained for the Roumanian front in October.

ROUMANIA.

1. Composed of the 26th, 27th, and 28th Bavarian Regiments, the division took part in the Roumanian campaign and fought in the region of Campolung (October-November, 1916).

2. In December it took part in the operations north of the road Buzeu-Rimnicu-Sarat.

1917.

FOCSANI.

1. Beginning with January, 1917, the 12th Bavarian Division remained in line north of Focsani.

2. In August it took part in the attacks launched against the Roumanians north of Focsani (from Batinesci to the Sereth) and suffered very heavy losses.

PANCIU.

3. Sent to rest after these engagements, it came back into line at the end of September, south of Panciu (Marasesti District).

4. In December it was in reserve in the Focsani District.

RECRUITING.

The division is recruited from the whole of Bavaria.

VALUE—1917 ESTIMATE.

It was on the Roumanian front from October, 1916. Its combat value is mediocre.

1918.

1. The division entrained at Ploesci on April 30 and traveled via Bucharest-Craiova-Budapest-Dresden-Frankfurt on the Main-Mainz-Mezieres to a station between Mezieres and Rethel, where it detrained after a journey of nine days. It rested near Vieil St. Remy (20 kilometers southeast of Mezieres), until May 24, when it marched toward the Aisne by Chateau Porcien, Asfeld, Avaux, and Neufchatel.

BATTLE OF THE AISNE.

2. The division crossed the old line near Berry au Bac on May 28 and followed the advance through Roucy, Montigny sur Vesle and Lagery. It was engaged on the 30th near Ville en Tardenois, with the Marne between Damery and Cumieres as its final objective. In that sector it stayed until July 13-14. Losses were heavy about the end of May and the 1st of June.

3. It was in reserve in the same sector on the 15th behind the 22d Division, on the 17th it attacked and until the end of July took part in the struggle for Epernay, toward which the division got as far as the Bois Courton.

4. Upon its relief on July 26 the division marched to the Ligny en Cambresis area in stages. There it rested until August 29, when it entrained at Solesmes and traveled via Valenciennes-Condes-Ath-Ghent to Roubaix. After two days' rest it reentrained and was railed via Courtrai to Isegheim, relieving the 6th Cavalry Division east of Ypres on the night of August 31-September 1.

FLANDERS.

5. In this sector the division sustained an attack by the British on September 28. It was thrown back on Moorslede with a loss of 3,000 prisoners. The division was relieved on October 1.

6. The division rested at Roubaix until October 17, when it returned to line southeast of Herseaux. It continued in this region until the armistice. The last identification was at Cordes.

VALUE—1918 ESTIMATE.

The division was rated as a third-class division. Its morale appears to have been low in the summer and fall of 1918.

13th Division.
COMPOSITION.

	1914		1915		1916		1917		1918	
	Brigade.	Regiment.	Brigade.	Regiment.	Brigade.	Regiment.	Brigade.	Regiment.	Brigade.	Regiment.
Infantry	25. 26. 11 Jag. Btn. (Oct. 1914–Mar. 1915).	13. 158. 15. 55.	25. 26.	13. 158. 15. 55.	26.	13. 15. 55.	26.	13. 15. 55.	26.	13. 15. 55.
Cavalry	16 Uhlan Rgt. (3 Sqns.).				16 Uhlans (2 Sqns.).		3 Sqn. 16 Uhlan Rgt.		3 Sqn. 16 Uhlan Rgt.	
Artillery	13 Brig.; 22 F. A. Rgt. 58 F. A. Rgt.		13 Brig.; 22 F. A. Rgt. 58 F. A. Rgt.		13 Brig.; 22 F. A. Rgt. 58 F. A. Rgt.		13 Art. Command: 58 F. A. Rgt.		13 Art. Command: 58 F. A. Rgt. 151 Ft. A. Btn. 856 Light Am. Col. 859 Light Am. Col. 861 Light Am. Col.	
Engineers and Liaisons.			1 Pion. Btn. No. 7: Field Co. 7 Pions. 13 Pont-Engs. 13 Tel. Detch.		1 Pion. Btn. No. 7: 1 Co. 7 Pions. 13 T. M. Co. 13 Pont-Engs. 13 Tel. Detch.		124 Pion. Btn. (1 Pion. Btn. No. 7): 1 Co. 7 Pions. 2 Co. 7 Pions. 13 T. M. Co. 7 Searchlight Section. 13 Tel. Detch.		7 Pion. Btn.: 1 Co. 7 Pions. 2 Co. 7 Pions. 13 T. M. Co. 13 Signal Command: 13 Tel. Detch. 5 Wireless Detch.	
Medical and Veterinary.							17 Ambulance Co. Field Hospital No. 73. Vet. Hospital.		17 Ambulance Co. 70 Field Hospital. 73 Field Hospital. 13 Vet. Hospital.	
Transports							M. T. Col.		546 M. T. Col.	
Attached							41 Anti-Aircraft Sect. M. G. S. S. Detch No. 75. 546 Supply Train. 265 A. Air. Sqn. 10 Air. Sqn. 37 Wireless Detch. 87 Labor Btn. 2 Co. 11 Labor Btn. 306 Wagon Train.			

HISTORY.

(7th Corps District—Westphalia.)

1914.

BELGIUM.

1. The 13th Division, forming with the 14th Division the 7th Army Corps, was a part, at the outbreak of the war, of the 2d Army (Von Buelow). It entrained in the vicinity of Eupen from the 9th to the 11th of August, and the 25th Brigade took part in the final operations of the siege of Liège. After the fall of this place the division reassembled, passed through Wavre, Nivelles, Seneffe, crossed the Sambre below Thuin (battle of Charleroi), entered France on August 25, and left the 26th Brigade in front of Maubeuge, where it remained until the city was taken (Sept. 7).

CHAMPAGNE.

2. The 25th Brigade, going forward, fought east of St. Quentin on the 29th, and was at Montmirail on September 6, where it took part in the battle of the Marne. After the 26th Brigade was released it reached Laon on the 10th, and on the 12th the entire 13th Division went into position north of Rheims, forming a part of the 7th Army (Von Heeringen). It remained there until the end of the month.

ARTOIS.

3. At the beginning of October the 13th Division was transferred to Artois, where it remained until the end of March, 1916. It fought in the sector Angres-Souchez in October and November, in that of Fromelles-Aubers in November and December.

1915.

ARTOIS.

In March and in June, 1915, the division underwent two heavy attacks at Neuve Chapelle and at Festubert. The battles from the 6th to the 29th of March, 1915, cost the 13th Infantry Regiment 21 officers and 1,301 noncommissioned officers in killed, wounded, and missing. (Official list of Prussian casualties.)

In March the division transferred the 158th Infantry Regiment to the 50th Division, a new formation.

1916.

VERDUN (HILL 304).

1. Relieved at the end of March, 1916, the 13th Division was sent to rest in the Cambrai area.

2. About the 5th of June the division entrained and was sent to the Verdun area by way of Montmédy–Stenay. It went into line in the sector of Hill 304, which it occupied until the month of September.

SOMME.

3. Transferred to the Somme, it took part in the battle on September 12 (south of Vouchavesnes-Cléry sur Somme). It suffered heavy losses there which necessitated its being relieved on September 19.

4. It was quickly reorganized in the Dun area and put back in the sector of Hill 304 (Oct. 10).

1917.

1. The 13th Division remained in line at Hill 304 until the middle of May, 1917. It was then relieved in this area and sent to the Aisne, where it remained at rest for three weeks near Laon.

CHEMIN DES DAMES.

2. On the 9th of June it began to take over the sector of Cerny. It launched an important attack on July 31 upon the Deimling salient, but was not able to retain the ground won. On August 2–3 it attacked again, but without success. The 13th and 15th Infantry Regiments each lost 600 men.

St. Gobain.

3. The 13th Division, very much exhausted, was relieved during the night of August 3–4. It was transferred by railroad to the St. Gobain area without having time to fill up its regiments, and went into line in the Deuillet-Servais sector, which it held from August 10 to September 17.

La Malmaison.

4. It was at rest in the area of Crépy en Laonnois (Sept. 20 to Oct. 11). The division was filled up from the recruit depots of neighboring divisions, although they were not Westphalians (5th Reserve Division, 29th Division, and 103d Division). About the 11th of October it again went into line on the Chemin des Dames east of Laffaux mill. Beginning with October 15, it suffered heavy losses from our artillery preparation. On the 23d it underwent the French attack. (Losses: 47 officers and 1,548 men prisoners, including 2 regimental commanders, a third being killed.) The division may be considered as exhausted at the Mennejean Farm.

5. It was sent to the Sedan area and reorganized. About November 10 it received 1,000 men from Russia as replacements (men at least 35 years of age).

Meuse.

6. About December 18 it occupied the sector of the Bois de Malancourt-Haucourt (and was still there on Jan. 23, 1918).

RECRUITING.

The 13th Division is a Westphalian Division, in addition to contingents from the two principalities of Lippe. These were even mentioned with honor in the German communique of July 1, 1917, a thing which would ordinarily be sufficient to identify the division.

It is manifest, however, that in 1917 the provincial character of the division had been very much changed. The replacements of September (1918 class) were taken from the recruit depots near by (5th Reserved Division, 29th Division, 103d Division), and introduced, especially in the 15th Infantry Regiment, men from Brandenburg, Baden, and Thuringia. Some Westphalians came in October, but they were mostly older men (classes 1892 to 1903 of the Landsturm), coming from Landsturm battalion of the 7th Corps District.

VALUE—1917 ESTIMATE.

In the Somme battle (September, 1916) the 13th Division put up a vigorous defense and did not yield any ground.

On the Aisne (June–July, 1916) its combat value was just as great; it attacked vigorously and put up a stubborn resistance to our counterattacks. Besides that, it is mentioned in the German communiques: September, 1916, for its valor on the Somme, December 20, 1916, and January 25, 1917 (Hill 304); January 29, 1917, the 15th and the 13th Infantry Regiments are praised for their heroic resistance. It may be considered as a good division.

It must be noticed, however, that on October 23, on the Chemin des Dames, in spite of stringent orders to hold its position, the 13th Division put up very little resistance; units surrendered en masse with their officers.

The 55th Infantry Regiment is probably only of mediocre worth since its reconstruction after the battle of Malmaison.

1918.

1. The division was relieved from the Verdun front about February 6 and went to rest in the vicinity of Arlon, and after February 15 at Valenciennes and Mons. It marched to the Somme front in four nights, and then rested at Clary for two days.

BATTLE OF PICARDY.

2. On March 21 it was in reserve of the 18th Division, during the advance toward Roisel. It was partially engaged on the 22d and 23d north of Marquaix and Peronne. Two days later the entire division was engaged north of the Somme, and on the 28th it passed to reserve near Morlancourt until April 4, when it returned to the battle front for four days, fighting at Dernancourt. Again the division retired to the second line, and was relieved on the 11th. The losses of the division in this offensive were about 40 per cent of its effectives.

AVRE.

3. After 10 days' rest (near Maricourt-Carnoy until the 18th and Caix until the 22d) during which it was reconstituted with returned wounded and 1919 recruits, it returned to line on the Avre (Castel) on April 23. The division executed attacks on Hill 82 and on Hailles on April 24. Other local attacks occurred on May 2 and 14. It was relieved on May 18. A further draft of 1,300 men was received on May 3.

THIRD BATTLE OF THE SOMME.

4. The division rested near Montdidier in June, probably at Moreuil. On July 1 it relieved the 77th Reserve Division northeast of Villers–Bretonneux. The British attack on the Somme threw the division back on Mericourt with a loss of 2,769 prisoners. On August 12 it was withdrawn.

5. It was in reserve near Mericourt during the middle of August. On the 24th it was reengaged east of Albert (Bazentin). About the 30th it was withdrawn. The total loss in prisoners was 3,400.

ALSACE.

6. The division was moved to Alsace for a rest. It entrained at Schlestadt on September 29 and was moved by Strasbourg, Metz, and Sedan.

BATTLE OF THE ARGONNE.

7. It went into line at Monthois–Challerange on September 30, remaining until October 3, when it went into support near Morel until the 8th, when it fell back toward Bourcq.

8. It was in support between Landres-Saint George and Bantheville on the 15th. It was engaged on the American front on the 16th in the Nantheville region. It was in line until the 30th, when it passed to reserve, but returned to line on the 2d. It continued to hold a sector until the armistice. An epidemic of Spanish fever greatly reduced the number of effectives in all the regiments. The 13th Regiment had less than 200 effectives at the end of October.

VALUE—1918 ESTIMATE.

The division was rated as a first-class division. Its performance was excellent in the March offensive, but after that it took no special part in any offensive. At the armistice the division had been used up through losses and sickness.

13th Reserve Division.
COMPOSITION.

	1914 Brigade.	1914 Regiment.	1915 Brigade.	1915 Regiment.	1916 Brigade.	1916 Regiment.	1917 Brigade.	1917 Regiment.	1918 Brigade.	1918 Regiment.
Infantry	25 Res. 28 Res. 7 Res. Jag. Btn.	13 Res. 56 Res. 39 Res. 57 Res.	25 Res. 28 Res. 7 Res. Jag. Btn.	13 Res. 56 Res. 39 Res. 57 Res. Jag. Btn.	28 Res. 7 Res. Jag. Btn.	13 Res. 39 Res. 57 Res. Jag. Btn.	28 Res.	13 Res. 39 Res. 57 Res.	28 Res.	13 Res. 39 Res. 57 Res.
Cavalry	5 Res. Hus. Rgt.		5 Res. Hus. Rgt.		5 Res. Hus. Rgt. (2 Sqns.).		3 Sqn. 5 Res. Hus. Rgt.		3 Sqn. 5 Res. Hus. Rgt.	
Artillery	13 Res. F. A. Rgt. (6 Btries.).		13 Res. F. A. Rgt.		13 Res. F. A. Rgt. (9 Btries.).		(?) Art. Command: 13 Res. F. A. Rgt. (9 Btries.).		100 Art. Command: 13 Res. F. A. Rgt. 99 Ft. A. Btn. 738 Light Am. Col. 812 Light Am. Col.	
Engineers and Liaisons.			2 Pion. Btn. No. 7: Res. Co. 7 Pions. 13 Res. Pont. Engs. 13 Res. Tel. Detch.		2 Pion. Btn. No. 7: 4 Co. 7 Pions. 213 T. M. Co. 13 Pont. Engs. 13 Tel. Detch.		(313) Pion. Btn.: 4 Co. 7 Pions. 287 Pion. Co. 213 T. M. Co. Tel. Detch.		313 Pion. Btn.: 4 Co. 7 Pions. 287 Pion. Co. 213 T. M. Co. 7 Searchlight Section. 413 Signal Command: 413 Tel. Detch. 164 Wireless Detch.	
Medical and Veterinary.							507 Ambulance Co. 33 Res. Field Hospital. 145 Field Hospital. Vet. Hospital.		507 Ambulance Co. 33 Res. Field Hospital. 34 Res. Field Hospital. 413 Vet. Hospital.	
Transports							712 M. T. Col.		712 M. T. Col.	
Attached									47 Art. Observation Section. 73 Balloon Sqn. 216 Pigeon Loft. 19 Reconnoissance Flight. 74 Antiaircraft Section. 128 Ft. A. Btn. Elements attached June, 1918.	

HISTORY.

(7th Corps District—Westphalia.)

1914.

At the beginning of the war the 13th Reserve Division and the 14th Reserve Division formed the 7th Reserve Corps.

MAUBEUGE-AISNE.

1. Assigned to the 2d German Army, the 13th Reserve Division arrived at Liège immediately after the city and the forts were taken (Aug. 14); reached Namur on the 25th, and took part in the siege and taking of Maubeuge. When it was released from this place it was quickly transferred to the front north of the Aisne; fought in the neighborhood of Pontavert-Craonne on September 15; fought near Cerny on the 16th, and took its position on the front of Braye–Cerny en Laonnois at the end of September.

2. On November 3 some elements of the division were engaged at Vailly.

3. The division occupied the sector of Braye en Laonnois until October, 1915.

1915.

1. January–October, 1915, the division occupied the sector Braye en Laonnois–Cerny.

2. At the end of October the 13th Reserve Division was relieved in the Laon area and transferred to the north, between Charleroi and Valenciennes. After a period of training in November and December, it entrained, about December 25, for the Verdun front.

1916.

1. At the beginning of January, 1916, the division was concentrated in the neighborhood of Damvillers (right bank of the Meuse). In January and February it was occupied in preparations for an attack.

VERDUN.

2. Beginning with February 21 some elements were engaged near Haumont, near Haumont wood. It took part in battles, from February 23 until March 10, in the region of Samogneux (sector of Vacherauville-Haudremont and Cote du Poivre). It lost 51 per cent of its infantry there.

3. From the middle of March to the 24th of October it occupied the same sector of Haudremont (west of Douaumont), and only took part in a few local engagements. It underwent the French attack on October 24 and suffered heavily.

4. Until December it held the sector included between the road of Louvemont-Bras and the Chaufour wood. It was relieved between December 8 and 12 and sent to rest in the Marville-Longuyon area.

5. Transferred to Champagne (Dec. 22–24), it went into line east of Rheims (Nogent l'Abbesse) about the 29th.

1917.

1. The division held the sector at Rheims (east of La Pomelle) until May 20, 1917.

CHAMPAGNE.

2. Concentrated, at this date, in the neighborhood of Epoye, it relieved the exhausted 242d Division at Cornillet (south of Nauroy). It went into action between Mont Cornillet and Mont Haut (about the end of May).

3. Between June 8 and 15 it returned into line in its former sector east of Rheims (south of Cernay), where it made several surprise attacks.

VERDUN.

4. Relieved about the end of August from the Rheims front, it was sent, after a few days of rest, to the right bank of the Meuse. On September 24 it attacked east of Beaumont, in the Bois le Chaume, and suffered very heavy losses. It made another attack on October 10 in the same sector, which it held until October 12–13.

5. It was sent to rest (Briey area) in the second half of October. In November it appeared on the front east of Verdun, where it was speedily relieved.

RECRUITING.

The division is recruited from Westphalia. In the course of 1917, however, a great number of its replacements came from other districts than Westphalia (9th, 10th, 11th Corps Districts).

VALUE—1917 ESTIMATE.

The 13th Reserve Division appears to be of mediocre quality.

It suffered heavy losses at Verdun. It showed very little brilliance there. During the French attack of October 24, 1916, it offered little resistance to the hostile troops.

On the Rheims front (January to May, 1917) it did not take part in any operation. Quite a large number of men who were captured in the course of raids in this sector surrendered with little resistance.

However, the 13th Reserve Division did not furnish a single prisoner or deserter during its second stay southeast of Rheims (from June 15 to the beginning of September), and on the Verdun front it showed itself quite active (September to October).

1918.

1. The division was relieved in the Avrocourt wood sector by the Bavarian Ersatz Division on the night of April 5–6 and went into rest billets at Villers near Montmedy. On the 16th it entrained at a station near Montmedy and traveled via Carignan–Sedan–Charleville–Givet–Dinant–Namur–Charleroi – Ath – Melle – Ghent – Deyuze to Thielt, where it detrained at 1 a. m. on April 19. After 10 days' rest at Coolscamp the division marched to Getsberg, and was to have gone into line in the Dixmude sector on April 22, but was suddenly entrained and moved via Roulers to Beythem. From there it marched to the Ledeghem area and rested until April 24, when it marched into line northwest of Wytschaete via Menin–Wervecq and Comines.

YPRES.

2. The division was engaged in the attack on Voormezeele on April 25. After three days' heavy fighting it was relieved by the 49th Reserve Division. After a few days in the second line the division came back and relieved the 49th Reserve Division. It remained in line until May 11. From the 11th to the 28th the division rested out of line. It was again engaged on May 28 southwest of Merris. It was relieved about June 12.

MERRIS.

3. The division went to rest in the area east of Bruges and later northwest of Ghent. It returned to its former sector west of Merris on July 9, relieving the 4th Bavarian Division. It held the sector until July 27 when its heavy losses at Meteren caused its relief by the 4th Division. Between the 27th and August 18 the division rested in the Douai area.

YPRES–BELGIUM.

4. In line the 18th–19th, it relieved the 35th Division in the sector east of Merckem. Here the division continued until September 29, when it was withdrawn from the line north of Staden after the loss of 1,500 prisoners and severe casualties. It rested two weeks, and on October 14 returned to the battle front at Cortemarck. It fought

until the 20th, when it retired for 10 days' rest in rear of the line. On the 30th it was reengaged near Deynze. The German communique of November 1 and 2 mentioned the 57th and 13th Reserve Regiments for their good work. The division was in line until the armistice. It was last identified at Nazareth on November 3.

VALUE—1918 ESTIMATE.

The 13th Reserve Division was rated as a first-class division. In 1918 it was almost wholly engaged in Belgium, taking a prominent part in the Armentiers offensive in April, and in the defense in October.

18th Landwehr Division.
COMPOSITION.

	1915 Brigade.	1915 Regiment.	1916 Brigade.	1916 Regiment.	1917 Brigade.	1917 Regiment.	1918 Brigade.	1918 Regiment.
Infantry	61 Res. / 60 Ldw.	60 Res. Cassel Landst Btn. (XI/2). Mayence Landst Btn. (XVIII/17). 60 Ldw. 71 Ldw.	61 Res. 60 Mixed Ldw.	15 Ldw. 82 Ldw. 60 Ldw. 71 Ldw. 8 Jäg. Btn.	60 Ldw.	15 Ldw. 60 Ldw. 82 Ldw.	60 Ldw.	15 Ldw. 60 Ldw. 82 Ldw.
Cavalry				5 Sqn. 6 Dragoon Regt.		5 Sqn. 6 Dragoon Regt.	5 Sqn. 6 Dragoon Regt.	
Artillery	1 Ers. Abt. 25 F. A. Regt. 1 Ers. Abt. 81 F. A. Regt.		1 Ers. Abt. of the 25 and 84 F. A. Regt. 2 Ers. Btry. (27 F. A. Regt.).		Art. command: 13 Ldw. F. A. Regt.		13 Ldw. F. A. Regt. 1414 Light Am. Col.	
Engineers and Liaisons.	1 Ldw. Pion. Co. (10 C. Dist.).		1 Ldw. Pion. Co. (10 and 15 C. Dist.). 313 T. M. Co.		413 Pion. Btn.: 1 Ldw. Co. 10 Corps Pions. 1 Ldw. Co. 15 Corps. Pions. 313 T. M. Co. 513 Tel. Detch.		413 Pion Btn.: 1 Ldw. Co. 10 C. Dist. Pions. 1 Ldw. Co. 15 C. Dist. Pions. 313 T. M. Co. 207 Searchlight Section. 513 Signal Command: 513 Tel. Detch. 22 Wireless Detch.	
Medical and Veterinary.					216 Ambulance Co. 102 Res. Field Hospital. 16 Ldw. Field Hospital. 513 Vet. Hospital.		216 Ambulance Co. 102 Res. Field Hospital. 513 Vet. Hospital.	
Transports.					782 M. T. Col. 809 M. T. Col.		782 M. T. Col.	
Attached.	115 Landst. Inf. Regt.		44 Art. Survey Section. 44 Labor Btn. 12 C. Dist. Landst. Btn. No. 1.					

HISTORY.

(15th Landwehr Regiment: 7th Corps District—Westphalia. 60th Landwehr Regiment: 21st Corps District—Lorraine. 82d Landwehr Regiment: 11th Corps District—Thuringia.)

1915.

LORRAINE.

1. The 13th Landwehr Division was formed in Lorraine about the middle of May, 1915. It was made up at this time of the 61st Reserve Brigade (60th Reserve Landsturm Battalions, Cassel and Mayence) and of the 60th Landwehr Brigade (the 60th Landwehr Regiment, and the 61st Landwehr Regiment). These elements were already in line on the Lorraine front before the formation of the division. The 71st Landwehr Regiment had been sent on August 10, 1914 (with the 82d Landwehr Regiment) to Strassburg as a garrison. The 60th Landwehr Regiment, beginning on August 11, was guarding the railroads of Lower Alsace. The 60th Infantry Regiment had been engaged in August in the Vosges.

2. The 13th Landwehr Division occupied the sector between Abaucourt and the Bezange woods from May, 1915, to February, 1917. Except for a few raids, it remained on the defensive during this long period.

3. At the end of June, 1915, the 82d Landwehr Regiment replaced the 60th Reserve Regiment.

In December the 15th Landwehr Regiment, which had formed the garrison of Thionville at the outbreak of the war, and was in the Vosges after a stay near Morhange, replaced the two battalions of Landsturm (which had been formed into the 115th Landsturm Regiment in July) sent to Serbia.

1916.

LORRAINE.

1. In 1916 the division held the sector Abaucourt–Bezange wood.

In August the 9th Jäger Battalion entrained for Galicia.

2. On September 15, 1916, the staff of the 61st Reserve Brigade and the 71st Landwehr Regiment were transferred to the 215th Division, a new formation. The 13th Landwehr Division then received its definite organization: 15th Landwehr Regiment, 60th Landwehr Regiment, 82d Landwehr Regiment (4 battalions each).

1917.

LORRAINE.

1. Relieved on the Lorraine front in the beginning of February, 1917, the 13th Landwehr Division was concentrated in the Chateau Salins front, entrained about the middle of February and sent by way of Metz–Longuyon–Montmedy–Sedan–Laon to the neighborhood of La Fère. It detrained at Versigny. One battalion was taken from each of its regiments to form the 328th Landwehr Regiment, destined to be a part of the 25th Landwehr Division.

2. Until March 18 the 13th Landwehr Division did work along the line Moy–La Fère–Fresne, where the German withdrawal was stopped.

FORET DE ST. GOBAIN.

3. On March 19, placed on the east bank of the Ailette, it covered the retreat of the 45th Reserve Division, and at the beginning of April occupied the sector Fresnes–Prémontré, where it was relieved about the 1st of May.

OISE LA FERE.

4. After a fortnight's rest in the forest of St. Gobain, it went back into line on the front south of Alaincourt north of Deuillet (May 16). It occupied the sector of the left bank of the Oise until the offensive of March, 1918.

VALUE—1917 ESTIMATE.

The 13th Landwehr Division is apparently considered by the German High Command as fit only to occupy a quiet sector (February, 1918).

Shock troops have been formed from its regiments, but the men appear to have been trained for patrol work rather than for making genuine assaults.

1918.

PICARDY.

1. The division was relieved about March 24. It passed the night at Versigny, and on the 25th reached Laon, passing by Crepy and Aulnois.

LAON.

2. On the 26th the division came into line south of Laon, relieving the 75th Reserve Division. It was engaged about Chevregny, Chavignon, and Urcil until May 27.

3. It did not advance in the Aisne offensive. The attacking divisions passed through, and it was withdrawn and transported to Lorraine at the beginning of June.

BATTLE OF ST. MIHIEL.

It entered the line in the Woevre in the Combres Les Eparges sector about the 1st of June and continued to hold the front until the armistice. In the American attack on the St. Mihiel salient the division lost about 800 men, principally prisoners. It was pushed back to Champlon and Marcheville, which sector it held until November 11.

VALUE—1918 ESTIMATE.

The division was rated as a fourth-class division. It was an inferior sector-holding unit of mediocre morale.

14th Division.
COMPOSITION.

	1914 Brigade	1914 Regiment	1915 Brigade	1915 Regiment	1916 Brigade	1916 Regiment	1917 Brigade	1917 Regiment	1918 Brigade	1918 Regiment
Infantry	27. 79.	16. 53. 56. 57.	27. 79.	16. 53. 56. 57.	79.	16. 56. 57.	79.	16. 56. 57.	79.	16. 56. 57.
Cavalry	16 Uhlan Rgt. (3 Sqns.)				4 Sqn. 16 Uhlan Rgt.		4 Sqn. 16 Uhlan Rgt.		5 Sqn. 16 Uhlan Rgt.	
Artillery	14 Brig.: 7 F. A. Rgt. 43 F. A. Rgt.		14 Brig.: 7 F. A. Rgt. 43 F. A. Rgt.		14 Brig.: 7 F. A. Rgt. 43 F. A. Rgt. 8 Trench Gun Detch.		14 Art. Command: 43 F. A. Rgt.		14 Art. Command: 43 F. A. Rgt. 1 Abt. 21 Ft. A. Rgt. (1 and 3 Btries) 1216 Light Am. Col. 1218 Light Am. Col. 1222 Light Am. Col.	
Engineers and Liaisons.			1 Pion. Btn. No. 7: Field Co. 7 Pions. 14 Pont. Engrs. 14 Tel. Detch.		1 Pion. Btn. No. 7: 2 Co. 7 Pions. 1 Co. 7 Pions. 14 T. M. Co. 14 Pont. Engrs. 14 Tel. Detch.		122 Pion. Btn.: 3 Co. 7 Pions. 5 Co. 7 Pions. 14 T. M. Co. 256 Searchlight Section. 14 Tel. Detch.		124 Pion. Btn.: 3 Co. 7 Pions. 5 Co. 7 Pions. 14 T. M. Co. 218 Searchlight Section. 14 Signal Command. 14 Tel.-Detch. 14 Wireless Detch.	
Medical and Veterinary.							18 Ambulance Co. 66 Field Hospital. 71 Field Hospital. Vet. Hospital.		18 Ambulance Co. 66 Field Hospital. 71 Field Hospital. 14 Vet. Hospital.	
Transports.							547 M. T. Col.		547 M. T. Col.	
Attached.					68 M. G. S. S. Detch.					

HISTORY.

(7th Corps District—Westphalia.)

1914.

FRANCE.

1. The 14th Division was mobilized at the outbreak of the war with two of its three peace-time brigades (27th and 79th Brigades) and sent its 28th Brigade to the 7th Reserve Corps (14th Reserve Division). The 27th Brigade (Cologne) was immediately sent against Liége, where it attacked with the five other brigades of five different army corps. On August 13 the entire division was before Liége, where the other division of the 7th Army Corps was on the 14th. With this latter division it formed part of the 2d Army (Von Buelow), of which it formed the right wing. It entered Belgium by way of Wavre and Nievelles, was engaged west of Charleroi, entered France by the valley of the Oise and took part in the battle of the Marne, at Petit Morin, southeast of Montmirail.

2. At the end of the retirement it stopped at the Chemin des Dames; was sent a short time afterwards to the area north of Rheims, from which place it was transferred, at the time of the race to the sea, to Lille, with the entire 7th Army Corps (at the beginning of October).

ARTOIS.

3. Beginning with November, 1914, it occupied different sectors around Lille, La Bassée, and Lens until the spring of 1916.

1915.

ARTOIS.

1. The losses of the 14th Division were not very important during the first two years of the war. However, in March, 1915, and in June, 1915, it underwent two strong British attacks at Neuve Chapelle and Festubert, which inflicted heavy losses upon it, following which it had to be reenforced. From March 7 to March 12 the 3d Battalion of the 16th Infantry Regiment had no less than 589 casualties, 16 of whom were officers (official list of casualties).

1916.

1. The 14th Division was relieved at the end of 1916 from the Artois sector and, after a long period of rest near Tournai, was transferred to the Verdun area.

VERDUN.

2. In June and July it occupied the Mort Homme sector.

3. At the end of July it crossed over to the right bank of the Meuse and held the sector of Thiaumont until August 25, where it suffered heavily.

4. It then returned to the left bank of the Meuse (Cumiéres) after a short rest. It was again sent to the rear area about the middle of October.

5. When the French attack of October 24 broke out the 14th Division went into action north of Douaumont on the 27th.

6. On December 16 it suffered the shock of the French offensive and had to be retired at the end of the month, very much weakened (65 per cent casualties).

1917.

1. After a month behind the Verdun front the 14th Division once more took over its former sector at the beginning of February, 1917, on the left bank of the Meuse, north of Chattancourt (Cumières, Mort Homme).

2. Relieved between April 14 and 20, it entrained between the 21st and the 25th at Sivry sur Meuse and Vilosnes and was transferred to the Aisne.

CHEMIN DES DAMES.

3. After a few days of rest in the Marchais area, at Sissonne Camp, it was brought back to the front, and on May 5 reenforced the sector between Ailles and Hurtebise, which was being held by guard divisions very much weakened by our attacks.

4. From May 7 to 12 it replaced the 1st Guard Division in line (west of Hurtebise) and then was sent to rest east of Laon. It remained in reserve, not taking part in any action as an entire division.

5. After a rest in the area northwest of Liesse, it came back into line in the sector Ailles–Hurtebise (June 20, 21) and there, on the 25th, underwent the French attack. It lost the Cave of the Dragon; the 57th Infantry Regiment lost 191 prisoners.

6. On July 26 the 14th Division attacked between Hurtebise and La Bovelle. Its efforts to regain the positions lost were futile. (On Aug. 1 the 1st Battalion of the 56th Infantry Regiment was commanded by a first lieutenant (document).

7. At the end of July, very much weakened by its losses, it was sent to rest in the Vervins area and reconstituted (principally by men of the 1918 class from the Bevelloo Camp). Between December 21, 1916, and August, 1917, no less than 326 men came as replacements to the 9th Company of the 56th Infantry Regiment.

8. On September 17 the 14th Division came back into line in the Laffaux area, underwent our attacks on October 23, suffered heavy losses from our preparation fire, and left to the French the greater part of its artillery and numerous prisoners (1,763 men and 43 officers).

9. An eye witness reckons the number of infantrymen left after the battle at not more than 1,400 (letter). It was filled up with returned wounded, men borrowed from Landsturm battalions of the 11th Corps District and men coming from the Russian front.

10. After being thus reorganized, in the Vervins area, the division was sent to Haye in the Flirey sector, where it was engaged from the 5th of November on. It was relieved January 13, 1918.

RECRUITING.

The 14th Division is recruited principally from the Rhine districts of the 7th Corps District, and it is for this reason that it is called "Troops from the Lower Rhine" in the German communiques of July 27, 1917.

This region, very populous, suffices for its own recruiting. It is to be noticed, however, that in the course of the year 1917, in spite of the growing tendency to emphasize the sectional character of the large units, the 14th Division received replacement troops from other districts besides the seventh; in May, men from the 6th Corps District trained in the fourth (class of 1918); in August, men from the third, fourth, and eighth (class of 1918); in October, Pomeranians from the 22d Landwehr Division. The seventh district hardly counts except in the replacements of October, with convalescents and men from the Westphalian Landsturm battalions. The heavy losses suffered since December, 1916 would explain, to a certain extent, this falling off in numbers. It may also be that the morale of an industrial region such as Westphalia had been sufficiently shattered to make a mixture advisable.

VALUE—1917 ESTIMATE.

During the French offensive of December 15, 1916, the 14th Division behaved very well.

South of Ailles (at the end of June, 1917) it attempted to regain lost ground with great tenacity.

It put up a strong resistance to the attacks of October 23.

"The 14th Division is a good division. It has just been withdrawn from a quiet sector to take part in a war of movement. It is a division destined to attack." (Jan. 18, 1918—note from the 1st French Army.)

1918.

1. The 14th Division was relieved in the Flirey sector (east of St. Mihiel) by the 78th Reserve Division during the night of January 13–14.

PICARDY.

2. After having gone through some maneuvers in the region of Mars la Tour the division entrained at that place (also Chambley) on March 27 and detrained at St. Quentin on the 29th. It remained in support for a few days and then reenforced the battle front west of Moreuil (northwest of Montdidier) on April 4. The same day attacked Rouvrel, but could make no progress. It suffered severely, and was withdrawn on the 11th, very much exhausted, to rest in the region of Bohain, where it was reconstituted, and went into intensive training for open warfare.

AISNE.

3. On May 27 the division entrained at Bohain, and detrained to the west of Laon, where it assembled in the forest of Coucy, and followed the offensive of the Aisne in the second line. It crossed the Aisne on May 30, and marched via Crécy au Mont to Hautebraye. Its objective was Vic sur Aisne, but it was completely checked with heavy losses. It was withdrawn about June 11.

4. On June 14 it relieved the 51st Reserve Division near St. Bandry (southwest of Soissons). It was badly shattered in the fighting that followed and was withdrawn about July 2.

5. On July 16 the division reinforced the front near Osly–Courtil (north of the Aisne— west of Soissons); it was withdrawn about the 26th of August.

CHAMPAGNE:

6. During the night of September 18–19 the division relieved the 3d Guard Division southeast of Aubérive; it was withdrawn about October 12 and went to rest in the area north of Rethel.

SOLESMES.

7. The division marched by easy stages, and entered line near Englefontaine (east of Solesmes) during the night of October 25–26. It was still in line at the time of the signing of the armistice.

VALUE—1918 ESTIMATE.

The 14th Division is rated as being in the second of four classes. Despite its two training periods (March and May), it did not distinguish itself on the offensive, being decidedly checked at Moreuil and Hautebraye. On the defensive, however, it fought tenaciously; it suffered heavy losses, the regiments being reduced to three companies. There is evidence supporting the view that there were not more than 1,800 rifles in the division the end of October.

14th Reserve Division.

COMPOSITION.

	1914 Brigade	1914 Regiment	1915 Brigade	1915 Regiment	1916 Brigade	1916 Regiment	1917 Brigade	1917 Regiment	1918 Brigade	1918 Regiment
Infantry	27 Res. 28.	16 Res. 53 Res. 39 Fus. 159.	27 Res. 28.	16 Res. 53 Res. 39 Fus. 159.	27 Res.	16 Res. 53 Res. 159.	27 Res.	16 Res. 53 Res. 159.	27 Res.	159. 16 Res. 53 Res.
Cavalry	8 Res. Hus. Rgt. (3 Sqns.).		8 Res. Hus. Rgt.		5 Res. Hus. Rgt. (? Sqns.).		1 Sqn. Res. Uhlan Rgt. (?).		1 Sqn. 5 Res. Hus. Rgt.	
Artillery	14 Res. F. A. Rgt. (6 Btries.).		14 Res. F. A. Rgt.		14 Res. F. A. Rgt. (8 Btries.).		(?) Art. Command: 14 Res. F. A.	Rgt. (9 Btries.).	102 Art. Command: 14 Res. F. A. Rgt. 1 Abt. 16 Ft. A. Btn. (1, 3, and 4 Btries.). 1169 Light Am. Col. 1170 Light Am. Col. 1193 Light Am. Col.	
Engineers and Liaisons	1 and 2 Res. Cos. 2 Pion. Btn. No. 7.		1 and 2 Res. Cos. 2 Pion. Btn. No. 7. 14 Res. Pont. Engrs. 14 Res. Tel. Detch.		1 and 2 Res. Cos. 2 Pion. Btn. No. 7. 282 Pion. Co. 214 T. M. Co. 14 Res. Pont. Engrs. 14 Res. Tel. Detch.		314 Pion. Btn.: 1 res. Co. 7 Pions. 2 Res. Co. 7 Pions. 214 T. M. Co. 414 Tel. Detch.		314 Pion. Btn.: 1 Res. Co. 7 Pions. 2 Res. Co. 7 Pions. 66 Searchlight Section. 414 Signal Command: 414 Tel. Detch. 150 Wireless Detch.	
Medical and Veterinary							521 Ambulance Co. 34 Res. Field Hospital. 35 Res. Field Hospital. (?) 414 Vet. Hospital.		521 Ambulance Co. 35 Res. Field Hospital. 38 Res. Field Hospital. 414 Vet. Hospital.	
Transport							M. T. Col.		713 M. T. Col.	

Attached	Electric Power Detch.	6 Bav. F. A. Rgt. 410 Ft. A. Btn. 2 Res. Ft. A. Btn. 19 Res. Ft. A. Btn. 74 Art. Observation Section. 23 Sound Ranging Section. 49 Balloon Sqn. 265 Reconnaissance Flight. (Elements attached, July, 1918; from German document.).

HISTORY.

(7TH CORPS DISTRICT—WESTPHALIA.)

1914.

BELGIUM.

1. The 14th Reserve Division belongs, like the 13th Reserve Division, to the 7th Reserve Corps. It was formed from the Reserve Brigade at the Senne Camp and from one brigade, surplus, of the 14th active division (28th Brigade). One regiment of this brigade, the 39th Fusiliers, from Dusseldorf, appeared in front of Liege on August 8, while the rest of the division was being assembled at Dueren.

MAUBEUGE.

2. Entering into Belgium by way of Vereiers, on August 16, the 14th Reserve Division then formed a part of the 2d German Army. It was in front of Namur on August 21, with the reserve corps of the Guard and the 11th Corps. After Namur was taken it went to invest Maubeuge with the 13th Division.

AISNE.

3. Set free on September 7 by the fall of this place, it left on the 10th to strengthen the Aisne front. About the 13th of September it occupied the heights around Cerny-en-Laonnois.

1915.

AISNE.

1. The division held the sector between Cerny and Craonne (north of Paissy) until the beginning of November, 1915. In March it gave the 39th Fusiliers to the 50th Division, a new formation.

2. About November 2 it was transferred to the Charleroi area where it rested and had further training.

3. At the end of December it was sent north of Verdun, near Romagne sous les Cotes.

1916.

VERDUN.

1. In January and until February 20, 1916, it was employed in works preparatory to the attack (Damvillers area).

2. On February 23 it was in line on the right bank of the Meuse. It took part, from the very beginning, in the German offensive against Verdun, attacked Samogneux, Poivre Hill, and the Hill of Talou and Vacherauville. (On the 3d of April, the 11th Company of the 16th Reserve Infantry Regiment had already received more than 118 men as replacements. On May 14, at least 153 had been sent to the 8th Company of the 53d Infantry Reserve Regiment.)

3. Until the end of December the 14th Reserve Division occupied this sector (of the Meuse (Champneuville) at Poivre Hill). On December 15, it underwent the French counteroffensive, to the west of Douaumont, which caused it to suffer very heavy losses. Then it took over the sector of Hill 344 for one week.

4. The division was relieved from December 22–25, concentrated in the Damvillers area and transferred to Champagne where it was reorganized.

1917.

CHAMPAGNE.

1. On January 1, 1917, it went into line north of Prunay and remained in this sector (quiet) until October 22–25.

2. In May the division sent some of its elements as reenforcements to units attacked at Cornillet and at Monthaut.

FORET DE COUCY.

3. It entrained on October 26 at Chatelet and was transferred to the area of Cerny-en-Laonnois. On the 28th it was interpolated between two divisions (the 10th Division and the 27th Division) on the front Bassoles-Fresnes, in the upper Coucy wood, which it occupied until the middle of February, 1918.

The 14th Reserve Division is recruited from Westphalia. As it suffered very little in 1917, the division probably did not receive in the course of that year the heterogeneous replacements which were sent—perhaps intentionally—to the other Westphalian divisions.

VALUE—1917 ESTIMATE.

The 14th Reserve Division did not participate in any important action in the course of the year 1917. It was thoroughly reorganized during its long stay in Champagne. It is composed for the most part of young men (20 to 30 years of age) and has suffered but few losses (a slight proportion of the 1918 class).

Its valor has not been put to any serious test since Verdun. It appears capable of serious effort.

1918.

LAON.

1. The division was withdrawn from line in the St. Gobain region and went to rest in the neighborhood of Laon. It was trained in open warfare during the weeks that followed.

· 2. On March 16 some equipment belonging to the 53d Reserve Regiment was found west of Laon, near Champs, but it is unlikely that the division was in line there; it was not identified in any other way. It was identified in line in that region, however, on the 6th of April. It was withdrawn on May 29.

AISNE.

3. The division went immediately to the Aisne battle front, where it was identified by prisoners in the Vierzy sector (south of Soissons) on May 31. It was withdrawn about the 10th of June and rested for a month in the region of Fére en Tardenois.

4. On July 8 it relieved the 47th Reserve Division near Chavigny (south of Soissons). The 47th Reserve Division relieved part of the 14th Reserve Division on the 12th, and the 14th Reserve seems to have come back in its entirety on the 16th. During this fighting, the division lost more than 1,500 prisoners. It was withdrawn on July 20, and went to rest and refit in the neighborhood of Mulhouse.

NESLE.

5. The division entrained on the 22d of August at Birnsweiler and traveled via Saarbruecken–Trier–Herbesthal–Liége–Namur–Charleroi–Condé, detraining at Tincourt the night of August 23–24. On the 26th it reinforced the front near Thilloy (southwest of Nesle). It was withdrawn on September 9, after losing some 1,300 prisoners, and went to rest in Alsace in the neighborhood of Oltingen.

CHAMPAGNE.

6. On October 9, it reinforced the front near Orfeuil (southwest of Vouziers).

7. On October 28, the division was moved eastward to Boult, so as to help to hinder the American advance. It was still in line on November 11.

VALUE—1918 ESTIMATE.

After the division's participation in the battle of the Aisne, Lieut. Gen. Loeb, its commander, was awarded the order Pour le Mérite. Again, the German communiqué of September 2 spoke highly of the fighting of the 56th Reserve Regiment. A captured regimental order mentions the fact that there had been many cases of the grippe. The division suffered such severe losses that most of the men from the 47th Reserve Division, dissolved in July, were sent to it. Nevertheless, the battalions were reduced to three companies in August. Despite its subsequent heavy losses (the 159th Regiment was reduced to 600 men, and the other regiment to about the same size), the division is still considered as being first class.

14th Landwehr Division.

COMPOSITION.

	1915 Brigade	1915 Regiment	1916 Brigade	1916 Regiment	1917 Brigade	1917 Regiment	1918 Brigade	1918 Regiment
Infantry	21 Ldw.	10 Ldw. 38 Ldw. 101 Ldw. 103 Ldw.	21 Ldw. 46 Ldw.	10 Ldw. 38 Ldw. 101 Ldw. 103 Ldw.	21 Ldw.	10 Ldw. 38 Ldw. 346.	....	337 (2 Btn.).
Cavalry	....		93 Cav. Regt.		2 Sqn. 6 Cuirassier Rgt. 2 Sqn. 93 Cav. Rgt.		1 Sqn. 17 Uhlan Rgt. 2 Sqn. 17 Uhlan Rgt. 1 Body Hus. Rgt.	
Artillery	82 F. A. Rgt. (1 Ers.-Abt.).		217 F. A. Rgt. 908 F. A. Bttry.		Art. Command: 217 F. A. Rgt.		253 Ldw. F. A. Rgt. (3d Btry. 1st Abt.	
Engineers and Liaisons.	....		1 Ers. Co. 28 Pions. 314 T. M. Co.		(414) Pion. Btn.: 2 Ldw. Co. 3 C. Dist. Pions. 1 Ers. Co. 28 Pions. 314 T. M. Co. 338 Searchlight Section. 514 Tel. Detch.		272 Searchlight Section. 514 Tel. Detch.	
Medical and Veterinary.	....				218 Ambulance Co. 143 Field Hospital. 257 Field Hospital. 170 Vet. Hospital.		257 Field Hospital. 167 Field Hospital.	
Transports	....				473 M. T. Col.		....	
Odd units	....		155 Cyclist Co.		155 Cyclist Co.		....	
Attached	....		10 Landst. Inf. Rgt.				....	

HISTORY.

(346th Infantry Regiment: 5th Corps District—Posen. 10th and 38th Landwehr Regiments: 6th Corps District—Silesia.)

1915.

RUSSIA–POLAND.

1. The 14th Landwehr Division appeared in Poland about the middle of July, 1915, in the Sierpec area.

It appeared to be made up at this time of the 21st Mixed Brigade of Landwehr (10th and 38th Landwehr Regiments, taken from the Breslau Corps), elements of the Graudenz Corps, the 46th Landwehr Brigade (Pfeil Brigade—101st and 103d Landwehr Regiments). At all events, the 14th Landwehr Division does not appear to have received its complete coherence until the stabilization of the front which followed the summer offensive against the Russians.

SMORGONI.

2. The division then took position in the Smorgoni sector (September). It remained there until February, 1918.

1916.

1. In 1916 the division remained in the Smorgoni sector.

1917.

1. In 1917 the division remained in the Smorgoni sector.

2. About the month of April, 1917, the 101st and 103d Landwehr Regiments (Saxon) were taken from the 14th Landwehr Division and assigned to the 46th Landwehr Division, a new formation on the Eastern Front. They were replaced in the 14th Landwehr Division by the 346th Regiment, which formerly belonged to the 87th Division.

VALUE—1917 ESTIMATE.

The division is of mediocre value.

1918.

MINSK.

1. At the beginning of 1918 the 14th Landwehr Division was still on the Smorgoni front, which it left about the middle of February to march farther toward the east. "We are advancing right into Russia," wrote a man of the 38th Landwehr Regiment on March 7. About the middle of March the division went into cantonment in the vicinity of Orcha and Kochanovo on the Minsk–Smolensk Railroad. It was still there at the end of April.

2. Sent to France during May, the 14th Landwehr Division arrived in Alsace with only two regiments, the 10th and 38th Landwehr Regiments. The division seems to have been dissolved soon afterwards, the 10th Landwehr seeming to be attached to the 301st Division and the 38th Landwehr to the 4th Cavalry Division.

3. The latter part of June the division was reconstituted on the Russian front after the departure of these two regiments for the West, with the following units: 103d Landwehr (from the 46th Landwehr Division), 343d Ersatz (from the 87th Division), and the 3d Landsturm (14th Landwehr Division). On the 30th of July the division was identified in the Orcha region. Late in September the division was identified in the same region.

VALUE.

The division was rated as fourth class.

14th Bavarian Division.

COMPOSITION.

	1916		1917		1918[1]	
	Brigade.	Regiment.	Brigade.	Regiment.	Brigade.	Regiment.
Infantry	8 Bav.	4 Bav. 8 Bav. 29 Bav.	8 Bav.	4 Bav. 8 Bav. 25 Bav.	8 Bav.	4 Bav. 8 Bav. 25 Bav.
Cavalry			4 Sqn. 8 Bav. Light Cav. Rgt.		4 Sqn. 8 Bav. Light Cav. Rgt.	
Artillery	23 Bav. F. A. Rgt.		14 Bav. Art. Command: 23 Bav. F. A. Rgt. (10 Btries.).		14 Bav. Art. Command: 23 Bav. F. A. Rgt.	
Engineers and Liaisons			14 Bav. Pion. Btn. 10 Bav. Res. Pion. Co. 11 Bav. Res. Pion. Co. 14 Bav. T. M. Co. 101 Searchlight Section. 14 Bav. Tel. Detch.		14 Bav. Pion. Btn.: 10 Bav. Res. Pion. Co. 11 Bav. Res. Pion. Co. 101 Searchlight Section. 14 Bav. T. M. Co. 14 Bav. Tel. Detch.	
Medical and Veterinary			14 Bav. Ambulance Co. 1 Bav. Field Hospital. 47 Bav. Field Hospital. Vet. Hospital.		14 Bav. Ambulance Co. 1 Bav. Field Hospital. 47 Bav. Field Hospital. Vet. Hospital.	
Transports			694 M. T. Col.		694 Bav. M. T. Col.	

[1] Composition at time of dissolution, Sept. 1, 1918.

HISTORY.

(4th and 8th Bavarian Infantry Regiments: Second Bavarian District. 25th Bavarian Infantry Regiment: Bavarian District.)

1916.

The 14th Bavarian Division was formed, at the beginning of August, 1916, with the 8th Bavarian Brigade (4th and 8th Bavarian Infantry Regiments), withdrawn from the 33d Reserve Division, and with the 29th Bavarian Infantry Regiment, formed at this time.

VERDUN.

1. The 14th Bavarian Division, going into line at the end of August, 1916, in the Vaux Chapitre wood, launched a violent attack on September 3 to the southwest of the fort of Vaux and continued to hold this sector until October 10.

At the end of October, the 29th Bavarian Infantry Regiment, whose losses in the Vaux sector were considerable, was dissolved and replaced by the 25th Bavarian Infantry Regiment, taken from the 192d Division, and raised from two to three battalions.

2. Having thus received its present composition, the 14th Bavarian Division went back into line on the Hauts de Meuse (Calonne trench) on October 22.

SOMME–ANCRE.

3. Relieved at the beginning of November and sent to rest, it was then sent to the Somme, where, about November 26, it took over the sector north of the Ancre.

1917.

1. The 14th Bavarian Division left the Ancre front at the end of January, 1917, passed the month of February at rest in the Denain area, and came back into line on the Somme, northeast of Gueudecourt, on February 26. It was withdrawn on March 20 at the time of the German retirement.

ARTOIS.

2. At the beginning of April it went into action against the British offensive in the Roclincourt (north of Arras) and suffered heavily (about 2,800 prisoners on Apr. 9).

RUSSIA–RIGA.

3. Sent to rest in Belgium, it remained for several days in the Ghent area, and then entrained for the Eastern Front (Apr. 26–28). About May 14 it went into line near Lipsk (south of Baranovitchi); in June it took over the sector of Tsirin, where it remained until the end of the August. It was then transferred to the Riga front (Sept. 1) and went into action on September 14 in the neighborhood of Uxkuell. It left there on September 18.

4. About September 20 it went into line west of Jakobstadt and took part in the action of the 21st.

5. At the end of October the 14th Bavarian Division was sent to Galicia. It was identified in the neighborhood of Tarnopol on November 1 and, for the last time, on December 14 (fraternizing).

FRANCE.

6. The division left the Tarnopol area on December 19 for the Western Front. Itinerary: Posen–Leipzig–Frankfort–Kreuznach–Thionville. It detrained at Wasigny and Saulces-Monclin (near Rethel) on December 23.

RECRUITING.

The 14th Bavarian Division is recruited from the 2d and 3d Bavarian Corps Districts.

The 8th Bavarian Brigade (4th and 8th Bavarian Infantry Regiments), which helped form the 14th Bavarian Division, is a strong body belonging, in peace times, to the garrison at Metz.

It distinguished itself at the battle of Eparges (March–April, 1915), at the attack of September 3, 1916 (Vaux–Chapitre wood).

The morale of the 14th Bavarian Division appears to be high. No deserter has been found since the arrival of the division on the Western Front (December, 1917). The 14th Bavarian Division has always been a good division (January, 1918).

1918.

CHAMPAGNE.

1. The 14th Bavarian Division embarked at Tarnopol on December 19 and traveled via Kalicz-Posen-Leipsic-Frankfort-Kreusnach-Thionville-Wassigny (north of Rethel), where it detrained on the 23d. On January 12 it relieved the 7th Reserve Division in the Mont Haut sector. It was relieved by the 80th Reserve Division on April 22.

PICARDY.

2. On the 26th the division entrained at Neuflize, detraining on the following day near Mericourt (northeast of St. Quentin). From there it marched via Bellenglise-Vermand-Mons en Chaussee-Brie-Foucaucourt to Framerville. On May 3 it relieved the 208th Division in the Hangard sector (southeast of Amiens). It was relieved on the 21st by the 225th Division.

3. The division remained in close support, and relieved the 15th Division one sector to the south on the 23d. It was withdrawn during the night of June 20–21, and rested in rear of the front for over a month.

4. About July 23, it relieved the 21st Division in the Castel sector (north of Hangard). In the fighting that followed the division suffered heavy losses, especially in the British attack of August 8. It was withdrawn about the 13th in a badly shattered condition, it having lost some 2,500 prisoners.

5. It was in line again on the 29th northwest of Villers-Carbonnel (southwest of Peronne), and was withdrawn about the 2d of September. Soon thereafter, the 14th Bavarian Division was disbanded—the 4th Bavarian went to the 4th Bavarian Division to replace the 5th Bavarian Reserves (dissolved); the 8th Bavarian went to the 16th Bavarian Division to replace the 21st Bavarian Reserves (dissolved); the 25th Bavarian went to the 6th Bavarian Reserves Division to replace the 17th Bavarian Reserves (dissolved). The commanding general and his staff were identified at Malineson October 24, but there is nothing to show what they were doing there, or where they went.

Previous to 1918 the 14th Bavarian was always considered a first-class division. Since then, however, it seems to have fallen off somewhat; it was not used in any of the German offensives, and it is significant that a battalion of the 2d Bavarian Division was used in its sector (south of Hailles) when it was desired to make a raid, and also that two of the divisions receiving regiments when the 14th Bavarian was disbanded were second class. The division lost over 2,000 prisoners, including all three regiment staffs and the staffs of several of the battalions.

15th Division.
COMPOSITION.

	1914 Brigade.	1914 Regiment.	1915 Brigade.	1915 Regiment.	1916 Brigade.	1916 Regiment.	1917 Brigade.	1917 Regiment.	1918 Brigade.	1918 Regiment.
Infantry......	29. 80.	25. 161. 65. 160.	29. 80.	25. 161. 65. 160.	29. 80.	Jan. to Aug., 1916. 25. 161. 65. 160. Aug. to Nov., 1916. 186. 160. 389. After Nov. 69. 160. 389.	80.	69. 160. 389	80.	69. 137. 160.
Cavalry......					7 Hus. Rgt.		2 Sqn. 7 Hus. Rgt.		2 Sqn. 7 Hus. Rgt.	
Artillery......	15 Brig.: 59 F. A. Rgt. 83 F. A. Rgt.		15 Brig.: 59 F. A. Rgt. 83 F. A. Rgt.		15 Brig.: 59 F. A. Rgt. 83 F. A. Rgt.		15 Art. Command: 59 F. A. Rgt.		15 Art. Command: 59 F. A. Rgt. 135 Ft. A. Btn. 707 Light Am. Col. 744 Light Am. Col. 1295 Light Am. Col.	
Engineers and Liaisons.			1 Pion. Btn. No. 8: Field Co. 8 Pions. 15 Tel. Detch. 15 Pont. Engs.		1 Pion. Btn. No. 8: 1 Co. 8 Pions. 5 Co. 8 Pions. 15 T. M. Co. 15 Pont. Engs. 15 Tel. Detch.		125 Pion. Btn. (1 No. 8): 1 Co. 8 Pions. 5 Co. 8 Pions. 15 T. M. Co. 15 Tel. Detch	Pion. Btn.	125 Pion. Btn. 1 Co. 8 Pions. 5 Co. 8 Pions. 15 T. M. Co. 108 T. M. Co. 41 Searchlight Section. 15 Signal Command: 15 Tel. Detch. 113 Wireless Detch.	

15th Division—Continued.

COMPOSITION—Continued.

	1914	1915	1916	1917	1918
Medical and Veterinary.				19 Ambulance Co. Field Hospital. Vet. Hospital.	19 Ambulance Co. 82 Field Hospital. 83 Field Hospital. 15 Vet. Hospital.
Transports				M. T. Col. No. 800.	548 M. T. Col.
Attached			69 Anti-Aircraft Section		

HISTORY.

(8th Corps District—Rhine Province.)

1914.

1. Upon mobilization, the 15th Division (Aix la Chapelle, Cologne, Bonn, etc.) formed with the 16th Division an organic part of the 8th Army Corps and was in the 4th Army (Duke of Wuerttemberg).

2. Temporarily detaching the 25th Infantry Regiment (Aix la Chapelle) from the corps at the siege at Liege, the 15th Division entered, on August 6, into Luxemburg, where it had been preceded by the 16th Division (Treves). It entered into Belgian Luxemburg on the 19th and 20th of August. Went into action on the 22d and 23d— Porcheresse, Graid, Bievre—and entered France on the 26th. While the 29th Brigade was crossing the Meuse at Sedan the 80th entered at Mezieres. Again uniting on the 30th, the 15th Division went through Champagne by way of Somme Py and Suippes and took part in the battle of the Marne at Vitry le Francois. It then withdrew to Souain and Perthes, where it remained as a whole until November.

CHAMPAGNE.

3. At this time the 29th Brigade was taken to the Ypres front until the end of December, at which date it went to the south of Alsace, making a part of the combined division of Fuchs. The separation of the two brigades lasted until May, 1915. The 29th Brigade lost heavily in Alsace, where the 25th Infantry Regiment was reduced to 600 men on March 26, 1915 (soldier's notebook).

1915.

1. The 15th Division, in which the 29th Brigade was temporarily replaced by the 1st Bavarian Landwehr Brigade, remained in Champagne until the beginning of April, 1915. At that date it went to reenforce the 3d Bavarian Corps near St. Mihiel in the Ailly wood.

ARTOIS.

2. At the end of May the 15th Division again had both its brigades (29th and 80th) and went into action at Artois until the middle of June. It suffered heavy losses. The 161st Infantry Regiment lost 31 officers and 1,653 men (official list of casualties).

AISNE.

3. From June, 1915, until June, 1916, the 15th Division occupied various sectors of the Aisne: Vailly–Pommiers (end of July), Nouvron (September), Ste. Marguerite–Bucy le Long (October).

1916.

SOMME.

1. July, 1916, the 15th Division was transferred to the Somme. It took part in the battle and participated in the attack at Biaches, where it suffered heavy losses.

2. At the end of August it again took over its sector, St. Marguerite–Bucy le Long. Its composition was modified by the temporary loss of the 160th Infantry Regiment, sent to the combined division of Dumrath (August) by the definite transfer of the 65th Infantry Regiment and the 161st Infantry Regiment to the 185th Division, and of the 25th Infantry Regiment to the 208th Division.

3. At the beginning of October it had received in exchange for the regiments transferred the 186th Infantry Regiment (temporarily) and the 389th Infantry Regiment, a new formation (men taken from various Rhine regiments), and received the 160th Infantry Regiment again (the Dumrath Division having been dissolved). It reappeared on the Somme front (Sailly–Saillisel), where it again suffered heavy losses.

AISNE.

4. At the end of October it returned to the Aisne and occupied the sectors of Nuvron-Moulin sous Touvent. It was reorganized finally in November and received its definitive composition.

RUSSIA.

5. About the middle of November the 15th Division was withdrawn from the front, entrained after a few days' rest, and transferred to the Eastern Front. It went into line north of Kisselin.

1917.

1. In February, 1917, the division was in Transylvania (upper valley of the Olta).

2. In April it was in reserve at Vladimir–Volynski.

FRANCE.

3. Transferred to the French front (entrained at Kovel, detrained at Vigneulles, at the end of April), the division occupied the sector of Vaux les Palameix (Meuse).

CALIFORNIE PLATEAU.

4. At the end of May it was relieved and sent (night of May 29–30) to the Vauclerc Plateau and the Californie Plateau. On June 2 and 3 it took part in the violent attack upon these plateaus. It renewed these attacks upon July 3 and again suffered heavy losses.

LORRAINE.

5. The division was relieved on the night of July 8–9 and then sent to the Lys area, from which it was transferred into the zone Richecourt–Avricourt. It was put in line (July 15) near Blamont.

FLANDERS.

6. It was relieved about September 4, sent to rest in the Verdun area, and transferred to Belgium on October 7, where it was in action and suffered heavily on the Ypres front (north of the Ypres–Menin road) until November 13.

7. The division was then sent to the rear (area of Bruges–Knocke).

8. It again went into line east of Ypres about December 18 (east of Passchendaele). In the middle of January, 1918, it was withdrawn from this sector and sent to the Bruges area.

RECRUITING.

The 15th Division is easily recruited from the populous districts of the Rhine Provinces. In case of heavy losses and urgent necessity for reenforcements, the need has been felt for having recourse to the rest of the Rhine country in the widest sense of the word, that is to say, Rhenish Hessia and the Grand Duchy of Baden, in return or reenforcements sent elsewhere. The frequence of the relation and the community of interests which unites these regions assures the 15th Division, under all circumstances, the advantages of regional homogeneity.

VALUE—1917 ESTIMATE.

The 15th Division, in spite of the lack of success of its efforts, has given the impression of being a good division.

On June 2 and 3, 1917, the 69th Infantry Regiment and the 389th Infantry Regiment, attacked vigorously upon the casemates and Californie Plateaus. The 389th Infantry Regiment, especially, showed a great deal of dash in the course of these actions (July, 1917).

The division is composed, for the most part, of young and well trained elements; it has the experience gained from a very active sector (September, 1917).

1918.

BELGIUM.

1. The division relieved the 25th Division east of Passchendaele on February 10 and occupied the sector until February 20–25 when it moved south and took over the Zonnebeke sector from the 31st Division. About March 21, it was relieved by the 39th Division. It entrained at Muelebeke on the 23d and detrained at Mons en Pevele (north of Douai). From there it went by marches to Cambrai (31st), Sailly Saillisel, Bray sur Somme and Suzanne. and Caix (Apr. 7–12).

PICARDY.

2. On April 12 it was engaged in the Bois Senecat, northwest of Moreuil. During the French attack of the 18th the division lost 700 prisoners. It was relieved about April 22.

3. It rested until mid-May near Busiginy. The 389th Regiment is known to have received 600 men as a draft at this time. On May 18, the division returned to line near Castel, and was engaged until May 22.

4. It rested in the Somme area (at Rosieres en Santerse June 1, and Peronne on the 9th), until June 17 when it came into line before Moreuil. It suffered heavy losses during the French attack of the 17th but continued in line until the 26th. It rested east of Roye in June and from the 3d to the 5th of July was in reserve south of Blerancourt.

BATTLE OF THE OISE-AISNE.

5. The division was engaged in the Nampcel–Autreches sector from July 5 until August 22. It was pushed back to Caisnes (Aug. 18) and as a result of the French attack lost 1,880 prisoners.

6. The division was moved to rest at Damvillers north of Verdun in early September. On the 26th it left that place and marched to Flabas, east of the Meuse.

MEUSE-ARGONNE.

7. On September 26 the division was in line in the Bois des Caures. It continued to hold a sector in the region until the armistice. The last identification was northwest of Ornes on November 10.

VALUE—1918 ESTIMATE.

The division was rated as second class. Its heavy losses at Moreuil in June and the ravages of the grippe in the summer lowered the morale. On the other hand, a document of October 4 indicated that the division had been congratulated by the Kaiser for its "heroic conduct."

15th Reserve Division.

COMPOSITION.

	1914 Brigade	1914 Regiment	1915 Brigade	1915 Regiment	1916 Brigade	1916 Regiment	1917 Brigade	1917 Regiment	1918 Brigade	1918 Regiment
Infantry	....	25 Res. 69 Res. 17 Res. 30 Res.	29 Res. 80 Res.	25 Res. 69 Res. 17 Res. 30 Res.	29 Res. 80 Res.	25 Res. 69 Res. 17 Res. 30 Res.	30 Res.	17 Res. 25 Res. 69 Res.	30 Res.	17 Res. 25 Res. 69 Res.
Cavalry	5 Res. Uhlan Rgt. (3 Sqns.).		5 Res. Uhlan Rgt.		5 Res. Uhlan Rgt.		5 Res. Uhlan Rgt. (? 3d Sqn.)		2 Sqn. 8 Cuirassier Rgt.	
Artillery	15 Res. F. A. Rgt. (6 Btries.).		15 Res. F. A. Rgt. (after Mar., 1915, 8 Btries.).		15 Res. F. A. Rgt. (8 Btries.).		104 Art. Command: 15 Res. F. A. Rgt. (9 Btries.).		104 Art. Command: 15 Res. F. A. Rgt. 125 Ft. A. Btn. (Staff, 1, 2, and 3d Btries.). 1064 Light Am. Col. 1066 Light Am. Col. 1067 Light Am. Col.	
Engineers and Liaisons.	4 Field Co., 2 Pion. Btn. No. 8.		4 Field Co., 2 Pion. Btn. No. 8. 15 Res. Pont. Engs. 15 Res. Tel. Detch.		4 Field Co., 2 Pion. Btn. No. 8. 2 Co. 31 Pion. Rgt. 5 Co. 31 Pion. Rgt. 215 T. M. Co. 15 Res. Pont. Engs. 15 Res. Tel. Detach.		315 Pion. Btn.: 4 Co. 8 Pion. 6 Co. 8 Pion. 215 T. M. Co. 257 Searchlight Section. 415 Tel. Detch.		315 Pion. Btn.: 4 Co. 8 Pions. 6 Co. 8 Pions. 53 Searchlight Section. 215 T. M. Co. 415 Signal Command: 415 Tel. Detch. 37 Wireless Detch.	
Medical and Veterinary.	....		....		....		508 Ambulance Co. 37 Res. Field Hospital. Vet. Hospital.		508 Ambulance Co. 37 Res. Field Hospital. 38 Res. Field Hospital. 415 Vet. Hospital.	
Transports.	....		....		....		M. T. Col.		714 M. T. Col.	
Odd units	....		....		78 Anti-Aircraft section.		....			

Attached

| 504 F. A. Rgt. (Staff, 2 and 3 Abt.).
3 Abt. 4 Ft. A. Rgt.
708 Transport Park.
30 Ammunition Col.
133 and 18 Bav. Supply Trains.
238 Reconnaissance Flight.
119 Balloon Sqn.
136 Labor Btn.
92 Art. Observation Section. | | | |

(Elements attached Oct. 12, 1918, from German document.)

HISTORY.

(25th Reserve Infantry Regiment, 69th Reserve Infantry Regiment: 8th Corps District—Rhine Province.   17th Reserve Infantry Regiment: 21st Corps District—Lorraine.)

1914.

1. In August, 1914, the 15th Reserve Division which was a part of the 8th Reserve Corps (with the 16th Reserve Division) and of the 4th Army, was concentrated on the Luxemburg frontier, which it crossed on the 19th.   Entering Belgium on the 21st, it fought on the 22d at Maissin and Paliseul, and between the 25th and 27th it crossed the Meuse near Sedan, losing heavily.   On August 28, the 2d Battalion of the 69th Reserve Infantry Regiment was reduced to 140 men (soldier's notebook).

CHAMPAGNE.

2. From this place, by way of le Chesne, Vouziers, Tahure, the division advanced as far as Marne Canal to the Rhine, at Vitry le Francois (Brusson Dompremy, Sept. 6), where it took part in the battle of the Marne.

3. The division retired between September 9 and September 16 by way of Suippes to Servon, Binarville, Massiges (Sept. 18 to 27), and established itself north of Massiges.

1915.

CHAMPAGNE.

1. The 15th Reserve Division occupied the front north of Massiges and of Mesnil les Hurlus in the Souain area.   In the course of various small actions, especially in May, it suffered heavily, so much so that by June 30, the losses suffered since the beginning of the campaign it amounted to 2,316 men for the 2d Battalion of the 17th Reserve Infantry Regiment (official list of casualties).

2. In September, 1915, the elements of the 15th Reserve Division divided between the Liebert Division (17th and 69th Reserve Infantry Regiments) and the Ditfurth Division (25th and 30th Reserve Infantry Regiments) took part in the battle of Champagne near Tahure, east of Somme Py (from Sept. 25 to the beginning of October). They suffered considerable losses.

AISNE.

3. Toward the end of October the 15th Reserve Division was relieved from the Tahure sector and reorganized.   At the beginning of November it went into line between Vailly and the Oise–Aisne Canal.

1916.

1. The division occupied the sector Chavonne-Soupir south of Braye en Laonnois until the end of June, 1916.

SOMME.

2. At the beginning of July, as soon as the Franco-British offensive began, the 15th Reserve Division detached some of its elements to reenforce divisions engaged along the Somme, especially at Flaucourt (July 2 and 3), Hem wood, and the Vermandovillers area (August).

AISNE.

3. Some of these elements returned to the Aisne and were reassigned to the Liebert (new 15th Reserve Division) and the Dumrath Division.

SOMME.

4. The 17th and 30th Reserve Infantry Regiments remained in the Somme area. Separated at first, at the end of August they formed the 32d Brigade reattached to the 35th Division which held the front in the area of Estrees-Ablaincourt (September).

5. At the beginning of October the 15th Reserve Division, once more reorganized its original elements, and occupied the lines between Fouquescourt and the north of Andechy.

6. The division was relieved from the Somme front about December 15.

1917.

SOMME.

1. Once more in line in the Fouquescourt sector, the division took part in the German withdrawal by way of Ercheu, Moyencourt (Mar. 17), Ham (Mar. 19).

2. It was sent to rest in the Maubeuge area (?) (end of March and April).

ARTOIS.

3. About May 2 it went into line in the Fresnoy sector (north of Arras), where it went into action about May 3.

4. It was withdrawn from the Artois front on May 10 and transferred to the Eastern Front (May 21 to May 28).

GALICIA.

5. Sent to Galicia, it occupied the sector south of Brzezany, where it underwent the Russian attack of July 1. Then it took part in the offensive against the Russians at the end of July, and suffered heavy losses near Husiatin, where it remained until August 24. Sent to the rear of Zbrucz it held this sector from September 15 to December 7.

FRANCE.

6. Relieved at this date, it remained in the Jablona area until December 19, and entrained on the 30th for the Western Front. Itinerary: Brest Litowsk-Warsaw-Karlish-Halle-Frankfort on the Main-Mayence-Sarrebruecken-Thionville-Sedan. It detrained on January 7, in the Dun area, where it went to rest.

The 15th Reserve Division suffered very heavy losses in Galicia (July and Aug., 1917).

At the end of February, 1918, these losses, according to the statements of deserters, had not yet been made good by sufficient replacements.

In Russia there was no exchange of the older men of the division for men of the 1919 class.

RECRUITING.

The 15th Reserve Division is recruited from the Rhine districts in general. The elements from the 9th Corps District, introduced by the assignment of one battalion of the 76th Landwehr Regiment to the 69th Reserve Infantry Regiment, have almost disappeared with the arrival of successive replacements.

1918.

1. During its occupancy of the Verdun sector the division underwent intensive training which was to fit it for operations on the Western Front. It was relieved about April 15. The division commenced entraining at Stenay about April 23 and traveled via Givet-Dinant-Namur-Charleroi-Braine le Comte-Ath-Tournai, and detrained between Tournai and Lille. One regiment marched to Haubourdin (12 miles), where it rested several days.

HINGE.

2. On the night of May 1-2 the division came into line east of St. Venant. It held this sector for 10 months. Toward the end of June it was relieved by the 23d Reserve Division.

ARRAS.

3. On July 11 the division entered the line southwest of Oppy. It was engaged at Gavrelle, Oppy, and Arleux until October 9 when the 187th Division relieved it.

4. The division returned to line on the 12th to reinforce the front east of Bohain and fought until the end of October in the region east of Wassigny. There was some talk in the division of the dissolution, as no drafts of importance were received during September or October.

5. On November 6 the division was again in line. In the closing days of the war it was engaged north of Beaurepaire, southeast of Limont-Fontaine, southwest of Aites and Obrechies (10th).

VALUE.

The division was rated as third class. During 1918 the division was almost constantly in line holding defensive sectors, which it did with fair success.

15th Landwehr Division.

COMPOSITION.

	1915 Brigade.	1915 Regiment.	1916 Brigade.	1916 Regiment.	1917 Brigade.	1917 Regiment.	1918 Brigade.	1918 Regiment.
Infantry	10 Ldw. 27 Ldw.	12 Ldw. 52 Ldw. 53 Ldw. 55 Ldw.	10 Ldw. 27 Ldw.	12 Ldw. 52 Ldw. 53 Ldw. 55 Ldw.	10 Ldw.	12 Ldw. 52 Ldw. 53 Ldw. 55 Ldw.	....	53 Ldw.
Cavalry		1 Ldw. Sqn. 3 C. Dist. 2 Ldw. Sqn. 7 C. Dist.	....		1 Sqn. 5 Hus. Rgt.			
Artillery		1 and 2 Landst. 3 C. Dist. F. A. Btries. Landst. F. A. Btry. 7 C. Dist.	15 Ldw. F. A. Rgt.		Art. Command: 15 Ldw. F. A. Rgt.		15 Ldw. F. A. Rgt. (Regt. Staff, 2 Abt. Staff, 2 and 4 and 6 Btries., 3 Abt. Staff, 7 and 9 Btries. not included).	
Engineers and Liaisons.			246 Pion. Co. 247 Pion. Co. 315 T. M. Co.		415 Pion. Btn.: 246 Pion. Co. 247 Pion. Co. 315 T. M. Co. 247 Searchlight Section. Tel. Detch.		109 Wireless Detch.	
Medical and Veterinary.					552 Ambulance Co. 3 Ldw. Field Hospital. 7 Ldw. Field Hospital.		7 Ldw. Field Hospital. 515 Vet. Hospital.	
Transports					M. T. Col.			
Attached			42 Art. Survey Section.					

1 The elements below are those grouped under the 797 Postal sector. Other elements belonging to the 15th Landwehr Division, but operating under other division staffs, are listed as attached to such division.

HISTORY.

(12th Landwehr Regiment: 3d Corps District—Brandenburg. 53d and 55th Landwehr Regiments: 7th Corps District—Westphalia.)

1915.

OISE.

1. The 15th Landwehr Division (Sack Division) was formed about the month of March, 1915, from two independent Landwehr brigades (the 10th and 27th) which had been holding, since September, 1914, the sectors of the Oise south of Noyon.

2. The 10th Brigade, entering Belgium on August 19, was at Tirlemont on September 1 and had been sent rapidly to the Oise at the beginning of the retreat from the Marne. It had gone into action at Blerancourt, Bellefontaine, Cuts, on September 15 and 16. The 27th Brigade, coming from Aix la Chapelle August 17, had advanced by way of Louvain, Douai, Cambrai, Bepaume, and Amiens and had likewise been in action on September 15 and 16 at Rivecourt and Nampcel.

3. After its formation the 15th Landwehr Division continued to occupy the Oise sector of Thiescourt (Ribecourt) until 1917.

1916.

1. The division held the Oise sector of Thiescourt (southwest of Noyon).

1917.

1. The Oise sector of Thiescourt was held by the division until 1917.

In the middle of March, 1917, the 15th Landwehr Division took part in the withdrawal of the German troops and retired southeast of St. Quentin by way of Salency, Chauny, and La Fere.

GALICIA.

2. Relieved at the end of March, it was transferred to the Eastern Front. Itinerary: Charleroi–Luxemburg–Treves * * * Breslau–Cracow–Lemberg. (Some elements of the division had already left before the withdrawal to the Hindenburg line and had entrained at Noyon.)

3. In Galicia the 15th Landwehr Division occupied the sector west of Brody until the beginning of 1918.

Almost immediately after its arrival the 52d Landwehr Regiment was withdrawn from the division (April, 1917).

Like the other Landwehr divisions on the Eastern Front, the 15th Landwehr Division at the end of 1917 had given its best elements to divisions operating in France (especially to the 111th Division).

VALUE—1917 ESTIMATE.

The division is purely a sector division.

1918.

UKRAINE.

1. Early in March the 15th Landwehr Division marched toward Rovno; from there it was transported to Kiev.

2. On May 11 the division was south of Ekaterinoslav; the 12th Landwehr Regiment at Sebastopol and the 53d Landwehr Regiment likewise being in the Crimea.

CAUCASUS.

3. Toward the end of May elements of the division were identified in the Kertch region, the 12th Landwehr Regiment, however, being on the Vardar front. The division was still here the latter part of September. During this time all of the younger men were sent to the Western Front.

VALUE—1918 ESTIMATE.

The division was rated as fourth class.

,15th Bavarian Division.

COMPOSITION.

	1917		1918	
	Brigade.	Regiment.	Brigade.	Regiment.
Infantry........	23 Bav.	30 Bav. 31 Bav. 32 Bav.	23 Bav.	30 Bav. 31 Bav. 32 Bav.
Cavalry..............	3 Sqn. 7 Bav. Light Cav. Rgt.		3 Sqn. 7 Bav. Light Cav. Rgt.	
Artillery..............	Art. Command: 7 Bav. F. A. Rgt.		7 Bav. F. A. Rgt. 23 Bav. Ft. A. Btn. 148 Bav. Light Am. Col. 152 Bav. Light Am. Col. 155 Bav. Light Am. Col.	
Engineers and Liaisons.	15 Bav. Pion. Btn.; 24 Bav. Pion. Co. 25 Bav. Pion. Co. 15 Bav. T. M. Co. 15 Bav. Tel. Detch.		15 Bav. Pion. Btn.; 24 Bav. Pion. Co. 25 Bav. Pion. Co. 15 Bav. T. M. Co. 15 Bav. Searchlight Section. 15 Bav. Signal Command: 15 Bav. Tel. Detch. 170 Wireless Detch.	
Medical and Veterinary	25 Bav. Ambulance Co. 64 Bav. Field Hospital. 65 Bav. Field Hospital. 15 Bav. Vet. Hospital.		25 Bav. Ambulance Co. 64 Bav. Field Hospital. 65 Bav. Field Hospital.	
Transport..............	696 M. T. Col.		696 M. T. Col.	

HISTORY.

(30th Bavarian Infantry Regiment: 1st Bavarian Corps District. 31st Bavarian Infantry Regiment: 2d Bavarian Corps District. 32d Bavarian Infantry Regiment: 3d Bavarian Corps District.)

1917.

The 15th Bavarian Division was formed in December, 1916, and January, 1917, at Nuremburg, of elements coming from the three Bavarian corps districts in the manner of the divisions 231-242; that is to say, a very large proportion of the men of the 1918 class, together with returned wounded and sick and men taken from units at the front.

1. From February 1 to March 1, 1917, the three regiments of the division received instruction for mountain troops in Upper Bavaria, near the Austrian frontier.

2. On March 1 the 15th Bavarian Division was transferred to the Charleroi area, where it remained one month; there it received training in the war of movement.

LORRAINE.

3. At the end of March it was transferred to Lorraine; it occupied the Leintrey sector (Parroy wood) until the beginning of May.

AISNE.

4. From Lorraine it went to the Laonnois area (Sissonne, La Selve, May 12); went into line southwest of Juvincourt on May 19-20; launched an attack on June 28-29 southeast of Corbeny, and left the front at the end of July.

5. After a rest in the Sedan area the division entrained on August 20 for the Verdun front.

MEUSE (HILL 304).

6. Detraining at Stenay and Dun (Aug. 22–24), it went into line north of Hill 304 (Forges Stream). The French attack on the 24th occasioned serious losses.

MEUSE (RIGHT BANK).

7. The 15th Bavarian Division was relieved from Hill 304 about October 16; went from there to the right bank of the Meuse, and then into line at Beaumont (Oct. 24).

RECRUITING.

The 15th Bavarian Division is recruited from all of Bavaria.

VALUE—1917 ESTIMATE.

In September, 1917, the 15th Bavarian Division appeared strong.

In the 31st Bavarian Infantry Regiment two-thirds of the men were recruits belonging to the 1918 class.

The division suffered few losses on the Verdun front after November, 1917.

1918.

1. During the spring the division made use of the quiet Bezouvaux sector to train the men in machine gun and assault tactics. It was relieved on July 23 and rested south of Longwy (Villers la Montagne) until July 4. It was moved to Sault St. Remy, by Carignan, Sedan, Rethel (July 4–5). Until the 11th it rested in a camp, when it marched by night toward the front.

BATTLE OF RHEIMS.

·2. On the 15th it was engaged in the offensive east of Prunay. It advanced to north of Thuizy, suffering very heavy losses, estimated to have been 30 to 40 per cent. It remained in line until mid-August. After 10 weeks' rest the division was again engaged about September 1 north of Prosnes until September 29.

MEUSE-ARGONNE.

3. The division was placed in line farther to the east, near Somme Py, where it remained until about September 29, at which time it was put in reserve north of Bouillon. In the fighting all three regiments were exhausted, but the losses of the 31st Bavarian Regiment were particularly heavy. Six hundred prisoners were taken from the division at this time.

4. The division rested from October 5 to 10. At this time the 18th Bavarian Reserve Regiment, from the disbanded Bavarian Ersatz Division, was divided among the three regiments of the division.

5. It came into line on October 13 east of Grandpre and was engaged on the United States front until November 11. It did not offer a vigorous resistance to the American attacks at first, but in late October and early November it did all in its power to check the American advance.

VALUE—1918 ESTIMATE.

The division was rated as a third-class. The heavy losses in Champagne in September and October, the prevalent sickness, political discontent, and dissatisfaction with Prussia continued to give the division a low morale.

16th Division.
COMPOSITION.

	1914		1915		1916		1917		1918	
	Brigade.	Regiment.	Brigade.	Regiment.	Brigade.	Regiment.	Brigade.	Regiment.	Brigade.	Regiment.
Infantry	30. 31.	28. 68. 29. 69.	30. 31.	28. 68. 29. 69.	30. 31.	28. 68. 29. 69.	30.	28. 29. 68.	30.	28. 29. 68.
Cavalry	8 Cuirassier Rgt.				8 Cuirassier Rgt. (3 and 4 Sqns.).		1 Sqn. 7 Hus. Rgt.		1 Sqn. 7 Hus. Rgt.	
Artillery	16 Brig.; 23 F. A. Rgt. 44 F. A. Rgt.		16 Brig.; 23 F. A. Rgt. 44 F. A. Rgt.		16 Brig.; 23 F. A. Rgt. 44 F. A. Rgt.		16 Art. Command: 23 F. A. Rgt.		16 Art. Command: 23 F. A. Rgt. 32 Ft. A. Btn. (3 Btries.). 1252 Light Am. Col. 1253 Light Am. Col. 1307 Light Am. Col.	
Engineers and Liaisons.	2 and 3 Field Cos. 1 Pion. Btn. No. 8.		1 Pion. Btn. No. 8: 2 Field Co. 8 Pions. 3 Field Co. 8 Pions. 16 Pont. Engs. 16 Tel. Detch.		1 Pion. Btn. No. 8: 2 Co. 8 Pions. 3 Co. 8 Pions. 16 T. M. Co. 16 Pont. Engs. 16 Tel. Detch.		125 Pion. Btn. (1 Pion. Btn. No. 8): 2 Co. 8 Pions. 3 Co. 8 Pions. 169 T. M. Co. 293 Searchlight Section. 16 Tel. Detch.		8 Pion. Btn.: 2 Co. 8 Pions. 3 Co. 8 Pions. 169 T. M. Co. 44 Searchlight Section. 16 Signal Command: 16 Tel. Detch. 120 Wireless Detch.	
Medical and Veterinary.							20 Ambulance Co. 80 Field Hospital. Vet. Hospital.		20 Ambulance Co. 78 Field Hospital. 80 Field Hospital. 16 Vet. Hospital.	
Transports							M. T. Col.		549 M. T. Col.	
Attached					113 Labor Btn.				188 and 417 Pigeon Lofts. 208 Balloon Sqn. 7 Reconnaissance Flight. 57 Art. Observation Section (Flash-spotters). 10 Co. 97 Labor Btn. 38 Div. Pont. Engs. 1294 Light Am. Col. (Elements attached July 17, 1918; from German documents.)	

HISTORY.

(8th Corps District—Rhine Province.)

1914.

ARDENNES–MARNE.

1. In August, 1914, the 16th Division (belonging to the 8th Army Corps, together with 16th Division) was a part of the 4th German Army (Duke of Wurttemberg). It entered Luxemburg at the beginning of August (28th Infantry Regiment), there received the rest of its reservists on the 7th, entered Belgian Luxemburg on the 20th, and went into action on the 23d at Bièvre and Gédinne. From there, by way of Sedan and Donchery (Aug. 26), forming the extreme right of the 4th Army, it went through Champagne, reached Suippes on September 3, and crossed the Marne near Vitry le François, where it came into contact with the French forces. It retired, having suffered heavily, by way of Somme–Yèvre–Herpont–St. Mard sur Auve–Somme Bionne, and stopped near Perthes les Hurlus, where it made a stand.

CHAMPAGNE.

2. The 16th Division occupied the sector Souain–Perthes during the winter of 1914 and 1915; it there withstood strong attacks.

BELGIUM.

3. In November and December, 1914, the division detached certain of its elements (31st Brigade, 29th and 69th Infantry Regiments) in Belgium, in the Langemarck area.

ALSACE.

4. In the middle of December the 31st Brigade was sent to Alsace for work near Mulhouse. It formed a part of the Fuchs Division, was in line north of Thann and rejoined the 30th Brigade opposite Perthes at the end of December.

1915.

ARTOIS.

1. Withdrawn from the Champagne front about April 18–19, 1915, the 16th Division was sent to rest in the Briey area, then transferred, about May 15, north of Arras.

2. It lost very heavily at Souchez and Neuville–St. Vaast, withstanding the offensive of May. The 69th Infantry Regiment lost 42 officers and 1,609 men. (Official List of Casualties.)

AISNE.

3. The division left Artois in the middle of June and, after a few days of rest near St. Quentin, went into line in the middle of July, east of Soissons (Chavonne–Soupir sector).

NOUVRON.

4. At the end of October it took over the sector of Nouvron, west of Soissons.

1916.

1. The 16th Division remained on the Aisne front until the end of July, 1916.

SOMME.

2. Entraining at Follembray, it was transferred to Ham and Nesle. After a short stay in the Maucourt sector (northwest of Roye) at the beginning of August, it took part in the battle of the Somme near Pozières–Thiepval, where it suffered very heavy losses (Aug. 10–24); the 3d Company of the 29th Infantry Regiment lost 131 men at Pozières (letter).

BERRY AU BAC.

3. In September the reorganized 16th Division (especially with men of the 1917 class) occupied a quiet sector west of Berry au Bac. In October the 69th Infantry Regiment was withdrawn from the 16th Division, which now has three regiments (30th Brigade).

SOMME.

4. Relieved about the 3d of October from the sector west of Berry au Bac, the division entrained at Laon and was transferred to the Somme. It went into line (Lesboeufs–Sailly–Saillsel) on October 9 and suffered heavy losses.

RUSSIA.

5. On October 26 the division left the Somme, returned for a few days (Nov. 5–16) to the front northwest of Soissons and entrained for Russia on November 20. Itinerary: Liege–Aix la Chapelle–Dusseldorf–Hanover–Magdeburg–Berlin–Skernewitzy–Warsaw–Brest Litowsk–Kovel–Turisk. It detrained on November 25.

1916.

GALICIA.

1. On the Russian front the 16th Division occupied the Kiselin sector, south of Kovel (until the beginning of May, 1917).

FRANCE.

2. On May 17, entraining near Kieslin, the division returned to France via Vladimir Volynski–Kovel–Brest Litowsk–Warsaw–Kalich–Cotthus–Leipzig–Cassel–Coblentz–Gerolstein–Sedan–Attigny, where it detrained on May 21.

FLANDERS.

3. After a rest at Ecordal, on June 4 the division was sent to Flanders. Detraining at Orchies, it marched to Wambrechies; it there remained for 12 days. On June 26 it went into line at Warneton, where the British attack of July 31 did not cause it any serious losses.

4. About the 23d of September the 16th Division was sent to rest in the Bruges area.

YPRES.

At the beginning of October it was sent to the Ypres front.

Some elements were engaged on October 3 and 4 against the British attacks east of Vonnebeke. On October 6 the division went to the southeast of Poelcappelle and supported the local offensives, against the British troops (Oct. 9–12).

The 16th Division remained behind the front from October 12 to November 24.

At this date it took over the sector north of Becelaere and a short time afterwards that of Passchendaele (east), where it was relieved about the middle of January, 1918.

RECRUITING.

The 16th Division is recruited almost exclusively from the Rhine Provinces.

VALUE—1917 ESTIMATE.

Before being engaged on the Somme the 16th Division had gained a wonderful reputation. It was known as the "Iron Division." In the battle of the Somme it did not, however, distinguish itself in any way.

At Warneton and at Ypres (June and October, 1917) it fought stubbornly in spite of its heavy losses.

1918.

YPRES.

1. The division was at rest in Belgium (Meulebeke area) until about March 1, when it was engaged east of Passchendaele until March 23.

2. It entrained at Pitthem and moved to reserve at Tourcoing until April 4. Later it was at Lille until April 10.

BATTLE OF THE LYS.

3. The division was engaged on April 4 north of Neuve Chapelle and south of Merville on the 12th. On the 17th the 68th Regiment was to attack but was unable to do so through weakness and lack of food. Two regimental commanders were included in the heavy casualties. It was relieved east of St. Venant on May 1.

MERVILLE.

4. The division rested in Belgium (Braine, south of Brussels) for about two weeks. On the 19th it was in line southwest of Merville. It was relieved by the 25th Division on the night of July 6–7. After 10 days' rest the division returned to its former sector and continued in line until August 18.

5. After leaving the line on August 18 it rested near Haubourdin until the 26th, when it entrained for Raches (north of Douai). It marched toward the front east of Arras by Douai and Vitry, entering the line near Vis en Artois on August 30.

THIRD BATTLE OF THE SOMME.

6. The division fought near Dury and Hendecourt until mid-September, losing more than 1,500 prisoners. It rested at Bruges until its return to line north of Lens on September 26. It was driven back toward Pont a Vendin and Courrieres, northwest of Orchies, Hollain, and Antoing. The division was withdrawn about November 6 from the Antoing area.

VALUE—1918 ESTIMATE.

The division was rated as a second-class division. During 1918 it fought entirely on the British front, chiefly on the defensive.

16th Reserve Division.
COMPOSITION.

	1914		1915		1916		1917		1918	
	Brigade.	Regiment.	Brigade.	Regiment.	Brigade.	Regiment.	Brigade.	Regiment.	Brigade.	Regiment.
Infantry	29 Res. 31 Res.	28 Res. 68 Res. 29 Res. 65 Res.	29 Res. 31 Res.	28 Res. 68 Res. 29 Res. 65 Res.	29 Res. 31 Res. 68 Res.	28 Res. 68 Res. 29 Res. 65 Res. Feb. to July. 28 Res. 68 Res. 25 Res. Aug. to Sept. 190. Hippe Rgt. Sept. to Dec. 190, 29 Res. 390.	31 Res.	29 Res. 30 Res. 68 Res.	31 Res.	29 Res. 30 Res. 68 Res.
Cavalry	2 Heavy Res. Cav. Rgt. (3 Sqns.).		2 Heavy Res. Cav. Rgt.		2 Heavy Res. Cav. Rgt.		2 (f) Heavy Res. Cav. Rgt.		4 Sqn. 8 Cuirassier Rgt.	
Artillery	16 Res. F. A. Rgt. (6 Btries.).		16 Res. F. A. Rgt. (8 Btries.).		16 Res. F. A. Rgt. (9 Btries.).		106 Art. Command: 16 Res. F. A. Regt. (9 Btries.)		106 Art. Command. 16 Res. F. A. Rgt. 127 Ft. Art. Btn. 724 Light Am. Col. 810 Light Am. Col. 1352 Light Am. Col.	
Engineers and Liaisons.	1 and 2 Res. Cos. 2 Pion. Btn. No. 8.		1 and 2 Res. Cos. 2 Pion. Btn. No. 8. 16 Res. Pont. Engs. 16 Res. Tel. Detch.		1 and 2 Res. Cos. 2 Piom. Btn. No. 8. 10 Co. 28 Pioms. 216 T. M. Co. 16 Res. Font. Engs. 16 Res. Tel. Detch.		(316) Pion. Btn.: 1 Res. Co. 8 Pioms. 2 Res. Co. 8 Pioms. 216 T. M. Co. 416 Tel. Detch.		316 Pion. Btn.: 1 Res. Co. 8 Pioms. 2 Res. Co. 8 Pioms. 8 Searchlight Section. 216 T. M. Co. 416 Signal Command: 416 Tel. Detch. 130 Wireless Detch.	

Medical and Veterinary.	512 Ambulance Co. Field Hospital. 416 Vet. Hospital.			512 Ambulance Co. 39 Res. Field Hospital. 40 Res. Field Hospital. 416 Vet. Hospital.
Transports	M. T. Col.			715 M. T. Col.
Attached				16 and 134 Art. Observation Section. 16 Balloon Sqn. 213 Reconnaissance Flight. 2,208 Pigeon Loft. (Elements attached Sept. 30, 1918; from German documents.)

HISTORY.

(8th Corps District—Rhine Province.)

1914.

1. At the outbreak of the war the 16th Reserve Division with the 15th Reserve Division was a part of the 8th Reserve Corps and belonged to the 4th Army (Duke of Wurttemberg).

CHAMPAGNE.

2. On August 14, 1914, it entered Luxemburg; on the 21st, Belgium. It went into action at St. Hubert on the 22d; at Matton on the 24th; crossed the Meuse at Sedan with heavy losses August 26–28. Entering Champagne by way of Vouziers, it took part in the battle of the Marne, along the canal from the Marne to the Rhine (Heiltz le Maurupt–Bignicourt–Le Buisson).

3. On September 9 it began its retreat, and retired by way of Suippes (Sept. 14) to Cernay en Dormois. About September 20 it stopped in the area of Minaucourt–Massiges and took up its position there.

4. The 16th Reserve Division occupied this sector of Champagne (north of Massiges) until the month of October, 1915. (On the 30th of January, 1915, the 29th Reserve Infantry Regiment had had a total of 79 officers and 3,090 men casualties.)

1915.

1. At the time of the French offensive in Champagne the 16th Reserve Division went into battle east of the road from Tahure to Perthes les Hurlus (Sept. 25). It was then a part of a new group under the orders of Gen. Ditfurth.

2. Having suffered heavily from these attacks, the 16th Reserve Division was relieved about October 15 and sent to the rest in the Chesne area. Between October 8 and 14 no less than 223 men came to the 5th Company of the 68th Reserve Infantry Regiment as replacements (in this number, recruits of the 1915 class who had had four months' instruction).

AISNE.

3. At the end of October the 16th Reserve Division was sent north of the Aisne, where it took over the sector between Soissons and Vailly.

1916.

1. The 16th Reserve Division remained in line east of Soissons until February 16, 1916.

AISNE.

2. In the middle of February it went to the west of Soissons, in the sector of Moulin sous Touvent–Autreches, which it occupied until the month of October.

3. In February the 16th Reserve Division lost two of its regiments, the 65th and 29th Reserve Infantry Regiments, which were replaced by a single regiment, the 35th Reserve Infantry Regiment. It was then composed of the 25th, 28th, and 68th Reserve Infantry Regiments.

4. At the beginning of the battle of the Somme, July 2, the 25th Reserve Infantry Regiment (2 battalions) was sent by itself as a reinforcement in the Barelaux area. The 28th Reserve Infantry Regiment left the 16th Reserve Division at the end of July to be attached to the 185th Division, likewise on the Somme.

5. The 16th Reserve Division, composed of the 68th Reserve Infantry Regiment and of two other regiments, the 190th Infantry Regiment and the Provisional Hippe Regiment, continued to occupy the sector of Moulin sous Touvent (August).

6. The 68th Reserve Infantry Regiment in its turn was sent to the Somme. It went into action near Deniécourt (September–October). One may calculate its losses

by the fact that the 5th Company received at least 55 men as replacements between October 2 and 6.

7. The 16th Reserve Division then comprised the 29th Reserve Infantry Regiment, once more attached to the division, the 190th Infantry Regiment, and the 390th Infantry Regiment, which replaced the Hippe Regiment above mentioned. Thus constituted, it was retained in the area Moulin sous Touvent–Autreches until the month of October.

SOMME.

8. Relieved on October 15, it entrained at Tergnier and was transferred to the Somme. It took part in the St. Pierre-Vaast wood in local operations, in the course of which it suffered heavily (Nov. 4 to 28).

9. About December 12 the 16th Reserve Division was sent north of the Aisne. It went into line in the Cerny en Laonnois area.

At this time the division was once more reorganized. It again received the 68th Reserve Infantry Regiment, which came back from the Somme. The 190th Infantry Regiment was transferred to the 47th Division, and the 390th Infantry Regiment, which was assigned to the 211th Division, was replaced by the 30th Reserve Infantry Regiment.

1917.

1. With this composition (29th, 68th, and 30th Reserve Infantry Regiments) the 16th Reserve Division occupied the sector of Cerny en Laonnois from January to April, 1917.

CHEMIN DES DAMES.

2. It underwent the French offensive of April 16 between Chivy and the Cerny sugar refinery, where it suffered very heavily (1,100 prisoners).

3. Relieved on the Aisne front about April 20, the division was sent to the Sissonne Camp, where it was reorganized (beginning of May).

LORRAINE.

4. About May 10 it went into line between the Sanon and Gondrexon, in Lorraine.

ALSACE.

5. The division was sent to Alsace about June 20 and remained in the Ferette area, where its training was vigorously carried out.

GALICIA.

6. On July 7, 1917, the 16th Reserve Division entrained for the Eastern Front.

7. Detraining on the 12th in the area of Rohatyn–Bourchtyn (Galicia), it went in to action on the 15th near Halucz, along the Dneister, and reached Khotin, where the Russian retreat halted.

8. At the end of August it occupied a new sector north of Bojan, east of Czernowitz (taking of Bojan, Aug. 27).

FRANCE.

9. The 16th Reserve Division was withdrawn from the front about November 15 and entrained for France near Czernowitz (Nov. 20). Itinerary: Kolomea–Stanislau–Lemberg – Przeymsl – Cracow – Oppeln – Breslau – Dresden – Chemnitz – Nuremberg–Karlsruhe – Haguenau – Saareguemines – Thionville – Sedan – Bucy les Pierrepont, where it detrained on November 29.

CAMBRAI.

10. Going into action southwest of Cambrai (Marcoing) on December 6, it was still in this sector at the beginning of March, 1918.

RECRUITING.

The 16th Reserve Division is recruited from the Rhine Province and all the Rhine districts. Thus, in October, 1916, it received men from the mining district of Westphalia, and also in March, 1917.

The 16th Reserve Division was a good division. It was very much exhausted on April 16 and 17, 1917, in the Cerny sector. During this action the 30th Reserve Infantry Regiment was remarkable for its desperate resistance and had only 50 prisoners taken.

During its stay in Lorraine (May and June, 1917) the 16th Reserve Division maintained a purely defensive attitude. The losses suffered on the Aisne and the nature of the replacements received appear to have sensibly diminished the combat value of the 30th Reserve Infantry Regiment.

In October, 1917, on the Galician front, the 16th Reserve Division was considered incapable of participating in active operations because of the large proportion of older men and the weakness of its effectives (according to prisoners statements).

1918.

PICARDY.

1. The division attacked on March 21 south of Marcoing. It was taken out on the 3d day of the offensive and sent to rest in the Ancre area. About April 10 the division relieved the 107th Division on the Ancre and held a sector until the 107th Division returned and relieved on April 27.

BATTLE OF THE SCARPE-SOMME.

2. The division rested near Puisieux until May 15, when it entered the line northwest of Beaumont Hamel and remained until about June 15. It rested in the neighborhood of Haplincourt until about July 4, when it returned to the Beaumont-Hamel sector. The British attack in August forced the division to retire through Muraumont (23d), Grandcourt (24th), Le Barque (25th), and Flers (27th). It was withdrawn on August 28, after suffering heavy losses.

3. The division again came into line on September 5 north of Equancourt. In five days' fighting it lost 600 prisoners. On September 10 it went to rest in the Bruges area, where it was until October 1.

BELGIUM.

4. On October 1 the division relieved the 16th Bavarian Division on the Ypres battle front, southeast of Staden. Throughout October it was engaged at Hooglede, Staden, and near Wynghene. It was withdrawn on October 28 and remained out of line in the Ghent area until the armistice.

The division was rated as second class. It was engaged as a sector-holding unit in active fronts during 1918.

16th Landwehr Division.
COMPOSITION.

	1915 Brigade.	1915 Regiment.	1916 Brigade.	1916 Regiment.	1917 Brigade.	1917 Regiment.	1918 Brigade.	1918 Regiment.
Infantry	2 Ldw.	3 Ldw. 374 (Jacobi Rgt.). 379 Ldw. (Tietz Rgt.). 378 (3 C. Dist.).	2 Ldw.	3 Ldw. 374. 379 Ldw.	2 Ldw.	3 Ldw. 374. 379 Ldw.	2 Ldw.	3 Ldw. 374. 379 Ldw.
Cavalry			94 Cav. Rgt.			2 Sqn. 8 Cuirassier Rgt. 5 Sqn. 94 Cav. Rgt. (?)	1 Sqn. 6 Cuirassier Rgt.	
Artillery			101 F. A. Rgt.		Art. Command: 101 F. A. Rgt.		101 F. A. Rgt. 791 Light Am. Col. 794 Light Am. Col. 1046 Light Am. Col.	
Engineers and Liaisons.			2 Ers. Co. 18 Pions.		(416) Pion Btn.: 2 Co. 34 Res. Pions. 3 Ers. Co. 18 Pions. 316 T. M. Co. 2 Light Fort Searchlight Section. Tel. Detch.		3 Ers. Co. 18 Pions. 1 Landst. Co. 8 C. Dist. Pions. 83 Searchlight Section. 516 Signal Command: 516 Tel. Detch.	
Medical and Veterinary.					71 Ambulance Co. 21 Field Hospital. 142 Field Hospital. 151 Field Hospital. Vet. Hospital.		71 Ambulance Co. 21 Field Hospital. 216 Vet. Hospital.	
Transport					996 M. T. Col.			
Odd units			157 Cyclist Co.					
Attached						1 C. Dist. Landst. Inf. Btn. No. 22.		

HISTORY.

(374th Infantry Regiment and 3d Landwehr Regiment: 1st Corps District—East Prussia. 379th Landwehr Regiment: 3d Corps District—Brandenburg.)

1915.

POLAND.

1. The 16th Landwehr Division (Landwehr Division of Koenigsberg, Sommer Division), providing the war garrison of Koenigsberg, took part in the battles on the East Prussian frontier in October, 1914, with a few of its future elements (1st Ersatz Battalion of the 12th Landwehr Regiment).

It was in the region of Mariampol from April until the end of August, 1915. It was identified in the Lipsk sector on August 30.

RUSSIA.

2. After the summer offensive it was sent to the sector between Krevo and Smorgoni (September).

1916.

1. The division was in the Krevo-Smorgoni sector during 1916.

1917.

1. Krevo-Smorgoni sector.

On July 22 and 23, 1917, the 16th Landwehr Division suffered very heavy losses withstanding Russian attacks in this area.

During the months which followed it gave its best elements to troops on the Western Front or to those assigned to the Western Front. At the end of November 70 per cent of the men of the 379th Landwehr Regiment were between the ages of 40 and 47 years (Russian interrogatory).

VALUE—1917 ESTIMATE.

The 16th Landwehr Division has always been on the Russian front. Its combat value appears mediocre.

1918.

1. The 16th Landwehr Division was still in line near Krevno in January. Moving then toward the east, it was near Orcha in April, and near Kharkov early in May. The 346th Infantry Regiment, which had remained in Russia after the departure for France of the two other regiments of the 14th Landwehr Division seems to have been attached to the 16th Landwehr Division.

SEA OF AZOV.

2. Early in September the division was identified in the Tanganrog region.

ROUMANIA.

3. The division left the Don region and went to Constantinople. It did not remain here however, but left immediately for Roumania, being identified at Constanza on October 28.

VALUE—1918 ESTIMATE.

The division was rated as fourth class.

16th Bavarian Division.

COMPOSITION.

	1917		1918	
	Brigade.	Regiment.	Brigade.	Regiment.
Infantry................	9 Bav.	11 Bav. 14 Bav. 21 Bav.	9 Bav.	8 Bav. 11 Bav. 14 Bav.
Calvary................	4 Sqn. 7 Bav. Light Cav. Rgt.		4 Sqn. 7 Bav. Light Cav. Rgt.	
Artillery................	Art. command: 3 Bav. F. A. Rgt.		8 Bav. F. A. Rgt. 1 Abt. 5 Bav. Ft. A. Rgt. 769 Light Am. Col. 130 Bav. Light Am. Col. 144 Bav. Light Am. Col. 161 Bav. Light Am. Col.	
Engineers and Liaisons.	(16 Bav.) Pion. Btn.: 14 Bav. Res. Pion. Co 15 Bav. Res. Pion. Co. 16 Bav. T. M. Co. 16 Bav. Tel. Detch.		16 Bav. Pion. Btn.: 14 Bav. Res. Pion. Co. 15 Bav. Res. Pion. Co. 16 Bav. Signal Command: 16 Bav. Tel. Detch. 104 Bav. Wireless Detch. 16 Bav. T. M. Co.	
Medical and Veterinary	8 Bav. Ambulance Co. 29 Bav. Field Hospital. Vet. Hospital.		8 Bav. Ambulance Co. 29 Bav. Field Hospital. 52 Bav. Field Hospital.	
Transports.............	Mt. Col.		697 M. T. Col.	

HISTORY.

(3d Bavarian Corps District.)

1917.

The 16th Bavarian Division was formed at the end of January, 1917, by taking three infantry regiments from existing Bavarian divisions—the 6th Bavarian Division furnished the 11th Bavarian Infantry Regiment; the 5th Bavarian Division the 14th Bavarian Infantry Regiment; the 6th Bavarian Reserve Division the 21st Bavarian Reserve Infantry Regiment. The 3d Field Artillery Regiment came from the 6th Bavarian Division.

ARTOIS.

1. On February 12, 1917, the 16th Bavarian Division replaced the 6th Bavarian Reserve Division south of Lens, opposite Souchez. It suffered serious losses there in February and March (raids by Canadian troops). After a period of rest, in March, in the Douai area, the division returned opposite Souchez and suffered in the British attack of April 9, which forced it back beyond Vimy Ridge. It was relieved on April 11, very much exhausted.

FLANDERS–MESSINES.

2. Toward the end of April the 16 Bavarian Division took over the calm sector of Armentieres (East), south of the Lys (Deulemont-Frelinghien). At the beginning of June, on account of the menace of the British attack on the Messines front, the division was transferred north of the Lys. During the battle which started on June 9 it

was not engaged as a whole; it sent some of its elements southeast of Messines to reenforce the 4th Bavarian Division.

3. The 16th Bavarian Division left the Lys sector, beginning of September, to go into reserve near Dadizeele, east of Ypres.

4. On September 20 it came up to replace the Bavarian Ersatz Division, which was very much exhausted by the British attack. It counterattacked north of the Lys. Its losses were such that it was relieved the next day.

5. After a period of rest at Bruges, the 16th Bavarian Division occupied the coast sector (Lombartzyde) from October 25 to November 22.

CAMBRESIS.

6. Transferred to the Cambrai front, it went into line on December 3 (Bullecourt–Queant) and launched a local attack on the 12th.

VALUE—1917 ESTIMATE.

The 16th Bavarian Division appears to be of good combat value. It may be compared with the best Bavarian Divisions. It was very much exhausted at Ypres in 1917, but in general its morale remained high.

1918.

BATTLE OF PICARDY.

1. The division did not participate in the initial attack of March 21, but remained in reserve of the front at Rumancourt. On the 23d it marched toward the front through Vaulx Vraucourt. The division was engaged at Sapignies on March 25, and on the 27th advanced on Gomiecourt, Courcelles, and Moyenneville. The division was relieved on April 7 and rested until the 26th.

YPRES.

2. It was reengaged south of the Scarpe, south of Feuchy, until May 19, when it moved north and took over a sector at Dranoutre. The route followed was through Cambrai–Tourcoing–Buskeque. On June 20 it went out to rest in the Lille area until the beginning of July. It returned to its former sector on July 4 and remained there until the end of July.

BATTLE OF THE SCARPE–SOMME.

3. It rested in the Lille area until August 20, when it moved south and was engaged west of Bapaume (Grevillers) in a German counterattack. It was thrown back on Avesnes les Bapaume (26th), Bancourt (30th), Villers au Flos (1st), until its relief on September 5. Losses of the division were heavy in this fighting.

4. The division went into reserve in Belgium at Iseghem until the 28th. At this time the 8th Bavarian Regiment, coming from the 14th Bavarian Division, replaced the 21st Bavarian Reserve, which was disbanded.

BATTLE OF DIXMUDE.

5. It was engaged north of Ypres and west of Roulers (Westroosebeke) from September 28 to October 5, with very heavy losses. The division was out of line for 10 days and then came back on the 15th southwest of Thourout. The Belgium advance forced it back southeast of Bruges (Oct. 18–19). On the 28th the division was relieved, but was obliged to return to line on November 3 and fought until the armistice.

VALUE—1918 ESTIMATE.

The division was rated as second class. It was engaged largely in holding defensive but active sectors on the British front in 1918.

17th Division.
COMPOSITION.

	1914 Brigade	1914 Regiment	1915 Brigade	1915 Regiment	1916 Brigade	1916 Regiment	1917 Brigade	1917 Regiment	1918 Brigade	1918 Regiment
Infantry	33. 34.	75. 76. 89 Gren. 90 Fus.	33. 34.	75. 76. 89 Gren. 90 Fus.	34.	75. 89 Gren. 90 Fus.	34.	75. 89 Gren. 90 Fus.	34.	75. 89. 90.
Cavalry	16 Dragoon Rgt. (3 Sqns.)				16 Dragoon Rgt. (3 Sqns.)		4 Sqn. 16 Dragoon Rgt.		4 Sqn. 16 Drag. Rgt.	
Artillery	17 Brig.: 24 F. A. Rgt. 60 F. A. Rgt.		17 Brig.: 24 F. A. Rgt. 60 F. A. Rgt.		17 Brig.: 24 F. A. Rgt. 60 F. A. Rgt.		17 Art. Command: 60 F. A. Rgt.		17 Art. Command: 60 F. A. Rgt. 1 Abt. 24 Ft. A. Rgt. (2, 3, and 4 Btries.). 940 Light Am. Col. 1329 Light Am. Col. 1270 Light Am. Col.	
Engineers and Liaisons.			1 Pion. Btn. No. 9: Field Co. 9 Pions. 17 Tel. Detch. 17 Pont. Engs		1 Pion. Btn. No. 9: 1 Co. 9 Pions. 17 T. M. Co. 17 Pont. Engs. 17 Tel. Detch.		126 Pion. Btn.: 1 Co. 9 Pions. 5 Co. 9 Pions. 17 T. M. Co. 17 Tel. Detch.		126 Pion. Btn.: 1 Co. 9 Pions. 5 Co. 9 Pions. 17 T. M. Co. 62 Searchlight Section. 17 Signal Command: 17 Tel. Detch. 138 Wireless Detch.	
Medical and Veterinary.							22 Ambulance Co. 84 Field Hospital. 89 Field Hospital. 17 Vet. Hospital.		22 Ambulance Co. 84 Field Hospital. 89 Field Hospital. 17 Vet. Hospital.	
Transports							550 M. T. Col.		550 M. T. Col.	
Attached					13 Anti-Aircraft Sections. 33 Balloon Sqn. 39 Labor Btn.		52 M. G. S. S. Detch. 13 Anti-Aircraft Section.			

HISTORY.

(9th Corps District—Hanseatic cities and Mecklenburg.)

1914.

Upon mobilization, the 17th Division with the 18th Division formed the 9th Army Corps (Schleswig-Holstein and Mecklemburg). It gave its 81st Brigade to the 17th Reserve Division (9th Reserve Corps) (new organization).

BELGIUM.

1. August, 1914, the 17th Division formed a part of the 1st German Army (Von Kluck). On the 3d of August it sent one of its brigades, the 34th (Mecklenburg), to Liege, where it was rejoined by its reservists and by the other brigade, the 33d (Hanseatic), (Aug. 9–13). On August 20 the division was with the 9th Corps of Louvain. It went into action against the British troops on the 24th. It went around Mauberge on the 25th and passed through Nesle, Roye, Vezaponin (north bank of the Aisne) September 1.

MARNE.

2. The division took part in the battle of the Marne at Châtillon sur Morin (Sept. 6), Esternay–Courgivaux (Sept. 7 and 8). It withdrew by way of Betz, Crépy en Valois Pierrefonds, crossed the Aisne at Rethondes (Sept. 11), and stopped in the area Carlepont, Nampcel, Audignicourt (Sept. 13). It went into action on the front Tracy le Mont east of Moulin sous Touvent (Sept. 16–21).

OISE.

3. In October it took up the position near Bailly (from the Oise to east of St. Mard) and remained there until the middle of November, 1915. Some of its elements occupied the right bank of the Oise near Connectancourt (Oct. 5 to Dec. 25).

4. November 17 it attacked Tracy le Val.

1915.

From January to October, 1915, it held the sector on the left bank of the Oise, east edge of the St. Mard wood. At the end of March the 76th Infantry Regiment was withdrawn and transferred to the 111th Division.

1. June 14 to 16 certain elements of the division counterattacked at Quennevières

CHAMPAGNE.

2. Withdrawn from the sector of the Oise (about Oct. 15), the division was transferred to Champagne. It occupied the front between the road Souain, Somme Py, and St. Hilaire, St. Souplet. It launched an attack on December 7.

1916.

1. The division was retained on the Champagne front northwest of Souain until June, 1916.

2. Relieved in the middle of June, it was sent to rest in the area southwest of Charleville (second half of June).

SOMME.

It entrained for the Somme between July 2 and 4. Certain elements of the 17th Division appeared in the sector of Biaches la Maisonnette, on July 9 and 10. The entire division was in line between Barleux and Belloy (July 10 to 25) and suffered heavy losses.

3. The division was withdrawn from the front and reorganized (end of July to Aug. 15).

4. From August 16 to August 20 to the middle of September it again occupied the sector of Barleux-Belloy.

ARTOIS.

5. At the beginning of October the division was sent to Artois. It held the line opposite Arras, between Roclincourt and Bailly, until December 24.

1917.

SOMME.

1. About January 9, 1917, the 17th Division occupied the sector of Py, south of the Ancre. Local combats in the neighborhood of Grandcourt and Miraumont (in January and February) caused it serious losses.

2. The division was withdrawn from the Somme front about March 20, at the time of the German retirement. It rested southwest of Douai (end of March and beginning of April).

ARTOIS.

3. On April 10 it was sent as a reenforcement to Arras to oppose the British offensive. It held the sector of Oppy–Gavrelle and suffered a great deal in the course of counterattacks. It was relieved on April 25. From March 27 to April 24 the 7th Company of 90th Fusiliers lost 115 men. (British Summary of Information.)

4. After a rest in the Tournai area until May 9 the 17th Division went into line in the sector of Boursies, Demicourt (west of Cambrai).

5. Relieved from this calm sector on May 28, it was sent to rest in the Cambrai area until June 9.

FLANDERS.

6. On this date it was transferred to Roulers by way of Valenciennes–Mons and put on the Ypres front north of Hooge. It was withdrawn three days before the British attack, on July 27, but suffered heavy losses from the bombardment.

7. For five weeks, until September 23, the division occupied the calm sector of Havrincourt (south of the road Bapaume–Cambrai).

8. On September 23 it again entrained for Flanders. Sent by way of Cambrai to Ledeghem, it went into action in the Polygon wood sector (northeast of Ypres). On September 26 it counterattacked without success and with great losses. It only remained in line for two days. In these engagements the 75th Infantry Regiment lost 30 officers and 1,000 men (British Summary of Information.)

9. Relieved on September 28 from the Flanders front, the 17th Division was sent south of Lens on October 17. It was still there on February, 1918.

RECRUITING.

The 17th Division is recruited from the Hanseatic towns and the Duchies of Mecklenburg. The sectional character was accentuated in June 1917, when the 89th Grenadiers took from the regiments of the 18th Division all the inhabitants of Mecklenburg who were in them. (Summary of Information, June 28.)

However, one must take into account a certain proportion of Poles from the 6th Corps District, received in the replacements of 1917.

VALUE—1917 ESTIMATE.

On July 11, 1916, the following appreciation was written of the 9th Army Corps:

"The 9th Army Corps gives the impression of a very good corps which would be a formidable adversary. The intellectual level of officers and men is appreciably higher than that ordinarily encountered in the German Army. This fact is due to the recruiting which, in most cases, is done in Hamburg, Bremen, and Luebeck."

After the last combats of Flanders (July and September, 1917), the 17th Division was considered as having its combative force perceptibly diminished on account of its losses.

In a general manner, the division has given a good account of itself in the course of its battles.

The Danes, who are numerous in its ranks, fight well and do not appear to occasion any weakness. (October, 1917.)

1918.

BATTLE OF PICARDY.

1. The division was relieved on the Acheville sector on February 17–18 by the 12th Reserve Division and went to rest near Douai until mid-March. On March 21 it was engaged near Lagnicourt and Moreuil (southeast of Arras), north of Vaulx-Vraucourt (22d), at Beliagnies and Lapigines (24th). The division was relieved on the 25th, after losing 50 per cent of its effectives. It rested until April 1, when it was reengaged near Bucquoy until the 10th.

2. The division was relieved by the 5th Bavarian Division, retired to the Favreuil-Sapignies-Beugnatre area on the 10th, and the next day went into billets near Cambrai. Later it moved to the Valenciennes area. On May 24 it left Bouchain and traveled via Marquion to Bapaume, where it came into line on that evening. While resting the division had undergone no special training. It is known to have received 1,300 men as a draft during this period.

3. It was reengaged in the Bucquoy sector from May 24 to June 23, when it returned to rest near Bouchain until July 17. The division was moved to Laon on July 24–25 and from there marched to the Vesle front by stage.

VESLE.

4. About August 1 the division went into line between Bazoches and Mont Notre Dame. It fell back on the Aisne toward Bourg et Comin from September 3–4, where it was relieved on September 15–16. The German communique of August 28 mentioned the 89th Grenadier Regiment for its conduct against the Americans at Bazoches.

AISNE–AILETTE.

5. The division was again in line on September 18 at Jouy–Aizy sector (north of Vailly). It retired to the Ailette on the 30th and shifted by rail to Semide.

CHAMPAGNE.

6. On October 4 it was engaged southeast of Machault (Somme Py road). The French attack forced it back to east of Attigny, where it was relieved on the 19th.

7. The division rested five days near Mouzon. It entrained on October 26 and moved to Rozoy, reaching there on the 27–28th.

ARDENNES.

8. It was put into line northwest of Chateau Porcien on the St. Fergeux–Recouvrance Road on October 28–29th. For its fighting east of Banonge on the 29th, the 90th Regiment was complimented by the German communique of the 30th. (558 prisoners were lost by the division on the 29th.) In November the division was driven back through Seraincourt, Remaucourt, Chaumont Porcien, Rocquigny, St. Jean aux Bois.

VALUE—1918 ESTIMATE.

The division was rated as first class. It was one of the best German divisions. Its conduct in the March offensive won the Kaiser's praise. Until August it was relatively fresh, but after that was engaged almost constantly in efforts to check the Allied offensive in Champagne. At the end the division was so reduced in numbers that it could muster but one or two battalions.

Its morale was excellent until late in the fall, when it was lowered noticeably. A mutiny and other acts of indiscipline were reported.

17th Reserve Division.

COMPOSITION.

	1914		1915		1916		1917		1918	
	Brigade.	Regiment.	Brigade.	Regiment.	Brigade.	Regiment.	Brigade.	Regiment.	Brigade.	Regiment.
Infantry	81. 33 Res.	162, 163, 75 Res., 76 Res.	81., 33 Res.	162, 163, 75 Res., 76 Res.	81. 33 Res.	162, 163, 75 Res., 76 Res.	81.	16, 162, 76 Res.	81.	162, 163, 76 Res.
Cavalry	6 Res. Hus. Rgt. (3 Sqns.).		6 Res. Hus. Rgt.		6 Res. Hus. Rgt.		1 Sqn. 6 Res. Hus. Rgt.		1 Sqn. 16 Res. Hus. Rgt.	
Artillery	17 Res. F. A. Rgt. (6 Btries.).		17 Res. F. A. Rgt. (8 Btries.).		17 Res. F. A. Rgt. (10 Btries.).		110 Art. Command: 17 Res. F. A. Rgt. (10 Btries.) (Nov. 4).		110 Art. Command: 17 Res. F. A. Rgt, 3 Abt. 26 Ft. A. Rgt. (7 and 9 Btries.). 703 Light Am. Col. 1245 Light Am. Col. 1299 Light Am. Col.	
Engineers and Liaisons.	4 Field Co. 2 Pion. Btn. No. 9.		4 Field Co. 2 Pion. Btn. No. 9. 17 Res. Pont. Engs. 17 Res. Tel. Detch.		4 Field Co. 2 Pion. Btn. No. 9. 340 Pion. Co. 217 T. M. Co. 17 Res. Pont. Engs. 17 Res. Tel. Detch.		(317) Pion. Btn.: 4 Co. 9 Pions. 340 Pion. Co. 217 T. M. Co. 255 Searchlight Section. 417 Tel. Detch.		317 Pion. Btn.: 4 Co. 9 Pions. 340 Pion. Co. 42 Searchlight Section. 417 Signal Command: 417 Tel. Detch. 111 Wireless Detch.	
Medical and Veterinary.							509 Ambulance Co. Field Hospital. Vet. Hospital.		509 Ambulance Co. 501 Field Hospital. 41 Res. Field Hospital. 417 Vet. Hospital.	
Transports							M. T. Col.		716 M. T. Col.	

HISTORY.

(9th Corps District.—Schleswig-Holstein and the Hanseatic cities.)

1914.

1. The 17th Reserve Division formed with the 18th Reserve Division, the 9th Reserve Corps. One of its brigades is a surplus brigade of the 9th Army Corps (the 81st).

2. During the first part of the month of August, 1914, the 17th Reserve Division was used to guard the coast of Schleswig-Holstein.

BELGIUM.

3. Entraining on August 23 for Belgium, it was at Louvain on the 25th, at Brussels on the 30th (until Sept. 3). It reached Termonde on September 4, and remained outside of Antwerp.

OISE.

4. On September 9, it was transferred in haste to the Valenciennes area and then sent to the Oise. It detrained on the 13th at Chauny and went into action on the right bank of the Oise, south of Noyon (Sept. 15 to 20).

5. About October 7 the 17th Reserve Division was sent to the vicinity of Roye, where it lost heavily.

6. About the middle of November the division occupied the front between the Avre and Roye. On December 20 it was in line between Ribécourt and Thiescourt.

1915.

On January 4, 1915, the 75th Reserve Infantry Regiment entrained at Noyon for Upper Alsace (Hartmannswillerkopf), and did not return to the division until May.

ROYE (SOMME).

1. On February 6 the division left the banks of the Oise to go back to the area south of the Avre, between Lassigny and Roye. It remained in this sector until the month of October.

2. Toward the end of September elements of the division formed a part of the Hartz Division in Artois (Sick and Balthasar Regiments).

ARTOIS.

3. In October the 17th Reserve Division was withdrawn from the front south of Roye and sent to Artois, near Lens (Liévin-Givenchy).

1916.

1. The 17th Reserve Division remained in Artois until the battle of the Somme. In February it launched several attacks.

SOMME.

2. About the beginning of July the 163d Infantry Regiment was sent, temporarily, to reinforce the 185th Division, engaged along the Somme near Cantalmaison.

3. The 17th Reserve Division was in line as a whole north of the Somme about July 25 (Bazentin-Pozières). It remained there until August 9–14.

4. It was sent to rest and to be reorganized near Valenciennes.

5. At the end of August it occupied the sector of Loos-Hulluch (north of Lens). In September the 75th Reserve Infantry Regiment was sent to the 211th Division.

6. About September 21 the division returned to the Somme (Le Transloy-Combles), where it lost heavily (losses, 51 per cent).

7. Relieved about October 10 it was transferred to Belgium.

8. From October 23–25 to the end of January, 1917, it was in line between Het Sas and the Ypres–Roulers railroad.

1917.

1. At the end of January, 1917, the 17th Reserve Division was sent for a month's rest near Bruges, and again took over its sector.

ARTOIS.

2. It left the Ypres salient at the end of March and went into line southeast of Arras. On April 9 it suffered very heavy losses from the British offensives (2,100 prisoners).

3. On April 12–13 the division was relieved and sent to rest and to be reorganized.

CAMBRESIS.

4. On April 27 it took over the sector of Havrincourt (southwest of Cambrai) and occupied it until June 1.

ARTOIS.

5. Transferred to the Arras front, the 17th Reserve Division went back into line in the sector Guémappe–Monchy le Preux, where it launched several violent battles during the month of June. At the end of July it extended its sector toward the north (south of the Scarpe).

6. Relieved at the end of August it went back into line at the beginning of September southeast of Arras (Vis en Artois). It lost especially heavy during the gas attacks. (It received, on Oct. 23, 40 men per company, coming from Hamburg and Beverloo, slightly trained, and on Nov. 10 men taken from the Russian front.) (Summary of Information, Dec. 2.)

7. The 17th Reserve Division left Artois in the middle of November.

FLANDERS.

8. Sent to Flanders the division took over the sector at Becelaere about November 18. The division was engaged against the British attack of December 3 and suffered heavy losses. It underwent violent attacks and left the front in the beginning of January, 1918.

RECRUITING.

The division is recruited in Schleswig-Holstein, the Hanseatic cities, and adjacent parts of Hanover. Some replacement troops were from Westphalia, and in September, 1916, men from Brandenburg of the 1917 class.

VALUE—1917 ESTIMATE.

During the year 1917 the 17th Reserve Division launched a great number of terrible attacks on the Arras front and in Flanders.

At Becelaere (Dec., 1917) it gave proof of great stubborness. The 162d Infantry Regiment carried out a successful attack in this sector on December 14. However, a few months before, on June 18, the 163d Infantry Regiment is said to have refused to advance. (Summary of Information, June 19.)

Although this division is not one of the best in the German Army and its morale is mediocre it is capable of offering serious resistance.

1918.

BATTLE OF THE LYS.

1. The northern sector was a fairly quiet front in the winter months and the division remained in line here until just before the German offensive on the Lys of April 9. Prior to this attack all of the division but one battalion of the 76th Reserve Regiment was withdrawn and sent hurriedly to the vicinity of Messines. It attacked there with other German divisions on the morning of April 9 under orders to take Messines by the evening of the 10th and to push ahead as far as possible. It gained considerable ground at heavy cost. Elements of the 7th Division relieved part of the 17th Reserve Division a few days later, but the bulk of the division remained in line until about

April 22, when it was relieved by the 13th Reserve Division and the 19th Reserve Division.

2. On April 24 the division arrived in the Maldeghem area for a long rest. While there the divisional and the brigade commanders were decorated for their part in the Lys offensive. Death notices published in the German newspapers disclosed the death of two battalion and many company commanders on the Lys. While at rest the division went through courses of training. On June 4 it entrained at Eecloo and moved via Mons and Marle to Tergnier. At this time the Noyon offensive (June 9) was being organized. The division marched at night to Boulogne la Grasse (10th) and went into line on the evening of the 11th near Mery, relieving the 227th Division.

OISE.

3. The division was in heavy fighting immediately and suffered severely in the successful French counteroffensive of June 16.

BATTLE OF THE MATZ.

4. The French attack in August threw the division back on Canny sur Matz and later north of Fresnieres. It passed to second line about August 31, but was reengaged on September 5 at Esmery–Hallon. It suffered heavy losses and was taken out on September 9.

5. The division was moved to Lorraine, where it rested a month and returned to Le Cateau on October 10.

6. The division was engaged at Le Cateau on October 11 and resisted the British attack until November 3. It fought near Le Cateau (Oct. 18), Bazuel (21st), Forest (23d), Landrecies (24th), and Bois L'Eveque (Oct. 27). The division received the men of the 265th Reserve Regiment (108th Division) as a draft in October.

7. The division was out of line from November 3 to the armistice.

VALUE—1918 ESTIMATE.

The division was rated as first class. Its effectives were generally young; 31 per cent belong to the 1919 class and 18 per cent to the 1918 class on October 1. It took a prominent part in the Lys and Noyon offensives, winning a reputation for its vigorous attacks. Its defensive work in October around Le Cateau was of a high order.

17th Landwehr Division.

COMPOSITION.

	1915		1916		1917		1918 [1]	
	Brigade.	Regiment.	Brigade.	Regiment.	Brigade.	Regiment.	Brigade.	Regiment.
Infantry.........	182 Ldw.	380 (Kurbatowski Rgt.) 381 (Nussbaum Rgt.) 23 Landst.	182 Ldw.	380. 381. 23 Landst.	182 Ldw.	380. 381. 23 Landst.	182 Ldw.	330. 380. 23 Landst.
Cavalry.........				1 Landst. Sqn. (1 C. Dist.).		1 Landst. Sqn. (1 C. Dist.).		
Artillery.........			235 F. A. Rgt.		Art. Command: 235 F. A. Rgt. 828 F. A. Btry.			
Engineers and Liaisons.					(417) Pion. Btn.: 2 Ers. Co. 23 Pion. 317 T. M. Co. 182 Tel. Detch.		87 Searchlight Section. 517 Signal command: 517 Tel. Detch.	
Medical and Veterinary.					206 Ambulance Co. 152 Field Hospital. 206 Field Hospital. Vet. Hospital.		206 Ambulance Co. 171 Field Hospital.	
Transports.........					M. T. Col.			
Attached.........	2d Cyclist Co. 1 Jag. Btn.		2 Cyclist Co. 1 Jag. Btn. 16 Cav. Brig. (7 and 8 Horse Jag, and 5 Res. Drag. Rgts.). 9 C. Dist. Landst. Inf. Btn. No. 13.		2 Cyclist Co. 1 Jag. Btn. 158 Cyclist Co. 91 Cav. Rgt. 7 C. Dist. Landst. Inf. Btn. No. 50. 9 C. Dist. Landst. Inf. Btn. No. 13.			

[1] The elements below are those listed under the 700th Postal Sector. Other elements belonging to the 17th Landwehr Division, but in other sectors, are listed as attached to whatever divisions may hold those sectors.

HISTORY.

(380th Infantry Regiment: 1st and 17th Corps Districts.   381st Infantry Regiment: 12th and 5th Corps Districts.)

1915.

1. The 17th Landwehr Division, formed on the Eastern Front in the Niémen Army, with the elements of the former Esebeck Brigade, appeared about the month of December, 1915.

RUSSIA.

2. Before forming a part of the 17th Landwehr Division the Esebeck Brigade took part in the offensive against the Russians north of Kovno (July–August, 1915), was east of Vilna about the end of September, and took up its position west of Kosiany (northwest of Postavy) in October.

POSTAVY.

3. The 17th Landwehr Division, being formed in this sector by the addition of the 23d Landsturm Regiment to the Esebeck Brigade, remained in line in the area of Vidzy-Postavy (Tveretch), from the end of 1915 to the beginning of 1918.

1916.

1. The Division remained in the Tveretch sector.

1917.

1. The Division remained in the Tveretch sector.

VALUE—1917 ESTIMATE.

The division is of mediocre value.

1918.

1. The 17th Landwehr Division was identified in the Tveretch region toward the end of January.

2. About the middle of March it advanced into Russia and was identified in the Polotsk-Vitebsk region in March, April, and June.

3. The division was identified on the Don on September 26.

VALUE—1918 ESTIMATE.

The division was rated as fourth class.

18th Division.
COMPOSITION.

	1914		1915		1916		1917		1918	
	Brigade.	Regiment.	Brigade.	Regiment.	Brigade.	Regiment.	Brigade.	Regiment.	Brigade.	Regiment.
Infantry	35. 36.	84, 86 Fus. 31, 85.	35. 36.	84, 86 Fus. 31, 85.	36.	31, 85, 86 Fus.	36.	31, 85, 86 Fus.	36	31, 85, 86.
Cavalry	16 Dragoon Rgt. (3 Sqns.).				16 Dragoon Rgt. (3 Sqns.).		2 Sqn. 16 Drag. Rgt.		2 Sqn. 16 Drag. Rgt.	
Artillery	18 Brig.: 9 F. A. Rgt. 45 F. A. Rgt.		18 Brig.: 9 F. A. Rgt. 45 F. A. Rgt.		18 Brig.: 9 F. A. Rgt. 45 F. A. Rgt.		18 Art. Command: 45 F. A. Rgt.		18 Art. Command: 45 F. A. Rgt. 2 Abt. 28 Ft. A. Rgt. (4 and 5 Btries.). 749 Light Am. Col. 753 Light Am. Col. 1,362 Light Am. Col.	
Engineers and Liaisons.			1 Pion. Btn. No. 9: Field Co. 9 Pions. 18 Pont. Enges. 18 Tel. Detch.		1 Pion. Btn. No. 9: 2 Co. 9 Pions. 18 T. M. Co. 18 Tel. Detch. 18 Pont. Enge.		1 Pion. Btn. No. 9: 2 Co. 9 Pions. 3 Co. 9 Pions. 18 T. M. Co. 18 Tel. Detch.		9 Pion. Btn.: 2 Co. 9 Pions. 3 Co. 9 Pions. 18 T. M. Co. 101 Searchlight Section. 18 Signal Command: 18 Tel. Detch. 54 Wireless Detch.	
Medical and Veterinary.							23 Ambulance Co. 90 Field Hospital. Vet. Hospital.		23 Ambulance Co. 90 Field Hospital. 92 Field Hospital. 18 Vet. Hospital.	
Transports							M. T. Col.		551 M. T. Col.	
Attached					57 Anti-Aircraft Section.		47 Anti-Aircraft Section. 505 Anti-Aircraft Btry.			

HISTORY.

(9th Corps District—Schleswig-Holstein.)

1914.

BELGIUM-MARNE.

1. At the outbreak of the war the 18th Division (of the 9th Army Corps, with the 17th Division) formed a part of the 1st Army (Von Kluck). Entraining at Aix la Chapelle August 8–10, it was before Liege on the 13th, went into action at Tirlemont on the 18th, at Mons on the 23d, entered France on the 25th, crossed the Marne at Chateau Thierry on September 3, and took part in the battle of the Marne on September 6 and 7, at Esternay and Courgivaux.

AISNE.

2. After the retreat it took up its position north of the Aisne, where it remained for more than a year in various parts of the sector.

1915.

In March, 1915, the 84th Infantry Regiment was taken from the 18th Division to help in the formation of the 54th Division.

AISNE.

1. Until October, 1915, the 18th Division occupied the sectors of the Aisne. On June 3 the 86th Fusiliers attacked at Quennevieres, suffering enormous losses. (Between June 18 and July 3 its 5th Company received at least 115 men as replacements; the 8th Company, 120.)

CHAMPAGNE.

2. From October, 1915, until June, 1916, the 18th Division was in Champagne (Souain area).

1916.

1. On February 25, 1916, the 31st Infantry Regiment suffered heavy losses south of St. Marie a Py; its 11th Company was entirely destroyed or captured.

SOMME.

2. From July to September, 1916, the 18th Division was in action along the Somme (south of the Somme). At Belloy, on September 4, the 4th Company of the 86th Fusiliers was destroyed with the exception of 23 men.

ARTOIS.

3. From October until the beginning of December the division was in the Arras area (east).

4. It left Artois about December 12 to take over a sector along the Somme (Grandcourt).

1917.

SOMME.

1. About February 18, 1917, the 18th Division was withdrawn from the front, then sent back into line at the beginning of March, at Puisieux-Gommecourt (Somme).

ARTOIS.

2. At the end of March it was transferred to Artois, north of the Scarpe, and went into action at Roeux and Fampoux, from April 10 to April 23.

3. Relieved at the end of April, it went back into line about May 8, in the area south of Arras, and from that date until the end of August occupied sectors in the vicinity of Cambrai (Villers-Plouich, Havrincourt, Marcoing).

FLANDERS.

4. On August 27 the 18th Division was relieved from the Cambrai front (Ribecourt-Marcoing sector) and entrained for Flanders, where it was made an army reserve in the Ruddervoorde (northeast of Thourout). It was there reorganized with replace-

ments coming from troops of the 9th Corps District stationed in Russia (taken from the 426th Infantry Regiment, the 31st Landwehr Regiment, and the 3d Ersatz Reserve Regiment).

5. It went into the sector Mangelaere about September 16 and underwent the Franco-British attack of October 9, which caused it rather serious losses.

RUSSIA.

6. The 18th Division was relieved about October 14 and transferred to Russia, where it made a rather short stay in the Vilna area.

ALSACE.

7. It was back in Upper Alsace about the end of November, in the region of Mulhouse, at the beginning of February, 1918.

RECRUITING.

The 18th Division is recruited from Schleswig-Holstein (Prussians and Danes). A certain proportion of Poles from Silesia appeared in the replacements of 1917 (especially in the 31st Infantry Regiment).

VALUE—1917 ESTIMATE.

The 18th Division has always passed as being a good division. However, in the course of the Franco-British attack of October 9, 1917, none of its elements carried out the counterattacks described by their leaders; however, in order to form a correct judgment of this, one must take account of the intensity of the bombardment, the state of the terrain, and the weakness of the effectives in line at that moment.

1918.

CAMBRAI.

1. The 18th Division left Alsace, entraining at Mulhouse, about the 12th of February, and traveled via Thionville and Sedan to Bertry, where it detrained after a journey of 2½ days. It relieved the 107th Division near Gonnelieu (south of Cambrai) the 16th. It was withdrawn the beginning of March, and had a few days' training near Ligny en Cambresis.

2. It left here on the 17th and marched to Malincourt, where it stayed three days.

ST. QUENTIN.

3. It reenforced the battle front near Hargicourt (north of St. Quentin) on March 21. The next day the division commander was killed. The division was withdrawn about the 26th.

SOMME.

4. During the night of March 29-30 the division relieved the 1st Division near Sailly le Sec (south of Albert). Here again heavy losses were suffered. The division received a draft of 500 men, mostly returned wounded. It is not clear just what happened during this period and as late as about the 18th of May, when the division was withdrawn, but it seems as though its regiments and the regiments of the 50th Reserve Division and the 199th Division interrelieved each other.

TOURNAI.

5. The division went to the Tournai region, where it rested, was completely reconstituted, and trained.

SOISSONS.

6. On August 1 it reenforced the battle front near Launoy (southwest of Soissons), after having left Tournai July 21 and having detrained at La Fere the following day. Toward the end of its tour in line (it was withdrawn during the night of Oct. 12-13), it retreated along the line Froidmont-Eppes.

OISE.

7. The division was transported by truck and relieved the 22d Reserve Division near Bernoville (northeast of St. Quentin) on October 15. On the 17th it withdrew to Grougis, and then to the Sambre Canal. During these operations it lost more than 500 prisoners. It was withdrawn about the 28th.

8. On November 4 the division reenforced the front near Hannapes (north of Guise) and withdrew, with the remainder of the line, through Iron, the Nouvion region, Boulogne sur Helpe, and Etroeung. It was still in line on the 11th.

VALUE—1918 ESTIMATE.

The 18th Division is rated as being first class. Since the spring, however, it has not been used to any great extent where heavy fighting was in progress, and it may well be it has deteriorated. It is known that part of the 6th Company of the 86th Regiment refused to go into line on October 25 until it was threatened with being shot.

18th Reserve Division.
COMPOSITION.

	1914 Brigade.	1914 Regiment.	1915 Brigade.	1915 Regiment.	1916 Brigade.	1916 Regiment.	1917 Brigade.	1917 Regiment.	1918 Brigade.	1918 Regiment.
Infantry	53 Res. 36 Res. 9 Res. Jag. Btn.	84 Res. 86 Res. 31 Res. 90 Res.	35 Res. 36 Res. 9 Res. Jag. Btn.	84 Res. 86 Res. 31 Res. 90 Res.	35 Res. 9 Res. Jag. Btn.	31 Res. 84 Res. 86 Res.	35 Res.	31 Res. 84 Res. 86 Res.	35 Res.	31 Res. 84 Res. 86 Res.
Cavalry	7 Res. Hus. Rgt. (3 Sqns.).		7 Res. Hus. Rgt.		7 Res. Hus. Rgt.		3 Sqn. 6 Res. Hus. Rgt.		2 Sqn. 16 Hus. Rgt.	
Artillery	18 Res. F. A. Rgt. (6 Btries.).		18 Res. F. A. Rgt. (8 Btries.).		18 Res. F. A. Rgt. (10 Btries.).		112 Art. Command: 18 Res. F. A. Rgt.		112 Art. Command: 18 Res. F. A. Rgt. 126 Ft. A. Btn. 757 Light Am. Col. 1250 Light Am. Col. 1304 Light Am. Col.	
Engineers and Liaisons.	1 and 2 Res. Cos. 2 Pion. Btn. No. 9.		1 and 2 Res. Coś. 2 Pion. Btn. No. 9. 18 Res. Pont. Engs. 18 Res. Tel. Detch.		1 and 2 Res. Cos. 2 Pion. Btn No. 9. 218 T. M. Co. 18 Res. Pont. Engs. 18 Res. Tel. Detch.		(318) Pion. Btn.: 1 Res. Co. 9 Pions. 2 Res. Co. 9 Pions. 218 T. M. Co. 9 Res. Searchlight Section. 418 Tel. Detch.		318 Pion. Btn.: 1 Co. 9 Res. Pions. 2 Co. 9 Res. Pions. 218 T. M. Co. 48 Searchlight Section. 418 Signal Command: 418 Tel. Detch. 115 Wireless Detch.	
Medical and Veterinary.							513 Ambulance Co. 400 Field Hospital. Vet Hospital.		513 Ambulance Co. 400 Field Hospital. 44 Res. Field Hospital. 418 Vet. Hospital.	
Transports							M. T. Col.		717 M. T. Col.	
Attached					95 Labor Btn. Anti-Aircraft Section.					

HISTORY.

(9th Corps District—Schleswig-Holstein and Mecklenburg.)

1914.

1. The 18th Reserve Division formed the 9th Reserve Corps, with the 17th Reserve Division.

BELGIUM.

2. From the outbreak of the war until August 22, 1914, the 18th Reserve Division was guarding the coast of Schleswig-Holstein. Entraining about this time, it went into Belgium, where it advanced rapidly. After taking and sacking Louvain (Aug. 25) it occupied Hamme (Sept. 1), Termonde (Sept. 4).

OISE.

3. On the 9th it was hastily transferred by way of Tournai and Valenciennes to the Oise area. Entraining on the 13th at Chauny, it reenforced the front south of Noyon and went into action between Carlepont and Lassigny (Sept. 15-21).

4. At the beginning of October the 18th Reserve Division was taken to the valley of the Avre. It fought in the vicinity of Roye (Laucourt, Oct. 2-3). At the beginning of November the division front extended between the Avre and Beuvraignes.

LASSIGNY.

5. On November 15 it bore to the south and held the region of the Loges-Lassigny wood.

1915.

In March, 1915, it gave the 90th Reserve Infantry Regiment to the 54th Division, a new formation.

1. The 18th Reserve Division occupied the Lassigny area until October, 1915, without any serious engagements. In October it took over elements of the Hartz Division (6th Army), among others the 3d Battalion of the 31st Infantry Regiment which contained four battalions from May, 1915, to September, 1916.

ARTOIS.

2. About October 23 the division was sent to Artois (Givenchy), where it launched several local attacks.

1916.

1. The 18th Reserve Division remained in the Lievin–Givenchy sector until July, 1916.

SOMME.

2. After a few days at rest, July 13 to July 28, it took part in the battle of the Somme, north of Pozieres, in several serious attacks.

3. It was reorganized in the Valenciennes area during the second half of August.

4. At the end of August, it was sent northeast of Lens (Pont a Vendin).

5. At the beginning of October the 18th Reserve Division again went into action along the Somme, north of Combles, (Morval, Sailly Saillisel). It suffered heavily in a series of local attacks.

FLANDERS.

6. Withdrawn from the front about October 12-16, the division was transferred to Belgium. On October 23-25 it went into line north of Ypres.

1917.

1. The 18th Reserve Division occupied the Ypres salient (Pilkem) until the end of March, 1917.

ARTOIS.

2. After a short rest at Roulers, the division was concentrated at Vitry en Artois (Apr. 1). Going into action southeast of Arras (Heninel), it underwent the British attack (Apr. 9), which caused it heavy losses (500 prisoners).

3. The division left the Artois front about April 15, and after a few days at rest took over the sector of Cherisy-Guemappe (southeast of Arras in May). .

4. At the beginning of June the 18th Reserve Division was relieved and sent to rest.

FLANDERS.

5. Transferred to Flanders about June 16, it first remained in reserve behind the Messines front. On July 3 the division was in action west of Houthem and suffered severe losses in consequence of local actions and bombardments.

6. Relieved about August 8, it was at rest in the Cambrai area until August 16. It then occupied the quiet sector of Queant (west of Cambrai) until the middle of October.

7. It was sent to Flanders again on October 20, and went into line near the Ypres–Menin railroad (Oct. 28–29).

RECRUITING.

The 18th Reserve Division is recruited in Schleswig-Holstein.

The Mecklenburgers, according to an order in 1917, had to return to their national regiment, the 90th Infantry Reserve Regiment, which no longer belonged to the division. A limited number of men from the 7th and 10th Corps districts (Westphalia and Hanover) is found.

VALUE 1917—ESTIMATE.

The 18th Reserve Division has the same value as the 17th Reserve Division. At the end of 1917 it is difficult to form an opinion as to its combat value. It has not been in any serious action since the battle of Arras, having arrived in Flanders when the autumn operations were about at an end. The morale of the division may be considered as passable. (British Summary of Information, February, 1918.)

1918.

1. The 18th Reserve Division was relieved by the 214th Division in the Gheluvelt sector on January 6. It went to rest in the vicinity of Menin and while there was intensively trained in open warfare.

YPRES.

2. On February 18 the division relieved the 214th Division in its former sector north of Gheluvelt (east of Ypres). It was relieved by the 7th Reserve Division about March 31.

LA BASSEE.

3. It reinforced the battle front near Locon (northwest of La Bassee) on April 9, and was withdrawn about the 18th, going to rest in the Sainghin area (southeast of Lille).

4. On May 14 it relieved the 25th Division west of Locon, and was relieved by the extension of fronts of the neighboring divisions about the 18th of June, when it went to rest in the region of Gondecourt (east of La Bassee). •

5. About the 14th of July it relieved the 1st Guard Reserve Division near Givenchy (north of the La Bassee Canal—west of La Bassee); relieved September 3, it went to rest in the region north of Denain.

CAMBRAI.

6. On the 29th of September the division reentered the line near Proville and Rumilly (south of Cambrai), and was still in line when the armistice was signed. It was thought that it had been withdrawn October 8, again on the 18th, and on the 4th of November, but considering the speed with which the German withdrawal was

executed, the confusion necessarily incident thereto, and the fact that the division always turned up a day or two later in the same relative position it had previously occupied, it seems best to assume that it was continuously in line.

VALUE—1918 ESTIMATE.

The 18th Reserve is considered a second-class division. It did not distinguish itself in the Lys offensive, and it is reported that thereafter it was to be used only as a holding division. At any rate, it engaged in no other German offensives, and, indeed, no other heavy fighting, until the beginning of October or sometime after practically the whole front had become active on account of the combined allied push.

18th Landwehr Division.
COMPOSITION.

	1914-15 Brigade	1914-15 Regiment	1916 Brigade	1916 Regiment	1917 Brigade	1917 Regiment	1918 Brigade	1918 Regiment
Infantry	19 Ldw.	19 Ldw. 47 Ldw. 72 Ldw. 133 Ldw.	20 Ldw. 28 Ldw.	19 Ldw. 47 Ldw. 133 Ldw. 57 Ldw. 72 Ldw.	19 Ldw.	47 Ldw. 57 Ldw. 72 Ldw.	19 Ldw.	47 Ldw. 57 Ldw. 72 Ldw.
Cavalry			Ers. Sqn. 1 Horse Jag. Rgt. Ers. Sqn. 1 Uhlan Rgt.		Ers. Sqn. 12 Drag. Rgt. Ers. Sqn. 2 Uhlan Rgt.		4 Sqn. 4 Drag. Rgt.	
Artillery			5 Ldw. F. A. Rgt. 835 F. A. Btry.		Art. Command: 5 Ldw. F. A. Rgt.		5 Ldw. F. A. Rgt.	
Engineers and Liaisons.			2 Res. Co. 1 Pions. 344 Pion. Co. 166 T. M. Co.		43 Pion. Btn.: 2 Res. Co. 1 Pions. 344 Pion. Co. 166 T. M. Co. 218 Searchlight Section. Tel. Detch.		2 Landst. Co. 3 C. Dist. Pions. 117 Searchlight Section. 518 Signal Command: 518 Tel. Detch.	
Medical and Veterinary.					258 Ambulance Co. 296 Field Hospital. 305 Field Hospital. 18 Ldw. Field Hospital. Vet. Hospital.		258 Ambulance Co. 305 Field Hospital. 18 Ldw. Field Hospital. 130 Vet. Hospital.	
Transports					534 M. T. Col.			
Odd Units			Cyclist Co.		60 Cyclist Co.			
Attached			43 Labor Btn.		43 Labor Btn.			

HISTORY.

(47th Landwehr Regiment: 5th Corps district.—Posen.) (57th Landwehr Regiment: 7th Corps district.—Westphalia.) (72d Landwehr Regiment: 4th Corps district.— Prussian Saxony.)

1914–15.

RUSSIA.

1. The 18th Landwehr Division is the former Bredow Division.

POLAND.

2. After being engaged in September, 1914, in the battle of the Mazurian Lakes, the Bredow Division fought in the Polish campaign: Battle of Warsaw (Oct. 9–19, 1914); battles on the Rawka (Oct. 22–28); near Czenstochow (Nov. 10–Dec. 15); between Pilica and Nidi, in the mountainous region of Kielce (December, 1914, to July, 1915).

3. In the middle of July, 1915, the division was in action near Sienno and before Ivangorod (breaking of the Russian front), crossed the Vistula (end of July), was in action between the Vistula and the Bug (Aug. 8–18), and advanced in action as far as Slonim and the Upper Chtchara (September). The front becoming stabilized in this area, the Bredow Division took up its position southeast of Novo-Grudok (near Goroditche in October and November). At the end of November it went into the sector southeast of Liakhovitchi (south of Baranovitchi). The number 18 appears to be given to the Bredow Division in December.

1916.

BARANOVITCHI.

1. The 18th Landwehr Division remained on the front south of Baranovitchi (Liakhovitchi) for more than two years (November, 1915, to the beginning of 1918). From July 2 to July 9, 1916, it withstood the Russian attacks in this area.

2. In June, 1916, two regiments of the division, the 57th Landwehr and the 133d Landwehr, were transferred to Volhyania (north of Lutsk), assigned to the Rusche Division and were in action against the offensive of Broussilov. The 57th Landwehr Regiment rejoined the 18th Landwehr Division near Baranovitchi in August. The 133d Landwehr Regiment was provisionally a part of the 92d Division.

1917.

1. The division held the sector Baranovitchi-Liakhovitchi.

2. In October 900 men from the 18th Landwehr Division, chosen from among the youngest, were entrained for the western front. In April a number had been taken from the 72d Landwehr Regiment for the 5th Reserve Division. In November the 47th Landwehr Regiment furnished men to the 15th Division. As the 18th Landwehr Division had received no replacements since the end of July, the trench strength of the 72d Landwehr Regiment had fallen, at the end of October, to 50–60 men per company (Russian interrogation).

VALUE—1917 ESTIMATE.

The division has been on the Russian front since the beginning of the war. Combat value appears to be mediocre.

1918.

1. In February, 1918, the 18th Landwehr Division advanced into the interior of Russia. The 72d Landwehr Regiment was identified between Mohilev and Gomel on February 2. In May the 57th Landwehr Regiment held the very long front from north of Kopys to south of Chklov.

2. In the middle of June the division was in the Orcha region. It was again identified in the region of Mohilev on the 22d of September.

3. There were rumors during October that the division had come to the Woevre, but since the division was never actually identified it is not believed that it left Russia.

VALUE—1918 ESTIMATE.

The division was rated as fourth class.

19th Division.
COMPOSITION.

	1914 Brigade.	1914 Regiment.	1915 Brigade.	1915 Regiment.	1916 Brigade.	1916 Regiment.	1917 Brigade.	1917 Regiment.	1918 Brigade.	1918 Regiment.
Infantry	37. 38.	78. 91. 73 Fus. 74.	37. 38.	78. 91. 73 Fus. 74.	37.	74. 78. 91.	37.	74. 78. 91.	37.	74. 78. 91.
Cavalry	17 Hus. Rgt. (3 Sqns.).		17 Hus. Rgt. (3 Sqns.).		17 Hus. Rgt. (2 Sqns.).		3 Sqn. 17 Hus. Rgt.		3 Sqn. 17 Hus. Rgt.	
Artillery	19 Brig.: 26 F. A. Rgt. 62 F. A. Rgt.		19 Brig.: 26 F. A. Rgt. 62 F. A. Rgt.		19 Brig.: 26 . A. Rgt. 6.. F. A. Rgt.		19 Art. Command: 26 F. A. Rgt.		19 Art. Command: 26 F. A. Rgt. 93 Ft. A. Btn. 740 Light Am. Col. 905 Light Am. Col. 1156 Light Am. Col.	
Engineers and Liaisons.			1 Pion. Btn. No. 10: Field Co. 10 Pions. 19 Pont. Engs. 19 Tel. Detch.		1 Pion. Btn. No. 10: 1 Co. 10 Pions. 19 T. M. Co. 19 Pont. Engs. 19 Tel. Detch.		(1/10 or 127) Pion. Btn.: 1 Co. 10 Pions. 5 Co. 10 Pions. 19 T. M. Co. 296 Searchlight Section. 19 Tel. Detch. 19 Pont. Engs.		127 Pion. Btn.: 1 Co. 10 Pions. 5 Co. 10 Pions. 19 T. M. Co. 50 Signal Command. 19 Tel. Detch. 4 Wireless Detch.	
Medical and Veterinary.							25 Ambulance Co. 6 Field Hospital. 95 Field Hospital. 97 Field Hospital. 19 Vet. Hospital.		25 Ambulance Co. 95 Field Hospital. 97 Field Hospital. 19 Vet. Hospital.	
Transports							M. T. Col.		552 M. T. Col.	

HISTORY.

(10th Corps District—Hanover and the Grand Duchy of Oldenburg.)

1914.

1. The 19th Division constituted, at the outbreak of the war, with the 20th Division, the 10th Army Corps (Hanover), which was a part of the 2d Army (Von Buelow).

BELGIUM-MARNE.

2. On August 3 one of its brigades, the 38th, was at Malmédy for the attack upon Liége, where it went into action on the 5th. After the fall of Liége the 19th Division, going around Namur on the north, fought at Charleroi on the 23d, entered France on the 25th, and went into action at Guise, at St. Quentin. It took part in the battle of the Marne on the right of the 20th Division, and then withdrew with that division to the northwest of Reims.

CHAMPAGNE.

3. In October it was in the same sector attached to the 7th Army (Von Heeringen) and remained during the winter of 1914–15.

1915.

RUSSIA.

1. In March, 1915, the 73d Fusiliers left the division to become a part of the 111th Division (a new formation).

2. In April the 19th Division was sent (with the 20th) to Galicia, where it took part in the offensive of Mackensen's army. This campaign caused heavy losses; in the 91st Infantry Regiment, between May and September, the casualties totaled 127 officers and 4,291 men. (Official List of casualties.)

3. Entraining at Warsaw on September 17 the 19th Division, together with the 20th, was taken to Antwerp, then, by way of Namur and Givet, to Champagne. There it remained behind the front to reinforce the 3d Army at the time of our attack on the Champagne front (September).

FRANCE.

4. It was relieved about October 17. After a few days rest in the area of Grandlup, Missy les Pierrepont, it occupied the Hurtebise–Vauclerc line at the end of October.

AISNE.

5. About December 19 it was withdrawn to the rear (Parfondru area). It remained in reserve of the army and received training.

1916.

1. The division again went into line at the beginning of January, 1916 (Hurtebise–Vauclerc sector) and remained there until the middle of May. Then it was sent to Sissonne and received training until June 7.

RUSSIA.

2. About June 8 it left Sissonne and entrained for the Eastern Front. Itinerary: Laon–Sedan–Trèves–Coblentz–Limberg–Marburg–Cassel–Leipzig – Breslau – Bautzen – Iwagorod–Kovel (June 12).

3. The division was retrained on the Russian front from June until November. It underwent the Broussliov offensive, and in November formed a part of the 4th Austrian Army in action on the Volhynia front.

FRANCE.

4. About November 8 it entrained and left Russia to return to the Western Front. Itinerary: Kovel–Brest–Litowsk–Warsaw–Thorn–Berlin–Hanover–Aix la Chapelle–Liége–Namur–Givet–Hirson.

5. After a few days of rest, the 19th Division entrained for Rethel. It was billeted in the vicinity until the end of December.

1917.

1. After a stay in Alsace (January, 1917) the 19th Division came into reserve in Champagne in February.

CHAMPAGNE.

2. On February 24 it occupied the sector Ripont, Cernay en Dormois.

3. On March 6 it was transferred to the Rheims front (Brimont, Cavaliers de Coucy in April and May). Only its right wing was engaged in the French offensive.

4. Relieved on the 10th of June and sent to rest, it was in action shortly afterwards southwest of Moronvilliers, then on the Cornillet-Monc St. Blond front, where it underwent the French attacks of July 14 and suffered heavy losses.

5. On July 20, it left this area and in two days marched to the sector north of Ville sur Tourbe.

MEUSE.

6. About September 7 it was sent to the Verdun area (Beaumont-Samogneux). It there launched several attacks.

7. Relieved from the Beaumont sector at the end of December, the 19th Division occupied the Forges sector (left bank of the Meuse) about January 6, 1918. There it was relieved by the 84th Division beginning of February.

RECRUITING.

The 19th Division is recruited from Hanover. The 91st Infantry Regiment is recruited in the Grand Duchy of Oldenburg. There were very few replacements from other corps districts.

VALUE—1917 ESTIMATE.

The 19th Division must be considered a good division (September, 1917).

1918.

1. The division rested at Stenay until March 6, when it entrained and traveled via Sedan-Charleville-Anor to Landrecies, going into billets at Hecq. On the 17th it marched to Croix and in the evening proceeded via Le Cateau to Honnechy. On the night of March 19-20 it marched to Brancourt, and on the 21st followed up the attack as far as Maissemy. The 91st Regiment crossed the Somme at Brie on the 25th and by the 28th had reached Harbonnieres.

BATTLE OF PICARDY.

2. It was in support until the 31st, when it was engaged near Marcelcaves. In the fighting in this locality between the 30th and April 6, the division lost 50 per cent of its effectives. The heaviest losses were incurred on March 31 at Brie where a battalion commander, ordered to attack, was unable to do so because of his losses.

3. The division rested until April 16 in the neighborhood of Proyart and Framerville. About 1,000 men were received as reinforcements at this time.

SOMME.

4. It was engaged on April 18, north of Hangard, until the 20th. Two days of rest at Harbonnieres followed, and it returned to line on the 24th. The French attack of the 26th caused the division severe losses and it withdrew on April 28. It was reengaged on the same sector on May 6 and in line until May 29. While in line the division received drafts of 1,200 men.

5. The division rested until the 1st of June in the vicinity of Cambrai. It marched toward the Lassigny front by night, passing through Ham (June 2), Esmery-Hallon, Tilloloy (June 7-8).

NOYON.

6. It was engaged on June 9 in the Lataule wood and was in line until the 14th. It entrained on the 21st and moved to Lorraine, where it relieved the 3d Guard Division at Bezanges on June 25. It rested on this quiet front until July 29, when the 81st Reserve Division from Flanders relieved it.

VESLE.

7. The division rested near Fort Brimont until mid-August, when it moved by stages to the Vesle front. It entered the line northeast of Fismes on September 1 and remained during the month. The division withstood the French attack of the 31st, losing about 700 prisoners. It was forced to retire on Ventelay and Chaudardes (Oct. 1), and later on Pontavert, Craonne, toward Sissonne (Oct. 11–12). It was in second line about the 13th to 18th.

LAON.

8. On October 19 it was again in line near Sissonne. In the retreat it retired by Boucourt, la Ville aux Bois, Montcornet. After November 4 it was identified near Renneval, Iviers, and Aubenton (Nov. 8).

VALUE—1918 ESTIMATE.

The division was rated as first class. It was regarded as one of the best German divisions. It resisted with great obstinacy the French counterattack at Hangard, April 26. Its morale remained good until the end of October.

19th Reserve Division.
COMPOSITION.

	1914		1915		1916		1917		1918	
	Brigade.	Regiment.	Brigade.	Regiment.	Brigade.	Regiment.	Brigade.	Regiment.	Brigade.	Regiment.
Infantry	37 Res. 39 Res.	73 Res. 78 Res. 74 Res. 92 Res. 79 Res.(2 Btns.) 10 Res. Jag. Btn.	37 Res. 39 Res.	73 Res. 78 Res. 74 Res. 92 Res. 79 Res.(2 Btns.) 10 Res. Jag. Btn.	37 Res. 39 Res.	73 Res. 78 Res. 79 Res.(2 Btns.) 74 Res. 92 Res.	39 Res.	73 Res. 78 Res. 92 Res.	39 Res.	73 Res. 78 Res. 92 Res.
Cavalry	6 Res. Dragoon Rgt. (3 Sqns.)		6 Res. Drag. Rgt.		6 Res. Drag. Rgt.		1 Sqn. 6 Res. Drag. Rgt.		3 Sqn. 6 Res. Drag. Rgt.	
Artillery	19 Res. F. A. Rgt. (6 Btries.).		19 Res. F. A. Rgt. (8 Btries.).		19 Res. F. A. Rgt. 2 Mountain Btry.		19 Res. F. A. Rgt.		19 Res. F. A. Rgt. 2 Abt. 3 Ft. A. Rgt. (Staff, and 5, 7, and 9 Btries.). 741 Light Am. Col. 742 Light Am. Col. 745 Light Am. Col.	
Engineers and liaisons.	1 and 2 Res. Cos. 2 Pion. Btn. No. 10.		1 and 2 Res. Cos. 2 Pion. Btn. No. 10. 19 Res. Tel. Detch. 19 Res. Pont. Engs.		1 and 2 Res. Cos. 2 Pion. Btn. No. 10. 6 Field Co. 1 Pion. Btn. No. 10. 219 T. M. Co. 19 Res. Tel. Detch. 19 Res. Pont. Engs.		319 Pion. Btn. 1 Res. Co. 10 Pions. 219 T. M. Co. 290 Searchlight Section. 419 Tel. Detch.		319 Pion. Btn. 1 Res. Co. 10 Pions. 2 Res. Co. 10 Pions. 54 Searchlight Section. 419 Signal Command: 419 Tel. Detch. 32 Wireless Detch.	
Medical and Veterinary.							510 Ambulance Co. 46 Res. Field Hospital. 47 Res. Field Hospital. 48 Res. Field Hospital. Vet. Hospital.		510 Ambulance Co. 46 Res. Field Hospital. 48 Res. Field Hospital. 200 Vet. Hospital.	
Transports.							M. T. Col.		718 M. T. Col.	

HISTORY.

(10th Corps District.—Hanover; Grand Duchy of Oldenburg; Duchy of Brunswick.)

1914.

BELGIUM-MARNE.

1. The 19th Reserve Division, constituting at the outbreak of the war, with the 2d Reserve Guard Division, the 10th Reserve Corps, was a part of the 2d Army (Von Buelow). It entrained near Cologne August 10–12, was concentrated at the Elsenhorn Camp and entered Belgium on the 15th by way of Spa. Going down the left bank of the Meuse near Liége, it crossed the Sambre west of Charleroi on the 22d; went into action on the 23d at Nalinnes; entered France on the 26th at Avesnes, and fought on the 29th and 30th between St. Quentin and Ribemont. Continuing on its way through Braine, it crossed the Marne at Dormans and took part in the battle of the Marne between Vauchamps and Montmirail (Sept. 6 to 7).

2. It retired on the 7th by way of Orbais, Vertus, Épernay, Rilly la Montagne (Sept. 10) Rheims (Sept. 12).

CHAMPAGNE.

3. It fought, in the middle of September, north of Rheims and established itself on the front Brimont-Courcy-Bétheny (October–December).

1915.

1. The division occupied the sector north of Rheims until the beginning of February, 1915.

PERTHES.

2. About February 2, elements of the division were transferred to the Somme Py and went into action in the Perthes les Hurlus area, where they took part in serious battles.

3. The division remained in Champagne (Souain-Perthes) until the month of April.

ALSACE.

4. About the end of April it was sent to Alsace (valley of the Fecht). At this time, the 10th Reserve Corps was broken up because of the employment of its two divisions on two separate fronts (19th Reserve Division, Vosges, 2d Reserve Guard Division, in the north). These two divisions are now independent. The 19th Reserve Division suffered very heavily in Alsace (valley of the Fecht) and lost 154 officers and 5,033 men (Official List of Casualties), of whom 60 officers and 1,964 men belong to the 74th Reserve Infantry Regiment.

CHAMPAGNE.

5. On September 30 the 37th Reserve Brigade entrained to reenforce the units engaged in the Tahure sector (Champagne), where it went into action on October 8.

ALSACE.

6. The 37th Reserve Brigade rejoined the 39th Reserve Brigade in Alsace at the beginning of November. At this time the entire division was concentrated in the vicinity of Mulhouse.

7. In December elements of the 19th Reserve Division took part in the struggle for the possession of Hartmannswillerkopf (Dec. 21–29).

1916.

1. The 19th Reserve Division remained in the Meuse area until March, 1916.

VERDUN.

2. About March 15 the division entrained and was transferred to Verdun. It went into action in the sector Douaumont-Haudremont-Thiaumont (Apr. 17 to June 21).

Its regiments made successive attacks and suffered heavily (attacks of Apr. 17, 24, May 7, and June 21). At the end of April and during the month of May, elements of the division were sent to rest in the vicinity of Montmédy.

ARGONNE.

3. At the beginning of July the 19th Reserve Division was withdrawn from the Verdun front and went into the Argonne (La Harazee). It had lost 79 per cent of its infantry at Verdun. From April 25 to July 19 the 4th Company of the 74th Infantry Regiment had received no less than 195 men as replacements; the 9th Company of the 73d Infantry Regiment, 211 men.

SOMME.

4. On October 10 it was transferred to the Somme (sector of Gueudecourt les Boeufs) and took part in limited actions which caused serious losses.

CÔTES DE MEUSE.

5. Relieved on October 26–28, it went into line on the Côtes de Meuse (Les Éparges) on October 31.

1917.

CHEMIN DES DAMES.

1. On February 18, 1917, the 19th Reserve Division left the Éparges sector for the front south of Laon. Concentrated in the region of Arrancy–Ste. Croix, it went into line about March 1, on the crest of the Chemin des Dames (Ailles-Hurtebise). It underwent the French attack of April 16, which caused it to suffer severely (900 prisoners).

On April 20 elements of the Division launched a counterattack (Poteau d' Ailles). The 19th Reserves Division remained in line until April 21.

RUSSIA.

2. After two weeks' rest in the vicinity of Sissonne, the division was transferred to Russia. It entrained at La Capelle on May 7. Itinerary: Charleroi–Namur–Liége–Aix le Chapelle-Dusseldorf-Hanover-Berlin-Bromberg-Koenigsberg-Shavli–Mitau; detraining at Gross-Ekkau on May 11, it was called on July 23 to help the exhausted 226th Division between Smorgoni and Krevo.

RIGA.

3. At the end of August or the beginning of September the division took part in the operations which began at the taking of Riga and of Duenamuemde (September).

FRANCE.

4. On September 11 the division entrained near Uxkull for the Western Front. Itinerary: Mitau – Shavli – Koenigsberg – Posen – Cottbus– Leipzig– Gotha– Mayence–Kreuznach–Luxemburg–Sedan–Hirson. It detrained at Vervins on September 17.

FLANDERS.

5. Transferred to Flanders (Sept. 20–24) it occupied the Polygon wood sector east of Ypres (Sept. 28). It underwent the British attack of October 4, when it lost very heavily. It was relieved immediately. (On Sept. 29 the 12th Company of the 92d Reserve Infantry Regiment had only 3 officers and 86 men.)

MEUSE.

6. After a rest near Sedan, in the course of which it was reorganized with mixed replacements from Beverloo and the recruit depot of the 228th Division, the division went northwest of Verdun in October (Malancourt sector).

7. Sent to rest in the Stenay area on December 22, the 19th Reserve Division occupied the Chaume wood sector on January 15, 1918. It was still there at the beginning of March.

RECRUITING.

The 19th Reserve Division is recruited from the 10th Corps District (Hanover, Oldenburg, Brunswick). There are few elements foreign to the district.

During the French offensive on the Chemin des Dames on April 16 the 19th Reserve Division gave the impression of having energetic and intelligent leadership. The attitude of the men was generally good.

The division suffered enormous losses on the Aisne.

The quality of the replacements received and its stay on the Russian front have diminished the value of this division, which was a good combat unit.

The presence of a certain number of Poles and Alsatians must be noted who are inclined to desertion (67 deserters from the 73d Reserve Infantry Regiment on Sept. 28, 1917). (November, 1917.)

1918.

1. About April 6 the division was relieved and moved to Belgium, entering line at Dixmude on April 17.

BATTLE OF THE LYS.

2. On the 25th the division moved south and reenforced the battle front at Vierstraat. It fought in the Ypres area until May 1, when it was relieved, after losing about 40 per cent of its effectives.

CHAMPAGNE.

3. The division appeared in Champagne on May 10, taking over the sector west of the Suippe from the 232d Division. About June 1 a battalion of the 78th Reserve Regiment was detached and took part in the attack on Rheims. Afterwards it returned and the complete division was in its sector on June 15. The division was withdrawn from Champagne just before the July offensive.

4. It was reengaged in Champagne on July 27 south of Le Mont sans Nom. It continued in this sector until the 1st of September.

5. The division moved directly from line in Champagne to line south of Concy le Chateau, where it was engaged until October 14. Withdrawn from the Selle front, elements of the division were immediately engaged on the Oise at Mont d'Origny (Oct. 17), but the bulk of the division was not identified until October 24, south of Catillon. Until the armistice the division fought in the vicinity of Catillon (Nov. 4) Fesmy (5th), Prisches (6th), Lemont Fontaine (8th).

The division was rated as first class. In 1918, except for the Lys offensive in April, the division was engaged only on the defensive.

19th Ersatz Division.
COMPOSITION

	1914 Brigade	1914 Regiment	1915 Brigade	1915 Regiment	1916 Brigade	1916 Regiment	1917 Brigade	1917 Regiment	1918 Brigade	1918 Regiment
Infantry	45 Mixed Ers. 47 Mixed Ers.	Ers. Btns.: 45 and 46. 63 and 64. 47 and 48. 88 and 89.	45 Mixed Ers. 47 Mixed Ers.	23 Ers. 32 Ers. 47 and 48 (Brig. Ers. Btns.). 88 and 89 (Brig. Ers. Btns.).	45 Mixed Ers. 47 Mixed Ers.	23 Ers. 32 Ers. 24 Ers. 40 Ers.	45 Ers.	23 Ers. 24 Ers. 32 Ers.	45 Ers.	23 Ers. 24 Ers. 32 Ers.
Cavalry						4 and 5 Sqns. 19 Hus. Rgt.	5 Sqn. 19 Hus. Rgt. 1 Ers. Sqn. 12 C. Dist.		5 Sqn. 19 Hus. Rgt.	
Artillery	1 Ers. Abtls. of the 28 and 48 F. A. Rgts. 1 Ers. Abtls. of 32 and 77 F. A. Rgts.		1 Ers. Abtls. of 28 and 48 F. A. Rgts. 1 Ers. Abtls. of 32 and 77 F. A. Rgts.		45 Ers. F. A. Rgt. 47 Ers. F. A. Rgt.		47 Ers. F. A. Rgt.		47 Ers. F. A. Rgt.	
Engineers and Liaisons.	1 Ers. Co. 12 Pions. 1 Ers. Co. 22 Pions.		1 Ers. Co. 12 Pions. 1 Ers. Co. 22 Pions. 254 Pion. Co.		1 Ers. Co. 12 Pions. 1 Ers. Co. 22 Pions. 254 Res. Pion. Co. 164 T. M. Co.		519 Pion. Btn.: 1 Ers. Co. 12 Pions. 1 Ers. Co. 22 Pions. 254 Pion. Co. 164 T. M. Co. 253 Searchlight Section. 569 Tel. Detch.		519 Pion. Btn.: 1 Ers. Co. 12 Pions. 1 Ers. Co. 22 Pions. 164 T. M. Co. 1 Searchlight Section. 569 Signal Command: 569 Tel. Detch. 47 Wireless Detch.	
Medical and Veterinary.							272 Ambulance Co. 506 Field Hospital. 507 Field Hospital. Vet. Hospital.		272 Ambulance Co. 506 Field Hospital. 518 Vet. Hospital.	
Transports							M. T. Col.		766 M. T. Col.	
Attached	5 Bav. Ldw. Brig. (4 Bav. Ldw. and 5 Bav. Ldw. Rgts.)		5 Bav. Ldw. Brig. (4 Bav. Ldw., 5 Bav. Ldw., and 60 Res. Rgts.). 100 Ldw. Inf. Rgt. 9 Jag. Btn.		21 Labor Btn. 85 Labor Btn. 4 Btn. 15 Ldw. Rgt. (Until April). 60 Res. Inf. Rgt. 100 Ldw. Inf. Rgt. (Until October.)					

HISTORY.

(12th and 19th Corps Districts—Saxony.)

1914.

VOSGES.

1. The 19th Ersatz Division (Saxon) detrained on August 18, 1914, before Strassburg. In action in the Vosges on the 20th, it went up the valley of the Bruche and fought on the Meurthe below St. Die, at St. Michel, and advanced to La Salle (Sept. 6).

LORRAINE.

2. Having suffered in these engagements, the division was withdrawn. On September 19 it was in the Blamont area, where it was reenforced by the 5th Bavarian Landwehr Brigade. It occupied the sector of Blamont-Ember-Menil-Parroy.

1915.

LORRAINE.

1. In 1915, and until October, 1916, it guarded the same front in Lorraine (from the canal of the Marne to the Rhine as far as the Cirey area).

2. About the month of April the 100th Landwehr was reattached to the division, the battalions of which were grouped in July into 4 Ersatz Regiments (Nos. 23, 32, 24, 40).

1916.

LORRAINE.

1. During its stay in Lorraine the 19th Ersatz Division was not engaged in any serious fighting. The 23d Ersatz alone took part in the affair of Thiaville, February 28, 1916.

COTES DE MEUSE.

2. Relieved in the area of Badonviller-Leintrey, at the beginning of October, 1916, the 19th Ersatz Division was reduced to three regiments (23d, 32d, 24th Ersatz) and sent to the Briey area (Oct. 8) and from there to Verdun (sector of Watronville-Damloup).

1917.

COTES DE MEUSE.

1. The 19th Ersatz Division remained in the same sector of the Cotes de Meuse for almost all of the year 1917. It lost very slightly.

2. Withdrawn from the sector Moranville-Watronville about November, the division was sent to rest in the Longwy area.

BEZONVAUX.

3. About December 8, it was assembled and sent to Spincourt where, on December 11, it went into line north of Bezonvaux.

RECRUITING.

The 19th Ersatz Division is recruited from the Kingdom of Saxony.

VALUE—1917 ESTIMATE.

The 19th Ersatz Division remained in Lorraine for a long time; it did not take part in any serious battles. After October, 1916, it only occupied quiet sectors on the Cotes de Meuse.

It can not be considered as an attack division.

1918.

1. The division occupied the quiet Beaumont sector until June 30, when it was put at rest near Longuyon until July 11. During this time the division was given training to fit it for a war of movement. On July 16 it was moved to the Rheims

front. Entrained at Montmedy on the 12th, the division reached Nouvion Porcien the next day, and went by stages to Bermericourt (northeast of Rheims), where it rested in reserve. On the 17th it moved to the vicinity of Rozoy.

BATTLE OF THE AISNE-MARNE.

2. From July 20 to 31 the division was engaged in severe fighting at Plessier-Huleu and Grand Rozoy.

3. It rested near Marle until the 21st of August undergoing reconstruction. It entrained on that date at Voyenne and reached La Fere the next day, from where it marched to Barisis and Folembray.

BATTLE OF THE AILETTE.

4. The division entered the line in the Quierzy-Manicamp-Champs area on August 23. It sustained a French attack on the 28th, losing nearly 500 prisoners. The division was withdrawn on September 3.

5. The division was moved by train from Voyenne to Haboudange via Marle Montcornet, Sedan, Montmedy, Longuyon, Audun le Roman, Thionville, Metz, and Benestroff. It marched to Hampont to the Huhnerwald Camp, where it rested until September 15.

LORRAINE.

6. It entered line at Arracourt on the 15th and occupied that quiet sector until the end of hostilities.

VALUE—1918 ESTIMATE.

The division was rated as third class. In 1918 it saw but two weeks' service on an active front.

125651°—20——20

19th Landwehr Division.

COMPOSITION.

	1916		1917		1918	
	Brigade.	Regiment.	Brigade.	Regiment.	Brigade.	Regiment.
Infantry	91 Res.	383 Ldw. 385 Ldw. 388 Ldw.	91 Res.	383 Ldw. 385 Ldw. 388 Ldw.		383 Ldw. 385 Ldw.
Cavalry			(?)		2 Sqn. 6 Res. Hus. Rgt.	
Artillery	281 F. A. Rgt.		Art. Command: 91 F. A. Rgt.			
Engineers and Liaisons			(419) Pion. Btn.: 303 Pion. Co. 319 T. M. Co. Tel. Detch.		519 Signal Command: 519 Tel. Detch.	
Medical and Veterinary			226 Ambulance Co. 396 Field Hospital. 91 Res. Field Hospital. 519 Vet. Hospital.		226 Ambulance Co. 396 Field Hospital. 10 Field Hospital.	
Transports			788 M. T. Col.		788 M. T. Col.	

HISTORY.

(383d Landwehr Regiment: 3d Corps District—Brandenburg.   385th Landwehr Regiment: 7th Corps District—Westphalia.   388th Landwehr Regiment: 12th Corps District—Saxony.)

1916.

BELGIUM.

1. The 19th Landwehr Division was formed at the same time as the divisions of the 200 Series (September–October, 1916).   It was formed at Cortemarck on September 29, 1916, by the union of the 383d, 385th, and 388th Landwehr Regiments.   These were made up of Landsturm battalions (Service of Supplies) of the 4th Army in Belgium, to which were added returned wounded.   The 3d Battalion of the 388th Landwehr Regiment (Saxon) is the old 4th Battalion of the 100th Landwehr.

DIXMUDE.

2. In the beginning of October, 1916, the 19th Landwehr Division replaced the 204th Division in the Dixmude–Steenstraat sector.   It remained there more than a year.

1917.

RUSSIA.

1. Relieved from the Dixmude front about the middle of October, 1917, the 19th Landwehr Division was transferred to Russia at the beginning of November.

RIGA.

2. Arriving in the Riga area about November 15, it went into line near the coast.

VALUE—1917 ESTIMATE.

The 19th Landwehr Division is made up either of elderly soldiers or those of mediocre physical strength, forming a body of men incapable, it appears, of an offensive effort.

In Belgium, however, the division organized an assault troop capable of making assaults.

1918.

LIVONIA.

1. The 19th Landwehr Division was identified on the shores of the Baltic in March. The 383d Landwehr Regiment was at Libau on May 8; the 385th Landwehr Regiment at Riga on the 15th.

FINLAND.

2. Toward the end of July all three regiments of the division were identified in Finland, but seem to have gone to Esthonia by August, where they were again identified in October.

VALUE—1918 ESTIMATE.

The division was rated as fourth class.

20th Division.
COMPOSITION.

	1914 Brigade.	1914 Regiment.	1915 Brigade.	1915 Regiment.	1916 Brigade.	1916 Regiment.	1917 Brigade.	1917 Regiment.	1918 Brigade.	1918 Regiment.
Infantry	39. 40.	79. 164. 77. 92.	39. 40.	79. 164. 77. 92.	40.	77. 79. 92.	40.	77. 79. 92.	40.	77. 79. 92.
Cavalry	17 Hus. Rgt. (3 Sqns.).				17 Hus. Rgt. (2 Sqns.).		5 Sqn. 17 Hus. Rgt.		5 Sqn. 17 Hus. Rgt.	
Artillery	20 Brig.: 10 F. A. Rgt. 46 F. A. Rgt.		20 Brig.: 10 F. A. Rgt. 46 F. A. Rgt.		20 Brig.: 10 F. A. Rgt. 46 F. A. Rgt.		20 Art. Command: 46 F. A. Rgt.		20 Art. Command: 46 F. A. Rgt. 155 Ft. A. Btn. 813 Light Am. Col. 921 Light Am. Col. 1339 Light Am. Col.	
Engineers and Liaisons.			1 Pion. Btn. No. 10: Field Co. 10 Pions. 20 Pont. Engs. 20 Tel. Detch.		1 Pion. Btn. No. 10: 2 Co. 10 Pions. 20 T. M. Co 20 Tel. Detch. 20 Pont. Engs.		(1/10 or 127) Pion. Btn.: 2 Co. 10 Pions. 3 Co. 10 Pions. 20 T. M. Co. (206) Searchlight Section. 20 Tel. Detch.		10 Pion. Btn.: 2 Co. 10 Pions. 3 Co. 10 Pions. 90 Searchlight section. 20 Signal Command: 20 Tel. Detch. 83 Wireless Detch.	
Medical and Veterinary.							24 Ambulance Co. Field Hospital. Vet. Hospital.		24 Ambulance Co. 100 Field Hospital. 93 Field Hospital. 20 Vet. Hospital.	
Transports									5'3 M. T. Col.	
Attached							3 Gleiwitz Landst. Depot Btn. (6 C. Dist. Btn. No. 26).			

HISTORY.

(10th Corps District—Hanover and Brunswick.)

1914.

The 20th Division and the 19th Division formed the 10th Army Corps (Hanover).
FRANCE.

1. At the outbreak of the war the 20th Division went to the Elsenborn Camp, August 8–10, and entered Belgium on the 11th. It was a part, with the 10th Corps, of the 2d Army (Von Buelow). It fought at Charleroi, at Guise, at St. Quentin. It took part in the battle of the Marne from September 6 to 9 (Congy, Mondement), after which it retired by way of Neufchâtel sur Aisne to the northwest of Rheims. It took up its position between the Aisne and Brimont.

1915.

At the beginning of 1915 it was still holding the lines in the vicinity of Rheims. At the end of March the 164th Infantry Regiment was transferred to the 111th Division (new formation).

GALACIA.

2. At the end of April, with its regiments raised to four battalions each, the 20th Division (as well as the 19th Division) was sent to Galacia, where it took part in the operation of Mackensen's army. It lost very heavily there. From July 28 to September 23 the 11th Company of the 77th Infantry Regiment received at least 133 men as replacements.

FRANCE.

3. Brought back to France in September, the 20th Division took part, in the month of October, in the battles in the Champagne.

4. From November, 1915, to June, 1916, it held a sector north of the Aisne (west of Craonne).

1916.

RUSSIA.

1. On June 8, 1916, the 20th Division, with all of the 10th Army Corps, was transferred again to the Eastern Front. In four days it arrived in the Kovel area by way of Berlin and Brest Litowsk.

2. On June 13 it was engaged in stopping the Russian advance and then occupied a sector near Kiselin. Its regiments were filled up in September and October.

From June to November the losses of the 92d Infantry Regiment had averaged 160 men per company. (Statements of deserters.) This is the number of the replacements received during the same period by the 9th Company of the 77th Infantry Regiment.

FRANCE.

3. The 20th Division was relieved on November 11 and entrained on the 15th for France. Itinerary: Warsaw–Kalich–Berlin–Dusseldorf–Aix la Chapelle–Liége–Namur. Billeted first in the area of Anor Hirson, the 20th Division was sent to the Sissonne Camp, where its regiments received training

4. At the end of December the division took over the sector of Moulin sous Touvent, Chevillecourt, where it was relieved on January 30, 1917.

1917.

1. In February, 1917, the 20th Division was transferred to Alsace (Sundgau) in anticipation of a French offensive.

2. In the beginning of March it was brought back to the Laon area, where it was billeted until the French attack of April 16; its regiments received some replacements.

CHEMIN DES DAMES.

3. In the night of April 16 all the units of the division were assembled. On April 17–18 they took their positions along the plateau of the Chemin des Dames on both sides of Cerny en Laonnois, relieving the 16th Reserve· Division, which had suffered heavy losses. Between April 18 and May 5 the three regiments of·the 20th Division suffered heavy losses from bombardments. On May 5 (renewal of the general attack by the French) the division again lost heavily. It was relieved immediately after the attack. (Apr. 27 to Aug. 10, the 10th Company of the 77th Infantry Regiment had received not less than 211 men as replacements.)

4. After a few weeks of rest, the division was put into line (end of May) in a sector of Champagne (Moronvilliers).

RUSSIA.

5. In the beginning of July it was relieved and transferred for a third time to the Russian front, first in Galicia and then in Courland. It remained there until September 19. At this date it entrained at Riga and was brought back to France by way of Chavli, Kovno, Grodno, Bromberg, Berlin, Hanover, Cologne, Aix la Chapelle, Mons, Valenciennes.

FLANDERS.

6. Arriving at Roulers on September 27, it immediately went into action in an attacking sector, north of Zonnebeke, without having any rest, on October 4.

ARTOIS.

7. Relieved almost immediately, it was put into line on October 17 in the Queant sector, where it still was at the beginning of February, 1918.

RECRUITING.

It is recruited from the Province of Hanover in the Duchy of Brunswick.

VALUE—1917 ESTIMATE.

It had very heavy losses on May 5, 1917 (many killed, 700 prisoners), which, joined to the preceding losses, lessened the value of the 20th Division very much.

It is to be noted that two weeks before the attack of May 5 the units of the division defended themselves obstinately.

1918.

CAMBRAI.

1. The division was relieved by the 119th Division about the middle of January; it, in turn, relieved the 119th Division during the first week in February. It was relieved by the 195th Division on February 16, and marched to Aubigny au Bac; it reached Basaecles (southeast of Tournai) the 18th. Here it was given a month's course of training in open warfare.

2. On March 14 the division marched to Peruwelz and then via St. Amand–Lourches–Bouchain, arriving at Pronville, where it entered line on the 20th. It advanced through Noreuil, Bapaume, Grevillers, Irles, and Miraumont. During this fighting the division suffered severely, its casualties amounting to 50 per cent of its effectives; very few officers left. It did not advance with the rest of the line during the night of the 24–25th, its place being taken by the 24th Division. It followed in support of the line, however, and relieved the 24th Division east of Colincamps on the 29th. A document captured on the 28th shows that the strength of the 3d Battalion of the 77th Regiment (excluding the machine gun company) was reduced to 214 men. Another battalion was reduced to 80 men and 1 officer.

WOEVRE.

3. The division was withdrawn early in April, and was sent to the Mars la Tour region, where it rested and was reconstituted. About the 20th it relieved the 82d Reserve Division in the Seuzey–Lamorville–Spada sector (north of St. Mihiel);

relieved toward the end of the month, it went to the Arlon area, where it received large drafts (in large part of the 1919 class), and where it was put through a long and thorough course of training. Toward the end of June it was transported to the Sedan area, from which it marched (about July 15) toward Soissons.

SOISSONS.

4. On the 21st of July the division reinforced the front near Villemontoire (south o. Soissons). Here heavy losses were again suffered. It was relieved by the 50th Reserve Division on the 29th and went to rest in the Chimay area, where it received a draft from the disbanded 260th Reserve Regiment (78th Reserve Division).

ARRAS.

5. On the night of the 27-28th of August the division moved up into the Drocourt–Queant line, south of Drocourt, and during the following days went into line in the Oppy sector (northeast of Arras), where a British attack was expected. The division was withdrawn again during the night of September 1-2.

6. On the 3d of September it came into line near Ecourt St. Quentin (south of Arleux), and covered the withdrawal across the Canal du Nord. It was withdrawn on the 10th.

CAMBRAI.

7. On the 12th it counterattacked in the Havrincourt sector (southwest of Cambrai). During the subsequent fighting the division suffered heavy losses. It was withdrawn on the 1st of October.

8. After a few days' rest it relieved the 21st Division in the Montbrehain sector (southeast of Cambrai), where it fought until the 13th, when it was relieved and went to the vicinity of Montmedy, where it rested for about three weeks. Losses, 70 per cent.

MEUSE.

9. The division was expected to enter line west of the Meuse, but the orders were changed suddenly, and it entered line to the east of it near Reville on November 5. It remained in line until the 11th, not being heavily engaged, however, all the prisoners captured subsequently stating that they were members of rear-guard detachments.

VALUE—1918 ESTIMATE.

The 20th is rated as a first-class division. It fought well throughout the year and suffered enormous losses. Besides the replacements already noted, the division received a large draft from its recruit depot in September (about 50 men per company); September 28, the 92d Regiment received 93 men; October 30, the companies received 30 men apiece from the 27th Reserve Regiment (197th Division, dissolved); the companies had a combat strength of 80 to 100 men.

20th Landwehr Division.

COMPOSITION.

	1916		1917		1918 [1]	
	Brigade.	Regiment.	Brigade.	Regiment.	Brigade.	Regiment.
Infantry		384 Ldw. 386 Ldw. 387 Ldw.	9 Ers.	384 Ldw. 386 Ldw. 387 Ldw.	9 Ers.	386 Ldw.
Cavalry			3 Sqn. 4 Res. Hus. Rgt.		3 Sqn. 4 Res. Hus. Rgt.	
Artillery			Art. Command: 282 F. A. Rgt.		282 F. A. Rgt. (Staff and 2 Abt.).	
Engineers and Liaisons			420 Pion. Btn.: 1 Ldw. Co. 9 Pions. 3 Ers. Co. 24 Pions. 320 T. M. Co. 520 (Wurtt.) Tel. Detch.		1 Ldw. Co., 9 C. Dist. Pions. 520 Signal Command: 520 Tel. Detch.	
Medical and Veterinary			227 Ambulance Co. 88 Field Hospital. 183 Field Hospital. Vet. Hospital.		227 Ambulance Co. 520 Vet. Hospital.	
Transport			M. T. Col.			

[1] The units below are those grouped under the divisional postal sector (660). Other units belonging to the 20th Landwehr Division, but operating under other divisions, are listed as attached to such division.

HISTORY.

(384th Landwehr Regiment: 4th Corps District—Prussian Saxony.   386th Landwehr Regiment: 9th Corps District—Mecklenburg.   387th Landwehr Regiment: (?).

1916.

BELGIUM.

1. The 20th Landwehr Division dates from September 29, 1916. It was formed at Roulers from the 384th, 386th, and 387th Landwehr Regiments. These regiments, formed at this time, respectively, at Menin, Renaix, and Cooescant, were formed two-thirds of men from the Landsturm battalions assigned to the Service of Supplies in Belgium, and one-third of returned wounded.

DIXMUDE.

2. At the beginning of October, 1916, the 20th Landwehr Division relieved the 206th Division in the sector Dixmude–Schoorbakke. It was retained there until the middle of November, 1917.

1917.

CAMBRAI.

1. Sent into line southwest of Cambrai (Nov. 1917), the division suffered heavily in the British offensive of November 20, when it lost 2,773 men as prisoners. It was relieved the day after this action.

RUSSIA.

2. Between November 28 and December 5, the 20th Landwehr Division was transferred to the Eastern Front.

VALUE—1917 ESTIMATE.

The division is of mediocre value.

1918.

PINSK–UKRAINE.

1. After having held the sector south of Pinsk from December, 1917, to February, 1918, the 20th Landwehr Division went into the Ukraine in March. The 384th Landwehr Regiment was in the region west of Gomel on April 23; the division was at Jitomir in May. The division was still in Ukraine on the 16th of October.

VALUE—1918 ESTIMATE.

The division was rated as fourth class.

21st Division.
COMPOSITION.

	1914 Brigade.	1914 Regiment.	1915 Brigade.	1915 Regiment.	1916 Brigade.	1916 Regiment.	1917 Brigade.	1917 Regiment.	1918 Brigade.	1918 Regiment.
Infantry	41. 42.	87. 88. 80 Fus. 81.	41. 42.	87. 88. 80 Fus. 81.	42.	80 Fus. 81. 87.	42.	80 Fus. 81. 87.	42.	80. 81. 87.
Cavalry	6 Uhlan Regt.				6 Uhlan Regt. (3 Sqns.).		(?) 5 Sqn. 6 Dragoon Rgt.		2 Sqn. 6 Drag. Rgt.	
Artillery	21 Brig.: 27 F. A. Rgt. 63 F. A. Rgt.		21 Brig.: 27 F. A. Rgt. 63 F. A. Rgt.		21 Brig.: 27 F. A. Rgt. 63 F. A. Rgt.		21 Art. Command: 27 F. A. Rgt.		21 Art. Command: 27 F. A. Rgt. 2 Abt. 14 Ft. A. Rgt. (5, 6, and 7 Btries.). 731 Light Am. Col. 1101 Light Am. Col. 1131 Light Am. Col.	
Engineers and Liaisons.			1 Pion. Btn. No. 21: Field Co. 21 Pions. 21 Pont. Engs. 21 Tel. Detch.		1 Pion. Btn. No. 21: 1 Co. 21 Pions. 5 Co. 21 Pions. 21 T. M. Co. 21 Tel. Detch. 21 Pont. Engs.		(1/21 or 131) Pion. Btn.: 1 Co. 21 Pions. 5 Co. 21 Pions. 21 T. M. Co. 21 Searchlight Section. 21 Tel. Detch.		21 Pion. Btn.: 1 Co. 21 Pions. 5 Co. 21 Pions. 18 Searchlight Section. 21 T. M. Co. 21 Signal Command: 21 Tel. Detch. 41 Wireless Detch.	
Medical and Veterinary.							46 Ambulance Co. 36 Field Hospital. 21 Vet. Hospital.		46 Ambulance Co. 154 Field Hospital. 303 Field Hospital. 21 Vet. Hospital.	
Transports							554 M. T. Col.		554 M. T. Col.	
Attached							54 M. G. S. S. Detch.			

HISTORY.

(18th Corps District—Hesse-Nassau, Hesse-Hombourg, Frankfort.)

1914.

The 21st Division belonged organically with the 25th Division of the 18th Army Corps District (Frankfort on the Main).

ARDENNES.

1. In August, 1914, it formed a part of the 4th Army (Duke of Wurttemberg). Entering Luxemburg on August 10, Belgium August 12, it fought on the 20th at Neuf Chateau, on the 22d at Bertrix and Orgeo, on the 24th at Matton, and crossed the Meuse on the 28th.

MARNE.

2. In September it took part in the battle of the Marne between Vitry and Sermaize (Etrepy, Pargny sur Saulx). From there it retired in the direction of Rheims, being in action northwest of the city from September 15 to 20.

3. In October it was reassigned with the 18th Army Corps to the 2d Army, which at this time formed the right flank of the German Army (vicinity of Roye).

1915.

SOMME.

1. It was retained with its army corps for a year in the vicinity of Roye (until Oct. 15, 1915). In March, the 25th Division transferred the 88th Infantry Regiment for the formation of the 56th Division.

2. On October 15, 1915, it was withdrawn from the front and sent for a long rest near St. Quentin.

1916.

The 80th Fusiliers took part in the attack at Frise on January 29, 1916. A few days afterwards the 21st Division was transferred north of Verdun.

VERDUN.

1. From February 27 to March 16 it was engaged at Verdun (Caures wood, Louvemont, Douaumont).

2. From March 17 to April 9 it was reorganized (imperial review on Apr. 1, at Marville).

3. From April 10 to 25 it again attacked at Verdun. One may judge of the losses by the replacements destined to make them good: From February 27 to May 10 the 1st Company of the 80th Fusiliers received at least 205 men; the 5th Company of the 81st Infantry Regiment at least 306 (Soldbuecher). The total losses of the 21st Division from March 15 to May 19, 1916, amounted to 8,549 officers and privates for the infantry alone. (Official List of Casualties.)

4. About May 15 the 21st Division occupied the sector west of Craonne, where it was relieved in September. Two battalions of the 87th Infantry Regiment were sent in haste to Fricourt at the time of the Somme offensive (July 2).

SOMME.

5. Between September 12 and 15 the 21st Division was transferred to the Somme (sectors of Clery–Bouchavesnes), where it suffered heavily.

6. At the beginning of October it was withdrawn from the Somme front and sent to the Cotes de Meuse in the Apremont area, which it occupied until November 10.

7. At the end of November it again went into action on the Somme (sector of Gomiecourt wood of Kratz) and remained there until February 10, when it went to rest near Chaumont Porcien.

1917.

AISNE.

1. On February 26, 1917, the 21st Division was taken to the front south of Berry au Bac, between the Godat and Loïvre.

2. The three regiments of the division were on line on April 16 and underwent our attack, which caused them very heavy losses (2,319 prisoners).

RUSSIA.

3. Relieved, about April 19, the 21st Division rested for a few days in the Neufchatel area and then entrained for the Eastern Front (about May 9). On the 16th it detrained at Vilna. After reorganization, it took over a sector, on June 14, in the neighborhood of Postavy (north of Lake Narotch), which it occupied until the end of September. There was no important operation during this period.

FRANCE.

4. On September 25 it was again transferred to France. Itinerary: Vilna–Posen–Leipzig–Frankfort on the Main-Saarebruecken-Luxemburg-Sedan.

5. Arriving from Russia on October 1, it went into line about the 28th, in the sector northeast of Rheims. After a rest in January, it returned there in February, 1918.

RECRUITING.

The 21st Division is recruited in Hesse-Nassau, Hesse-Homburg, and Frankfort. They have borrowed very few from other districts, except from the 8th (Rhine Province), its neighbor.

VALUE—1917 ESTIMATE.

The 21st Division showed itself, in the course of our attack of April 16, 1916, as a good division, which put up a serious resistance.

The 81st Infantry Regiment, however, was criticised for its conduct on April 4. (Order of the 42d Brigade, of Apr. 9.) (See Appendix to the British Summary of Information of May 12, 1917.)

On the Russian front, according to the statement of a deserter (Nov. 7, 1917), the attempts at fraternization and exchange of the Russians were badly received by order of the German commanders.

1918.

1. The division held the Clonay–La Pompelle sector until April 23. A local operation was attempted on March 1, with the demolition of Fort La Pompelle as the objective.

2. When relieved on April 23, the division rested several days at Warmeriville before being transported to St. Quentin. From there it marched by stages to Rosieres en Santerre (May 1) and later to the Avre front.

PICARDY.

3. It relieved the 2d Bavarian Division, on May 3–4 in the sector south of Thennes and held that sector for five weeks. On June 12, the division moved into second line, and reappeared in line west of Castel–Bois Senecat in mid-June. During local operations, June 26 and July 2, the division lost a number of prisoners. It was relieved about the end of July.

BATTLE OF THE SOMME.

The division returned to line on August 13 to oppose the British drive on the Somme. It was engaged north of Lihons (13th) and east of Proyart. Toward the end of August it was forced to retreat through Cappy, Frise, Clery, and Le Mont St. Quentin, until its relief on September 1. Twelve hundred prisoners were lost during the fighting.

LA CHATEAU.

5. On September 9, the division was reengaged northwest of Jeancourt for four days, again losing heavly in prisoners. From the 13th to the 30th the division rested in the vicinity of St. Quentin, close to the front. It was put back in line at Bellicourt on the 30th and remained in until October 7.

6. The division rested in the Charleroi area and later at Ghent. It was brought back to the front by stages and reengaged east of Deynze (Petegem-Ouest de Nazareth) on October 31. In the closing days, the division was identified south of Heurne (Nov. 5), Gelsen (8th), Wendle (8th), south of Ghent (10th).

VALUE—1918 ESTIMATE.

The division was rated as first class. In 1918 it was used entirely on the defensive. At the end the regiments had been reduced to two battalions of three companies. Morale was very low in the fall. Between August 14 and the middle of October the division lost 2,473 prisoners on the Somme battle front.

21st Reserve Division.

COMPOSITION.

	1914		1915		1916		1917		1918	
	Brigade.	Regiment.	Brigade.	Regiment.	Brigade.	Regiment.	Brigade.	Regiment.	Brigade.	Regiment.
Infantry	41 Res. 42 Res.	80 Res. 87 Res. 81 Res. 88 Res.	41 Res. 42 Res.	80 Res. 87 Res. 81 Res. 88 Res.	41 Res. 42 Res.	80 Res. 87 Res. 81 Res. 88 Res.	41 Res.	80 Res. 87 Res. 83 Res.	41 Res.	80 Res. 87 Res. (?).
Cavalry	7 Res. Drag. Rgt. (3 Sqns.).		7 Res. Drag. Rgt.		7 Res. Drag. Rgt.		3 Sqn. 4 Res. Drag. Rgt. 1 Sqn. 7 Res. Drag. Rgt.		3 Sqn. 4 Res. Drag. Rgt.	
Artillery	21 Res. F. A. Rgt. (6 Btries.).		21 Res. F. A. Rgt.		21 Res. F. A. Rgt. (9 Btries.).		Art. Command: 21 Res. F. A. Rgt. (9 Btries.).		126 Art. Command: 21 Res. F. A. Rgt. 136 Ft. A. Btn. 808 Light Am. Col. 1286 Light Am. Col. 1350 Light Am. Col.	
Engineers and Liaisons.	4 Field Co. 2 Pion. Btn. No. 11.		4 and 5 Field Cos. 2 Pion. Btn. No. 11. 21 Res. Pont. Engs. 21 Res. Tel. Detch.		4 and 5 Field Cos. 2 Pion. Btn. No. 11. 221 T. M. Co. 21 Pont. Engs. 21 Tel. Detch.		(321) Pion. Btn.: 4 Co. 11 Pions. 5 Co. 11 Pions. 221 T. M. Co. 421 Tel. Detch.		11 Pion. Btn.: 4 Co. 11 Pions. 5 Co. 11 Pions. 221 T. M. Co. 27 Searchlight Section. 421 Signal Command: 421 Tel. Detch. 129 Wireless Detch.	
Medical and Veterinary.							517 Ambulance Co. 51 Res. Field Hospital. 52 Res. Field Hospital. Vet. Hospital.		517 Ambulance Co. 51 Res. Field Hospital. 69 Res. Field Hospital. 421 Vet. Hospital.	
Transports.							749 M. T. Col.		719 M. T. Col.	

Attached	44 Anti-aircraft Section.	21 Bav. Ft. A. Btn. (Staff, 1 and 3 Btries.), 1 Ft. A. Rgt. (Staff, 5 and 6 Btries.), 821 Light Am. Col. 90 Artillery Observation Section. (Flash Spotters.) 103 Sound Ranging Detch. 202 Balloon Sqn. 208 Reconnaissance Flight. 237 Carrier Pigeon Loft. 364 Carrier Pigeon Loft. Elements attached Aug. 24, 1918.

HISTORY.

(18th Corps District—Hesse-Nassau and the south of Westphalia.)

1914.

1. At the outbreak of the war the 21st Reserve Division formed, with the 25th Reserve Division, the 18th Reserve Corps. It belonged to the 4th Army (Prince Albrecht of Wurttemberg). Detraining near Saarburg (Rhine Province) on August 10–12, it passed to the north of Luxemburg and entered Belgian Luxemburg, by Martelange.

ARDENNE.

2. After fighting at Neufchateau on August 22, the 21st Reserve Division reached Carignan on the 25th, fought at Mouzon on the 28th, crossed the Meuse at that point, and from there, by Grandpré, skirting the Argonne to the west, it arrived at the Marne–Rhine Canal on September 6.

ARGONNE–CHAMPAGNE.

3. At the battle of the Marne it went into action on the Saulx in the vicinity of Mognéville (Sept. 7–10, south of Revigny). It effected its retreat by way of the Givry en Argonne, Ste. Menehould, Vienne la Ville, and stopped on the heights to the south of Cernay en Dormois on September 14.

4. The 21st Reserve Division established its positions in the sector of Ville sur Tourbe and remained there until June, 1916.

1915.

CHAMPAGNE.

1. From January to December, 1915, the division was in the sector of Ville sur Tourbe north of Massiges à L'Aisne.

2. In September the division took part in the Champagne battle.

1916.

1. The 21st Reserve Division continued to occupy the Massiges sector from January to June, 1916.

VERDUN.

2. After a rest in the Briey area from the end of June until July 15, the division was sent to Verdun (sector of Fumin wood) where it went into action from July 15–25 to the beginning of September. During this period it suffered heavy losses, which made it necessary to give men as replacements on August 12, taken from the 83d Landwehr Regiment and the 36th Reserve Infantry Regiment, taken in haste from the Argonne; at the end of August it received conscripts of the 1917 class who had only been called up in May, many of whom came from depots in Baden.

CHAMPAGNE.

3. At the beginning of September, the 21st Reserve Division came back into its own sector of Ville sur Tourbe. A short time afterwards it gave the 81st Reserve Infantry Regiment to the 222d Division a new formation.

4. In the middle of October it was sent to rest in the Rethel area.

VERDUN.

5. On August 26 and 27 it was concentrated in the vicinity of Senon–Foameix. It occupied the sector of Hardaumont until December 7. After a few days' rest it was brought back into line at Verdun (Bezonvaux, on Dec. 16).

1917.

1. The division left the Verdun front on January 11, 1917, very much exhausted.

LORRAINE.

2. On February 24, 1917, it took over the sector Letricourt-Moucel in Lorraine.

AISNE.

3. After a few days' rest at Morhange it entrained on April 14 for the Aisne. Detraining between Hirson and Vervins, it was concentrated in the vicinity of Prouvais-

Amifontaine. On April 18 and 19, after the French advance of April 16 in the vicinity of Juvincourt, it took up its position between the Miette and the Aisne as a reenforcement division, and then to replace units in the line. It attacked on May 18, near the Mauchamp Farm, and suffered heavy losses.

4. Relieved between the 27th and 30th of May, it was sent to rest and reorganized (June replacements; mostly men of the 1918 class).

CHAMPAGNE.

5. It then occupied a sector in Champagne southwest of Nauroy from July 19–20 to October 22.

CAMBRAI.

6. After a rest in the vicinity of Cambrai in November, it went into action at the end of November, east of Cambrai (southeast of Bourlon). It remained in line south of the Bapaume-Cambrai road until the end of December.

RECRUITING.

The division is recruited in Hesse-Nassau and the extreme southern part of Westphalia. It received few outside elements except under exceptional circumstances (e. g., on Aug. 12, 1916, at Verdun).

VALUE—1917 ESTIMATE.

The 21st Reserve Division is a good division. (October, 1917.)

On the Aisne front (April to May, 1917) the 21st Reserve Division held a difficult sector. The unsuccessful counterattacks which it launched there diminished its offensive value. Nevertheless, on the whole, it gave a good account of itself.

In Champagne (August to October, 1917) its activity was limited to a few assaults carried out energetically.

1918.

1. In the March offensive the division advanced from la Vacquerie to Beaumont Hamel, which it reached on March 27. Here the line stabilized and it held this sector throughout April, May, and June. It was relieved by the 16th Reserve Division on the night of July 3–4.

BATTLE OF THE SOMME.

2. The division rested in the Bapaume area until it returned to line northwest of Hamelincourt on August 6–7, relieving the 5th Bavarian Division. It met the British attack in the region and was driven back through Croisilles, Cherisy, and St. Leger until its withdrawal on August 30. Nine hundred prisoners were lost in the engagement.

3. The division rested in the Tournai area until September 18, when it reenforced the front south of Villers-Guislain. About this time the 81st Reserve Regiment was broken up and distributed among the regiments of the 21st Reserve Division. The division fought at Gouzeaucourt (28th), Gonnelieu (30th), Banteux (30th), Gouy (Oct. 3), Beaurevoir (5th), Villers Outreaux (8th), Clary (9th), Le Cateau (11th). After losing 1,550 prisoners the division was withdrawn on October 17. According to a divisional order of October 1, the strength was so low as to warrant the reduction in half of the normal allotment of kitchen and supply wagons.

4. The division returned from close reserve on October 23 northeast of Haussy. In the closing days it fought at Vendegies (24th), Ruesnes (24th), Orsinval (Nov. 2), southwest of Wargnies le Grand (4th), east of Villers Pol and in the Gommegnies sector (5th). The division withdrew on November 8.

VALUE—1918 ESTIMATE.

The division was rated as second class. During 1918 its service was entirely in the area north and south of the Somme, where it saw a great deal of heavy fighting.

21st Landwehr Division.

COMPOSITION.

	1917		1918	
	Brigade.	Regiment.	Brigade.	Regiment.
Infantry...............	11 Ldw.	20 Ldw. 35 Ldw. 435 Ldw.	11 Ldw.	20 Ldw. 35 Ldw. 435 Ldw.
Cavalry................	4 Sqn. 6 Cuirassier Rgt.		4 Sqn. 6 Cuirassier Rgt.	
Artillery...............	Art. Command: 253 Ldw. F. A. Rgt.		(?)	
Engineers and Liaisons.	(421) Pion. Btn.: 1 Landst. Co. 14 C. Dist. Pions. 406 T. M. Co. 521 Tel. Detch.		414 Pion. Btn.: 1 Ldw. Co. 3 C. Dist. Pions. 1 Landst. Co. 15 C. Dist. Pions. 80 Searchlight Section. 521 Signal Command: 521 Tel. Detch. 175 Wireless Detch.	
Medical and veterinary.	553 Ambulance Co. 54 Res. Field Hospital. 105 Res. Field Hospital. Vet. Hospital.		553 Ambulance Co. 54 Res. Field Hospital.	
Transports.............	797 M. T. Col............................		797 M. T. Col.	

HISTORY.

(20th and 35th Landwehr Regiments: 3d Corps District—Brandenburg.   435th Landwehr: Mixed—11th and 14th Corps Districts.)

1917.

BELGIUM.

1. The 21st Landwehr Division was formed in April, 1917, by the addition of the
435th Regiment to the two regiments of the 11th Landwehr Brigade. This brigade,
until then independent, had come to Belgium the 2d of August, 1914, had detached
certain of its elements in Picardy, from the end of September to the end of November,
and had fought near Ypres in November and December. From March to October,
1915, it acted as garrison at Brussels and Antwerp. At the end of December, 1915,
it reappeared on the Belgian front between Dixmude and Ypres (from Steenstraate
to the Ypres-Zonnebeke road).

RUSSIA.

2. In May, 1917, the 21st Landwehr Division was identified in the vicinity of Arras.
On May 16 it entrained for the Eastern Front. Itinerary: Liege-Aix la Chapelle-
Paderborn-Halle-Posen-Warsaw. Detraining at Brest-Litovsk on May 21, it remained
in training for 10 days, was then sent to the Niémen front, and occupied the Vichnev
sector until March, 1918.

VALUE—1917 ESTIMATE.

The 21st Landwehr Division did work in the service of supplies in Belgium and held
very calm sectors in Russia. Its offensive value seems mediocre.

On the Russian front in January, 1918, the 20th Landwehr Regiment received 600
men of the 1919 class in exchange for its men of 25 to 35 years of age sent to the Western

?ront.   Before being brought back to France in March, 1918, the 35th Landwehr
Regiment left its older men in Russia and received 900 men of 19 to 30 years of age.

1918.

1. The division held the Badonviller sector from April 29 until the armistice.   The
division was strong in the number of effectives, but their quality and morale was low.
The division was rated as a fourth-class division.

22d Division.
COMPOSITION.

	1914 Brigade.	1914 Regiment.	1915 Brigade.	1915 Regiment.	1916 Brigade.	1916 Regiment.	1917 Brigade.	1917 Regiment.	1918 Brigade.	1918 Regiment.
Infantry	43. 44.	82. 83. 32. 167.	43. 44.	82. 83. 32. 167.	43.	82. 83. 167.	43.	82. 83. 167.	43.*	82. 83. 167.
Cavalry		6 Cuirassier Rgt. (3 Sqns.).		......		6 Cuirassier Rgt. (2 Sqns.).		2 Sqn. 6 Cuir. Rgt.		6 Sqn. 6 Cuirassier Rgt.
Artillery	22 Brig.: 11 F. A. Rgt. 47 F. A. Rgt.		22 Brig.: 11 F. A. Rgt. 47 F. A. Rgt.		22 Brig.: 11 F. A. Rgt. 47 F. A. Rgt.		22 Art. Command: 11 F. A. Rgt.		22 Art. Command: 11 F. A. Rgt. (not including 4 and 5 Abt.). 50 Ft. A. Btn. 1140 Light Am. Col. 1141 Light Am. Col. 1142 Light Am. Col.	
Engineers and Liaisons.			1 Pion. Btn. No. 11: Field Co. 11 Pions. 22 Pont. Engs. 22 Tel. Detch.		1 Pion. Btn. No. 11: 2 Co. 11 Pions. 22 T. M. Co. 22 Pont. Engs. 22 Tel. Detch.		(1/11 or 128) Pion. Btn.: 1 Co. 11 Pions. 2 Co. 11 Pions. 22 T. M. Co. 51 Searchlight Section. 22 Tel. Detch.		128 Pion. Btn.: 1 Co. 11 Pions. 2 Co. 11 Pions. 235 T. M. Co. 51 Searchlight Section. 22 Signal Command: 22 Tel. Detch. 169 Wireless Detch.	
Medical and Veterinary.							Ambulance Co.: 103 Field Hospital. 107 Field Hospital. 110 Field Hospital. Vet. Hospital.		25 Ambulance Co.: 103 Field Hospital. 107 Field Hospital. 148 Vet. Hospital.	
Transports							52 Supply Train. 51 Supply Train. M. T. Col.			
Attached					2 Cyclist Co. (11 Jag. Btn.). 35 Air Sqn. 109 Labor Btn.		2 Cyclist Co. (11 Jag. Btn.).			

HISTORY.

(11th Corps District—Electorate of Hesse.)

1914.

1. The 22d Division formed a part of the 11th Army Corps (Cassel) with the 38th Division.

BELGIUM.

2. One of its brigades, the 43d, was sent to Liege and entrained on August 2–3, 1914. The other rejoined it there and after the surrender of the city the 22d Division, with the rest of the 11th Army Corps, formed a part of the 3d Army (Von Hausen). It went to Namur and then to Eastern Prussia.

RUSSIA.

3. In October the 22d Division (and the 11th Army Corps) was in Poland, where it remained until May, 1915. It took part in the violent attacks along the Bzura and the Rawka.

1915.

RUSSIA.

1. In April, 1915, the division gave the 32d Infantry Regiment to the 103d Division (a new formation).

2. In July it was separated from the 38th Division. It took part in the offensive of the 11th Army (Mackensen), and arrived on the Styr in October. It then formed a part of the 4th Austrian Army.

1916.

1. In the spring of 1916 the 22d Division was in the rear of Vilna (May), after having been at Mitau. On June 11 it entrained at Mitau for Vilna.

GALICIA.

2. It then formed a part of the troops destined to withstand the Russian offensive in Galicia and took up its position on the Lipa.

ROUMANIA.

3. In December it was sent to Roumania and operated in Moldavia.

1917.

GALICIA.

1. It returned in January, 1917, to the 4th Austrian Army on the Lipa.

2. At the beginning of July it was in Volhynia (Mikolajow, northwest of Brody).

3. On July 7–9 the division was relieved and sent to the area south of Tarnopol. It arrived there on July 15 and took part in the offensive against the Russians. It suffered rather heavy losses in the beginning, the Russians having resisted for several days.

4. The 22d Division remained in this area until October 7. On this date it was relieved and entrained for the Western Front (itinerary: Brzezany–Torgau–Erfurt–Frankfort on the Main–Mayence–Sarrebrucken–Thionville–Montmedy), detraining at Douzy (east of Sedan) about October 14.

At the end of October the division, after a few days of rest, was put in line in the Forges sector (Verdun area), where it had a few losses (November, December). January 1918, it was on the front north of Verdun (right bank of the Meuse).

RECRUITING.

The 22d Division is recruited from the electorate of Hesse. Alsace-Lorrainers were numerous during its stay on the Eastern Front.

The 22d Division, coming from Russia, where it had had rather easy victories, appeared to have a relatively good morale. Its spirit, however, did not appear very combative (Nov. 1917).

1918.

1. The division was in line on the right bank of the Meuse (Samogneux–Cote 344) from January, 1918, to the end of May, when it was relieved by the 6th Bavarian Division.

2. It was in reserve southwest of Reims on June 16, and came into line at Anthenay on June 20. About the 1st of July the 103d Division relieved the 22d Division, which went to rest in the neighborhood of Fismes and Hourges.

BATTLE OF THE MARNE.

3. The division was engaged southeast of Ville en Tardenois (Chambrecy, Champlat, Velval) July 15–26. It fell back in the line Romigny–Ville en Tardenois and was relieved on August 7. About 400 prisoners were lost in this fighting.

BATTLE OF THE SOMME.

4. The division rested in the Cambrai area until August 29, when it was moved up to the line. On the 1st of September it was engaged on the Arras–Cambrai road near Bullecourt. The British attack rolled it back on Inchy and Marquion, where it was withdrawn on the 10th. The division lost 1,100 prisoners in the week of fighting.

THE SCARPE.

5. It rested until September 28, when it came into line north of Cambrai (Epinoy), Sancourt, Blecourt. About October 1 it was moved north and relieved the 48th Reserve Division north of the Scarpe. In the sector it fought until October 23 (southeast of Lille, St. Amand, southwest of Odomez).

6. Upon its relief, the division marched from Thulin, west of Mons, on October 24 to the Le Quesnoy area, and on the next day relieved the 185th Division east of, Ghissegnies. In November it was in the fighting around Le Quesnoy and Gommegnies until its withdrawal on November 7.

The division was rated as third class. It was employed in the July offensive, but made little headway. On the defensive the division appears to have done better than many divisions of a higher rating.

22d Reserve Division.

COMPOSITION.

	1914		1915		1916		1917		1918	
	Brigade.	Regiment.	Brigade.	Regiment.	Brigade.	Regiment.	Brigade.	Regiment.	Brigade.	Regiment.
Infantry	43 Res. 44 Res. 11 Res. Jag. Btn.	71 Res. 94 Res. 32 Res. 82 Res.	43 Res. 44 Res. 11 Res. Jag. Btn.	71 Res. 94 Res. 32 Res. 82 Res.	43 Res. 11 Res. Jag. Btn.	71 Res. 82 Res. 94 Res.	43 Res.	71 Res. 82 Res. 94 Res.	43 Res.	71 Res. 82 Res. 94 Res.
Cavalry	1 Res. Horse Jag. Rgt. (3 Sqns.).		1 Res. Horse Jag. Rgt.		1 Res. Horse Jag. Rgt.		3 Sqn. 1 Res. Jag. Horse Rgt. 2 Sqn. 1 Res. Heavy Cav. Rgt.		1 Sqn. 2 Uhlan Rgt.	
Artillery	22 Res. F. A. Rgt. (6 Btries.).		22 Res. F. A. Rgt.		22 Res. F. A. Rgt. (9 Btries.).		Art. Command: 22 Res. F. A. Rgt. (9 Btries.).		22 Res. F. A. Rgt. 43 Ft. A. Btn. (Staff, and 1, 2, and 3 Btries.). 737 Light Am. Col. 1379 Light Am. Col. 1380 Light Am. Col.	
Engineers and Liaisons.	1 and 2 Res. Cos. 2 Pion. Btn. No. 4.		1 and 2 Res. Cos. 2 Pion. Btn. No. 4. 22 Res. Pont. Engs. 22 Res. Tel. Detch.		1 and 2 Res. Cos. 2 Pion. Btn. No. 4. 222 T. M. Co. 22 Res. Pont. Engs. 22 Res. Tel. Detch.		(322) Pion. Btn.: 1 Res. Co. 4 Pions. 2 Res. Co. 4 Pions. 222 T. M. Co. 27, 251, and 271 Search-light Sections. 422 Tel. Detch.		322 Pion. Btn.: 1 Res. Co. 4 Pions. 2 Res. Co. 4 Pions. 103 Searchlight Section. 422 Signal Command: 422 Tel. Detch. 35 Wireless Detch.	
Medical and Veterinary.							511 Ambulance Co. 21 Res. Field Hospital. 50 Res. Field Hospital. Vet. Hospital.		511 Ambulance Co. 23 Res. Field Hospital. 50 Res. Field Hospital. 422 Vet. Hospital.	
Transports.							M. T. Col.			

HISTORY.

(11th Corps District—Electorate of Hesse and Thuringia.)

1914.

1. At the beginning of the war the 22d Reserve Division formed the 4th Reserve Corps with the 7th Reserve Division. It was a part of the 1st Army (Von Kluck).

BELGIUM.

2. Concentrated at Dusseldorf (Aug. 10) the 22d Reserve Division reached Brussels by way of Aix la Chapelle, Tongres, and Louvain. The 94th Reserve Infantry Regiment remained at Brussels until September 5, when it was hastily called to rejoin the division. The 71st Reserve Infantry Regiment remained there until August 31 and then figured in the battle of the Marne on September 6.

MARNE.

3. The 44th Reserve Brigade joined to the 7th Reserve Division went to Ath, Conde, Amiens (Aug. 30–31), and Creil (Sept. 2), almost without combat, but by forced marches to the extreme right flank of the 1st Army. In action on the right bank of the Ourcq, it withdrew to the north of the Aisne.

4. The 43d Reserve Brigade, of which only one regiment had fought with the 44th from September 6 to 9 was filled upon the 9th and went to Peronne. On September 11, strengthened by the 72d Reserve Regiment, detached from the 7th Reserve Division, it was concentrated north of Compiegne.

TRACY LE MONT.

5. Until September 20 the 43d Reserve Brigade fought in the vicinity of Tracy le Mont with some elements of the 7th Reserve Division. The 44th Reserve Brigade was engaged with the majority of this division on the Nouvron Plateau.

NOUVRON.

6. On September 20 the 43d Reserve Brigade rejoined the 44th (Hautebraye-Chevillecourt).

7. On November 12 elements of the division took part in the attack on the Nouvron Plateau and suffered rather heavy losses.

1915.

AISNE.

1. The 22d Reserve Division occupied the lines between the Aisne and the Oise until the autumn of 1915.

2. In January, 1915, elements of the division took part in the battle around Soissons. In April, 1915, the 32d Reserve Infantry Regiment became a part of the 113th Division.

CHAMPAGNE.

3. At the end of October the 22d Reserve Division left the area northwest of Soissons to go to Champagne (Souain sector).

1916.

1. The 22d Reserve Division left Champagne at the end of January, 1916; it went to rest at Attigny, which it left on February 29.

VERDUN.

2. From March 1 to 5, at the height of the Verdun offensive, the division was reassembled between Dun and Vilosnes behind the front. On March 6 it attacked on the left bank of the Meuse. In took part in the operations in this sector (valley of the Forges and Corbeaux wood) until the middle of April. In the first attacks of March the 6th Company of the 82d Reserve Infantry Regiment required replacements of 90 men, among whom were recruits from the 1916 class. After a few days of rest

he 22d Reserve Division again attacked at Verdun, south of Corbeaux wood and
ear the Mort Homme (May 23 to beginning of June). It lost very heavily. Its
ttacks at Verdun had cost it 90 per cent of its infantry. From April 24 to June 26
he 1st and 4th Companies of the 11th Battalion of Reserve Chasseurs had each
eceived at least 204 men as replacements; the 6th Company of the 94th Reserve
nfantry Regiment, from March 9 to June 15, 217 men; the 8th Company, 207 men.

3. The division rested and was reorganized in the vicinity of Fourmies-Hirson; it
as then sent between St. Quentin and Tergnier.

OMME.

4. At the beginning of the Somme offensive the 22d Reserve Division was con-
entrated southeast of Peronne on July 2. It went into action south of the Somme
Biaches-Belloy), and suffered heavy losses (1,500 prisoners between July 2 and
uly 10).

HAMPAGNE.

5. Transferred to Champagne, it rested for a few days and then went into line east
f Rheims (Auberive sector) and in the Prosnes sector at the end of August.

6. At the end of October, after it had rested in the Rethel–Vouziers sector until
[ovember 10, the division was placed behind the Cambrai–St. Quentin sector.

OMME.

7. It went back to the Somme at the beginning of December east of Rancourt and
emained there until December 20.

1917.

1. The 22d Reserve Division passed the month of January, 1917, at rest in the
alenciennes area.

2. In February it took over the Saillisel sector, where it took part in secondary
ction. In March the division took part in the withdrawal and established itself in
ie Hindenburg line between Gonnelieu and Le Catelet.

3. About May 20 the 22d Reserve Division went to rest in the neighborhood of
ens and Tourcoing.

LANDERS.

4. On June 14 it went into line in the Comines sector, west of Warneton, where it
emained until the end of June.

5. After a period of rest north of Lille (end of June to July 23–24) it went into action
utheast of Zillebeke, where it underwent the British attack of July 31, and suffered
ery heavily.

6. Relieved immediately after the attack, the division was sent to the Bullecourt
ctor (Aug. 10–Sept. 22).

7. Until October 5 it rested in the vicinity of Courtrai. At this date it occupied
ie Becelaere sector as a counterattacking division, supporting the 4th Guard Division,
id suffered heavily from bombardments (Oct. 5–21).

ORRAINE-ALSACE.

8. At the beginning of November it was in line in Lorraine, southwest of Delme,
ien in Alsace (sector of Aspach south of the Rhone-Rhine Canal in December).

RECRUITING.

The 22d Reserve Division is recruited from the Electorate of Hesse and Thuringia.
i case of emergency replacements are occasionally furnished by neighboring corps
stricts (8th Corps in June, 1916). At the end of October, 1917, unequally trained
en were received from the Eastern Front (the 71st Infantry Reserve Regiment
ceiving men from the depot of the 146th Infantry Regiment, men from the Service
Supplies, convalescents, or men of mediocre physical quality).

The 22d Reserve Division is a mediocre division (December, 1917). The units of the 11th Corps District have generally fought well during the entire war.

The 22d Reserve District lost very heavily in the battles of Verdun and the Somme and from artillery fire at Ypres.

1918.

BATTLE OF THE LYS.

1. The division left Alsace about April 6 and came into the Lys battle line on April 16 northeast of Bailleul. Its former sector in the Vosges was taken over by an extension of the neighboring divisions. The route of the division lay through Strasbourg, Treves, Cologne, Verviers, Liege, Brussels, Courtrai–Roubaix, a journey of two days. The division participated in heavy fighting about Kemmel until its relief on May 1.

2. When relieved by the 117th Division, it marched to Roubaix, where it rested for two days. From there it marched to Waereghem, where the 82d Reserve Regiment rested for about eight days. About May 11 the 22d Reserve Division entrained at Audenarde and was railed to Rieux, 5 miles east of Cambrai. The division marched via Cambrai to the Montauban–Longueval–Gullemont area, where it went into rest billets. On the night of May 31–June 1 the 1st Battalion, 82d Reserve Regiment, reenforced the 122d Fusilier Regiment (243d Division) near Avelcy.

VERDUN.

3. The division entrained in the Cambrai area on June 8 and traveled via Valenciennes–Mons Charleroi–Dinant–Mezieres–Sedan to Ligny sur Meuse, where it detrained on June 9. The next day it relieved the 53d Reserve Division east of Bethincourt. It held the sector until about July 25.

CHAMPAGNE.

4. Entraining at Brieulles, the division moved by Sedan and Vouziers to St. Morel and Savigny sur Aisne, where it rested until August 5. On the 6th it came into line in the St. Souplet–Somme Py sector, which it held until August 23.

5. The division left Champagne and moved from Semide by Laon–La Fere–Tergnier to the Noyon area. Relieved August 24–27, it detrained at Flavy le Martel and La Fere, and rested a day at Cugny, Petit Detroit, Bois de Genlis, and Bois de Frieres before moving east of Noyon to cover the retreat of elements of the 71st Division and the 105th Division.

NOYON.

6. On August 29 it came into line and held the sector Mont St. Simeon–Baboeuf. The division resisted the French attack until September 3, when it fell back slowly toward the Crozat Canal, offering resistance at Behericourt–Baboeuf (4th), Cuivry–Caillouel–Crepigny–Bethancourt (5th), and Villequier Aumont (6th). It was relieved on the night of September 7–8 by the 11th Division and rested at Ribemont and then farther north in the billets at Fontaine Notre Dame, Regny, and Homblieres.

ST. QUENTIN.

7. From September 10 to 12 the division was relieving the 75th Reserve Division in the sector Castres–Contescourt–Hill 98. The division held in this vicinity until September 28 when the British advance north of St. Quentin compelled it to retreat. Between October 2 and 5 the division held the line Harley–Neuville–St. Amand. On the 8th it was again forced to retreat. The division was relieved on October 15–16. In this fighting the division lost at least one-third of its effectives. The battalion had but three companies, and the effective strength of the infantry companies averaged about 35. The entire division had but about 1,300 infantry combatants.

8. After its relief by the 18th Division on the night of October 15–16, the division remained near the front at Grand Verly, Hannappes, and Lesquielles. It was suddenly alerted on October 17 and obliged to return to support the 18th Division west

of Petit Verly.   It put up a stiff resistance on October 18, but was thrown back eas
of the Sambre Canal, losing a large number of prisoners.

In the closing week the division was at Favril (5th), Marvilles (6th).

VALUE—1918 ESTIMATE.

The division was rated as second class.   It was heavily engaged at Kemmel ir
April, after which it did not appear in an active front until the autumn.   The divisior
resisted the Allied advance on the St. Quentin area in September and October witl
great tenacity.

22d Landwehr Division.

COMPOSITION.

	1917		1918 [1]	
	Brigade.	Regiment.	Brigade.	Regiment.
Infantry	6 Ldw.	34 Ldw. · 49 Ldw. 10 Landst. (4 Btns.).		34 Ldw. (3d Btn.). 49 Ldw. (2d Btn.).
Cavalry		(z)		
Artillery	Art. Command: 219 F. A. Rgt.		219 F. A. Rgt. (Staff and 3 Abt.).	
Engineers and Liaisons.	(422) Pion. Btn.: (322) T. M. Co. 30 Searchlight Section. 284 Searchlight Section. Tel. Detch.		522 Signal Command: 522 Tel. Detch.	
Medical and Veterinary.	551 Ambulance Co. Field Hospital. Vet. Hospital.		11 Res. Field Hospital. 139 Vet. Hospital.	
Transports	M. T. Col.			

[1] The units below are those grouped under the 22d Landwehr Division Postal Sector (380). Other units of the 22d Landwehr Division, but functioning with other divisions, are carried as attached to such division.

HISTORY.

(2d Corps District—Pomerania.)

1917.

RUSSIA.

1. The 22d Landwehr Division was formed on the Eastern Front in the vicinity of Riga, at the end of March, 1917. The 6th Landwehr Brigade, which entered into its composition, had belonged to the 1st Landwehr Division (former Jacobi Division), then had become independent when the latter left the Riga front to go to Volhynia. It is then that the addition of the 10th Landsturm Battalion to the Mitau group made the 22d Landwehr Division from the 6th Landwehr Brigade.

COURTLAND.

2. From April to October, 1917, the 22d Landwehr Division remained on the Riga front (vicinity of Olaï).

VOLHYNIA.

3. In October, it was transferred to the west of Kachovka (Volhynia), where it remained until February, 1918.

VALUE—1917 ESTIMATE.

The 22d Landwehr Division remained on the Russian front from the time of its formation, March, 1917.

1918.

UKRAINE.

1. In February, 1918, the 22d Landwehr Division advanced into the Ukraine, where it was between Kiev and Koursk on the 24th of March. On May 9 the division was near Jitomir. The 219th Field Artillery Regiment was at Kiev on the 24th of May. On September 7 the division was identified near Stochod.

VALUE—1918 ESTIMATE.

The division was rated as fourth class.

23d Division.

COMPOSITION.

	1914 Brigade.	1914 Regiment.	1915 Brigade.	1915 Regiment.	1916 Brigade.	1916 Regiment.	1917 Brigade.	1917 Regiment.	1918 Brigade.	1918 Regiment.
Infantry	45. 46. 12 Jäg. Btn.	100 Gren. 101 Gren. 108 Fus. 182.	45. 46.	100 Gren. 101 Gren. 108 Fus. 182.	45.	100 Gren. 101 Gren. 108 Fus.	45.	100 Gren. 101 Gren. 108 Fus.	45.	100. 101. 108.
Cavalry	20 Hus. Rgt.				18 Hus. Rgt. (3 Sqns.).		3 Sqns. 20 Hus. Rgt.		1 Sqn. 20 Hus. Rgt.	
Artillery	23 Brig.: 12 F. A. Rgt. 48 F. A. Rgt.		23 Brig.: 12 F. A. Rgt. 48 F. A. Rgt.		23 Brig.: 12 F. A. Rgt. 48 F. A. Rgt.		23 Art. Command: 12 F. A. Rgt.		23 Art. Command: 12 F. A. Rgt. 1 Abt. 19 Ft. A. Rgt. (1 and 3 Bries.), 891 Light Am. Col. 950 Light Am. Col. 1100 Light Am. Col.	
Engineers and Liaisons.			1 Pion. Btn. No. 12: Field Co. 12 Pions. 23 Pont. Engs. 23 Tel. Detch.		1 Pion. Btn. No. 12: 1 Co. 12 Pions. 23 T. M. Co. 23 Pont. Engs. 23 Tel. Detch.		(1/12) Pion. Btn.: 1 Co. 12 Pions. 3 Co. 12 Pions. 6 Co. 12 Pions. 23 T. M. Co. 23 Tel. Detch.		23 Pion. Btn.: 1 Co. 12 Pions. 3 Co. 12 Pions. 23 T. M. Co. 125 Searchlight Section. 23 Signal Command: 23 Tel. Detch. 12 Wireless Detch.	
Medical and Veterinary.							30 Ambulance Co. Vet. Hospital.		30 Ambulance Co. 114 Field Hospital. 117 Field Hospital. 23 Vet. Hospital.	
Transports.							M. T. Col.			

HISTORY.

(12th Corps District—Saxony.)

1914.

BELGIUM.

1. The 23d Division, on mobilization, was a part of the 12th Army Corps with the 32d Division (2d Army, Von Hausen). It detrained on August 9–11, 1914, at Eifel, north of Treves, and entered Belgium on the 18th by the north of Luxemburg.

MARNE.

2. It went into action on August 23 at Dinant, crossed the Meuse on the 24th, entered France on the 26th, went to the west of Chalons and took part in the battle of the Marne on September 7 at Sompuis (west of Vitry ¹e Francois).

AISNE.

3. The 23d Division, with the 2d Army Corps, established itself in the area north-west of Rheims.

1915.

AISNE.

1. The division held the front Craonne–Berry au Bac until July, 1916. In this sector the losses were very slight.

2. In March, 1915, some of its elements were in Champagne for a short time. In April, the 182d Infantry Regiment was taken for the 123d Division (a new formation).

1916.

SOMME.

1. On July 3, 1916, at the beginning of the Franco-English offensive, the 23d Division detached some elements of the 101st and 108th Regiments to reinforce the divisions engaged in the attack (region of Sovecourt–Vermandovillers).

2. From the end of July and until the 1st of September the 100th Grenadier Regiment was incorporated in a new division (Franke Division), which held the front from Deniecourt to Vermandovillers.

3. The other regiments of the 23d Division continued to occupy the sector of Craonne-Berry au Bac until the end of August.

4. On September 4 the 101st and 108th Regiments, coming from Berry au Bac, were sent to the Somme. They suffered considerable losses.

5. About September 15 the 23d Division was regrouped with its normal elements (the Franke Division being dissolved) and received 2,700 men as replacements (men of the Landstrum called in April and May and young men of the 1917 class, most of them having had not more than two or three months' service. The 12th Company of the 100th Grenadier Regiment received at least 108 men as replacements on September 20).

6. From October 1 to 6 the 23d Division went back into line between the Chaulnes Railroad and the south of Vermandovillers. It again lost very heavily during the time it remained in line until October 20. (The 2d Company of the 108th Riflemen received, on Oct. 27, replacements of at least 97 men, most of whom were returned wounded and convalescents. Since Sept. 17 it had received at least 198 newcomers; the same holds true for the 4th Company of the 104th Grenadier Regiment).

7. Relieved about October 25, the division was sent to a sector in the Roye (Beu-vraignes) area in November.

1917.

CHAMPAGNE.

1. It occupied this sector (between Armancourt and Roye) until the moment of the German retirement and retired to St. Quentin on March 25, 1917.

2. Relieved and sent to rest at the beginning of April in the Sedan area, it went up in the middle of the month to the sector in Champagne between Hill 232 (east of Nauroy) and the Suippe.

3. On April 19 the 101st and 108th Infantry Regiments counterattacked energetically and in very good order between the Teton and the Suippe and obtained some local success for a short time. On April 20 the 100th Infantry Regiment went into action in its turn.

4. Upon the conclusion of these operations, the 23d Division took up its position on the new front (west of Auberive) and remained there until the beginning of December, after making up for the heavy losses suffered in April. At the beginning of January, 1918, the 23d Division went to occupy the sector of Loivre, northwest of Rheims, and in February the sector of Courcy.

RECRUITING.

The 23d Division is purely Saxon.

VALUE—1917 ESTIMATE.

The 23d Division is very good.

It lost very heavily at the time of the offensive, April, 1917, in Champagne, but still appeared good.

1918.

In February, 1918, the morale of the division seemed high.

1. The division continued in the sector northwest of Rheims (Courcy-Brimont) until about February 20, where it was relieved by the 213th Division and moved toward the Somme front.

2. It was transported to Neufchatel on the 23d. From there it proceeded by stages to north of Guise (Esqueheries, La Neuville-le-Dorengt). It rested and underwent training in this area until March 18. It marched by night toward the front by way of Bohain, Fresnoy le Grand (where the Kaiser inspected it), Le Verguier (evening of Mar. 21–22).

BATTLE OF THE SOMME.

3. The division followed the advance in third line from March 22 to 29 through Holnon, Beauvois, Athies, St. Christ, Chaulnes, Rosieres, Beaucourt en Santerre. It was engaged from March 29 to April 3 (Mezieres, Villers aux Erables, La Neuville Sire Bernard). Its advance continued to a line east of Mailly-Rainval, Sauvillers. It was in second line from April 2 to 7, when it returned to line near Grievesnes until April 13. The division's losses were estimated to have been about 70 per cent in the fighting.

CHAMPAGNE.

4. When withdrawn from the Somme, on the 13th, the division was moved to Champagne and took over a quiet sector east of Auberive on the 31st, which it held until June 6. While in line the division was reconstituted.

5. The division rested in the vicinity of Bazoches from June 5 to 15, undergoing intensive training. It came into line on the night of June 19–20 at St. Pierre Aigle, relieving the 45th Reserve Division. It was retired from the front at Villers Cotterets about July 1. It rested near Braisne until the 12th, when it marched toward the Marne front (Foret de Ris) on July 12.

SECOND BATTLE OF THE MARNE.

6. It reinforced the battle front southwest of Dormans on the 15th. It crossed the Marne east of Courcelles north of Sawigny and advanced to La Chapelle Monthodon. On the 17th it was checked and rolled back by the Foret de Fere to Fresnes (south of Fere en Tardenoise, July 26).

ARTOIS.

7. The division was withdrawn about the end of July and went to Chimay to rest. On August 13 it entrained and moved to the Douai area via Valencennes, where it

came into line on August 24 southwest of Arras. The British attack forced it to give way to the line Beugny–Morchies, with a loss of 700 prisoners. On the 5th the division withdrew from line.

8. The division rested until September 27, when it appeared in line northeast of Bixschoote, southeast of the forest of Houthulst. After five days of heavy fighting it was withdrawn from line. Eight hundred prisoners were taken from the division. It was at rest near Gits until the 14th, when it was again engaged north of Roulers until October 20. On that date it passed to second line southeast of Ghent, where it was again in contact with the Allies on November 8. The last identification was at Sommersaeke, Aecke, on November 9.

VALUE—1918 ESTIMATE.

The division was rated as a third-class division. Its use in two offensives of 1918 and its constant employment on active sectors in the last six months of the war would seem to warrant a higher rating.

At the end the effectives of the division was very much reduced.

23d Reserve Division.

COMPOSITION.

	1914 Brigade.	1914 Regiment.	1915 Brigade.	1915 Regiment.	1916 Brigade.	1916 Regiment.	1917 Brigade.	1917 Regiment.	1918 Brigade.	1918 Regiment.
Infantry	45 Res. 46 Res. 12 Res. Jäg. Btn.	100 Res. Gren. 101 Res. 102 Res. 103 Res. 12 Res. Jäg. Btn.	45 Re,. 46 Res. 12 Res. Jäg. Btn.	100 Res. Gren. 100 Res. 102 Res. 103 Res. 12 Res. Jäg. Btn.	45 Res. 46 Res. 12 Res. Jäg. Btn.	100 Res. Gren. 101 Res. 102 Res. 103 Res. 12 Res. Jäg. Btn.	45 Res.	100 Res. Gren. 102 Res. 392.	46 Res.	100 Res. 102 Res. 392.
Cavalry	Res. Hus. Rgt. (3 Sqns.).				Res. Hus. Rgt.		2 Sqn. Res. Hus. Rgt. (Saxon).		2 Sqn. 18 Res. Hus. Rgt.	
Artillery	23 Res. F. A. Rgt. (9 Btries.).		23 Res. F. A. Rgt. (6 Btries.). 32 Res. F. A. Rgt. (6 Btries.).		23 Res. F. A. Rgt. 32 Res. F. A. Rgt.		118 Art. Command: 23 Res. F. A. Rgt. (9 Btries.).		118 Art. Command: 23 Res. F. A. Rgt. 1 Abt. 15 Res. Ft. A. Rgt. 875 Light Am. Col. 1002 Light Am. Col. 1003 Light Am. Col.	
Engineers and Liaisons.			(?) Res. Co. 2 Pion. Btn. No. 12. 23 Res. Pont. Engs. 23 Res. Tel. Detch.		4 Field Co. 2 Pion. Btn. No. 12. 2 Res. Co. 2 Pion. Btn. No. 12. 223 T. M. Co. 23 Res. Pont. Engs. 23 Res. Tel. Detch.		323 Pion. Btn.: 4 Co. 12 Pions. 2 Res. Co. 12 Pions. 5 Res. Co. 12 Pions. 223 T. M. Co. 423 Tel. Detch.		323 Pion. Btn. 4 Co. 12 Pions. 4 Res. Co. 22 Pions. 223 T. M. Co. 133 Searchlight Section. 423 Signal Command: 423 Tel. Detch. 143 Wireless Detch.	
Medical and Veterinary.							270 Ambulance Co. (Sax.). 520 Ambulance Co. 4 Res. Field Hospital. 8 Res. Field Hospital. 423 Vet. Hospital.		270 Ambulance Co. 4 Res. Field Hospital. 8 Res. Field Hospital. 423 Vet. Hospital.	
Transports							721 M. T. Col.		721 M. T. Col.	

HISTORY.

(12th Corps District—Saxony.)

1914.

BELGIUM–ARDENNES–CHAMPAGNE.

1. The 23d Reserve Division, forming on mobilization the 12th Reserve Corps, with the 24th Reserve Division, was a part in 1914 of the 3d German Army (Von Hausen). It detrained on August 12–13 at Wengerohr (Coblentz–Treves line), remained for a few days on the frontier north of Luxemburg, and entered Belgium on the 19th. It crossed the Meuse at Antree, below Dinant (Aug. 23), and entered France on the 27th by way of Phillipville (Marienburg and Couvin). It went across Champagne by Chateau Porcien, Tagnon, and Le Chatelet (Sept. 1), went to the east of Rheims, crossed the Marne east of Epernay, and reached the railroad from Sezanne to Vitry le Francois between Vassimont and Sommesous on September 8.

MARNE.

2. Engaged in the battle of the Marne, on the extreme right of the 3d Army, the 23d Reserve Division suffered heavy losses (Sept. 8–9).

CHAMPAGNE.

3. It retired, by way of Mourmelon, to the region of Monronvilliers Auberive and took up its position there (end of September).

1915.

CHAMPAGNE.

1. The 23d Reserve Division occupied the Champagne front (Auberive sector) until the month of July, 1916.

2. On September 25 it received the French offensive, which caused it very heavy losses. At this time the 103d Reserve Infantry Regiment was detached from the 23d Reserve Division and assigned to the Liebert Division. In October it rejoined the 23d Reserve Division after being reorganized. Its losses in the Champagne battle had been 140 killed, 751 wounded, and 1,369 missing. On October 2 at least 115 men had been sent to the 8th Company of the 103d Infantry Regiment as replacements.

1916.

1. The 23d Reserve Division was relieved from the sector of Auberive–St. Souplet sector between July 15 and 20, 1916, and transferred to the north of Peronne.

SOMME.

2. It was engaged in the battle of the Somme (north of Hem to the Monacu Farm) until August 12–14. The 100th Reserve Grenadier Regiment lost 1,700 men there (letter). The 7th Company of the 103d Infantry Regiment received at least 113 men as replacements between August 1 and 17.

ARTOIS.

3. After a rest in the vicinity of Douai, the division was sent south of Lens (Angres–Souchez from the beginning of September to Oct. 20). Its composition was modified by the substitution of the 392d Infantry Regiment, formed by men taken from various Saxon regiments, for the 103d Reserve Infantry Regiment.

SOMME.

4. About the middle of October it was again on the Somme (north of Gueudecourt). It remained there for five weeks and suffered very little.

ARTOIS.

5. Relieved from the Somme on December 3 and 4 the 23d Reserve Division remained at rest for a few days near Cambrai, and then took over the sector east of Arras (between Roclincourt and Beaurains). The 101st Reserve Infantry Regiment was transferred to a new Saxon Division, the 119th, and the 23d Reserve Division was reduced to three regiments.

1917.

1. The division occupied the Artois front during the winter of 1916–17.

2. It was withdrawn at the end of March to go to Belgium.

FLANDERS.

3. Sent to rest in the Bruges area for a fortnight; it then went in line for a month north of Ypres (calm sector).

4. It was in reserve in June and then went to the front on July 10 between the railroad from Ypres to Staden and the Ypres-Roulers Railroad. In the course of its relief (July 31) it suffered heavily from the bombardment which preceded the British attack.

5. Retained in Flanders, it took part on September 22 in the fighting in the Passchendaele sector and underwent the British attack of September 26, which caused it heavy losses. (The 2d Company of the 100th Reserve Infantry Regiment was reduced to 25 men.)

RUSSIA.

6. After five days in line the 23d Reserve Division was relieved and transferred to Russia, where it arrived on October 8.

7. It appeared in the Vilna area between October 10 and 17. In the middle of November it was identified near Postavy, where it still was at the end of January, 1918.

RECRUITING.

The 23d Reserve Division is purely Saxon.

VALUE—1917 ESTIMATE.

The 23d Reserve Division was not seriously engaged during the first half of 1917, but has suffered heavily since that time.

After the losses which it suffered in July, 1917, it received mediocre replacements (elderly men and returned convalescents.)

If one adds to that the heavy losses which it suffered at Passchendaele in September, and in its four months' stay on the Eastern Front, one may rest assured that the morale and general quality of the division had diminished in value for more than a year. (British Summary of Information, Feb., 1918.)

1918.

ARTOIS.

1. In March the division was transferred to the Western Front. It entrained near Dvinsk on March 16 and traveled via Vilna-Koenigsberg-Marienburg-Schneidemuhl-Berlin-Hanover-Menden-Krefeld-Aix la Chapelle-Hasselt-Louvain-Brussels-Courtrai-Lille, and detrained at Libercourt (16 km. south of Lille) on March 22. It left for the front on March 26.

It came into line in the Oppy sector on March 28. In the attack on this day all three regiments of the division suffered heavy casualties. The division continued in line in the vicinity until about June 25.

FLANDERS.

2. When relieved in the Arras sector the division marched north and relieved the 15th Reserve Division near Calonne sur la Lys about June 27. In later August the division extended its sector to the south to include the front southwest of Vielle Chapelle, southeast of Merville and east of Laventie.

The division held this front through August and September. On September 30 the resting regiment of the division—the 100th Reserve Regiment—was sent up to reenforce the Ypres front. It was engaged for two weeks in the vicinity of Ledeghem. In

October the division was engaged in the Little area until about the 20th.   It was taken out of line north of Tournai and sent to relieve the 6th Bavarian Reserve Division on the night of October 22–23 at Octeghem.   It remained in line until a few days before the armistice.   The last identification was at Audenarde on November 2.

VALUE—1918 ESTIMATE.

The division was rated as third class.   Its record of more than eight months' constant service in line in fairly active sectors indicated considerable power of resistance.

23d Landwehr Division.

COMPOSITION.

	1917		1918	
	Brigade.	Regiment.	Brigade.	Regiment.
Infantry................	14 Ldw.	27 Ldw. 26 Ldw. 66 Ldw.	13 Ldw.	26 Ldw. 27 Ldw. 66 Ldw.
Cavalry.................	(?)		6 Sqn. 10 Hus. Rgt. 43 Res. Cav. Detch. 91 Ldw. Cav. Rgt. (Schutz.).	
Artillery..............	Art. Command: 103 F. A. Rgt.			
Engineers and Liaisons.	(423) Pion. Btn.: 347 Pion. Co. (323) T. M. Co. 523 Tel. Detch.		1 Landst. Co. 7 C. Dist. Pions. 264 Searchlight Section. 283 Searchlight Section. 112 Searchlight Section. 523 Signal Command: 523 Tel. Detch.	
Medical and veterinary.	558 Ambulance Co. 70 Res. Field Hospital. Vet. Hospital.		558 Ambulance Co. 99 Field Hospital. 70 Res. Field Hospital. 106 Res. Field Hospital. 523 Vet. Hospital.	
Transports.............	M. T. Col.		760 M. T. Col.	

HISTORY.

(4th Corps District—Prussian Saxony.)

1917.

1. The 23d Landwehr Division, formed at the end of April, 1917, in the Argonne, was composed of the independent 13th Landwehr Brigade (26th and 27th Landwehr Regiments) and of the 66th Landwehr Regiment taken from the 5th Landwehr Division. This latter division furnished the staff of its infantry brigade (14th Landwehr Brigade).

2. After being assigned to the 23d Landwehr Division, the 13th Landwehr Brigade occupied the sector of Boureuilles north of Vienne la Ville in the Agonne. It was in the Argonne from September 1914.

RUSSIA.

3. Almost as soon as it was formed the 23d Landwehr Division was transferred to the Eastern Front (entraining of the 26th Landwehr Regiment on May 19). Itinerary: Carignan–Liége–Coblentz–Cassel–Halle–Cottbus–Gnessen–Graudenz–Koenigsberg–Chavli–Poneviej. Going into line about May 25 in the vicinity of Illukst (Courland) the division remained in this sector until February, 1918. It was too much weakened to contribute replacements to the division destined to operate in France, as, for example, the 87th Division. On December 28 the 1st and 2d Companies of the 347th Infantry Regiment each received some 75 to 80 men from the 23d Landwehr Division.

VALUE.

The 23d Landwehr Division is composed entirely of elderly men; in May 1917, the recruit depots of the division furnished men from 40 to 46 years of age. At the end of 1917 the best elements had been taken for use on the Western Front.

1918.

DVINSK.

1. Beginning in February, the 23d Landwehr Division occupied the Dvinsk region. A man of the division wrote from that city under date of March 15: "We have been here since the 20th of February. The 23d Landwehr Regiment, to which I belong, is to remain in Russia for guard duty. We hold the new frontier." The 26th Landwehr and 27th Landwehr Regiments and divisional headquarters were identified here on May 9. On the 18th of May, elements of the 27th Landwehr Regiment were in the vicinity of Riejitsa.

VALUE—1918 ESTIMATE.

The division was rated as fourth class.

24th Division.
COMPOSITION.

	1914 Brigade.	1914 Regiment.	1915 Brigade.	1915 Regiment.	1916 Brigade.	1916 Regiment.	1917 Brigade.	1917 Regiment.	1918 Brigade.	1918 Regiment.
Infantry	47. 48.	139. 179. 106. 107.	47. 48.	139. 179. 106. 107.	47.	139. 133. 179.	89.	133. 139. 179.	89.	133. 139. 179.
Cavalry	18 Uhlan Rgt.				(?) Squ. 19 Hus. Rgt.		1 Squ. 19 Hus. Rgt.		1 Sqn. 19 Hus. Rgt.	
Artillery	24 Brig.: 77 F. A. Rgt. 78 F. A. Rgt.		21 Brig.: 77 F. A. Rgt. 78 F. A. Rgt.		24 Brig.: 77 F. A. Rgt. 78 F. A. Rgt.		24 Art. Command: 77 F. A. Rgt.		24 Art. Command: 77 F. A. Rgt. 96 Ft. A. Btn. (Staff, and 1, 2, and 3 Btries.). 818 Light Am. Col. 1277 Light Am. Col. 1278 Light Am. Col.	
Engineers and liaisons.			1 Pion. Btn. No. 22: Field Co. 22 Pions. 24 Tel. Detch. 24 Pont. Engs.		1 Pion. Btn. No. 22: 1 Co. 22 Pions. 24 T. M. Co. 24 Tel. Detch.		(1/22) Pion. Btn.: 2 Co. 22 Pions. 5 Co. 22 Pions. 2 Ers. Co. 24 Pions. 24 T. M. Co. 22 Searchlight Section. 24 Tel. Detch.		22 Pion. Btn.: 2 Co. 22 Pions. 5 Co. 22 Pions. 134 Searchlight Section. 24 Signal Command: 24 Tel. Detch. 98 Wireless Detch.	
Medical and Veterinary.							47 Ambulance Co. 307 Field Hospital. (?) 24 Vet. Hospital.		47 Ambulance Co. 307 Field Hospital. 311 Field Hospital. 21 Vet. Hospital.	
Transports							M. T. Col.			
Attached					24 Art. Survey Section. 58 Labor Btn.					

HISTORY.

(19th Corps District—Saxony.)

1914.

1. The 24th Division belongs to the 19th Army Corps. It is recruited in the western part of the Kingdom of Saxony (Leipzig).

MARNE.

2. At the outbreak of the war it formed a part with the 19th Army Corps, of the 3d German Army (Von Hausen). One of its brigades, the 48th, sent away secretly, detrained on August 4 at Pruem (Eifel), and entered the north of Luxemburg on the 5th. The division concentrated in the Houffalize on August 11, arrived on the banks of the Meuse on the 22d, which it crossed on the 24th and 25th above Dinant. It was at Châlons on September 5, and took part in the battle of the Marne on the 7th and 8th between Vitry le François and Maisons en Champagne. From there it returned to St. Hilaire le Grand.

FLANDERS.

3. In October, 1914, the 24th Division went over to the 6th Army (Crown Prince of Bavaria), and took up its position, which crosses the Lys (Flanders).

1915.

FLANDERS.

1. In March, 1915, the 106th and 107th Infantry Regiments were transferred to the 58th Division. The 24th Division, reduced to two regiments, was filled up by taking the 133d Infantry Regiment from the 40th Division. The 19th Army Corps retained the Lys sector until the month of August, 1917. It detached elements from its divisions to reenforce other sectors at various times.

2. In January, 1915, the 24th Division had elements in action at L'Epinette.

3. At the battle of Neuve Chapelle (March, 1915) and at Festubert (May–June, 1915), it reinforced the 7th Army Corps.

4. At the time of the Franco–British offensive in Artois, units of the 24th Division again acted as reenforcements at La Bassée–Souchez (June and October, 1915).

1916.

SOMME.

1. Relieved at the beginning of August, 1916, in the sector of the Lys, the 19th Army Corps was sent, about August 8, to the Somme, north of Pozières, where it suffered considerable losses.

2. At the end of August it was placed for several weeks in the sector of Neuve Chapelle–La Bassée, then of Le Sars–Butte de Warlencourt. It took part a second time in the battle of the Somme (October).

The two divisions of the corps suffered very heavily during these two engagements in the Franco–British offensive. The 24th division lost 6,217 men; that is, 69 per cent of its effectives.

3. The 24th Division was withdrawn from the Somme about November 11 and transferred to Flanders, where it occupied the line between the Ypres–Comines Canal and the Douve (December and the first months of 1917).

1917.

FLANDERS.

1. When the British offensive was being prepared on the Wytschaete-Messines front, the 24th Division was withdrawn from the Ypres-Comines sector and stationed behind Lille (beginning of April, 1917).

On the 7th of June it was sent toward the front; the 179th Infantry Regiment was in action east of Wytschaete on the 8th, and the division occupied the sector of Hollebeke, where it was retained until June 27.

During this period the division suffered heavily.

2. Relieved and sent to rest at the end of June, it went back into line in Belgium (sector southwest of Houthem) during the month of August.

3. It left the line at the beginning of October, and, after a few days of rest, again took over a sector in the area southeast of Ypres northwest of Zandvoorde—west of Gheluvelt. It left there at the end of October to go to the south of the Scarpe, at Monchy le Preux, where it was still in line at the beginning of February, 1918

RECRUITING.

The 24th Division is purely Saxon.

VALUE—1917 ESTIMATE

In a general manner, the attitude of the 19th Army Corps has been rather passive since trench warfare succeeded the war of movement.

We may say that the Saxon is a courageous adversary.

The 24th Division is good.

1918.

1. The division held the Monchy le Preux sector until about February 11, when it was relieved by the 185th Division and transferred to the area north of Valenciennes to rest and train. On March 16 it began to march toward the Cambrai front. The route lay through Raismes, Haveluy, Wallers, Aniche, Aubigny au Bac, Marquion. It reached the original German front line on March 22 at 9 a. m.

BATTLE OF THE SOMME.

2. The division followed the advance in reserve until the night of March 24–25, when it came in line south of Bapaume (Ligny-Tilloy). It advanced in first line by Grevillers (26th) Achiet le Petit, Hebuterne (27th and 29th). From March 30 to April 5 it was in reserve. On the 6th the division was reengaged near Hebuterne and Bucquoy until April 15.

According to the German press, the Kaiser on March 27 telegraphed the King of Saxony felicitating him on the success of the 24th Division.

3. The division was at rest from April 15 to the end of May, first at Bapaume and later at Valenciennes.

PICARDY.

4. The division was engaged from May 28 to June 16 in the sector of the Bois d'Aveluy (north of Albert). When relieved from this front it went by railroad to the Cambrai area. The 139th Regiment went into camp at Eswars and St. Martin; the 133d, at Raillencourt; the 179th, at Ramillies and Escaudoewres. The division underwent training and executed divisional maneuvers. Between the 5th and 10th of July the division marched by Cambrai, Flesquieres, Havrincourt, Bertincourt to the region Haplincourt Bus for the purpose of reengaging in the Aveluy sector where the Germans expected an attack by the English. It remained a week in the region and returned to its cantonments in the Cambrai area.

About July 18 an order was issued placing the division at the disposition of the 6th Army for a projected offensive in Flanders. This order was revoked, and about July 20 the division entrained at Ivuy and Sancourt and moved to Chaulnes (via Peronne). It remained in the vicinity several days and then moved to Quesnel by narrow-gauge railroad.

AVRE.

5. From the 1st of August until the 17th the division opposed a lively resistance to the French attack in the Avre. In this fighting the division lost 800 prisoners.

LAON.

6. ·The division rested a week west of Ham. It was engaged west of Coucy le Chateau (Champs Folembray) from August 30 to September 9. It retreated about the 9th to Baresis. On October 3 the division was relieved north of the St. Gobain-Baresis railroad.

ST. QUENTIN.

7. It was moved by trucks to Fontaine-Uterte (north of St. Quentin) and engaged on October 4 near Sequehart. The division was forced back on Monthrehain and Andigny. Three hundred and forty-five prisoners were lost on the 8th. Two days later the division was relieved. On the 17th the division was again identified in line at Vaux-Audigny, but was withdrawn in a day or two.

8. It arrived in an area northeast of Fourmies on October 23 and was still there on the 26th. No later identification was secured.

VALUE—1918 ESTIMATE.

The division was rated as a third-class division. Its conduct in the March offensive and in the defensive in August and October was above the average and would warrant a higher rating.

24th Reserve Division.
COMPOSITION.

	1914 Brigade.	1914 Regiment.	1915 Brigade.	1915 Regiment.	1916 Brigade.	1916 Regiment.	1917 Brigade.	1917 Regiment.	1918 Brigade.	1918 Regiment.
Infantry........	47 Res. 48 Res.	104 Res. 106 Res. 13 Res. Jäg. Btn. 107 Res. 133 Res.	47 Res. 48 Res.	104 Res. 106 Res. 13 Res. Jäg. Btn. 107 Res. 133 Res.	48 Res.	104 Res. 107 Res. 133 Res.	48 Res.	104 Res. 107 Res. 133 Res.	48 Res.	104 Res. 107 Res. 133 Res.
Cavalry........		Saxon Res. Hus. Rgt.		Saxon Res. Hus. Rgt.		3 Sqn. Saxon Res. Hus. Rgt.		3 Sqn. Saxon Res. Hus. Rgt.		3 Sqn. 18 Res. Hus. Rgt. (Saxon).
Artillery......		24 Res. F. A. Rgt. (9 Btries.)		24 Res. F. A. Rgt.		24 Res. F. A. Rgt. (6 Btries.) 40 Res. F. A. Rgt. (6 Btries.)		120 Art. Command: 40 Res. F. A. Rgt. (9 Btries.).		120 Art. Command: 68 F. A. Rgt. 5 Btry. 7 Res. Ft. A. Rgt. 64 (Saxon) Ft. A. Btn. 1115 Light Am. Col 1116 Light Am. Col 1117 Light Am. Col
Engineers and Liaisons.			Res. Co. 2 Pion. Btn. No. 12. 24 Res. Pont. Engs. 24 Res. Tel. Detch.		3 Res. Co. 12 Pions. 4 Res. Co. 12 Pions. 224 T. M. Co. 24 Res. Pont. Engs. 24 Res. Tel. Detch.		324 Pion. Btn.: 5 Res. Co. 12 Pions. 6 Res. Co. 12 Pions. 224 T. M. Co. 424 Tel. Detch.		324 Pion. Btn.: 1 Res. Co. 12 Pions. 6 Res. Co. 12 Pions. 126 Searchlight Section. 424 Signal Command: 424 Tel. Detch. 138 Wireless Detch.	
Medical and Veterinary.							271 Ambulance Co. 1 Res. Field Hospital. 424 Vet. Hospital.		271 Ambulance Co. 1 Res. Field Hospital. 7 Res. Field Hospital. 424 Vet. Hospital.	
Transports....							M. T. Col.		722 M. T. Col.	
Attached......					28 Labor Btn.				50 M. G. S. Detch. 207 Reconnaissance Flight. 50 Balloon Sqn. 17 Sound Ranging Section. 40 Art. Observation Section. (Elements attached June, 1918. German document, June 15–16, 1918.)	

HISTORY.

(19th Corps District—Saxony.)

1914.

1. The 24th Reserve Division (12th Reserve Corps with the 23d Reserve Division) belonged at the outbreak of the war to the 3d German Army (Von Hausen).

2. Detraining on August 12–13, 1914, northeast of Trèves, (Coblentz–Trèves railroad), entering Belgium by way of Viel–Salm on the 19th, it advanced into France by way of the Ardennes and Champagne and from there to Sompuis (west of Vitry le François, Sept. 8).

MARNE.

3. Going into action on September 8 and 9 in the vicinity of Mailly, it retired by way of Mourmelon and Sept–Saulx to the east of Rheims (Moronvilliers–Vaudesin-court). It made a stand in this sector and established its position there (end of September).

1915.

CHAMPAGNE.

1. The 24th Reserve Division remained in line on the Champagne front (north of Souain, south of St. Souplet–Moronvilliers) from September, 1914, until the beginning of July, 1916. In April, 1915, the 106th Reserve Infantry Regiment was transferred to the 123d Division, a new formation.

2. At the end of September, 1915, it suffered very heavy losses while opposing the French offensive.

1916.

SOMME.

1. Relieved from its sector in Champagne about the beginning of July, 1916, the 24th Reserve Division was transferred to the Somme. It went into action between Longueval and Hardecourt, from the middle to the end of July.

2. Some elements of the division were still fighting on the Somme (near Martin-puich in September).

ARTOIS.

3. About September 21, the 24th Reserve Division was put in line north of Arras (area from Lievin to Roclincourt).

SOMME.

4. It left Artois in the middle of November to return to the Somme, south of Bapaume (Le Transloy–Gueudecourt). It remained there until December 12, then returned to Artois (sector east of Arras) at the end of December.

1917.

ARTOIS.

1. The 24th Reserve Division occupied the sector east of Arras until March 25, 1917. Relieved at this date, it was sent to rest northeast of Ghent.

GALICIA.

2. On April 26 it entrained for the Eastern Front. Itinerary: Herbestal–Aix la Chapelle–Dusseldorf–Barmen–Leipzig–Dresden–Georlitz–Lemberg. Detraining in Galicia, it went into line south of Brzezany, at the beginning of May. It underwent the Russian offensive at the beginning of July, in the course of which prisoners of the three regiments and a part of the artillery of the division were left in the hands of the Russians (366 prisoners from the 133d Reserve Infantry Regiment).

3. Withdrawn from the front and reorganized, the 24th Reserve Division again went into action on July 20 (German counterattack). It advanced as far as Zbrucz and suffered new losses.

4. About August 16 it took over the sector of Skala.

5. Entraining for the Western Front on October 24, it detrained at Bruges on the 31st.   Itinerary: Stanislau–Lemberg–Breslau–Dresden–Leipzig–Cassel–Trèves–Brussels.

CAMBRAI.

6. After a rest in Belgium during the month of November, the 24th Reserve Division fought at Cambrai (end of November).   It remained in the sector Flesquières–Graincourt until the end of February, 1918.

VALUE—1917 ESTIMATE.

The 24th Reserve Division took part in numerous battles; it is a fairly good division.

1918.

1. The division was relieved in the Cambrai sector on February 6 by the 27th Division and went to rest in the Ivny area.   On the 28th it marched via Cambrai— Sains Inchy to Prouville and went into line.

BATTLE OF THE SOMME.

2. It took part in the initial attack and by the 22d had reached Boursies.   On the following day, the division advanced through Hermies to Ruyaulcourt and was relieved in the evening.   The division rested until April 6 when it came into line north of Hangard where it was engaged until April 19, when the 19th Division relieved it.   The division suffered very heavily from artillery and machine gun fire in this sector.

3. The division was at rest until May 1, when it returned to the front south of the Somme, relieving the 1st Division.   About the 24th of May the division sideslipped north and took the sector astride the Somme.   It was relieved about the middle of June.

SECOND BATTLE OF THE MARNE.

4. The division rested in the Cambrai area undergoing training.   It left Cambrai about July 19 and was engaged west of Fere en Tardenois on July 24.   The division took part in the fighting on the Aisne until about September 5.   It passed to second line for about two weeks and returned to line at Pinon on September 20.   Until the armistice, it was constantly engaged in resisting the Allied advance.   It was identified at Verneuil (Oct. 19), Chalaudry (21st), Mortiers (26th), Crecy (28th), and south of Landouzy on November 7.

VALUE—1918 ESTIMATE.

The division was rated as third class.   It was used as an attack division in March, but thereafter was engaged entirely on the defensive.   It appears to have resisted as well as the average German division.

24th Landwehr Division.

COMPOSITION.

	1917		1918[1]	
	Brigade.	Regiment.	Brigade.	Regiment.
Infantry	9 Landwehr	24 Landwehr. 48 Landwehr. 427.		24 Landwehr. 48 Landwehr.
Artillery	Art. Command: 250 Ldw. F. A. Rgt.			

[1] The 24th Landwehr Division is considered as dissolved.

HISTORY.

(24th and 48th Landwehr Regiments: 3d Corps District—Brandenburg.)

1917.

RUSSIA.

1. The 24th Landwehr Division was formed on the Eastern Front about October, 1917, by the transformation of the 9th Landwehr Brigade (24th and 48th Landwehr Regiments).

This brigade, after forming a part of the war garrison of Koenigsberg (August, 1914), then of the Sommer Division, had gone over to the new 10th Landwehr Division in 1915.

Becoming independent, it held the sector of Lake Svir until September, 1915.

SPIAGLA.

2. Made up of the 24th and 48th Landwehr Regiments, to which was temporarily joined the 427th Infantry Regiment coming from the 205th Division, the 24th Landwehr Division occupied the sector south of Lake Narotch-Spiagla until February, 1918.

VALUE—1917 ESTIMATE.

The 24th Landwehr Division is of mediocre quality.

1918.

1. In January, 1918, the division was reduced to two regiments, the 427th Regiment having been sent to the Western Front.

LIVONIA.

2. In March the division advanced into Russia and was identified about the middle of May in the Ostrov-Reijitsa region. The 427th Regiment was dissolved, but the 48th Landwehr Regiment was identified in Russia on the 19th of September. It seems possible that the divisional staff was also disbanded and that the 9th Landwehr Brigade, with the 48th Landwehr Regiment under its orders, again became independent.

VALUE—1918 ESTIMATE.

The division was rated as fourth class.

25th Division.
COMPOSITION.

	1914		1915		1916		1917		1918	
	Brigade.	Regiment.	Brigade.	Regiment.	Brigade.	Regiment.	Brigade.	Regiment.	Brigade.	Regiment.
Infantry	49. 50.	115 Body Gd. Inf. 116. 117 Body Inf. 118.	49. 50.	115 Body Gd. Inf. 116. 117 Body Inf. 118.	49.	115 Body Gd. Inf. 116. 117 Body Inf.	49.	115 Body Gd. Inf. 116. 117 Body Inf.	49.	115. 116. 117.
Cavalry	6 Dragoon Rgt.		......		6 Dragoon Rgt. (3 Sqns.)		3 Sqn. 6 Drag. Rgt. (?)		1 Sqn. 6 Drag. Rgt.	
Artillery	25 Brig.: 25 F. A. Rgt. 61 F. A. Rgt.		25 Brig.: 25 F. A. Rgt. 61 F. A. Rgt.		25 Brig: 25 F. A. Rgt. 61 F. A. Rgt.		25 Art. Command: 61 F. A. Rgt.		25 Art. Command: 25 F. A. Rgt. 1 Abt. 24 Res. Ft. A. Rgt. 823 Light Am. Col. 866 Light Am. Col. 1294 Light Am. Col.	
Engineers and Liaisons.			1 Pion. Btn. No. 21: Field Co. 21 Pions. 25 Tel. Detch. 25 Pont. Engs.		1 Pion. Btn. No. 21: 2 Co. 21 Pions. 89 Res. Pion. Co. Field Co. 25 Pions. 25 T. M. Co. 25 Tel. Detch. 25 Pont. Engs.		(1/21 or 134) Pion. Btn.: 2 Co. 21 Pions. 3 Co. 21 Pions. 89 Res. Pion. Co. 25 T. M. Co. 25 Tel. Detch.		129 Pion. Btn.: 3 Co. 21 Pions. 89 Res. Pion. Co. 68 Searchlight Section. 25 Signal Command: 25 Tel. Detch. 7 Wireless Detch.	
Medical and Veterinary.			......				45 Ambulance Co. Field Hospital. Vet. Hospital.		45 Ambulance Co. 298 Field Hospital. 304 Field Hospital. 25 Vet. Hospital.	
Transports			......				M. T. Col.			
Attached			......		14 Anti-Aircraft Section.		14 Anti-Aircraft Section 16 Anti-Aircraft Section (3.7 cm. automatic guns).			

HISTORY.

(18th Corps District—Grand Duchy of Hesse.)

1914.

LUXEMBURG.

1. The 25th Division, also known as the Hessian Grand Ducal Division, formed, in August, 1914, with the 21st Division, the 18th Army Corps. On August 3 its 50th Brigade set out for Koenigsmacher, near Thionville, as covering troops. On August 10 and 11 the 25th Division entered the Grand Duchy of Luxemburg, which it crossed, and entered Belgian Luxemburg on the 19th.

ARDENNES.

2. It formed a part of the 4th Army (Duke of Wurttemberg) and fought at Maissin, northwest of Neufchâteau on August 22. On August 24, it entered France; on the 27th it crossed the Meuse below Mouzon. (On Aug. 31 the losses had been such that the remnants of the 116th Infantry Regiment formed only four companies.)

MARNE.

3. On September 6 and the days immediately following the 25th Division took part in the battle of the Marne between Vitry and Sermaize. In the middle of the month, it was northwest of Rheims, on the Aisne-Marne Canal. On September 26 it entrained at Laon for Ham.

SOMME.

4. In October the 18th Army Corps was reattached to the 2d Army which formed at this time the extreme right flank of the German Army (Péronne area) and the division went into line—the Lihons–Chaulnes road to the banks of the Avre.

1915.

SOMME.

1. The 25th Division was retained in this sector north of the Avre until October 15, 1915. During this time it did not take part in any important action. In March it ceded the 118th Infantry Regiment to the 56th Division, a new formation.

2. After a long rest in the St. Quentin area (the staff of the 18th Army Corps was at Fresnoy le Grand in December, 1915, and that of the 25th Division at Busigny in January, 1916) the 25th Division was transferred to the sector north of Verdun at the beginning of February, 1916.

1916.

VERDUN.

1. On February 21, 1916, it took part in the general attack north of Verdun. After advancing rapidly, the 18th Army Corps was stopped in the area west of Douaumont. On March 9 it failed in its attacks on the Haudremont Farm.

2. The Army Corps was then sent to rest in the rear area to be reorganized.

3. About April 10, the 18th Army Corps reappeared in line (Caillette wood). The 25th Division suffered very heavy losses in its attacks.

4. Relieved about April 25, it was put in line about the middle of May in the vicinity of Craonne.

SOMME.

5. It was withdrawn from this sector about the 1st of September and transferred to the Somme, where it went into action from September 15 to October 1, and again lost very heavily.

6. At the beginning of October the 25th Division left the Somme to occupy the sector Apremont–Ailly wood in the Woevre.

7. Again transferred to the Somme at the end of November, it was put into line in the area north of Chaulnes (sector from Kratz wood to the Demi-Lune). It was in this sector at the time of the retirement on March 16, 1916.

1917.

1. On this date it carried out its retreat by way of Villecourt–Matigny–Douchy–Roupy, in the direction of St. Quentin.

ST. QUENTIN.

2. On March 20 it began to withstand our advance on the line. Savy–Dallon–Giffecourt, and when the front was stabilized on April 4 it occupied the sector in front of St. Quentin and did not leave until the end of May, after having pillaged the town.

3. It spent the month of June at rest (area of Neuvillette–Bernot).

4. On July 2 it went into line (Itancourt sector), and on July 18 launched an attack upon the salient Moulin de Tous Vents (south of St. Quentin).

FLANDERS.

5. Relieved about the middle of September, it was sent to the active sector of Flanders (north of Zandvoorde).

6. At the beginning of October it was sent to rest in the Ghent area.

7. It reappeared on the front, near Passchendaele, in the middle of November, and remained there except for a few short intervals until its relief on February 10, 1918.

RECRUITING.

The 25th Division is recruited from the Grand Duchy of Hesse. Men are furnished principally from the rest of the 18th Corps District and the Rhine District (7th and 8th Corps Districts).

VALUE—1917 ESTIMATE.

The 18th Army Corps has been considered one of the best corps in the German Army.

In September, 1917, the morale of the 25th Division appeared good. At this time, as the division had not taken part in any important actions since September, 1916, it was difficult to form a judgment as to the combat value of this organization.

Its local operation on the salient of Moulin de Tous Vents (July 18, 1917) was carried out energetically.

1918.

1. The reports concerning the location of the 25th Division during January and early February are conflicting, mention being made in some of two reliefs; it seems most likely, however, that the division was not relieved until February 10, when the 15th Division took over its sector east of Passchendaele.

MONS.

2. On the 15th it entrained at Iseghem and traveled via Courtrai–Ath–Mons to Givry; from here it marched to Bavai (southwest of Mons), where it underwent a course of intensive training in open warfare; cooperation with tanks was featured.

ST. QUENTIN.

3. The division marched from Pommereuil on the 16th, via Le Cateau and Busigny, to Becquigny, and from there, on the 19th, to Wiancourt, reenforcing the battle front near Le Verguier (northwest of St. Quentin) on the 21st. It was relieved about the 30th, after having suffered heavy losses.

AMIENS.

4. On April 1 it went back into line southeast of Hangard en Santerre (southeast of Amiens); it was withdrawn about the 12th and moved by easy stages to the Lille area, where, on account of its good fighting on the St. Quentin and Amiens fronts, it was inspected by the Kaiser on April 20. The commander of the 115th Regiment received Pour le Mérite at the same time.

BETHUNE.

5. During the night of the 26–27th of April it relieved the 240th Division near Hinges (north of Bethune); relieved by the 36th Reserve Division on the 10th of May, it went to rest in the area north of Douai.

LYS.

6. On July 4 the division moved up into close reserve in the Laventie–Estaires area, and during the night of the 6–7th it relieved the 16th Division near Merville, north of the Lys. On the 20th it was withdrawn, the 16th Division coming back into line, and went to the Lille area.

SOMME.

7. After about a month's rest it reenforced the front near Montauban (southeast of Albert). The front was being forced back here, and so the division passed successively through Hardecourt, Combles, and the St. Pierre–Vaast wood, where it was withdrawn September 5, after losing about 900 prisoners, and went to rest in the Bohain–Malincourt area.

CAMBRAI.

8. The division reenforced the front near Briastre (east of Cambrai) on October 11, and was withdrawn about the 28th.

VALENCIENNES.

9. On November 1 it came back into line north of Valenciennes, and had not been withdrawn on the 11th.

VALUE—1918 ESTIMATE.

The 25th is rated as a first-class division. It did very well in the large amount of heavy fighting in which it participated during 1918, and as a result suffered exceedingly heavy losses, especially in officers. It received numerous large drafts, and so the division's strength was rather larger than the average.

25th Reserve Division.

COMPOSITION.

	1914 Brigade	1914 Regiment	1915 Brigade	1915 Regiment	1916 Brigade	1916 Regiment	1917 Brigade	1917 Regiment	1918 Brigade	1918 Regiment
Infantry	....	116 Res. 118 Res. 83 Res. 168.	49 Res. 50 Res.	116 Res. 118 Res. 83 Res. 168.	50 Res.	83 Res. 118 Res. 168.	50 Res.	83 Res. 118 Res. 168.	50 Res.	168. 83 Res. 118 Res.
Cavalry	4 Res. Dragoon Rgt. (3 Sqns.).		4 Res. Dragoon Rgt........	....	4 Res. Dragoon Rgt. (2 Sqns.).		2 Sqn. 4 Res. Dragoon Rgt.		2 Sqn. 4 Res. Drag. Rgt. 4 Sqn. 4 Res. Drag. Rgt.	
Artillery	25 Res. F. A. Rgt. (6 Btries.).		25 Res. F. A. Rgt. 13 F. A. Rgt.		25 Res. F. A. Rgt. (9 Btries., Nos. 4-12).		127 Art. Command: 25 Res. F. A. Rgt. (9 Btries.).		127 Art. Command: 25 Res. F. A. Rgt. (6 4-gun and 6 4-how. Btries.).	
Engineers and Liaisons.	1 and 2 Res. Cos., 2 Pion. Btn. No. 11.		1 and 2 Res. Cos., 2 Pion. Btn. No. 11. 25 Res. Pont. Engs. 25 Res. Tel. Detch.		1 and 2 Res. Cos., 2 Pion. Btn. No. 11. 1 Co. 29 Pions. 2 Co. 29 Pions. 225 T. M. Co. 25 Res. Tel. Detch. 25 Res. Pont. Engs.		(325) Pion. Btn.: 1 Res. Co. 11 Pions. 2 Res. Co. 11 Pions. 225 T. M. Co. 20 Ldw. Field Searchlight Section. 425 Tel. Detch.		2 Pion. Btn. No. 11: 1 Res. Co. 11 Pions. 2 Res. Co. 11 Pions. 286 Pion. Co. 225 T. M. Co. 425 Tel. Detch. 151 Wireless Detch.	
Medical and Veterinary.							518 Ambulance Co. 67 Field Hospital. 68 Field Hospital. Vet. Hospital.		518 Ambulance Co. 67 Res. Field Hospital. 68 Res. Field Hospital. Vet. Hospital.	
Transports.							518 M. T. Col.		M. T. Col.	

[1] Composition at time of dissolution, October, 1918.

HISTORY.

(168th and 118th Reserve Regiments: 18th Corps District—Grand Duchy of Hesse.
83d Reserve Regiment: 11th Corps District—Electorate of Hesse.)

1914.

1. At the outbreak of the war the 25th Reserve Division, forming with the 21st Reserve Division the 18th Reserve Corps, belonged to the 4th Army (Duke of Wurttemberg).

BELGIUM-ARGONNE.

2. It detrained August 9–11 at Hermeskeil (southeast of Treves); entered Luxemburg the 16th (by way of Remich); crossed Luxemburg on the 19th; entered Belgium on the 20th. On the 22d it fought at Neufchateau; on the 22d, at Tremblois; crossed the Meuse on the 28th. To the west of the Argonne the 25th Reserve Division advanced to the area of Revigny. At the battle of the Marne it fought on the Saulx, in the neighborhood of Brabant le Roy (Sept. 7–10). It retired by way of Ste. Menehould, Moinemout, to the south of Cernay en Dormois (Sept. 14).

FLANDERS.

3. In October the 25th Reserve Division was sent to Flanders, south of the Lys. Toward the end of November it occupied a sector north of Wytschaete.

RUSSIA.

4. In December the division was transferred to the Eastern Front, It took part, with the Fabeck Corps, in the operations on the Bzura (December, 1914, to February, 1915).

1915.

GALICIA.

1. At the end of February, 1915, it was engaged in the Carpathians north of the Dniester (Von der Màrwitz Detachment); in June at Przemysl, then at Lemberg.

BREST-LITOWSK.

2. In July, the 25th Reserve Division took part in the offensive on Brest-Litowsk. Its successes occasioned it heavy losses; the 5th Company of the 168th Infantry Regiment received not less than 199 men as replacements from June 19 to August 17.

SERBIA.

3. The division took part in the Serbian campaign (October–November).

FRANCE.

4. It was transferred to the Western Front at the beginning of December, 1917. It entrained at Weisskirchen (Hungary). Itinerary: Temesvar–Budapest–Vienna–Ulm–Stuttgart–Spire–Deux Ponts–Saarbrucken–Sedan (detrained on Dec. 11).

ARGONNE.

5. On December 18, the 25th Reserve Division went into line on the Argonne (La Harazee).

1916.

1. The division remained in the Argonne until the end of July, 1916.

VERDUN.

2. At the beginning of July it was transferred to the Verdun area. It was engaged in the sector of Thiaumont (July–August); in the Nawe wood (August) and suffered heavy losses. It was again very much exhausted resisting the French attack of October 24.

CHAMPAGNE.

3. Relieved after this attack, the 25th Reserve Division was sent to rest in vicinity of Jametz and was reorganized. On November 16 it went into line east of Auberive.

In the course of November it received important replacements, including a large proportion of the 1917 class. Its reconstitution was not completed until February, 1917.

1917.

1. The division was retained on the Champagne front (Auberive) until the end of January, 1917.

MEUSE.

2. On February 27 it went into line on the right bank of the Meuse (sector of Louvemont–Chambrettes–Caurieres wood) and remained there, without any important losses, until June 20.

3. After resting until July 6 in the vicinity of Juvigny, Jametz, Marville, the 25th Reserve Division again occupied the front near Verdun (north of Vacherauville). North of Louvemont it withstood the French attack of August 20, which caused it to suffer very heavy losses (47 officers and 1,150 men prisoners, of whom 1,012 belonged to 168th Infantry Regiment).

VOSGES.

4. The 25th Reserve Division, already weakened by an epidemic of dysentery, was almost completely exhausted, when it was relieved on August 25 on the Verdun front. Sent to rest in the vicinity of Sarreburg, it took over a sector of the Vosges (Blamont), about September 4.

CHAMPAGNE.

5. Relieved on September 25 and entraining on the 27th at Rechicourt, the division was transferred to Champagne, where it occupied the sector Nogent–l'Abbesse (Nov. 11 to beginning of February, 1918).

RECRUITING.

The 25th Reserve Division is recruited from the Grand Duchy of Hesse, the Electorate of Hesse, and Hesse–Nassau. At times replacements were furnished from the Rhine districts, including the Grand Duchy of Baden (especially in 1916).

VALUE—1917 ESTIMATE.

The 25th Reserve Division put up a splendid defense against the French at the time of the attack on August 20, 1917.

It was an excellent organization at the outbreak of the campaign, but it seems (in spite of recent assertions of prisoners that it is still unfit to attack and was put in the fourth class, Arbeits Division) that the 25th Reserve Division, although it is exhausted by too long stays in line, is capable of rendering services even on an active front. Therefore it must be considered as a good division of the second class until more detailed information is received (Mar. 30, 1918).

1918.

1. The 25th Reserve Division was relieved by the 21st Division in the Nogent–l'Abbesse sector on February 6, and went to the Vouziers area, where it was put through a course of training, but not in open warfare.

AISNE.

2. On the 20th it relieved the 10th Reserve Division near Juvincourt (northwest of Rheims); it was withdrawn on April 11.

MONTDIDIER.

3. The division moved north by easy stages, and relieved the 6th Bavarian Reserve Division, west of Montdidier, on the 21st. Here it lost near Cantigny (north) heavily while trying to prevent Cantigny from falling to the Americans. It also lost even more heavily during the offensive of August 9, and was pushed back to Dancourt (southwest of Roye). It was withdrawn about the 18th.

St. Quentin.

4. On September 1 it reenforced the front near Voyennes (west of St. Quentin). In the fighting that followed the division was forced back to the Holnon wood (west of St. Quentin); it was withdrawn here about the 20th.

5. On the 30th, it again reenforced the front in the Lehaucourt sector (north of St. Quentin). It was withdrawn on October 11, and dissolved. 168th Regiment was transferred to the 21st Reserve Division. 83d Reserve Regiment was disbanded and drafted to the 22d Division. 87th Reserve Regiment was disbanded and drafted to the 48th Reserve Division.

VALUE—1918 ESTIMATE.

Until 1918 the 25th Reserve had been considered a second-class division. It is to be noted, however, that although it was trained in February, the training it received was not in open warfare—not to fit it to become an attack division. Prisoners captured soon after stated that the Germans considered it as little better than "a labor division." It was not used in any of the offensives made by the Germans, and was not very tenacious on the defense in any sector that was at all active. Moreover, two of the divisions that received replacements from the division when it was disbanded were second class and the other was rated as a fourth-class division. It was probably a third-class division.

25th Landwehr Division.
COMPOSITION.

	1916		1917		1918	
	Brigade.	Regiment.	Brigade.	Regiment.	Brigade.	Regiment.
Infantry	25 Mixed Ldw.	13 Ldw. 16 Ldw.	32 Res.	13 Ldw. 16 Ldw. 328 Ldw.	32 Res.	13 Ldw. 16 Ldw. 328 Ldw.
Cavalry	2 Sqn. 6 Res. Drag. Rgt.		2 Sqn. 6 Res. Drag. Rgt.		2 Sqn. 6 Res. Drag. Rgt.	
Artillery	254 F. A. Rgt.		244 Art. Command: 254 F. A. Rgt.		244 Art. Command: 254 Ldw. F. A. Rgt.	
Engineers and Liaisons	407 T. M. Co. 525 Tel. Detch.		425 Pion. Btn.: 1 Res. Co. 21 Pions. 4 Co. 27 Pions. 407 T. M. Co. 525 Tel. Detch.		425 Pion. Btn.: 4 Co. 27 Pions. 3 Landst. Co. 6 C. Dist. Pions. 12 Searchlight Section. 525 Signal Command: 525 Tel. Detch. 81 Wireless Detch.	
Medical and Veterinary			554 Ambulance Co. 414 Field Hospital. 6 Ldw. Field Hospital. 525 Vet. Hospital.		554 Ambulance Co. 414 Field Hospital. 6 Ldw. Field Hospital. 525 Vet. Hospital.	
Transports	M. T. Col.		M. T. Col.		790 M. T. Col.	

HISTORY.
(7th Corps District—Westphalia.)
1916.
AISNE.

1. The 25th Landwehr Division was organized in part from the former 25th Mixed Landwehr Brigade, independent (13th and 16th Landwehr Regiments), which entered Belgium on August 20, 1914, and went immediately after the battle of the Marne to the Laon area, where it occupied the Craonne–La Ville aux Bois sector from the end of September, 1914, until almost the end of 1916.

2. In October, 1916, the 25th Landwehr Brigade was transformed into the 25th Landwehr Division by the addition of a third regiment, the Schuster Regiment, which had existed for only a short time.

3. The division was then sent to the west and sent into line between Vailly and Chavonne (October).

1917.
CHEMIN DES DAMES.

1. At the beginning of February, 1917, the 186th Infantry Regiment was added as a third regiment to the 25th Landwehr Division. The division was still occupying the sector east of Vailly when the French offensive was launched on April 16. The division suffered heavy losses, retiring to the Chemin des Dames by way of Ostel, Aizy, Jouy (Apr. 16-22).

UPPER ALSACE.

2. Relieved north of the Aisne about April 25, the 25th Landwehr Division was transferred to Upper Alsace. At the beginning of May it went into line near the Swiss frontier (Hirtzbach, Largitzen, Bisel). It did not leave this sector since that time.

3. In May the 186th Infantry Regiment was replaced by a new regiment, the 328th Landwehr Regiment, formed by taking one battalion of each of the three regiments of the 13th Landwehr Division.

RECRUITING.

The division has a marked sectional quality; the infantry and field artillery come entirely from Westphalia.

VALUE—1917 ESTIMATE.

This is purely a sector division. The 25th Landwehr Division has been in line near the Swiss frontier for more than a year.

Since its arrival in Upper Alsace (May, 1917) the division has possessed an assault detachment supposed to carry out raids (June, 1918).

1918
ALSACE.

1. The division remained in the Hirzbach–Swiss frontier sector all through the year until the signing of the armistice.

VALUE—1918 ESTIMATE.

The 25th Landwehr Division is rated as a fourth-class division, as being fit to hold only a quiet sector. On the 11th of November, soon after the hour fixed for the suspension of hostilities, a number of men came over to the French lines to fraternize; they were taken prisoners. It seems that there had been a great deal of revolutionary agitation in the division. On October 8 a doctor had had his epaulettes cut to pieces; on the 9th the Soldiers' Council had come together and had elected representatives; on the 10th the company commander (of at least one company) had read the program for the organization of the Soldiers' Council. Prisoners state that the causes of this state of mind were the recent defeats suffered by the German forces, the weariness caused by four years of war, and the Kiel disturbances. From the 10th of November on none of the advanced posts had been occupied, and the men refused to do any work, the war having come to an end, to their mind.

26th Division.

COMPOSITION.

	1914 Brigade.	1914 Regiment.	1915 Brigade.	1915 Regiment.	1916 Brigade.	1916 Regiment.	1917 Brigade.	1917 Regiment.	1918 Brigade.	1918 Regiment.
Infantry	51. 52.	119 Gren. 125. 121. 122 Fus.	51. 52.	119 Gren. 125. 121. 122 Fus.	51.	119 Gren. 121. 125.	51.	119 Gren. 121. 125.	51.	119. 121. 125.
Cavalry	20 Uhlan Rgt.		20 Uhlan Rgt.		20 Uhlan Rgt. (3 Sqns.).		20 Sqn. 20 Uhlan Rgt. (?).		2 Sqn. 19 Uhlan Rgt.	
Artillery	26 Brig.: 29 F. A. Rgt. 65 F. A. Rgt.		26 Brig.: 29 F. A. Rgt. 65 F. A. Rgt.		26 Brig.: 29 F. A. Rgt. 65 F. A. Rgt.		26 Art. Command: 29 F. A. Rgt. (9 Btries.).		26 Art. Command: 29 F. A. Rgt., 2 Abt. 5 Ft. A. Rgt. (5, 6, and 13 Btries.). 1376 Light Am. Col. 1377 Light Am. Col. 1378 Light Am. Col.	
Engineers and Liaisons.	1 Field Co. 1 Pion. Btn. No. 13		1 Field Co. 1 Pion. Btn. No. 13: 26 Pont.Engs. 26 Tel. Detch.		1 and 5 Field Cos. 1 Pion. Btn. No. 13: 26 T. M. Co. 26 Pont. Engs. 26 Tel. Detch.		(1/13 or 129) Pion. Btn.: 1 Co. 13 Pions. 5 Co. 13 Pions. 26 T. M. Co. 311 Searchlight Section. Tel. Detch.		143 Pion. Btn.: 1 Co. 13 Pions. 5 Co. 13 Pions. 26 T. M. Co. 140 Searchlight Section 26 Signal Command: 26 Tel. Detch. 70 Wireless Detch.	
Medical and Veterinary.							3 Ambulance Co. 33 Ambulance Co. 250 Field Hospital. 259 Field Hospital. Vet. Hospital.		33 Ambulance Co. 250 Field Hospital. 259 Field Hospital. 26 Vet. Hospital.	
Transports							599 (?) M. T. Col.			

HISTORY.

(13th Corps District—Wurttemberg.)

1914.

LORRAINE–ARGONNE.

. 1. At the outbreak of the war the 26th Division formed the 13th Army Corps, with the 27th Division, and was a part of the 5th Army (German Crown Prince), and went into action on August 22 at Baranzy, northwest of Longwy, and on August 24 near Longuyon.   On August 31 it crossed the Meuse in the vicinity of Sassey, proceeded between the Meuse and the Argonne by way of Epinonville, Cheppy, Clermont, and Thiaucourt, fought on September 6, 7, 8, and 9 near Pretz and Beauzée, and retired toward Evre, Wally, and the Argonne (Apremont–Grurie wood).   (On Sept. 11 the 8th Company of the 119th Grenadier Regiment had already had 3 officers and 168 men as casualties; the 10th Company was reduced to 2 officers and 59 men.'

FLANDERS.

2. Separated then from the 27th Division, which remained in the Argonne, the 26th Division was transferred west of Lille on October 8, and fought at Fromelles, Aubert, and Maisnil from October 20 to 28.

3. At the end of the month it went north and took part in the attacks upon Messines on October 31.

RUSSIA.

4. At the end of November the division entrained for Russia with the 25th Reserve Division, these two divisions forming the reorganized 13th Army Corps.

POLAND.

5. In December and January, 1915, it was a part of the Fabeck Corps, and fought in Poland on the Bzura and the Rawka where it suffered heavily.

1915.

1. In March, 1915, the 26th Division was sent to the front north of Prasnysz.   It then composed the 13th Army Corps, with the 4th Guard Division and the 3d Division. In May it gave the 122d Fusilier Regiment to the 105th Division, a new formation. In June and July it took part in the offensive upon the Narew.

SERBIA.

2. Assigned to the army of Gen. von Koevess, it took part in the campaign against Serbia (October) and advanced along the Morava to Kragujevatz.

BELGIUM.

3. Sent to rest at Belgrade, at the end of November, before its departure for the Western Front, it entrained at Semlin on November 26 and was transferred to Belgium.   (Itinerary: Budapest–Vienna–Munich–Ulm–Deux Ponts–Saarbrücken; detraining at Bertrix on Nov. 20.)

4. In December it was concentrated in the vicinity of Courtrai, where the 27th Division was and again formed the 13th Army Corps with this division as it had done originally.

1916.

1. In January, 1916, the 26th Division went into line southeast of Ypres (between Hooge and the south of Sanctuary wood).   It held this sector until the month of July and suffered heavy losses July 2 (Zillebeke).

SOMME.

2. At the end of July the division was sent to the Somme and opposed the British troops on the Longueval front.   It lost very heavily while resting at Guillemont. (Aug. 18–19).

FLANDERS.

. 3. Relieved on August 25, it took over the sector of Wytschaete (September to November 11).

SOMME.

4. About November 11 the division left Flanders and returned to the Somme. It occupied the Transloy sector from December 7 to the beginning of March, 1917.

1917.

ARTOIS.

1. The division was in reserve during the month of March behind the Artois front; went into action south of the Scarpe at the time of the British offensive. On April 25 it launched a counterattack at Monchy le Preux.

2. Relieved in a fortnight and sent to rest, it went back to the same sector (south of the Scarpe); remained there from May 31 to the end of July without any important losses and went to rest near Cambrai during the first half of August.

FLANDERS.

3. From August 16 to September 4 it occupied the sector north of Langemerck, where the artillery caused it heavy losses.

LORRAINE.

4. Sent to rest in Lorraine, it was trained and was outfitted for mountain warfare and then sent to the Italian front at the end of September.

ITALY.

5. It formed a part of the Berrer Corps (14th German Army) on October 20, fought northwest of Tolmino on October 24, entered Udine on the 28th, and reached the Tagliamento on the 29th.

RECRUITING.

The 26th Division is recruited entirely in Wurttemberg.

VALUE—1917 ESTIMATE.

The 26th Division conducted itself well in the numerous battles in which it took part. It is to be especially noted that at Poelcappelle, in August, 1917, some units mutinied and left the first line vacant, when the relief did not arrive quickly enough. This weakening of the morale of the 26th Division was probably only temporary and will disappear, no doubt, after a period of rest. (British Summary of Information, October, 1917.)

1918.

FRANCE.

1. The 26th Division, after having done very well in Italy, was transported to the Western Front, detraining in the Freiburg region (southeast of Dieuze), and remaining here until March 10.

CAMBRAI.

2. The division entrained at Strassburg on the 11th and 12th, and detrained near Peruwelz on the 13th and 14th, remaining in the neighborhood of Valenciennes until the 17th; from here it proceeded by night marches via Denain and Aniche to the Estrées-Ecourt-St. Quentin region (south of Douai), where it arrived on the 20th. On the 26th it went into close reserve near Fontaine les Croisilles, and the next day it entered line near Hamelincourt (south of Arras). It attacked the next day, but made no headway. It was relieved by the 111th Division on the 31st, and rested near Croisilles until April 3.

3. Then it marched via Bapaume and Miraumont and entered line south of Hébuterne (south of Arras), taking part in the unsuccessful attack of the 5th. It was relieved about the 12th of May by the 16th Reserve Division, and went to the Denain region to rest and refit. On June 15 it was in army reserve in the Roye–Carrépuis area.

364 DIVISIONS OF GERMAN ARMY WHICH PARTICIPATED IN WAR.

RHEIMS.

4. About July 3 it went to the vicinity of Neuflize (northeast of Rheims); the 15th it entered line north of Prosnes (southeast of Rheims), and was withdrawn on the 17th.

5. By traveling in trucks, the division reached Bazoches on the 21st; it remained in reserve the 23d and 24th, and relieved the 45th Reserve Division east of Saponay (northwest of Fére-en-Tardenois during the night of July 25–26. The Allied push forced the front back here, and the division was identified north of Saponay on August 2, northeast of Fismes on the 18th, east of Braine on the 20th. It was relieved about the 10th of September and went to rest north of Pont Arcy (northwest of Fismes).

6. On the 3d of October it came back into line north of Soupir (east of Vailly), and was still in line on November 11.

VALUE—1918 ESTIMATE.

The 26th is rated as a first-class division. While it was in Alsace (January, February, and the first part of March) it was thoroughly trained in open warfare, and so it was used as a shock division, but it did not succeed in making much headway in its first two engagements. It did fight tenaciously, however, then and in subsequent fighting, and was mentioned in the German communiqués of October 27 and November 2 as having particularly distinguished itself. It suffered heavy losses, so that despite the large numbers of reenforcements sent it from time to time, its battalions were reduced to three companies.

26th Reserve Division.
COMPOSITION.

	1914		1915		1916		1917		1918	
	Brigade.	Regiment.	Brigade.	Regiment.	Brigade.	Regiment.	Brigade.	Regiment.	Brigade.	Regiment.
Infantry......	51 Res. 52 Res.	121 Res. 180, 99 Res. 119 Res. 120 Res.	51 Res. 52 Res.	121 Res. 180, 99 Res. 119 Res. 120 Res.	51 Res. 52 Res.	119 Res. 180, 121 Res. 99 Res.	51 Res.	119 Res. 121 Res. 180.	51 Res.	180, 119 Res. 121 Res.
Cavalry......	Wurtt. Res. Drag. Rgt. (3 Sqns.).		Wurtt. Res. Drag. Rgt.		Wurtt. Res. Drag. Rgt.		2 Sqn. 20 Uhlan Rgt.		2 Sqn. 20 Uhlan Rgt.	
Artillery......	26 Res. F. A. Rgt. (9 Btries.).		26 Res. F. A. Rgt.		26 Res. F. A. Rgt. (6 Btries.). 27 Res. F. A. Rgt. (6 Btries.).		122 (Wurtt.) Art. Command; 26 Res. F. A. Rgt. (9 Btries.).		122 Art. Command: 26 Res. F. A. Rgt. 59 Ft. A. Btn. 1261 Light Am. Col. 1262 Light Am. Col. 1316 Light Am. Col.	
Engineers and Liaisons.	4 Field Co. 2 Pion. Btn. No. 13.		4 Field Co. 2 Pion. Btn. No. 13. 26 Res. Pont. Engs. 26 Res. Tel. Detch.		4 Field Co. 13 Pions. 6 Field Co. 13 Pions. 226 T. M. Co. 26 Res. Pont. Engs. 26 Res. Tel. Detch.		326 Pion. Btn.: 4 Co. 13 Pions. 6 Co. 13 Pions. 226 T. M. Co. 426 Tel. Detch.		326 Pion. Btn.: 4 Co. 13 Pions. 6 Co. 13 Pions. 226 T. M. Co. 36 Searchlight Section. 426 Signal Command: 426 Tel. Detch. 139 Wireless Detch.	
Medical and Veterinary.							522 Ambulance Co. 502 Field Hospital. 505 Field Hospital. 146 Vet. Hospital.		522 Ambulance Co. 502 Field Hospital. 245 Vet. Hospital.	
Transports......							M. T. Col.			
Odd Units......							2 (Wurtt.) Cyclist Co......			

HISTORY.

(13th Corps District—Wurttemberg.)

1914.

VOSGES.

1.. At the beginning of the war the 26th Reserve Division, forming the 14th Reserve Corps with the 28th Reserve Division, was a part of the 7th German Army. While the 99th Reserve Infantry Regiment formed in Alsace and at once went to the valley of the Bruche, the 180th Infantry Regiment went to Ste. Marie aux Mines on August 8. The three reserve regiments (119th, 120th, 121st) detrained between Freiburg and Neubreisach on August 8-11 and fought at the Donon and in the valley of the Bruche from August 17 to 24. Going then to the western slope of the Vosges, the division reached St. Die on August 28, then advanced as far as Rougiville, from which place it was sent to Ste. Marie aux Mines.

SOMME.

2. On September 11 the 26th Reserve Division was sent to the Somme and assigned to the 2d Army. It went into action on both banks of the Ancre, near Thiepval, near Mirmaumont and Beaumont Hamel, beginning on the 27th.

3. It occupied this sector of the front (south of Hebuterne, north of Ovillers) until July, 1916. During this period it did not take part in any important action.

1915.

ARTOIS.

1. In March, 1915, the 120th Reserve Infantry Regiment was given to the 58th Division, a new formation.

2. In May, 1915, elements of the 26th Reserve Division were sent to Artois on detached service and fought at Neuville-St. Vaast. In June some units of the 99th Reserve Regiment (3d and 4th Battalions) and the 180th Infantry Regiment took part in the battles around Arras (Le Labyrinthe).

SOMME.

3. At the beginning of July these elements rejoined the division, which continued to hold the Somme sector before Bapaume.

1916.

SOMME.

1. On July 1, 1916, the 26th Reserve Division withstood the Franco–British offensive north and south of the Ancre (Beaumont Hamel, Ovillers, Thiepval). (The total of the losses on the Somme amounted to 10,042 men.) The 99th Reserve Infantry Regiment lost 48 officers and 2,070 men. (Official List of Casualties.)

ARTOIS.

2. Relieved along the Somme about October 6, the division was sent south of Arras (Monchy aux Bois) on October 10. Some elements of the division were still engaged on both banks of the Ancre in November.

1917.

HINDENBURG LINE.

1. After having occupied the calm sector of Artois for the winter of 1916–17, the 26th Reserve Division took part in the withdrawal of the German troops about March 20. It left the front of Monchy aux Bois and retired southeast of Croisilles (Lagnicourt-Ecoust-St. Main). It fought along this line until April 7-13 and suffered some losses (Noreuil, Apr. 2).

2. After a rest of a month in the vicinity of Valenciennes, in the course of which it sent some elements south of St. Quentin (Itancourt, May 4-11), the 26th Reserve Division went back into line between Arras and St. Quentin (Bullecourt-Queant) about May 17.

FLANDERS.

3. On August 10 the division was withdrawn from the front and entrained at Aubigny au Bac (south of Douai) for Belgium. It went into action north of Langemarck (Aug. 19–Sept. 16). It was then sent to rest (vicinity of Bohain, northeast of St. Quentin) until October 14.

4. About October 17 the 26th Reserve Division went back into line north of Ypres (The Ypres-Staden railroad—Houthulst wood) until October 23.

5. Sent to rest south of Cortemarck, it was transferred at the end of October to Eerneghem, where it was first in reserve.

6. In the middle of November the 26th Reserve Division took over the calm sector of Merckem, which it occupied until February, 1918, after a short rest in the middle. of December.

RECRUITING.

Since the departure of the 99th Reserve Infantry Regiment, the 26th Reserve Division is made up entirely of Wurttembergers.

VALUE—1917 ESTIMATE.

The 26th Reserve Division is a very good division, of a combative value equal to that of the majority of the active divisions. In the battle of the Somme, in 1916, it opposed a stubborn resistance to the British advance and launched vigorous counterattacks.

The division has not been seriously engaged since 1916; it was thoroughly rested on the Flanders front. Not having been exposed to violent battles and not having any great losses, its morale has not been shaken. (British Summary of Information, February, 1918.)

1918.

BELGIUM.

1. The 26th Reserve Division was withdrawn from the Merckem sector on the 20th of February, and went to the area west of Antwerp. Here, it was very probably trained in open warfare, but the fact has not been definitely established.

ARRAS.

2. It left about March 11 and entered line near Henin (southeast of Arras) on the 24th. Its mission was to protect the troops engaged in the main attack farther to the south against a flanking movement by the British troops massed around Arras. In so doing, it became heavily engaged, and is reported to have lost 60 per cent of its strength. It was relieved on May 14, and went to rest in the Arleux area (south of Douai).

3. On June 9 it relieved the 41st Division east of Hebuterne. A week or so later it extended its sector toward the south so as to relieve the 16th Reserve Division. It was relieved about July 23 by the 183d Division, and went to rest in the Bapaume area, after having suffered severe losses.

SOMME.

4. On August 10 the division reenforced the front astride the Braye–Corbie road (north of the Somme). It did not become heavily engaged this time; withdrawn about the 18th, and went to rest in the Douai area. Battalions were reduced to three companies.

ARRAS.

5. It reenforced the front near Vis en Artois (on Arras–Cambrai road) on August 27. After suffering heavy losses it was withdrawn on the 31st to region north of Cambrai.

CAMBRAI.

6. It came back into line on the 29th of September, after having rested and thoroughly refitted, reenforcing the front near Tilloy (northwest of Cambrai). It was

heavily engaged, and fought very well. A few days later Gen. von Beulow (commanding the 17th Army) sent a telegram to the King of Saxony saying that the division had fought in an exemplary manner at Cambrai, where it had several times reestablished the situation by its counterattacks on the 29th, inflicting enormous losses on the enemy, and thus preventing the town from falling into their hands. It was withdrawn about the 9th of October.

VALENCIENNES.

7. On the 13th it relieved the 22d Division near Herin (west of Valenciennes). It had not been withdrawn on the 11th of November.

VALUE—1918 ESTIMATE.

The 26th Reserve is rated as a first-class division. It did not distinguish itself in the fighting during 1918 (except on the Cambrai front, as already noted), still it could be depended upon and on the whole fought well. In this connection it is to be noted that the 26th Division had been held in reserve to relieve the 26th Reserve in the March offensive, but the relief was considered unnecessary.

26th Landwehr Division.

COMPOSITION.

	1917		1918	
	Brigade.	Regiment.	Brigade.	Regiment.
Infantry...........	51 Ldw.	119 Ldw. 123 Ldw. 124 Ldw.	51 Ldw.	119 Ldw. 123 Ldw. 124 Ldw.
Cavalry............	3 Sqn. 20 Uhlan Rgt.		3 Sqn. 20 Uhlan Rgt.	
Artillery............	Art. Command: 116 F. A. Rgt.		116 F. A. Rgt.	
Engineers and Liaisons.	(426) Pion. Btn.: 4 Ldw. Co. 13 Pions. 6 Ldw. Co. 13 Pions. 326 T. M. Co. 526 Tel. Detch.		(426) Pion. Btn.: 4 Ldw. Co. 13 C. Dist. Pions. 3 Searchlight Section. 526 Signal Command: 526 Tel. Detch. 180 Wireless Detch.	
Medical and Veterinary	569 Ambulance Co. Field Hospital. Vet. Hospital.		569 Ambulance Co. 251 Field Hospital. 256 Field Hospital.	
Transports............	M. T. Col.			

HISTORY.

(13th Corps District—Wurttemberg.)

1917.

1. The 26th Landwehr Division was formed on the Alsatian front at the beginning of the year 1917. Two of its regiments, the 119th and 123d Landwehr, forming the 51st Landwehr Brigade, had belonged to the 7th Landwehr Division until that time. Its 3d Regiment, the 124th Landwehr, came from the 2d Landwehr Division.

UPPER ALSACE.

2. Since its formation the 26th Landwehr Division has continually occupied the Upper Alsace front (north of Cernay, Hartmannswillerskopf).

RECRUITING.

The division is entirely recruited from Wurttemberg.

VALUE—1917 ESTIMATE.

The 26th Landwehr Division is purely a sector division. Each regiment has an assault troop composed of young men.

1918.

ALSACE.

1. The 26th Landwehr Division remained in the sector north of Cernay (southwest of Colmar, throughout 1918).

VALUE—1918 ESTIMATE.

In view of the division having been kept so long in what was probably the most quiet sector on the whole front (only 1 prisoner was taken after Dec. 15, 1917), when, the need for troops was so great that fourth-class divisions were frequently used on very active fronts, it would seem that the 26th Landwehr was one of the poorest divisions in the German Army.

125651°—20——24

27th Division.
COMPOSITION.

	1914		1915		1916		1917		1918	
	Brigade.	Regiment.	Brigade.	Regiment.	Brigade.	Regiment.	Brigade.	Regiment.	Brigade.	Regiment.
Infantry	53. 54.	123 Gren. 124. 120. 127.	53. 54.	123 Gren. 124. 120. 127.	53. 54.	123 Gren. 124. 120. 127.		123 Gren. 120. 124.	53.	120. 123. 124.
Cavalry	19th Uhlan Rgt.		19th Uhlan Rgt.		19th Uhlan Rgt. (3 Sqns.).		5th Sqn. 19th Uhlan Rgt.		5 Sqn. 19 Uhlan Rgt.	
Artillery	27th Brig. 13 F. A. Rgt. 49th F. A. Rgt.		27th Brig. 13th F. A. Rgt. 49th F. A. Rgt.		27 Brig. 13 F. A. Rgt. 49 F. A. Rgt.		27 Artillery Command, 49 F. A. Rgt.		27 Art. Command: 13 F. A. Rgt. 4 Abt. 13 Ft. A. Rgt. (11, 12, and 13 Btries.). 1289 Light Am. Col. 1290 Light Am. Col. 1291 Light Am. Col.	
Engineers and Liaisons.			1 Pion. Btn. No. 13. Field Co. 13 Pions. 27 Tel. Detch. 27 Pont. Engs.		1 Pion. Btn. No. 13. 2 Co. 13 Plons. 1 Res. Co. 24 Plons. Co. 29 Plons. 27 T. M. Co. 27 Tel. Detch. 23 Pont. Engs.		129 Pion. Btn. (former 1 Pion. No. 13). 2 Co. 13 Pions. 3 Co. 13 Pions. 52 Searchlight Co. 27 Tel. Detch.		12 (Saxon) Pion. Btn.: 3 Co. 13 Pions. 27 T. M. Co. 137 Searchlight Section. 27 Signal Command: 27 Tel. Detch. 154 Wireless Detch.	
Medical and Veterinary.							31 Ambulance Co. 253 Field Hospital. Vet. Hospital.		31 Ambulance Co. 253 Field Hospital. 255 Field Hospital. 27 Vet. Hospital.	
Transports							560 M. T. Col.		560 M. T. Col.	
Attached					68 Anti-Aircraft.		3, 34, and 99 Anti-Aircraft.			

HISTORY.

(13th Corps District—Wurttemberg.)

1914.

The 27th Division belongs to the 13th Army Corps (Royal Wurttemberg), with the 26th Division.

LORRAINE.

1. At the beginning of the war it formed a part of the 5th Army (German Crown Prince). It was engaged in the battle of Longwy, August 22, 1914 (between Longwy and Virton); on the 23d, north of Longuyon. On August 30, at Dun and Sassey, it crossed the Meuse and went south with the 5th Army between the Meuse and the Argonne. It fought at Pretz and Vaubécourt on September 6 and 7. Following the retirement to the north, it took up its positions in the Argonne.

2. At the beginning of October the 13th Army Corps was broken up and the two divisions were separated for more than a year.

ARGONNE.

3. The 27th Division remained in the Argonne until the end of 1915.

1915.

ARGONNE.

1. In the Argonne (Binarville–Grurie wood) the 27th Division was engaged in mine warfare. In August, 1915, it took part in the local offensive of the Army of the Crown Prince.

2. In September, at the time of the French offensive, elements of the 53d Brigade were sent to Champagne (northwest of Massiges), where they remained in reserve.

3. In December the 27th Division entrained at Grandpré for the Courtrai area, where the 13th Army Corps was re-formed as in the beginning, the 26th Division having returned from Serbia.

1916.

YPRES.

1. From January to July, 1916, the 13th Army Corps was in line southeast of the Ypres salient. The 27th Division was on the left of the 26th, between Sanctuary wood and the Ypres–Comines Canal. On February 24 units of the 27th Division gained possession of the British trenches of Bluff (north of the canal), but lost them on March 2. In this action the 123d Grenadier Regiment lost very heavily.

On June 2 the two divisions of the corps made a violent attack upon the Canadians in the Cillebeke sector. They gained possession of Observation Ridge, but were forced to abandon it by a counterattack. In these battles the regiments lost heavily.

SOMME.

2. At the end of July the 13th Army Corps was withdrawn from the Ypres salient and transferred to the Somme front. On August 1 the 27th Division went into line in the Guillemont sector. It put up a successful resistance to the attacks upon the village, but had serious losses.

3. It was relieved on August 25 and put in the Wytchaete sector, where it remained for about two and one-half months (until Nov. 11).

4. In the middle of November the 27th Division returned to the Somme a second time, north of Sailly Saillisel.

1917.

1. The 27th Division was retained on the Somme until the beginning of 1917. On this date it was sent east of Cambrai. During the month of March it was in line in the Roisel area.

ARTOIS.

2. After a short rest in the vicinity of Valenciennes it went into action in the Bullecourt sector (southeast of Arras), where it had very heavy losses (Apr. 7 to May

11). The dissolution of the 627th Infantry Regiment, formed in Wurttemberg, served to make up a part of its losses, and 600 men from this regiment came to the 27th Division.

3. Withdrawn about May 11 from the Arras front, the 27th Division occupied a sector in the vicinity of Le Catelet (between Gonnelieu and Honnecourt) at the beginning of June.

4. At the beginning of August it was relieved; entrained on August 12 at Caudry, and was transferred to Flanders by way of Lille–Tourcoing–Menin–Ledeghem–Roulers.

5. On August 26 it went into action northeast of Ypres (southeast of St. Julien). In this sector it did not take part in any important attack but suffered heavily from artillery fire.

The division was sent to the rear on September 12–13 and rested for a month northeast of Ghent.

On October 11 it went back into line northeast of Ypres (near the Ypres–Thourout railroad) and remained there until November 11. It was sent almost immediately to Alsace, where it arrived between November 16 and 18.

RECRUITING.

The 27th Division is recruited entirely from Wurttemberg.

VALUE—1917 ESTIMATE.

The 27th Division has fought well ever since the beginning of the war. It seems that the heavy losses which it has suffered have weakened its morale to a slight extent. Nevertheless, it may be considered as a very good division (Dec. 9, 1917).

1918.

CAMBRAI.

1. The 27th Division remained in the region of Schlettstadt (north of Colmar) until February 2. While here it received some 1919-class recruits. It then went to Cambrai, where it arrived on the 4th. On the 6th it relieved the 24th Reserve Division west of Graincourt (southwest of Cambrai). It was relieved by the 53d Reserve Division early in March and went to the neighborhood of Avesnes le Sec (southwest of Valenciennes), where it was trained in open warfare.

2. Subsequently it was transferred to the Cambrai region. Between the evening of March 20 and 5 a. m. on the 21st, it marched nearly 20 miles, when it came into line near Villers–Guislain (south of Cambrai). It was immediately heavily engaged and suffered severe losses. The 6th Company of the 124th Regiment had lost 84 men by the time it had reached Fins. A draft of 30 men was received at Guinchy. Withdrawn the 23d.

3. On April 4 it relieved the 54th Reserve Division near Aveluy (north of Albert). Fighting on the 5th, the 6th Company of the 124th Regiment lost 50 per cent of its effectives. All three regiments suffered heavy losses. One battalion of the 120th Regiment was practically annihilated. It was relieved by the 3d Naval Division on the 24th and went to rest south of Tournai.

4. The division left on July 24 and marched via Landas–Marchiennes–Neuville sur l'Escaut (south of Denain, rest)–St. Vaast (east of Cambrai, rest)–Fins–Nurlu (rest)–Peronne, into line in the Morlancourt sector (south of Albert), where it relieved the 107th Division about the 3d of August. In the heavy fighting that ensued it was forced back through Bray and Suzanne. It was withdrawn the 28th after leaving more than 1,400 prisoners in the hands of the British. It went to rest in the vicinity of Briastre (south of Solesmes), and while here received as a draft the dissolved 248th Reserve Regiment (54th Division disbanded).

MEUSE.

5. The division now became army and corps reserve.   On September 6 it entrained and traveled to Spincourt, arriving on the 10th.   It then marched to Camp Priester (near Loison), where it remained 14 days as army reserve.   About the 26th it entered line near Flabas (north of Verdun).   Five days later it was withdrawn and went back to the camp and remained eight days.

6. Then it went to the Jaeger Lager near Billy (south of Longuyon).   About the 11th of October it entered line near Douaumont (north of Verdun).   On the 29th it was relieved and marched to the Jaeger Lager, and then by truck via Stenay to a farm about 10 kilometers away.

7. On November 1 it reenforced the front near Tailly (southwest of Stenay); it was still in line on the 11th.

VALUE—1918 ESTIMATE.

The 27th has always been considered one of the very best German divisions, and its conduct in the fighting during 1918 confirms its rating as a first-class shock unit. It suffered severely, especially in the spring, but not a great deal later on.   Its moves toward the end of the war seem to indicate that it was to form part of the reserve with which the Germans hoped to regain the initiative.

28th Division.
COMPOSITION.

	1914 Brigade	1914 Regiment	1915 Brigade	1915 Regiment	1916 Brigade	1916 Regiment	1917 Brigade	1917 Regiment	1918 Brigade	1918 Regiment
Infantry	55. 56.	109. Body Gren. 110 Gren. 40 Fus. 111.	55. 56.	109. Body Gren. 110 Gren. 40 Fus. 111.	55. 56.	109. Body Gren. 110 Gren. 40 Fus. 111.	56.	109. Body Gren. 40 Fus. 110 Gren.	55.	40. 109. 110.
Cavalry	5th Jag. z. Pf.		....		5th Jag. z. Pf.		2d Sq. 5th Jag. z. Pf.		2 Sqn. 5 Horse Jag. Rgt.	
Artillery	28 Brig. 14 F. A. Regt. 50 F. A. Regt.		28 Brig. 14 F. A. Regt. 50 F. A. Regt.		28 Brig. 14 F. A. Regt. 50 F. A. Regt.		28 Art. Command: 14 F. A. Regt.		28 Art. Command: 14 F. A. Regt. 55 Ft. A. Btn. 801 Light Am. Col. 991 Light Am. Col. 1129 Light Am. Col.	
Engineers and Liaisons	....		1 Pion. Bn. No. 14: Field Co. 14 Pions. 28 Tel. Detch. 28 Pont. Engs.		1 Pion. Bn. No. 14: 1 Co. 14 Pions. 3 Co. 36 Pions. 28 T. M. Co. 28 Tel. Detch. 28 Pont. Engs.		130 Pion. Bn. (former 1 Pion. No. 14): 2 Co. 14 Pions. 3 Co. 14 Pions. 28 T. M. Co. 28 Tel. Detch.		14 Pion. Btn.: 2 Co. 14 Pions. 3 Co. 14 Pions. 94 Searchlight Section. 28 Signal Command: 28 Tel. Detch. 55 Wireless Detch.	
Medical and veterinary	....						35 Ambulance Co. 262, 292 Field Hospitals. Vet. Hospital.		35 Ambulance Co. 261 Field Hospital. 262 Field Hospital. 28 Vet. Hospital.	
Transports	....						67th Truck Train. Light Mun. Col.		561 M. T. Col.	
Attached	....		....		29 Antiaircraft 1st Bav. Labor Bn.		40th M. G. Detch.	Sharpshooters		

HISTORY.

(14th Corps District—Northern part Grand Duchy of Baden.)

1914.

ALSACE-LORRAINE.

1. The 28th Division formed a part of the 14th Army Corps with the 29th Division, also from Baden. At the beginning of the campaign went to Upper Alsace to reenforce the 29th Division; fought at Mulhousen on August 9, and on the 13th west of Altkirch. Returning to Mulhousen on the 14th, it entrained at Muelheim on the 16th for Petite Pierre. The 14th Army Corps was placed on the left flank of the 6th Army and took part with it in the battle of the 20th. The 28th Division then crossed the frontier and advanced to Mortagne at the beginning of September, On September 11 it recrossed the frontier and went to the west of Pont à Mousson, where it went into action between September 20 and 29.

ARTOIS.

2. Withdrawn from La Haye at the end of the month, it entrained on October 4 at Metz, detrained at Mons, and from there marched to the front—La Bassée, Ablain, St. Nazaire.

1915.

ARTOIS.

1. From October, 1914, to May, 1915, its regiments were exhausted one after the other on the plateau of Notre Dame de Lorette. (On November 30, 1914, the 110th Grenadier Regiment acknowledged casualties of 58 officers and 3,814 men since the beginning of the campaign.) The 28th Division again suffered very heavily during the winter (especially the 110th Grenadiers and the 40th Fusileers); finally it lost very heavily from April 9 to May 3 (Carency-Ouvrages-Blancs). In the course of these battles the 111th Infantry Regiment was almost completely destroyed. On May 10 its first battalion had only 3 officers and 272 men. (Notebook of the captain commanding the battalion.) The Casualty Lists report 32 officers and 1,737 men as casualties.

2. The division was relieved on May 15, sent to rest in the area Lens, Pont à Vendin, Héuin-Liétard, and reorganized.

3. About May 25 it was put back into line (Ablain-Lorette) and again suffered very heavy losses.

CHAMPAGNE.

4. Withdrawn from Artois about June 13, it was transferred to the northeast of Reims. Beginning with June 18, it occupied the front between Bétheny and the Sillery-Beine road. In this sector it had only a few local actions and very few losses.

5. During the offensive of September, 1915, the division detached two battalions (one from the 109th Grenadiers and one from the 110th Grenadiers) to act as reinforcements in the Somme Py area.

6. On October 19 and 20 a gas attack was rather poorly carried out by the Badensian Infantry (La Pompelle-Prosnes front).

7. The 28th Division was relieved about November 10. At the beginning of December it went into the sector of Tahure-Butte du Mesnil which it occupied for the entire winter without any notable action.

1916.

1. About the end of April, 1916, the 28th Division left the sector of the Butte du Mesnil. It was sent to rest for a week in the Vouziers area, and about May 5 went back into line (sector of Maisons de Champagne-La Justice). During this time the units received intensive training.

SOMME.

2. During the first half of July the regiments of the division (minus the 109th Infantry Regiment, which had remained in Champagne) were successively relieved and transferred by way of Charleville, Hirson, and St. Quentin to the Biaches area (Somme). Between July 16 and 20 they established their positions between the Somme and the Barleux.

3. The 28th Division was retained in this sector until the beginning of October. It suffered heavy losses there, which were partially covered by reenforcements sent from the depots of the 14th Army Corps (1915 and 1916 classes).

4. At the beginning of October the division was sent to Champagne, into the sector east of Tahure. It left this about the 20th and reoccupied it from December until the end of January, 1917.

1917.

MEUSE.

1. At this time the 28th Division was transferred to the Verdun area. It was sent into line in the Caurières wood sector and remained until the beginning of September. It took part in the attacks on this front in the middle of August.

ALSACE.

2. Withdrawn from the Verdun area about the middle of September the division was sent to Alsace, northwest of Altkirch and was in the front line on October 20. It soon left this for the Montmedy area, then for Laon, and finally for the Cambrai front where it fought at Gonnelieu on November 30. Relieved at the beginning of December, it was sent to rest in the Ardennes and, at the beginning of February, 1918, occupied a sector at Mount Cornillet.

RECRUITING.

The 28th Division is recruited almost exclusively from Baden. A slight admixture from the 4th Corps District. The 40th Fusileers, although a Prussian regiment. was recruited in the Grand Duchy of Baden.

VALUE—1917 ESTIMATE.

The 28th Division has always given a good account of itself and must be considered a good division (July, 1917).

At the beginning of March, 1917, it carried out an attack against the Caurières wood with a great deal of vigor. A division order (dated Mar. 3, 1917) found on a corpse praises the heroism of the valiant troops of the 28th Division and calls its regiments "The conquerors of Lorette."

1918.

AISNE.

1. The division held the Butte du Mesnil sector continuously until May 13, when it rested for 10 days in the vicinity of Vouziers. On May 23 the division entrained at Montcornet and was moved to the region of Laon. It came into line on May 31, reenforcing the Aisne battle front between Chateau de Maucreux and Troesnes. It was relieved on June 8 by the 10th Reserve Division.

SECOND BATTLE OF THE MARNE.

2. Its stay out of line was short, for on June 13 it again relieved the 50th Division near Varneuil; about this time the divisional commander, Lieut. Gen. Hahn, was decorated. The division was withdrawn from the Marne front about July 1. It returned to reenforce the battle line near Chaumuzy, southwest of Rheims on July 24. It fell back to the Vesle, where it held the line until August 26.

WOEVRE.

3. The division then went to rest in the vicinity of Baroucourt for three weeks. It left that place on September 14 and marched via Amermont–Offleville–Gondre-

court Rouvers-Etain to a position in line near Grimacourt and Hermeville, relieving the 8th Landwehr Division which side slipped to the south. It held this sector until October 19, when it was withdrawn and moved from Conflans, via Arlon, to Flanders on October 22.

MONS.

4. On November 1, the division came into line at Maresches in which area it fought until the armistice. The last identifications were at Sebourg (Nov. 4), west of Roisin (6th), and Dour (9th).

VALUE—1918 ESTIMATE.

The division was rated as second class. It was not greatly used in 1918, spending most of the time on quiet fronts. After the Vesle fighting in August, the battalions of the division were reduced to three companies.

28th Reserve Division.

COMPOSITION.

	1914		1915		1916		1917		1918	
	Brigade.	Regiment.	Brigade.	Regiment.	Brigade.	Regiment.	Brigade.	Regiment.	Brigade.	Regiment.
Infantry	55 Res. 56th Res.	109 Res. 110 Res. 40 Res. 111 Res. 9 Res. Jag. Bn. 14 Res. Jag. Bn	55 Res. 56 Res.	109 Res. 110 Res. 40 Res. 111 Res. 8 Res. Jag. Bn. 14 Res. Jag. Bn 55 Ldw. Brig. Ers. Bn.	55 Res.	109 Res. 110 Res. 111 Res.	56 Res.	109 Res. 110 Res. 111 Res.	56 Res.	109 Res. 110 Res. 111 Res.
Cavalry	8 Res. Drag.		8 Res. Drag.		8 Res. Drag.		3d Sq. 22d Drag.		3 Sqn. 22 Drag. Rgt.	
Artillery	29 Res. F. A. Rgt. (9 btries.).		29 Res. F. A. Rgt. (29 btries.).		28 Res. F. A. Rgt. (6 btries.). 29 Res. F. A. Rgt. (6 btries.). 1 Ers. Abt. of 76 F. A. Rgt.		29 Res. F. A. Rgt. (9 btries.).		29 Res. F. A. Rgt. 2 Abt. 1 Gd. Ft. A. Rgt. (7 and 9 btries.). 766 Light Am. Col. 918 Light Am. Col. 1366 Light Am. Col.	
Engineers and Liaisons.	1 and 2 Res. Cos. 2 Pion. Bn. No. 13.		1 and 2 Res. Cos. 2 Pion. No. 13. 28 Res. Pont. Engs. 28 Res. Tel. Detch.		1 and 2 Res. Cos. 2 Pion. No. 13. 228 T. M. Co. 28 Res. Pont. Engs. 28 Res. Tel. Detch.		328 Pion. Bn. 1st Co. 16th Pion. 4 Co. 16 Pion. 228 T. M. Co. 428 Tel. Detch.		328 Pion. Btn.: 4 Co. 16 Pions. 1 Ers. Co. 16 Pions. 72 Searchlight Section. 428 Signal Command: 428 Tel. Detch. 160 Wireless Detch.	
Medical and Veterinary.							514 Ambulance Co. 56, 57 Res. Field Hospitals. Vet. Hospital.		514 Ambulance Co. 56 Res. Field Hospital. 57 Res. Field Hospital. 428 Vet. Hospital.	
Transports.							725 Light Mun. Col.		725 M. T. Col.	

HISTORY.

(14th Corps District—Baden.)

1914.

VOSGES.

1. At the beginning of the war the 28th Reserve Division formed in the Grand Duchy of Baden, and constituting the 14th Reserve Corps, with the 26th Reserve Division, belonged to the 7th Army (Von Heeringen). The division detraining near Emmendingen (Baden), entered Alsace by way of Markolsheim on August 10. It was engaged in the valley of the Bruche beginning on the 15th, fought at Donon on the 20th, and went down toward the Meurthe, where it fought until September 5 (Nompatelize and la Bourgonce), suffering heavy losses (two-thirds of the effectives of the 111th Reserve Infantry Regiment).

SOMME.

2. After September 5 the 28th Reserve Division retired toward Blamont on September 15. On September 22 and 23 it entrained at Teterchen (Lorraine) for Cambria, where it detrained on September 26 and 27. It was assigned to the 2d Army with the other division of the 14th Reserve Corps.

1915.

1. The division occupied the sector crossed by the Albert–Baupaume road (Ovillers to Fricourt) until July, 1916.

In April, 1915, the 28th Reserve Division lost the 40th Reserve Infantry Regiment, which went to the 115th Division, and its two battalions of Chasseurs left it—one in January, the other in May.

2. In August and September, 1915, elements of the division were in reserve in the area south of St. Quentin.

1916.

SOMME.

1. The 28th Reserve Division did not have any great losses on the Somme between October, 1915, and July, 1916. Its combat activity was weak during this period.

2. On July 1, 1916, the Division supported the entire weight of the British offensive north of the Somme, and suffered very heavy losses (casualties of the 111th Reserve Infantry Regiment, 39 officers and 1,821 men).

3. On July 4 the division was withdrawn from the front, sent to rest, and reorganized.

CHAMPAGNE.

4. Transferred to Champagne on July 10, it took over the sector west of Auberive (July 14 to the beginning of October).

SOMME.

5. The 28th Reserve Division was brought back to the Somme at Thiepval about October 5; it was in action until the end of October and lost heavily. On the one day of October 24 the 9th Company of the 111th Reserve Infantry Regiment noted the arrival of 134 men as replacements.

MEUSE (AVOCOURT).

Relieved about October 28, the division was sent to the Stenay area and reorganized. Beginning of November, it occupied, at Verdun, the Avocourt sector at Hill 304.

1917.

1. On the Avocourt front the 28th Reserve Division took part in a few local engagements. It left this sector between April 7 and April 15.

CALIFORNIE PLATEAU.

2. Concentrated in the area northwest of Montfaucon, the division entrained about April 16 at Brieulles sur Meuse, Dun, Romagne and was transferred to Rozoy sur Serre; from there it marched to the sector east of Californie Plateau (Apr. 21). It underwent the French attack of May 4, which caused it heavy losses. Elements of the division lost very heavily counterattacking on the days following.

3. The division was relieved on May 18 and reorganized hastily (replacements of 1,100 men including 25 per cent of the 1918 class and men from the 626th Infantry Regiment dissolved). It was sent to Verdun to the Talou sector on May 20.

VERDUN.

4. The division, weakened by an epidemic of dysentery, was withdrawn from the front on July 8 and sent to rest in the area of Marville-Jametz until the beginning of August.

5. It went back into line at this date, on the right bank of the Meuse (Talou, Hill 344). It lost very heavily from the French attack of August 20 (47 officers and 1,150 men as prisoners) and was relieved on August 30.

CHAMPAGNE.

6. At the beginning of September it occupied the sector of Ville sur Tourbe in Champagne.

RECRUITING.

The 28th Reserve Division is recruited mostly from Baden. In addition, there are men from Rhenish-Hesse and the Rhine districts. There was also a small number of men from the 4th Corps District (1918 class).

VALUE—1917 ESTIMATE.

The combat value of the 28th Reserve Division appears mediocre.

During the entire time that it spent on the Somme (October, 1914–July, 1916), the division remained on the defensive.

Having lost very heavily on the Somme, it showed no great activity on the Somme (August–October, 1916).

On the Californie Plateau (May, 1917), the 28th Reserve Division appeared very much inferior to the guard.

At Hill 344 (Aug. 20), the attitude of the regiments of the 28th Reserve Division was rather passive, and the resistance was quite weak.

1918.

1. The division was relieved south of Beine (Champagne) on February 16. It entrained on the following day for Cartignies, near Avesnes, where it underwent training for offensive operations. It remained there until the 14th of March, when it commenced to march by night to the front via Etreux-Fresnoy-Le Nouvion-Wassigny-Essigny le Petit Remancourt, arriving in line on March 20.

BATTLE OF THE SOMME.

2. The division was in the front line of the attack at Fayet on the 21st. On the 23d it passed through Savy and reached Vaux. On the 26th it passed through Parvillers and Erches, proceeding on the 27th via Warsy to Becquigny. The division distinguished itself in the fighting, though at a heavy cost. Some companies are known to have lost 75 per cent of their effectives. When withdrawn from the front line on March 29, the division was held in reserve on the front at Davenscourt, Warsy, and Gruny until April 17. Two thousand five hundred men, with a large percentage of the 1919 class, were received at this time as reinforcements.

BATTLE OF THE AISNE.

3. The division rested in the Avesnes–Maubeuge area until May 22, when it marched via Marle–Ste. Preuve–Montaigu May 22–27. The division was used as an attack division to break through on the Aisne front. It attacked southwest of Craonne on the 27th and advanced by Corbeny, southwest of Craonne, Merval, east of Fismes, Treloup (30th) and Jaulgonne. Prince von Buchau, the divisional commander, was killed on May 30. In the advance to the Marne the division covered 60 kilometers.

CHATEAU THIERRY.

4. The division was out of line June 3 to 7. On the 8th, it reentered line before Bouresches (west of Chateau Thierry) where it opposed the 2d United States Division until July 3. Heavy losses were received in the fighting in the Bois Belleu on June 10–11. The division received a draft of 200 men in June. The division was withdrawn on July 3 and rested southwest of Soissons from July 7 to 18.

SOISSONS.

5. It was alerted on July 18 and engaged south of Soissons (Berzy–Courmelles) on the next day. It was heavily engaged until August 1, when it entrained north of Laon and moved to north of Vouziers on August 1. Here the division rested until the middle of August. A draft of 400 men was received early in August.

CHAMPAGNE.

6. The division was engaged in the sector north of Mesnil les Hurlus about August 20 until the end of the month, when it was withdrawn.

7. After leaving the line at Tahure the division was shifted back and forth behind the Argonne and Meuse sectors ready to be thrust into line. It was moved from Juniville to Longuyon on September 5 and stayed at St. Jean les Buzy (west of Conflans) until the 26th. From there it moved to the Damvillers region, and on October 1 was sent to Milly and Villers devant Dun.

MEUSE–ARGONNE.

8. The division was engaged near Cunel from October 3 to 18, when it was withdrawn to Stenay where it received replacements. The company strength was brought up to 40–50 men. On the 24th it was again in line near Bantheville and continued in to the end. It fell back north of Villers devant Dun on November 1–2, where it was last identified.

VALUE—1918 ESTIMATE.

The division was rated as first class. It was one of the best of the German divisions. It was used as an assault division in the Somme and Aisne offensives and met with great success. Following the attack it received in June in the Bois de Belleu, the division was not seriously engaged until it was thrown in the Argonne in an effort to stop the American advance. Its morale remained high up to the last though its effectives dwindled.

29th Division.
COMPOSITION.

	1914 Brigade	1914 Regiment	1915 Brigade	1915 Regiment	1916 Brigade	1916 Regiment	1917 Brigade	1917 Regiment	1918 Brigade	1918 Regiment
Infantry	57. 58. 84.	113. 114. 112. 142. 169. 170.	57. 58. 84.	113. 114. 112. 142. 169. 170.	57. 58.	113. 114. 112. 142.	58.	112. 113. 142.	58.	112. 113. 142.
Cavalry	22 Drag.				5th Jag. z. Pf.		4 Sq. 5th Jag. z. Pf.		4 Sqn. 5 Horse Jag. Rgt.	
Artillery	29 Brig. 30 Regt. 76 Regt.		29 Brig. 30 Regt. 76 Regt.		29 Brig. 30 Regt. 76 Regt.		29 Art. Command: 30 Regt.		29 Art. Command: 30 F. A. Regt. 2 Abt. 9 Res. Ft. A. Regt. 734 Light Am. Col. 827 Light Am. Col. 932 Light Am. Col.	
Engineers and Liaison.			1 Pion. No. 14. Field Co. 14 Pion. 29 Tel. Detch. 29 Pont. Engs.		1 Pion. No. 14. 2 Co. 14 Pion. 29 T. M. Co. 29 Tel. Detch. 29 Pont. Engs.		130 Pion. Btn. 1 and 514 Pion. 29 T. M. Co. 29 Tel. Detch.		130 Pion. Btn. 1 Co. 14 Pion. 5 Co. 14 Pion. 29 T. M. Co. 185 Searchlight Section. 29 Signal Command: 29 Tel. Detch. 31 Wireless Detch.	
Medical and Veterinary.							36 Ambulance Co. 263, 266 Field Hospitals. 29 Vet. Hospital.		36 Ambulance Co. 263 Field Hospital. 266 Field Hospital. 29 Vet. Hospital.	
Transports					562 Light Mun. Col.		562 Light Mun. Col.		562 M. T. Col.	
Attached					29 Div. M. G. Co. 60 Labor Btn.					

HISTORY.

(14th Corps District—Southern part Grand Duchy of Baden and Upper Alsace.)

1914.

ALSACE-LORRAINE.

1. The 29th Division is a division of Baden, like the 28th, with which it formed the 14th Army Corps. Entering the campaign with its three brigades, it fought at Mulhouse on August 9, 1914. On August 14 taken to the right bank of the Rhine, it entrained for Zabern and took part in the battle of the 20th, after which it crossed the French frontier of Lorraine. Suffering heavily on the Meurthe, it retired to Dieuze, from which place it was sent to the front at La Haye west of Pont a Mousson.

ARTOIS.

2. It was transferred to the area north of Arras at the beginning of October, 1914 (front of La Bassee, Ablain, St. Nazaire).

1915.

ARTOIS.

1. From October, 1914, to May, 1915, all the regiments of the 29th Division suffered heavy losses on the plateau of Notre Dame de Lorette. On January 28, 1915, the 3d Company of the 196th Infantry Regiment had only 38 men left (letter). The 58th Brigade, especially, which contained a greater number of Alsace-Lorrainers than the others, lost very heavily in the course of this winter. At the end of November, 1914, the 142d Infantry Regiment had already had casualties of 44 officers and 2,603 men. On February 24, 1915, the 2d Company of the 142d Infantry Regiment had already received 358 men as successive replacements. But it was from May 8 to 13 that the regiments of the division suffered most heavily (1,000 men of the 114th Infantry Regiment). In March the 84th Brigade was taken from the 28th Division and transferred to the 52d Division (a new formation).

2. About May 15 the division was withdrawn from the front and sent to the area of Lens, Pont a Vendin, Henin-Lietard.

3. Sent back into line about May 25 (Souchez–Fond de Buval–Chateau de Carleul), it again suffered heavy losses.

CHAMPAGNE.

4. The division was again relieved about June 13 and sent northeast of Rheims (sector between the Sillery–Beine road and Prosne), on June 18. It held these lines until the beginning of November.

5. During its stay in the Rheims area, the 29th Division sent one battalion of the 113th Infantry Regiment into the Champagne battle.

6. On October 19 and 20 the 112th and 142d Infantry Regiments attempted a gas attack upon the sector La Pompelle–Prosnes. During this period (June to November, 1915) the losses of the division were insignificant.

7. About November 10 the 29th Division left this sector to go farther east, to the Tahure–Butte du Mesnil (Nov. 23). It occupied this sector until the end of September, 1916.

1916.

1. During the entire winter of 1915–16 the 29th Division held the front of Tahure–Butte du Mesnil without any notable action. In the course of their period of rest in the Vouziers area its battalions continued their training.

SOMME.

2. At the end of September, the division was transferred to the Somme. After this time the two divisions of the 14th Army Corps seemed to have become "flying divisions." The 114th Infantry Regiment was withdrawn from the division and assigned to the 212th Division, later to 199th Division.

3. On October 4 the 29th Division went into action on the Somme east of Cléry. It was retained in this area until the beginning of February, 1917. On January 31, its regiments, each of which contained four battalions since the autumn of 1916, were reduced to three, the men of the 4th battalion being assigned to the other three.

1917.

1. On February 15, 1917, the 29th Division was sent to rest north of St. Quentin, where it worked on the Hindenburg line.

CHAMPAGNE.

2. Transferred to the Rethel area on April 1, it was engaged south of Nauroy (west of Cornillet) on the 17th, where it lost heavily. It was relieved about April 20 and filled up with men of the 1918 class and of the 626th Infantry Regiment, dissolved at the end of April.

3. From May 10 until about the middle of June, it occupied the sector of Tahure-Butte du Mesnil.

4. About June 14 it was sent to the rear and rested in the area east of Vouziers-Attigny. The three regiments were filled up with important replacements (men of the 1918 class and the last of the 1917 class incorporated in the army in October, 1916).

VERDUN.

5. About July 10-12, the 29th Division entrained for the Verdun front and was sent into the sector of Avocourt wood. It underwent the French attack the 17th which caused it great losses.

6. On August 1 the 29th Division launched an attack to retake the positions lost on the 17th. Taken to the rear at the beginning of August, it was again engaged at the time of the French offensive of August 20 and counter attacked unsuccessfully (west of Hill 304) suffering heavy losses.

7. Relieved on October 24-25, it went to rest in the area of Joeuf (Landres, St. Georges, and vicinity), where it was reorganized. The gravity of its losses caused conscripts of the 1918 class called out in June, having only two months' instruction, to be sent to it (5th company of the 142d Infantry Regiment for example).

8. About October 6, the division went back into line on the right bank of the Meuse (north of Hill 344). It remained there until the last of December.

RECRUITING.

The 29th Division is recruited almost exclusively in Baden, the regional character being accentuated by the return of the men from the 14th Corps District who had been serving in the regiments of the 4th Corps District.

VALUE—1917 ESTIMATE.

Until the attacks of April, 1917, the 29th Division was considered a good division, well trained and well officered. The cohesion of the troops appears to have suffered from the large proportion of raw replacements, in consequence of their losses.

On August 21, 1917, the 142d Infantry Regiment launched a counter attack (west of Hill 304) which failed because of lack of cohesion and liaison between the different units and because of the heavy losses caused by the French machine guns.

1918.

VERDUN.

1. The division held the Beaumont sector until about April 1, when it was relieved by the 19th Ersatz Division. It rested in the Montmedy-Virton area (Meix) from April 6 to 25. The division was high in effectives at this time, the companies averaging 180 to 200 men.

2. On April 25-28 the division was railed to Belgium via Sedan-Charleville-Namur-Bruxelles-Courtrai. It marched to Wervieq, rested there until April 30 and marched into line northeast of Mount Kemmel on the night of May 1-2

. **Lys.**

3. The division was in line until May 15 at Kemmel. Losses from artillery fire were considerable. It was relieved by the 8th Division and rested at Oostroosebeke (north of Courtrai) until June 14.

4. On the night of the 14–15, the division entered line east of Langemarck, relieving the 49th Reserve Division. On July 15, the 49th Reserve Division returned and relieved the 29th Division, which rested near Gits (Roulers) until the 25th. Then it entrained and moved to the Laon district, detraining at Malmaison. From there the division was taken in trucks on the Vesle front.

Aisne.

5. It held the Courlaudon sector (east of Fismes) from August 1 to 31, when it retreated to the Aisne (Maizy). It was withdrawn about September 8. It rested near Laon until the 15th, when it was reengaged north of the Aisne (Allemant) from September 16 to 24. It retreated behind the Ailette Canal (east of Anizy and Chavignon) and was relieved on October 1.

6. The division left Laon on October 2 and was brought by rail and truck to Fresnoy le Grand, coming into line on October 6 in that area. On the 7th and 8th French attacks forced the division to withdraw by Croix Fonsomme, Seboncourt. On the 13th the division was relieved by elements of the 81st Reserve Division and held in rear of the line. On the 18th it was reengaged south of Le Cateau (Ribeauville). In November the division retreated on the axes Fresmy, Prisches, in the direction of Avesnes, where it was last identified on November 7.

VALUE—1918 ESTIMATE.

The division was rated as first class. In 1918 it was used to hold active defensive sectors. In the middle of October its effectives had greatly diminished.

125651°—20——25

29th Landwehr Division.

COMPOSITION.

	1914		1915		1916		1917		1918	
	Brigade.	Regiment.	Brigade.	Regiment.	Brigade.	Regiment.	Brigade.	Regiment.	Brigade.	Regiment.
Infantry	29 (Mixed) Ldw.	28 Ldw. 29 Ldw.	29 (Mixed) Ldw.	28 Ldw. 29 Ldw. (427).	29 Ldw.	28 Ldw. 29 Ldw.			29 Ldw.	28 Ldw. 29 Ldw. (?)
Cavalry					5 Sqn. 8 Uhlan Rgt.				4 Sqn. 8 Uhlan Rgt.	
Artillery	1 Ldst. Btry. 8 Corps.		247 Rgt.		247 Art. Command.					(?)
Engineers and Liaisons.					Pion. Bn. 182 T. M. Co. 289 Wireless. 302 Wireless.					(?)
Medical and Veterinary.					Ambulance Co. Field Hospital. Vet. Hospital.				555 Ambulance Co. 327 Field Hospital. 140 Vet. Hospital.	
Attached			11th Ldst. Bn.							

HISTORY.

(8th Corps District—Rhine Province.)

1915.

1. The 29th Landwehr Division was formed from the 29th Landwehr Brigade. The latter was transformed into a division on the Russian Front about November 1917.

FRANCE.

2. Entering Belgium on August 20, 1914, at Charleroi on the 31st, at Berry au Bac at the end of September, then attached to the 18th Army Corps north of St. Quentin, then to the 14th Reserve Corps, the 29th Landwehr Brigade was transferred to the Eastern Front at the end of March, 1915. In April and May it was in Poland south of Rawa; it was then attached to the Posen Corps (9th Corps).

COURLAND.

3. The German offensive in the summer of 1915 sent the 28th Landwehr Regiment to Courland (vicinity of Toukkoum, in August). This regiment took up its position in October in the vicinity of Kalnzem (north of Mitau). The 29th Landwehr Regiment, after taking part in the operations at Vilna, was brought to the east of Olai, in October, and rejoined the 28th Landwehr Regiment in the vicinity of Kalnzem, at the beginning of November.

1916.

COURLAND.

1. The 29th Landwehr Brigade remained on the Mitau Front (Kalnzem-Chmarden) during the whole of the year 1916 and until March, 1917. It then formed a part of the Winecken detachment. In October it received a new regiment, the 427th Infantry Regiment, which was taken from it in January, 1917.

1917.

COURLAND.

1. About the middle of March, 1917, the 29th Landwehr Brigade was relieved north of Mitau and sent west of Jakobstadt. It appears to be in reserve in this sector at the time of the operations against Riga. It then came into line north of Kreuzburg (vicinity of Jakobstadt).

2. About the month of November the 29th Landwehr Brigade was transformed into the 29th Landwehr Division, which did not prevent the taking of men from the division to reinforce its neighbor, the 77th Reserve Division.

VALUE—1917 ESTIMATE.

On the Russian Front since 1914, the elements of the 29th Landwehr Division can have only a mediocre combat value.

1918.

ESTHONIA.

1. The 29th Landwehr Division occupied a very extended sector north of Kreuzburg until March,.1918. The division was sent then to the Polotsk-Vitebsk region and then to the Baltic Provinces. It was in Esthonia at the beginning of May; to the west of Reval early in June. "I have been in Esthonia three weeks now for guard duty," a man wrote on May 19. The division was identified here several times subsequently, the last identification being on the 5th of September.

VALUE—1918 ESTIMATE.

The division was rated as fourth class.

30th Division.
COMPOSITION.

	1914 Brigade	1914 Regiment	1915 Brigade	1915 Regiment	1916 Brigade	1916 Regiment	1917 Brigade	1917 Regiment	1918 Brigade	1918 Regiment
Infantry	60. 85.	99. 143. 105. 136. 8 Jag. Bn. 14 Jag. Bn.	60. 85.	99. 143. 105. 136.	60.	99. 105. 143.	60.	99. 105. 143.	68.	99. 105 (Saxon). 143.
Cavalry	3 Jag. z. Pf.				8 Res. Hussars (2 Sqns.)		8 Res. Hussars (?).		5 Sqn. 7 Drag. Rgt.	
Artillery	30 Brig. 51 Regt. 84 Regt.		30 Brig. 51 Regt. 84 Regt.		30 Brig. 51 Regt. 84 Regt.		30 Art. Command: 84 Regt.		30 Art. Command: 84 F. A. Rgt. 10 Bav. Ft. A. Btn. 885 Light Am. Col. 1369 Light Am. Col. 1394 Light Am. Col.	
Engineers and Liaisons.			1 Pion. No. 15. Fld. Co. 15 Pion. 30 Pont. Engs. 30 Tel. Detch.		1 Pion. No. 15. 1 Co. 15 Pion. 30 T. M. Co. 30 Pont. Engs. 30 Tel. Detch.		131 Pion. Bn. 1, 5/15 Pion. 30 T. M. Co. 30 Tel. Detch.		15 Pion. Btn.: 1 Co. 15 Pions. 5 Co. 15 Pions. 182 Searchlight Section. 30 Tel. Detch. 161 Wireless Detch. 30 Signal Command.	
Medical and Veterinary.							37 and 39 Ambulance Cos. Field Hospital. Vet. Hospital.		30 Ambulance Co. 275 Field Hospital. 276 Field Hospital. 30 Vet. Hospital.	
Transports							Light Mun. Col.			
Attached					30 Antiaircraft Detch.		30 Antiaircraft Detch.			

HISTORY.

(15th Corps—District, Alsace.)

1914.

ALSACE–LORRAINE.

The 30th Division constituted the 15th Army Corps (Strassburg) with the 39th Division.

1. At the beginning of the campaign the 30th Division formed a part of the 7th Army (Von Heeringen). Entraining on August 8, 1914, for Upper Alsace, it fought there until the 13th. It was transferred from there to south of Sarreburg and crossed the French frontier after the battle of the 20th. It advanced by way of Raon l'Étape across the Meurthe. At the beginning of September it was concentrated near Avricourt and went to Tergnier; from there to Craonne and Hurtebise. It fought there from the middle of September to the middle of October.

2. Concentrated at Laon on October 20, the 30th Division (as well as the 39th Division) arrived on the Lys on the 29th.

FLANDERS.

3. The 15th Army Corps, now a part of the 6th Army, went into action southeast of Ypres, an area in which it remained for almost 15 months (October, 1914–January. 1916).

1915.

FLANDERS.

1. Before our attacks of 1915, the 30th Division was attached, with the 15th Army Corps to the 4th Army. It went into action south of Ypres.

The 136th Infantry Regiment left it in April and became a part of the 115th Division (a new formation).

1916.

VERDUN.

1. Toward the end of January, 1916, elements of the 30th Division were transferred to Verdun to take part in the February offensive.

2. On February 24 the 15th Army Corps, which was on the western wing of the German attacking forces, went into action on the front of Maucourt-Warcq.

3. The regiments of the 30th Division suffered slightly during this period, the battle having been less intense in the Woëvre. Only the 105th Infantry Regiment, in action as a reenforcement of the 3d Army Corps, suffered very heavy losses.

4. The 30th Division was not relieved after the battles of February and the beginning of March. It remained in the sector and, on July 11, the 99th and 143d Infantry Regiments took part in a new offensive. On August 8 the 143d Infantry Regiment attacked the works of Thiaumont and was decimated. At this time the regiments were filled from day to day by irregular replacements. (Between July 7 and 19 more than 136 men were sent to the 11th Company of the 99th Infantry Regiment.)

SOMME.

5. About the end of September the 30th Division was relieved and sent to rest in the Cambrai area. It went into line a short time afterwards, on the Somme at Sailly Saillisel and remained there one month. It again lost very heavily (the 143d Infantry Regiment lost half of its effectives).

6. Relieved at the end of November, the 30th Division was sent back to the Verdun front.

MEUSE.

7. After a rest near Dun sur Meuse, it went into line in the vicinity of the Mort Homme, then of the Côte du Poivre and east of Louvemont (from Dec. 15 to the end of January, 1917) without taking part there in any important offensive or defensive engagement.

1917.

CHAMPAGNE.

1. On March 1, 1917, it went into line in the sector east of Auberive and was still there at the time of our spring offensive in Champagne. It underwent this attack at the beginning of May and occupied the sector until the middle of August. During this time, between April 17–20 and the beginning of May, 1917, the losses of the 30th Division were very great. The effectives of the 105th Infantry Regiment were reduced to 400 men; this regiment had to be reorganized in the Argonne.

MEUSE.

2. About August 25 the 30th Division was again transferred to the Meuse and occupied the trenches in the vicinity of Forges-Bethincourt, where its losses were slight.

CAMBRAI.

3. About October 24 the division was relieved. The British attack on the Cambrai front on November 20 caused it to be recalled in haste. It was sent into line on the 23d, and remained there until about December 10.

CHAMPAGNE.

4. At rest in the Sedan area, it was sent to the Champagne front, northwest of Auberive, about the middle of January, 1918.

RECRUITING.

Of the three regiments of the division, one, the 105th Infantry Regiment, is Saxon. Stationed in Alsace since 1871, it has represented Saxony in the occupation of the Reichsland, and continues to draw its recruits from Saxony. The other two, Prussian, are composed mostly of Westphalians.

VALUE—1917 ESTIMATE.

The 30th Division is a good division and well commanded.

The morale, which is good in the 99th and 143d Infantry Regiments, would seem to be mediocre in the 105th Infantry Regiment (Saxon) in November, 1917.

This last regiment, very much exhausted on April 17, 1917, was accused by the other regiments of having given way. It was withdrawn from the division for a month.

1918.

CHAMPAGNE.

1. The middle of January the 30th Division relieved the 28th Reserve Division near Ville sur Tourbe; it was relieved about the 20th of March by the 52d Reserve Division, entrained near Vouziers and traveled via Hirson and Marle to the area northwest of Laon.

MONTDIDIER.

2. On the 27th it left and marched via Achery-Vendeuil-Jussy-Flavy le Meldeux, Freniches-Libermont-Solente-Gruny, reaching Framicourt on the 12th of April, and entered line the following day south of Cantigny (west of Montdidier). It was withdrawn on May 16.

3. The division had suffered casualties amounting to 30 per cent of its total effectives, and so when it was withdrawn, it moved to the region south of Roye to refit. Here each company received between 40 and 50 1919-class recruits, after which the division was trained. On June 12 it reinforced the front near Courcelles (south of Montdidier). It suffered heavy losses in the fighting that followed, and was withdrawn about the 22d.

CHAMPAGNE.

4. During the night of June 28–29 the division relieved the 1st Bavarian Division astride the Souain–Sommey road. It seems to have been "leap-frogged" by the 2d

Bavarian Division on the 15th—the opening day of the Champagne offensive—but it relieved the 2d Bavarian Division on the 19th.   It was relieved by the 22d Division on August 10, and went to rest in the Lens area.

CAMBRAI.

5. On the 23d of September it left and moved to the Cambrai area, where it arrived the following day.   On the 27th it reenforced the battle front south of Villers Guislain (south of Cambrai).   It was pushed back steadily in the ensuing weeks, and was withdrawn about the 28th of October, southeast of Englefontaine (south of Quesnoy), and went to rest in Maubeuge.

VALUE—1918 ESTIMATE.

Until this year the 30th had always been considered a first-class division.   During 1918, however, it was not used nearly so much as other shock units.   The fact that, although it was in line only a fortnight after more than a month's rest, it was not used in the attack of July 15 in Champagne, but was put back into line as soon as it was seen that the offensive there was a failure, is significant.   It would seem that the German High Command considered it as only a second-class division.

30th Bavarian Reserve Division.

COMPOSITION.

	1914		1915		1916		1917		1918	
	Brigade.	Regiment.	Brigade.	Regiment.	Brigade.	Regiment.	Brigade.	Regiment.	Brigade.	Regiment.
Infantry	84 Ldw. 5 Bav. Ers. 10 Bav. Res.	70 Res. 7 and 8 Brig. Ers. Bn. 11 Bav. Res. 14 Bav. Res.	5 Bav. Ers. 10 Bav. Res. 84 Ldw.	2 Bav. Ers. 4 Bav. Ers. 11 Bav. Res. 14 Bav. Res. 70 Res.	5 Bav. Ers. 10 Bav. Ers. 84 Ldw.	2 Bav. Ers. 4 Bav. Ers. 11 Bav. Res. 70 Res.	5 Bav. Ers.	8 Bav. Ldw. 15 Bav. Ldw. 4 Bav. Ers.	5 Bav. Ers.	8 Bav. Ldw. 15 Bav. Ldw. 4 Bav. Ers.
Cavalry	9 Res. Hus.		9 Res. Hus.		9 Res. Hus.		2d Sq. 9 Res. Hus.		1 Sq. 1 Bav. Res. Cav. Rgt.	
Artillery	1st Frs. Abt. 13, 31, and 80 F. A. Regts.		239 F. A. Rgt.		239 F. A. Rgt. 252 Ldw. F. A. Rgt. 1 Mountain F. A. Abt.		8 Bav. F. A. Rgt. (Elements).		4 Bav. F. A. Rgt.	
Engineers and Liaisons.	4 Co. 15 Pions. 2 Ldw. Co. 15 Corps Pions.		4 Co. 15 Pions. 2 Ldw. Co. 15 Corps Pions.			2 Ldw. Co. 15 Corps Pions. 249 Pion. Co. 88 Res. Pion. Co. 230 T. M. Co.		22 Bav. Pion. Btn. 13 Bav. Res. Pion. Co. 5 Bav. Ldw. Pion. Co. 230 T. M. Co. 430 Bav. Tel. Detch.	22 Bav. Pion. Btn.: 13 Bav. Res. Pion. Co. 5 Bav. Ldw. Pion. Co. 22 Bav. Searchlight Section. 430 Signal Command. 430 Tel. Detch.	
Medical and Veterinary.							23 Bav. Ambulance Co. 5 Bav. Field Hospital. 30 Bav. Vet. Hospital.		23 Bav. Ambulance Co. 5 Bav. Field Hospital. 36 Bav. Field Hospital.	
Transports							Light Mun. Col.			
Odd Units			30 Res. Cyc. Co.		30 Res. Cyc. Co.					
Attached	1st Ldst. Btn. Kempton. 1st Bav. Corps No. 13.				1 Ldst. Btn. Passau, 1st Bav. Corps No. 5. 1 Ldst. Btn. Mindelheim, 1 Bav. Corps No. 14. 1st Ldst. Btn. Neustadt, 2 Bav. Corps No. 4. 1 Ldst. Btn. Eisenach, 11 Corps No. 12.		54 Ldst. Foot Art. Vtn. 2d Btry/5 Bav. F. A. Rgt. 4 Btry/5 Bav. F. A. Rgt. 9 Btry/5 Bav. F. A. Rgt. 1 Ldst. Btn. Bruchsal, 14 Corps No. 3.			

HISTORY.

(Bavaria.)

1914.

ALSACE.

1. The 30th Bavarian Reserve Division, constituted in August, 1914, half of Prussian and half of Bavarian troops, operated in the Vosges beginning with August 17, and entered St. Dié on the 27th.

In 1915, with the 39th Reserve Division, formed after it, it made up the Eberhardt Corps, since then the 15th Reserve Corps. These 2 divisions comprised a total of 25 battalions, reserve units, Landwehr or Ersatz, Bavarian for the most part, to which were subordinated Landsturm Battalions.

They were scattered, after the retirement of the first part of September, 1914, among the valleys of the Plaine and the Liepvrette (Ste. Marie aux Mines).

The predominance of Bavarian troops in these Divisions had the effect of causing both to be officially called Bavarian. As a matter of fact, they were afterwards almost exclusively filled by Bavarian contingents.

1915.

1. In 1915 the 30th Bavarian Reserve Division continued to occupy the same sector of the Vosges, south of the valley of the Plaine. It remained there until May, 1917. The 39th Bavarian Reserve Division was at its left, holding the lines as far as Ste. Marie aux Mines.

2. In the spring of 1915, the Brigade Ersatz Battalions of the divisions were grouped into regiments and became the 2d and 4th Bavarian Ersatz Regiments, forming the 5th Bavarian Ersatz Brigade.

3. The two Brigades of the 30th Bavarian Reserve Division took an active part in the battles of La Fontenelle in June and July, 1915.

1916.

1. Vosges sector (south of the Valley of the Plaine, Senones, Le Ban-de-Sapt).

2. In October, 1916, the 11th and 14th Bavarian Reserve Regiments went to the 1st Bavarian Landwehr Division and to the 9th Bavarian Reserve Division.

The 30th Bavarian Reserve Division received, in November, the 8th Bavarian Landwher Regiment from the 1st Bavarian Landwehr Division, and in December the 15th Bavarian Landwehr Regiment, taken from the 39th Bavarian Division, which received the 2d Bavarian Ersatz Regiment in exchange.

1917.

LORRAINE.

1. In April, 1917, the 30th Bavarian Reserve Division was relieved from the Vosges sector, which it had occupied since its formation, and sent into line on the Lorraine front (sector of the Seille).

2. At the end of October, it was transferred to Upper Alsace (north of the Rhone-Rhine Canal), where it relieved the 3d Reserve Division.

VALUE—1917 ESTIMATE.

The 30th Bavarian Reserve Division is a sector division, as it has occupied the front either in Lorraine or Alsace since its formation. Its offensive value is mediocre.

In the 8th Bavarian Landwehr and the 4th Bavarian Ersatz Regiments, the average age of the men is 38 years. The men of the machine gun companies are younger, according to the ordinary rule. In the 15th Bavarian Landwehr Regiment the majority of the men are more than 30 years old.

Each battalion of the 8th Bavarian Landwehr Regiment possesses an assault troop composed of young men averaging 24 years of age.

There is also a Divisional Assault Company.

1918.

HAUTE ALSACE.

1. The division remained in line north of the Rhine–Rhone Canal until the armistice was signed.

VALUE—1918 ESTIMATE.

The division possesses very little fighting value. The men are, for the most part, old, and the fathers of several children. Then, too, a great many are those—untrained landstrum—who usually, for physical defects, were not inducted into the army when their classes were called to the colors; these men complain of the hard work. Moreover, Bavarians came to believe that Prussia was "using" them. It was found necessary to establish shock detachments with each battalion, and these do all of the necessary patrolling.

31st Division.
COMPOSITION.

	1914 Brigade.	1914 Regiment.	1915 Brigade.	1915 Regiment.	1916 Brigade.	1916 Regiment.	1917 Brigade.	1917 Regiment.	1918 Brigade.	1918 Regiment.
Infantry	32. 62.	70. 174. 60. 137. 166.	32. 62.	70. 174. 137. 166.	32.	70. 174. 166.	32.	70. 174. 166.	32.	70. 166. 174.
Cavalry	7 Uhlan Rgt.				5 Sqn. 7 Uhlan Rgt.				5 Sqn. 7 Uhlan Rgt.	
Artillery	31 Brig.: 31 F. A. Rgt. 67 F. A. Rgt.		31 Brig.: 31 F. A. Rgt. 67 F. A. Rgt.		31 Brig.: 31 F. A. Rgt. 67 F. A. Rgt.		31 Art. Command: 31 F. A. Rgt.		31 Art. Command: 31 F. A. Rgt. 44 Ft. A. Btn. 1005 Light Am. Col. 1011 Light Am. Col. 1012 Light Am. Col	
Engineers and liaisons.			1 Pion. Btn. No. 27. Field Co. 27 Pion. 31 Pont. Engs. 31 Tel. Detch.		1 Pion. Btn. No. 27. 1 and 2 27 Pion. 31 T. M. Co. 31 Tel. Detch. 31 Pont. Engs.		136 Pion. Btn.: 1 Co. 27 Pion. 31 T. M. Co. 505 Searchlight Section. 31 Tel. Detch.		93 Pion. Btn.: 1 Co. 27 Pion. 3 Co. 32 Res. Pion. 31 T. M. Co. 40 Searchlight Section. 31 Signal Command: 31 Tel. Detch. 116 Wireless Detch.	
Medical and veterinary.							262 Ambulance Co. Field Hospital. Vet. Hospital.		262 Ambulance Co. 326 Field Hospital 333 Field Hospital 161 Vet. Hospital.	
Transports							Light Mun. Col.		564 M. T. Col.	

31st Division.—Continued.

COMPOSITION.—Continued.

	1914	1915	1916	1917	1918
Attached			Field Recruit Depot 31 Div. 153 Cyclist Co.		24 M. G. S. S. Detch. 2 and 3d Abt. 44 F. A. Rgt. 121 Ft. A. Rgt. 1 Abt. 44 Ft. A. Rgt. 2 Abt. 6 Ft. A. Rgt. 1 Abt. 74 Ft. A. Rgt. 134 Art. Observation Section. 75 Sound Ranging Detch. 134 Balloon Squn. 105 Balloon Squn. 286 Reconnaissance Flight. (Elements attached May 15, 1918. German document.)

HISTORY.

(21st Corps District—Lorraine, part of Lower Alsace, and southern portion of the Rhine Province.)

1914.

Upon mobilization, the 31st Division, with the 42d Division, constituted the 21st Army Corps.

LORRAINE.

1. At the beginning of the war the 31st Division was a part of the 6th Army (Prince Rupprecht of Bavaria). In August, 1914, it was on the Lorraine frontier; on the 12th of August at Chateau Salins, Rechicourt. It fought at Dieuze on August 20, where the 174th Infantry Regiment lost half of its effectives. The division was at Luneville on the 23d, marched upon Rehainviller, Gerbeviller on the 24th; at Rozelieure Essey on the 26th; in the vicinity of Moyen–Domptail at the beginning of September; it withdrew to Dieuze about September 11.

SOMME.

2. Transferred to the vicinity of St. Quentin–Vermand, about September 18, the division occupied the vicinity of Fouquescourt on September 26 and 27; attacked in the direction of Bouchoir on October 6. At the end of October the division took over the front of Fouquescourt–Chaulnes and kept it until the end of January, 1915. At this date the losses of the 174th Infantry Regiment, since the beginning of the war, amounted to 81 officers and 3 521 men. (Official List of Casualties.)

1915.

RUSSIA.

1. About January 25, 1915, the 31st Division left the Somme for the Eastern Front, leaving the 60th Infantry Regiment in France, and detrained at Tilsit.

2. Concentrated in Eastern Prussia, at the beginning of February, it was a part of the Hindenburg Army.

3. On February 14 it left the region of Augustowo to advance to the east. It reached Sopockin on the 20th and took up its position with the 21st Army Corps on the line Sopockin–Chatbine (north of Grodno). On the 9th of March, in a counterattack of the Russians, it suffered heavy losses.

4. From March 29 to April 24 it took part in the battles in the vicinity Kalwariia–Mariampol.

5. At the end of April it was withdrawn from the front and reorganized. From the time of its arrival in Russia until April 10, the first battalion of the 166th Infantry Regiment had lost 17 officers and 1,022 men, the 1st Company alone losing 5 officers and 336 men.

6. At the end of July the division again occupied the lines near Mariampol.

VILNA.

7. In the month of August it took part in the offensive upon Vilna. It advanced to Kovno on August 19, to Vilna at the end of September, and reached the area Smorgoni–Soly, where it stopped in October.

8. The division was relieved on October 6. It went back into line about October 24, in the sector of Postawy–Lake Narotch.

NAROTCH.

1. The 31st Division occupied the vicinity of Lake Narotch until its departure for the Western Front in December, 1917.

2. At the end of March, 1916, it opposed the Russian offensive in the vicinity of this lake; it lost very heavily.

1917.

BELGIUM.

1. On December 5, 1917, it was relieved from the Russian front, and after a few days rest at Vilna entrained for Belgium on December 16. (Itinerary: Wirballen–Koenigsberg–Elbing–Dirschau–Ramberg (?) Aix la Chapelle Verviers.) It detrained about the 21st, in the vicinity of Ghent and took up its position at the end of January, 1918 south of the Ypres-Roulers line where it alternated with the 12th Reserve Division.

RECRUITING.

The 31st Division is recruited mostly from the vicinity of Sarrebrucken and St. Wendel in the Rhine Province. Most of the replacements are furnished by Westphalia

VALUE—1917 ESTIMATE.

The 31st Division was on the Russian front from February, 1915 to December 1917. The quality is mediocre.

1918.

YPRES.

1. From January 19 to February 4 the division held the Moorslede sector (south of Ypres–Roulers railway). The division rested until the 14th in the vicinity of Lendelede. It relieved the 12th Reserve Division on the 14th in its old sector at Moorslede which it held until March 3, and again from March 21 until April 4.

BATTLE OF THE LYS.

2. About April 4 the division was withdrawn and marched to the Messines front. The route lay through Menin, Werwicq, Comines, Warneton. It was engaged on April 10 to 12 in the Bois de Ploegsteert. For its fighting in this area the division was mentioned by the German communique of April 13. From the 12th to the 17th, it was in second line. It fought south and southwest of Kemmel from April 18 to 24 when it passed into close support until the 26th. The division's losses were large in this severe engagement. The 3d Battalion of the 174th Regiment is known to have lost from 60 to 70 per cent of its effectives.

3. When relieved in the Kemmel area, the division rested north of Tourcoing until May 6, undergoing reconstitution. It returned to line north of Kemmel on the night of May 6–7, relieving the Alpine Corps. It suffered heavily from the French attack of May 21, losing many prisoners. It was relieved on May 24, and rested in the Courtrai–Menin area until June 15. It was engaged in the sector south of Ypres from June 15 until July 27.

WOEVRE.

4. Following its arduous service on the Ypres front, the division was moved to a quiet sector on the Woevre. It was moved from Belgium by way of Brussels, Namur, Charleville, Sedan to Mars la Tour from where it marched to the front and took over the St. Mihiel sector on July 29, which it held until September 3.

BATTLE OF ST. MIHIEL.

5. The division was resting in the area north of Dampvitoux when the American attack was made on the St. Mihiel salient. It was brought into line north of Thiavcourt on the 14th and held this sector until October 28.

MEUSE—ARGONNE.

6. On the 31st, the division was engaged at Imecourt (northeast of Grandpre) and took part in the final combats in that area. It was still in line on November 11.

VALUE—1918 ESTIMATE.

The division was rated as third class. In spite of its relatively low quality it appears to have been used as an attack division in the Lys offensive. The losses in the spring and the presence of numerous Lorrainers in its composition lowered the value of the division after May, 1918.

32d Division.
COMPOSITION.

	1914 Brigade.	1914 Regiment.	1915 Brigade.	1915 Regiment.	1916 Brigade.	1916 Regiment.	1917 Brigade.	1917 Regiment.	1918 Brigade.	1918 Regiment.
Infantry	63. 64.	102. 103. 177. 178.	63. 64.	102. 103. 177. 178.	64.	102. 177. 108.	63.	102. 177. 108.	63.	102. 103. 177.
Cavalry	18 Hus. Rgt.				20 Hus. Rgt. (3 Squadrons).		4 Sqn. 20 Hus. Rgt.		4 Sqn. 20 Hus. Rgt.	
Artillery	32 Brig.: 28 F. A. Rgt. 64 F. A. Rgt.		32 Brig.: 28 F. A. Rgt. 64 F. A. Rgt.		32 Brig.: 28 F. A. Rgt. 64 F. A. Rgt.		32 Art. Command: 64 F. A. Rgt.		32 Art. Command: 64 F. A. Rgt. 80 Ft. A. Btn. 942 Light Am. Col. 1063 Light Am. Col. 1266 Light Am. Col.	
Engineers and Liaisons.			1 Pion. Btn. No. 12: Field Co. 12 Pion. 32 Pont. Engs. 32 Tel. Detch.		1 Pion. No. 12: 2 Co. 12 Pion. 32 T. M. Co. 32 Tel. Detch. 32 Pont. Engs.		140 Pion. Btn.: 2 and 5 Cos. 12 Pion. 32 T. M. Co. 32 Tel. Detch.		140 Pion. Btn.: 2 Co. 12 Pions. 5 Co. 12 Pions. 3 Res. Co. 12 Pions. 32 T. M. Co. 220 Searchlight Section. 32 Signal Command: 32 Tel. Detch. 20 (Saxon) Wireless Detch.	
Medical and Veterinary.							28 Ambulance Co. 308 Field Hospital. Vet. Hospital.		28 Ambulance Co. 308 Field Hospital. 116 Field Hospital. 32 Vet. Hospital.	
Transports							Light Mun. Col.		565 M. T. Col.	
Attached					115 Labor Btn.		61 M. G. Sharpshooter Detachment.			

HISTORY.

(12th Corps District—Saxony.)

1914.

BELGIUM-MARNE.

1. Upon the declaration of war the 32d Division, with the 23d Division, formed the 12th Army Corps (1st Saxon Army Corps). On the night of August 2, 1914, its 64th Brigade entrained for the frontier north of Luxemburg to act as covering troops. The 32d Division was concentrated there on the 10th and entered Belgium on the 13th. In August, it marched with the 3d Army (von Hausen), fought on the right bank of the Meuse on August 23 near Dinant, went into action on the 28th at Signy l'Abbaye, and from there went down to Chalons. It took part in the battle of the Marne to the left of the Guard at Lenharree on the extreme right flank of the 6th Army and retired by way of Chalons, Mourmelon, Betheniville to the northwest of Rheims.

CHAMPAGNE.

2. Reattached to the 7th Army (Von Heeringen), it took part in the attacks in the vicinity of Rheims (northwest).

3. When the front became stabilized it retained the sector of Berry au Bac Craonne and remained there until the month of July, 1915.

1915.

AISNE.

1. Sector Berry au Bac-Craonne. (During this period the losses of the division were very small.) In April, 1915, the 178th Infantry Regiment was taken from the 32d Division and assigned to the 123d Division (a new formation).

1916.

1. Retained in the same calm sector and having taken part in no important affair since October, 1914, the 32d Division retained its combat value intact at the end of June, 1916.

SOMME.

2. During the first days of the Franco-British offensive on the Somme the 32d Division sent one battalion from reserve there, which went into action from July 4 to July 7 in the vicinity of Belloy.

3. Toward the end of July two of its regiments (102d and 103d Infantry Regiments) helped to form (with elements from the 23d Division) the provisional Franke Division, which fought on the Somme until September 10 (Deniecourt-Vermandovillers). The losses were very heavy.

4. On the 4th of September the 177th Infantry Regiment was sent up in its turn, but was in action only a few days in the vicinity of Vermandovillers from September 4 to 10. Its losses were enormous (1,600 men in 6 days).

5. The Franke Division was withdrawn on September 10 and dissolved.

ARGONNE.

6. The 32d Division, reformed (102d, 103d, 177th Infantry Regiments) and reorganized, was sent north of Rheims and then to the Argonne (Four de Paris and Avocourt wood).

SOMME.

7. Relieved at the beginning of November, it entrained on the 3d and 4th near Grandpre, detrained at Hirson, and on November 15 began to occupy the sector between Bouchavesnes and northeast of Clery.

1917.

1. The 32d Division was retained in the Bouchaevesnes sector until the time of e German retirement in March, 1917.
2. It left the Somme front at the end of March.

IAMPAGNE.

3. After a period of rest in the vicinity of Sissonne, the division went into action the sector of Mont sans Nom (4 kilometers west of Vaudesincourt on Apr. 17 and 18). aving lost heavily, the 3 regiments were withdrawn on the 19th.
4. On May 5 the division again went into line west of Tahure.

.ANDERS.

5. About June 10 it was relieved, and after a few days of rest entrained at Machault r Flanders. There it went into line near the Ypres–Menin road.
6. At the beginning of September it was withdrawn from the Ypres front and sent rest, then took over the sector Warneton–Messines and was not relieved until the iddle of January, 1918.

RECRUITING.

The 32d Division is exclusively Saxon.

VALUE—1917 ESTIMATE.

In June, 1917, the morale of the division was very low because of the losses suffered Mont Haut.

However, during the division's stay in the Tahure sector from May to June, 1917, .ere were only two desertions.

Besides, Gen. von Der Decken is considered an energetic commander and it is ry probable that under his influence the morale has become more satisfactory eptember, 1917).

1918.

ATTLE OF THE LYS.

1. The division was relieved on January 15 by the 49th Reserve Division and sted near Tournai until the beginning of March. It was railed to Wambrechies d entered the line northwest of Lille about March 1. About the 4th of April it is moved south and on April 9 was engaged at Fleurbaix. It was withdrawn to st on the 16th to Armentieres and returned to line on the 18th, relieving the 117th ivision. It was in line until May 8, during which time it suffered heavy losses. replacement of 450 men was received on April 17.
2. Relieved by the 35th Division, it rested in rear of the Lys front until May 26, 1en it took over the sector west of Merville and held it until the end of June.

OEVRE.

3. It was relieved about July 1 and railed to Lorraine, detraining near Spincourt July 4. About this time, the division received a draft of 1500 men. It was in 1e at Eix-Bezonveaux from July 15 to October 1, a very quiet sector. The troops 2re marched to the rear on that date and rested in the Eton-Loison area for two days. 1 the 3d the division marched to Penard-Tilly, where it rested until the 5th, and that night marched to Breville. It came into line on October 9 on the right bank the Meuse, and was engaged in the Bois de Moirey region until October 24. Losses 2re heavy, some companies being reduced to 15 men. On November 3 the division appeared in its former sector of Bezonvaux, relieving the 106th A. H. D. It held is sector until the armistice.

VALUE—1918 ESTIMATE.

The division was rated as third class. It did well on the Lys in April, but after at was not seriously engaged except for a few days in October, when it was brought) to resist an American attack east of the Meuse. In the fighting it did not dis- nguish itself. The morale of the division was low in the latter half of 1918.

33d Division.
COMPOSITION.

	1914		1915		1916		1917		1918	
	Brigade.	Regiment.	Brigade.	Regiment.	Brigade.	Regiment.	Brigade.	Regiment.	Brigade.	Regiment.
Infantry......	66. 67.	98. 130. 135. 144.	66. 67.	98. 130. 135. 144.	66. 67.	98. 130. 135. 144.	66.	98. 135. 130.	66.	98. 130. 135.
Cavalry........	12 Jag. z. Pf.				4 Sqn. 12 Jag. z. Pf.		4 Sqn. 12 Jag. z. Pf.		4 Sqn. 12 Horse Jag. Rgt.	
Artillery......	33 Brig.: 33 Rgt. 34 Rgt.		33 Brig.: 33 Rgt. 34 Rgt.		33 Brig.: 33 Rgt. 34 Rgt.		33 Art. Command: 283 Rgt.		33 Art. Command: 283 F. A. Rgt. 76 Ft. A. Btn. 883 Light Am. Col. 1372 Light Am. Col. 1373 Light Am. Col.	
Engineers and liaisons.			1 Pion. Btn. No. 16: Field Co. 16 Pion. 33 Tel. Detch. 33 Pont. Engs.		1 Pion. Btn. No. 16: 1 Co. 16 Pion. Field Co. 20 Pion. 33 T. M. Co. 33 Tel. Detch. 33 Pont. Engs.		132 Pion. Btn.: 1 and 5 Cos. 16 Pion. 1 Res. Co. 16 Pion. 33 T. M. Co. (16) Searchlight Section. 33 Tel. Detch.		16 Pion. Btn.: 5 Co. 16 Pions. 1 Res. Co. 16 Pion. 34 Searchlight Section. 33 Signal Command: 33 Tel. Detch. 74 Wireless Detch.	
Medical and veterinary.							42 Ambulance Co. 280, 282 Field Hospitals. Vet. Hospital.		42 Ambulance Co. 282 Field Hospital. 33 Vet. Hospital.	
Transports......							Light Mun. Col.			

HISTORY.

(16th Corps District—Lorraine.)

1914.

At the beginning of the war the 33d Division, with the 34th Division, formed the 16th Army Corps (Metz). Reservists began arriving on July 29 (Soldbuecher).

1. At the outbreak of hostilities the 33d Division was a part of the 5th Army (German Crown Prince). It invaded France by way of Audun le Roman, went around by the north of Verdun, crossed the Meuse at Givry on September 1 and advanced as far as Rambluzim and Heippes (20 kilometers south of Verdun).

ARGONNE.

2. After the battle of the Marne it took up its position in the Argonne. Its advance had been costly. On September 24 the new commander of the 98th Infantry Regiment found it reduced 13 officers and 982 men (document).

1915.

ARGONNE.

1. The 33d Division remained without interruption in the Argonne from September, 1914, to about the middle of August, 1916.

1916.

VERDUN.

1. About August 10, 1916, the division was relieved from the Argonne and, after a short rest behind the front, was sent into the line at Verdun, east of Fleury.

2. In this sector, the division lost rather heavily. It remained there until the middle of September, at which time it took its place in the sector Vauquois, giving the 144th Infantry Regiment to the 223d Division, a new formation.

ARGONNE.

3. During this latter period, which extended up to the middle of December, the division was reorganized and absorbed the 4th Battalion, suppressed, on October 31, in the 27th Landwehr Regiment. At the same time, the 4th Battalions which the regiments of the division possessed, were broken up.

SOMME.

4. Transferred to the Somme about December 15, it there occupied the sector east of Beaumont–Hamel and did not leave it until February 8, 1917. During these two months, its losses were rather serious.

1917.

ARGONNE.

1. Sent to rest in the Sedan area, the 33d Division went back into its old sector Vauquois at the end of February, 1917. No important event marks its stay in the Argonne after that time.

CHAMPAGNE.

2. On May 3, it was relieved and transferred to Champagne. It marched as far as Pont Faverger and went into line at Cornillet and Mont Blond. It took part in the battle on this front and suffered some losses (172 prisoners from the 130th Infantry Regiment on May 20).

ARGONNE.

3. Withdrawn from this region at the end of May, it was again sent to the Argonne (Boureuilles–Vauquois), about June 7.

CHAMPAGNE.

4. At the end of September it came out of the Argonne, and about October 4 went to the area of Tahure, where it remained in line until February, 1918.

Not being able to utilize the regional system of recruiting from annexed Lorraine, the 33d Division is composed almost entirely of Westphalians from the 7th Corps District.

VALUE—1917 ESTIMATE.

The 16th Army Corps, of which the 33d Division is a part, has always had the reputation of being one of the best corps of the German Army.

Although the 33d Division lost very heavily during the offensive of April and May, 1917, it still appeared strong (October, 1917).

1918.

1. The division was relieved on January 4 by the 28th Reserve Division and went to rest and train in the area northwest of Sedan. On March 14 it was railed to the vicinity of Rozoy sur Serre and rested a week north of Montcornet. From there the division proceeded by night marches via Montcornet–Crecy sur Serre–Monceau le Neuf–Ribemont–Mezieres–Moy ly Fontaine–Gibercourt–Montescourt–Jussy–Flavy le Martel, where it arrived on March 23. On the following night the division was billeted in Villeselve and came into line astride the Ham–Noyon road on March 24.

BATTLE OF PICARDY.

2. On the 25th the division fought its way through Noyon and on the following days was engaged in heavy fighting about Suzoy and Mont Renaud, which it failed to capture in spite of heavy sacrifices. It was withdrawn on April 15.

3. The division rested from April 15 to May 24 in the vicinity of Dercy, Mortiers, Pierrepont, and Barenton sur Serre undergoing reconstitution. It marched to the Aisne front by Coucy les Eppes, Bruyeres, and Chamouille.

BATTLE OF THE AISNE.

4. The division was engaged on May 27 in the front line of the attack and advanced by Pancy, Courtecon, Verneuil, Pont-Arcy, Dhinzel, Courcelles, Jouaignes (20th), Oulchy la Ville, south of Neuilly St. Front, Dammard. In this last region losses were heavy on June 2. It was relieved by the 78th Reserve Division on June 3.

SECOND BATTLE OF THE MARNE.

5. The division rested south of Soissons from June 7 to July 11, when it marched to the Marne front by Braisne, Fere en Tardenois, Foret de Ris. It was in reserve on the 15th on the north of the Marne, west of Dormans. On the 17th–18th it fell back on Beuvardes and Grisolles and was engaged the next day southeast of Neuilly St. Front. In the heavy fighting of the following days the division was thrown back south of Oulchy le Chateau toward Fere en Tardenois (July 21–23). The division withdrew until the Vesle was reached when it was relieved about July 31.

VERDUN.

6. The division entrained southeast of Montcornet on August 6 and was moved to Avocourt via Sedan–Charleville–Montmedy. It rested southeast of Stenay until August 15. Replacements were received from the dissolved 33d Reserve Division in August. On August 21, the division entered line near Ornes (north of Verdun) where it remained until the armistice.

VALUE—1918 ESTIMATE.

The division was rated as first class. It was used as an assault division in the Somme and Aisne offensives of 1918. It was disorganized by its losses in the Marne retreat and never recovered its offensive value.

33d Reserve Division.

COMPOSITION.

	1914 Brigade	1914 Regiment	1915 Brigade	1915 Regiment	1916 Brigade	1916 Regiment	1917 Brigade	1917 Regiment	1918¹ Brigade	1918¹ Regiment
Infantry	66 Res. 8 Bav.	67 Res. 130 Res. 4 Bav. 8 Bav.	66 Res. 8 Bav.	67 Res. 130 Res. 4 Bav. 8 Bav.	66 Res. 8 Bav.	67 Res. 130 Res. 4 Bav. 8 Bav.	66 Res.	67 Res. 130 Res. 364.	66 Res.	364. 67 Res. 130 Res.
Cavalry	2 Res. Hus. Rgt. (3 Sqns.).		2 Res. Hus. Rgt.		2 Res. Hus. Rgt.			4 Sqn. 19 Hus. Rgt		
Artillery	4 Ers. Abts. of 33, 34, 69, 70 F. A. Rgts.		Ers. Abts. of 33,34,69,70 F. A. Rgts. combined into 33 Res. F. A. Rgt.		33 Res. F. A. Rgt.		33 Res. F. A. Rgt.		33 Res. F. A. Rgt.	
Engineers and liaisons.			3 Pion. Btn. No. 16: 1 Ers. Co. 20 Pion. 1 Ldw. Pont. Co. 4, Corps. 33 Res. Pont. Engs. 33 Res. Tel. Detch.		4 Field Co. 16 Pion. Btn.: 1 Ldw. Pion. Co. 4, corps. 233 T. M. Co. 33 Pont. Engs. 33 Res. Tel. Detch.		233 Pion. Btn.: 1 Ers. Co. 20 Pion. 1 Ldw. Co. 4 Pion. 233 T. M. Co. 14 Searchlight Section. 433 Tel. Detch.		333 Pion. Btn.: 333 Pion Co. 1 Ldw. Co. 4 C. Dist. Pions. (in 3 Pion. Btn. No. 16). 14 Searchlight Section. 233 T. M. Co. 433 Tel. Detch.	
Medical and veterinary.							274 Ambulance Co. 47 and 51 Field Hospitals. Vet. Hospital.		273 Ambulance Co. 51 Field Hospital. Vet. Hospital.	
Transports							873 Light Mun. Col.		M. T. Col.	
Odd units									646 Supply Depot.	
Attached	Battery of 8 Ft. A. R. 3 Abt. 18 Ft. A. R. (elements). 2 Btry. 8 Res. Ft. A. R. 1 and 2 Btries. 2 Abt. 16 Ft. A. R. 2 Abt. 2 Bav. Res. Ft. A. R. (elements).				4 Anti-Aircraft Detch.				47 F. A. Rgt.	

¹ Composition at the time of dissolution September, 1918.

HISTORY.

(16th Corps District—Lorraine.)

1914.

LORRAINE.

1. Formed at Metz with the 8th Bavarian Brigade and the 66th Reserve Brigade, he 33d Reserve Division was a part of the 5th Army (German Crown Prince) at the outbreak of the war. In August, 1914, it took part in the battles of Nomèny and went o Verdun by way of Gondrecourt, Rouvres, Étain. On August 24 and 25 it was in ction at Étain and suffered heavily. On August 26 the 10th Company of the 8th Bavarian Regiment had only 75 men left (notebook).

At the beginning of September, it occupied both banks of the Moselle south of Pont à Mousson, and about September 15 the vicinity of Thiaucourt.

VOËVRE—LES ÉPARGES.

2. At the end of September and the beginning of October it went back into the ector south of Étain (Riaville, Bracquis). On October 8 the 8th Bavarian Brigade ttacked Champlon and Fresnes; the 67th Reserve Regiment attacked the Ville en Voëvre on October 9. After these battles, the 33d Reserve Division took up its osition on the Côtes de Meuse (Combres, Les Éparges).

3. In November the 66th Reserve Brigade was in Flanders—on the Yser Canal rom November 16 to 24, and left for Lorraine on November 25.

1915.

CÔTES DE MEUSE.

1. The 33d Reserve Division remained in line on the Côtes de Meuse until the nd of July, 1916.

2. About January 17, 1915, elements of the 66th Reserve Brigade were sent to the Bois le Pretre and suffered heavy losses. They rejoined the division on the Côtes t the end of January.

LES ÉPARGES.

3. From February to the end of April, 1915, the 33d Reserve Division took part a the battles of Combres and of Les Éparges; it lost very heavily there, especially a the actions of February 17 to 20. From April 15 to May 1 no less than 140 men vere sent as replacements to the 12th Company of the 67th Reserve Regiment.

4. After reorganization the 33d Reserve Division went to the calmer sector of 'aux les Palameix, Lamorville.

CALONNE.

5. The division once more suffered heavy losses in the Calonne trench in May, 915.

6. On July 17, 1915, the 130th Reserve Infantry Regiment was sent in support of n attack on Les Éparges. After this period the 33d Reserve Division occupied the ector south of Vaux les Palameix (Chevaliers wood, Bouchot wood) without taking art in any important engagement.

1916.

1. On July 25, 1916, the division was relieved from the Côtes de Meuse and sent o rest until August 25 in the area north of Briey. At this time the 8th Bavarian Brigade was detached from the 33d Reserve Division to serve in forming the 14th Bavarian Division and the 33d Reserve Division was reorganized with three regiments, with the 66th Reserve Brigade and the 364th Infantry Regiment (coming om the 8th Ersatz Division).

VERDUN.

2. On August 26 the division went into line on the front north of Verdun, southest of the fort of Vaux. It took part in the battles from September 2 to 9 in the

Vaux Chapitre wood and suffered very heavy losses. The 12th Company of the 67th Reserve Infantry Regiment received at least 142 men as replacements from September 13 to 21.

3. After being reorganized the division underwent the French attack of October 24, which again caused it considerable losses. Upon its relief the 2d Battalion of the 130th Reserve Infantry Regiment was reduced to 45 combatants. (Notebook of an aspirant officer.)

4. Withdrawn from the front on November 1, the 33d Reserve Division was sent to rest and to be reorganized. It had suffered so heavily that among the reenforcements at the beginning of 1917 we find untrained men of the Landsturm II Ban.

LORRAINE.

5. The division was then sent to Lorraine to the Blamont sector.

1917.

1. The division held the Lorraine front until March 10, 1917.

CHEMIN DES DAMES.

2. After a month's rest in the vicinity of Sarreburg, the 33d Reserve Division was transferred to Marle (Apr. 16–19). On April 21 and 22 elements of the division were distributed upon different points of the Aisne front to replace the units exhausted by the French attack of April 16, and soon afterwards were regrouped north of Laffaux Mill. The 33d Reserve Division suffered very heavy losses withstanding the French attack of May 5 and counterattacking on the days following (May 5–7) (1,000 prisoners); almost the entire 2d Battalion of the 67th Reserve Infantry Regiment was captured.

3. Withdrawn in part from the Aisne front on May 12, the 33d Division again had some of its units in action between the Aisne Canal and Laffaux Mill until May 23 (German attack of May 16, where the 130th Reserve Infantry Regiment suffered heavy losses).

4. At the end of May the 33d Reserve Division returned to the vicinity of Sarreburg to rest and be reorganized. It received recruits not only from the recruit depot of Beverloo, but also from the depot at Warsaw.

LORRAINE.

5. About June 10 it again took over its former sector in Lorraine (Blamont-Leintry).

VERDUN.

6. On August 23 the division went into action on the Verdun front (sector of Baumont-Chaume wood). It underwent the French attack of the 26th where it suffered heavily. It again had recourse to the Warsaw recruit depot which sent it, among other reenforcements, untrained men of the Landsturm second Ban.

7. Relieved about September 10, the 33d Reserve Division was transferred to Galicia by way of Metz, Frankfort, Erfurt, Dresden, Breslau, Cracow.

GALICIA.

8. It was identified in Galicia at the beginning of October.

RECRUITING.

After the 8th Bavarian Brigade was withdrawn the 33d Reserve Division was exclusively Prussian. Its regiments were recruited almost entirely from the Rhine Province and Westphalia. In May, 1917, however, following the losses suffered on the Chemin des Dames, a great number of young men came from Western Prussia (1918 class), coming from the large depots of Beverloo and Warsaw. At the end of August the Warsaw depot sent untrained men from the Landsturm II Ban from the 9th and 10th Corps' Districts.

The 33d Reserve Division is a good division.

At Verdun elements of the division fought vigorously and made the French advance very difficult on October 24, 1916.

Between May 5 and May 7, 1917, the division launched very violent counterattacks against Laffaux Mill. Elements of the 364th Infantry Regiment succeeded in capturing the Chateau de la Motte. In the sector of Beaumont at Verdun the 1st Battalion of the 364th Infantry Regiment put up a very stubborn resistance to the French on August 26, 1917.

The 33d Reserve Division was very much exhausted by the attacks on the Aisne. The reenforcement which it received on May 4, 1917, were mostly men belonging to the 1918 class. On August 26, 1917, more than one-fourth of the prisoners belonged to this class.

In January, 1918, it already counted among its ranks young men of the 1919 class, who had arrived on January 14.

Taking into account its recent long rest and its intensive training in offensive warfare and the declarations of prisoners captured in March, 1918, who all declare that their division is an assault division destined to take part in a great breaking through offensive, we must conclude that the 33d Reserve Division has again become an organization of high quality (Mar. 30, 1918).

1918.

BATTLE OF THE AISNE.

1. The division continued to hold its sector northwest of Rheims until the Aisne offensive in May. It advanced with the rest of the line, having as its objective the Marne River. It progressed through Cauroy (27th), St. Thierry (28th), and Vrigny (31st). Here the line was stabilized. The division was withdrawn June 20.

CHAMPAGNE.

2. On June 25 the division relieved the 88th Division in the Mont Tetu sector (Eastern Champagne). It was on the extreme left of the German attack east of Rheims on July 15, and suffered so heavily that it was withdrawn on July 20.

3. In mid-August the division was broken up. The 364th and 67th Reserve Regiments were drafted to the 16th and 34th Divisions.

VALUE—1918 ESTIMATE.

The 33d Reserve Division was rated as fourth class. As a result of its failure in the Aisne and Champagne offensives, it was disbanded in August, 1918.

34th Division.
COMPOSITION.

	1914		1915		1916		1917		1918	
	Brigade.	Regiment.	Brigade.	Regiment.	Brigade.	Regiment.	Brigade.	Regiment.	Brigade.	Regiment.
Infantry	68. 86.	67. 145. 30. 173.	68. 86.	67. 145. 30. 173.	68. 86.	67. 145. 30. 173.	68.	67. 30. 145.	68.	30. 67. 145.
Cavalry	16 Uhlan Rgt.				5 Sqn. 12 Jag. z. Pf.		5 Sqn. 12 Jag. z. Pf.		5 Sqn. 12 Horse Jag. Rgt.	
Artillery	34 Brig.: 69 Rgt. 70 Rgt.		34 Brig.: 69 Rgt. 70 Rgt.		34 Brig.: 69 Rgt. 70 Rgt.		34 Art. Command: 70 Rgt.		34 Art. Command: (?) F. A. Rgt. 116 Ft. A. Btn. 1174 Light Am. Col. 1191 Light Am. Col. 1192 Light Am. Col.	
Engineers and Liaisons.			1 Pion. Btn. No. 16: Field Co. 16 Pion. 34 Tel. Detch. 34 Pont. Engs.		1 Pion. Btn. No. 16: 2 Co. 16 Pion. 34 T. M. Co. 34 Tel. Detch. 34 Pont. Engs.		132 Pion. Btn.: 2 and 3 Cos. 16 Pion. 34 T. M. Co. 259 Searchlight Section. 34 Tel. Detch. 34 Pont. Engs.		132 Pion. Btn.: 2 Co. 16 Pion. 3 Co. 16 Pion. 34 T. M. Co. 193 Searchlight Section. 34 Signal Command: 34 Tel. Detch. 18 Wireless Detch.	
Medical and Veterinary.							Ambulance Co. 281–283 Field Hospitals. Vet. Hospital.		41 Ambulance Co. 281 Field Hospital. 283 Field Hospital. 34 Vet. Hospital.	
Transports							Light Mun. Col.		567 M. T. Col.	
Attached					Labor Btn. 34 Div.				44 M. G. S. S. Abt. 249 Reconnaissance Flight. 119 Art. Observation Section. 83 Balloon Sqn. 534 Carrier Pigeon Loft. (Elements attached June 6, 1918. German documents.)	

HISTORY.

(16th Corps District—Lorraine.)

1914.

Upon mobilization, the 34th Division and the 33d Division were organic parts of the 16th Army Corps (Metz).

MEUSE.

1. At the outbreak of the war the 34th Division marched with the 5th Army (German Crown Prince), entered France on August 21, by Audun le Roman and by way of Nouillon Pont, and reached the Meuse, which it crossed at Vilosnes and Sivry on September 1. It advanced as far as Beauzée and Seraucourt.

ARGONNE.

2. After the battle of the Marne it retired to the north and took up its position in the Argonne.

1915.

ARGONNE.

1. The 54th Division remained in the Argonne without interruption from September, 1914, until about August 15, 1916. It took part there in the offensives of January and July, 1915, where it suffered heavy losses. On January 18, 1915, the 30th Infantry Regiment had already lost 56 officers and 2,723 men. (Official List of Casualties.)

2. After these violent battles, it received fairly large replacements. The division suffered no serious losses in this sector during the period which followed these engagements until its relief on Aug. 15, 1916.

1916.

VERDUN.

1. On this date the 34th Division was transferred to the right bank of the Meuse at Verdun.

2. It went into action in the Chiaumont sector at the end of August, 1916, and during the month of September, took part in some very severe battles in this vicinity.

3. On September 20, its losses were very great because of our attack. The regiments of the 34th Division again lost heavily in the course of our offensive of October 24, which succeeded in recapturing the Douaumont Fort and the Thiaumont Works; on that day, their resistance was rather weak. The 67th Infantry Regiment received about 71 men for its 8th Company in the week of October 28–November 5.

VOSGES.

4. On October 29 the 34th Division was relieved. Beginning with November 14, it occupied a calm sector in the Vosges, southwest of Senones. At this time it received fairly large replacements. The 173d Infantry Regiment was transferred to the 223d Division, a new formation.

1917.

ARGONNE.

1. At the beginning of February, 1917, the division returned to the Argonne. It remained there a short time. In the middle of March, it was relieved and transferred to the region north of Rheims (beginning of April).

CHAMPAGNE.

2. Immediately after our offensive of April 16, the 67th and 30th Infantry Regiments went into action in the vicinity of Brimont, while the 145th Infantry Regiment was sent to Cornillet as a reenforcement from April 18 to 20.

3. About April 25, the 34th Division was again concentrated in the Brimont sector, where it relieved the 43d Reserve Division.

4. About the middle of June it extended its sector to include the stretch from the Champ du Seigneur to the Verrerie of Courcy. During the attacks of April the divi-

sion suffered very heavy losses; the 145th Infantry Regiment lost about one-third of its effectives.

FLANDERS.

5. On July 21 the 34th Division was relieved from the Rheims front and sent to Flanders on August 7. It remained in reserve in the vicinity of Dadizeele until August 12. It then went into action near the Ypres-Menin road, where it had heavy losses.

WOËVRE.

6. On August 24, it left this front for La Haye, where it went into line southeast of Thiaucourt (vicinity of Flirey) and remained until October 31.

CAMBRAI.

7. At the beginning of November, it was in the vicinity of Cambrai. It took part in the German counterattack of November 30.

LAONNOIS.

8. After a rest in December, the 34th Division occupied the sector of Grandelain, on the Ailette, until January 7, 1918.

RECRUITING.

Because of the difficulty of recruiting in its own corps district (Lorraine), the 34th Division is composed mostly of Westphalians and men from the Rhine Province. The name of "Magdeburg" given to the 67th Infantry Regiment has only a historic value.

The men, as a rule, belong to the classes of 1912 to 1918.

The replacements received by the division in Lorraine (September, 1917) brought in an undetermined number of men more than 25 years of age, especially those of the Landsturm of about 30 years of age, withdrawn from the Russian front and trained for a while in a depot in the interior.

VALUE—1917 ESTIMATE.

The 34th Division was one of the good Divisions of the German Army. Nevertheless, at the time of our attack upon Thiamont on October 24, 1916, it had a period of genuine weakness.

Its attitude in the Brimont sector in April and May, 1917, was such that it must still be classed among the good divisions.

At Ypres, in August, 1917, charged with the defense of one of the most important sectors, it did not realize the hopes of the German High Command.

According to the interrogation of a prisoner (February, 1918), the 34th Division is a shock division destined to attack.

1918.

LAON.

1. Early in January the division which had been resting near Laon, relieved the 3d Bavarian Division near Courtecon (south of Laon); withdrawn toward the end of February, it went to rest near Liesse (northeast of Laon), where it remained until March 15.

PICARDY.

2. Then it marched toward the front via Marcy (west of Marle) and Ribemont. On the 21st it entered line south of St. Quentin, took Benay, which was its objective, crossed the canal, and took Jussy on the 23d. It continued its advance as far as Pontoise (southeast of Noyon). It was withdrawn on April 2, after having lost 50 per cent of its total effectives, and went to rest in the area southeast of Roye. While here it received 1,000 replacements.

3. On the 10th, it came back into line south of Guiscard (north of Noyon). It was withdrawn about the 20th, the 50th Division taking over its sector.

4. After spending about 10 days near Beaumont en Beine (southeast of Ham) training in close and open order and in rifle practice, the division relieved the 223d Division south of Appilly (east of Noyon) on May 1. On the 15th, it received 15 replacements per company. It was relieved by the 9th Bavarian Reserve Division on the 20th, and went to rest, first in the region east of Chauny, and then in the St. Gobain forest (south of La Fère).

AISNE.

5. After having been in reserve four days near Pernant (west of Soissons), the division reenforced the front near Ambleny (west of Soissons) on June 12, attacking, the same day, with the Coeuvres–Vic sur Aisne road as its objective. It could make no headway at all, and suffered losses of about 30 per cent of its strength. It was withdrawn about the 6th of July.

6. On the 19th, it came back into line near Vauxbuin (southwest of Soissons), and was withdrawn on the 22d after suffering severely; over 300 in prisoners alone. It went to rest in the Guise area; later, it moved to the vicinity of Coucy le Château. While here, it received as a draft the dissolved 67th Reserve Regiment (33d Reserve Division disbanded).

AILETTE.

7. The division reenforced the front near Cuts (southeast of Noyon) on August 15. It was withdrawn on September 25.

ST. QUENTIN.

8. It entrained the same day north of St. Gobain, and detrained in the St. Bohain region the next day; it rested here for two days, and was transported by truck to St. Quentin on the 28th. The following day, it relieved the 221st Division southwest of that town. On the 30th, it was forced to relinquish St. Quentin to the French. It continued to withdraw, but fighting stubbornly, and was relieved on the 9th of October near Fontaine–Uterte (northeast of St. Quentin). It rested for a week between Avesnes and Maubeuge.

GUISE.

9. It moved to the Petit Verly–Grougis region (northwest of Guise) on the 17th, in support of the 81st Reserve Division, but that unit being placed hors de combat by the attack of the 18th, the 34th Division found itself in the front line, and even lost nearly 100 prisoners. It was relieved on the 23d after losing nearly 700 more prisoners. It then rested about a week in the Vervins region.

10. On November 1, it returned to line near Puisieux (south of Guise), and withdrew along the line Marly, Romery, Sommeron. It was still in line on the 11th.

VALUE—1918 ESTIMATE.

The 34th has always been considered as one of the best second-class divisions. As a result, however, of its heavy losses during the spring, it contained large numbers of boys of the 1919 class. Having been engaged without rest from the middle of August until the end of the war, it was reduced to the point where it has less than 1,000 effectives left. In all probability, it would soon have been dissolved had the war continued.

35th Division.

COMPOSITION.

	1914		1915		1916		1917		1918	
	Brigade.	Regiment.	Brigade.	Regiment.	Brigade.	Regiment.	Brigade.	Regiment.	Brigade.	Regiment.
Infantry	70. 87.	21. 61. 141. 176.	70. 87.	21. 61. 141. 176.	87.	141. 61. 176.	87.	141. 61. 176.	87.	61. 141. 176.
Cavalry	4 Jäg. z. Pf.				5 Ilus. Rgt. (2 sqns.).		2 Sqn. 5 Hus. Rgt.		2 Sqn. 5 Hus. Rgt.	
Artillery	35 Brig.: 71 Rgt. 81 Rgt.		35 Brig.: 71 Rgt. 81 Rgt.		35 Brig.: 71 Rgt. 81 Rgt.		35 Art. Command: 71 Rgt.		35 Art. Command: 71 F. A. Rgt. 1 Abt. 18 Res. Ft. A. Rgt. 715 Light Am. Col. 716 Light Am. Col. 1305 Light Am. Col.	
Engineers and Liaisons.			1 Pion. Btn. No. 17: Field Co. 17 Pion. 35 Tel. Detch. 25 Pont. Engs.		1 Pion. Btn. No. 17: 1 Co. 17 Pion. 4 Co. 36 Pion. 35 T. M. Co. 35 Tel. Detch. 35 Pont. Engs.		133 Pion Btn.: 1 and 2 17 Pion. 35 T. M. Co. 35 Tel. Detch. 36 Pont. Engs.		133 Pion. Btn. 1 Co. 17 Pions. 2 Co. 17 Pions. 35 T. M. Co. 223 Searchlight Section. 35 Signal Command: 35 Tel. Detch. 121 Wireless Detch.	
Medical and Veterinary.							44 Amb. Co. 289, 293 Field Hospts. 35 Vet. Hospital.		44 Ambulance Co. 289 Field Hospital. 293 Field Hospital. 35 Vet. Hospital.	
Transports							568 Light Mun. Col.		568 M. T. Col.	
Attached					2 Assault Detch.					

HISTORY.

(17th Corps District—Western Prussia.)

1914–15.

EAST PRUSSIA.

1. The 35th Division formed with the 36th Division the 17th Army Corps (Danzig). It remained on the Eastern Front from the beginning of the war until October, 1915. It took part in the battles of Gumbinnen and Tannenberg, then in the two German offensives upon Warsaw. It participated in the operations on the Bzura and the Narew, where it remained until August 1, 1915.

RUSSIA.

2. It was sent to rest near Bielostok, and at the end of September, 1915, the decision was made to send it to the Western Front.

3. It entrained at Grodno about October 6, and arrived about the 10th in the vicinity of Péronne where it was filled up. The 9th Company of the 176th Infantry Regiment received no less than 60 men between October 3 and 13.

FRANCE.

4. In the middle of October it went into the Roye sector and remained there during the entire winter of 1915–16.

1916.

SOMME.

1. About May 25, 1916, it went slightly to the north and occupied the sector between the Chaulnes-Amiens railroad and the south of Soyécourt.

2. At the beginning of July, when the Somme battle began, the 35th Division was holding the front from west of Vermandovillers to the south of Chilly. The 176th Infantry Regiment was sent into line in the sector of Herbécourt-Estrées on July 2 and lost 170 prisoners to the French. This regiment lost heavily in the French attack of July 20 between Belloy and the Étoilé wood.

3. On September 4 and the days following the 35th Division was effecting a relief at the time of the French offensive and suffered considerably because of this (almost 2,000 prisoners, 39 of whom were officers).

4. It had to be retired from the front on September 8 and sent to rest at Ham. Between October 15 and 20 it again went into line from the southwest of Chaulnes to the southwest of Chilly.

5. According to official calculations, the 35th Division had casualties of 6,102 men, 68 per cent of the effectives engaged, in the course of the battle of the Somme.

1917.

ST. QUENTIN.

1. The 35th Division remained in the vicinity of Chaulnes until the German retirement. It took part in the retreat and established itself in the Hindenburg Line south of St. Quentin at the end of March.

ARTOIS.

2. After a few days of rest in the vicinity of Guise at the beginning of April, the division took part in the battle of Arras in the second half of April. At this time it lost about 50 per cent of its fighting men. The 141st Infantry Regiment received in May 135 to 140 men per company to make up for its losses (1918 class and men liberated by the dissolution of the 618th Infantry Regiment).

FLANDERS.

3. Sent to rest for the entire month of May in the vicinity of Lille and filled up by replacements of 3,000 men coming from the recruit depot at Warsaw on May 9, the 35th Division was sent into Belgium and occupied, on May 31, the banks of the Ypres-Comines Canal. On June 7 it lost heavily there (5,000 to 6,000 men, of whom 1,272 were prisoners).

4. Reorganized on June 11 in the vicinity of Cambrai, by replacements mostly made up of returned convalescents and wounded, the division was then sent into line in a calm sector north of St. Quentin, where it remained from June 21 to October 20.

FLANDERS.

5. On October 22 and 23 it reappeared on the Flanders front in the sector of the Houthulst wood. It had rather serious losses between October 22 and 25.

It was relieved on January 22, 1918, and sent to rest east of Bruges.

RECRUITING.

The 35th Division is recruited from western Prussia with some help from the 6th Corps District, especially in June, 1916 (important replacements made up of miners from Silesia). There is a rather large proportion of Poles, not only from the 17th Corps District, but also from the 5th and 6th Corps Districts.

VALUE—1917 ESTIMATE.

The 35th Division has taken part in numerous battles. Its quality has been greatly weakened by the incorporation of recruits of the 1918 class, and by the increase of the Polish elements.

The 35th Division appears to be a mediocre division (July, 1917).

The morale of the 141st Infantry Regiment, 50 per cent of which are Poles, appears poor. (November, 1917.)

1918.

YPRES.

1. The division was at rest east of Bruges (Maldeghem) until about February 17, when it was engaged in the vicinity of Merckem until March 20.

BATTLE OF THE LYS.

2. It entrained at Pitthem on the 22d and moved to Carvin. It was in reserve at Evin-Malmaison until March 27, and later in reserve south of Lens (near Rouvroy) until April 1. It was moved to Lille and engaged from April 8-9 to the 14th at Neuve-Chapelle, Lestrem, Locon, Neuf Berquin. In the fighting on April 12 the division lost heavily. It was withdrawn on April 14.

FLANDERS.

3. The division rested near Armentiers until May 5, during which period it was reviewed by the Kaiser. It was in the sector north of Bailleul from May 8 to July 3. At this time the company effectives of the division seems to have been about 50 men. The division rested at Bruges from the 5th to the 17th, when it returned to the Merckem sector and occupied it until August 18. Considerable replacements were received in mid-August by the division.

ARTOIS.

4. It rested near Lille (Aug. 19-24), and on August 25 was railed to Douai. On the 26th the division occupied the Drocourt–Queant line and fought in the area until about September 30, when it was relieved after losing 800 prisoners.

BATTLE OF CAMBRESIS.

5. The division was reengaged on October 1 northwest of Cambrai. It withdrew to Abancourt (9th), Hem-Lenglet (11th), Denain north of Maing, Famars (28th), northwest of Maresches (Nov. 1). It passed to second line about the 1st of the month, returning on November 9 near Harchies. The division was not in line on November 11.

VALUE—1918 ESTIMATE.

The division was rated as second class. It was considered as a good sector-holding division in 1918.

35th Reserve Division.

COMPOSITION.

	1914 Brigade.	1914 Regiment.	1915 Brigade.	1915 Regiment.	1916 Brigade.	1916 Regiment.	1917 Brigade.	1917 Regiment.	1918 Brigade.	1918 Regiment.
Infantry	5 Ldw. (z)	2 Ldw. 9 Ldw. 107 Ldw.	5 Ldw. (z)	2 Ldw. 9 Ldw. 107 Ldw.	5 Ldw. (Mixed)	2 Ldw. 9 Ldw. 107 Ldw.	167.	420. 421. 438.	167.	420. 438.
Cavalry	3d Res. Heavy Cavalry		3d Res. Heavy Cavalry		3d Res. Heavy Cavalry		2 Sq. 4 Jag. Pf		Staff, 4 Horse Jag. Rgt. 2 Sqn. 4 Horse Jag. Rgt.	
Artillery	Ers. Abt. 35, 81 F. A. Rgt.		35 Res. F. A. Rgt.		35 Res. F. A. Rgt.	833d Battery.	Art. Command: 35 Res. F. A. Rgt.			(z)
Engineers and Liaisons.	2 Pion. Btn. No. 17.		2 Pion. Btn. No. 17.		235 T. M. Co.		335 Pion. Btn. 1 Res. Co. 17 Pion. 235 T. M. Co. 35 Res. Searchlight Section. Tel. Detch.		335 Pion. Btn. 1 Res. Co. 17 Pions. 149 Searchlight Section. 435 Signal Command: 435 Tel. Detch.	
Medical and Veterinary.							238 Ambulance Co. Field Hospital. Vet. Hospital.		238 Ambulance Co. 291 Field Hospital. 435 Vet. Hospital.	
Transports							Light Mun. Col.			
Attached					5 Ldst. Pion. Co. 9th Corps		93 Brig. reenforced by 20 and 24 Ldst. Btns.			

HISTORY.

(420th Infantry Regiment: 1st Corps District—East Prussia. 421st Infantry Regiment: 2d Corps District—Pomerania. 438th Infantry Regiment: 14th Corps District—Grand Duchy of Baden.)

1914.

The 35th Reserve Division is a Landwehr division. It has always occupied the Eastern Front.

POLAND.

1. At the outbreak of the war the 35th Reserve Division fought (Aug. 25–28) on the southern frontier of East Prussia, which it crossed. It took part in the Polish campaign—southwest of Warsaw in October and November, 1914, in the vicinity of Czenstochow in December.

1915.

GALICIA.

1. From January to March, 1915, the division was in line south of the Pilica. From April to June it took part in the operations in the Carpathians, then in the vicinity of Lemberg.

RUSSIA.

2. In the middle of July it was replaced near Sokal (Galicia) by the 39th Austrian Division and went south of Grabowiec. The pursuit of the Russians led it north of Cholm in the beginning of August, east of Brest-Litovsk, near Kobrin in September, then to the Chtchara at the mouth of the Oginski Canal in October.

3. It took up its position along the canal north of Logischin.

1916.

OGINSKI CANAL.

1. The 35th Reserve Division remained in line along the Oginski Canal for more than two years (Oct., 1915 to Feb., 1918).

2. About October, 1916, the 5th Landwehr Brigade (2d and 9th Landwehr Regiments) was assigned to the 226th Division (being formed in the Smorgoni sector). The 35th Reserve Division received two new regiments—the 420th and 421st Infantry Regiments.

1917.

OGINSKI CANAL.

1. The division was in the same sector.

In July, 1917, the 438th Infantry Regiment became a part of the 35th Reserve Division to replace the 107th Saxon Landwehr Regiment, which had been transferred to the 45th Landwehr Division (Saxon).

VALUE—1917 ESTIMATE.

Composed of Landwehr and Landsturm elements, retained for more than two years in a calm sector of the Russian front, later in the Ukraine, the 35th Reserve Division has only a mediocre military value.

1918.

UKRAINE.

1. In March the division advanced into Ukraine, after having furnished men to the 10th Landwehr Division, which was about to leave for the Western Front. In this advance the division saw some fighting and consequently suffered some losses. In April the division was identified in the Gomel region. The division was identified in Ukraine early in October, and so its reported presence in Flanders on September 20 appears incorrect.

VALUE—1918 ESTIMATE.

The division was rated as fourth class.

125651°—20——27

36th Division.
COMPOSITION.

	1914		1915		1916		1917		1918	
	Brigade.	Regiment.	Brigade.	Regiment.	Brigade.	Regiment.	Brigade.	Regiment.	Brigade.	Regiment.
Infantry	69. 71.	129. 175. 5 Gren. 128.	69. 71.	129. 175. 5 Gren. 128.	71.	5 Gren. 175. 128.	71.	5 Gren. 175. 128.	71.	5. 128. 175.
Cavalry	5 Hus. Rgt.				4 Sq. 5 Hus. Rgt.		4 Sq. 5 Hus. Rgt.		4 Sq. 5 Hus. Rgt.	
Artillery	36 Brig.: 36 Rgt. 72 Rgt.		36 Brig.: 36 Rgt. 72 Rgt.		36 Brig.: 36 Rgt. 72 Rgt.		36 Art. Command: 36 Rgt.		36 Art. Command: 36 F. A. Rgt. 1 Abt. 4 Res. Ft. A. Rgt. 824 Light Am. Col. 1209 Light Am. Col. 1229 Light Am. Col.	
Engineers and Liaisons.			1 Pion. Btn. No. 17: Field Co. 17 Pion. 36 Tel. Detch. 36 Pont. Engs.		1 Pion. Btn. No. 17: 2 Co. 17 Pion. 3 and 4 Cos. 35 Pion. 3 Co. 36 Pion. 36 T. M. Co. 36 Tel. Detch. 36 Pont. Engs.		1 Pion. Btn. No. 17: 3 and 5 Cos. 17 Pion. 36 T. M. Co. 36 Tel. Detch.		17 Pion. Btn.: 3 Co. 17 Pions. 5 Co. 17 Pions. 36 T. M. Co. 206 Searchlight Section. 36 Signal Command: 36 Tel. Detch. 62 Wireless Detch.	
Medical and Veterinary.							43 Ambulance Co. 288, 290 Field Hospts. 36 Vet. Hospital.		43 Ambulance Co. 238 Field Hospital. 230 Field Hospital. 36 Vet. Hospital.	
Transports									569 M. T. Col.	

HISTORY.

(17th Corps District—West Prussia.)

1914.

The 36th Division (with the 35th Division) was a part of the 17th Army Corps (Danzig).

EAST PRUSSIA—RUSSIA.

1. The 17th Army Corps, which comprises the 35th and 36th Divisions, was sent to East Prussia in August, 1914, where it belonged to the 8th Army, soon placed under the command of Von Hindenburg. With this army it took part in the battle of Tannenberg on August 30, and in the battle of Loetzen on September 9, then with the 9th German Army (Mackensen), in the battle of Radom, on October 6.

2. In the battles which mark the advance upon Warsaw and then the retreat, the regiments of the 36th Division, and especially the 5th Grenadier Regiment, suffered considerable losses (principally at Lodz between Nov. 23 and Dec. 6).

1915.

1. During the winter of 1914–15 the 36th Division, with the 17th Army Corps, took part in the actions along the Bzura until June. In July it was on the Narew, later on the right bank of the Bug, and at the beginning of September on the Chtchara River.

2. At the end of September, 1915, at the time of the pressure exerted by the Franco-British offensive, the 17th Army Corps entrained for the Western Front.

FRANCE.

3. Detraining at Peronne on October 10, it was sent to rest in the vicinity of Ham until October 16. At this date it went into line in the Roye sector. Until the battle of the Somme it was not seriously engaged.

1916.

SOMME.

1. Upon the outbreak of the Franco-British offensive on the Somme in July, 1916, the 36th Division occupied the sector included between the south of Chilly and the north of Andechy. It was not engaged as a whole until October, the time when the battle front extended as far as the Chaulnes-Chilly sector. Until then it had only sent detached units to reenforce certain points south of the river.

2. About the end of September it occupied the front from north of Fouquescourt to the Chaulnes railroad. Relieved between October 15 and 20, and sent to rest between Nesle and Ham, it had to go back into line on October 24–25 to replace, in the sector south of Ablaincourt-Chaulnes wood, the divisions which our attacks north of Chaulnes had exhausted. Its regiments lost heavily during this period. The 128th Infantry Regiment lost more than the others, especially on November 7, 10, and 11.

3. On December 8 the 36th Division left the front north of Chaulnes and was sent north of Roye to the Fouqescourt sector.

1917.

ST. QUENTIN.

1. On March 17, 1917, it was included in the retirement and withdrew to the Hindenburg Line, where it established itself, on March 23, south of St. Quentin.

ARTOIS.

2. After a month's rest (Apr. 9–May 9) behind the front, the 36th Division went into line southeast of Arras in the Guemmape sector. It had only a few local engagements there and did not suffer any great losses.

3. It then spent a part of June at rest in the Douai area and took up its position on July 4 in the sector of Oppy-Gavrelle (Artois). It did not take part in any serious engagements there.

YPRES.

4. Relieved at the end of August, it entrained at Douai on the 28th for Courtrai and Isegsem. Sent on September 10–11 into the sector of Poelcapelle, it had to be replaced there on the 23d because of the heavy losses which it received from the British attack.

5. The division left Flanders on September 27 to occupy a calm sector west of St. Quentin, where it still was at the beginning of February, 1918.

RECRUITING.

The 36th Division is recruited from the same region as the 35th Division.

VALUE—1917 ESTIMATE.

The 36th Division was an excellent combat division.

In the battles of the Somme and of Arras the 36th Division gave a good account of itself.

On the Ypres front the combat spirit of the division was less energetic than in the preceding battles. The British Artillery, however, had reduced its effectives by one-half.

1918.

BATTLE OF PICARDY.

1. The division was relieved in the sector north of St. Quentin about February 1 and entered the sector south of St. Quentin within a few days. It was in line when the Somme offensive came off and advanced in the front line by Essigny le Grand, Clastres, Brouchy, Guiscard, Campagne, Candor. From the 23d to the 25th it was in second line. On the 25th it was reengaged in the Lassigny area. The division was relieved on April 8.

2. The division rested in close support southeast of Roye until April 20. A draft of 300 men was received about this time.

3. On April 20 the division was engaged southeast of Montdidier (Rollet) until April 28. It was in reserve from the 28th to the beginning of May in the vicinity of Roye. A draft of 1,000 men was received on April 29. On May 9 the division was moved to Wasigny, where it rested until the 22d. It marched toward the Aisne front by night from May 22 to 27 via Rozoy sur Sene, Montcornet, Liesse, Montaigv.

BATTLE OF THE AISNE.

4. The division had in line on the 27th only one battalion of the 128th Regiment (near Winterberg). The rest of the division followed the advance in reserve, passing through Villers en Prayeres, Fismes, Villers sur Fere. It was engaged from May 29 to the middle of June at Courmont, Fresnes (29th), Jaulgonne (31st), east of Chateau Thierry. The division withdrew from the sector east of Chateau Thierry about June 30.

SECOND BATTLE OF THE MARNE.

5. It rested in the salient (near Fere en Tardenois) until July 14, undergoing reconstitution. On that date it marched to the front and was engaged the next day. It crossed the Marne and penetrated south of Charteves, but was stopped and thrown back on Mezy and Fossoy. From July 20 to 22 it was in second line. Reengaged south of the Ourcq on 22d, the division fought at Rocourt and Villeneuve sur Fere until July 27.

BATTLE OF THE SOMME.

6. The division rested near Laon in early August. It was brought up to resist the British attack north of Bapaume on August 24. It was still under strength and was unable to check the advance. It was forced to fall back on Vaulx Vraucourt, Ecoust

St. Mein (27th–30th), Pronville, and Inchy (Sept. 2–3). The losses in prisoners amounted to 800 in this fighting.

7. On the 16th of September the division was again in line south of La Bassee. Beginning October 1 it retreated on Bauvin, Pont a Vendin, Provin (16th), Attiches (18th), and toward the south of Tournai. It was last identified at Bany on November 10.

VALUE—1918 ESTIMATE.

The division was rated as second class. It was heavily engaged in 1918 as a follow-up division in the attacks and to hold important defensive sectors.

36th Reserve Division.
COMPOSITION.

	1914 Brigade.	1914 Regiment.	1915 Brigade.	1915 Regiment.	1916 Brigade.	1916 Regiment.	1917 Brigade.	1917 Regiment.	1918 Brigade.	1918 Regiment.
Infantry	69 Res. 70 Res.	21 Res, 61 Res, 5 Res, 54. 2 Res. Jag. Btn.	69 Res. 70 Res.	21 Res, 61 Res, 5 Res, 54. 2 Res. Jag. Btn.	69 Res. 70 Res.	21 Res, 61 Res, 5 Res, 54.	69 Res.	5 Res, 61 Res, 54.	69 Res.	54. 5 Res. 61 Res.
Cavalry	1 Res. Hus. Rgt. (3 Sqns.).		1 Res. Hus. Rgt.		....		5 sq. 2 Guard Dragoon. 1 and 2 Sqns. 1st Res. Uhlan Rgt.		5 Sqn. 2 Gd. Drag. Rgt.	
Artillery	36 Res. Rgt. (6 Btries.).		36 Res. Rgt. (7 Btries.).		36 Res. Rgt. (7 Btries.).		72 Art. Command: 36 Res. Rgt. (9 Btries.).		72 Art. Command: 36 Res. F. A. Rgt. 3 Abt. 4 Res. Ft. A. Rgt. 833 Light Am. Col. 1252 Light Am. Col. 1306 Light Am. Col.	
Engineers and Liaisons.	1 Res. Co. 2, Pion. No. 2.		1 Res. Co. 2, Pion. No. 2. 2 Co. 32 Res. Pion. 36 Res. Pont. Engs. 36 Res. Tel. Detch.		1 Res. Co. 2, Pion. No. 2. 236 T. M. Co. 36 Res. Pont. Engs. 36 Res. Tel. Detch. 80 Art. Survey Section. 24 Sound Ranging Section.		336 Pion. Btn. 1 Res. Co. 2 Pion. 236 T. M. Co. 436 Tel. Detch.		2 Pion. Btn. 1 Co. 2 Pions. 1 Res. Co. 2 Pions. 236 T. M. Co. 45 Searchlight Section. 436 Signal Command: 436 Tel. Detch. 119 Wireless Detch.	
Medical and Veterinary.	....		....		....		515 Ambulance Co. 398 Field Hospital. Vet. Hospital.		515 Ambulance Co. 10 Res. Field Hospital. 12 Res. Field Hospital. 138 Vet. Hospital.	
Transports	....		....		....		Light Mun. Col.			
Attached	....		....		217 Anti-Aircraft Detch.		....			

HISTORY.

(17th Corps District—Western Prussia and the eastern part of Pomerania.)

1914.

EAST PRUSSIA.

1. At the outbreak of the war the 36th Reserve Division constituting, with the 1st Reserve Division, the 1st Reserve Corps, was engaged in East Prussia in the vicinity of Gumbinnen-Angerburg.

BZURA.

2. Assigned to the 9th German Army (Mackensen), it fought on November 6 on the left bank of the Vistula and on the Bzura at the beginning of December.

1915.

1. At the beginning of 1915 the 36th Reserve Division took part in the engagements on the line Bzura-Rawka-Bolimov (Jan. 4 and Feb. 5).

PRASNYSZ.

2. On February 13 the division entrained, with the entire 1st Reserve Corps, to reenforce the right wing of the Germany Army, which was pushing back the Russians from East Prussia. Detraining at Ostrolenka, it attacked in the vicinity of Mlawa, then near Prasnysz (April), where the Russian counterattacks caused it to suffer heavy losses.

COURLAND.

3. In May, it took part in the Hindenburg offensive in Courland. First occupying the sector of Jurburg, north of Niemen, it reached Ponieviej in July and from there pushed on to the vicinity of Dvinsk. The division suffered heavily during this period. On October 15, the 61st Reserve Infantry Regiment had an average of only 80 men per company (letter).

FRIEDRICHSTADT.

4. In December, the 36th Reserve Division occupied the sector of Friedrichstadt, southeast of Riga.

1916.

1. The division remained in its Courland sector (Friedrichstadt) until September 24, 1916.

GALICIA.

2. At the end of September and the beginning of October, it entrained at Libau and was transferred to Galicia. The 54th Infantry Regiment was engaged on October 3 east of Brzezany to oppose the advance of the Russians. The rest of the division rejoined the rest of the 54th Infantry Regiment on October 19, and remained in this area.

1917.

1. About the end of May, 1917, the 36th Reserve Division was relieved from the sector south of Brzezany and entrained near Rohatyn (Galicia) for the Western Front. Itinerary: Lemberg-Cracow-Oppeln-Munich-Karlsruhe.

LORRAINE.

2. Detraining in Lorraine on the 1st of June, the division received training until June 24. At this date, it took over a calm sector in Haye for a fortnight.

ARTOIS.

3. Sent to the vicinity of Lens in July, the 36th Reserve Division occupied the sector of Mericourt until the beginning of October.

FLANDERS.

4. About October 20, it went into line east of Ypres (north of Becelaere).

The 36th Reserve Division is recruited from West Prussia and the eastern part of Pomerania. It contained a large number of Alsace-Lorrainers during its stay on the Western Front.

In Russia the 36th Reserve Division took part in several major operations. It did not come to the Western Front until June, 1917.

1918.

BATTLE OF THE LYS.

1. The division was relieved in the Foret de Holthust on April 4 by the 1st Landwehr Division, and marched via Amersveld to Cortemarch, where it entrained and arrived at Courtrai on April 5.   It left Courtrai on the 8th and marched toward Armentieres. On the 10th the division followed up the German advance in support of an assault division, and on the 11th came into action north of Armentieres.   Losses were severe and the division retired about April 13 to rest.   It returned in the Ploegsteert area on April 17 and went to rest in the Roulers area.   On May 11, the division came back to line for the third time north of Hinges.

2. It was withdrawn about May 25, rested behind the front until June 11, when it relieved the 235th Division northwest of Bethune, which sector it held until about June 22.

LENS.

3. On June 26 the division entered line in Artois area, southeast of Loos.   It held this quiet sector until October 2.

BELGIUM.

4. On the night of October 4–5 the division relieved tbe 16th Bavarian Division southwest of Roulers.   From then until about November 4, the division fought first in the Roulers area, and after October 15, at Thielt (17th), Deynze (26th), Ecke (Nov. 2).   It was withdrawn from line about November 4 and did not reenter.

The division was rated as third class.   It was heavily engaged on the Lys in the spring without achieving much success.   Thereafter the division was employed on the defensive.

37th Division.
COMPOSITION.

	1914 Brigade	1914 Regiment	1915 Brigade	1915 Regiment	1916 Brigade	1916 Regiment	1917 Brigade	1917 Regiment	1918 Brigade	1918 Regiment
Infantry	73. 75.	147. 151. 146. 150.	73. 75.	147. 151. 146. 150.	73.	147. 151. 150.	73.	147. 151. 150.	73.	147. 150. 151.
Cavalry	11 Drag. Rgt.				11 Drag. Rgt. (3 Squadrons).		3 Sq. 10 Jag. z. Pf.		3 Sqn. 10 Mounted Jag. Rgt.	
Artillery	37 Brig.: 73 Rgt. 82 Rgt.		37 Brig.: 73 Rgt. 82 Rgt.		37 Brig.: 73 Rgt. 82 Rgt.		37 Art. Command: 73 Rgt.		37 Art. Command: 73 F. A. Rgt. 2 Abt. 16 Ft. A. Rgt. (2, 9 and 10 Btries.). 846 Light Am. Col. 924 Light Am. Col. 1184 Light Am. Col.	
Engineers and Liaisons.			1 Pion. Btn. No. 26: Field Co. 26 Pion. 37 Tel. Detch. 37 Pont. Engs.		1 Pion. Btn. No. 26: 1 Co. 26 Pion. 37 T. M. Co. 37 Tel. Detch. 37 Pont. Engs.		134 Pion. Btn.: 3 Co. 26 Pion. 250 Pion Co. 37 T. M. Co. 250 Searchlight Section. 37 Tel. Detch.		134 Pion. Btn.: 3 Co. 26 Pions. 250 Pion Co. 37 T. M. C. 63 Searchlight Section. 37 Signal Command: 37 Tel. Detch. 82 Wireless Detch.	
Medical and Veterinary.							40 Ambulance Co. 317, 318 Field Hospital. Vet. Hospital.		49 Ambulance Co. 317 Field Hospital. 318 Field Hospital. 194 Vet. Hospital.	
Transports.							Light Mun. Col.			

HISTORY.

(20th Corps District—East Prussia.)

1914.

Upon mobilization, the 37th Division, with the 41st Division, formed the 20th Army Corps (Allenstein).

RUSSIA.

1. At the beginning of the war the 37th Division was engaged on the Eastern Front. It took part in the battle of Tannenberg at the end of August, in the attempt against Warsaw in October, and in the battles on the Rawka during the winter of 1914 and 1915.

1915.

RUSSIA.

1. In April, 1915, the 37th Division was on the Narew. In May it ceded the 146th Infantry Regiment to the 101st Division, a new formation. The battles lasted until the end of July on the Narew, which was crossed on the 31st. The division was at Bielostok at the end of August, and entered Grodno on September 2.

2. In the course of September, it advanced from Niemen to the Berezina, and in October it occupied a sector in the vicinity of Dvinsk (Lake Sventen) on the stabilized front. It remained there until its departure for the Western Front in December, 1916.

1916.

1. One of its regiments, the 150th Infantry Regiment, was temporarily detached at the time of the Russian offensive of 1916 on the Stokhod and then made a part of the 91st Division.

FRANCE.

2. After taking part in the terrible battles on the Stokhod, in the course of which it suffered enormous losses, the 150th Infantry Regiment was transferred to Galicia at the end of September, 1916, and then returned to the 37th Division. The division was sent to the Western Front on December 10, 1916. Itinerary: Cracow–Breslau–Dresden–Leipzig–Nuremburg–Karlsruhe–Rastatt–Strassburg–Colmar–Neu Breisach.

1917.

UPPER ALSACE.

1. Regrouped with its three regiments in Upper Alsace (vicinity of Ferrette) at the end of 1916, the 37th Division spent some time at rest and, in the middle of January, 1917, went into line in the sector which extends from Niederlarg to the Swiss frontier.

The division occupied this sector until the month of May.

2. About May 1 it was relieved, entrained south of Mulhouse and sent to Charleville by way of Strassburg, Sarrebruecken, and Sedan, from which place it went to the vicinity of Gizy (6 kilometers from Sissonne).

AISNE.

3. After a week's rest, it went into line on the Aisne at the Chemins des Dames, in the sector of Courtecon, which it occupied until the end of July.

4. During these two months (May 25 to the end of July), the 37th Division did not play an important role. However, units of the division carried out several local operations in the course of this period. On July 14, units from the three regiments aided by the assault troops of the 5th Assault Battalion, succeeded, at the expense of very heavy losses, in reducing a salient near the Cerny sugar refinery.

ST. GOBAIN.

5. On July 31 the 37th Division was relieved, and about August 3 went into line in the St. Gobain sector (in front of Coucy le Chateau) which it occupied until the end of November. On October 23 it suffered losses (Mont des Singes) from our bombardments. On the 24th the division withdrew its units across the canal and occupied the sector included between the Brancourt-Quincy road and Anizy.

RECRUITING.

The 37th Division is recruited from East and West Prussia. During its stay on the Eastern Front it contained a large number of Alsace-Lorrainers. Because of its circumscribed territorial extent, the 37th Division contains an admixture of elements coming from other districts (5th and 6th Corps Districts among others). Nevertheless, and in spite of their official designations (from Moravia, from Ermeland), its regiments are called "East Prussian" in the German communique of July 15, 1917.

VALUE—1917 ESTIMATE.

On July 14 and 15, 1917, the 37th Division attacked with great energy. At that time, it seemed to be of good quality and of high morale. However, according to statements of prisoners of the 151st Infantry Regiment made in September, October, and November, the morale appears to have weakened (Jan. 18, 1918).

LAON.

1. During January and early February the 37th Division and the 14th Reserve Division relieved each other in the St. Gobain sector (north of Soissons). It seems probable (though the fact has never been proved) that during one of its periods out of line, the 37th Division was given a course of training in open warfare. On February 20, the 37th relieved the 14th Reserve in the same sector, and it was in turn relieved by the 14th Reserve about the 9th of March.

PICARDY.

2. On March 21 the division reinforced the front near Benay (south of St. Quentin) attacking with such dash that it received special mention by Prof. Wegener in the Koelnische Zeitung. It was withdrawn on the 30th.

3. The division rested for a few days between Champs and Folembray (north of Soissons), and then entered line north of Thiescourt (west of Noyon) on the 9th of April. It was withdrawn about the 20th, and went to rest and refit in the area southeast of Avesnes.

AISNE.

4. On May 27, the first day of the battle of the Aisne, the division attacked near Presles (south of Laon), and advanced via Braine (the 28th) as far as the Troesnes-Longpont sector (east of Villers Cotterets). It was relieved by the 115th Division on the 4th of June, and went to the area northeast of Braine to rest and to be thoroughly trained.

MARNE.

5. It set out the evening of the 12th of July, and in two night marches, reached its point of assembly in the woods north of Verneuil (northeast of Dormans). It was planned that the 37th with three other divisions, forming the v. Conta Group, should "leap-frog" the divisions in line, and to sweep up the valley of the Marne, beginning with the line Vincelles-Antheney and ending at a line passing north of Avenay and north of Moslins. It was thought that this movement, combined with the push of the units to the east of Rheims, would result in the fall of that city and also of the Montagne de Rheims to the south. The division attacked on the 15th, crossed the Marne, reached the Bois du Chataignier (south of Mareuil-east of Dormans); and was stopped

there.   It delivered its last counterattack on the 19th, and the order having been given, crossed the Marne, and continued its retreat toward the north.   It was identified by prisoners for the last time on the 28th in the vicinity of Champvoisy (north of Dormans).   It then went to the Charleville area to rest and refit; the 10th Landwehr Division having been disbanded, the 372d Regiment was drafted to the regiments of the 37th Division.

VERDUN.

6. During the night of the 12th–13th of August, it relieved the 231st Division to the north of Avocourt (north of Verdun).   It was relieved by the 117th Division about the 20th of September, and moved to the vicinity of Billy (south of Longuyon,) where it rested for about a week.

ARGONNE.

7. On September 26, it reinforced the 117th Division near Montfaucon, where they counterattacked the same day.   It was heavily engaged until withdrawn October 1.

8. It moved some kilometres to the west, in the vicinity of Exermont, in anticipation of the American attack of October 4, and came into line in that region on the 5th.   It was engaged in a number of minor actions, that proved quite costly; its losses in prisoners alone was 962.   It was withdrawn on the 18th, and went to rest near Verpel (northeast of Grandpre).

9. On November 9, the division came back into line near Abaucourt (northeast of Verdun); it had not been withdrawn on the 11th.

VALUE—1918 ESTIMATE.

The 37th has always been considered a first-class shock division.   It did very well in the offensives in which it took part (Somme, Aisne, Marne), and one of its regiments, the 147th, "The Marshal von Hindenburg Regiment" was particularly mentioned in the German Communique for its work on October 10.   It suffered such heavy losses throughout the year that, despite numerous large drafts of replacements, the regiments were reduced to four companies of 80 men each at the end of the war.

38th Division.
COMPOSITION.

	1914 Brigade	1914 Regiment	1916 Brigade	1916 Regiment	1916 Brigade	1916 Regiment	1917 Brigade	1917 Regiment	1918 Brigade	1918 Regiment
Infantry	76. 83.	71. 95. 94. 96.	76. 83. 11 Jäg. Btn.	71. 95. 94. 96.	83.	94. 95. 96.	83.	94. 95. 96.	83.	94. 95. 96.
Cavalry	6 Cuir. Rgt. (3 Sqns.).		6 Cuir. Rgt. (3 Sqns.).		2 Sqn. 6 Cuir. Rgt.		3 Sqn. 6 Cuir Rgt.		3 Sqn. 6 Cuir. Rgt.	
Artillery	38 Brig.: 19 Rgt. 55 Rgt.		38 Brig.: 19 Rgt. 55 Rgt.		38 Brig.: 19 Rgt. 55 Rgt.		38 Art. Command: 19 Rgt. (9 Btries).		38 Art. Command: 19 Ft. A. Rgt. 61 Ft. A. Btn. (Staff, 1, 2, and 3 Btries.) 704 Light Am. Col. 726 Light Am. Col. 1258 Light Am. Col.	
Engineers and Liaisons.	3 Field Co., 1 Pion. No. 11.		3 Field Co., 1 Pion. No. 11. 38 Pont. Engs. 38 Tel. Detch.		3 Field Co., 1 Pion. No. 11. 38 T. M. Co. 38 Pont. Engs. 38 Tel. Detch.		128 Pion. Btn. 3 Co. 11 Pion. 285 Pion Co. 38 T. M. Co, Tel. Detch.		125 Pion. Btn.: 3 Co. 11 Pions. 285 Pion. Co. 46 Searchlight Section. 38 Signal Command: 38 Tel. Detch. 118 Wireless Detch.	
Medical and Veterinary.							Ambulance Co. 108 Field Hospital. Vet. Hospital.		27 Ambulance Co. 104 Field Hospital. 108 Field Hospital. 38 Vet. Hospital.	
Transports							Light Mun. Col.		571 M. T. Col.	
Attached					25 Labor Btn.					

HISTORY.

(11th Corps District—Thuringian States.)

1914.

BELGIUM.

1. At the outbreak of the war the 38th Division, forming the 11th Army Corps with the 22d Division, belonged to the 3d Army (Von Hausen), which went through the Belgian Ardennes. It halted in front of Namur until the surrender of this place.

EAST PRUSSIA–POLAND.

2. In consequence of the invasion of East Prussia, the 38th Division as well as the 22d Division, left Belgium about August 27. Going by way of Aix la Chapelle, it detrained in East Prussia, where it fought from September 9 to 11. From that place it was taken to the southern part of Poland (Pinczow, Sept. 28; Opatow, Oct. 4). The enveloping movement of the Russians obliged it to retire from the Lodz front with the army group to which it was attached. It was assigned to the 9th Army (Mackensen) in November and to the 10th Army in December.

3. During the winter of 1914 and 1915 it took part in several important engagements on the Bzura and the Rawka, as well as on the Pilica.

1915.

POLAND.

1. Returning to the 9th Army (Von Fabeck), at the beginning of 1915, the 38th Division fought in the vicinity of Rava, on March 6 and 7. It was then separated from the 22d Division and rejoined the army detachment of Von Gallitz, north of Warsaw. In May it transferred the 71st Infantry Regiment to the 103d Division, a new formation.

2. During the summer offensive it took part in numerous battles from July 13 to September 19, advanced to the southeast of Bielostok, reached the Svislotch on September 1 and marched beyond this until September 19.

FRANCE.

3. At the end of September the 38th Division was concentrated in the vicinity of Grodno and entrained for France on September 25. (Itinerary: Lyck–Graudenz–Berlin–Hanover–Minden–Cologne–Aix la Chapelle–Liege–Namur–Douai.) Detraining on October 1, it completed its reorganization. Between August 30 and October 8 the 5th Company of the 94th Infantry Regiment had received not less than 161 men as replacements.

OISE.

4. Sent to the south of the Oise, the 38th Division went into line in the sector of Tracy le Val., which it held until the beginning of May, 1916, without any serious engagements.

1916.

VERDUN.

1. On May 11, 1916, the division entrained at Tergnier and was transferred to the Verdun front.

2. On May 13 it took over the sector of Hill 304, which it did not leave until October 10, seriously weakened by the battles which it had sustained for five months (losses, 52 per cent of the infantry).

SOMME.

3. Sent to the Somme on October 12, it went into action on October 12; it went into action on October 22 at Thiepval–Grandcourt, and remained there only three weeks, because of the severe losses which it suffered.

FLANDERS.

4. It left the front on November 13 to go to rest and to be reorganized on the coast of Flanders, between Ostend and the Dutch frontier.

5. On December 19 it was brought back to the Somme.

1917.

SOMME.

1. In January, 1917, elements of the division were sent as reenforcements north of Courcelette and southwest of Serre.

2. On January 17 the entire 38th Division went into line in the vicinity of Puisieux-Hébuterne, where it was relieved about March 8 without any serious losses.

3. On March 17 the division replaced the 4th Guard Division near Beugny Bertin-court, which had lost heavily at the beginning of its retirement to the Hindenburg Line, and the 38th Division itself continued to withdraw by way of Beaumetz and Doignies. It took up its position between Demicourt and Boursies, west of Cambrai, and remained there until the end of April.

ARTOIS.

4. After a period of rest in the Cambrai–Douai area during the first half of May, the 38th Division took over the sector east of Arras (north of the Scarpe), on May 16. It left this front on May 31, after having been greatly weakened on the 16th, during the counterattacks on the village of Rouex (800 men were sent to make up these losses from the dissolved 624th Infantry Regiment).

FLANDERS.

5. The division remained at rest at Douai, until June 8; at this time, it was transferred to the vicinity of Gheluwe and sent into reserve to reenforce finally the Messines front.

6. On July 27, before the British attack, the 38th Division went into line east of Ypres (Hooge). It suffered heavy losses on July 31, the day of the attack, and also the three days preceding.

7. Relieved on August 1, it was sent to Antwerp for rest and reorganization (August).

ARTOIS.

8. On September 2, it took over the sector of Monchy le Preux, south of the Scarpe, where it again lost heavily from artillery fire.

FLANDERS.

9. Withdrawn from the front on November 2, the 38th Division after a week's rest in the vicinity of Douai, again took over the lines north of Ypres (Staden) from November 19 to November 25, then north of Passchendaele where on December 3, a British attack inflicted heavy losses upon it.

10. The division was relieved on November 19 and sent to rest in the vicinity of Bruges.

RECRUITING.

The 38th Division is recruited from the small Thuringian States. At the beginning of 1917, it included a rather large number of men from Baden, almost all of whom have been withdrawn.

VALUE—1917 ESTIMATE.

The 38th Division is a good division.

As a rule it gave a good account of itself in the numerous battles in which it took part. On June 13, 1916, however, at the Mort Homme, the 94th Infantry Regiment is said to have refused to go over the top (letter).

The heavy losses which it suffered at the end of 1917 in the course of the attack upon Ypres, were made up by the replacements composed, for the most part, of the 1918 class.

This element did not have a good effect upon the morale of the division.

1918.

BATTLE OF THE LYS.

1. The division remained in Passchendaele area until its relief by the 58th Division about April 5. It rested in the Lille area until the night of April 15–16 when it entered the line at Meteren to reenforce the battle line. It was withdrawn about May 8.

2. The division rested at Provin after May 12. It entered line north of Givenchy on May 21 and held that sector until July 5, when it was relieved by the 1st Guard Reserve Division. It rested at Lille until August 6, when it was alerted and railed to Cambrai, remaining there until August 9. The division moved from Cambrai by motor trucks on August 10 and came into line on the battle front near Lihons on the same day.

SOMME.

3. Until September 22, the division was engaged in resisting the allied advance. It held a sector south of Chaulnes until August 20, when it retired to the St. Christ area (22d). After the 8th of September the division was falling back in a northeasterly direction by Péronne toward Le Catelet. It was withdrawn from line near Hargicourt on September 22.

CAMBRAI.

4. After a rest of only one week, the division was brought back to reenforce the Cambrai battle front at Rumilly (Oct. 1). It was heavily engaged until October 16 when it went to reserve in the Cambrai area. Since August 11 the division had lost more than 2,000 prisoners.

BELGIUM.

5. On October 29, the division returned to line northeast of Roubaix. It remained in line until the armistice. The last identification was at Renaix on November 8.

VALUE—1918 ESTIMATE.

The division was rated as second class. Its worth as a defensive division was proved by the extent to which it was used in the last three months of the war.

38th Landwehr Division.

COMPOSITION.

	1914		1915		1916		1917		1918	
	Brigade.	Regiment.	Brigade.	Regiment.	Brigade.	Regiment.	Brigade.	Regiment.	Brigade.	Regiment.
Infantry	38 Ldw. (mixed).	77 Ldw. 78 Ldw.	38 Ldw. (mixed).	77 Ldw. 78 Ldw.	38 Ldw. (mixed).	77 Ldw. 78 Ldw.	38 Ldw.	79 Res. 85 Ldw. 77 Ldw. 78 Ldw.	38 Ldw.	425. 79 Res. 77 Ldw. 78 Ldw.
Cavalry									2 Squ. 17 Hus. Rgt.	
Artillery					1st Mobile Ers. Abt. 59 F. A. Rgt.		145 Art. Command. 255 Ldw. Rgt.		255 Ldw. F. A. Rgt.	
Engineers and Liaisons.							438 Pion. Btn. 5 Ldst. Btn, 9 Army Corps. 338 T. M. Co. 538 Tel. Detch.		438 Pion. Btn.: 2 Landst. Co., 2 C. Dist. Pions. 5 Landst. Co, 9 C. Dist. Pions. 338 T. M. Co. 243 Searchlight Section. 538 Signal Command: 538 Tel. Detch. 9 Wireless Detch.	
Medical and Veterinary.							557 Ambulance Co. 109 Res. Field Hospital. 12 Ldw. Field Hospl. Vet. Hospital.		557 Ambulance Co. 109 Res. Field Hospital. 12 Ldw. Field Hospital. 538 Vet. Hospital.	
Transports							Light Mun. Col.			

HISTORY.

(38th Landwehr Division: 10th Corps District—Hanover.)

1914.

The grouping of the 38th Landwehr Brigade (77th and 78th Landwehr Regiments) and of a mixed regiment, 79th Reserve Infantry Regiment, formed the 38th Landwehr Division in April, 1917.

1. The 38th Landwehr Brigade remained independent until it was assigned to the 38th Landwehr Division.

FLANDERS.

2. Arriving at Liége on October 21, 1914, the 38th Brigade remained there about two months. Transferred to Flanders on October 27, it held the sector north of the Passchendaele Canal (Nieuport) until the beginning of November.

3. After occupying the front of Ypres near Becelaere, the brigade came into line before Passchendaele at the end of December.

1915.

FLANDERS.

1. In April, 1915, the 38th Landwehr Brigade took part in the second battle of Ypres near Zonnebeke.

2. On May 18 it was transferred from Roulers to La Bassée (Festubert) to reenforce the 7th Army Corps.

3. After a rest at Lille it went into line south of the Lys (Frelinghien-Houplines) at the end of August.

1916.

ARTOIS.

1. Relieved from the north of Armentieres in March, 1916, the 38th Landwehr Brigade was sent south of Arras (sector Wailly-Blaireville).

FLANDERS.

.2. In the middle of September it returned to the Armentieres front (from the Armentières-Lille railroad to Aubers). It occupied this sector for a year and a half.

1917.

1. In 1917 sector south of Armentières.

In April, 1917, the 38th Landwehr Brigade was transformed into the 38th Landwehr Division by the addition of a third regiment, the 79th Reserve–85th Landwehr, a composite regiment (1st and 2d Battalions of the 85th Landwehr Regiment, four companies of the 79th Reserve Regiment, the eight others having entered into the composition of the 440th Reserve Regiment of the 183d Division).

VALUE—1917 ESTIMATE.

The 38th Landwehr Division, formed of fairly old men, constitutes an organization of the third class. It held an honorable position in the battles of Ypres in 1914 and 1915, but, as a rule, its rôle was limited to occupying calm sectors. (Belgian Summary of Information, February, 1918.

1918.

FLANDERS.

1. The 38th Landwehr Division was relieved on January 16 in the sector south of Armentieres by the 187th Division and went to rest in the region east of Bruges.

2. After a week's rest it relieved the 8th Bavarian Reserve Division north of Dixmude on January 22. It was relieved by the 214th Division on February 20.

3. On March 3 it relieved the 2d Naval Division east of Ramscappelle (north of Bruges) in the sector just north of the one it previously occupied.

4. About the 10th of May the division side slipped toward the south, and in so doing relieved the 19th Reserve Division.

5. About the middle of October it side slipped southward. It was still in line on the 11th of November, although it was forced with the rest of the German line in Flanders, to withdraw considerably.

VALUE—1918 ESTIMATE.

The 38th Landwehr is rated as a fourth-class division. It could be and was used only to hold a quiet sector. Most of the men were nearly 40 years of age, and so it was found necessary to have a divisional "Stosstrupp" for purposes of patroling.

On November 1 the Franco-American forces in Belgium started an offensive in conjunction with the British 2d Army farther to the south. On the same day, according to the Belgium communique, "The Belgian Army carried out successful minor operations along the drainage canal," and the German communique said, "The 57th (13th Reserve Division) and the 79th Reserve (38th Landwehr Division) Infantry Regiments distinguished themselves in the course of this fighting."

39th Division.

COMPOSITION.

	1914 Brigade	1914 Regiment	1915 Brigade	1915 Regiment	1916 Brigade	1916 Regiment	1917 Brigade	1917 Regiment	1918 Brigade	1918 Regiment
Infantry	61. 82.	126. 132. 171. 172. 8 Jag. Btn. 14 Jag. Btn.	61. 82.	126. 132. 171. 172.	61.	126. 132. 172.	61.	126. 132. 172.	61.	126. 132. 172.
Cavalry	14 Drag. Rgt.				H Res. Hus. Rgt. (2 Sqns.).		1 and 2 Sqns. 8 Res. Hus. Rgt.		5 Sqn. 9 Drag. Rgt.	
Artillery	39 Brig.: 66 Rgt. 80 Rgt.		39 Brig.: 66 Rgt. 80 Rgt.		39 Brig.: 66 Rgt. 80 Rgt.		39 Artillery Command: 80 Rgt.		39 Art. Command: 80 F. A. Rgt. 406 Ft. A. Btn. 869 Light Am. Col. 1324 Light Am. Col. 1325 Light Am. Col.	
Engineers and Liaisons.	2 and 3 Field Cos. 1 Pion. Btn No. 15.		2 and 3 Field Cos. 1 Pion. Btn. No. 15. 39 Pont. Engs. 39 Tel. Detch.		2 and 3 Cos. 1 Pion. Btn. No. 15. Btn. No. 15 39 T. M. Co. 39 Pont. Engs. 39 Tel. Detch.		131 Pion. Btn. 2 and 3 Cos. 15 Pions. 39 T. M. Co. Tel. Detch.		136 Pion. Btn.: 2 Co. 15 Pions. 3 Co. 15 Pions. 39 T. M. Co. 58 Searchlight Section. 30 Signal Command: 39 Tel. Detch. 84 Wireless Detch.	
Medical and Veterinary.							38 Ambulance Co. 270, 271, 272 Field Hospitals. Vet. Hospital.		33 Ambulance Co. 270 Field Hospital. 272 Field Hospital. 39 Vet. Hospital.	
Transports							Light Mun. Col.		572 M. T. Col.	

HISTORY.

(15th Corps District—Alsace.)

1914.

ALSACE AND THE VOSGES.

1. Upon mobilization, the 39th Division and the 30th Division formed the 5th Army Corps (Strassburg).

At the beginning of the campaign the 39th Division was a part of the 7th Army (Von Herringen). In the first days of August it fought in the pass of the Bonhomme. On the 9th it went into Cernay and Mulhouse and was transferred to Dabo (Vosges) on October 19. On August 20 it took part in the battle of Albreschwiller and crossed the frontier on the 31st. It advanced to a point between the Meurthe and the Mortagne and then retreated fighting.

CHAMPAGNE.

2. Entraining on September 9, it was transferred to the northwest of Rheims, where it fought between Craonne and Ailles until October.

FLANDERS.

3. At the end of October it became a part of the 6th Army (Crown Prince of Bavaria), of which the 15th Army Corps formed the right wing (north of Lille) until the summer of 1915.

1915.

FLANDERS.

1. Before our attacks of 1915 it was attached to the 4th Army (Duke of Wurttemberg), south of Ypres. At this time the 15th Army Corps became the left wing of the 4th Army. In April the 39th Division gave the 171st Infantry Regiment to the 115th Division, a new formation.

2. The 39th Division was retained in the vicinity of Ypres until the month of February, 1916. One of its regiments, the 172d Infantry Regiment, suffered heavy losses there on September 25 (its 8th Company received at least 111 men as replacements between September 28 and October 16).

1916.

VERDUN.

1. At the beginning of 1916 various elements of the 15th Army Corps were transferred to the vicinity of Verdun and concentrated on the right bank of the Meuse, in the area Piennes–Etain–Ornel–Senon.

2. At the beginning of the German offensive on February 24, the 39th Division suffered relatively few losses, the battle being less intense in the Woevre. But little by little all its units were engaged. On March 8, the 132d Infantry Regiment took part in the attacks upon Douaumont, and on the 18th upon the Caillette wood. Its losses were enormous. On July 11 the 126th Infantry Regiment was in action with two regiments of the 30th Division. Almost all its battalions went successively to the active sectors in the vicinity of Vaux (Aug. 18). At Verdun the division lost 69 per cent of its infantry.

SOMME.

3. On October 20 the 39th Division was relieved from the Verdun front and transferred to the Somme. On the 29th it occupied the sector of Sailly Saillisel. In the attack of Sailly Saillisel by the French troops the three regiments of the division were all put into line simultaneously and acted especially with the assault troops. In these battles the losses of the division were very great (an average of 80 men per company). In the 126th Infantry Regiment, the 4th Company received at least 82 men as replacements between November 16 and 23; the 3d Company, 106 men.

VERDUN.

4. Withdrawn from the Somme, about November 11, the 39th Division was again sent to Verdun. Between December 8 and December 12 it went into the sector between the Louvemont road and the Chaufour wood and there sustained our attack of December 15. It was relieved on the 20th, very much exhausted, and went for reorganization near Vouziers.

1917.

ARGONNE.

1. About January 10, 1917, the division went into line in the sector of Ville sur Tourbe (Argonne). It was withdrawn at the beginning of March. In the course of this month, it was engaged in Champagne, in the attack of March 27 at Cernay en Dormois. It remained in the sector of Massiges until the beginning of May.

CHAMPAGNE.

2. It then went to the vicinity of Rheims (Loivre–Berry au Bac sector) from May 11 to the beginning of July.

ARTOIS.

3. Sent to rest near Asfeld, it then went into line west of Fontaine les Croisilles (middle of July). Withdrawn from the Arras front, it occupied the Loos sector in September.

FLANDERS.

4. At the end of October, it went to Flanders, Passchendaele sector, then Becelaere sector.

ARTOIS.

5. At the end of November, it was again in Artois, north of La Bassee Canal, a position which it was still occupying February, 1918.

RECRUITING.

The 171st and 172d Infantry Regiments are recruited in the Rhine District, in the widest sense of the word (Grand Duchy of Baden, Rhenish Hesse, Rhine Province), and from Westphalia.

The 126th Infantry Regiment, in Alsace since 1871, represents the participation of Wurttemberg in the guard of the Reichsland. Besides its maintenance by the younger recruiting classes, at the end of 1916 it took some of the best elements from the 123d, 125th, and 126th Landwehr Regiments (young Landsturm classes, then having at least 20 to 22 months of service).

VALUE—1917 ESTIMATE.

In spite of its relatively high losses, the 39th Division did well on the Somme (October to November, 1916). During its second engagement at Verdun, the Division was much less brilliant. Its resistance was weak (December, 1916).

1918.

LA BASSEE.

1. During the night of February 25–26 the 39th Division was relieved by the 44th Reserve Division and went to rest near Sequedin (west of Lille), where it is presumed to have been trained in open warfare.

PICARDY.

2. About the middle of March, when the Germans were concentrating their reserves on the Cambrai–St. Quentin front, the 39th Division left the Lille area for the Cambrai front. On the 21st of March, when the initial attack was delivered, the 39th Division was in reserve to the 20th Division and only came into action on the evening of that day, at Beaumetz (west of Cambrai). Encountering fighting of the severest kind, the division had to be withdrawn to reserve by the evening of the 23d.

3. The division reappeared in line on the 28th and continued to make slow progress until it reached the area south of Hebuterne (west of Bapaume). It was relieved on the 6th of April by the 26th Division and went to rest in the Cambrai area.

LYS.

4. It left this area about the 12th and marched by stages to the Lys battle front, arriving on the 17th in the Estaires area (west of Lille). The German attacks in this area had been successfully held up by the British by this time and the division was not immediately required. On the 30th it came into line northwest of Merville (west of Lille) and relieved the 12th Reserve Division. The division was not heavily engaged in this sector; it was relieved by the 44th Reserve Division on May 26 and went to rest in the vicinity of Lille.

5. On the 3d of July it relieved the 48th Reserve Division in the Vieux Berquin sector (east of Hazebrouck), and was relieved by the 187th Division during the night of July 13–14. It went to the Haubourddin area (southwest of Lille) and there received training as an assault division.

ARRAS.

6. During the night of August 2–3 it relieved the 185th Division south of Neuville–Vitasse (south of Arras). In the heavy fighting that followed the division lost over 1,300 prisoners and was driven back as far as Cherisy, where it was withdrawn on the 30th and went to rest near Aniches (east of Douai).

CAMBRAI.

7. On September 18 the division reenforced the front near Ecourt–St. Quentin (northwest of Cambrai). It was driven back as far as Palluel, where it was relieved by the 58th Division on the 28th.

YPRES.

9. The division entrained at Roulers and detrained at Menin, entering line east of Gheluvelt (north of Menin) all on the same day. About the 25th of October it was withdrawn from line near Vichte (east of Courtrai) to which point it had been driven back. It rested then for about a week in the region of Audenarde.

10. During the night of October 31–November 1 the division relieved the 23d Reserve Division in the Nukerke sector (south of Audenarde); it was identified in line there on the 9th and was probably still there on the 11th.

VALUE—1918 ESTIMATE.

The 39th is rated as a second-class division. With the exception of a statement in the German communique of October 2, that the 132d Regiment had displayed "unusual fighting ability" in the operations north of Menin, there is nothing to show that the division had distinguished itself in any way in the fighting during 1918.

39th Bavarian Reserve Division.
COMPOSITION.

	1915 Brigade	1915 Regiment	1916 Brigade	1916 Regiment	1917 Brigade	1917 Regiment	1918 Brigade	1918 Regiment
Infantry	1 Bav. Ers. 52 Ldw. 8 Jag. Btn.	1 Bav. Ers. 3 Bav. Ers. 81 Ldw. 80 Ldw. 29 Ers.	1 Bav. Ers. 9 Bav. Ers.	1 Bav. Ers. 3 Bav. Ers. 5 Bav. Ers. 15 Bav. Ldw.	1 Bav. Ers.	1 Bav. Ers. 2 Bav. Ers. 5 Bav. Ers.	1 Bav. Ers.	1 Bav. Ers. 2 Bav. Ers. 5 Bav. Ers.
Cavalry			1 Sqn. 2 Chev. Rgt.		1 Sqn. 2 Chev. Rgt.		1 Sqn. 2 Bav. Light Cav. Rgt.	
Artillery	1 Ers. Abt. 51 Rgt.		10 Bav. Res. Rgt. 5 Mountain Gun Abt.		Artillery Command: 10 Bav. Res. Rgt.		11 Bav. Res. F. A. Rgt. 111 Bav. Light Am. Col. 112 Bav. Light Am. Col. 165 Bav. Light Am. Col.	
Engineers and Liaisons			2 Ers. Co. 1 Pion. 410 T. M. Co.		23 Bav. Pion. Btn. 20 Bav. Res. Pion. Co. 21 Bav. Res. Pion. Co. 410 T. M. Co. 9 Bav. Searchlight Section. 430 Bav. Tel. Detch.		23 Bav. Pion. Btn. 20 Bav. Res. Pion. Co. 21 Bav. Res. Pion. Co. 23 Bav. Searchlight Section. 9 Bav. Searchlight Section. 439 Bav. Signal Command: 439 Bav. Tel. Detch. 106 Bav. Wireless Detch.	
Medical and Veterinary					524 Ambulance Co. 2 Bav. Field Hospital. 24 Bav. Vet. Hospital. 227 Vet. Hospital.		20 Bav. Ambulance Co. 2 Bav. Field Hospital. 51 Bav. Field Hospital.	
Transports					40, 41, and 49 Bav. Light Mun. Cols.			
Attached	1 Ldst. Btn. Duren. 8th Corps No. 18.		8 Jag. Btn. (2d Cyc. Co.). 1 Ldst. Btn. Rosenheim (1 Bav. Corps No. 4). Ldst. Btn. Landshut (1 Bav. Corps No. 7). Ldst. Btn. Esslingen (13 Corps No. 18). Ldst. Btn. Passau 2 (1 Bav. Corps No. 6)		1 Ldst. Btn. Ldst. Btn. Mosbach I (14 Corps No. 1). Ldst. Btn. Passau II (1 Bav. Corps No. 6).			

HISTORY.

(Bavaria.)

ALSACE.   1915.

1. The 39th Bavarian Reserve Division was formed in February, 1915, on the Alsace front in the vicinity of Ste. Marie aux Mines. (See 30th Bavarian Reserve Division.)

It then comprised the 52d Landwehr Brigade, consisting of the 80th Landwehr Regiment and 29th Ersatz Regiment (since become the 61st), and the 1st Bavarian Ersatz Brigade (81st Landwehr Regiment, 3d and 1st Bavarian Ersatz Regiments). After October, 1915, we find them officially designated "Bavarian."

2. During 1915 and until the beginning of November, 1916, the 39th Bavarian Reserve Division occupied the sector included between the Ban de Sapt and Ste. Marie aux Mines. The elements of the division took part in several local attacks in this region (south of Lusse in February. 1915; at La Fontenelle in June and July, 1915).

ALSACE.   1916.

1. 1916 same sector of Alsace (Ban de Sapt and Ste. Marie aux Mines).

2. In March, 1916, the composition of the 39th Bavarian Reserve Division was modified—the 81st Landwehr Regiment was replaced by the 15th Bavarian Landwehr Regiment, coming from the 1st Bavarian Landwehr Division. In July the division comprised the 1st Bavarian Ersatz Brigade (1st and 3d Bavarian Ersatz Regiments) and the 9th Bavarian Ersatz Brigade (the 15th Bavarian Landwehr Regiment and the 5th Bavarian Ersatz Regiment, the latter having been formed in July).

3. In October the 3d Bavarian Ersatz Regiment was assigned to the 9th Bavarian Reserve Division and the 29th Ersatz Regiment to the 223d Division, both being new formations. From that time on the 39th Bavarian Reserve Division was entirely Bavarian.

In November the 15th Bavarian Landwehr Regiment went over to the 30th Bavarian Reserve Division, which sent the 2d Bavarian Ersatz Regiment in its place to the 39th Bavarian Reserve Division.

VERDUN.

4. Relieved from its sector in the Vosges about November 6, 1916, the 39th Bavarian Reserve Division was sent to the Verdun front in the vicinity of Vaux. It underwent the French attack of December 15, during which certain of its units (5th Bavarian Ersatz Regiment) suffered heavily. It was withdrawn on December 17.

ALSACE.   1917.

1. In the middle of January, 1917, the 39th Bavarian Reserve Division was sent back to its former sector in the vicinity of Ste. Marie aux Mines (Wisembach, Lusse, Provenchères) which it occupied from then on without changing.

VALUE—1917 ESTIMATE.

Except in December, 1916, at Verdun, the 39th Bavarian Reserve Division has always occupied the same sector of the Vosges. Its combat value appears mediocre.

The average age of the men in the 1st and 5th Bavarian Ersatz Regiments is between 30 and 40 years (April to July, 1918).

In February and March, 1918, all the younger elements (20 to 26 years) were withdrawn from the division and sent to active and reserve regiments.

ALSACE.   1918.

1. The 39th Bavarian Reserve Division was still in its sector in Alsace, northwest of Ste. Marie aux Mines, on the 11th of November.

VALUE—1918 ESTIMATE.

It is rated as a fourth-class division. Most of the men are old, the younger men having been combed out in February and March to be sent to other organizations, and although the companies are large—the average ration strength seems to be 200 men—the division has very little combat value.

40th Division.
COMPOSITION.

	1914 Brigade.	1914 Regiment.	1915 Brigade.	1915 Regiment.	1916 Brigade.	1916 Regiment.	1917 Brigade.	1917 Regiment.	1918 Brigade.	1918 Regiment.
Infantry	88. 89. 13 Jag. Btn.	104. 181. 133. 134. 13 Jag. Btn.	88. 89. 13 Jag. Btn.	104. 181. 133. 134. 13 Jag. Btn.	88. 13 Jag. Btn.	104. 181. 134. 13 Jag. Btn.	88.	104. 181. 134.	83.	104. 134. 181.
Cavalry	19 Hus. Rgt.		19 Hus. Rgt.		19 Hus. Rgt. (3 Sqns.).		2 Sqn. 19 Hus. Rgt.		2 Sqn. 19 Hus. Rgt.	
Artillery	40 Brig.: 32 Rgt. 68 Rgt.		40 Brig.: 32 Rgt. 68 Rgt.		40 Brig.: 32 Rgt. 68 Rgt.		40 Artillery Command: 32 Rgt.		40 Art. Command: 32 F. A. Rgt. 403 Ft. A. Btn. 877 Light Am. Col. 960 Light Am. Col. 1408 Light Am. Col.	
Engineers and Liaisons.	1 and 2 Field Cos. 1 Pions. No. 32.		1 and 2 Field Cos. 1 Pion. No. 22. 40 Pont. Engs. 40 Tel. Detch.		1 and 2 Cos. 1 Pion. No. 22. 40 T. M. Co. 40 Pont. Engs. 40 Tel. Detch.		141 Pion. Btn.: 1 and 3 Cos. 22 Pions. 40 T. M. Co. 310 Searchlight. 40 Tel. Detch.		141 Pion. Btn.: 3 Co. 22 Pions. 54 Res. Pion. Co. 40 T. M. Co. 131 Searchlight Section. 40 Signal Command: 40 Tel. Detch. 171 Wireless Detch.	
Medical and Veterinary.							48 Saxon Ambulance Co. 306, 309 Field Hospitals. Vet. Hospital.		48 Ambulance Co. 306 Field Hospital. 309 Field Hospital. 40 Vet. Hospital.	
Transports							Light Mun. Col.			
Attached					Anti-Aircraft Detch.					

HISTORY.

(19th Corps District—Saxony.)

1914.

BELGIUM-MARNE

1. The 40th Division (4th Saxon) formed, with the 24th Division (2d Saxon), the 19th Army Corps, which, at the outbreak of the war, was a part of the 3d Army (Von Hausen). Detraining north of Trèves August 10–12, the division entered the north of Luxemburg on the 13th, Belgium on the 18th. It crossed the Meuse on the 23d above Dinant, and entered France by way of Fumay. If fought on August 30 at Chesnois, reached Semide on September 1, Somme Py on September 2, Châlons on September 4. On liaison with the right wing of the 4th Army, it took part in the battle of the Marne west of Vitry le François. After the battle it retired to Souain.

FLANDERS.

2. At the beginning of October the 19th Army Corps was transferred to Lille. It belonged to the 6th Army (Crown Prince of Bavaria). Attacked by the British troops, it was forced back upon the line between Ploegsteert wood and Grenier wood.

At the end of October the 9th Company of the 107th Infantry Regiment (24th Division) had only 38 men left (letter).

1915.

1. In 1915 and until August 1916 the two divisions of the 19th Army Corps were retained in the zone of Ploegsteert and Grenier wood.

2. Elements of the 40th Division were sent as reenforcements in the battles of Neuve Chapelle (March 1915), of Festubert (May to June 1915) and upon the occasion of the Franco-British offensives in Artois (La Bassee–Souchez, June to October 1915). In March 1915, the 40th Division was definitely reduced to three regiments, having given the 133d Infantry Regiment to the 24th Division.

1916.

SOMME.

1. On August 8, 1916, the 40th Division took part in the battle of the Somme in the region north of Pozières. It was in violent battles and was withdrawn, very much exhausted.

ARTOIS.

2. At the end of August, it went from the Somme front to the sector of Neuve Chapelle–La Bassée Canal, where it remained for six weeks.

SOMME.

3. About the middle of October, it returned to the Somme (sector north of Le Sars–Butte de Warlencourt) for a second period of three weeks during which its losses were again very heavy (the total losses of the 40th Division in August and October on the Somme were 6,127 men).

On October 30, the 7th Company of the 104th Infantry Regiment received at least 75 men as replacements (1917 class) who had had only three months of service.

4. Relieved from the Somme, the Division went into the sector of St. Eloi–Messines about November 11.

1917.

1. The division left the Messines front about March 26, before the beginning of the British offensive at Arras, and remained at rest in the area of Renaix.

FLANDERS.

2. It returned to line on April 23 in the same sector, and was subjected to the artillery preparation for the battle of Messines, which caused it extremely heavy losses. The 104th Infantry Regiment lost 224 men as prisoners.

On June 7, the first day of the attack, it was withdrawn from the front and sent to rest in the vicinity of Bruges and Thielt until July 19.

3. On July 22 it went into line north of Ypres in the sector of Steenstraat–Het–Sas. It suffered the bombardment in the attack of July 31.

ST. QUENTIN.

4. After a rest, in the course of which it was reorganized, it spent several weeks in the sector of Itancourt, in the vicinity of St. Quentin. During the months of August and September it received 2,300 men as replacements. A large number came from the Russian front (244th Reserve Infantry Regiment, 350th Landwehr Regiment, the 19th Landsturm Battalion from the garrison of Posen; besides these, Saxons were withdrawn from the 428th Infantry Regiment and the 8th Landsturm).

FLANDERS.

5. On October 12 the 40th Division was transferred to Flanders for a second time. From October 17 to 27 it occupied the sector of Langewaade-Zevecoten, northeast of Bixschoote, and there underwent the attack of October 27, which again caused it heavy losses.

RUSSIA.

6. The division was then sent to Russia, where it arrived at the end of November. It was there assigned to the 10th Army and took up its position south of Smorgoni, where it still was at the beginning of January, 1918.

RECRUITING.

The 40th Division is purely Saxon.

VALUE—1917 ESTIMATE.

The attitude of the division has generally been passive (especially during the attack of July 31, 1917, north of Ypres).

In the 104th Infantry Regiment (July 22–28) the men scattered under fire, sometimes with their noncommissioned officers, and fled to a distance of 8 kilometers behind the front.

The same thing happened for the period October 17–27. In the 134th Infantry Regiment, which was considered the best regiment of the division, one-half of the 6th Company left the front line on October 24.

Only the assault detachment offered any energetic resistance on October 27, 1917.

1918.

RUSSIA.

1. The 40th Division was identified in the region of Lake Narotch-Niemen for the last time on the 15th of January. It then went into reserve in the vicinity of Vilna.

FRANCE.

2. The division was not identified between the 4th of February, when it was stated as being "on the Eastern front," and the 20th of March, when it was in Lorraine. It very probably came from the East about the end of February.

WOEVRE.

3. On April 15 it relieved the 4th Bavarian Division near Regnieville (west of Pont à Mousson). During this time whenever units were out of line they were intensively trained. It was withdrawn on June 1, its place being taken by the 183d Division.

MARNE.

4. The division entrained at Jaulny the following day and traveled via Rembercourt-Waville-Onville-Chambley-Mars la Tour–Jarny–Conflans–Montmedy–Sedan–Mézières–Rethel, detraining at Asfeld la Ville on the 3d. On the 16th it relieved the 2d Guard Division near Troësnes. This sector was a quiet one until the beginning

of the Allied counteroffensive of July 18. The 40th Division was caught in this drive and was driven northward. On the 24th it was relieved by the Bavarian Ersatz Division and went to rest near Oisy le Verger (northwest of Cambrai).

ARRAS.

5. On the 22d of August the division entered line near Courcelles le Comte (south of Arras), counterattacking the same day. It was withdrawn on the 31st.

YPRES.

6. After a short rest near Roubaix, it relieved the 236th Division southeast of Ypres on September 10. After losing nearly 1,300 prisoners, the division was withdrawn from line near Wervicq, October 8, and went to the Courtrai area, where it rested six days.

7. On the 15th it reenforced the front near Gulleghem (northeast of Menin). It was withdrawn from line in the Vichte sector (east of Courtrai), about the 26th.

8. On November 8 the division returned to line near Avelghem (northeast of Roubaix), and was still in line on the 11th.

VALUE—1918 ESTIMATE.

Until 1918 the 40th (Saxon) Division had been considered as being a second-class unit. It was soon noticed that practically all Saxon troops were not fighting as well as before, and this was particularly true of the 40th Division, for although its men were young and the number of effectives high, it was used in none of the German offensives. It must be considered a third-class division.

41st Division.

COMPOSITION.

	1914 Brigade	1914 Regiment	1915 Brigade	1915 Regiment	1916 Brigade	1916 Regiment	1917 Brigade	1917 Regiment	1918 Brigade	1918 Regiment
Infantry	72. 74.	18. 59. 148. 152.	72. 74.	18. 59. 148. 152.	74. 9 Ldst. Btn.	18. 148. 152.	74.	18. 148. 152.	74.	18. 148. 152.
Cavalry	10 Dragoon Rgt.				10 Drag. Rgt. (3 Sqns.).		1 Sq. 10 Dragoons.		4 Sqn. 10 Drag. Rgt.	
Artillery	41 Brig.: 35 Rgt. 79 Rgt.		41 Brig.: 35 Rgt. 79 Rgt.		41 Brig.: 35 Rgt. 79 Rgt.		41 Art. Command: 79 Rgt.		41 Art. Command: 79 F. A. Rgt. 2 Abt. 15 Ft. A. Rgt. (5, 7, and 8 Btries.). 835 Light Am. Col. 1235 Light Am. Col. 1236 Light Am. Col.	
Engineers and Liaisons.	2 Field Co. 1 Pion. No. 26.		2 Field Co. 1 Pion. No. 26. 41 Pont. Engs. 41 Tel. Detch.		2 Field Co. 1 Pion. No. 26. 41 T. M. Co. 41 Pont. Engs. 41 Tel. Detch.		135 Pion. Btn. 1 and 2 Cos. 26 Pion. 41 T. M. Co. Tel. Detch.		26 Pion. Btn.: 1 Co. 26 Pions. 2 Co. 26 Pions. 41 T. M. Co. 37 Searchlight Section. 41 Signal Command: 41 Tel. Detch. 96 Wireless Detch.	
Medical and Veterinary.							Ambulance Co. 316, 321, 323d Field Hospitals. Vet. Hospital.		261 Ambulance Co. 316 Field Hospital. 323 Field Hospital. 145 Vet. Hospital.	
Transports							Light Mun. Col.		574 M. T. Col.	

Attached.....	41 Cyc. Co.	10 Btry. 7 Res. Ft. A. Rgt. 41 Ft. A. Btry. 65 Carrier Pigeon Loft. 574 Carrier Pigeon Loft. 72 Balloon Sqn. 219 Reconnaissance Flight. 8, 29, and 245 M. T. Col. 140 Art. Observation Section. (Elements attached Aug. 18, 1918. German document.)

HISTORY.

(20th Corps District—Eastern portion of West Prussia.)

1914.

At the outbreak of the war the 41st Division and the 37th Division formed the 20th Army Corps.

RUSSIA.

1. At the beginning of hostilities the 41st Division was engaged against Russia, first in East Prussia, then in Poland, beginning with October. It was at Lodz at the beginning of December, at Skiernewice on the 20th, and fought on the Rawka in January, 1915.

1915.

RUSSIA.

1. In February, 1915, transferred north of the Vistula, it operated until summer between Prasnysz and the valley of Bobr-Narew. From there it was taken to the northern frontier of East Prussia in July and advanced as far as Mitau, from there to Jakobstadt.

1916.

RUSSIA.

1. Until October, 1916, the division occupied the same sector on the Dvina, between Friedrichstadt and Jakobstadt. It underwent a Russian offensive in March, 1916, and took part in an attack on May 10. In these two actions it suffered serious losses.

ROUMANIA.

2. On October 21, the 41st Division, destined to take part in the Roumanian campaign, entrained southeast of Friedrichstadt, traveled by way of Mitau, Grodno, Warsaw, Oppeln, Budapest, Temesvar, and detrained on November 5 at Pay, south of Hatszeg. It went into action in the vicinity of Jiu and advanced almost without fighting. It entered Bucarest on December 6. On the 7th it again took up the pursuit of the Roumanians. On reaching the Sereth the 41st Division encountered the Russians. It remained in line until February 8, 1917. The losses of the division, slight in the battles with the Roumanians, were greater in the Russian attacks.

1917.

FRANCE.

1. Between February 8 and February 15 the 41st Division entrained at Zilibia for the Western Front. (Itinerary: Bucarest – Salzberg – Munich – Ulm – Augsburg – Thionville.) It detrained in Lorraine (Arsweiler, Ruxweiler, Audun le Roman) on February 20.

2. After a month of rest and training in Lorraine, during which it was reorganized (the 148th Infantry Regiment received 600 men as replacements), the division went into line, at the beginning of May, at Bois le Prêtre.

3. Between May 6 and May 9 it was transferred by way of Sedan to Rethel, from which place it marched to the vicinity of Sissonne.

CALIFORNIE PLATEAU.

4. Sent into line in the sector of Hurtebise for a very short stay (May 25–26 to May 28–29), it went into action on the 21st in the vicinity of Chevreux. It took part there in the attack of June 3 upon Californie Plateau, in the course of which its losses were serious (50 to 60 men per company in the 152d Regiment, heavy losses in the 148th Infantry Regiment).

5. The 42d Division remained in the sector of Chevreux until June 25. About July 3 it went to the east of the Butte du Mesnil. It remained in this sector, without any notable occurrences, until the beginning of November.

FLANDERS.

6. On November 12 it was in the vicinity of Staden, Houthulst wood, where it alternated with the 38th Division. Relieved on January 14, 1918, it went to rest near Bruges.

RECRUITING.

The 41st Division is recruited principally from West Prussia. As the region is not very large and has a relatively small population, the 41st Division borrows from other districts (especially the 6th Corps District). It contained a large number of Alsace-Lorrainers during its stay on the Russian front

VALUE—1917 ESTIMATE.

The 41st Division, coming from the Russo-Roumanian front, where it had remained until the beginning of February, 1917, appears to have only a mediocre military value.

In the course of the attack of June 3, 1917, on the Californie Plateau, the retreat of the 148th Infantry Regiment was carried out in a state of extreme confusion.

During its stay on the Champagne front the 41st Division showed no offensive activity. (July 3–November, 1917.)

1918.

FLANDERS.

1. The 41st Division was relieved in the sector north of Ypres by the 38th Division toward the end of January, and went to rest near Bruges. While here the artillery received new guns, and it seems probable that the division was put through a course of training.

2. During the night of February 25–26 the division relieved the 2d Guard Reserve Division south of Westroosebeke (northeast of Ypres). About the 4th of March it was relieved by the 38th Division and went to rest in the Turcoing area.

ARRAS.

3. On the 26th of March the division was identified near Oppy (northeast of Arras). Here it was heavily engaged, and the attack which it attempted broke down through heavy casualties.

ALBERT.

4. The division was identified in the same area on the 28th, but not afterwards, and so it was very likely withdrawn during the next day or two. Early in April the division moved up in support of the 21st Reserve Division in the Beaumont-Hamel region (north of Albert), and during the night of the 7th–8th it relieved the 1st Guard Reserve Division a little farther to the north in the Puisieux sector (east of Hébuterne). On the 14th of April the division extended its front to the south so as to relieve the 24th Division. On the 11th of June it was relieved by the 26th Reserve Division and went to rest and refit in the Douai area.

5. On the 9th of July it relieved the 108th Division east of Villers-Bretonneux (east of Amiens). Here it was caught in the Allied drive of August 8, and after losing over 1,700 prisoners was withdrawn on the 10th.

6. After resting a fortnight immediately behind the front, it came back into line near Cappy (southeast of Bray) on the 25th. In the fighting that followed the division lost more than 800 prisoners, and even more killed and wounded. It was relieved early in September and went to rest and to be reconstituted near Château Salins (northeast of Nancy). On September 8 it received as a draft what was left of the dissolved 18th Reserve Regiment (225th Division disbanded).

ARGONNE.

7. Leaving Metz on October 6 and traveling via St. Juvin, the division reenforced the front near Sommerance (east of Grandpré) on the 9th to meet the American push of the 8th. It was withdrawn on the 31st after having suffered very heavy losses.

8. It rested a day or two immediately in rear of the front, and on the 3d it was thrown in near Nouart (southwest of Stenay), the Americans having attacked again on the 1st. It was again withdrawn on the 8th, and did not come back into line.

VALUE—1918 ESTIMATE.

The 41st has been considered a second-class division. With the exception of its engagements in the spring near Albert and in the Argonne in October and November, it has not done a great deal of fighting during the year; during this fighting, however, it suffered very severely, so that when it was withdrawn on the 8th of November its companies did not have an average combatant strength of 25. On June 6 the commanding general issued an order indicating an increase in the number of instances in which subordinates emphatically refused to accompany their units into line and in which officers neglected to enforce obedience to orders, and insisting that the evil be remedied even though the men had to be shot.

42d Division.

COMPOSITION.

	1914 Brigade.	1914 Regiment.	1915 Brigade.	1915 Regiment.	1916 Brigade.	1916 Regiment.	1917 Brigade.	1917 Regiment.	1918 Brigade.	1918 Regiment.
Infantry	59. 65.	97. 138. 17. 131.	59. 65.	97. 138. 17. 131.	65.	17. 131. 138.	65.	17. 131. 138. Gd. Res. Jäg. Btn.	65.	17. 131. 138.
Cavalry	7 Uhlan Rgt.		1 Sqn. 7 Uhlan Rgt.		1 Sqn. 7 Uhlan Rgt.		1 Sqn. 7 Drag. Rgt.		1 Sqn. 7 Drag. Rgt.	
Artillery	42 Brig.: 8 F. A. Rgt. 15 F. A. Rgt.		42 Brig.: 8 F. A. Rgt. 15 F. A. Rgt.		42 Brig.: 8 F. A. Rgt. 15 F. A. Rgt.		42 Art. Command: 15 F. A. Rgt.		42 Art. Command: 15 F. A. Rgt. 2 Abt. 15 Ft. A. Rgt. (4, 11, and 12 Btries.). 804 Light Am. Col. 1044 Light Am. Col. 1045 Light Am. Col.	
Engineers and Liaisons.	3 Field Co. (1 Pion. Btn. No. 27).		3 and 5 Field Cos. (1 Pion. Btn. No. 27). 42 Pont. Engs. 42 Tel. Detch.		3 and 5 Field Cos. (1 Pion. Btn. No. 27). 42 T. M. Co. 42 Tel. Detch. 42 Pont. Engs.		(1/27 or 136 Pion. Btn.): 3 Field Co. 27 Pions. 5 Field Co. 27 Pions. 42 T. M. Co. 229 Searchlight Section. 345 Searchlight Section. Tel. Detch.		27 Pion. Btn.: 3 Co. 27 Pions 5 Co. 27 Pions. 42 T. M. Co. 14 Searchlight Section. 42 Signal Command: 42 Tel. Detch. 147 Wireless Detch.	
Medical and Veterinary.							263 Ambulance Co. Field Hospital. Vet. Hospital.		263 Ambulance Co. 269 Field Hospital. 368 Field Hospital. 162 Vet. Hospital.	
Transports							M. T. Col.		575 M. T. Col.	

HISTORY.

(21st Corps District—Lorraine.)

1914.

LORRAINE.

1. Upon mobilization, the 42d Division and the 31st Division formed the 21st Army Corps.

It was a part of the 6th Army (Prince Rupprecht of Bavaria), and fought, at the beginning of August, 1914, across the Lorraine frontier, in the vicinity of Château Salins, Dieuze, Rechicourt (Aug. 5–12). Engaged on the 20th northeast of Dieuze, the 42d Division reached Lunéville on the 22d and attacked Rehainviller and Gerbeviller on the 24th. These days had been very costly. On August 26 the 121st Infantry Regiment was reduced to 31 officers and 1,562 men. (Official Document.)

2. At the beginning of September it was sent to reenforce the 2d Bavarian Corps. On September 3 it was in the vicinity of Moyen–Domptail. It retired to Dieuze (Sept. 11–13) and entrained at Boulay on the 18th, for Cambrai.

SOMME.

3. On September 24 it was on the Somme. If fought at Gruny, Maucourt, in the vicinity of Chaulnes-Pressoire (end of September to beginning of October). It took up its position on the Chaulnes front, along the road from Amiens to St. Quentin (November–December).

1915.

1. The 42d Division occupied the lines north of Chaulnes until the end of January, 1915. On December 26, the losses of the 131st Infantry Regiment since the beginning of the campaign amounted to 87 officers and 3,233 men. (Official List of Casualties.)

2. About January 25 the 42d Division was relieved and entrained for the Eastern Front with the 31st Division (21st Army Corps).

3. Concentrated in East Prussia at the beginning of February, it formed a part of the Hindenburg Army which was to force the Russians across the frontier.

4. From the vicinity of Augustowo (Feb. 14) it advanced rapidly to the east; it reached Sopockin on the 20th, and took up its position with the 21st Army Corps on the line Sopockin–Chtabine (north of Grodno). On March 9 the violent Russian counterattacks caused it heavy losses.

MARIAMPOL.

5. At the beginning of March the 42d Division bore to the north; it was at Kalwarjia on March 26; occupied the vicinity of Mariampol on April 2. It fought in this sector from March 29 to April 24 and remained there until August. (On Apr. 13 the losses of the first two battalions of the 131st Infantry Regiment since the 6th of February had been 1,672 men, according to the Official Casualty List. The 7th Company had only 65 men left on Apr. 7.)

VILNA.

6. Renewing its forward march, the division reached Vilna on August 30; continuing toward the east, it reached Herviaty–Vorniany on September 20, then went toward Lake Narotch, vicinity of Postavy, where the front became stable.

In the autumn the 97th Infantry Regiment was transferred to the 108th Division, a new formation.

1916.

LAKE NAROTCH.

1. The 42d Division held its positions at Lake Narotch until April, 1917.

2. At the end of March, 1916, it sustained the Russian attacks and suffered great losses.

1917.

GALICIA.

1. On April 24, 1917, the 42d Division was relieved from the sector of Lake Narotch and entrained at Vilna for the Western Front. The activity along the Galician front caused its itinerary to be modified, and from Warsaw it was sent to Lemberg. In reserve first, it went into action on July 20 in the German counteroffensive of Brzezany, which took it to the region south of Tarnopol (Grjimalov, July 31).

RIGA.

2. Withdrawn from the Galician front at the beginning of August, it entrained at Lemberg on the 24th, and was transferred to Neugut (between Mitau and Jakobstadt) on August 27. It took part in the advance to Riga; one of its regiments crossed the Dvina, in the vicinity of Uxkull, on September 1.

OESEL ISLAND.

3. At the end of September it was sent to Libau, where important forces were being concentrated for the occupation of the islands in the Baltic. On October 12 the 131st Infantry Regiment landed on the Oesel Island, which it occupied until November 1. The 138th Infantry Regiment remained at Moon until October 25. At the beginning of November the 42d Division was transferred to the vicinity of Kovel. At the end of November it took over a calm sector in the vicinity of Kachovka.

FRANCE.

4. Entraining at Kovel on December 23, it arrived in France on December 28. (Itinerary: Warsaw–Thorn–Posen–Leipzig–Dortmund–Cologne–Herbestal–Brussels. It detrained at Ascq on the 28th.)

5. After a stay in the vicinity of Lille, it relieved the 4th Division east of Armentières on January 23, 1918.

RECRUITING.

As the regional system of recruiting could not furnish dependable elements, the 42d Division is principally recruited from Westphalia and the Rhine Province. The Alsace-Lorrainers were fairly numerous, however, during the stay of the division on the Russian front.

VALUE—1917 ESTIMATE.

The 42d Division occupied the Eastern Front from February, 1915, until the end of December, 1917.

In the offensive operations in which the 42d Division took part in 1917 the successes appear to have been fairly easy. The greater part of the time it has not had to sustain any serious action and its losses have been comparatively slight.

1918.

BATTLE OF THE LYS.

1. The division held the Armentiéres sector until it was relieved about March 22 by the 32d Division. On April 9 it reenforced the battle front near Merris. It was engaged in heavy fighting, and between April 9 and 16 the losses of the division amounted to 50 per cent of the strength. On April 17 it was relieved by the 12th Division.

2. The division came in on the quiet Lens sector on April 25–26, relieving the 220th Division. It held the sector until June 25, when it was relieved by the 36th Reserve Division and moved to the region southwest of Soissons, where on June 30 it relieved the 14th Division. It suffered from the French attack of July 18, losing 1,400 prisoners. It was withdrawn about July 22.

3. The division rested nearly a month undergoing reconstitution by elements from the dissolved 211th Division. The 390th Regiment was completely merged with the 42d Division. From Laon the division moved to Rethel.

CHAMPAGNE.

4. From its entry into the Champagne line on August 22 in relief of the 28th Division until October 1 it was engaged in resisting the French offensive operations in Champagne, during which period it lost about 2,000 prisoners. The division was withdrawn on October 1. After two weeks in the second line the division returned to line about October 14 near Olizy. It continued in line until the armistice. After November 3 the division was opposite the left flank of the American front.

VALUE—1918 ESTIMATE.

The division was rated as third class. It was used as an attack division in the Lys offensive, but thereafter was employed solely on the defensive. The division had a good composition with a large percentage of men of the younger classes.

43d Reserve Division.

COMPOSITION.

	1914		1915		1916		1917		1918[1]	
	Brigade.	Regiment.	Brigade.	Regiment.	Brigade.	Regiment.	Brigade.	Regiment.	Brigade.	Regiment.
Infantry	85 Res. 86 Res. 15 Res. Jag. Btn.	201 Res. 202 Res. 203 Res. 204 Res. Jag. Btn.	85 Res. 86 Res. 15 Res. Jag. Btn.	201 Res. 202 Res. 203 Res. 204 Res. Jag. Btn.	85 Res. 86 Res. 15 Res. Jag. Btn.	201 Res. 202 Res. 203 Res. 204 Res. Jag. Btn.	85 Res.	201 Res. 202 Res. 203 Res.	85 Res.	201 Res. 202 Res. 203 Res.
Cavalry	43 Res. Cav. Detch.		43 Res. Cav. Detch.		43 Res. Cav. Detch.		43 Res. Cav. Detch. 2 Sqn. 17 Hus. Rgt.		43 Res. Cav. Detch.	
Artillery	43 Res. F. A. Rgt. (9 Btries.).		43 Res. F. A. Rgt.		43 Res. F. A. Rgt.		Art. Command: 43 Res. F. A. Rgt.		(?) Art. Command: 43 Res. F. A. Rgt.	
Engineers and Liaisons.	43 Res. Pion. Co.		43 Res. Pion. Co. 43 Res. Pont. Engs.		43 Res. Pion. Co. 243 T. M. Co. 43 Res. Pont. Engs.		343 Pion. Btn.: 43 Res. Pion. Co. 4 Field Co. 17 Pion. Btn. 243 T. M. Co. 443 Tel. Detch.		343 Pion. Btn.: 4 Co. 2 Pion. Btn. No. 17. 1 Res. Co. 23 Pions. 43 Res. Pion. Co. 243 T. M. Co. 443 Tel. Detch.	
Medical and Veterinary.			43 Res. Ambulance Co.				525 Ambulance Co. 72 Res. Field Hospital. 73 Res. Field Hospital. Vet. Hospital.		525 Ambulance Co. 72 Res. Field Hospital. 237 Vet. Hospital.	
Transports							730 T. M. Col.		730 M. T. Col.	

[1] Composition at the time of dissolution, September, 1918.

HISTORY.

(From all of the Prussian territory, by selection, in the same manner as the guard.)

1914.

1. The 43d Reserve Division (first series of reserve divisions engaged in October, 1914) formed at this time, with the 44th Reserve Division, the 22d Reserve Corps. It was formed from the regimental recruit depots of the guard, and has preserved from that time a selective system of recruiting from the whole of the Prussian territory.

2. Going into training at the camp of Doeberitz at the beginning of September, the 43d Reserve Division entrained on October 13 for Belgium, and on the 19th it began fighting in the vicinity of Dixmude, Merckem, Bixschoote, etc. It was in action there until the end of November.

YSER.

3. After the battle of the Yser the elements of the division occupied different parts of the front between Ypres and Nieuport.

1915.

FLANDERS.

1. At the beginning of January, 1915, the 86th Reserve Brigade was in line at Westende.

2. About the end of February the 43d Reserve Division was reconcentrated and then sent to rest in the vicinity of Menin–Roulers until April 25.

ARTOIS.

3. In May elements of the division were holding the sector Bixschoote–Boesinghe (North of the Ypres salient). Another part of the division was sent as a reenforcement north of Arras (Souchez) to oppose the French offensive. The 202d Reserve Infantry Regiment lost 76 officers and 1,320 men at Notre Dame de Lorette (Official List of Casualties).

RUSSIA.

4. About the beginning of July the 86th Reserve Brigade was transferred to Russia and took part in the offensive of Mackensen in Poland. Between May 15 and September 29 the 204th Reserve Infantry Regiment listed as casualties 63 officers and 3,511 men. (Official List of Casualties.)

CHAMPAGNE–SERBIA.

5. The 85th Reserve Brigade, sent to Lorraine (Xivray), then to Woevre (July to September), took part in the battle of Champagne (end of September), and then rejoined the rest of the division in Serbia, where the 43d Reserve Division took part in the campaign in October.

1916.

FRANCE.

1. The division left Serbia to return to France at the end of January and beginning of February, 1916.

VERDUN.

2. After a rest in the vicinity of Valenciennes (February–March) it was sent to the Verdun front at the end of March, and went into action west of the Meuse on April 10 (attacks of Bethincourt and the Mort Homme), where it suffered heavy losses between April 10 and May 25. The 12th Company of the 201st Reserve Infantry Regiment received not less than 185 men as replacements during the month of May. (Document.)

3. Toward the end of May the 43d Reserve Division was withdrawn from the front and sent to rest in the Thionville area. At Verdun it had lost 50 per cent of its infantry.

RUSSIA.

4. At the middle of June it entrained at Novion Porcien and was again sent to Russia. (Itinerary: Charleville–Trèves–Cassel–Leipzig–Dresden–Breslau–Cracow–

Lemberg–Stojanow (southwest of Sokal.) The 204th Reserve Infantry Regiment detrained on June 19.

5. On the Russian front the division was engaged west of Loutsk in the German counteroffensive in June. (Its losses may be estimated from the fact that the. 12th Company of the 201st Reserve Infantry Regiment received replacements of 152 men in July and August, the 3d Company at least 145 men from July 9 to 29.)

FRANCE.

6. On November 15 the division was brought back to the Western Front. (Itinerary. Oderberg–Leipzig–Frankfort–Mayence–Thionville–Sedan–Thourout.) Reduced to three regiments by the assignment of the 204th Reserve Infantry Regiment to the 218th Division, a new formation, it was at rest for almost a month in the vicinity of Rethel.

VERDUN.

7. In consequence of the French attack of December 15 north of Verdun, the division was concentrated in the vicinity of Azannes. On December 17 it relieved the remnants of the 10th Division in the Chambrettes sector.

1917.

1. The 43d Reserve Division remained at Verdun until January 31, 1917, without being engaged in any important action. However, it suffered rather heavy losses there.

CHAMPAGNE.

2. After a rest in Alsace, the division was sent to Champagne, where, on February 22, it reenforced the front between Loivre and east of the Cavaliers du Courcy. The French attack of April 16 caused it serious losses.

ARGONNE.

3. Relieved at the end of April, and reorganized, it went back into line in the calm sector of Vauquois about May 9; the 12th Company of the 201st Reserve Infantry Regiment was filled up by the arrival of 100 men (1918 class; men from the 613th and 614th dissolved Infantry Regiments).

4. At the end of May the division was withdrawn from the Argonne. It was rested and reorganized first in the Ardennes, then in the vicinity of Laon.

CHEMIN DES DAMES.

5. From July 18 to 20, it went into the sector Panthéon–Épine du Chevregny (south of Pargny–Filain) and almost at once underwent the artillery preparation and the French attack of July 30 which caused it heavy losses, increased by the counterattacks which it attempted on July 31 and August 10. On July 30 the 12th Company of the 202d Reserve Infantry Regiment had only 5 noncommissioned officers and 56 men left (document). On August 10 the 201st Reserve Infantry Regiment was almost completely destroyed and left 124 men as prisoners south of La Royère.

6. The 43d Reserve Division was relieved from the Chemin des Dames on August 23 and sent to rest until the end of September in the vicinity of Laon. It was filled up and reorganized.

LA MALMAISON.

· 7. Receiving training at the beginning of October in view of an offensive which was to anticipate the expected French attack, the elements of the 43d Reserve Division were engaged, beginning with October 15, to reenforce weakened divisions at Vaudesson, La Malmaison, and Bruyères. They underwent the attack of October 23, which caused them heavy losses (53 officers, 2,190 men, prisoners). The remnants of the division were relieved on the Ailette on October 28.

RUSSIA.

8. The division was sent to Russia soon afterwards, where it detrained on November 11, in the vicinity of Baranovitchi, after five days' travel. It then relieved the 201st Division, scheduled to go to France.

The 43d Reserve Division was recruited, as was the guard in which it had its origin, from the whole of the Prussian territory. The trained men (returned, wounded, and sick), who figure in the reenforcements which it received, had the same origin (Guard, 1st Reserve Guard Division, 261st and 262d Reserve Guard Ersatz Divisions, Guard Landsturm Battalions, etc.). In April, 1917, the division absorbed a part of the 613th and 614th Regiments formed from the Guard recruit depots and dissolved on March 31.

VALUE—1917 ESTIMATE.

The 43d Reserve Division has always been considered a very good organization (December, 1917).

On August 10, 1917, south of La Royère, the 201st Ersatz Regiment attacked "with very great energy."

In October, 1917, at La Malmaison, the 43d Reserve Division was brought up for reenforcement as an attacking division.

Because of its recent losses (in the attack of Oct. 3) the 43d Reserve Division needs to be completely reorganized before going into action (December, 1917).

It is to be noted that all the recruits of the division come from the Guard recruit depots. (After the losses suffered on Apr. 16, 1917, the division received 3,000 men from the depots of Brandenburg.)

The human material at the disposition of the division is of high quality.

1918.

1. The division left Russia on February 9 and arrived at the Camp Alten-Grabon near Magdeburg about the middle of February. After resting there about five weeks the division entrained on March 18 and traveled via Bielefeld–Gladbach–Aachen–Visé – Hasselt - Louvain - Brussels - Denderleeuw –Audenarde – Courtrai – Tourcoing to Lille, where the regiment detrained on the 22d, billeting at Loos. On the night of April 1–2 the 202d Reserve Infantry Regiment marched via Emmerin and Wattignies to Herrin, continuing on the night of April 2–3 via Chemy–Camphin–Ostricourt to Malmaison and thence to Herrin-Lietard. On April 4 the regiment proceeded to Noyelles-Godault, on the 5th back to Malmaison, and thence on the 7th to Billy Berclau.

La Bassee Canal.

2. The division was engaged at Festubert on April 9. The objective of the division was to break through the enemy's positions, force the passage of the Lawe and the La Bassee Canals, and capture the heights of Hinges and the town of Bethum. It was held up by British resistance at Festubert and did not penetrate farther. On April 29 it was relieved by the 9th Reserve Division.

Somme.

3. After its relief, the division rested in the area south of Lille until June 24, when it relieved the 24th Reserve Division at Bouzencourt. Until August 8, it held the sector on the Somme. In the fighting in August, the division lost 600 prisoners. On August 20 it returned to line at Bray and was engaged until the end of the month. The total number of prisoners lost by the division in these two engagements was 1,100.

4. Early in September the division was broken up. The 203d Reserve Regiment was turned into the Guard Ersatz Division, the 202d Reserve Regiment to the 2d Guard Division.

VALUE—1918 ESTIMATE.

The division was rated as third class. Its complete failure on the La Bassee attack in April and its subsequently long retention in line on the Somme prepared the way for its dissolution about the first of September.

44th Reserve Division.

COMPOSITION.

	1914		1915		1916		1917		1918	
	Brigade.	Regiment.	Brigade.	Regiment.	Brigade.	Regiment.	Brigade.	Regiment.	Brigade.	Regiment.
Infantry	87 Res. 88 Res. 16 Res. Jag. Btn.	205 Res. 206 Res. 207 Res. 208 Res.	87 Res. 88 Res. 16 Res. Jag. Btn.	205 Res. 206 Res. 207 Res. 208 Res.	87 Res. 88 Res. 16 Res. Jag. Btn.	205 Res. 206 Res. 207 Res. 208 Res.	87 Res.	205 Res. 206 Res. 208 Res.	87 Res.	205 Res. 206 Res. 208 Res.
Cavalry	44 Res. Cav. Detch.		44 Res. Cav. Detch.		44 Res. Cav. Detch.		44 Res. Cav. Detch.		4 Sqn. 7 Drag. Rgt.	
Artillery	44 Res. F. A. Rgt. (9 Btries.)		44 Res. F. A. Rgt.		44 Reg. F. A. Rgt.		(?) Art. command: 44 Res. F. A. Rgt.		44 Res. F. A. Rgt. 2 Abt. 21 Ft. A. Rgt. (4 and 6 Btries.). 706 Light Am. Col. 828 Light Am. Col. 1322 Light Am. Col.	
Engineers and liaisons.	44 Pion. Co.		44 Res. Pion. Co. 44 Res. Pont. Engs.		44 Res. Pion. Co. 5 Field Co. 29 Pion. Rgt. 244 T. M. Co. 44 Res. Pont. Engs.		344 Pion. Btn. 44 Res. Pion. Co. 5 Field Co. 29 Pion. Btn. 244 T. M. Co. 306 Searchlight Sect. 444 Tel. Detch.		344 Pion. Btn.: 5 Co. 29 Pions. 44 Res. Pion. Co. 244 T. M. Co. 21 Searchlight Section. 250 Searchlight Section. 444 Signal Command: 444 Tel. Detch. 86 Wireless Detch.	
Medical and Veterinary.	....		44 Res. Ambulance Co.		....		526 Ambulance Co. 73 Res. Field Hospital. 238 Vet. Hospital.		526 Ambulance Co. 71 Res. Field Hospital. 75 Res. Field Hospital. 238 Vet. Hospital.	
Transports	....		....				M. T. Col.		731 M. T. Col.	

HISTORY.

(3d Corps District—Brandenburg.)

1914.

YSER.

1. The 44th Reserve Division, formed between August and October, 1914, like the other division of the 22d Reserve Corps (43d Reserve Division), was trained at Jueterbog Camp and entrained on October 12. Detraining at Termonde, it was in action at Dixmude and at Bixschoote in October and November and lost very heavily. On November 9 the 3d Battalion of the 205th Reserve Infantry Regiment was reduced to 153 men. (Notebook.)

2. After the battle of the Yser, it occupied several sectors north of Ypres.

1915.

NIEUPORT.

1. The 44th Reserve Division remained on the Flanders front until the month of June, 1915.

2. On June 7 the division was relieved from the Lombartzyde-Nieuport sector and transferred to the Eastern Front.

RUSSIA.

3. Arriving in Russia in the middle of June, it took part in the Mackensen offensive— battles of pursuit on the Galician frontier (June 22–July 16); battle of Krasnostaw (July 19–28) and of Biskupice (July, 29–30); battles up to the Bug (July 31 to Aug. 19); taking of Brest-Litovsk on August 26.

SERBIA.

4. In October it was sent to Serbia and went through the entire campaign.

5. At the end of December, it was sent to rest in Hungary.

1916.

FRANCE.

1. At the end of January, 1916, the 44th Reserve Division entrained for France. (Itinerary: Inddis–Budapest–Vienna–Rosenheim–Cologne–Charleroi.) It detrained at Landrecies–Valenciennes on February 6. It did some work on the Somme front (the 306th Reserve Infantry Regiment near Peronne; the 208th Reserve Infantry Regiment remained at Mesle until Mar. 14) and then entrained at Landrecies on March 24.

VERDUN (MORT-HOMME).

2. Concentrated in the vicinity of Buzancy, at the end of March, the division went to the left bank of the Meuse. On April 11 the 86th Reserve Brigade went into line in the Mort-Homme sector. The 44th Reserve Division was in action beginning with April 25, and suffered very heavy losses (April–May).

3. On June 5 the 44th Reserve Division was withdrawn from the front, reorganized, and sent to rest in the vicinity of Sedan (replacements from the 3d and 5th Corps Districts).

SOMME.

4. Transferred to the Somme (July 2 and 3), the division sent some of its elements into action on the Estrees-Belloy front on July 4. It underwent the French attacks between these two villages (July 6–10) and launched a violent counterattack on the 7th and 8th. These engagements caused it severe losses (9 officers and 522 men as prisoners).

LASSIGNY.

5. Relieved on July 10, it spent a few days at rest, and on July 20 entered the line in the sector of Lassigny–Beuvraignes.

Between June 1 and July 15 the 205th Reserve Infantry Regiment, after it had received men from the Beverloo depot, had received at least 145 men for its 5th Company, 167 for its 8th; on July 14 the 1st Company of the 206th Infantry Regiment received at least 128 men; some (1917 class) had only been in the service since May 5.

SOMME.

6. Sent to rest in the middle of September, the 44th Reserve Division again went into action on the Somme (Berny en Santerre–Genermont), between October 9 and October 28, and again lost very heavily.

7. It then came back into the Lassigny sector, where it was reorganized (reinforcements of 300 to 400 men per regiment). It transferred the 207th Reserve Infantry Regiment to the 228th Division, a new organization.

1917.

LASSIGNY (RETREAT).

1. In March, 1917, the 44th Reserve Division took part in the German retreat and left the lines at Lassigny to take up its position between La Fère and Moy (Mar. 25).

LA MALMAISON (WOËVRE).

2. Sent into the reserve of the army at the end of March in the vicinity of Marle St. Gobert, the division was concentrated on April 15 in the vicinity of Monampteuil–Filain (Apr. 20). On the 21st, on both banks of the Oise–Aisne Canal, it relieved the remnants of the division decimated by the French offensive of April 16 and at La Malmaison received the new attack of May 5. Very much exhausted (1,670 prisoners), it was replaced at once (night of May 5–6) and transferred to the Woëvre first and then to the Côtes de Meuse northeast of St. Mihiel, where the division took over the sector of Chevaliers after being reorganized. It was withdrawn October 25.

FLANDERS.

3. On November 10 it went into line in Flanders, north of Passchendaele.

ARTOIS.

Relieved at the end of the month, it was sent to the sector of Neuve Chapelle. It was still there March 19, 1918.

RECRUITING.

The 44th Reserve Division was mixed at the time of its formation (one regiment from Hanover), but has since become purely Brandenburg by its reduction to three regiments. However, this does not prevent the occasional introduction of extraneous elements—for example, in July, 1916 (urgent call for available reserve at Beverloo). The 1917 class then made its appearance on July 12, 1916 (in the 208th Reserve Infantry Regiment); the 1918 class on April 13, 1917 (in the 205th Reserve Infantry Regiment).

VALUE—1917 ESTIMATE.

The 44th Reserve Division has been designated an assault division.

The 44th Reserve Division has not shown any great military value in the course of the battles which it went into north of the Aisne. Certain elements, however, fought well. One must note that the combat effectives of the division were very much reduced by the artillery preparation before the attack of May 5, 1917.

After the battle of the Aisne, the division made up for its losses with elements from the field recruit depots and two replacements, one coming from Warsaw (1917 class), and the other from the 5th Corps District (mostly returned wounded).

1918.

LA BASSEE CANAL.

1. About April 1st, the division was retired to the second line, from which it eturned on the night of April 12–13 to attack near Locon on the 13th. It held a sector n that region until its relief by the 220th Division on May 6–7.

2. The division rested at Courrieres for three weeks. On May 26 it relieved the 9th Division west of Vieux Berqum. Here it remained until July 4, when it was elieved by the 207th Division.

SOMME.

3. The division moved to the area northwest of Tournai early in July. There it ested and received drafts until its return to line northeast of Martinpuich on August 6. The division fell back on Flers (27th), Beaulencourt (1st), Villers au Flos (2d), Ruyaulcourt (3d), southwest of Havrincourt (7th). It was withdrawn from line on September 10 after losing 700 prisoners.

4. It was out of line for four weeks and unconfirmed reports indicated its presence t Metz. However, it again appeared in line on the Cambrai-St. Quentin front on October 10, north of Montay. It fought around Le Cateau until the end of the month vhen it was withdrawn from line north of Robersart. About the fourth of November he division was back in line at Locquignol and in the closing days of the war it fell back to Maubeurge.

VALUE—1918 ESTIMATE.

The division was rated as first class. It was not used in any of the major offensives of 1918.

44th Landwehr Division.

COMPOSITION.

	1916		1917		1918		1918	
	Brigade.	Regiment.	Brigade.	Regiment.	Brigade.	Regiment.	Brigade.	Regiment.
Infantry	Rosenberg.	93 Ldw. 382 Ldw.	44 Ldw.	81 Ldw. 93 Ldw. 382 Ldw.	44 Ldw.	81 Ldw. 93 Ldw. 382 Ldw.	(?)	81 Ldw. 93 Ldw. 382 Ldw.
Cavalry					3 Sqn. 2 Uhlan Rgt.		3 Sqn. 2 Uhlan Rgt.	
Artillery			Art. Command: 270 F. A. Rgt.		134 Art. Command: 4, 5, 6, and 8 Abtl. 254 Ldw. F. A. Rgt. 828 and 837 F. A. Btries.		134 Art. Command. 61 Res. F. A. Rgt. 822 Light Am. Col. 1268 Light Am. Col. 1321 Light Am. Col.	
Engineers and Liaisons.			(444) Pion. Btn.: 411 T. M. Co. 544 Tel. Detch.		(444) Pion. Btn.: 2 Landst. Co. 7 C. Dist. Pions. 4 Landst. Co. 7 C. Dist. Pions. 411 T. M. Co. 544 Tel. Detch.		444 Pion. Btn.: 4 Landst. Co. 7 C. Dist. Pions. 244 Searchlight Section. 544 Signal Command: 544 Tel. Detch. 63 Wireless Detch.	
Medical and Veterinary.			274 Ambulance Co. 380 Field Hospital Vet. Hospital.		274 Ambulance Co. 268 Field Hospital. 360 Field Hospital. Vet. Hospital.		274 Ambulance Co. 360 Field Hospital.	
Transports			M. T. Col.		M. T. Col.			

HISTORY.

81st Landwehr Regiment: 18th Corps District—Grand Duchy of Hesse and Hesse-Nassau.   93d Landwehr Regiment: 4th Corps District—Prussian Saxony.   382d Landwehr Regiment: 7th Corps District—Westphalia.

1916.

LORRAINE.

1. The 44th Landwehr Division was formed in April, 1917, by the grouping of the 4th Landwehr Brigade (93d and 382d Landwehr Regiments) and the 81st Landwehr Regiment.   The latter regiment had been successively attached to the 39th Reserve Division (area of St. Dié until the spring of 1916), to the Bavarian Ersatz Division near Verdun until the end of 1916) and finally to the 54th Division (Flirey).

2. The 44th Landwehr Brigade, called the Rosenberg Brigade until July, 1916, united in December, 1915, on the left bank of the Moselle, the 1st Landwehr Ersatz Regiment, afterwards the 382d Landwehr Regiment (formerly attached to the Norroy Brigade) and the 93d Landwehr, former Von Gundlach Regiment of the Graudenz Corps, formed from two of the six surplus Landwehr battalions of the 4th Corps District and of the 38th Landwehr Brigade Ersatz Battalion (Hanover), identified Jean-lelize in June, 1915.   It was attached to the 8th Ersatz Division at the beginning of 1916.

3. The 44th Landwehr Brigade held the Moselle front on the left bank of the river until it was transformed into the 44th Landwehr Division.

1917.

BOIS LE PRÊTRE.

1. The formation of the 44th Landwehr Division in April, 1917, had no effect upon the position of the elements which entered into its composition.   They continued to hold the left bank of the Moselle (Bois le Prêtre) until October, 1917.

2. In this sector the 44th Landwehr Division gave signs of its presence only by a few unimportant raids.

UPPER ALSACE.

3. On October 13, 1917, the 44th Landwehr Division was relieved from Bois le Prêtre, entrained on the 16th at Arnaville, Pagny, Bayonville, and was transferred to Alsace, detraining at Sierentz and Bartenheim.   During the night of the 18th–19th it went into line on both banks of the Rhône-Rhine Canal.

On November 7 the division suffered some losses at Schoenholz.

VALUE—1917 ESTIMATE.

Composed for the most part of elderly men accustomed to holding calm sectors, the 44th Landwehr Division is the antithesis of an attack division.   However, it knows how to organize and maintain a position and there is reason to believe that it would do well on the defensive.

Each of its regiments possesses an assault troop.

1918.

1. The division held the Altkirch sector throughout 1918 until the armistice.   The sector remained absolutely quiet.

VALUE—1918 ESTIMATE.

The division was rated as fourth class.

45th Reserve Division.
COMPOSITION.

	1914 Brigade.	1914 Regiment.	1915 Brigade.	1915 Regiment.	1916 Brigade.	1916 Regiment.	1917 Brigade.	1917 Regiment.	1918 Brigade.	1918 Regiment.
Infantry	89 Res. 90 Res. 17 Res. Jag. Btn.	209 Res. 212 Res. 210 Res. 211 Res.	89 Res. 90 Res. 17 Res. Jag. Btn.	209 Res. 212 Res. 210 Res. 211 Res.	89 Res. 90 Res. 17 Res. Jag. Btn.	209 Res. 212 Res. 210 Res. 211 Res.	90 Res.	210 Res. 211 Res. 212 Res.	90 Res.	210 Res. 211 Res. 212 Res.
Cavalry	45 Res. Cav. Detch.		45 Res. Cav. Detch.		45 Res. Cav. Detch.		45 Res. Cav. Detch.		45 Res. Cav. Detch.	
Artillery	45 Res. F. A. Regt. (9 Btries.).		45 Res. F. A. Rgt.		45 Res. F. A. Rgt.		(?) Art. Command: 45 Res. F. A. Rgt.		45 Res. F. A. Rgt. 1 Abt. 20 Ft. A. Rgt. (1, 2, and 4 Btries.). 773 Light Am. Col. 839 Light Am. Col. 1210 Light Am. Col.	
Engineers and Liaisons.	45 Pion. Co.		45 Res. Pion. Co. 45 Res. Pont. Engs.		45 Res. Pion Co. 90 Res. Pion. Co. 245 T. M. Co. 45 Res. Pont. Engs.		II/21 or 345 Pion. Btn.: 6 Co. 21 Pions. 45 Res. Pion. Co. 245 T. M. Co. 294 Searchlight Section. 23 Res. Searchlight Section. 445 Tel. Detch.		345 Pion. Btn.: 6 Co. 21 Pions 45 Res. Pion. Co. 245 T. M. Co. — Searchlight Section: 445 Signal Command: 445 Tel. Detch. 141 Wireless Detch.	
Medical and Veterinary.			45 Res. Ambulance Co......				527 Ambulance Co. 75 Res. Field Hospital. 76 Res. Field Hospital. 77 Res. Field Hospital. Vet. Hospital.		527 Ambulance Co. 76 Res. Field Hospital. 77 Res. Field Hospital. 445 Vet. Detch.	
Transports.							732 M. T. Col.		732 M. T. Col.	

HISTORY.

(2d Corps District—Pomerania.)

1914.

1. The 45th Reserve Division (forming the 23d Reserve Corps with the 46th Reserve Division) belongs to the series of divisions formed between August and October, 1914. t received its training at the Jueterbog Camp, entrained on October 12, and detrained t Alost in Belgium.

YSER.

2. On October 21, 1914, the 45th Reserve Division was engaged in the battle of the Yser in the vicinity of Noordschoote-Steenstraat, and suffered serious losses in the course of the battles, which were prolonged until November (from Oct. 15 to Nov. 11 i2 officers and 1,669 men in the 212th Reserve Infantry Regiment, according to the Official List of Casualties).

3. In December elements of the division were in line in the vicinity of Bixschoote.

1915.

FLANDERS.

1. The division remained in Belgium and in the vicinity of Armentières during he entire year of 1915 and the first half of 1916.

2. On April 22, 1915, it attacked in the Steenstraat sector and occupied the village of Lizerne, which counter attacks obliged it to abandon.

1916.

FLANDERS.

1. The 45th Reserve Division continued to occupy the zone north of Ypres (Steenstraat-Boesinghe) until March 3, 1916. The 209th and 212th Reserve Infantry Regiments were temporarily detached (from the end of January to the beginning of March) and assigned to the 26th Division in the Becelaere sector.

MESSINES.

2. On March 12 the division took over the sector of Messines, south of Ypres. Until he month of September it did not take part in any important action.

SOMME.

3. At the beginning of September it was withdrawn from Flanders, sent to the Somme, and engaged in the sector of Thiepval-Martinpuich (Sept. 9 to 24). On September 15 it withstood the British attack between Courcelette and Thiepval, where t lost very heavily.

OISE.

4. After a short rest in the vicinity of Bapaume the division was sent to the Noyon rea. It transferred the 209th Reserve Infantry Regiment to the 207th Division, a new formation. At the beginning of October it went into line on the left bank of he Oise at Tracy le Val. In the interval, in order to fill up its regiments, it had o borrow from the Landsturm battalions of the 2d Corps District (men of the Landsturm 2d Ban, trained and untrained from the classes 1892 to 1894).

1917.

1. January 22, 1917, the 45th Reserve Division left the sector of Tracy le Val for he Sissonne Camp, and received training there for three weeks. Its regiments had been practically re-formed. Between September 24, 1916, and February 21, 1917, he 210th Reserve Infantry Regiment had received 79 noncommissioned officers and ,522 men.

2. On February 12 it went into the sector Osly–Courtil–Chevillecourt, west of Soissons. In March it retired in the direction of Coucy le Château; it was put in reserve

AISNE–CHEMIN DES DAMES.

3. On April 10, in anticipation of the French attack, the elements of the division were concentrated near Filain. On the 7th the 210th Reserve Infantry Regiment was in action south of the Ailette Canal (east of Vauxaillon). The other regiments were sent west of the Oise–Aisne Canal toward Braye en Laonnois. All the units underwent the attack of April 16, and were relieved between April 20 and 22, having suffered very heavy losses.

4. Concentrated and reorganized north of Laon (Crecy sur Serre), the division again went into action near the Oise–Aisne Canal (Froidmont Farm–Malval Farm, on May 3). Its losses were again very severe during the new French attack of May 5. It was withdrawn from the front on the 6th.

VERDUN.

5. Transferred to the vicinity of Conflans and reorganized, the division went into line on the Côtes de Meuse (Calonne les Éparges) on May 27.

6. After three months in the sector on the Côtes, the 45th Reserve Division entrained at Conflans (Sept. 26) for Flanders.

FLANDERS.

7. On September 22 it went into position in the Zonnebeke sector as a counterattacking division. Elements of the division were engaged on October 1 (Polygon wood), on the 4th (Zoonebeke), and from the 9th to the 12th as reinforcements on the Passchendaele front. After the British attack of October 12 the division, very much exhausted by these battles, was relieved.

VERDUN.

Transferred to the rear of the Côtes de Meuse, sent into line on the heights northeast of St. Mihiel in November; it was sent to the vicinity of Bohain in December.

RECRUITING.

Mixed at the time of its formation (1 Hanseatic Regiment), the 45th Reserve Division was recruited almost entirely from Pomerania, in theory at least, after its reduction to three regiments. Like the other units recruited from this province (4th Division), at the end of 1915 and several times since then, it has received a relatively large proportion of elderly men (1892 to 1894 classes, trained and untrained).

VALUE—1917 ESTIMATE.

The 45th Reserve Division fought well on the Somme. It put up a vigorous defense on the Aisne in the course of its two engagements of April 16 and May 6, 1917.

The Pomeranians, who formed the greater part of its effectives, have a military reputation to sustain. However, according to the statements of prisoners, when the 212th Reserve Infantry Regiment came from the Verdun front to Flanders it refused to attack on September 30, 1917. (British Summary of Information, Oct. 4.)

1918.

ST. QUENTIN.

1. Toward the end of January the division relieved the 36th Division near Faye (north of St. Quentin), the latter division side slipping toward the south. It remained here and took part in the initial attack of the Somme offensive; it was withdrawn about the 24th of March. It was not entirely withdrawn on that date, however, for besides still having some elements in line, the rest of the division was in close support as a "follow up" division. In this fighting it lost heavily.

MONTDIDIER.

2. A few days later it went to rest in the Montdidier area. Early in April it entered line near Assainvillers (east of Montdidier), where it was identified on the 6th, and was relieved by the 206th Division on the 18th, going to rest and refit in the region of Vouziers.

AISNE.

3. On the 1st of June the division was in reserve northeast of Fère en Tardenois, and on the 3d it reinforced the front near Chaudun (southwest of Soissons); it was relieved by the 23d Division and went to rest near Oulchy le Château (west of Fère en Tardenois).

MARNE.

4. The allied counteroffensive having started on July 18, the division was hurried into line near Montron (east of La Ferté Milon) to meet it. Here it was heavily engaged and suffered severe losses. It was relieved by the 26th Division on July 27.

5. It did not have an opportunity to rest, however, for it relieved the 201st Division north of Fère en Tardenois two days later. It was relieved on August 3, and went to rest in the Maubeuge region. It was identified here on the 23d, but a few days afterwards the Germans, fearing an American attack in Alsace, it was dispatched to the vicinity of Muelheim, where it arrived prior to September 3.

CHAMPAGNE–ARGONNE.

6. The division entrained on the 24th for Flanders, but was ordered to detrain when it reached St. Morel (south of Vouziers) on the 26th and remained there until midnight. Then the 212th Reserve Regiment entered line in the Aire valley near Baulny, while the remainder of the division moved farther to the west and entered line to the north of Fontaine en Dormois (northeast of Suippes). On October 8 these elements came to the east and the division was in line as a whole northwest of Châtel Chéhéry. It was withdrawn on the 25th and went to rest in Lorraine in the vicinity of Conflans (southwest of Briey).

7. On the 4th of November it came back into line near Woël (northeast of St. Mihiel); it was still here on the 11th.

VALUE—1918 ESTIMATE.

The 45th Reserve has been considered a second-class division. Heavily engaged on the Somme (three times), on the Aisne, against the Allied counteroffensive, and in the battle of the Meuse-Argonne, it has done a great deal of heavy fighting during 1918, without, however, ever particularly distinguishing itself. It suffered exceedingly heavy losses. Early in September, the 212th Regiment received as a draft the 397th Regiment of the disbanded 222d Division. About the 16th of October it received a very large draft of replacements among which were a considerable number of elements of decidedly Bolshevistic tendencies. Men deserted to the rear, to the enemy, and quite a few were punished for insubordination to officers, and some for refusing to fight. The morale of the whole division was very low.

45th Landwehr Division.

COMPOSITION.

	1917		1918	
	Brigade.	Regiment.	Brigade.	Regiment.
Infantry..............	45 Ldw.	107 Ldw. 133 Ldw. 350 Ldw.	45 Ldw.	107. Ldw. 133 Ldw. 350 Ldw.
Cavalry..............	(?)		4 Sqn. Gd. (Saxon) Cav. Rgt. 23 Drag. Rgt.	
Artillery..............	Art. Command: 408 F. A. Rgt.		498 F. A. Rgt. 1027 Light Am. Col. 1043 Light Am. Col.	
Engineers and Liaisons.	(445) Pion. Btn.: 4 Res. Co. 22 Pions. 345 T. M. Co. 545 Tel. Detch.		183 Pion. Co. 4 Landst. Co. 9 C. Dist. Pions. 221 Searchlight Section. 545 Signal Command: 545 Tel. Detch.	
Medical and Veterinary	Ambulance Co. 355 Field Hospital. Vet. Hospital.		639 Ambulance Co. 355 Field Hospital. 45 Vet. Hospital.	
Transports.............	562 M. T. Col.			

HISTORY.

(19th Corps District—Saxony.)

1917.

1. The 45th Landwehr Division was formed on the Eastern Front in April, 1917. The 107th Landwehr Regiment was taken from the 35th Reserve Division; the 133d Landwehr Regiment from the 92d Division; and the 350th Landwehr from the 91st Division, after having been a part of the 88th Division.

VOLHYNIA.

2. Until February, 1917, the 45th Landwehr Division occupied a sector in Volhynia, near the Kovel-Rovno railroad.

VALUE—1917 ESTIMATE.

The 45th Landwehr Division has been on the Eastern Front since its formation. It appears to have only a mediocre offensive value.

1918.

UKRAINE.

1. In February, 1918, the division advanced toward Kiev. A man of the 133 Landwehr Regiment wrote from the Wolczek Camp (southeast of Kovel) on the 15th of March: "Our regiment continues its march forward. It is said to have suffered heavy losses. We are fighting against the Bolsheviks; the Ukrainians are on our side." Divisional headquarters were at Poltava in April.

2. In May the three regiments of the division were in the vicinity of Kharkov. The division was again identified here on October 13.

VALUE—1918 ESTIMATE.

The division was rated as fourth class.

46th Reserve Division.

COMPOSITION.

	1914 Brigade	1914 Regiment	1915 Brigade	1915 Regiment	1916 Brigade	1916 Regiment	1917 Brigade	1917 Regiment	1918[1] Brigade	1918[1] Regiment
Infantry	91 Res. 92 Res. 18 Res. Jag. Btn.	213 Res. 214 Res. 215 Res. 216 Res.	91 Res. 92 Res. 18 Res. Jag. Btn.	213 Res. 214 Res. 215 Res. 216 Res.	91 Res. 92 Res. 18 Res. Jag. Btn.	213 Res. 214 Res. 215 Reg. 216 Res.	92 Res.	214 Res. 215 Res. 216 Res.	92 Res.	214 Res. 215 Res. 216 Res.
Cavalry	46 Res. Cav. Detch.		46 Res. Cav. Detch.		46 Res. Cav. Detch.		46 Res. Cav. Detch.		46 Res. Cav. Detch.	
Artillery	46 Res. F. A. Rgt. (9 Btries.).		46 Res. F. A. Rgt.		46 Res. F. A. Rgt.		(?) Art. command: 46 Res. F. A. Rgt.		(?) Art. command: 46 Res. F. A. Rgt.	
Engineers and liaisons.	46 Res. Pion. Co.		46 Res. Pion. Co. 46 Res. Pont. Engs.		46 Res. Pion. Co. 1 Res. Co. 25 Pions. 246 T. M. Co. 46 Res. Pont. Engs.		(346) Pion. Btn.: 46 Res. Pion. Co. (23 Res. Pions.) 246 T. M. Co. 446 Tel. Detch.		46 Res. Pion. Co. 1 Ldw. Co. 3 Bav. C. Dist. Pions. 23 Res. Searchlight Section. 246 T. M. Co. 446 Tel. Detch.	
Medical and Veterinary.			46 Res. Ambulance Co.				528 Ambulance Co. 335 Field Hospital. 78 Res. Field Hospital. Vet. Hospital.		528 Ambulance Co. 335 Field Hospital. Vet. Hospital.	
Transports.							733 M. T. Col.		733 M. T. Col.	
Attached.					60 Anti-Aircraft Section. 3 Balloon Sqn.		214 Res. Rgt. T. M. Co. (Doc.).			

[1] Composition at the time of its dissolution, August, 1918.

HISTORY.

. (9th Corps District—Hanseatic Cities and Grand Duchies of Mecklenburg.)

1914.

YSER.

1. The 46th Reserve Division (belonging to the 23d Reserve Corps with the 45th Division), formed between August and October, 1914, was trained at the Lockstedt Camp, and entrained for Belgium on October 12. It went into action in the battle of the Yser between Dixmude and Bixschoote on October 21, 1914.

FLANDERS.

2. After these battles, which lasted until about November 15, and in the course of which it suffered heavy losses, the division remained in Flanders and occupied the area of Bixschoote. On November 21 only 1 officer remained in the 3d Battalion of the 214th Reserve Infantry Regiment (letter); the 11th Company, which started with 253 men, had only 90 left.

1915.

FLANDERS.

1. Between April 22 and April 27, 1915, the 46th Reserve Division, which was still holding the front north of Ypres, took part in the battles launched around Lizerne, Het-Sas, Steenstraat.

2. During the rest of the year 1915 and until March, 1916, the 46th Reserve Division (as well as the 45th Reserve Division) held the lines between Dixmude and Ypres, without any important action, with periods of rest in the vicinity of Bruges and Thourout.

1916.

ST. ELOI WYTSCHAETE.

1. Relieved north of Ypres at the end of February, 1916, the 46th Reserve Division was transferred to Werwicq, from which place on March 14 it went to the sector of St. Eloi, near Messines.

2. The division lost very heavily in this sector, at the beginning of April. After a short period of rest it took over the same line from May to September.

SOMME.

3. At the beginning of September it left the area south of Ypres to go to the Somme. It went into action on September 8 between Vermandovillers and the Chaulnes railroad and suffered rather heavy losses, especially during the French attack of September 17; the 2d Battalion of the 214th Reserve Infantry Regiment was almost completely destroyed (letter).

4. Sent behind the front for a short time, about October 8, in the vicinity of Ham, it came back into line on October 17–20 minus the 213th Reserve Infantry Regiment, which was transferred to the 207th Division, a new organization. It supported the attacks of the 21st, between Ablaincourt and Chaulnes wood, where certain of its units lost very heavily. After launching a counterattack on the 22d the division was relieved on October 24–25.

CHAMPAGNE.

5. In November and December the reorganized division took over the sector east of Rheims.

1917.

1. In January, 1917, the 46th Reserve Division was at rest in Lorraine. On January 28 it entrained at Lorquin and was transferred to the Oise, by way of Sarreburg, Thionville, Luxemburg, Namur, Maubeuge, St. Quentin, Tergnier, Chauny.

MOULIN SOUS TOUVENT.

2. On January 30 it went into the sector of Moulin sous Touvent–Autrèches, which it left about March 18 to retire to Barisis, Folembray, and the lower Coucy wood.

Forêt de St. Gobain.

3. Established in the St. Gobain sector in April and May, it was relieved on May 20 and sent to rest in the area of Marle and Vervins.   It was reorganized there (the 216th Reserve Infantry Regiment received 500 men from the depot of the 76th Reserve Infantry Regiment at Hamburg).

Chemin des Dames.

4. On June 13 the division went into line on the Chemin des Dames, took part in the German attack of June 22 at the Épine de Chevregny-Royère Farm, and in the attack of July 8 on the front Panthéon–Froidmont.   In these two actions it had heavy losses.   It made up for these in part by men taken from the 94th Division in Russia.

5. Withdrawn from the Laon front on July 24, the division was sent to rest and to be reorganized in the area of Montmédy.

6. On August 12 it was transferred to Spincourt and placed in reserve on the right bank of the Meuse during the French attack of August 20.

Verdun.

7. Engaged on August 22 at the Fosse wood–Chaume wood, it lost heavily by the attack of August 26 and by its counterattack upon Beaumont.

8. Relieved at once, it was reorganized and sent to rest in the vicinity of Sedan–Longuyon from August 26 to the end of September.

Meuse.

9. The 46th Reserve Division reappeared from October 3 to November 10 in the sector of Fosse wood–Chaume wood, where some elements launched an attack on November 9 and suffered heavy losses.

10. The division was at rest in the vicinity of Longwy from November 10 to December 15.

Lorraine.

11. About December 17 it took over the sector west of Nomény (Cheminot–Eply) in Lorraine.   It was still there at the beginning of April, 1918.

RECRUITING.

Composed at the beginning of equal contingents from the 9th and 10th Corps Districts (Schleswig-Holstein, Hanseatic cities, and Mecklenburg; Hanover, Brunswick, Oldenburg), the division, since its reduction to three regiments, is filled up from the Hanseatic cities and the Grand Duchies of Mecklenburg.   It has ceased, therefore, to be Prussian, a thing which has a certain practical interest in its designation in communiques, etc., and has not been able to develop any regional sentiment or cohesion.   It is to be noted that the reinforcements of 1917 have been rather mixed (Poles, men from the 2d, 3d, and 5th Corps Districts), partly because of their being taken from the Russian front, and, during its recent stay in Lorraine, from the neighboring depot of the 99th Infantry Regiment.

VALUE—1917 ESTIMATE.

The 46th Reserve Division may be considered a good division.

The attack of July 8, 1917, was carried out energetically.   The assault troops attacked with "extraordinary fury."

The division fought bravely at Verdun in August, 1917.

Weakened by battles and by an epidemic of dysentery (October–November), it was sent to Lorraine for rest and reorganization.

The division received intensive training and it would seem that in spite of new, untrained recruits it will quickly regain its value.

1918.

NOYON.

1. The division was relieved about April 25 in Lorraine and transferred to the Montdidier area, where it was at rest until June 10. On that day it reenforced the Montdidier-Noyon battle front northeast of Gournay. In the course of the attacks the division suffered considerable losses. About July 2 it was relieved. It rested in rear of the Noyon front.

SOISSONS.

2. On July 20 the division reenforced the battle front near Buzancy, south of Soissons. It lasted but one week and was then withdrawn.

3. The effectives of the division was very low, due to the failure to receive drafts. Early in August the division was disbanded. The 214th Reserve Regiment was transferred to the 4th Division, the 216th Reserve Regiment to the 18th Reserve Division, and the 215th Reserve Regiment was turned into the 4th Ersatz Division. The divisional commander, Maj. Gen. Wasielewski, was retired.

VALUE—1918 ESTIMATE.

The division was rated as second class. Although it was not heavily engaged in 1918, its effective strength was allowed to dwindle to a very low level and dissolution followed.

46th Landwehr Division.

COMPOSITION.

	1917		1918 [1]	
	Brigade.	Regiment.	Brigade.	Regiment.
nfantry	46 Ldw.	101 Ldw. 103 Ldw. 105 Ldw.		101 Ldw. (?) 105 Ldw.
Cavalry	4 Sqn. 17 Uhlan Rgt.			
Artillery	Art. command: 246 F. A. Rgt.		246 F. A. Rgt. (Rgt. Staff).	
Engineers and Liaisons.	(446) Pion. Btn.: 346 T. M. Co. 546 Tel. Detch.		546 Signal Command: 346 Tel. Detch. (Except 1st Zug)	
Medical and veterinary.	638 Ambulance Co. 315 Field Hospital. 46 Vet. Hospital.		638 Ambulance Co. 46 Vet. Hospital.	
Transports	M. T. Col.			

[1] The elements below are those grouped under the Division Postal Sector (728). Other units of the 46th Landwehr Division, operating in other divisional sectors, are carried as attached to such divisions.

HISTORY.

(12th Corps District—Saxony.)

1917.

The 46th Landwehr Division, composed of the 101st and 103d Landwehr Regiments (taken from the 14th Landwehr Division) and of the 33d Landsturm Battalion (taken from the 3d Reserve Division), was formed on the Eastern Front about May, 1917.

SMORGONI.

1. It occupied the sector of Smorgoni-Lake Narotch until the beginning of 1918.

2. About the month of September, 1917, it received a new regiment, the 105th Landwehr, formed in 1917, at the time of the withdrawal of the Saxon battalions from the Prussian regiments of which they had been a part (345th and 374th Infantry Regiments). In December a great number of the young men were taken from the division to reenforce the 40th Division (Saxon) before its departure for France.

VALUE—1917 ESTIMATE.

The use made of the 46th Landwehr Division allows us to form an appreciation of its value; it held a calm sector on the Russian front in 1917; occupied the Ukraine in 1918.

1918.

VOLHYNIA.

1. In January the division was on the Volhynian front, next to the 10th Landwehr Division.

UKRAINE.

2. In February it moved into the Ukraine, leaving behind elements whose duty it was to gather the matériel which had been abandoned in the Russian positions.

3. About the middle of March the division held the sector north of Mohilev. The 103d Landwehr Regiment was along the Berezina in April. The 101st Landwehr Regiment was reported in the vicinity of Minsk early in May. The whole division was identified in the Minsk region the end of the month, and also toward the end of September.

47th Reserve Division.
COMPOSITION.

	1914		1915		1916		1917		1918 [1]	
	Brigade.	Regiment.	Brigade.	Regiment.	Brigade.	Regiment.	Brigade.	Regiment.	Brigade.	Regiment.
Infantry	93 Res. 94 Res. 19 Res. Jag. Btn.	217 Res. 218 Res. 219 Res. 220 Res.	93 Res. 94 Res. 19 Res. Jag. Btn.	217 Res. 218 Res. 219 Res. 220 Res.	93 Res. 94 Res. 19 Res. Jag. Btn.	217 Res. 218 Res. 219 Res. 220 Res. 13 (Wurtt.) Landst. Btn.	94 Res.	217 Res. 219 Res. 220 Res.	94 Res.	218 Res. 219 Res. 220 Res.
Cavalry	47 Res. Cav. Detch.		47 Res. Cav. Detch.		47 Res. Cav. Detch.		....		4 Sqn. 4 Horse Jag. Rgt.	
Artillery	47 Res. F. A. Rgt. (9 Btries.)		47 Res. F. A. Rgt.		47 Res. F. A. Rgt.		47 Art. Command: 47 Res. F. A. Rgt.		47 Art. Command: 47 Res. F. A. Rgt.	
Engineers and Liaisons.	47 Res. Pion. Co.		47 Res. Pion. Co. 47 Res. Pont. Engs.		47 Res. Pion. Co. 91 Res. Pion. Co. 247 T. M. Co. 47 Res. Pont. Engs.		(347) Pion. Btn.: 47 Res. Pion. Co. 91 Res. Pion. Co. 247 T. M. Co. 335 Searchlight Section. 447 Tel. Detch.		47 Res. Pion. Co. 91 Res. Pion. Co. 42 Res. Searchlight Section. 247 T. M. Co. 447 Tel. Detch. 117 Wireless Detch.	
Medical and Vetorinary.			47 Res. Ambulance Co.				529 Ambulance Co. Field Hospital. 199 Vet. Hospital.		529 Ambulance Co. 78 Res. Field Hospital. 81 Res. Field Hospital. 82 Res. Field Hospital. 199 Vet. Hospital.	
Transports							M. T. Col.		M. T. Col.	
Attached					839 F. A. Btry. 84 Anti-Aircraft Section. 80 Labor Btn.					

[1] Composition at the time of dissolution, July, 1918.

HISTORY.

(7th Corps District—Westphalia.)

1914.
WOEVRE.

1. The 47th Reserve Division, formed between August and October, 1914, and composing the 24th Reserve Corps with the 48th Reserve Division, was concentrated in the vicinity of Metz about October 20, sent to the Woevre, south of Etain, on the 26th, went into action at Magnaville on the 31st, and at Maucourt on November 6 to 11.

RUSSIA.

2. On November 23 the 47th Reserve Division entrained for the Eastern Front.

DUNAJEC.

3. Detraining in the vicinity of Cracow at the beginning of December, it went into action on the Dunajec (Neu-Sandec) west of Tarnow on the 8th, where it suffered serious check on December 20.

1915.

1. On January 10, 1915, the 47th Reserve Division was identified on the Dunajec–Gorlice front.

GALICIA.

2. From the end of January to the month of April it occupied the front west of Tarnow, near the Tarnow–Cracow railroad.

POLAND.

3. It took part in the spring and summer offensive of 1915. On July 2 it was on the right bank of the Vistula, in the vicinity of Janow. From July 20 to August 9 it took part in the advance from the Wysnica to the Wieprz, reached the Bug on October 19, the Jaselda on September 8, and fought along this last river until the 12th. On the 13th it was at Slonim.

4. At the end of September it went to the vicinity of Baranovitchi. On October 19 it held the lines near Lipsk.

1916.
RUSSIA.

1. The 47th Reserve Division remained in the sector of Lipsk–Baranovitchi during the entire year of 1916 and until May, 1917, when it entrained for France. On July 23 the 217th Reserve Infantry Regiment was withdrawn from the division to aid in the formation of the 225th Division.

1917.
FRANCE.

1. At the beginning of May, 1917, the 47th Reserve Division was transferred to the Western Front. (Itinerary of the 219th Reserve Infantry Regiment: Entrained on May 3 at Baranovitchi, Warsaw, Lodz, Lissa, Glogau, Leipzig, Erfurt, Frankfort, Metz; detrained at Bouillonville, near Thiaucourt, on May 7.)

AISNE.

2. After a stay in the Woevre, at Bois le Prêtre, until the beginning of June, and a short rest near Marle, the 47th Reserve Division went into line north of Braye en Laonnois (west of the Épine de Chevregny) on June 20. It took part in the attacks launched in this sector and suffered heavy losses from June 22 to July 8. Some of its elements were engaged in the French attack of October 23, after which they retired to the village of Chevregny.

3. The 47th Reserve Division was relieved at the end of October.

FORÊT DE ST. GOBAIN.

4. After a rest in the villages of the Serre valley, it took over the sector of Septvaux

Mixed at the time of its formation, the division has become entirely Westphalian since its reduction to three regiments.   The levies from the Russian front in the course of 1917, however, introduced outside elements (men from the 1st, 2d, and 3d Corps District in May, coming from the 406th, 420th, and 421st Infantry Regiments).   Thirteen prisoners (220th Reserve Infantry Regiment) captured on October 1, 1917, north of Braye en Laonnois, came from the following Provinces in Germany: 4 from Westphalia, 2 from Hanover, 3 from East Prussia, 1 from the Rhine Province, 1 from Oldenburg, 1 from Silesia, and 1 from Pomerania.

VALUE—1917 ESTIMATE.

The 47th Reserve Division is a mediocre division more fitted for defense than attack, but still capable of effort after rest and reorganization.   It had won some reputation in the offensive at Poland and Courland.

Its effectives include a large proportion of Poles.

In the sector of Chevregny, Froidmont (June-July), it gave a good account of itself, although sanitary conditions were very defective (Dec. 1, 1917).

1918.

1. About the beginning of February the division was relieved by the 3d Bavarian Division and went to train near Vervins.

BATTLE OF PICARDY.

2. It was engaged in the Somme offensive on March 21 near Tergnier and participated in the attack until the 25th.   It was reengaged on April 1 southwest of Lassigny and held that sector until May 2, when it was relieved by the extension of the 206th Division.

3. The division entrained at Ham on May 6 and moved to St. Quentin area.   From May 27 onward it followed up the advance behind the 113th Division, and finally relieved that division on June 1 near Vierzy.   It was relieved on June 20.

MARNE.

4. This division, although greatly weakened, was returned to line without having been reconstructed, in the vicinity of Longpont.   At this time the division had not more than 40 to 50 rifles to a company.   It again suffered heavy losses, and about July 27 was retired to rest.

5. The division was dissolved at Mainbresson on June 30.   The 218th Reserve Regiment was formed into one battalion, which became the 3d Battalion of the 53d Reserve Infantry Regiment.   The 219th Reserve Regiment was drafted to the 159th Regiment.

VALUE—1918 ESTIMATE.

The division was rated as second class.   Its dissolution was occasioned by its low effective strength following its losses and failure to receive drafts.

47th Landwehr Division.

COMPOSITION.

	1914		1915		1916		1917		1918	
	Brigade.	Regiment.	Brigade.	Regiment.	Brigade.	Regiment.	Brigade.	Regiment.	Brigade.	Regiment.
Infantry......	47 Ldw.	104 Ldw. 106 Ldw.	47 Ldw.	104 Ldw. 106 Ldw.	47 Mixed Ldw.	104 Ldw. 106 Ldw.	47 Ldw.	100 Ldw. Gren. 104 Ldw. 106 Ldw.	47 Ldw.	100 Ldw. 104 Ldw. 106 Ldw.
Cavalry......					Ldw. Sqn. 18 Uhlan Rgt. Sqn. 21 Uhlan Rgt.		2 Sqn. 20 Hus. Rgt. 2 Ldw. Sqn. 19 C. Dist. Cav.		Staff, 20 Hus. Rgt. 2 Sqn. 20 Hus. Rgt.	
Artillery......	19 C. Dist. Landst. F. A. Btry.		19 C. Dist. Landst. F. A. Btry.		19 Ldw. F. A. Rgt.		Art. Command: 19 Ldw. F. A. Rgt.		19 Ldw. F. A. Rgt. (except 3d Abt).	
Engineers and Liaisons.							447 Pion. Btn.: 6 Co. 22 Pions. 1 Res. Co. 22 Pions. 347 T. M. Co. Tel. Detch.		6 Co. 22 Pions. 547 Signal Command. 547 Tel. Detch.	
Medical and Veterinary.							562 Ambulance Co. 24 Ldw. Field Hospital. Vet. Hospita.		562 Ambulance Co. 24 Ldw. Field Hospital. 547 Vet. Hospital.	
Transport......							104 M. T. Col.			
Attached......							136 Labor Btn......			

˙HISTORY.

(12th and 19th Corps District—Saxony.)

1914.

The 47th Landwehr Division came from the 47th Landwehr Brigade (104th and 106th Landwehr Regiments) which was independent at first under the command of Lieut. Gen. Mueller, and was made a division in the autumn of 1915.

CHAMPAGNE.

1. Detraining at Bourcy (northeast of Bastogne) on August 18, 1914, the 47th Landwehr Brigade arrived on the Champagne front immediately after the battle of the Marne.

2. On September 14, 1914, the brigade was in line in the vicinity of Moronvilliers. It remained in Champagne until the beginning of 1917.

1915.

CHAMPAGNE.

1. About the month of May, 1915, it left the sector Prosne Moronvilliers for the north of Rheims, from Loivre to the Rheims–Witry road.

2. Reenforced by the 113th Infantry Regiment, later by the 29th Reserve Infantry Regiment, it formed the Mueller Division in October.

3. At the end of September one battalion of the 104th Landwehr Regiment was sent as a reenforcement into action south of Ste. Marie à Py to help out the 133d Reserve Infantry Regiment during the French offensive.

1916.

CHAMPAGNE.

1. The 47th Landwehr Brigade continued to occupy the Rheims sector (Courcy-Betheny) during 1916.

2. In the month of July it was made a division (47th Landwehr Division) and received a 3d Regiment, the 391st Infantry Regiment (Saxon).

1917.

OISE LA FÈRE.

1. Withdrawn from the Rheims front about February 23, 1917, the 47th Landwehr Division was sent into line west of La Fère during the retirement of the German Army to the Hindenburg Line (Quessy–Travecy, Mar. 23). It remained in the sector at La Fère until May 16.

RUSSIA.

2. In the middle of May the division was transferred to the Eastern Front, where it occupied the sector Goroditche–Tsirin. It exchanged with the 219th Division, the 391st Infantry Regiment for the 100th Landwehr Granadier Regiment.

VALUE—1917 ESTIMATE.

The 47th Landwehr Division is a mediocre division. Its retention on the Russian front is a sufficient indication of its value.

1918.

UKRAINE.

1. In February the 47th Landwehr Division left the Tsirin region and took part in the advance into the Ukraine. On the 27th of April it was between Gomel and Briansk; on the 5th of June, in the Kiev region. It was identified in the same region several times subsequently, the last date of identification being September 30.

VALUE—1918 ESTIMATE.

The division was rated as fourth class.

48th Reserve Division.

COMPOSITION.

	1914 Brigade.	1914 Regiment.	1915 Brigade.	1915 Regiment.	1916 Brigade.	1916 Regiment.	1917 Brigade.	1917 Regiment.	1918 Brigade.	1918 Regiment.
Infantry	95 Res. 96 Res. 20 Res. Jag. Btn.	221 Res. 222 Res. 223 Res. 224 Res.	95 Res. 96 Res. 20 Res. Jag. Btn.	221 Res. 222 Res. 223 Res. 224 Res.	95 Res. 96 Res. 20 Res. Jag. Btn.	221 Res. 222 Res. 223 Res. 224 Res.	96 Res.	221 Res. 222 Res. 223 Res.	96 Res.	221 Res. 222 Res. 223 Res.
Cavalry	48 Res. Cav. Detch.		48 Res. Cav. Detch.		48 Res. Cav. Detch.		5 Sqn. 1 Drag. Rgt.		5 Sqn. 1 Gd. Drag. Rgt.	
Artillery	48 Res. F. A. Rgt. (9 btries.).		48 Res. F. A. Rgt.		48 Res. F. A. Rgt.		(?) Art. Command: 48 Res. F. A. Rgt.		48 Res. F. A. Rgt. 1 Abt. 23 Ft. A. Rgt. (1 and 3 btries.). 752 Light Am. Col. 954 Light Am. Col. 1382 Light Am. Col.	
Engineers and Liaisons.	48 Res. Pion. Co.		48 Res. Pion. Co. 48 Res. Pont. Engs.		48 Res. Pion. Co. 274 Pion. Co. (?) 2 Ldw. Pion. Co. 6 C. Dist. 248 T. M. Co. 48 Res. Pont. Engs.		(348) Pion. Btn.: 48 Res. Pion. Co. 1 Res. Co. 26 Pion. Btn. 248 T. M. Co. 448 Tel. Detch.		348 Pion. Btn.: 1 Res. Co. 26 Pions. 48 Res. Pion. Co. 248 T. M. Co. 214 Searchlight Section. 448 Signal Command: 448 Tel. Detch. 69 Wireless Detch.	
Medical and Veterinary.			48 Res. Ambulance Co.				530 Ambulance Co. 79 Res. Field Hospital. Vet. Hospital.		530 Ambulance Co. 102 Field Hospital. 79 Res. Field Hospital. 448 Vet. Hospital.	
Transport							587 M. T. Col.		735 M. T. Col.	

HISTORY.

(18th Corps District—Hesse–Nassau and the Grand Duchy of Hesse.)

1914.

The 48th Reserve Division (belonging to the 24th Reserve Corps with the 47th Reserve Division) was formed between August and October, 1914, and trained at the Oberhofen Camp.

ARTOIS.

1. Concentrated near Metz in the middle of October, the 48th Reserve Division was transferred on the 25th to the area between Armentières and La Bassée (Fromelles), while the 47th Reserve Division was sent to the Woevre.

2. On November 1 the division held the line at Neuve Chapelle. Some elements were sent farther north, west of Wytschaete, in the middle of November.

RUSSIA.

3. At the end of November the 48th Reserve Division left the Western Front for Russia.

POLAND.

4. On December 3 it was identified in Poland in the vicinity of Kalisch It then made a part of the X Army and fought west of the Rawka, near Warsaw, at the end of December.

1915.

1. The 48th Reserve Division was engaged in Poland (Rawka) until January 28, 1915.

CARPATHIANS.

2. On February 2 elements of the division fought in the Carpathians, southeast of Beskides. It was then assigned to the German Army of the South (Von Linsingen) and was opposed to the Russians in the vicinity of the Uzsok Ridge (February–May).

GALICIA.

3. Taking part in the spring and summer offensive of 1915, it marched to Halicz in May; crossed the Dniester in the middle of June; advanced to Brzezany-Tarnopol and was on the Zlota-Lipa at the end of July. One of its regiments, the 224th Reserve Infantry Regiment, was renewed several times; the list of losses from August to October show casualties of 70 officers and 4,712 men, 3,100 of whom were reported as missing. The greater part of these were Alsace-Lorrainers who had succeeded in deserting.

4. When the offensive was resumed in October and November the 48th Reserve Division formed a part of the Bothmer Army and progressed from the Zlota-Lipa as far as the Stripa.

1916.

1. The 48th Reserve Division was retained at the Stripa, west of Tarnapol, during the winter and spring of 1916; it was still in this sector at the time of the Russian attack (Broussilow offensive, June to September).

ROUMANIA.

2. In the beginning of October the division went into action with the Falkenheim Army against Roumania, and fought in the vicinity of Hermannstadt, then at Préoéal in November.

GALICIA.

3. It then left the Transylvanian front and went to eastern Galicia, where it was a part of the Bothmer Army. It took up its position between Brzezan, and the Dniester.

1917.

1. At the beginning of 1917 the 224th Reserve Infantry Regiment left the division and was transferred to the 215th Division, in process of reorganization.

FRANCE.

2. The 48th Reserve Division was relieved from its sector in May, 1917, and transferred to the Western Front (Itinerary: Lemberg–Jaroslav–Cracow–Oppeln–Breslau–Leipzig–Erfurt–Gotha–Eisenach–Frankfort–Worms–Sarrebruecken–Thionville–Montmedy–Dun sur Meuse). It rested in the vicinity of Stenay from May 27 to June 28.

VERDUN.

3. It was first behind the Verdun front, on the left bank of the Meuse. Toward the end of June it sustained the artillery preparation for the French offensive of July 17, and sent some of its elements in as reenforcements (Hill 304–Morthomme) on the day of the attack.

4. Sent to rest and reorganized in the Stenay area at the end of July. By an important draft of men of the 1918 class, it went back into the same sector (Hill 304–Corbeaux wood) on August 20, at the time of the new French attack, and lost heavily reenforcing and relieving units of the 6th Reserve Division.

5. Withdrawn from the front on August 24, it was employed on various works until September 3 and then sent into the area of Damvillers.

6. On September 12 it went into line north of Hill 344, which it left at the end of the month to go to rest in the vicinity of Morhange.

LORRAINE–ALSACE.

7. After holding the lines in Lorraine (middle of October to the middle of November) northeast of Arracourt, the 48th Reserve Division was sent to Alsace and went to rest for two months in the vicinity of Enisheim.

RECRUITING.

Mixed upon formation (1 Thuringian Regiment), the division became, in theory, a Hessian Division. The Alsace–Lorrainers were very numerous during its stay on the Russian front, whence the desertions en masse from the 224th Infantry Regiment in the summer of 1915.

VALUE—1917 ESTIMATE.

At the end of June, 1917, the 48th Reserve Division, coming from the Russian front, went into line at Hill 304, after a month's rest near Stenay. But as the men were not accustomed to the activity of the western front and were unable to sustain artillery fire for a long time, they could only be kept in this sector for a few days.

During the French attack of August 20 the 48th Reserve Division played only a passive rôle.

The 48th Reserve Division must be classed among the mediocre divisions (December, 1917).

1918.

1. About March 1 the division was relieved by the 22d Reserve Division and went into reserve in Alsace. It left that sector about April 1 and came into line on the 14th southwest of Vieux Berquin. It was engaged in that locality until its relief on the night of May 26–27 by the 32d Division.

VIEUX BERQUIN.

2. The division rested in the Lille area until June 28, when it returned to its former sector at Vieux Berquin. Its stay here was short. On July 3 it was relieved by the 39th Division and entrained at Laventie the next day for Douai.

SCARPE.

3. On the night of July 6-7 the division relieved the 187th Division southwest of Gavrelle. Throughout August and September the division held this sector. It was relieved north of the Scarpe on the night of October 5-6 and moved south.

4. The division was used to reenforce the Cambrai–St. Quentin front near Cambrai on October 7. Thereafter almost until the day of the armistice the division was engaged in opposing the British advance. The direction of its retreat was through Awoingt (10th), Saulzoir (13th), Montrecourt (14th), north of Haussy (17th), Vendegies (24th), Maresches (Nov. 1), Jenlain (4th). The division received drafts from the dissolved 118th Reserve Regiment (25th Reserve Division) in late October. It was withdrawn from line about November 5.

VALUE—1918 ESTIMATE.

The division was rated as second class. In 1918 it was engaged entirely in defensive sectors and performed with credit.

48th Landwehr Division.

COMPOSITION.

	1917		1918		1918	
	Brigade.	Regiment.	Brigade.	Regiment.	Brigade.	Regiment.
Infantry		38 Landst. 39 Landst. 47 Landst.	1 Landst.	38 Landst. 40 Landst. 47 Landst.	1 Landst.	38 Landst. 40 Landst. 47 Landst.
Cavalry						3 Sqn. 14 Uhlan Rgt. 1 Sqn. Gd. Res. Uhlan Rgt.
Artillery	(?)		Art. Command: 264 F. A. Rgt.		264 F. A. Rgt.	
Engineers and Liaisons			1/28 Pion. Btn.: 1 Landst. Co. 3 C. Dist. Pions. 455 T. M. Co. 590 Tel. Detch.		224 Pion. Btn.: 1 Ldw. Co. Gd. C. Dist. Pions. 1 Landst. Co. 3 C. Dist. Pions. 210 Searchlight Section. 548 Signal Command: 548 Tel. Detch. 67 Wireless Detch.	
Medical and Veterinary			Ambulance Co. 80 Res. Field Hospital. Vet. Hospital.		602 Ambulance Co. 51 Field Hospital. 80 Res. Field Hospital. 570 Vet. Hospital.	
Transport			800 M. T. Col.		800 M. T. Col.	
Attached			2 Ratisbonne Landst. Inf. Btn. (3 Bav. C. Dist. Btn. No. 14).			

HISTORY.

(38th Landsturm: Brandenburg and Alsace.   40th Landsturm: Prussian Saxony, Westphalia and the Rhine Province.   47th Landsturm: Hesse and Thuringia.)

1917.

LORRAINE.

1. The 48th Landwehr Division appears to have been formed on the Lorraine front
in September, 1917, by the grouping of three new regiments—the 38th Landsturm,
the 39th Landsturm (Wurttemberg), and the 47th Landsturm—the elements of which
had previously been employed behind the front or in calm sectors.

2. In September, 1917, the 48th Landwehr Division occupied the sector of Avricourt (Leintrey-Gondrexon, Embermenil).

VALUE—1917 ESTIMATE.

The 48th Landwehr Division is composed of troops of mediocre value.

The average age of the men is 40 years.   A certain number of young soldiers of the
1918 class are to be found in most of the units.   Sent into these Landsturm divisions
because of their reduced physical fitness, they left them for active or reserve units as
soon as they became hardened.

There is a divisional assault company which has never shown any offensive activity
(July, 1918).

1918.

1. The division continued to hold the Delme sector until the armistice.   Nothing
occurred to disturb the tranquility of that part of the front.

VALUE—1918 ESTIMATE.

The division was rated as fourth class.   The average age of its effectives was near
40 years.   At no time did the division take part in any fighting.

49th Reserve Division.
COMPOSITION.

	1914 Brigade	1914 Regiment	1915 Brigade	1915 Regiment	1916 Brigade	1916 Regiment	1917 Brigade	1917 Regiment	1918 Brigade	1918 Regiment
Infantry	97 Res. 98 Res. 21 Res. Jag. Btn.	225 Res. 226 Res. 227 Res. 228 Res.	97 Res. 98 Res. 21 Res. Jag. Btn.	225 Res. 226 Res. 227 Res. 228 Res.	97 Res. 21 Res. Jag. Btn.	225 Res. 226 Res. 228 Res.	97 Res.	225 Res. 226 Res. 228 Res.	97 Res.	225 Res. 226 Res. 228 Res.
Cavalry	49 Res. Cav. Detch.		49 Res. Cav. Detch.		49 Res. Cav. Detch.		49 Res. Cav. Detch. (?)		2 Sqn. (?) Drag. Rgt.	
Artillery	49 Res. F. A. Rgt. (9 Btries.).		49 Res. F. A. Rgt.		49 Res. F. A. Rgt.		(?) 49 Art. command: 49 Res. F. A. Rgt.		49 Art. command: 49 Res. F. A. Rgt. 1 Abt. 25 Ft. A. Rgt. (1, 2, and 4 Btries.). 788 Light Am. Col. 972 Light Am. Col. 1,318 Light Am. Col.	
Engineers and Liaison.	49 Res. Pion. Co.		49 Res. Pion. Co. 49 Res. Pont. Engs.		49 Res. Pion. Co. 249 T. M. Co 49 Res. Pont. Engs.		(349) Pion. Btn.: 49 Res. Pion. Co. 249 T. M. Co. 449 Tel. Detch.		349 Pion. Btn.: 43 Res. Pion. Co. 49 Res. Pion. Co. 249 T. M. Co. 188 Searchlight Section. 449 Signal command: 449 Tel. Detch. 110 Wireless Detch.	
Medical and veterinary.			49 Res. Ambulance Co.				531 Ambulance Co. 85 Res. Field Hospital. 155 Vet. Hospital.		531 Ambulance Co. 83 Res. Field Hospital. 85 Res. Field Hospital. 155 Vet. Hospital.	
Transports							M. T. Col.			
Odd units							49 Res. Cyclist Co.			

HISTORY.

(4th Corps District—Prussian Saxony and part of Thuringia.)

1914.

EAST PRUSSIA.

1. The 49th Reserve Division, forming the 25th Reserve Corps with the 50th Reserve Division, was formed between August and October, 1914, trained at the Warthe Camp, and sent to East Prussia on October 14, 1914, as a part of the 8th Army (Von Hindenburg).

POLAND.

2. It took part in the offensive in Poland between the Vistula and the Warta at the end of October, escaped from the enveloping movement attempted by the Russians before Lodz (Nov. 25), and fought on the front of the Bzura, Rawka, Bolimow, where it was repulsed in December.

1915.

POLAND.

1. At the beginning of January, 1915, the 49th Reserve Division was again engaged on the Bzura and remained in this area until the summer of the same year. In June it transferred the 227th Reserve Infantry Regiment to the 107th Division, a new formation.

2. Advancing in August with the Hindenburg offensive, it entered Warsaw on August 7, took part in the pursuit of the Russians in the sector of Skierniewicz, and stopped near Baranovitchi (Tsirin).

1916.

1. The 49th Reserve Division was still occupying the sector north of Baranovitchi when the Russian offensive broke out in this region in July, 1916. At this time elements of the division were sent to reenforce the 35th Austrian Division between Baranovitchi and the north of Pripet. This latter division was relieved a short time afterwards by the 49th Reserve Division.

GALICIA.

2. Sent into Galicia, the division held the lines southwest of Brody at the beginning of October. At this time the 225th Reserve Infantry Regiment was sent to Roumania.

CARPATHIANS.

3. Made up only of the 226th and 228th Reserve Infantry Regiments, the 49th Reserve Division opposed the Russians on the Narajowka, then, at the beginning of December and until January, 1917, fought in the Carpathians in the vicinity of Worochta.

1917.

ROUMANIA.

1. In January, 1917, the 49th Reserve Division rejoined the 225th Reserve Infantry Regiment (Roumania) in the valley of Uz.

2. In the middle of January it was transferred to the Western Front. (Itinerary: Szekely-Udvarhely – Goborin – Budapest – Oderberg – Oppeln – Breslau – Goerlitz-Dresden–Leipzig–Halle–Liege–Mons–St. Ghislain, detraining on Jan. 22.)

FRANCE.

3. After a rest of two months in the vicinity of Mons, then in the vicinity of Lille, the 49th Reserve Division went into line east of Armentières, south of Frelinghien on March 20.

ARTOIS.

4. Relieved at the end of April, it was engaged almost at once in the sector of Fontaine les Croisilles, Bullecourt (southeast of Arras), where it suffered very heavily

from May 1 to May 21. On June 16, after reorganization, the ranks of the 228th Reserve Infantry Regiment contained more than two-fifths new recruits; more than one-fifth of the men belonged to the 1918 class.

FLANDERS.

5. Sent to rest and to be reorganized during the month of June in the vicinity of Tournai-Audenarde, it went into line at the end of June in the sector of Steenstraat-Bixschoote (north of Ypres), and suffered heavy losses during the artillery preparation which preceded the Franco-British attack of July 21. On July 28 it was withdrawn from the front before the attack.

ARTOIS.

6. The 49th Reserve Division rested and was reorganized in the month of August between Lille and Tournai, and in September took over its old Artois sector (Croisilles-Bullecourt), from which place it was relieved at the end of October.

7. After occupying the sector south of the Ypres-Menin road until November 21, it went into action about November 26 in the same sector of Croisilles-Bullecourt (Cambrai attack).

8. At the end of December, the 49th Reserve Division was resting in the Tourcoing area.

RECRUITING.

Formed at the beginning by contingents from the 5th and 6th Corps Districts (Posen and Silesia) the Division, beginning with the summer of 1915, received most of its reenforcements from the 4th Corps District. At the present time it is entirely Saxo-Thuringian.

VALUE—1917 ESTIMATE.

The 49th Reserve Division is considered a good division.

It fought well in Artois in May 1917. North of Ypres it suffered heavily by the Franco-British bombardment at the end of July, 1917. It is to be noted that under artillery fire units in the first line scattered and fled. The remnants of the advanced elements deserted (30 men).

On July 25, 1917, the 226th Reserve Infantry Regiment received replacements of 500 to 700 men, principally of the 1918 class.

1918.

MESSINES.

1. About April 6 the division temporarily withdrew to reserve. It returned on the 11th and carried out a divisional attack on Messines. It was engaged until about April 25.

YPRES.

2. Two days later the division relieved the 13th Reserve Division south of Ypres, which in turn relieved it about May 2. It remained in rear of the front while resting and was engaged east of Bixschoote on May 10. Here the division remained until June 14, when the 29th Division relieved it. The division rested in the Bruges area until July 10, when it returned to its former sector northeast of Ypres. It held this sector until about August 27, when the 11th Bavarian Division relieved it.

3. The division entrained at Hooglede August 27 and traveled to Courtrai, where it halted one day. On August 28 it moved to Iwuy, from where it marched to Lallaing (near Douai) two days later. On September 1 the division came into line near Fremicourt. It was engaged until about September 16.

SCARPE–SOMME.

4. The division rested in the Cambrai area until September 27, where it was identified in line west of Gaincourt. It again retired from the front about October 1 and

rested in the Eswars area.   On the Scarpe–Somme front in September the division lost 1,100 prisoners.

5. On the night of October 11–12 the division was again in line at Courcelles les Lens. After holding this rather quiet sector for a week the division moved north and on October 29 appeared on the Ypres front at Anseghem in relief of the 7th Cavalry Division.   It continued in line until the armistice.   The last identification was west of Audenarde on November 2.

VALUE—1918 ESTIMATE.

The division was rated as second class.   It was used as a holding division in important sectors on the British front during 1918.

50th Division.
COMPOSITION.

	1915 Brigade.	1915 Regiment.	1916 Brigade.	1916 Regiment.	1917 Brigade.	1917 Regiment.	1918 Brigade.	1918 Regiment.
Infantry	100.	39 Fus. 53. 158.	100.	39 Fus. 53. 158.	100.	39 Fus. 53. 158.	100.	39 Fus. 53. 158.
Cavalry	2 Sqn. mounted Jäg. Rgt. 3 Sqn. mounted Jäg. Rgt.		1 Sqn. 16 Uhlan Rgt.		1 Sqn. 16 Uhlan Rgt.		1 Sqn. 16 Uhlan Rgt.	
Artillery	50 Brig.: 99 F. A. Rgt. (6 Batteries). 100 F. A. Rgt. (6 Batteries, 3 are Hows.).		50 Brig.: 99 F. A. Rgt. 100 F. A. Rgt.		50 Art. Command: 99 F. A. Rgt. (9 Batteries).		50 Art. Command: 99 F. A. Rgt. 95 Ft. A. Btn. 1178 Light Am. Col. 1179 Light Am. Col. 1204 Light Am. Col.	
Engineers and Liaisons.	99 Pion. Co. 100 Pion. Co.		99 Pion. Co. 100 Pion. Co. 4 Co. 23 Pions. 1 T. M. Co. 50 T. M. Co. 50 Pont. Engs. 50 Tel. Detch.		50 Pion Btn.: 99 Pion. Co. 100 Pion. Co. 50 T. M. Co. 99 Searchlight Section. 50 Tel. Detch.		50 Pion Btn.: 99 Pion. Co. 100 Pion. Co. 50 T. M. Co. 50 Signal Command: 50 Tel. Detch. 13 Wireless Detch.	
Medical and Veterinary.					50 Ambulance Co. 337 Field Hospital. 338 Field Hospital. 340 Field Hospital. Vet. Hospital.		50 Ambulance Co. 337 Field Hospital. 338 Field Hospital. 132 Vet. Hospital.	
Transports					M. T. Col.			
Odd units			50 Cyclist Co.					
Attached	1 Ldw. 7 C. Dist. Pion. Co.		80 Antiaircraft Section. 2 Res. Co. 2 Pion. Btn. No. 27.					

HISTORY.

(7th Corps District—Westphalia.)

1915.

The 50th Division (one of the new divisions in the 50 to 58 series) was formed in March, 1915, by taking three regiments from the three divisions of the 7th Corps and 7th Reserve Corps (the 13th Division giving the 158th Infantry, the 14th Division the 53d, and the 14th Reserve Division the 39th Fusileer Division), all Westphalian Regiments.

1. At the end of March, 1915, the 158th and 53d Infantry Regiments were identified at Hirson (Aisne), while the 39th Fusileer Regiment was still between Perthes and Tahure. In April the division was concentrated and was identified in Champagne, May 14 (area south of Somme-Py).

CHAMPAGNE.

2. From June to October it occupied the sector of Tahure (north of Perthes and Mesnil les Hurlus). It there underwent the French offensive of the end of September, which caused it very heavy losses—infantry, 130 officers and 7,849 men casualties; the 100th Company of Pioneers lost 5 officers and 135 men.

3. Sent to rest and reorganized in the vicinity of Vouziers and of Juniville (end of October to the end of November), it reappeared on November 7 north of Prosnes (east of Reims).

1916.

CHAMPAGNE.

1. In April, 1916, the division left the sector of Prosnes-Prunay, for the front northeast of Verdun (Ornes).

VERDUN–VAUX.

2. Going into action, at the beginning of May, north of Vaux, it took part in the attacks launched upon the line Caillette wood–Damloup (June 1 to June 3), which ended in the capture of the fort of Vaux by the 158th Infantry Regiment on June 4.

3. Very much exhausted by these battles, the division was sent to rest and reorganized in the vicinity of Étain in June and July.

4. In July elements of the division occupied the calm sectors of the Woëvre.

5. At the end of July the 50th Division went back into line at Verdun, south of the fort of Vaux. It launched an attack on August 1 (La Lauffée), underwent the French offensives of August 8 and October 24, suffering heavy losses, and held this sector until November.

ARGONNE.

6. Sent to the Argonne, it took over the sector of Vauquois.

1917.

1. Withdrawn from the Argonne on February 15, 1917, the division remained at rest in the area of Saulces-Champenoise until the end of March, then in the camp at Sissonne, then at Thenailles, near Vervins (beginning of April).

AISNE.

2. Concentrated on April 8, it went into action on the 15th at Juvincourt and there underwent the French attack of April 15. After heavy losses it was relieved between April 29–April 27 and went for reorganization to Nizy le Comte, near the Sissonne Camp.

CHEMIN DES DAMES.

3. About May 10, the division went back into line east of Allment on the Chemin des Dames.

4. It was sent to rest in July in the vicinity of Mons en Laonnois, Coucy les Eppes, Parfondru.

5. At the beginning of August, it came back to the Chemin des Dames (vicinity of Ailles), where, on October 15, the 9th Company of the 158th Infantry Regiment was reduced to 50 men, including officers (letter). Following the French offensive upon La Malmaison, the 50th Division retired on November 1, to the north of the Ailette toward Neuville (outside of Chamouille) and was still occupying this sector in December.

RECRUITING.

Upon its formation the division was composed of Westphalian troops. The recruiting is still almost exclusively Westphalian.

VALUE—1917 ESTIMATE.

Since the battle of Vaux in June, 1916, the division likes to consider itself a shock division.

Its prolonged stay on the Ailette front (August to December) seems to mean that it had to be put at rest for a fairly long time before being engaged in an active sector.

It must be regarded as a good division, capable of putting up a vigorous defense (December).

1918.

1. The 50th Division was withdrawn from line near Ailles (west of Craonne) on January 9, the neighboring divisions extending their fronts, and moved by easy stages to the Chimay area, where it arrived on the 14th. It remained here for a month during which time it was thoroughly trained in open warfare and brought up to strength. It then moved to the La Capelle–Fontenelle area for rest and further training.

St. Quentin.

2. The middle of March the division moved up to the front, and on the 21st attacked in the front line southwest of St. Quentin; it captured Holnon during the day, Etreillers on the 22d, Hangest en Santerre on the 29th, and reached Moreuil on the 30th. It was withdrawn about April 1, after having suffered severely heavy losses, and went to rest, refit, and train in the Lassigny region.

Aisne.

3. On May 27, the division attacked near Craonne, reached Pontavert toward noon and crossed the Aisne. The following day it crossed the Vesle west of Breuil sur Vesle and continued to the south, where a French counterattack was repelled. On the 30th it reached Goussancourt, and then the Marne east of Dormans. After having suffered severe losses, it was relieved by the 28th Reserve Division during the night of June 12–13, and went to rest in the Laon region.

Rheims.

4. On the 19th of July the division was thrown into line just southwest of Rheims to meet the Allies' tightening at the bases of the Chateau-Thierry salient. It was withdrawn early in August.

5. About the 30th of September it came back into line northwest of Rheims, near Prouilly and Cormicy. It remained here, and was driven back—fighting stubbornly—passing near Brimont, Guignicourt, and Banogne, where it was withdrawn on the 7th of November.

Meuse.

6. After a day's rest, the division was put back into line on the 8th near Mezières; it had not been withdrawn when the armistice was signed.

VALUE—1918 ESTIMATE.

The 50th is rated as a first-class division. It distinguished itself in the fighting during 1918. After the Somme offensive, it was praised by Prof. Wegener in the Koelnische Zeitung. Immediately after the battle of the Aisne Maj. Fritsch, in command of the 158th Regiment, was awarded Pour le Mérite. After the Allied counteroffensive, Lieut. Gen. v. Engelhuhten, the division commander, was decorated and made governor of Riga, and the commander of the 53d Regiment was also decorated. The 58th Regiment was mentioned as having particularly distinguished itself in the fighting near Banogne in the German communique of October 30. Losses suffered throughout the year were enormous, but the High Command did all in its power to make these good. There are no desertions of record since July 1, 1917. The morale was very good, everything being taken into consideration.

50th Reserve Division.

COMPOSITION.

	1914 Brigade	1914 Regiment	1915 Brigade	1915 Regiment	1916 Brigade	1916 Regiment	1917 Brigade	1917 Regiment	1918 Brigade	1918 Regiment
Infantry	99 Res. 100 Res.	229 Res. 230 Res. 231 Res. 232 Res. 22 Res. Jäg. Btn.	99 Res. 100 Res.	229 Res. 230 Res. 231 Res. 232 Res. 22 Res. Jag. Btn.	99 Res.	229 Res. 230 Res. 231 Res.	99 Res.	229 Res. 230 Res. 231 Res.	99 Res.	229 Res. 230 Res. 231 Res.
Cavalry	50 Res. Cav. Detch.		50 Res. Cav. Detch.		50 Res. Cav. Detch.		50 Res. Cav. Detch.		50 Res. Cav. Detch.	
Artillery	50 Res. F. A. Rgt. (9 Btries.).		50 Res. F. A. Rgt.		50 Res. F. A. Rgt.		(z) Art. Command: 50 Res. F. A. Rgt.		68 Art. Command: 50 Res. F. A. Rgt., 81 Ft. A. Btn. (Staff, 1, 2, and 3 Btries.), 705 Light Am. Col., 902 Light Am. Col., 923 Light Am. Col.	
Engineers and liaisons.	50 Res. Pion. Co.		50 Res. Pion. Co. 50 Res. Pont, Engs.		50 Res. Pion. Co. 250 T. M. Co. 50 Res. Pont. Engs.		(350) Pion. Btn.: 50 Res. Pion. Co. 2 Res. Co. 19 Pion. Btn. 250 T. M. Co. 325 Searchlight Section. 450 Tel. Detch.		350 Pion. Btn.; 2 Res. Co. 19 Pions. 50 Res. Pion. Co. 250 T. M. Co. 30 Searchlight Section. 450 Signal Command: 450 Tel. Detch. 60 Wireless Detch.	
Medical and veterinary.			50 Res. Ambulance Co...				532 Ambulance Co. Field Hospital. Vet. Hospital.		532 Ambulance Co. 21 Res. Field Hospital. 84 Res. Field Hospital. 450 Vet. Hospital.	
Transports							M. T. Col.		737 M. T. Col.	

HISTORY.

(10th Corps District—Hanover and Brunswick.)

1914.

1. The 50th Reserve Division (belonging to the 1st series of divisions created between August and October, 1914), formed a part of the 25th Reserve Corps with the 49th Reserve Division. It received its training, at the time of its formation, in the Alten-Grabow Camp in the 4th Corps District.

POLAND.

2. In the middle of October the 50th Reserve Division and the 49th Reserve Division belonged to the 8th Army (Von Hindenburg) and took part in the second German offensive in Poland (battles between the Vistula and the Warta in October, Lodz in November, on the Bzura–Rawka front in December).

Since November the 25th Reserve Corps has belonged to the 9th Army.

1915.

1. Engaged in the operations along the Bzura (region of Bolimow) during the winter and spring of 1915, the 50th Reserve Division took part in the summer offensive of Von Hindenburg and pursued the Russians to the vicinity of Baranovitchi. In June it transferred the 232d Reserve Infantry Regiment to the 107th Division, a new formation.

2. In September the 25th Reserve Corps was dissolved—the 49th Reserve Division remained in Russia, the 50th Reserved Division was transferred to the Western Front. The division entrained at Kovno on October 7. (Itinerary: Koenigsberg–Marienburg–Stettin–Hamburg–Bremen–Osnabrueck–Muenster–Aix la Chapelle–Namur–Givet.) It detrained at Rethel October 13–14.

FRANCE–CHAMPAGNE.

3. On October 16 the 50th Reserve Division was sent to Champagne. It cooperated in the gas attack of October 27 in the vicinity of Rheims and remained in line until December 19.

ARTOIS.

4. Entraining at Witry les Rheims for Douai on December 21, it took over the sector Roclincourt, east of Neuville–St. Vaast.

1916.

1. Having lost heavily at Neuville–St. Vaast, the 50th Reserve Division was withdrawn from from this sector in March, 1916, and south of Armentières (Grenier wood), from April to September. It rested in this calm sector.

SOMME.

2. About December 16 the division was relieved and went into action on the Somme (Martinpuich–Flers), from September 20 to 28. It suffered very heavily there.

3. From October 6 to November 11 it occupied the sector south of the canal of La Bassée (northeast of Vermelles).

4. The division returned to the Somme, on both banks of the Ancre (near Miraumont, Grandcourt), about November 20, and remained in this active sector until December 22.

5. At the end of December it went to rest in the vicinity of Valenciennes.

1917.

1. In January, 1917, the elements of the 50th Reserve Division were in reserve at Achiet le Petit.

SOMME.

2. At the end of January the 50th Reserve Division came back into line north of the Ancre (Beaumont-Hamel); it lost heavily there (200 prisoners) on February 11.

3. Withdrawn from the Somme front at the beginning of March, it went into line east of Transloy (south of Bapaume) on March 13. It withdrew to the Hindenburg Line, near Metz en Couture (southwest of Cambrai), and remained there from the end of March to April 18.

ARTOIS.

4. After a rest in the vicinity of Douai until the middle of May, the division took over the sector of Oppy–Gavrelle, northeast of Arras, where it did not take part in any important action (May 18 to June 10).

FLANDERS.

5. Transferred to the Ypres front about June 11, in anticipation of the British attack, it was kept in reserve in the vicinity of Roulers until July 24.

6. On July 31 the 50th Reserve Division went into action in St. Julien and suffered heavy losses while fighting for the possession of the village (Aug. 1–2).

7. Relieved on August 10 it was sent to rest in the vicinty of Mons and went back into line on September 20, was engaged on the 26th in the vicinity of Gheluvelt, and left the Ypres front on October 3, after serious losses—the 1st Company of the 231st Reserve Infantry Regiment was reduced to 15 men after September 21, the 6th Company to 28. (British Summary of Information, Oct. 24.)

LILLE.

8. At the end of October it took over a sector in the vicinity of Lille (Fromelles) (until the middle of December).

CAMBRAI.

9. It then occupied the lines before Cambrai south of Marcoing and Masnières (Dec. 21–Jan. 31, 1918).

RECRUITING.

At the beginning the 50th Reserve Division was composed of drafts from Silesia and Prussian Saxony, but after the end of 1915 it received most of its replacements from the 10th Corps District. The 229th Reserve Infantry Regiment is from Brunswick; the two others from Hanover. In certain documents we find the division designated as "troops from lower Saxony."

VALUE—1917 ESTIMATE.

The 50th Reserve Division took part in a great number of battles.

Its morale was shaken by the heavy losses which it suffered; it has improved very much.

The division fought comparatively well at Ypres.

1918.

1. The 50th Reserve Division was withdrawn from line south of Marcoing on the 31st of January, the neighboring divisions extending their fronts, and went to the area east of Cambrai, where it received training in open warfare.

PICARDY.

2. On the 13th of March the division marched from Cagnoncles via Carnières and Cattenières to Esnes, and on the 17th proceeded to Villers Outréaux. On the 20th it came into line southwest of Cambrai and took part in the attack of the 21st. The division suffered very heavy losses and was relieved by the 9th Reserve Division on the 22d, going to rest at Liéramont (northeast of Pèronne).

3. On the 23d the division followed up the advance behind the 9th Reserve Division via St. Pierre–Vaast wood (24th), Rancourt–Combles (25th), Montauban (26th), Fricourt (27th), and on the following day went into line southwest of Albert, carrying out an unsuccessful attack. In another attack against the ridge west of Dernancourt on April 5 the division was beaten back with heavy losses. It was relieved on the 9th and went to rest at Maricourt.

4. During the night of April 17–18 it relieved the 18th Division near Morlancourt (south of Albert). It was relieved by the 199th Division early in May and went to rest and refit in the Solesmes area.

5. On the 24th of May it traveled by rail to Montauban (south of Albert), marched via Maricourt to Carnoy the following day, and came into line during the night of May 27th–28th south of Albert. It was relieved by the 54th Reserve Division on June 28 and went to rest near Cambrai.

SOISSONS.

6. On the 19th of July the division entrained at Le Cateau and traveled via St. Quentin to Chauny, where it was loaded on trucks and sent to the Forêt de Pinon. On the 28th it relieved the 20th Division near Buzancy (south of Soissons). Here it was gradually forced to retire toward the northeast, was finally withdrawn to the north of Braine about the 20th of August, and went to the region between Laval and Laon.

7. The presence of elements of the 231st Reserve Regiment was reported the 4th of September west of Vauxaillon, and on the 6th to the south of Neuville sous Margival, the rest of the regiment being in the Urcel–Laval region.

8. On September 14 the whole division went back into line east of Soissons near the Mennejean Farm. This was surrounded by the French on the 15th. The following day Sancy fell to them, too. The same day the plateau to the east and northeast of the Mennejean Farm was captured. On the 18th the division lost still more ground and prisoners; it was withdrawn on the 21st and went to rest near St. Pierre a Arnes (south of Machault).

RHEIMS.

9. On the 2d of October the division came back into line northeast of Rheims, near Bétheny, and went through very heavy fighting. It was still in line on November 11.

VALUE—1918 ESTIMATE.

On October 11 the following was written: "The division did fairly well in its recent encounters, the men, though lacking in enthusiasm, seeming possessed by a dogged determination to do what they conceived to be their duty. The morale, which was good, has been very much lowered by recent losses." That this statement is erroneous seems to be proved by the fact that the German communiqués of October 22, November 1 and 2, say that the division "had shown particular merit in the recent fighting, retook their position in counterattack and repulsed hostile attacks," "bore the brunt of the fighting * * * without showing signs of weariness," and "again maintained their positions against heavy attacks." Therefore, although the division suffered heavy losses, especially in the spring, it is still to be considered as second class.

51st Reserve Division.

COMPOSITION.

	1914 Brigade	1914 Regiment	1915 Brigade	1915 Regiment	1916 Brigade	1916 Regiment	1917 Brigade	1917 Regiment	1918 Brigade	1918 Regiment
Infantry	101 Res. 102 Res. 23 Res. Jag. Btn.	233 Res. 234 Res. 235 Res. 236 Res.	101 Res. 102 Res. 23 Res. Jag. Btn.	233 Res. 234 Res. 235 Res. 236 Res.	101 Res. 102 Res. 23 Res. Jag. Btn.	233 Res. 234 Res. 235 Res. 236 Res.	102 Res.	234 Res. 235 Res. 236 Res.	102 Res.	234 Res. 235 Res. 236 Res.
Cavalry	51 Res. Cav. Detch.		51 Res. Cav. Detch.		51 Res. Cav. Detch.		51 Res. Cav. Detch.		51 Res. Cav. Detch.	
Artillery	51 Res. F. A. Rgt. (9 Btries.).		51 Res. F. A. Rgt.; Mobile Ers. Detch. of 26 F. A. Rgt.		51 Res. F. A. Rgt.		(?) Art. Command: 61 Res. F. A. Rgt.		51 Res. F. A. Rgt. 1 Abt. 11 Res. Ft. A. Rgt. 896 Light Am. Col. 897 Light Am. Col. 1395 Light Am. Col.	
Engineers and Liaisons.	51 Res. Pion. Co.		51 Res. Pion. Co. 51 Res. Pont. Engs.		51 Res. Pion. Co. 25 T. M. Co. 51 Res. Pont. Engs.		(351) Pion. Btn.: 7 Co. 28 Pions. 51 Res. Pion. Co. 251 Searchlight Section. 451 Tel. Detch.		351 Pion. Btn.: 7 Co. 28 Pions. 51 Res. Pion. Co. 33 Searchlight Section. 451 Signal Command: 451 Tel. Detch. 85 Wireless Detch.	
Medical and Veterinary.			51 Res. Ambulance Co.				263 Vet. Hospital. 533 Ambulance Co. 87 Res. Field Hospital. 90 Res. Field Hospital.		533 Ambulance Co. 87 Res. Field Hospital. 88 Res. Field Hospital. 263 Vet. Hospital.	
Transports.							738 M. T. Col.		738 M. T. Col.	
Odd units.					Cylist Co.		Cylist Co.			

HISTORY.

(11th Corps District—Electorate of Hesse and Thuringia.)

1914.

FLANDERS.

1. The 51st Reserve Division (of the series of divisions created between August and October, 1914), forming the 26th Reserve Corps with the 52d Reserve Division, went into action northeast of Ypres in the middle of October. It fought on the line Cortemarck–Moorslede on the 22d, reached Langemarck on the 24th, and finally took up its position near Poelcappelle.

1915.

YPRES.

1. The division remained in the area northeast of Ypres (Poelcappelle, Langemarck, St. Julien) during the entire year of 1915, and until September, 1916. In September, 1916, it transferred the 233d Reserve Infantry Regiment to the 195th Division, a new formation, in consequence of the Russian advance in Galicia.

1916.

SOMME.

1. On September 16, 1916, the 51st Reserve Division was relieved from the sector of Wieltje (north of the Ypres–Zonnebeke road) and transferred to the Somme. It went into action between Combles and Morval about December 18 and suffered very heavy losses from the British attack of the 26th.

CHAMPAGNE.

2. After occupying the Lille front (Neuve Chapelle) for a few days, the division was sent to Champagne at the beginning of October.

It took over the sector of Tahure-Rouvroy (south of Ripont) in the middle of October.

1917.

CHAMPAGNE.

1. The 51st Reserve Division remained on the Massiges front until the middle of May, 1917, with a short rest at the end of February.

2. It was engaged in the attacks on Maisons de Champagne in March, and suffered quite heavily.

3. In the middle of May it went into line near Nauroy and Moronvilliers (Casque–Mont Haut), where it lost heavily.

4. Withdrawn from the front about June 8, it returned, after a short rest in the vicinity of Marbaux, to the sector east of Tahure (June 22–Aug. 10).

MEUSE.

5. Brought back to the right bank of the Meuse, after a rest in the vicinity of Sedan–Montmedy, the division occupied the sector of Samogneux–Hill 344, about August 22, and lost heavily (French attack of Aug. 25, German attack of Sept. 9).

CHAMPAGNE.

6. It was relieved about September 12 and sent to rest behind the Champagne front.

RECRUITING.

Mixed at the time of its formation, the division is actually recruited in the 11th Corps District (Electorate of Hesse and Thuringia), and is so designated in various documents. Beginning with March 13, 1917, it has received young men of the 1918 class who have less than four months' training (236th Reserve Infantry Regiment).

VALUE—1917 ESTIMATE.

The 51st Reserve Division was good at the beginning of the war, but now appears mediocre.

Health conditions seem to be poor (August, 1917).

1918.

CHAMPAGNE.

1. The 51st Reserve Division remained in the Vouziers being trained until about the 20th of January, when it relieved the 52d Division near the Butte du Mesnil. It was relieved early in March and went to the Vouziers-Rethel area, where it received some more training in open warfare.

PICARDY.

2. On the 20th it entrained, and arrived at Etreux (north of Guise) the following day. From there it marched via St. Quentin-Ham-Roye-Faverolles to Montdidier, where it arrived on the 30th. The following day it reenforced the front near Ayencourt (south of Montdidier), relieving the 9th Division. It was relieved by the 2d Division during the night of the 1st-2d of May and went to rest in the Chimay area.

AISNE.

3. On the 30th of May the division, thoroughly rested and brought up to strength, reenforced the battle front near Vauxbuin (southwest of Soissons). Here it became heavily engaged and suffered severe losses, especially the first two days. It was relieved near Cutry (southwest of Soissons) on June 16, and went to rest near Oulchy le Chateau.

4. During the night of July 19-20, the division reenforced the front near Blanzy (south of Soissons). Here it became heavily engaged. It was forced back by the Allied counteroffensive, and was withdrawn from line south of Braine early in August. It went to rest near Marle.

CHAMPAGNE.

5. On September 28 the division entered line near Somme-Py (north of Suippes). Here it was badly handled and had to be withdrawn on the 4th of October, when it had been driven back to St. Etienne à Py. It then rested for a day or two near Vouziers.

OISE.

6. On the 6th it entrained at Vouziers and Vrizy and arrived at La Ferté-Chevresis two days later. It was then put on trucks and moved up to the front, taking over the Bernot-Origny sector (east of St. Quentin) on the 8th. It was withdrawn about the 15th.

CHAMPAGNE.

7. After having rested a fortnight between the Oise and the Aisne, the division entered line east of Rethel on the 31st, remaining in line until the signing of the armistice.

VALUE—1918 ESTIMATE.

The 51st Reserve is to be considered a good second-class division. It did not distinguish itself by any brilliant fighting, but it did acquit itself in the battles of the Somme and the Aisne and during the Allied counteroffensive. It suffered exceedingly heavy losses, but these were in large measure made good by drafts of 1919 class recruits.

52d Division.
COMPOSITION.

	1915		1916		1917		1918	
	Brigade.	Regiment.	Brigade.	Regiment.	Brigade.	Regiment.	Brigade.	Regiment.
Infantry	104.	66. 169. 170.	104.	66. 169. 170.	56.	111. 169. 170.	56.	111. 169. 170.
Cavalry	(2) Sqn. 16 Uhlan Rgt.		2 Sqn. 16 Uhlan Rgt.		4 Sqn. 16 Uhlan Rgt.		4 Sqn. 16 Uhlan Rgt.	
Artillery	52 Brig.; 103 F. A. Rgt. (6 Btries.) 104 F. A. Rgt. (6 Btries., 3 of which are Hows.).		52 Brig.; 103 F. A. Rgt. 104 F. A. Rgt.		52 Art. Command: 104 F. A. Rgt. (9 Btries.).		52 Art. Command: 104 Ft. A. Rgt. 84 Ft. A. Btn. (Staff, 1, 2, and 3 Btries.). 892 Light Am. Col. 917 Light Am. Col. 1371 Light Am. Col.	
Engineers and Liaisons.	103 Pion. Co. 104 Pion. Co.		103 Pion. Co. 104 Pion. Co. 52 T. M. Co. 52 Tel. Detch. 52 Pont. Engs.		137 Pion. Btn.; 103 Pion. Co. 104 Pion. Co. 52 T. M. Co. 103 Searchlight Section. 52 Tel. Detch.		137 Pion. Btn.; 103 Pion. Co. 104 Pion. Co. 52 T. M. Co. 32 Searchlight Section. 52 Signal Command: 52 Tel. Detch. 46 Wireless Detch.	
Medical and Veterinary.					52 Ambulance Co. 341 Field Hospital. 342 Field Hospital. 343 Field Hospital. 205 Vet. Hospital.		52 Ambulance Co. 341 Field Hospital. 342 Field Hospital. 205 Vet. Hospital.	
Transport.							577 M. T. Col.	

Odd units......	52 Cyclist Co.	52 Cyclist Co. 577 Divisional Supply Co.
Attached......	1 & 2 Potsdam Landst. Inf. Btn. (3 C. Dist.). 2 Co. 24 Pions.	147 Giant Periscope Sect. 209 Field Sig. Section. 210 Field Sig. Section. Pigeon Loft. 107 Wireless Detch. 57 Wireless Compass Station. 52 Trench Wireless Detch. Power Buzzer Section. 16 M. G. S. S. Detch. Staff of 203 Ft. A. Rgt. Staff of 3 Abdl. 27 Ft. A. Rgt. 1 Btry. 94 Ft. A. Btn. 1 Btry. 14 Ft. A. Rgt. 1 Btry. 4 Ft. A. Rgt. 4 Naval Gun Btry. 237 Close-range Btry. (3 7-cm. guns). 44 Art. Survey Section. The following is according to a captured German document dated June 4, 1917: 87 Supply Train. 103 M. T. Col. 274 M. T. Col. 725 M. T. Col. 944 M. T. Col. 2 Ammunition Train. 4 Ammunition Train. 136 Ammunition Train (new pattern). 65 Supply Train. 663 Supply Depot. 665 Supply Depot. 107 Balloon Sqn. 8 Air Sqns. (Protective Flight). 205 Air Sqn. (Reconnaissance Flight). 1 Co. 14 Labor Btn. 2 Co. 14 Labor Btn. 3 Co. 14 Labor Btn. 1 Co. 56 Road Const. Btn. 6 Co. 56 Road Const. Btn.

HISTORY.

(14th Corps District —Grand Duchy of Baden.)

1915.

The 52d Division (of the even 50 to 58 series) was formed in March, 1915, by taking the 169th and 170th Infantry Regiments from the 29th Division (14th Army Corps, Baden), and the 66th Landwehr Regiment from the 7th Division (4th Army Corps). On April 6, 1917, the last-named regiment was replaced by the 111th Infantry Regiment (the 4th Regiment of the 28th Division, also from Baden).

ARTOIS.

1. In April, 1915, the 52d Division was in line south of Arras (Monchy aux Bois, Hebuterne). It occupied this sector until September, 1916.

1916.

SOMME.

1. During the Franco-English offensive on the Somme the 52d Division bore to the south and held the sector Hebuterne, Beaumont–Hamel, north of Thiepval (September–November, 1916).

2. On November 26 the division was withdrawn from the front and sent to rest in the vicinity of Bouchain (December).

1917.

ALSACE.

1. On January 13, 1917, the 52d Division was sent to Alsace (northwest of Bale).

2. About the middle of January it took over the sector of Altkirch (Carspach–Hirtzbach), which it held until the end of March.

3. After a few days at rest (at the beginning of April) in the Grand Duchy of Baden south of Muellheim, it entrained on April 16 north of Bale and was transferred to the Aisne, already including men of the 1918 class in its ranks.

AISNE.

4. On April 21 it went into line south of Juvincourt. It occupied this sector until July 10, with a period of rest from June 1 to 15.

CALIFORNIE PLATEAU.

5. About July 24 it went back into line on the Californie Plateau, where it launched an attack on September 14.

6. Sent into rest in the vicinity of Sissonne about the end of September, it appeared in the vicinity of Pinon about the middle of October, where it went into action and lost heavily on the 23d.

CHAMPAGNE.

7. After a rest in the vicinity of Chimay (beginning of November), it went into line on the Champagne front (Butte du Mesnil-Maisons de Champagne); it remained there until December 15.

8. From December 15 until January, 1918, it was at rest in the vicinity of Vouziers.

RECRUITING.

Since April, 1917, the 52d Division has been almost purely Badensian. Besides the Badensians, who form almost all of the drafts, we find men from the neighboring districts of the Empire (Rhine Province, Hesse-Nassau).

VALUE—1917 ESTIMATE.

In general the morale of the 52d Division has appeared rather high. In the sector of Juvincourt (April to July, 1917) the troops of the division showed nerve and dash in the course of the local operations in which they took part.

The division had few losses until the month of September.

However, it lost heavily on October 23 (the battle of La Malmaison), especially the 170th Infantry Regiment.

1918.

CHAMPAGNE.

1. The 52d Division, which had been resting near Vouziers since December 15, relieved the 52d Reserve Division near Tahure (northeast of Suippes) on the 10th of January. During the time the division held this sector the elements not actually in the front line were being trained in open warfare. Early in March it was relieved by the 52d Reserve Division and went to the Vouziers area, where it received still more intensive training in the war of movement.

PICARDY.

2. The division entrained near Vouziers on the 22d of March, and detrained on the following day near Bohain. On the 24th it left and marched via Fresnoy le Grand–Holnon wood (26th)–Bethenicourt (27th)–Etalon–Liancourt-Fosse to Fresnoy les Roye. It relieved the 28th Division near Hangest en Santerre (northwest of Mont-didier) on the 28th. It was relieved by the 76th Reserve Division on the 14th of April and went to rest in the Sedan area

AISNE.

3. Here it was thoroughly reconstituted. It entrained on the 22d of May, arriving at La Malmaison (southeast of Laon) the same day. On the 26th it went into line near Juvincourt (east of Craonne), and took part in the initial attack on the following day. It crossed the Aisne between Pontavert and Gernicourt; proceeding via Bouvancourt and Guyancourt, it crossed the Vesle at Jonquery on the 28th, reached Faverolles on the 29th, Olizy on the 31st, and the Marne, in the region of Verneuil, on June 2. The division was at first ordered to cross the same day, but the order was subsequently rescinded. It was withdrawn, after having suffered severely, about the 10th, and was reported to be at rest in the Sedan area on the 15th. On the 20th it was reported in reserve in the Tournai region.

LENS.

4. During the night of July 12–13 it relieved the 119th Division in the Avion sector (south of Lens). It was relieved about the 5th of August by the extension of fronts of flanking divisions.

ARMENTIERES.

5. During the night of the 6th–7th it relieved the 207th Division near Vieux Berquin (southwest of Bailleul), the 207th Division taking over the sector just vacated by the 52d Division. On the 17th it was withdrawn, the neighboring divisions extending their fronts.

BAPAUME.

6. Five days later it reenforced the battle front near Miraumont (west of Bapaume). It was withdrawn about the 4th of September, after having lost over 1,300 prisoners, and went to rest in the Courtrai area. Here the battalions were reduced to three companies, the strength of which was further made up by drafts of the 29th Ersatz Regiment (223d Division disbanded).

ARGONNE.

7. On September 28 the division reenforced the front near Exermont (southeast of Grandpre). In the heavy fighting that followed the division was driven back to Landres et St. Georges, where it was withdrawn about the 14th of October after having suffered heavy losses (almost 600 in prisoners alone).

8. During the night of October 31–November 1 the division, which had received large numbers of replacements during its two weeks' rest, relieved the 41st Division east of Busancy (north of Grandpre). It was still in line on the 11th.

VALUE—1918 ESTIMATE.

The 52d is rated as one of the best German divisions. It was in a great deal of heavy fighting during 1918 (as in preceding years) and acquitted itself most creditably.

52d Reserve Division.
COMPOSITION.

	1914 Brigade	1914 Regiment	1915 Brigade	1915 Regiment	1916 Brigade	1916 Regiment	1917 Brigade	1917 Regiment	1918 Brigade	1918 Regiment
Infantry	103 Res. 104 Res. 24 Res. Jag. Btn.	237 Res. 238 Res. 239 Res. 240 Res.	103 Res. 104 Res. 24 Res. Jag. Btn.	237 Res. 238 Res. 239 Res. 240 Res.	103 Res. 104 Res. 24 Res. Jag. Btn.	237 Res. 238 Res. 239 Res. 240 Res.	104 Res.	238 Res. 239 Res. 240 Res.	104 Res.	239 Res. 239 Res. 240 Res.
Cavalry	52 Res. Cav. Detch.		52 Res. Cav. Detch.		52 Res. Cav. Detch.				52 Res. Cav. Detch.	
Artillery	52 Res. F. A. Rgt. (9 Btries.).		52 Res. F. A. Rgt.		52 Res. F. A. Rgt.		(?) Art. Command: 52 Res. F. A. Rgt.		69 Art. Command:	52 Res. F. A. Rgt. 51 Ft. A. Btn. 894 Light Am. Col. 1365 Light Am. Col. 1393 Light Am. Col.
Engineers and Liaisons.	52 Res. Pion. Co.		52 Res. Pion. Co. 52 Res. Pont. Engs.		52 Res. Pion. Co. 1 Ldw. Pion. Co. (9 C. Dist.). 2 Ers. Co. 24 Pions. 252 T. M. Co. 52 Res. Pont. Engs.		(352) Pion. Btn.: 8 Co. 28 Pions. 52 Res. Pion. Co. 252 T. M. Co. (?) 312 T. M. Co. 452 Tel. Detch.		253 Pion. Btn.: 8 Co. 28 Pions. 52 Res. Pion. Co. 252 T. M. Co. 184 Searchlight Section. 452 Signal Command: 453 Tel. Detch. 23 Wireless Detch.	
Medical and Veterinary.			52 Res. Ambulance Co.				534 Ambulance Co. 88 Res. Field Hospital. Vet. Hospital.		534 Ambulance Co. 89 Field Hospital. 90 Field Hospital. 264 Vet. Hospital.	
Transports							M. T. Col.			

HISTORY.

(8th Corps District—Rhine Province.)

1914.

FLANDERS.

1. The 52d Reserve Division (belonging to the 26th Reserve Corps with the 51st Reserve Division), formed between August and October, 1914, was trained at the Senne Camp and entrained for Belgium on October 12.

The division was engaged in the first battle of the Ypres about October 22.

It fought in October and November in the vicinity of Langemarck-Passachendaele and suffered heavy losses. Between October 18 and 28, the 240th Reserve Infantry Regiment listed casualties of 28 officers and 1,360 men. (Official List of Casualties.)

1915.

YPRES.

1. The division remained on the front north of Ypres (Pilckem, St. Julien, Zonnebeke) during the year 1915 and until the month of September, 1916. Certain of its regiments lost very heavily in April and May—25 officers and 1,268 men casulaties in the 240th Reserve Infantry Regiment. (Official List of Casulaties.)

1916.

SOMME.

1. About September 14, 1916, it was transferred to the Somme minus the 237th Reserve Infantry Regiment, sent to Galicia for the formation of the 199th Division.

It was engaged in the Lesboeufs sector (Sept. 16–29) and lost very heavily in the British attack of the 26th.

CHAMPAGNE.

2. Sent to Champagne, it went into line at the Butte de Souain on October 6, then on November 6 entered St. Marie à Py and the vicinity of Tahure.

1917.

CHAMPAGNE.

1. The 52d Reserve Division occupied the Tahure front south of Rouvroy until April 20, 1917. It suffered losses at Maisons de Champagne, at the end of March, which caused hasty replacements of the 1918 class with only four months' training to be sent.

SAPIGNEUL.

2. Relieved between April 15 and 20, it went to the vicinity of Rethel and passed in review at Asfeld on May 3; went into line on the 5th southeast of Berry au Bac and underwent the French attack of the 7th south of Sapigneul. (The 239th Reserve Division had 107 prisoners taken.) On May 31 it again lost heavily while attacking Hill 108.

YPRES.

3. The division was withdrawn from the Aisne front at the beginning of July and transferred to Belgium. It went into action on the Ypres-Menin road on the 31st, the day of the British offensive, and lost heavily. The attacks of August 10 again caused serious losses—the remnants of the 1st Battalion of the 238th Reserve Infantry Regiment formed only two companies at the time of their relief. (British Summary of Information, Aug. 11.)

CHAMPAGNE.

4. About August 11 the 52d Reserve Division left the Belgian front for Champagne, where it again took over its own sector east of the Butte de Souain about August 26. It remained there until the end of December.

At the time of its formation the 52d Reserve Division was made up of one Rhenish Regiment and three from Baden; to-day it is entirely Rhenish.

VALUE—1917 ESTIMATE.

In May and June, 1917, the 52d Reserve Division held a very difficult sector south of Berry au Bac where it apparently lost very heavily. However, it acted like a good division.

During its rest in the vicinity of Vouziers, at the end of January, 1918, it was given very intensive training. It was considered as an attack division. (Interrogation of prisoners, February, 1918.)

1918.

CHAMPAGNE.

1. The 52d Reserve Division was relieved by the 52d Division in the Tahure sector on January 10 and went to the vicinity of Vouziers, where it was intensively trained in open warfare.

2. Early in March it returned to line and relieved the 52d Division. It was relieved on the 23d of April by the 1st Bavarian Division.

YPRES.

3. It proceeded to march to Vouziers, where it entrained on the 28th and, traveling via Mezières–Signy–Hirson–Mons–Tournai, detrained at Mouscron on the 30th. On May 4 it marched to Wervicq, and on the following day moved into line via Warneton and Messines, relieving the 3d Guard Division in the Voormezeele sector (south of Ypres). In the fighting before Dickebusch on the 8th heavy losses were suffered. It was withdrawn about the 25th, and went to rest near Menin.

4. During the night of the 13th–14th of June it relieved the 58th Division near Locre (south of Ypres). It was relieved on the 1st of July, the flanking divisions extending their fronts, and went to rest in the region southwest of Courtrai.

5. On the 6th of August it came back into line, relieving the 58th Division in the Kemmel sector (south of Ypres). It was withdrawn about the 26th.

CAMBRAI.

6. About the 2d of September it reenforced the front in the Bertincourt sector (east of Bapaume). After having suffered severe losses in killed and wounded, besides losing over 1,000 prisoners, it was relieved by the 6th Division near Havrincourt on the 16th.

COURTRAI.

7. About the 27th it entered line near Moorslede (southwest of Roulers). It suffered severe losses here, and was withdrawn early in October.

8. On October 14 it relieved the Guard Ersatz Division in the Iseghem sector (north of Courtrai). It was heavily engaged here, and was finally withdrawn on the 25th. It did not reenter line.

VALUE—1918 ESTIMATE.

The 52d was rated as a second-class division, but it was probably not so good as other divisions similarly rated, for although it was intensively trained for use as a shock unit for almost two months in Champagne early in the year it was not used in any of the German offensives. It is to be noted, however, that the German communique of October 24 said, "Southwest of Deynze the veteran 52d Reserve Division, which has been in battle daily since October 14, repulsed the renewed attacks of the enemy along the Deynze–Waregem railway."

53d Reserve Division.

COMPOSITION.

	1914		1915		1916		1917		1918 [1]	
	Brigade.	Regiment.	Brigade.	Regiment.	Brigade.	Regiment.	Brigade.	Regiment.	Brigade.	Regiment.
Infantry	105 Res. 106 Res. 25 Res. Jäg. Btn.	241 Res. 242 Res. 243 Res. 244 Res.	105 Res. 106 Res. 25 Res. Jäg. Btn.	241 Res. 242 Res. 243 Res. 244 Res.	105 Res. 106 Res. 25 Res. Jäg. Btn.	241 Res. 243 Res. 242 Res. 244 Res.	105 Res.	241 Res. 242 Res. 243 Res.	105 Res.	241 Res. 242 Res. 243 Res.
Cavalry	53 Res. Cav. Detch.		53 Res. Cav. Detch.		53 Res. Cav. Detch.		53 Res. (?) Cav. Detch.		53 Res. Cav. Detch. (Saxon).	
Artillery	53 Res. F. A. Rgt. (9 Btries.).		53 Res. F. A. Rgt.		53 Res. F. A. Rgt.		(?) Art. command: 53 Res. F. A. Rgt.		(?) Art. Command: 53 Res. F. A. Rgt. (Saxon).	
Engineers and Liaisons.	53 Res. Pion. Co.		53 Res. Pion. Co. 53 Res. Pont. Engs.		53 Res. Pion. Co. 53 Res. Pont. Engs. 253 T. M. Co.		(353) Pion. Btn.: 53 Res. Pion. Co. 279 Pion. Co. 253 T. M. Co. 453 Tel. Detch.		53 Res. Pion. Co. (Saxon). 279 Pion. Co. 253 Searchlight Section. 453 Tel. Detch.	
Medical and Veterinary.			53 Res. Ambulance Co.				Ambulance Co. 94 Res. Field Hospital. Vet. Hospital.		535 (?) Ambulance Co. 92 Res. Field Hospital (Saxon). 453 Vet. Hospital.	
Transports							M. T. Col.		M. T. Col.	

[1] Composition at the time of dissolution, October, 1918.

HISTORY.

(241st and 242d Reserve Infantry Regiments: 12th Corps District—Saxony. 243d Reserve Infantry Regiment: 19th Corps District—Saxony.)

1914.

FLANDERS-YPRES.

1. The 53d Reserve Division (of the 27th Reserve Corps with the 54th Reserve Division), formed between August and October, 1914, were sent to Belgium, and detrained on August 14 at Ath. It was engaged, with the divisions of the same series, in the battle of Ypres, against the British Army. Beginning on October 21, it fought on the front Poelcappelle-Becelaere; southeast of Gheluvelt on October 29, and near the Ypres-Menin road at the time of the great attack of November 11.. It suffered very heavy losses—the 25th Reserve Chasseurs Battalion, already reduced to 225 men on October 31, had only 73 on November 4 (notebook). On November 25 the 6th Company of the 241st Reserve Infantry Regiment had only 7 of the men left who constituted it upon its departure from Saxony (letter).

1915.

FLANDERS.

1. The division remained in line north of Ypres during the winter of 1914-15, alternating with the 54th Reserve Division in the sector Broodseinde-Polygon wood.

2. It took part in the second battle of Ypres, near Frezenberg and Gravenstafel, where it again lost heavily.

3. In June it occupied the sector of Wytchaete-St. Éloi and returned northeast of Ypres (Verlorenhoek) in the middle of July.

CHAMPAGNE AND FLANDERS.

4. At the beginning of October the 105th Reserve Brigade was sent to Champagne to reenforce the lines near Tahure. The 106th Reserve Brigade took over the sector of the Lys.

5. In November the division was regrouped and sent to rest in the vicinity of Ingelmunster (north of Courtrai). It remained behind the front during the winter of 1915-16 in the vicinity of Roulers.

1916.

LA BASSEE.

1. At the end of March, 1916, the 53d Reserve Division left Flanders and went into line on both banks of the La Bassee Canal.

SOMME.

2. Sent to the Somme at the end of August, it was engaged southeast of Maurepas (Le Forest) at the time of the French attack of September 3, which ended in the capture of Le Forest and of Clery. It suffered heavy losses in counterattacking and in withstanding the new French offensive of September 13. Between September 6 and 12 the 241st Reserve Infantry Regiment listed 12 officers and 1,502 men as casualties. On September 3 the 244th Reserve Infantry Regiment had lost 400 prisoners.

LOOS.

3. Relieved on September 14, it was transferred to the Loos front (between Hulluch and the Lens-Béthune railroad), from September 21 to October 5.

CHAMPAGNE.

4. On October 9 it was in Champagne, where it occupied the sector of Prosnes, east of Rheims.

GALICIA.

5. Withdrawn from the Champagne front, the 53d Reserve Division entrained for the Eastern Front on November 17. (Itinerary: Bétheniville-Rethel-Sedan-Trèves-

Coblenz-Ems-Cologne-Halle-Cotthus-Liegnitz-Breslau-Cracow-Tarnow-Jaroslaw-Przemysl-Lemberg-Rohatyn.) It detrained at Pukow (south of Lemberg) on the 26th.

6. It was sent into reserve behind the line of the Narajowka in December. In the autumn of 1916 the 244th Reserve Infantry Regiment was transferred to the 215th Division; later it was transferred to the 96th Division (Saxon).

1917.

1. At the beginning of January, 1917, the 53d Reserve Division went into line at the junction of the Narajowka and the Dniester, and remained in this sector until the middle of June without any important engagement.

2. Relieved and sent to rest in June, it took part in the German counteroffensive begun on July 20 and advanced north of the Dniester. It was identified on August 3 east of Krjivtche.

3. The division was withdrawn from the front at the end of November and entrained for Belgium in the middle of December.

RECRUITING.

The 53d Reserve Division is purely Saxon.

VALUE—1917 ESTIMATE.

The 53d Reserve Division spent a year on the Eastern Front (November, 1916, to November, 1917). It is of mediocre quality.

1918.

1. The division was relieved in the Houthulst forest on February 12 and went to rest in the Bruges area.

BATTLE OF PICARDY.

2. On March 1-2 it relieved the 27th Division northeast of Flesquieres. It took part in the initial attack on March 21, was withdrawn on the 22d and went to rest near Bourlon wood. The division was in General Headquarters reserve and on March 27 marched via Havrincourt-Ruyanlcourt-Moislains-Bouchavesnes, crossing the Somme at Clery, and continued to march via Raincourt to Rosieres en Santerre. The 241st Reserve Regiment went into line near Moreuil on the night of April 1-2 and relieved the 426th Regiment (88th Division); the 242d Reserve Regiment went into line on the night of April 3-4, relieving the 100th Body Grenadier Regiment (23d Division). On the morning of April 4 the division attacked in the vicinity of Arriese Cour wood. The division at this date was operating under the 18th German Army. About the middle of April it was withdrawn from the Moreuil sector.

VERDUN.

3. About May 1 the division was resting in rear of the Verdun front. It relieved the 84th Division west of Bethincourt in the first week of May. It held that quiet sector until the 11th of June, when a tired division took its place and the 53d Reserve Division returned to an active front.

SOISSONS.

4. The division detrained near Laon on June 14-15, and the next night relieved the 6th Bavarian Reserve Division north of Le Port. Here it participated in heavy fighting in July and August until its relief about August 10. In this engagement the 243d Reserve Regiment was reduced to three companies per battalion as a result of heavy losses.

5. The division was taken to the region in rear of the Argonne front and the process of dissolution begun. Before its completion the American offensive in the Argonne began and elements of the division were used on the United States front between September 29 and October 15.

According to the available evidence, the 242d Reserve Regiment was drafted to the 24th and 58th Divisions, the 241st Regiment to the 23d Division, and the 243d Reserve Regiment to the 40th and 58th Divisions.

VALUE—1917 ESTIMATE.

The division was rated as third class. It participated in the spring Somme offensive, but thereafter did not play an important part in the fighting. The low effective strength was directly responsible for the dissolution of the division.

54th Division.
COMPOSITION.

	1915 Brigade	1915 Regiment	1916 Brigade	1916 Regiment	1917 Brigade	1917 Regiment	1918 Brigade	1918 Regiment
Infantry	108.	27 Res. 90 Res. 84.	108.	84. 27 Res. 90 Res.	108.	84. 27 Res. 90 Res.	(?)	84. 27 Res. 90 Res.
Cavalry		(?)	17 Hus. Rgt. (Sqn.).		1 Sqn. 17 Hus. Rgt.		1 Sqn. 17 Hus. Rgt.	
Artillery	54 Brig.: 107 F. A. Rgt. (6 Btries.). 108 F. A. Rgt. (6 Btries.).		54 Brig.: 107 F. A. Rgt. 108 F. A. Rgt.		54 Art. Command: 108 F. A. Rgt. (9 Btries.).		55 Art. Command: 108 F. A. Rgt. 54 Ft. A. Btn. 746 Light Am. Col. 955 Light Am. Col. 966 Light Am. Col.	
Engineers and liaisons.	107 Pion. Co. 108 Pion. Co.		107 Pion. Co. 108 Pion. Co. 54 T. M. Co. 54 Pont. Engs. 54 Tel. Detch.		Pion. Btn.: 107 Pion. Co. 108 Pion. Co. 1 Ldw. Co., 16 Pions. 54 T. M. Co. 107 Searchlight Section. 54 Tel. Detch.		138 Pion. Btn.: 107 Pion. Co. 108 Pion. Co. 97 Searchlight Section. 54 Signal Command: 54 Tel. Detch. 87 Wireless Detch.	
Medical and Veterinary.					54 Ambulance Co. 345 Field Hospital. 348 Field Hospital. Vet. Hospital.		54 Ambulance Co. 345 Field Hospital. 348 Field Hospital. 54 Vet. Hospital.	
Transport					578 M. T. Col.		578 M. T. Col.	
Oddu nits			54 Cyclist Co.					
Attached	54 Ft. A. Btn.		24 Labor Btn.		119 Labor Btn.			

HISTORY.

(84th and 90th Reserve Infantry Regiments: 9th Corps District—Schleswig-Holstein and Mecklenburg.   27th Reserve Infantry Regiment: 4th Corps District—Prussian Saxony.)

1915.

1. The 54th Division was formed in March, 1915, by the removal of regiments from divisions engaged at this time between the north of Noyon and east of Soissons.

Two of these regiments, the 84th (18th Division) and the 90th Reserve (18th Reserve Division), came from the 9th Corps District (Schleswig-Holstein and Mecklenburg); the third regiment, the 27th Reserve (7th Reserve Division) was originally from Prussian Saxony (4th Corps District).

CHAMPAGNE.

2. Concentrated in March near Guise, the 54th Division was sent to Champagne in the middle of April (vicinity of Perthes), where it remained until July, 1915.

RUSSIA.

3. In July it was transferred to Russia.   It fought on the Narew (July and August) . and on the Niemen, southeast of Grodno, in September.

FRANCE–OISE.

4. Brought back to France at the beginning of October, it went into line on the 12th on the left bank of the Oise (Quennevières–Moulin sous Touvent).

1916.

1. Withdrawn from the Oise front in January, 1916, the 54th Division rested in the vicinity of La Fère until May.   During this time it was occupied in defensive works in the vicinity of Soissons–Craonne.

VERDUN.

2. In May it was transferred to Verdun.   It occupied the sector of Hill 304 on May 14.

3. About September 11 it crossed to the right bank of the Meuse and advanced north of Fleury.   On October 24 it was dislodged by the French attacks and thrown back with heavy losses north of Douaumont Fort.   It was relieved at the beginning of November.

LORRAINE.

4. Having scarcely made good its losses, it went back into line on November 5 north of Flirey en Haye.

1917.

1. The division remained in the calm sector of Flirey during the winter of 1916–17.

AISNE.

2. Relieved in the middle of April, 1917, it was sent behind the Champagne front (vicinity of Asfeld).   On April 21 it reenforced the lines at Berry au Bac.   It underwent the French attack of May 4, to which it opposed a serious resistance on the Juvincourt Ridge, but suffered heavy losses (650 prisoners).

3. It was withdrawn from the Aisne front on May 10.

CHAMPAGNE.

4. Sent to the east of Rheims, the division occupied the sector south of Somme Py from May 15 to July 24.   It was filled up there in June by several reenforcements, totaling about 2,000 men.

YPRES.

5. On July 25 it entrained at Machault (southwest of Vouziers) for Charleville, from which place it went to Belgium after a short rest.   It was in action east of Ypres from August 5 to 19, and suffered new losses during the British attack of August 16.   One company of the 90th Reserve Infantry Regiment was reduced to one officer and four men.

CAMBRAI.

6. Sent back into line at the end of August on the Cambrai front (Havrincourt-Villers Plouich), the division again lost very heavily in this sector, principally in the course of a tank attack on November 20 (2,789 prisoners).

LORRAINE.

7. Relieved immediately after this attack, it was sent to rest in Lorraine and reorganized. Between August and November the division received more than 3,000 replacements. (British Summary of Information.)

RECRUITING.

Mixed upon its formation (Schleswig-Holstein, Mecklenburg, Prussian Saxony,) the 54th Division remained so with a tendency, nevertheless, to make the 90th Reserve Infantry Regiment a pure Mecklenburg regiment and to reserve the drafts from the rest of the 9th Corps District for the 84th Infantry Regiment.

In January 1918, the 1919 class did not seem to be represented; the 90th Reserve Infantry Regiment had just received replacements made up of men put back in the 1917 and 1918 classes who entered the service in September, 1917.

VALUE—1917 ESTIMATE.

The 54th Division held the most active sectors on the Western front; it has everywhere given proof of great energy in its resistance, especially at Cambrai in November, 1917. However, before the affair of Cambrai rather frequent desertions proved that the losses incurred at Ypres had weakened the morale of the troops; besides, the replacements received in Lorraine were mostly composed of returned wounded of all ages.

However, the 54th Division tried, during its stay in Lorraine, to amalgamate all these elements and to renew their combat value by intensive training and careful instruction (March, 1918).

1918.

BATTLE OF PICARDY.

The division was relieved in the sector north of Nancy about February 17 by the 48th Landwehr Division. It remained in Lorraine in March undergoing training for open warfare. It entrained near Dieuze on the 24th and traveled via Metz–Sedan–Charleville–Mons–Valenciennes to a place about 10 miles east of Douai. The division expected to come into line near Arras, but after resting one night at Douai it marched off toward Peronne and arrived at Rosieres on April 2. It moved up to the line north of Moreuil on the night of April 3–4, taking part in the attack. The division withdrew on the night of the 5th–6th. It returned to line south of Thennes on April 10 and stayed in about eight days.

SOMME.

2. The division rested at Cambrai until the night of May 22–23, when it relieved the 183d Division near Ville sur Ancre. It was relieved on June 20 by the 107th Division. Following its relief, the division rested north of the Somme until August 3, when it was engaged near Antheuil. About September 1 the division left its sector near Lassigny and relieved the 105th Division northeast of Noyon. Here it was relieved on September 10.

CAMBRAI–ST. QUENTIN.

3. The division rested 15 days before it entered line northeast of Hargicourt on September 25, relieving the 232d Division. It fought in the Le Cateau area until October 12, when it retired to reserves in the vicinity of Landrecies. On November 2 it was reengaged at Ors and continued in line until the armistice. The last identification was at Lemont-Fontaine on the 8th.

VALUE—1918 ESTIMATE.

The division was rated as second class. In the last year its service was largely on the defensive in active sectors. In this capacity it was almost constantly in line.

54th Reserve Division.

COMPOSITION.

	1914 Brigade	1914 Regiment	1915 Brigade	1915 Regiment	1916 Brigade	1916 Regiment	1917 Brigade	1917 Regiment	1918[1] Brigade	1918[1] Regiment
Infantry	107 Res. 108 Res. 26 Res. Jäg. Btn.	245 Res. 246 Res. 247 Res. 248 Res.	107 Res. 108 Res. 26 Res. Jäg. Btn.	245 Res. 246 Res. 247 Res. 248 Res.	107 Res. 108 Res. 26 Res. Jäg. Btn.	245 Res. 247 Res. 246 Res. 248 Res.	107 Res.	246 Res. 247 Res. 248 Res.	107 Res.	246 Res. 247 Res. 248 Res.
Cavalry	54 Res. Cav. Detch. (Wurtt.)		54 Res. Cav. Detch.		54 Res. Cav. Detch.		54 Res. Cav. Detch.		54 Res. Cav. Detch. (Wurtt.).	
Artillery	54 Res. F. A. Rgt. (9 Btries., 1-3 Sax., 4-9 Wurtt.).		54 Res. F. A. Rgt., Ers. Abtl. 59 F. A. Rgt.		54 Res. F. A. Rgt.		(?) Art. command: 54 Res. F. A. Rgt. (9 Btries. Wurtt.).		(?) Art. command:	54 Res. F. A. Rgt. (Wurtt.).
Engineers and Liaisons.	54 Res. Pion. Co. (Saxon).		54 Res. Pion. Co. 54 Res. Pont. Engs.		54 Res. Pion. Co. 254 T. M. Co. 54 Pont. Engs.		(354) Pion. Btn.: 1 Res. Co. 13 Pions. 2 Res. Co. 13 Pions. 254 T. M. Co. 312 Searchlight Section. 454 Tel. Detch.		1 Res. Co. 13 Pions. 2 Res. Co. 13 Pions. 312 Searchlight Section. 254 T. M. Co. 454 Tel. Detch.	
Medical and Veterinary.			54 Res. Ambulance Co.				536 Ambulance Co. (Wurtt.). 92 Res. Field Hospital. Vet. Hospital.		536 Ambulance Co. (Wurtt.). 93 Res. Field Hospital(Wurtt.). 94 Res. Field Hospital(Wurtt.). 246 Vet. Hospital.	
Transport							M. T. Col.		M. T. Col.	

[1] Composition at the time of dissolution, September, 1918.

HISTORY.

(13th Corps District—Wuerttemberg.)

1914.

BELGIUM.

1. The 54th Reserve Division, forming the 27th Reserve Corps with the 53d Reserve Division, was formed of men from Wurttemberg, with the addition of one infantry regiment and one battalion of chasseurs from Saxony. Trained at the Muensingen Camp, it went into action for the first time on October 21, 1914, in Belgium at the battle of Ypres. On October 29, it made an unsuccessful attack south of Gheluvelt; going slightly to the north, it took part in the general attack of November 11 in the vicinity of Zonnebeke, where it lost very heavily. From October 21 to November 20 the 248th Reserve Infantry Regiment listed 32 officers and 1,395 men as casualties. (Official List of Casualties.)

1915.

1. The division remained in Flanders during the entire year of 1915, occupying the front Becelaere–Polygon wood, between the Ypres–Menin wood and the Roulers railroad.

2. In April and May it suffered heavy losses during the second battle of Ypres (Frezenberg, Verlorenhoek, Hooge).

1916.

1. At the end of January and beginning of February, 1916, the 54th Reserve Division was withdrawn from the Ypres salient, concentrated in the vicinity of Thielt, Ghent, and Hasselt and sent for training to the Beverloo Camp (February–March).

ARTOIS.

2. Toward the end of March it took over the sector south of Neuve Chapelle (north of La Bassée) where it did not take part in any important action.

SOMME.

3. Relieved at the end of August, it was sent to the Somme (sector of Combles–La Forest) and suffered very heavy losses between September 8 and 18.

LORRAINE.

4. After a short stay in the Loos salient (Vermelles–Hulluch road) at the beginning of October the 54th Reserve Division was transferred to Lorraine and sent into line in the vicinity of Blamont.

5. At this time, the 245th Reserve Infantry Regiment (Saxon) was taken from it to be assigned to the 192d Division.

VERDUN.

6. At the end of November the division left Lorraine, was sent during the course of December behind the front northwest of Cambrai, then to the Meuse, where it went into line on December 22, west of Bezonvaux (Les Chambrettes), after the French attack of December 16.

1917.

CHAMPAGNE.

1. Withdrawn from the Verdun front about January 23, 1917, the 54th Reserve Division took over, in Champagne, the sector included between the Navarin Farm and the Tahure Hill.

2. In March it sent one battalion of the 246th Reserve Infantry Regiment into the attacks of Maisons de Champagne on March 27.

3. At the beginning of May the division went as a reenforcement south of Moronvilliers. It went into action from May 15 to June 10 (Téton, Mont Haut) and lost heavily.

4. About June 10–15, without any rest, it again took over the sector west of Tahure, which it occupied until August 20–25.

HILL 304.

5. Suddenly transferred to the Verdun area, the 54th Reserve Division went into line on August 24, north of Hill 304; it remained there until October 18.

FLANDERS.

6. Sent to Flanders, it was in the Dixmude sector from October 29 until March 1918.

RECRUITING.

Mixed at the time of its formation, the 54th Reserve Division became exclusively Wurttemberg, by the departure of its Saxon elements.

VALUE—1917 ESTIMATE.

Since the number of prisoners of the 54th Reserve Division in Champagne, as in the vicinity of Verdun, March to October 1917, was very slight, it has been practically impossible to obtain information concerning this division (November 1918).

1918.

BATTLE OF PICARDY.

1. The division which had been holding the Dixmude sector entrained at Bruges on March 14, and detrained at Cambrai on the following day. On March 20 it marched to Seranvillers, and a day later proceeded via Ledsain to the high ground west of Honnecourt. On the 22d it reached Gouzeaucourt; on the 23d it passed through Lechelle, Bus, and Sailly Saillisel; on the 24th it progressed north of Mametz wood, being engaged near Rozieres on the 25th and at Ovillers on the 26th. The division was relieved on April 4 by the 27th Division after suffering heavy losses at Aveluy.

SOMME.

2. The division was in reserve in immediate rear of the front until the night of April 10-11, when it relieved the 13th Division at Ville sur Ancre. The division held this sector until May 27 and again from June 28 until August 25. It was withdrawn in the Mametz area where it had fallen back upon the British attack.

3. Early in September the division was dissolved. Prisoners stated that the 248th Reserve Regiment was drafted to the 27th Division.

VALUE—1918 ESTIMATE.

The division was rated as second class. Its efforts in the Somme offensive were unsuccessful. Thereafter the effectives were used up and the division dissolved.

56th Division.

COMPOSITION.

	1915 Brigade	1915 Regiment	1916 Brigade	1916 Regiment	1917 Brigade	1917 Regiment	1918 Brigade	1918 Regiment
Infantry	112.	35 Fus. 88. 118.	112.	35 Fus. 88. 118.	112.	88. 118. 186.	112.	88. 118. 186.
Cavalry	(?)		17 Hus. Rgt. (Sqn.).		4 Sqn. 17 Hus. Rgt.		4 Sqn. 17 Hus. Rgt.	
Artillery	56 Brig.: 111 F. A. Rgt. (6 Btries.), 112 F. A. Rgt. (6 Btries.).		56 Brig.: 111 F. A. Rgt. 112 F. A. Rgt.		56 Art. Command: 112 F. A. Rgt. (9 Btries.)		56 Art. Command: 112 F. A. Rgt. 56 Ft. A. Btn. 855 Light Am. Col. 858 Light Am. Col. 893 Light Am. Col.	
Engineers and Liaisons.	111 Pion. Co. 112 Pion. Co.		111 Pion. Co. 112 Pion. Co. 6 Field Co. 23 Pions. 2 Res. Co. 23 Pions. 56 T. M. Co. 56 Pont. Engrs. 56 Tel. Detch.		Pion. Btn.: 111 Pion. Co. 112 Pion. Co. 56 T. M. Co. 111 Searchlight Section. 56 Tel. Detch.		139 Pion Btn.: 111 Pion. Co. 112 Pion. Co. 56 T. M. Co. 186 Searchlight Section. 56 Signal Command: 56 Tel. Detch. 165 Wireless Detch.	
Medical and Veterinary.					56 Ambulance Co. 349 Field Hospital. 351 Field Hospital. Vet. Hospital.		56 Ambulance Co. 349 Field Hospital. 56 Vet. Hospital.	
Transports					M. T. Col.			
Odd units			56 Cyclist Co.		56 Cyclist Co.			

HISTORY.

(18th Corps District—Grand Duchy of Hesse and Hesse Nassau.)

1915.

The 56th Division was formed in March, 1915, of surplus regiments—the 35th Fusileer Regiment from the 6th Division (3d Corps District, Brandenburg), the 88th and 118th Infantry Regiments from the 21st and 25th Divisions (18th Corps District, Hesse Nassau and the Grand Duchy of Hesse). In May, 1917, the 35th Fusileer Regiment was replaced by the 186th Infantry Regiment (from the 25th Landwehr Division) recruited from Hesse.

CHAMPAGNE.

1. Concentrated in March, 1915, near Vouziers, the 56th Division went to the Champagne front, south of Ripont, in April.

GALICIA.

2. At the beginning of May it was transferred to the Eastern Front. It took part in the Galician offensive (battles of Jaroslau, on May 18, and of Rudka, on June 18), where it lost heavily.

FRANCE.

3. In June the division was brought back to the Western Front. Entraining at Jaroslau on June 28, it detrained in the vicinity of Valenciennes, where it remained at rest for a month.

LORRAINE.

4. On July 28 the division went to Lorraine and remained as a reserve troop in the vicinity of Pfalzburg–Zabern–Schirmeck.

CHAMPAGNE.

5. On September 25 it was sent to Champagne to oppose the French offensive. It was engaged in the sector of Maison de Champagne, but was soon retired on account of its losses. The infantry had casualties of 107 officers and 5,968 men. (Official List of Casualties.)

6. After reorganization, it went into line north of Massiges and took part in the attack of Mont Têtu at the beginning of November. It was relieved in the middle of November.

7. In December it returned to the Champagne front.

1916.

CHAMPAGNE.

1. The 56th Division occupied the same calm sector south of Rouvroy during the entire winter of 1915–16.

2. Relieved on April 25, 1916, it was sent to rest in the vicinity of Sedan.

VERDUN–MORT HOMME.

3. On May 26–27 it was sent into line on the left bank of the Meuse, at the Mort Homme. It received a vigorous attack there on May 31, had heavy losses, and continued to hold this sector until the middle of July.

ARTOIS.

4. After a short rest in the vicinity of Sedan, it went to the Vimy Ridge, in Artois (end of July–end of August).

SOMME.

5. On August 24–25 it was engaged in the battle of the Somme, in Belleville wood. On August 31 it launched a counterattack northeast of the wood. It left the Somme on September 9.

CHAMPAGNE.

6. It then took over a quiet sector east of Rheims at Cernay–La Pompelle. In the middle of November it returned to the Somme front (Pys) until January 7, 1917.

1917.

1. In January, 1917, the 56th Division was sent to rest in the vicinity of St. Quentin.

SOMME–HINDENBURG LINE.

2. About February 11 it went back into line south of the Somme in the vicinity of Biaches, retired at the end of March to the north of St. Quentin, and from there went to Courrières in the vicinity of the Lens mines.

LENS.

3. On April 10 it took over the sector of Lens, where it suffered important losses from raids and local conflicts. It absorbed 1,000 men from the 624th Infantry Regiment, dissolved, and some from the 625th (Hessian).

MEUSE (RIGHT BANK).

4. Withdrawn from the Lens front at the end of June, it remained at rest in the vicinity of Buzancy and Grandpré in July, near Carignan, at the beginning of August; spent the second half of August in the Woevre, reenforcing the Verdun front east of Vaux. In September it occupied the sector north of the Chaume wood–Baumont, where it was relieved at the end of October.

MEUSE (LEFT BANK).

5. About November 10 the 56th Division occupied the sector of Cheppy wood, on the left bank of the Meuse, where it remained until March 20, 1918.

RECRUITING.

Since the substitution of the 186th Infantry Regiment for the 35th Fusileers, the division has become entirely Hessian. By analogy with the 9th Landwehr Division, we sometimes find it designated as "Rhine troops"; the Rhine Provinces in general cooperate with Hesse and Hesse–Nassau in sending its replacements.

In the first months of 1918 the reenforcements received comprised men from the 3d and 4th Corps Districts (Berlin and Silesia) belonging to the industrial classes.

VALUE—1917 ESTIMATE.

Having suffered heavily in the Galician campaign in 1915, and in Champagne and at Verdun, the 56th Division had serious losses at Lens between April and June, 1917. The 186th Infantry Regiment had heavy losses during the battle of the Aisne (April, 1917) before joining the 56th Division. The division had few losses on the left bank of the Meuse from January to March, 1918.

Of 84 prisoners coming from three regiments of the 56th Division, captured on March 16 and 17, 1918, more than half belong either to the active or to the reserve.

1918.

1. The division was relieved west of the Meuse about March 19 by an extension of the front of the 13th Reserve Division and underwent a course of training for open warfare. At this time the companies had about 180 to 200 effectives. It had no men of the 1919 class and few Alsatians or Poles. The quality of men in the division was high. On April 18 the division entrained at Cesse (northwest of Stenay) and traveled via Sedan–Dinant–Charleroi–Braine le Comte–Tournai–Roubaix, from where it marched to Croix. On the 21st the 118th Regiment proceeded via Mouveaux–Bondues–Roucq to Halluin, where it rested until the 23d. On the following day the regiment marched via Wervicq–Comines to Messines.

KEMMEL.

2. The division came into line on the 25th and captured the village of Kemmel. It was engaged in this vicinity until May 2, when it was relieved by the 29th Division, and went to rest in the area north of Menin. It returned to line on the night of May 11–12, relieving the 13th Reserve Division on the Voormezeele sector. The division remained in line South of Ypres until the night of June 3–4.

BELGIUM.

3. After its relief the division rested in the Bruges area until its return to line northeast of Bailleul on July 2. From then until October 19 the division remained in line on this front. It had fallen back east of Roubaix when it was withdrawn.

4. After several days in reserve the division was again in line near St. Genois. The German communiqué of October 26 praised the fighting of the 118th Regiment. The last identification of the division was on November 8, when it was east of Avelghem.

VALUE—1918 ESTIMATE.

The division was rated as second class. It was very actively engaged during almost the entire last year of the war on the British front.

58th Division.
COMPOSITION.

	1915		1916		1917		1918	
	Brigade.	Regiment.	Brigade.	Regiment.	Brigade.	Regiment.	Brigade.	Regiment.
Infantry	116.	106. 107. 120 Res.	116.	106. 107. 120 Res.	116.	106. 107. 103 Res.	116.	106. 107. 103 Res.
Cavalry	4 Sqn. 18 Uhlan Rgt.		2 Sqn. 18 Uhlan Rgt.		4 Sqn. 18 Uhlan Rgt.		4 Sqn. 18 Uhlan Rgt.	
Artillery	58 Brig.: 115 F. A. Rgt. (Saxon) (6 Btries.). 116 F. A. Rgt. (Wurt.) (6 Btries.).		58 Brig.: 115 F. A. Rgt. 116 F. A. Rgt.		58 Art. Command: 115 F. A. Rgt. (9 Btries.).		58 Art. Command: 115 Ft. A. Rgt. 97 Ft. A. Btn. 711 Light Am. Col. 832 Light Am. Col. 931 Light Am. Col.	
Engineers and Liaisons.	115 Pion. Co. (Saxon). 116 Pion. Co. (Wurt.).		115 Pion. Co. 116 Pion. Co. 58 T. M. Co. 58 Tel. Detch. 58 Pont. Engs.		Pion. Btn.: 2 Res. 22 Pions. 115 Pion. Co. 404 Pion. Co. 58 T. M. Co. 115 Searchlight Section. 58 Tel. Detch.		142 Pion. Btn.: 115 Pion. Co. 404 Pion. Co. 58 T. M. Co. 127 Searchlight Section. 58 Signal Command. 58 Tel. Detch. 135 Wireless Detch.	
Medical and Veterinary.					58 Ambulance Co. 353 Field Hospital. 354 Field Hospital. 58 Vet. Hospital		58 Ambulance Co. 353 Field Hospital. 354 Field Hospital. 58 Vet. Hospital.	
Transports.					M. T. Col.		580 M. T. Col.	
Odd Units.			58 Cyclist Co.					
Attached.			7 Labor Btn.					

HISTORY.

(19th Corps District—Saxony.)

1915.

The 58th Division was formed on March 7, 1915, at Roulers, of surplus regiments taken from old divisions—the 106th and 107th Infantry Regiments, Saxon, came from the 24th Division; the 120th Reserve Infantry Regiment (Wurttemberg), from the 26th Reserve Division. At the end of 1916 the last-named regiment was replaced by the 103d Reserve Regiment (Saxon). The provincial homogeneity is thus realized.

1. The division remained at Roulers until the beginning of May.

ARTOIS.

2. On May 12, 1915, the 58th Division took part in the battle of Artois (Carency, May 12–15) and suffered heavy losses. On May 12 and 14 the 1st Battalion of the 106th Infantry Regiment had casualties of 22 officers and 642 men. (Official List of Casualties.) The casualties of the division amounted to 116 officers and 4,194 men.

3. At the beginning of June the division fought at Neuville St. Vaast (Le Labyrinthe.)

4. It was at rest in the middle of June in the vicinity of Douai.

RUSSIA.

5. On July 21 the division was transferred to Russia. (Itinerary: Roubaix–Sedan–Longwy–Thionville – Trèves – Coblentz – Cassel – Berlin – Marienburg – Koenigsberg–Loetzen.)

6. It took part in the offensive against the Russians in August and September (Narew, Bobr, Bielostok, Vilna) as far as Lake Narotch.

FRANCE.

7. Brought back to France between October 16 and 22 (itinerary: Vilna–Kovno–Koenigsberg – Berlin – Hanover – Cassel – Frankfort – Mayence – Coblentz – Trèves – Sarrebreucken), it took over a sector in Lorraine (Leintrey–Domèvre) in November and December.

1916.

1. In January and February, 1916, the 58th Division was at rest in the vicinity of Sarreburg.

LORRAINE.

2. About February 25 it returned to the sector of Leintrey–Embermenil and remained there until the middle of March. It celebrated its first anniversary there—150 days of fighting, 1,200 kilometers on foot, 4,400 by railroad (notebook).

VERDUN.

3. Brought back to Verdun at this time, it took part in the attack of Caillette wood, near Douaumont, on April 2.

CHAMPAGNE.

4. The division was withdrawn from the Verdun front about April 7 and sent to rest in the vicinity of Rethel. On April 30 it went to Champagne, where it occupied the sector east of Rheims (Bétheny–Cernay, La Pompelle).

SOMME.

5. In September the division was engaged on the Somme (Barleux). The 2d Company of the 20th Reserve Infantry Regiment, 177 strong, was destroyed, with the exception of 22 prisoners.

6. After occupying a calm sector on the Yser from September 29 to October 23, it again fought on the Somme (Courcelette–Grandcourt) in November.

7. On December 20 the division was withdrawn and reorganized—the 120th Reserve Infangry Regiment left the division for the 204th Division, a new formation, and went to Belgium.

1917.

VERDUN.

1. In January and February, 1917, the 58th Division became exclusively Saxon (106th, 107th, 103d Reserve Infantry Regiments). It went to the Verdun front and remained to the end of March, 1917.

CHAMPAGNE.

2. The latter part of March it went into line at Auberive, and suffered heavy losses in the attack of April 16-17. Because of these losses, the 8th Company of the 103d Infantry Regiment required a minimum reenforcement of 70 men.

RUSSIA–LAKE NAROTCH.

3. Relieved about April 20, the 58th Division entrained on the 24th for Russia. (Itinerary: Coblentz–Giessen–Halle–Lissa–Lodz–Warsaw–Brest-Litowsk (Apr. 28).) It held the sector south of Lake Narotch from the beginning of May until the beginning of October.

BELGIUM.

4. On October 6 it was brought back to France. (Itinerary: Vilna–Koenigsberg–Luebeck–Hamburg–Crefeld–Aix la Chapelle–Liége–Ghent–Bruges–Thourout (Oct. 11).)

HOUTHULST WOOD.

•5. On October 17 it took over the sector south of Houthulst wood and received the attack of October 22; it was relieved on the 24th.

6. On October 31 it again occupied the sector which it left at the end of November.

7. It spent December at rest in the vicinity of Bruges.

RECRUITING.

Mixed at the beginning (Saxon and Wurttemberg), like the 54th Reserve Division, the division became homogeneous by exchanging its Wurttemberg troops for Saxon units.

VALUE—1917 ESTIMATE.

When the 58th Division was on the Russian front, a division school was formed in the month of June, 1917, with the purpose of teaching men the method of attack.

The division school was dissolved a few days before the departure for Russia. As soon as they arrived on the Western Front it was made an assault detachment of the division.

On the Flanders front the 58th Division did not show any high combat value. Rather frequent cases of abandoning the front line have been proved (October, 1917).

1918.

YPRES.

1. About April 3 the division extended its left flank and relieved the 38th Division. At that time the division was holding two divisional sectors. About May 19, it was relieved by the 49th Reserve Division and moved to the Locre sector where it relieved the 31st Division a day later. This sector was held by the division until the night of June 13-14 when it was relieved by the 52d Reserve Division.

2. It rested in the Courtrai area until July 7 when it returned to line west of Dranoutre in relief of the 121st Division. The 52d Reserve Division again relieved it on August 9.

SCARPE–SOMME.

3. The division entrained at Menin on August 25 and detrained at Sancourt on the evening of the 26th coming into line on August 28 near Hardecourt and Bullecourt. It sideslipped south about the 1st of September and replaced the 52d Division which had been withdrawn. About September 10 the division was withdrawn from the

battle front after suffering heavy losses.   About this time the regiments of the division were reduced to two battalions of three companies each.

4. On September 27, the division relieved the 39th Division north of Ecourt–St. Quentin.   It retreated by Arleux to a point west of Valenciennes where it was relieved about October 22.   Two days later it came into line farther south at Ghent and fought until November 7.   The final identifications were at Hecq (Nov. 4), north of Berlaimont (Nov. 5) and north of Pont-sur-Sambre (Nov. 6).

VALUE—1918 ESTIMATE.

The division was rated as second class.   It was used as a strong defensive division exclusively on the British front during 1918.

75th Reserve Division.

COMPOSITION.

	1915 Brigade.	1915 Regiment.	1916 Brigade.	1916 Regiment.	1917 Brigade.	1917 Regiment.	1918 Brigade.	1918 Regiment.
Infantry	75 Res.	249 Res. 250 Res. 251 Res.	75 Res.	249 Res. 250 Res. 251 Res.	75 Res.	249 Res. 250 Res. 251 Res.	75 Res.	249 Res. 250 Res. 251 Res.
Cavalry	75 Res. Cav. Detch.		75 Res. Cav. Detch.		1 Sqn. 2 Uhlan Rgt.		3 Sqn. 2 Drag. Rgt.	
Artillery	75 Res. Brig.; 55 Res. F. A. Rgt. (6 Btries.). 57 Res. F. A. Rgt. (6 Btries.).		75 Res. Brig.: 55 Res. F. A. Rgt. 57 Res. F. A. Rgt.			(?) Art. Command: 55 Res. F. A. Rgt. (9 Btries.).	55 Res. F. A. Rgt. 82 Ft. A. Btn. 826 Light Am. Col. 1189 Light Am. Col. 1190 Light Am. Col.	
Engineers and Liaisons.	75 Res. Pion. Co. 75 Res. Pont. Engs.		75 Res. Pion. Co. 275 T. M. Co. 75 Res. Pont. Engs.		(375) Pion. Btn.: 75 Res. Pion. Co. 384 Pion. Co. 275 T. M. Co. 333 Searchlight Section. Tel. Detch.		375 Pion. Btn.: 384 Pion. Co. 75 Res. Pion. Co. 275 T. M. Co. 65 Searchlight Section. 475 Signal Command: 475 Tel. Detch. 145 Wireless Detch.	
Medical and Veterinary.	1 Ambulance Co.				537 Ambulance Co. 95 Res. Field Hospital. 99 Res. Field Hospital. Vet. Hospital.		537 Ambulance Co. 98 Res. Field Hospital. 99 Res. Field Hospital. 169 Vet. Hospital.	
Transports	75 Res. Train Detch.				586 M. T. Col.		742 M. T. Col.	
Odd units	75 Res. Cyclist Co.		75 Res. Cyclist Co.		75 Res. Cyclist Co.			
Attached			Ers. Field Btn. of the 75th Res. Div. Balloon Sqn. of the 75th Res. Div. 90 Labor Btn.					

HISTORY.

(249th and 250th Reserve Infantry Regiments, 14th Corps District—Grand Duchy of Baden. 251st Reserve Infantry Regiment; 11th Corps District—Electorate of Hesse.)

1915.

RUSSIA.

1. The 75th Reserve Division, trained at the Heuberg Camp in Baden, included two regiments of the 14th Corps District and one from the 11th Corps District. The first two were formed from the six field battalions from Baden, Nos. 61 to 66; the third, from three Thuringian field battalions, Nos. 58 to 60.

2. Forming a part of the 38th Reserve Corps with the 76th Reserve Division, it was sent to the Eastern Front at the end of January, 1915.

3. On February 17 it was in the vicinity of Augustowo, after taking part in the battle of Mazurian Lakes, where it lost heavily (250th Reserve Infantry Regiment).

4. At the end of February and the beginning of March it occupied the front near Chtabin.

5. On March 9 it attacked north of Ostrolenka and marched to Ossowiec. It remained in the region north of Ostrolenka until the end of April.

6. In the summer, it took part in the march upon Vilna and advanced beyond this by way of Wileisk (Sept. 24), south of Lake Drisviaty (Oct. 6).

7. At the end of October, the 75th Reserve Division went somewhat to the south and took over the sector of Spiagla, south of Lake Narotch.

1916.

LAKE NAROTCH.

1. The division remained in line in the vicinity of Lake Narotch until the end of July, 1916. In the spring of 1916, it received the Russian offensive in this area.

2. At the beginning of August, it was transferred to the Stokhod. We find it south-west of Sviniouki on October 1; south of Kisselin on November 9 (except the 251st Reserve Infantry Regiment sent to Galicia on Oct. 30).

GALICIA.

3. At the end of November, the entire division was in Galicia, where it occupied the sector of the Narajowka (north of Halicz, Rohatyn).

1917

GALICIA.

1. The 75th Reserve Division was retained in the vicinity of Halicz, and of Brzezany until July, 1917 (in reserve from the end of March to the end of May).

COURLAND.

2. On July 25 the division left Galicia to go to Smorgoni, from which place it was transferred to the Riga sector (Uxkull) at the end of August. After the taking of Riga, it advanced beyond the Dvina and took up its position on the Meloupe.

FRANCE.

3. On December 1 the division entrained for France. (Itinerary: Riga–Mitau–Kovno–Marienburg–Berlin–Hanover–Cassel–Cologne–Coblentz–Trèves–Thionville–Metz–Charleville–Hirson–Vervins.) It detrained at St. Gobert and Vervins about December 7.

1917.

AISNE.

4. Sent to rest near Vervins, about December 26, the division took over the sector of Chavignon-Urcel on the 27th.

RECRUITING.

The divisions formed in 1915 were not homogeneous. The 75th Reserve Division consists of two regiments from Baden and one from the Electorate of Hesse.

Since the 75th Reserve Division comes from Russia and has only been on the French front since the end of December 1917, it is difficult to form a judgment as to the combat value of this organization.

At the end of December elements of the division took part in maneuvers supported by tanks (at Voulpaix, west of Verdun). (Interrogation of prisoner, Feb. 20, 1918.)

At the beginning of February the 251st Reserve Infantry Regiment took part in a division maneuver in which the infantry had to fight simulated tanks. (Interrogation of prisoner, Mar. 11, 1918.)

DISCIPLINE.

It is to be noted that during the trip from Russia to France 40 men belonging to the Minenwerfer and pioneer companies, were reported missing. (Interrogation of prisoner, Jan. 31, 1918.)

1918.

PICARDY.

1. The division was relieved south of Laon on March 26 and went to Laon. By way of Champignon (west of Crepy), Charmes, it marched to Chauny, where it went into line on March 30. It was engaged until about April 14, and then went to rest north of St. Gobain.

BATTLE OF THE MATZ.

2. It returned to line southeast of Canny sur Matz on the night of May 16–17 and took part in the battle of Noyon in June. It was relieved about June 20 and rested until July 2. It was in line at Courcelles from that date until August 18. Prior to the French attack on August 18, the division counted about 3,000 combatants. It suffered important losses between the 8th and 18th.

3. The division rested in the Bois de Champien and Bois de Glandon until August 23 and then in the Bois du Tunnel. On the 27th it went to Ham. On the night of August 31–September 1 it relieved the 1st Reserve Division in the sector Libermont–Bois du Tunnel. It fell back across the Canal du Nord on September 3 and continued its retreat through Sommette, Dury, Bray St. Christophe until it reached a position at Happencourt on September 7. It was relieved on the 13th by the 22d Reserve Division. The attack of August and September had completely disorganized the division and greatly reduced its morale.

LE CATEAU.

4. The division returned to line west of Bellenglise on September 20 and was heavily engaged for 10 days.

WOEVRE.

5. On November 10 the division came into line near Jamez on the American front.

VALUE—1918 ESTIMATE.

The division was rated as third class. Throughout 1918 its morale appears to have been low, and after the battle of Matz its effectives were greatly reduced.

76th Reserve Division.

COMPOSITION.

	1915 Brigade	1915 Regiment	1916 Brigade	1916 Regiment	1917 Brigade	1917 Regiment	1918 Brigade	1918 Regiment
Infantry........	76 Res.	252 Res. 253 Res. 254 Res.	76 Res.	252 Res. 253 Res. 254 Res.	76 Res.	252 Res. 253 Res. 254 Res.	76 Res.	252 Res. 253 Res. 254 Res.
Cavalry........	76 Res. Cav. Detch.		76 Res. Cav. Detch.		3 Sqn. 1 Res. Uhlan Rgt.		3 Sqn. 13 Uhlan Rgt.	
Artillery........	76 Res. Brig.: 56 Res. F. A. Rgt. (6 Btries.). 58 Res. F. A. Rgt. (6 Btries.).		76 Res. Brig.: 56 Res. F. A. Rgt. 58 Res. F. A. Rgt.		(7) Art. Command.: 56 Res. F. A. Rgt. 58 Res. F. A. Rgt.		76 Art. Command: 56 Res. F. A. Rgt. 2 Abt. 24 Ft. A. Rgt. (5th and 7th Btries.). 763 Light Am. Col. 1081 Light Am. Col. 1082 Light Am. Col.	
Engineers and Liaisons.	76 Res. Pion. Co. 76 Res. Pont. Engs.		76 Res. Pion. Co. 276 T. M. Co. 76 Res. Pont. Engs.		(376) Pion. Btn.: 76 Res. Pion. Co. 77 Res. Pion. Co. 276 T. M. Co. 344 Searchlight Section. Tel. Detch.		378 Pion. Btn.: 77 Res. Pion. Co. 76 Res. Pion. Co. 76 Searchlight Section. 476 Tel. Detch. Signal Command: 476 Tel. Detch. 188 Wireless Detch.	
Medical and Veterinary.	1 Ambulance Co.		....		538 Ambulance Co. 100 Field Hospital (Res.). 101 Field Hospital (Res.). Vet. Hospital.		538 Ambulance Co. 100 Res. Field Hospital. 101 Res. Field Hospital. 146 Vet. Hospital.	
Transports......	76 Res. Train Detch.		....		M. T. Col.		743 M. T. Col.	
Odd Units......	76 Res. Cyclist Co.		76 Res. Cyclist Co.		76 Res. Cyclist Co.			

HISTORY.

(11th and 18th Corps District—Hesse Electoral. Hesse-Nassau, and Grand Duchy of Hesse.)

1915.

RUSSIA.

1. The 76th Reserve Division (included in the 38th Reserve Corps with the 75th Reserve Division), formed in January, 1915, grows out of three field battalions (Feld bataillone), Nos. 55–57 of the 11th Corps District, and out of six field battalions, Nos. 67–72 of the 18th Corps District. It was sent toward Russia at the beginning of February, 1915.

2. On February 13 it was identified in the region of Gumbinnen. It was really part of the group which operated in the region of Wylkowyszki-Mariampol.

3. On March 2 it was on the Sopotzkyn–Chtabin front.

4. In March it was northeast of Prasnysz.

5. In April it was in the region of Suwalki-Augustowo.

6. In May it was north of Suwalki.

7. On June 23 the 76th Reserve Division went to the Dubissa area.

8. On June 30, region of Eydtkuhnen.

9. The summer offensive of 1915 brought it, through the region of Vilia, to Kovno Aug. 16) and then to the south of Smorgoni (Oct. 6–10).

It was withdrawn from the front about October 15 and was at Vilna on November 1 and in the region of Mitau on December 5.

1916.

COURLAND.

1. Then moved toward the north, the 76th Reserve Division took up a sector on the Dvina, opposite Uxkull (Jan.-Aug., 1916).

ROUMANIA.

2. From the 10th to the 20th of September the division was moved to the Roumanian front.

3. In October it took part in the battles in the regions of Hermannstadt and Brasso (Kronstadt).

4. At the end of October or beginning of November it occupied the vicinity of Campolung. At the end of December, to the south of Rimnicu-Sarat.

1917.

ROUMANIA (FOCSANI).

1. With the stabilization of the Roumanian front, it was in line to the north and east to Focsani, where it remained from January to April, 1917.

2. In May it was in reserve. At about this time it seems to have been brought to the rear of the French front.

3. The division reappeared in Roumania, in the vicinity of Focsani, from August 6 to 14. It attacked on the 15th and suffered heavy losses.

4. Put in reserve, near Focsani, it went back into line at the beginning of October to the north of Iresti. It was still in that region at the beginning of January, 1918.

RECRUITING.

The 252d Regiment in Thuringe, 253d Regiment in Hesse-Nassau, and 254th Regiment in the Grand Duchy of Hesse. These last two regiments may be termed Rhenish regiments.

VALUE—1917 ESTIMATE.

The 76th Reserve Division was at all times used on the eastern front.

125651°—20——34

1919.

1. The division was moved to the Western Front in the spring after exchanging its older men for younger men from the divisions remaining in Roumania. It entrained at Focsani on March 7 and traveled by way of Hermannstadt, Budapest, Breslau, Erfurt, Fulda, to Metz, where it detrained on March 15. The 254th Reserve Regiment was in cantonments a few days at Fort Luitpold and then went to Norroy le Veneur where it remained about 12 days. It entrained on March 31 and proceeded by way of Sedan and Charleville to Hirson (Apr. 1). From there it marched via Remigny-Golancourt–Roye–Narvillers–Hangest–Plessier–Rozainvillers, where it went into cantonments for three days.

MONTDIDIER.

2. On the night of April 12–13 the division relieved elements of the 23d Division between Malpart and La Chappelle–St. Aignan. About May 2 the division extended its front to the north and relieved a part of the 240th Division. This was a defensive sector at this time. On May 9 the French made an attack on Grivesnes Park while the 76th Reserve Division was holding it. The attack was a complete surprise and caused many casualties. Between April 10 and May 8 the losses averaged 30 to 35 men per company and the number of combatants on May 9 was about 75 per company. It was relieved in the middle of May.

VERDUN.

3. The division entered line in the Verdun region to the south of Bezonvaux on June 21. It was withdrawn from the quiet sector in mid-July, and on the 29th relieved the 46th Reserve Division southwest of Soissons. Until August 2 it was not involved in the attack. It defended the flanks of the German retreat energetically until its withdrawal on September 8. A week later its regiments were used singly to support the units in line in delaying the French advance on the line Coucy le Chateau–Ferny–Sorny. The losses in the fighting were considerable, including 575 prisoners. It showed itself a good defensive division.

4. On September 25 the division came in line on the extreme left of the American line in the Argonne. On October 10 all three regiments were opposite the United States troops in Grandpre. It remained in line until November 8 before it was finally withdrawn.

The excessive use of the division gave rise to serious internal discontent. The rifle strength of the regiments was down to less than 300 by October 24, and the troops were demanding a rest. Some companies refused to enter the line in mid-October. The divisional commander was obliged to issue an appeal to the division on October 21 to hold out. The entire rifle strength of the 2d Battalion, 254th Reserve Regiment, was but 3 officers and 75 men on October 28.

VALUE—1918 ESTIMATE.

The division was rated as third class. As a defensive sector holding unit the division showed a power of sustained resistance that warranted a higher classification. By the end the division had been completely used up.

77th Reserve Division.

COMPOSITION.

	1915		1916		1917		1918 [1]	
	Brigade.	Regiment.	Brigade.	Regiment.	Brigade.	Regiment.	Brigade.	Regiment.
Infantry........	77 Res.	255 Res. 256 Res. 257 Res.	77 Res.	255 Res. 256 Res. 257 Res.	77 Res.	255 Res. 256 Res. 257 Res.	77 Res.	332, 257 Res. 419.
Cavalry........	77 Res. Cav. Detch.		77 Res Cav. Detch.		4 Sqn. 2 Horse Jag. Rgt. (?) 77 Res. Cav. Detch. (?)		4 Sqn. 2 Horse Jag. Rgt.	
Artillery........	77 Res. Brig.; 59 Res. F. A. Regt. (6 Btries.). 60 Res. F. A. Rgt. (6 Btries.).		77 Res. Brig.; 59 Res. F. A. Rgt. 60 Res. F. A. Rgt.		(?) Art. Command: 59 Res. F. A. Rgt. (9 Btries.).		(?) Art. Command: 59 Res. F. A. Rgt.	
Engineers and Liaisons.	77 Res. Pion. Co. 77 Res. Pont. Engs.		77 Res. Pion. Co. 277 T. M. Co. 77 Res. Pont. Engs.		(377) Pion. Btn.: 78 Res. Pion. Co. 277 T. M. Co 39 Res. Searchlight Section. 477 Tel. Detch.		1 Co. 1 Pions. 1 Ldw. Co. 7 C. Dist. Pions. 39 Res. Searchlight Section. 277 T. M. Co. 477 Tel. Detch.	
Medical and Veterinary.	1 Ambulance Co.....				539 Ambulance Co. 103 Field Hospital (Res.), 104 Field Hospital (Res.), Vet. Hospital.		539 Ambulance Co. 103 Res. Field Hospital. 104 Res. Field Hospital. 105 Res. Field Hospital. Vet. Hospital.	
Transport......	77 Res. Train Detch.....				M. T. Col.		744 M. T. Col.	
Odd units.....	77 Res. Cyclist Co.		77 Res. Cyclist Co		77 Res. Cyclist Co.		77 Res. Cyclist Co.	
Attached......							403 Pion. Btn. (?)	

[1] Composition at the time of dissolution.

HISTORY.

(255th Regiment: 7th Corps District—Westphalia.   257th Regiment, 332d Regiment: 8th Corps District—Rhenish Province.)

1915.

The 77th Reserve Division was formed at the Senne Cantonment (7th Corps Region) in January, 1915, with six field battalions (Nos. 31–36) of the 7th Corps Region and three of the 8th, (Nos. 37–39.)   With the 78th Reserve Division, it composed the 39th Reserve Corps.

RUSSIA.

1. Brought to the Eastern Front at the beginning of February, detraining at Insterburg, it was a part of the army operating in Eastern Prussia after February 12.

2. At the beginning of March it was engaged on the Sopotzkyn-Chtabin front in the region of Simmo; on March 9 it covered the retreat of the 21st Corps and fell back to Seiny, Suwalki and Augustowo (Mar. 10 to 31).

3. During May and June the 77th Reserve Division took part in the Courland raid. On May 5 it was identified as being on the Rossieny-Beisagola front (to the South of Chavli).

GRODNO.

4. Taking part in the summer offensive, it advanced through the regions of Grodno, Olita (Aug 30) and Vileiki (Sept 27).

5. At the beginning of November it established itself in the vicinity of Kchtchava, east of Novo-Alexandrovsk.

1916.

COURLAND.

1. The 77th Reserve Division stayed in the region north of Kchtchava—and south of Dvinsk during all of 1916 and until August 1917.   In August of 1916 it gave one of its regiments—the 256th—to the Mitau group and later to the 218th Division.

1917.

COURLAND.

1. At the end of August, 1917, the 77th Reserve Division was transferred from the region of the Dvinsk to the Riga front, being brought up to strength by the addition of the 332d Regiment, the latter having originally come from the 83d Division after having successively been part of the 11th Landwehr Division and the 8th Cavalry Division.

2. In October the 77th Reserve Division appeared in the vicinity of Friedrichstadt; near Jakobstadt, at the end of October.   The 255th Regiment may have participated about this date in the occupation of the island of Oesel.

3. On November 5 the division is identified in the region of Libau; on January 20, the 257th Regiment at Mitau; and to the northwest of the Novo-Alexandrovsk-Dvinsk railway, the 255th Regiment on February 10.   On March 1 the 332d Regiment of Infantry was to leave "in order to advance in the East" (letter).

RECRUITING.

Principally Westphalia for the 255th Regiment; Rhenish provinces for the 257th and 332d Regiments.   Numerous recruits from Lorraine and Alsace.   Poles in the 332d Regiment, which received the Ersatz Battalion of the 19th Infantry at the time it was formed.

VALUE—1917 ESTIMATE.

The 77th Reserve Division did not leave the Russian front.   One of its present regiments, the 332d, is a former regiment of the Posen garrison, of which two of the three battalions were Rhenish Landsturm battalions. Successive replacements gave this regiment the appearance of an ordinary regiment. In January, 1918, the older and sickly men were released.

1918.

1. The division left Russia about April 1 and traveled via Magdebourg–Hildesheim–Cologne – Gerolstein – Gouvy – Bastogne – Lebramont – Sedan – Liart – Rozay – Montcornet, detraining in the vicinity of Laon on April 4. It marched by stages toward Villers–Carbonnel–Athies, where it rested and trained from April 11 to 19. On April 20 it entered the line north of Hangard and was engaged until the end of the month.

Somme.

2. It returned to line east of Villers-Bretonneux on May 18 and held that sector until July 4.

Woevre.

3. The division was moved to the Woevre by Hirson and Montmedy and on July 14 relieved the 183d Division in the Flirey sector. It held that sector until the American attack on St. Mihiel on September 12. The division suffered very heavy losses in prisoners, but had few other casualties, the prisoners stating that they were completely cut off by the American barrage. It was withdrawn on September 16 and did not thereafter return to line.

4. What remained of the 77th Reserve Division was reassembled at Pagny and was occupied in organizing the ground between Pagny and Prenay. A report of October 11 stated that the division passed through Berlin on its way to the Balkan front on October 2. The division was then considered as withdrawn from the Western Front.

VALUE—1918 ESTIMATE.

The division was rated as third class. It was not seriously engaged except in the St. Mihiel attack, which practically destroyed the division. Its morale was only mediocre. Deserters from the Alsace-Lorraine element in the division were numerous.

78th Reserve Division.

COMPOSITION.

	1915		1916		1917		1918 [1]	
	Brigade.	Regiment.	Brigade.	Regiment.	Brigade.	Regiment.	Brigade.	Regiment.
Infantry	78 Res.	258 Res. 259 Res. 260 Res.	78 Res.	258 Res. 259 Res. 260 Res.	78 Res.	258 Res. 259 Res. 260 Res.	78 Res.	258 Res. 259 Res. 260 Res.
Cavalry	78 Res. Cav. Detch.		78 Res. Cav. Detch.		2 Sqn. 16 Hus. Rgt.		78 Res. Cav. Detch. 2 Sqn. 16 Hus. Rgt.	
Artillery	78 Res. Brig.: 61 Res. F. A. Rgt. (6 Btries). 62 Res. F. A. Rgt. (6 Btries).		78 Res. Brig.: 61 Res. F. A. Rgt. 62 Res. F. A. Rgt.		78 Art. Command: 62 Res. F. A. Rgt. (9 Btries.).		(?)Art. Command: 62 Res. F. A. Rgt.	
Engineers and Liaisons.	78 Res. Pion. Co. 78 Res. Pont. Engs.		78 Res. Pion. Co. 2 Landst. Pion. Co. (2 C. Dist.). 278 T. M. Co. 78 Res. Pont. Engs.		378 Pion. Btn.: 79 Res. Pion. Co. 80 Res. Pion. Co. 278 T. M. Co. (299 Searchlight section). 478 Tel. Detch.		79 Res. Pion. Co. 80 Res. Pion. Co. 299 Searchlight Section. 278 T. M. Co. 478 Tel. Detch.	
Medical and Veterinary.	1 Ambulance Co.				540 Ambulance Co. 107 Res. Field Hospital. 108 Res. Field Hospital. Vet. Hospital.		540 Ambulance Co. 106 Res. Field Hospital. 107 Res. Field Hospital. 108 Res. Field Hospital. Vet. Hospital.	
Transports	78 Res. Train Detch.				M. T. Col.		745 M. T. Col.	
Odd units	78 Res. Cyclist Co.		78 Res. Cyclist Co. 83 Labor Btn.		78 Res. Cyclist Co.			

1 Composition at the time of dissolution.

HISTORY.

(258th Regiment: 8th Corps District—Rhenish Province. 259th Regiment: 10th Corps District—Grand Duchy of Oldenberg. 260th Regiment: 10th Corps District—Hanover.)

1915.

The 78th Reserve Division which, with the 77th Reserve Division, constituted the 39th Reserve Corps as one of the reserve divisions created during the winter of 1914–15. One of its regiments—the 258th—grew out of three field battalions of the 8th Corps Region (Nos. 40–42) and the 259th and the 260th out of six field battalions (Nos. 49–54) of the 10th Corps District. All three regiments were trained at the Alten-Grabow cantonment (4th Corps District).

RUSSIA.

1. In action on the Russian front to the north of Grodno, near Simno, Kalvariia and Suwalki in March, 1915, it took part in the Courland raid (region of Chavli) in May. It was engaged in the operations on the Dubissa to the northeast of Rossieny from the end of May to the middle of July.

2. In July, with the Army of Niemen (Beulow) it took part in the offensive against Russia, occupied the region of Poneviej, to the west of Kupichki (August) arrived before Dvinsk in September and held a position near the Illukst (September–December).

1916.

COURLAND.

1. The 78th Reserve Division remained in the Illukst (region of Dvinsk) during the whole year 1916 and until the month of April, 1917.

1917.

COURLAND.

1. Relieved from the Illukst region on April 14, 1917, the division was transferred to the Western Front. It entrained on April 15 (itinerary: Kovno–Wirballen–Allenstein–Posen–Leipzig–Nuremberg–Karlsruhe–Friberg–Muelheim) and detrained near Mulhausen on the 19th.

FRANCE (ALSACE).

2. On April 25 it went into line in the Burnhaupt sector to the north of the Rhône-Rhine Canal.

AISNE (AILETTE).

3. Relieved on May 11, it was sent into the Aisne. For 10 weeks it occupied (May 23–Aug. 5) the sector south of the Ailette, where it did not participate in any action of importance. Beginning with June 19 it made a series of local attacks in which the 258th Regiment suffered some fairly big losses (especially on June 20, to the east of Vauxaillon).

VERDUN.

4. Sent toward the Verdun front as a reserve at the time of the French offensive of August 20, it was engaged to the north of Caurières (southwest of the Ornes) on September 10. On September 13 it executed a counterattack and continued to occupy this difficult sector until the middle of October.

LORRAINE.

5. Withdrawn from Verdun, the division immediately went into line along the banks of the Seille (between Cheminot and Abaucourt) on October 14. Its stay in Lorraine was devoid of any particular event.

HAYE.

' 6. Toward the middle of December it was withdrawn from the Abaucourt sector and put at rest for instruction in the region of Chambley–Mars la Tour (Dec. 18 to Jan. 11, 1918), then sent to Seicheprey toward the middle of January. It was identified as still there on March 29.

RECRUITING.

One of the three regiments, the 258th, was Rhenish; the 259th was an "Oldenberger" Regiment, while the 260th was a Hanoverian and Brunswickian organization, terms found in documents, as well as the designation Lower Saxony, a more general term.

The neighboring corps districts (7th, Westphalia, and 9th, Schleswig–Holstein) were occasionally called upon for replacements.

VALUE—1917 ESTIMATE.

The 78th Reserve Division showed up well on the Eastern Front and on the French front.

After a hard stay opposite Verdun, the division seems to have gone through a moral crisis; relatively high number of desertions took place in the 258th, and especially in the 259th Regiment. The intention of the High Command in sending the division into Lorraine (October–December, 1917) is said to have been done with an idea or giving its chiefs an opportunity of getting their units well in hand again.

Nevertheless, the vigorous command and the fairly high number of effectives, taken for the greater part from the younger classes, make the 78th Reserve Division a combat division worthy of consideration. At Jonville at the end of December, 1917, the division took part in assault practice.

It is to be noted that a certain number of recruits were from Alsace and Lorraine.

1918.

CHATEAU THIERRY.

1. The division was relieved in the Woevre about May 11 by the 8th Bavarian Reserve Division. It came into line on June 4 west of Dammard (Ourcq region). It was engaged until about July 20 and then withdrawn.

2. The division was disbanded at Montcornet on August 12. The 259th Reserve Regiment was broken up and one battalion of it sent to each regiment of the 2d Guard Division. The 260th Reserve Regiment was turned as a draft to the 20th Division.

VALUE—1918 ESTIMATE.

The division was rated as third class. After about two weeks of heavy fighting on the Marne salient, the division was dissolved.

79th Reserve Division.
COMPOSITION.

	1915 Brigade	1915 Regiment	1916 Brigade	1916 Regiment	1917 Brigade	1917 Regiment	1918 Brigade	1918 Regiment
Infantry	79 Res.	261 Res. 262 Res. 263 Res.	79 Res.	261 Res. 262 Res. 263 Res.	79 Res.	261 Res. 262 Res. 263 Res.	79 Res.	261 Res. 262 Res. 263 Res.
Cavalry	79 Res. Cav. Detch.		79 Res. Cav. Detch.		3 Sqn. 16 Hus. Rgt.		3 Sqn. 16 Hus. Rgt.	
Artillery	79 Res. Brig.; 63 Res. F. A. Rgt. 64 Res. F. A. Rgt.		79 Res. Brig.; 63 Res. F. A. Rgt. 64 Res. F. A. Rgt.		79 Art. Command; 63 Res. F. A. Rgt. (9 Btries.).		79 Art. Command: 63 Res. F. A. Rgt. (6 and 8 Btries.) 2 Abt. 20 Ft. A. Rgt. 718 Light Am. Col. 719 Light Am. Col. 1354 Light Am. Col.	
Engineers and Liaisons.	79 Res. Pion. Co. 79 Res. Pont. Engs.		79 Res. Pion. Co. 83 Res. Pion. Co. 279 T. M. Co. 79 Res. Pont. Engs.		379 Pion. Btn.; 81 Res. Pion. Co. 1 Ers. Co. 24 Pions. 279 T. M. Co. 40 Res. Searchlight Sections. 50 Searchlight Sections. 51 Searchlight Section. 79 Searchlight Sections. 79 Res. Pont. Engs.		379 Pion. Btn.: 81 Res. Pion. Co. 1 Ers. Co. 24 Pions. 25 Searchlight Section. 479 Signal Command: 479 Tel. Detch. 64 Wireless Detch.	
Medical and Veterinary.	1 Ambulance Co.				541 Ambulance Co. 110 Field Hospital. 111 Field Hospital. 112 Field Hospital. Vet. Hospital.		541 Ambulance Co. 110 Res. Field Hospital. 111 Res. Field Hospital. 164 Vet. Hospital.	
Transports	79 Res. Train Detch.				746 M. T. Col.		746 M. T. Col.	
Odd Units	79 Res. Cyclist Co.		79 Res. Cyclist Co.					

HISTORY.

(261st and 262d Reserve Regiments: Entire Prussian territory by selection, in the same manner as the Guard. 263d Reserve Regiment: 4th Corps District—Prussian Saxony.

1915.

EASTERN PRUSSIA.

1. The 79th Reserve Division was one of the divisions formed in the winter of 1914–15, and, with the 80th Reserve Division, formed the 40th Reserve Corps. It grew out of six field battalions of the Guard and three field battalions. (Nos. 19–21) of the 4th Corps District. It was trained at the Doeberitz cantonment and sent to Eastern Prussia at the beginning of February, 1915, where it took part in the battle of the Masure Lakes from the 7th to the 17th.

RUSSIA.

2. It was identified in the vicinity of Lyck on February 13, as marching toward Augustowo on the 14th and to the south of the Forest of Augustowo on the 24th.

POLAND.

3. From the end of February until the end of March it was engaged on the Bobr, to the north of the Fortess of Ossoviec. At the end of March, having come back in the northeast, it held the passes in the lakes to the east of Suwalki-Augustowo.

4. At the beginning of May the 40th Reserve Corps advanced toward Kalwariia-Mariampol.

KOVNO.

5. On June 9 the 79th Reserve Division appeared before Kovno; it took part in the siege and the taking of this town (July–Aug. 18).

SMORGONI.

6. The offensive against the Russians took it through Ochmiana (?) to the south of Smorgoni (Aug. 27). The division took a position in this region.

SMORGONI–KREVO.

7. The division occupied the Krevo–Smorgoni (south of Vilna) sector from the end of August, 1915. until some time in November, 1916.

1916.

RUSSIA–FRANCE.

1. Relieved from the Smorgoni sector at the end of November, 1916, the 79th Division was transferred to the Western Front. It entrained at Mitau (Itinerary: Chavli–Grodno–Bielostok–Varsovie–Lodz–Kalisz–Glogau–Cottbus–Halle–Paderborn–Duesseldorf-Aix la Chapelle–Herbesthal–Liege–Louvain–Brussels) and detrained at Ascq (east of Lille) on December 10.

LILLE.

2. Remained there at rest.

1917.

LA BASSEE.

1. About January 10, 1917, it took over the La Bassee-Vermelles sector (up to Jan: 28).

LENS–VIMY.

2. At the end of February it appeared in the Lens sector and on March 3 on the Vimy front. On April 9 it was sorely tried by the British attack on the heights of Vimy, where it lost 1,660 prisoners.

3. It was relieved about April 14 and put at rest.

LILLE.

4. On May 3 the division entered the line again in the quiet sector to the southwest of Lille (between Boutillerie and Fauquissart). It stayed there until July 8.

FLANDERS.

5. After a few days rest at Templeuve it was transferred to Flanders, where it was again at rest (east of Bruges) (July).

LANGEMARCK.

6. At the beginning of the British offensive at Ypres (July 31) it was brought to Langemarck as a "counterattack" division. Engaged on August 6 it suffered very heavy losses and abandoned Langemarck during the attack of the 16th. It was relieved on the 16th, having lost 75 per cent of its strength. It was put at rest east of Cambrai and reorganized.

ST. QUENTIN.

7. On September 1 it took over the sector northwest of St. Quentin (Pontruet-Gricourt), which it occupied until November 28.

CAMBRAI.

8. On November 21, by reason of the British offensive, it hastily put two battalions in action at Masnières.

9. At the beginning of December the 79th Reserve Division went into line to the east of Gouzeaucourt. It was relieved in January, 1918, reappeared on the front at the beginning of February near Gonnelieu, and went back to rest at the end of the month.

RECRUITING.

The 261st and 262d Regiments were taken from depots of the Guard and were recruited like the latter, from all sections of Prussia. The 263d Regiment was a "Magdeberg" unit (Prussian Saxony).

VALUE—1917 ESTIMATE.

The 79th Division, already sorely tried at Vimy in April, was much used at Ypres in August, 1917.

The 261st and 262d Regiments were completely demoralized during the British attack and fled to the rear. According to an officer this panic was due to the lack of combat spirit displayed by the 1918 class, which made up an important part of the strength of the soldiers engaged.

It arrived in a very worn out condition in the St. Quentin sector and left it on November 28 with nearly full strength and replacement of material. It should (December, 1917) be capable of putting forth an appreciable effort.

The soldiers from Alsace and Lorraine, formerly numerous in this division, were withdrawn from this unit when it was sent to the French front. Ninety-three of them remained in the 252d Regiment, who were mostly sent to the Eastern Front on July 3, 1917 (German order).

1918.

BATTLE OF PICARDY.

1. The division reenforced the Somme battle front on March 21 near Ronssoy. It advanced west of Epehy on March 22 and was withdrawn to second line a day later. It followed up the advance and took part in the attack near Meaulte on April 5, after which it was withdrawn.

BAILLEUL.

2. It rested in Belgium for five weeks, and on May 26 entered the line northwest of Bailleul. It was relieved on the night of June 19–20.

3. The division rested in Roubaix area until July 20, when it was transferred by rail to Tergnier (west of La Fère) and then marched to Guny, west of Coucy le Chateau, where it remained in army reserve. On August 8 the division was alarmed, and at mid-day was transferred in motor busses via Chauny–Ham–Nesle to Rethonvillers, arriving before dawn on the 9th. It came into action on the following day at 4 kilometers northeast of Andechy.

SCARPE–SOMME.

4. At once the division was heavily engaged with all nine battalions in line. On the 13th its place was taken by the 121st Division, and it rested for three or four days in the area southwest of Nesle. On the 16th the division relieved the 204th Division on the line east of Goyencourt–Hill 81, west of Roye–Avre. It was heavily engaged in opposing the French attacks until August 31, when it was withdrawn east of Roye.

5. On September 5 the division relieved the Alpine Corps at Epenancourt. It fell back in a northeasterly direction by Atilly, southeast of Vermand, southeast of Maissemy, Pontruet, and Gricourt. It was relieved about October 8 after losing 2,200 prisoners in August and September.

SCARPE.

6. When relieved, the division went to the Fres–Sancourt area (north of St. Gobain), where it was in reserve. About the 14th it was taken to La Ferte–Chevresis to construct rear positions. It was moved in trucks on the 18th by Sains–Richaumont–Wiege–Villers les Guise–Iron near Etreux. It went into line on the evening of the 18th, relieving elements of the 81st Division. It was engaged until the armistice. The line of retreat was through Boue, Boulogne, Avesnes, Sobre le Chateau. In the last place it was identified on November 10.

At the end the effective strength of the division was greatly diminished, although it had received drafts from the dissolved 201st and 202d Regiments.

VALUE—1918 ESTIMATE.

The division was rated as third class. Throughout 1918 the division was extensively used in important defensive sectors, in which it did fairly well.

80th Reserve Division.
COMPOSITION.

	1915 Brigade.	1915 Regiment.	1916 Brigade.	1916 Regiment.	1917 Brigade.	1917 Regiment.	1918 Brigade.	1918 Regiment.
Infantry	80 Res.	264 Res. 265 Res. 266 Res.	80 Res.	264 Res. 266 Res. 34 Res.	80 Res.	264 Res. 266 Res. 34 Res.	80 Res.	34 Res. 264 Res. 266 Res.
Cavalry	80 Res. Cav. Detch.		80 Res. Cav. Detch.		4 Sqn. 16 Hus. Rgt.		4 Sqn. 16 Hus. Rgt.	
Artillery	80 Res. Brig.: 65 Res. F. A. Rgt. (6 Btries.). 66 Res. F. A. Rgt. (6 Btries.).		80 Res. Brig.: 65 Res. F. A. Rgt. 66 Res. F. A. Rgt.		74 Art. Command: 66 Res. F. A. Rgt. (9 Btries.).		74 Art. Command: 66 Res. F. A. Rgt. 3 Abt. 27 Ft. A. Rgt. (8 and 10 Btries.). 899 Light Am. Col. 900 Light Am. Col. 1370 Light Am. Col.	
Engineers and Liaisons.	80 Res. Pion. Co. 80 Res. Pont. Engs.		80 Res. Pion. Co. 281 T. M. Co. 80 Res. Pont. Engs.		(380) Pion. Btn.: 82 Res. Pion. Co. 83 Res. Pion. Co. 280 T. M. Co. 308 Searchlight Section. 480 Tel. Detch.		380 Pion. Btn.: 82 Res. Pion. Co. 83 Res. Pion. Co. 280 T. M. Co. 96 Searchlight Section. 240 Searchlight Section. 480 Signal Command: 480 Tel. Detch. 24 Wireless Detch.	
Medical and Veterinary.	1 Ambulance Co.				542 Ambulance Co. 59 Res. Field Hospital. 114 Res. Field Hospital. Vet. Hospital.		542 Ambulance Co. 113 Res. Field Hospital. 114 Res. Field Hospital. 165 Vet. Hospital.	
Transports	80 Res. Train Detch.				T. M. Col.			
Odd Units	80 Res. Cyclist Co.		80 Res. Cyclist Co.					

HISTORY.

(264th Regiment; 4th Corps District—Prussian Saxony and part of Thuringia. 266th
Regiment, 9th Corps District—Grand Duchies of Mecklenberg. 34th Regiment,
2d Corps District—Pomerania).

1915.

EASTERN PRUSSIA.

1. Organized during the winter of 1914–15, this division and the 79th Reserve Division
formed the 40th Reserve Corps. The 80th Reserve Division was formed out of three field
battalions of the 4th Corps District (Nos. 22–24) and six field battalions (Nos. 43–48)
of the 9th Corps District. After training at the Lockstedt cantonment it was sent
to Eastern Prussia at the beginning of February, 1915. There it took part in the battle
of the Lakes of Masura from the 7th to the 17th.

POLAND.

2. From the end of February to the beginning of March it was actively engaged in
the region of the fortress of Ossoviec and took part in combats along the Polish frontier
before the Russian retreat in Eastern Prussia. In March it was brought back to the
frontier of Eastern Prussia and fought in the zone of the Suvalki government until
July. It exchanged the 265th Regiment for the 34th Regiment.

SMORGONI.

3. At the time of the Summer offensive the division participated in the taking of
Kovno (Aug. 18), fought on the Niémen (Aug. 19, Sept. 8th) and entered Vilna.
It occupied the new front in the region of Smorgoni and held this sector until March,
1916.

1916.

NAROTCH LAKE.

1. In March, 1916, the division opposed the Russian offensive on the Narotch Lake
front and occupied this sector until the month of December.

FRANCE.

2. On December 23 it entrained for the Western Front. (Itinerary: Lyntuny
(northeast of Vilna)–Vilna–Kovno–Koenigsberg–Danzig–Stettin–Hamberg–Hanover–
Cologne–Aix la Chapelle–Liège–Mons.) It detrained at Douai on the 29th and 30th
of December and was put at rest at Waziers (northeast of Douai) until the middle of
January, 1917.

1917.

ARTOIS.

1. January 18, 1917, it went into line before Neuve Chapelle (north of the canal of
la Bassée).

2. Relieved at about the beginning of March, it took over a sector to the south of
Lens (Mar. 14). Obliged to fall back to the Méricourt–Avion line after the capture
of the heights of Vimy by the British troops (Apr. 9), it suffered serious losses in the
course of that operation.

FLANDERS.

3. On May 16 it was relieved from the Lens front and sent to rest in the region of
Trent until May 29.

4. From May 29 to June 22 it held the Boesinghe–Wieltje sector, where it took part
in no engagements.

MEUSE.

5. After resting, in July, in the region of Sedan–Montmédy, the 80th Reserve Division was brought (July 20) as a reserve to the left bank of the Meuse, and at the
beginning of August to the right bank (region of Juvigny–Jametz–Etraye).

VERDUN.

6. On August 14 it drew near the front and on August 20 reenforced, near Hill 344,
the units strained by the French attack. On the 23d it sustained very heavy losses
and gave up the counter attack.

CHAMPAGNE.

7. At the beginning of September the division entrained for Champagne. It occupied the Tahure sector the first half of September.

ARGONNE.

8. At the beginning of October it took over the Boureuilles–Vauquois sector, which it left on January 23, 1918, going to the Semide cantonment for training.

RECRUITING.

The 264th Regiment was recruited in the 4th Corps District and is sometimes called an Altenberg regiment. The 266th Regiment is a Mecklenberg unit. The 34th Regiment is Pomeranian in theory with a fairly heterogeneous make-up like the greater number of the units from Pomerania.

VALUE—1917 ESTIMATE.

The 80th Reserve Division, which seems to have had a high morale while opposite the English front, did not come up to expectations on August 20, 1917, while opposite Verdun. It proved incapable of counter attacking. It is reported that there were desertions and mutiny among the men which resulted in the relieving of the general commanding the brigade and of the commanding officer of the 264th Regiment.

The 34th Regiment was completely exhausted during the attacks of August 20.

In Argonne the losses of this division were very slight. At the Semide cantonment (Jan. 23 to Feb. 20, 1918) the division went through various maneuvers connected with open warfare.

1918.

1. The division was relieved in the Vauquois sector by the 237th Division from Russia about March 18. It rested and trained until March 27, when it traveled by St. Quentin–Ham–Roye to the vicinity of Moreuil.

PICARDY.

2. It reenforced the battle front north of Sauvillers on April 3, but was withdrawn on the 7th and rested at Ribemont. Losses were heavy during the brief engagement of the division.

CHAMPAGNE.

3. The division relieved the 14th Bavarian Division on April 21–22 in the sector Cornillet–Mont Blond. It remained there until the July 15 offensive, but did not take part in that action. On July 27 it returned to line near Moronvillers and held that sector until August 22.

AILETTE–AISNE.

4. It marched to Paris and went into line there. Two days later it was hastily relieved and marched to Chavignon. It entered line on the night of September 2–3 northwest of Crouy. It was withdrawn on September 21.

CHAMPAGNE.

5. The division returned to Champagne and relieved the 213th Division on September 27 at Loivre. It was engaged near Orainville, Aumenancourt, Pont Givart until October 11. It was again in line on October 17 at Nanteuil sur Aisne. It continued in line until the end of hostilities. The last identification was near Wasigny on November 7.

VALUE—1918 ESTIMATE.

The division was rated as third class. In general, it was used to hold less important defensive sectors.

81st Reserve Division.
COMPOSITION.

	1915 Brigade	1915 Regiment	1916 Brigade	1916 Regiment	1917 Brigade	1917 Regiment	1918 Brigade	1918 Regiment
Infantry	81 Res.	267 Res. 268 Res. 269 Res.	81 Res.	267 Res. 268 Res. 269 Res. 39 Ldw.	81 Res.	267 Res. 268 Res. 269 Res.	81 Res.	267 Res. 268 Res. 269 Res.
Cavalry	81 Res. Cav. Detch. 4 Sqn. 7 Drag. Rgt.		81 Res. Cav. Detch.		81 Res. (?) Cav. Detch.		2 Sqn. 1 Drag. Rgt.	
Artillery	81 Res. Brig.; 67 Res. F. A. Rgt. (6 Btries.). 68 Res. F. A. Rgt. (6 Btries.).		81 Res. Brig.; 67 Res. F. A. Rgt. 68 Res. F. A. Rgt.		(?) Art. Command: 67 Res. F. A. Rgt. (9 Btries.).		(?) F. A. Rgt.: 2 Abt. 26 Ft. A. Rgt. (4 and 6 Btries.). 980 Light Am. Col. 1019 Light Am. Col. 1034 Light Am. Col.	
Engineers and Liaisons.	81 Res. Pion. Co. 81 Res. Pont. Engs.		81 Res. Pion. Co. 84 Res. Pion. Co. 281 T. M. Co. 81 Res. Pont. Engs.		(381) Pion. Btn.: 84 Res. Pion. Co. 85 Res. Pion. Co. 95 T. M. Co. 281 T. M. Co. 14 Res. Searchlight Section. 380 Searchlight Section. 481 Tel. Detch.		41 Pion. Btn.: 84 Res. Pion. Co. 85 Res. Pion. Co. 281 T. M. Co. 56 Searchlight Section. 481 Signal Command: 481 Tel. Detch. 137 Wireless Detch.	
Medical and Veterinary.	1 Ambulance Co..........				543 Ambulance Co. Field Hospital. Vet. Hospital.		543 Ambulance Co. 120 Res. Field Hospital. 302 Field Hospital. 220 Vet. Hospital.	
Transports	81 Res. Train Detch.				M. T. Col.			
Odd Units	81 Res. Cyclist Co.		81 Res. Cyclist Co.		81 Res. Cyclist Co.			
Attached			47 Labor Btn.					

HISTORY.

(267th Regiment: 2d Corps District—Pomerania. 268th Regiment: 6th Corps District—Silesia. 269th Regiment: 3d Corps District—Brandenburg.)

1915.

The 81st Reserve Division was formed out of six field battalions of the 2d Corps District (Nos. 7–12) and three field battalions (Nos. 13–15) of the 3d Corps District. The first six were used to form the 267th and the 268th and the last named three were used to form the 269th Regiment. The division was instructed at the Warthe cantonment (5th Corps District) before being sent to the Western Front.

1. The 81st Reserve Division (with the 82d Reserve Division it constituted the 41st Reserve Corps), was transported to Belgium and detrained at Courtrai January 21, 1915.

SOMME.

2. Sent to the Somme district, it was engaged to the north of Chaulnes (Jan. 27–Mar. 28).

3. At the end of March the division was sent toward the Eastern Front.

GALICIA—RUSSIA.

The division was found on the Galician front in May (Jaslo, May 9); took part in operations on the San, near Jaroslav (between San and the Jaroslav-Przeworsk railway on May 15) then on the Bug (region of Krylov in July). Going down the Bug by Vladova (August) it advanced up to the west of Logitchin and the Oginsky Canal (north of Pinsk) in September. The front becoming fixed, the division established itself in that region.

1916.

PINSK.

1. The 81st Reserve Division stayed for more than two years in the Oginski–Iasälda Canal sector (Sept., 1915–Dec., 1917).

2. At the beginning of July, 1916, the 269th Regiment was identified between the Styr and the Stokhod, doubtlessly as a reserve for the units engaged against the Russian offensive.

1917.

RUSSIA—FRANCE.

1. In December, 1917, the division was relieved from its sector to the north of Pinsk and transported to the Western Front. It entrained on December 20 at Ivanovo (itinerary: Soldau–Bromberg–Schneide-Muehl–Berlin–Sarrebruck–Sedan–Cambrai), and detrained at Lille on December 26. After resting in the vicinity of Lille it went into line to the south of Fleurbaix (Jan. 24–25, 1918). It again occupied the same sector at the beginning of April.

RECRUITING.

The 267th and the 268th Regiments were originally Pomeranian and became quite heterogeneous like all regiments from this province. The 268th Regiment was in theory recruited in Silesia which contributes to a maintenance of the mixed character of its personnel. The 269th is a Brandenburg unit.

VALUE—1917 ESTIMATE.

On the Eastern Front from May, 1915, to the end of December, 1917.

1918.

BATTLE OF THE LYS.

1. The division was relieved on the night of April 8–9 by the 35th Division at Neuve Chapelle. It moved northward and on the 12th reenforced the battle front south of Meteren. In the attacks in this area the 268th and 269th Reserve Regiments suffered heavy losses. It was relieved by the 11th Reserve Division on April 28.

METEREN.

2. On May 18 the division returned to its former sector at Meteren. It held this sector until May 28, and again from June 6 to 12 and from June 18 to July 19.

LORRAINE.

3. It entrained on the 22d at Roubaix and detrained at Haboudange on the 24th. The itinerary was Courtrai–Ghent–Louvain–Liege–Herbestal–Gerolstein–Treves–Sarreguemines. After several days of rest near Chateau Salins it relieved the 19th Division on the night of July 28–29. It held this quiet sector until October 5, when it was relieved by the 87th Division.

4. It entrained on the 6th and detrained at Guise about October 8. On the night of the 10th–11th it came into line near Seboncourt and was heavily engaged until October 20, when it was withdrawn east of Bohain. The division suffered heavy losses in this engagement.

5. On October 26 the division reenforced the line south of Guise and fought until the armistice. The last identification was south of Guise on November 3.

VALUE—1918 ESTIMATE.

The division was rated as third class. Its services in Flanders was of a mediocre character. In the St. Quentin area in October it put up a good resistance.

82d Reserve Division.
COMPOSITION.

	1915		1916		1917		1918	
	Brigade.	Regiment.	Brigade.	Regiment.	Brigade.	Regiment.	Brigade.	Regiment.
Infantry	82 Res.	60. 270 Res. 271 Res. 272 Res.	82 Res.	270 Res. 271 Res. 272 Res.	82 Res.	270 Res. 271 Res. 272 Res.	82 Res.	270 Res. 271 Res. 272 Res.
Cavalry	82 Res. Cav. Detch.		82 Res. Cav. Detch.		82 Res. Cav. Detch.		3 Sqn. 1 Drag. Rgt.	
Artillery	82 Res. Brig.: 69 Res. F. A. Rgt. (6 Btries.). 70 Res. F. A. Rgt. (6 Btries.).		82 Res. Brig.: 69 Res. F. A. Rgt. 70 Res. F. A. Rgt.			(?) Art. Command: 69 Res. F. A. Rgt. (9 Btries.).	70 Res. F. A. Rgt. 1 Abt. 18 Ft. A. Rgt. (2, 3, and 13 Btries.). 755 Light Am. Col. 1224 Light Am. Col. 1225 Light Am. Col.	
Engineers and Liaisons.	84 Res. Pion. Co. 82 Res. Pont. Engs.		86 Res. Pion. Co. 82 Res. Pont. Engs. 282 T. M. Co.		(382) Pion. Btn.: 86 Res. Pion. Co. 246 Pion. Co. 282 T. M. Co. 287 Searchlight Section. Tel. Detch.		382 Pion. Btn.: 348 Pion. Co. 86 Res. Pion. Co. 106 Res. Pion. Co. 482 Signal Command: 482 Tel. Detch. 174 Wireless Detch.	
Medical and Veterinary.	1 Ambulance Co.				544 Ambulance Co. 118 Res. Field Hospital. Vet. Hospital.		544 Ambulance Co. 115 Res. Field Hospital. 119 Res. Field Hospital. 221 Vet. Hospital.	
Transport	82 Res. Train Detch.				M. T. Col.		749 M. T. Col.	
Odd units	82 Res. Cyclist Co.		82 Res. Cyclist Co.		82 Res. Cyclist Co.			
Attached			40 Labor Btn.		46 Labor Btn.			

HISTORY.

(270th Regiment: 3d Corps District—Brandenburg.   271st and 272d Regiments: 6th
Corps   District—Silesia.)

1915.

1. Formed during November, 1914–January, 1915, with three field battalions of
the 3d Corps District and six of the 6th Corps District (Nos. 25–30) it was trained
at the Jueterbog cantonment.   The 82d Reserve Division (which with the 81st Reserve
Division formed the 41st Reserve Corps) entrained on January 21 for the Somme.   It
included an additional regiment—the 60th Infantry—which the 21st Corps had left
in France before leaving for Russia.

SOMME.

2. It was engaged in February and March, 1915, to the north of Chaulnes.

3. About March 28 it was transferred to the Eastern Front minus the 60th Infantry,
which joined the 121st Division.

GALICIA–RUSSIA.

4. In May, 1915, the 82d Reserve Division as well as the 81st Reserve Division took
part in the German offensive along the San, which resulted in the breaking up of
the Russian front in Galicia.   It was identified in region of Jaslo (May 9) to the south
of Radymno (May 12–21) and at Medyka (June 4).   Its pursuit of the Russians brought
it together with the 41st Reserve Corps to the Bug, in the vicinity of Grubeszow
(July) and to the northeast of Pinsk (September–October).   During that offensive
the division suffered heavy losses.

PINSK.

5. The Russian retreat being halted, the 82d Reserve Division took its position in
the Pinsk region (Nobel Lake, October–December).

1916.

PINSK–NOBEL LAKE.

1. The division remained the entire year in the Nobel Lake sector and up to November, 1917.   A soldier of the 270th Regiment wrote on November 8, 1917: "I have not
loaded my gun since the middle of March."

1917.

RUSSIA–FRANCE.

1. In November, 1917, the 82d Reserve Division was relieved by some Landsturm
units and re-formed (elimination of soldiers from Alsace and Lorraine, etc.).

2. At the beginning of December the division was transported to the Western Front.

3. The division entrained at Ivanovo on December 4 (itinerary: Brest-Litowsk–
Varsovie – Kalisz – Glogau – Cottbus – Halle – Frankfort – Mainz – Kreuznach – Sarrebrueck–Metz–Conflans) and detrained at Mars la Tour about December 10.

RECRUITING.

In theory Brandenburg and Silesia.   Very mixed personnel, seemingly including
men from Pomerania and the eastern Provinces of the Empire.

VALUE—1917 ESTIMATE.

In January, 1918, the 82d Reserve Division took part in maneuvers in the vicinity of
Thuméréville (northwest of Conflans).   After these maneuvers Lieut. Gen. Fuchs is said
to have said that the division could be put in class 3 of the combat units (Kampf
Truppen, 3) a classification which is just above that of labor troops.   (Interrogation
of prisoner, Mar. 4, 1918.   See Bull. Rens. Second Army (French), No. 744.)

The make-up of the division is heterogeneous and of mediocre quality and includes returned wounded men, Landsturm, former railway guards, dismounted troopers, and few recruits of the 1918 class. (Interrogation, Jan. 22, 1918.)

After a two-year stay in the Pinsk sector the 82d Reserve Division lacked training when it returned on the Western Front (December, 1917).

1918.

CANTIGNY.

1. The division was relieved on April 20 in the Woevre and marched by Conflans-Briey–Mairy to Landres, where it entrained. It moved via Longuyon–Mezieres–Hirson and arrived at Wassigny, where it detrained on May 5. On May 16 the division relieved the 30th Division west of Cantigny. It was thrown out of the city by the American attack at the end of the month. The division was withdrawn about July 22.

THIRD BATTLE OF THE SOMME.

2. To reenforce the Somme battle front the division came into line on August 9 between Hangest and Arvillers. It was withdrawn on the 18th northwest of Roye, but a week later returned to its former sector. The division fell back on the Canal du Nord on August 27, and on September 2 took up a position between the Chaulnes–Ham railroad and a point north of Moyencourt. It again retreated on the night of September 4–5 and occupied a position at Etreillers–Roupy before the Siegfried-Stellung.

The division was constantly engaged, resisting strongly, but being gradually forced back. On the 28th it retired to the line of the St. Quentin Canal. On October 8, a surprise attack threw it back to Fontaine Notre Dame. Here it resisted fiercely. It was relieved about October 10 and went to the Guise area.

In this fighting the division lost 2,000 men. Its combatant strength was estimated to be about 1,200 men on October 7.

3. On October 14 the division reenforced the line east of Bernot and fought for three days. It returned to the Guise area, but intervened again west of Pleine–Selve on October 25. Until the armistice it was engaged south of Guise, east of La Capelle, and at Liessies.

VALUE—1918 ESTIMATE.

The division was rated as third class. After August it was almost constantly in line in the St. Quentin area until its effectives were almost completely consumed.

83d Division.
COMPOSITION.

	1915 Brigade	1915 Regiment	1916 Brigade	1916 Regiment	1917 Brigade	1917 Regiment	1918 Brigade	1918 Regiment
Infantry	Doussin (1 Garrison Brig., now 165). Rudiger (2 Garrison Brig., now 166).	1 Garrison Rgt. (329). 2 Garrison Rgt. (330). 3 Garrison Rgt. (331). 4 Garrison Rgt. (332).	165. 166.	329. 330. 331. 332.	165.	329. 330. 331.	165.	255 Res. 4 Ldw. 346.
Cavalry			2 Sqn. 92 Ldw. Cav. Rgt.	2 Sqn. 92 Ldw. Cav. Rgt.....	83 Heavy Cav. Rgt. 2 Sqn. 92 Ldw. Cav. Rgt.		3 Sqn. 11 Drag. Rgt.	
Artillery	Von Conta F. A. Rgt. (F. A. Rgt.).	249 F. A. Rgt. (Ers. Abt. 61	249 F. A. Rgt.		Art. Command: 249 F. A. Rgt.		80 Art. Command: 249 F. A. Rgt. 3 Abt. 28 Ft. A. Rgt. (7th to 9th Btries.). 796 Light Am. Col. 798 Light Am. Col. 951 Light Am. Col.	
Engineers and Liaisons.			83 T. M. Co. 83 Pont. Engs. 83 Tel. Detch.		83 Pion. Btn.: 1 Ldw. Co. 1 Pions. 246 Pion. Co. 83 T. M. Co. 316 Searchlight Section. 83 Tel. Detch.		83 Pion. Btn.: 1 Ldw. Co. 1 C. Dist. Pions. 1 Ldw. Co. 5 C. Dist. Pions. 123 Searchlight Section. 83 Signal Command: 83 Tel. Detch. 185 Wireless Detch.	
Medical and Veterinary.					83 Ambulance Co. 49 Field Hospital. 165 Field Hospital. Vet. Hospital.		83 Ambulance Co. 49 Field Hospital. 165 Field Hospital. 83 Vet. Hospital.	
Transport					M. T. Col.		581 M. T. Col.	

Attached......			26 Bav. Ft. A. Btn. (1, 2, and 4 Btries.). 3 Abt. 5 Ft. A. Rgt. (6, 10, and 11 Btries.). 1 Art. Observation Section. 121 Sound Ranging Section. 8 Bav. Pion. Co. 4 Co. 10 Labor Btn. 2 Co. 35 Labor Btn. 77 Balloon Sqn. (Elements attached, Aug. 14, 1918. German document.)

HISTORY.

(329th and 331st Regiment: 5th Corps District—Posen and Lower Silesia. 330th Regiment: 7th Corps District—Westphalia.)

1915.

The 83d Division was formed out of the garrison of defense of Posen which went under the name of Posen Corps. It was engaged on the Eastern Front from the beginning of the war.

The Posen Corps composed of depot battalions of active regiments, of reserve, of Landwher, and even battalions of Landsturm, was divided into four brigades. Its strength was distributed into two divisions, the 83d and 84th, in June, 1915, and the battalions, which were at first formed into regiments bearing the names of the respective commanders of these regiments, were numbered 329 to 336, inclusive.

RUSSIA–POLAND.

1. From March to June, with the Posen Corps, the regiments which were to form the 83d Reserve Division took part in the Poland campaign to the north of Pilica and on the Bzura.

VICHNEV.

2. The 83d Division took part in the summer offensive against the Russians. Leaving the Ostrolenka region (July) it advanced by way of Grodno, Lipnichki (northeast of Lida, September) up to Vichnev (October), where it established its position.

1916.

VICHNEV.

1. The division stayed in the Vichnév sector during the entire year 1916 and until the month of April, 1917.

1917.

1. About the middle of April, 1917, the 83d Division was transferred from Vichnev to Baranovitchi, where it was held some time as a reserve and then to the northeast of Halicz, from which place it was transported by automobiles to the Stanislau region (June 5).

GALICIA.

2. At the beginning of July it was attacked by the Russians to the west of Stanislau (serious losses on July 9, particularly 690 prisoners). It afterwards took part in the German counteroffensive and advanced through the Dniester valley up to the west of Chotin (beginning of August.)

3. Relieved about the middle of September, the 83d Reserve Division was sent to rest in the Czernovitz region and then put back in line to the northeast of Bojan (October–November).

4. At the end of November the division left the Bojan sector and became a reserve for the Bothmer Army in back of the Czernovitz front. Before leaving for the Western Front the 4th Division had sent it men from Alsace and Lorraine (middle of December when the 36th Division had left the former some months before.)

RECRUITING.

Recruiting was mostly from Posen and Silesia with some support from Westphalia and the Rhine Province. Coming from Galicia as late as March, 1918, the 83d Division could not come without the soldiers coming from Alsace and Lorraine which other divisions which had left before had transferred to it.

VALUE—1917 ESTIMATE.

Mediocre division, formed to the extent of one third by older men. Appears for the first time on the Western Front in April, 1918.

1918.

YPRES.

1. The division held the sector north of Ypres until July 18. After its relief it rested a few days in Roulers and then entrained at Lichterfelde for the Douai area. On August 16 it traveled via Cambrai and detrained near Ruyanlcourt. Here it spent the night, moving up to Flers the next morning. The division came into line on the 19th, when it relieved the 3d Naval Division north of Albert.

SCARPE–SOMME.

2. It was engaged at Thiepval, Bazentin le Grand, Courcelette, and Martinpuich until about April 26, when it was withdrawn.

3. On September 10, the division came into line in Lorraine with an entirely new composition. It then included the 255th Reserve Regiment, the 346th Regiment, and the 4th Landwehr Regiment grouped under the brigade and divisional staff of the 83d Division. The 329th Regiment, one of the former regiments of the division, was sent to Esthonia on September 5. It had lost 700 casualties in the August fighting. The reconstructed division held the Embermenil sector until the armistice.

VALUE—1918 ESTIMATE.

The division was rated as fourth class. After its transfer to the Western Front, the division held a quiet sector except for a short time on the Scarpe in August.

84th Division.
COMPOSITION.

	1915 Brigade	1915 Regiment	1916 Brigade	1916 Regiment	1917 Brigade	1917 Regiment	1918 Brigade	1918 Regiment
Infantry	Hoffmann, afterward Schutze (3 Garrison Brig.) (167). Reisswitz (4 Garrison Brig.) (168).	5 Garrison Rgt. (333). 6 Garrison Rgt. (334). 7 Garrison Rgt. (335). Schutze, afterwards Kroebel, Rgt. (8 Garrison Rgt. "336").	168.	334. 335. 336.	168.	335. 336. 423.	163.	335. 336. 423.
Cavalry		84 Cav. Rgt. (Ers. Sqns. 8 Drag., 3 Uhlan Rgts., and 2 and 4 Landst. Sqn. 5 C. Dist.).	84 Cav. Rgt.			1 Sqn. 84 Cav. (Heavy) Rgt.	3 Sqn. 16 Drag. Rgt.	
Artillery			248 F. A. Rgt. 847 F. A. Btry. 854 F. A. Btry.		Art. Command: 248 F. A. Rgt. 903 F. A. Btry.		54 Art. Command: 248 F. A. Rgt. 3 Abt. 25 Ft. A. Rgt. (8 to 10th Btries.). 1007 Light Am. Col. 1008 Light Am. Col. 1009 Light Am. Col.	
Engineers and Liaisons.			272 Pion. Co. 1 Ldw. Pion. Co. (12 C. Dist.). 3 Labdst. Pion. Co. (13 C. Dist.). 84 T. M. Co. 84 Pont. Engs. 84 Tel. Detch.		(?) Pion. Btn.: 272 Pion. Co. 1 Ldw. Co. 12 Pions. 84 T. M. Co. 347 Searchlight Section. 84 Tel. Detch.		84 Pion. Btn.: 2 Res. Co. 1 Pions. 272 Pion. Co. 84 T. M. Co. 52 Searchlight Section. 84 Signal Command: 84 Tel. Detch. 166 Wireless Detch.	

Medical and Veterinary.		84 (?) Ambulance Co. 21 Ldw. Field Hospital. 156 Field Hospital.	84 Ambulance Co. 77 Field Hospital. 21 Ldw. Field Hospital. 156 Vet. Hospital.
Transports.		1008 M. T. Col.	
Attached.	1 Haguenau Landst. Inf. Btn. (21 C. Dist. Btn. No. 12).	1 Anklam, Landst. Inf. Btn. (2 C. Dist. Btn. No. 1). 7 Posen Landst. Btn. (5 C. Dist. Btn. No. 7). 1 Glogau Landst. Btn. (5 C. Dist. Btn. No. 15). 1 Cottbus Landst. Ers. Btn. (3 C. Dist. Btn. No. 23). 2 Dresden Landst. Inf. Btn. (12 C. Dist. Btn. No. 2).	

HISTORY.

(335th and 336th Regiments: 5th Corps District—Posen.   423d Regiment: 5th Corps District—Lower Silesia.)

1915.

The 84th Division with the 83d Division formed the Posen Corps and was engaged on the Eastern Front from the beginning of the war. (See 83d Division.) It was organized in June, 1915.

RUSSIA.

1. After having fought in Poland to the north of Pilica (February to June, 1915) the elements of the 84th Division operated in the region of Bleudow.

2. The 84th Division took part in the offensive against the Russians. It advanced through the region of Bug (Aug. 17), through the southeast of Bielsk (end of August) north of Slonim (September, battle from the 13th to the 18th), up to the south of Novogrodek (Sept. 22). The front having become stationary, the division took a position in the vicinity of Deliatitchi (north of the Niemen). In December it gave up the 333d Regiment of Infantry to the 89th Division, then recently organized.

1916.

RUSSIA.

1. The 84th Division stayed in the sector in the vicinity of the Niemen (Liubtcha, Deliatitchi) during the entire year 1916.

2. From July to October the 334th and 335th Regiments were detached as reenforcements between Goroditche and Baranovitchi to meet the Russian offensive.

1917.

1. In 1917 the division still occupied the same sectors along the Niemen (Deliatitchi, Negnevitchi) until its departure for the Western Front (December).

2. About the month of June the 334th Infantry was transferred to the 94th Division and replaced by the 423d Infantry, to which the former transferred some of its men.

In December the division absorbed another lot of men from the 334th Infantry and some from the Landsturm Battalion V. 15. Its strength had since November included some young men of the class of 1919.

3. At the end of December the division was transported to France. The 3d Battalion of the 423d Regiment entrained at Novogrodek on December 31. (Itinerary: Varsovie–Leipzig—Frankfort on the Main–Thionville) and detrained at Arrancy (south of Longuyon) on January 7. The 2d Battalion of the 336th Regiment entrained on December 28 and detrained at Landres on January 3.

RECRUITING.

The division was for the most part recruited from the 5th and the 7th Corps Districts. This was but slightly changed by the incorporation of the men of the Landsturm Battalion V.15 which consisted mostly of soldiers from Brandenburg and of the addition of those belonging to the class of 1919 which came from the 4th Corps District.

VALUE—1917 ESTIMATE.

The 84th Division had been on the Eastern front since 1914. Its offensive value was mediocre.

On the Russian front it began to fraternize at the end of December. The Germans were only allowed to do so in the presence of their officers. In November and about December 20 the men in the division who were over 40 years of age were transferred into Landsturm battalions or into regiments staying in Russia, and replaced by young men nearly all belonging to the class of 1919 (250 to the 84th Division in November).

1918.

MONTDIDIER-NOYON.

1. The divison was relieved by the 53d Reserve Division about May 1. It moved west and on May 25 relieved the 3d Bavarian Division in the Lassigny sector. It was taken out in early June and rested until the 9th, when it returned to attack at Courcelles. It again retired on June 20 and rested until July 2.

LASSIGNY.

2. On that date it was in line southeast of Belloy, where it was engaged until mid-July. It rested near Antheuil until August 12, when it reenforced the battle front south of Thiescourt. Then it was engaged until about August 22.

OISE.

3. One regiment—the 423d—entered line on the Oise on August 22 and by September 4 all the division was in line near Quierzy. It was withdrawn on September 15.

4. On September 30 the division entered line at Trouquoy and south of Sequehart. In the fighting in the first week of October the elements of the division were badly mixed with other divisions. They were taken out about October 9 and re-formed.

5. It was reengaged on October 27 in the vicinity of Sissonne and fought until the armistice. The last identification was east of Bucy les Pierrepont on November 6.

VALUE—1918 ESTIMATE.

The division was rated as fourth class. It was a very mediocre unit, composed largely of Landsturm elements and of young recruits. It was decimated by the fighting in the fall and its morale became very bad. A contributing factor was a draft of 300 prisoners returned from Russia.

85th Landwehr Division.
COMPOSITION.

	1915		1916		1917		1918	
	Brigade.	Regiment.	Brigade.	Regiment.	Brigade.	Regiment.	Brigade.	Regiment.
Infantry	60 Ldw.	17 Ldw. 21 Ldw. 61 Ldw. 99 Ldw.	169 Ldw. 170 Ldw.	61 Ldw. 99 Ldw. 17 Ldw. 21 Ldw.	170 Ldw.	17 Ldw. 21 Ldw. 99 Ldw.	169 Ldw.	17 Ldw. 21 Ldw. 99 Ldw.
Cavalry	85 Cav. Rgt. (4 Sqns.).		85 Cav. Rgt.		5 Sqn. 6 Cuirassier Rgt. (?) Sqn. 85 Cav. Rgt. Ers. Sqn. 12 Dragoon Rgt.		5 Sqn. 6 Cuir. Rgt.	
Artillery	Ers. Abts. of the 36, 71, and 73 F. A. Rgts.		85 F. A. Rgt. 93 F. A. Rgt. 844 F. A. Btry.		(?) 844 F. A. Btry.		275 Field Artillery Rgt.	
Engineers and Liaisons.					(485) Pion. Btn.: 2 Ers. Co. 26 Pions. 385 T. M. Co. 22 Heavy Field Searchlight Section. Tel. Detch.		1 Ldst. Pion. 4 Army Corps. 585 Tel. Detch.	
Medical and Veterinary.					85 Ambulance Co. Field Hospital. Vet. Hospital.		320 Field Hospital. 181 Vet. Hospital.	
Transport					M. T. Col.			
Odd units					85 Cyclist Co.			
Attached			Zittau Landst. Inf. Btn. (12 C. Dist. No.7).		Zittau Landst. Inf. Btn. (12 C. Dist. Btn. No. 7). Osterode Landst. Inf. Btn. (20 C. Dist. Inf. Btn. No. 8).			

HISTORY.

(17th Landwehr: 21st Corps District—Lorraine. 21st Landwehr: 17th Corps District—
Western Prussia. 99th Landwehr: 15th Corps District—Alsace.)

1915.

The 85th Landwehr Division is the old Breugel Division, which at the beginning of the war, together with the Woernitz Division (86th Division), formed the Graudenz Corps (also known as the Zastrow Corps and in 1915 the 17th Reserve Corps), and operated on the Eastern Front.

RUSSIA.

1. Two of the regiments, the 17th Landwehr and the 99th Landwehr, went to the Eastern Front, the former at the beginning of the war and the latter in the spring of 1915.

POLAND.

1. Until July, 1915, the Breugel Division was engaged in Poland (Prasnysz, region of Mlawa).

2. In July it took part in the offensive against the Russians, advancing to the west of Pultusk (middle of July); besieged Novo-Georgievsk; was on the Bug (beginning of August) and near Bielsk (end of August). The 61st Landwehr entered Warsaw on August 22 and remained there during the month of September.

3. With the stabilization of the front the former Breugel, now the 85th Landwehr Division occupied the Vichnev sector (to the south of Krevo) on the Little Berezina.

1916.

VICHNEV.

1. The 85th Landwehr Division remained on the Vichnev-Deliatitchi front for more than two years (September, 1915–October, 1917). In September, 1917, it gave up the 61st Landwehr Regiment to the 217th Division, then newly organized.

1917.

VICHNEV.

1. About the 15th of October, 1917, the 85th Landwehr Division moved to the north. It left the Niemen region to go to the south of Dvinsk, near the lake of Drisviaty. In December it extended its sector toward the south (Vidzy).

RECRUITING.

The 21st Landwehr was recruited in the 17th Corps District, or more generally in western Prussia. There were numerous soldiers from Alsace and Lorraine in the division. Frequent desertions on the part of the men from Lorraine and men from the mining region of the Sarre in 1914 on the French front led to the decision which sent the 17th Landwehr to Russia.

VALUE—1917 ESTIMATE.

Remained a long while in quiet sectors on the Russian front. The 85th Landwehr Division had but a very mediocre combat value.

1918.

COURLAND.

1. Toward the end of January the men of the 85th Landwehr Division were still fraternizing in the Vidzy region. The 17th Landwehr Regiment was in the vicinity of Jakobstadt in April and the 99th Landwehr Regiment participated at this time in the operations in Finland.

UKRAINE.

2. Early in May the whole division, with the exception of some elements (14th Jaeger Battalion, 1st Guard Uhlan Regiment, 229th Mounted Machine Gun Co.), moved to the Polotsk region. Regiments of the division were identified in this area early in September. There was a rumor that the division had been transferred to the Western Front early in October, but this seems unlikely.

VALUE—1918 ESTIMATE.

The division was rated as fourth class.

86th Division.
COMPOSITION.

	1915 Brigade	1915 Regiment	1916 Brigade	1916 Regiment	1917 Brigade	1917 Regiment	1918 Brigade	1918 Regiment
Infantry	Grossman (171). Windhelm (172).	Reinhard (341). Krause (342). Hoebel (343). Gropp (344).	171. 172.	341. 342. 343. 344.	172. 4 Jag. Btn.	341. 343. 344.	172.	341. 343. 344.
Cavalry	86 Cav. Regt. (Ers. Sqns. 11 Drag., 4 Horse Jag. Rgts., 1 Ldw. Sqn. 17 C. Dist. Cav., and Res. Ers. Sqn. 17 C. Dist. Cav.				3 Sqn. 7 Uhlan Rgt.		3 Sqn. 7 Uhlan Rgt.	
Artillery	86 F. A. Rgt.		86 F. A. Rgt. 220 F. A. Rgt.		Art. Command: 86 (?) F. A. Rgt.		86 F. A. Rgt. 404 F. Art. Btn. 971 Light Mun. Col. 973 Light Mun. Col.	
Engineers and Liaisons.			86 T. M. Co. 86 Pont. Engs. 86 Tel. Detch.		Pion. Btn.: 3 Ers. Co. 26 Pions. 2 Co. 34 Res. Pions. 86 T. M. Co. 328 Searchlight Section. Tel. Detch.		Pion. Btn.: 3 Ers. 26th Pion. 3 Pion. Btn. No. 34. 19th Searchlight Section. 86 Div. Signal Command. 86 Tel. Detch. 157 Div. Wireless Detch.	
Medical and Veterinary.					86 Ambulance Co. 81 Field Hospital. 129 Field Hospital. Vet. Hospital.		86 Ambulance Co. 81 and 129 Field Hospitals. 182 Vet. Hospital.	
Transport.					797 M. T. Col. 971 M. T. Col.		583 M. T. Col.	
Odd units.					86 Cyclist Co.			
Attached.			110 Labor Btn. Briesen Landst Inf. Btn. (17 C. Dist. No. 1). Neufahrwasser Landst. Inf. Btn. (17 C. Dist. No. 8).		2 Cologne Landst. Inf. Btn. (8 C. Dist. Btn. No. 15). 7 Munst. Landst. Inf. Btn. (7 C. Dist. Btn. No. 69).			

HISTORY.

(341st Regiment: 20th Corps District—Eastern part of Western Prussia. 343d and 344th Regiments: 17th Corps District—Western Prussia.)

1914.

The 86th Division was organized during the summer of 1915 with the elements of the Woernitz Division. The latter with the 85th Landwehr Division, constituted the Suren Corps coming from the garrisons of Graudenz, Kulm, and Marienberg, which was used on the Eastern Front from the beginning of the war. There were 11 battalions of mobile depots (active, reserve, and Landwehr) and two companies of depots of chasseurs (jaeger).

POLAND.

1. After having participated in the operations on the Polish front from September to December, 1914, the troops which were to be formed into the 86th Division were then used in the region of Mlawa (trench warfare) from the end of December, 1914, to the middle of May, 1915. Some of the units were sorely tried. At Koslau (Nov. 12 to Dec. 25), then at Prasnysz, the 4th Company of the mobile Ersatz battalion of the 18th Infantry lost 2 officers and 266 men. (Casualty Report.)

1915.

RUSSIA.

1. From July, 1915, on the Woernitz Division, now the 86th Division, took part in the German offensive and helped to break up the Russian front near Prasnysz (July 13–17). Following up its advance, it fought on the Narew after the taking of Pultusk. It took part in the battles of Ostrowo (Aug. 8–10), of Bielsk (Aug. 19–25) and on the Niemen (September).

2. When the Russian front became stationary it found itself on the Little Berezina and took a position to the east of Deliatitchi.

1916.

RUSSIA.

1. The 86th Division remained in the sector near the Little Berezina until March.

2. From the 18th of March to the 30th of April it took part in the battle of Narotch, and until the month of July, occupied the Krevo–Smorgoni sector. It then went on the Chtchara (July 9–26), opposed the Russian offensive near Kovel from July 28 to November 4 and finally established itself on the upper Styr and on the Stokhod, reduced in strength by the transfer of the 342d Regiment to the 93d Division, then just formed.

1917.

ZOLHYNIA.

1. After having occupied the Stokhod front in front of Kovel until April, 1917, the 86th Division put into line on April 22, to the south of Kisselin. It remained there until January, 1918.

RECRUITING.

Division sufficiently homogeneous (Prussian Provinces) with relatively no other numerous elements from other Provinces. Having left the Russian front at a late date, the division could not leave the soldiers coming from Alsace and Lorraine behind.

VALUE—1917 ESTIMATE.

The 86th Division seemed to be a good division, composed of young and vigorous men (March, 1918).

On the Eastern Front it was rated as a first-class division.

125651°—20——36

1918.

VOLHYNIA.

1. The 86th Division left its sector in the Kiselin area toward the end of January. It entrained at Rogozwo on the 29th and traveled via Brest–Litowsk–Kalisch–Cottbus–Eisenach–Frankfort–Sarrebruecken–Metz–Sedan–Rethel, and detrained at Le Chatelet on the 4th of February.

RHEIMS.

2. It then marched via Neuflize–Isles–Boult–Fresnes, and entered line near Betheny (northeast of Rheims) on the 27th, when it relieved the 242d Division. It was withdrawn about the 21st of May, and went to rest near Asfeld.

3. On the evening of the 26th it left and marched toward the front; the 27th it was in reserve; on the 28th it attacked near Trigny (west of Rheims) and succeeded in advancing about 5 kilometers. On the 6th of June the 86th and 232d Divisions, supported by the 33d Reserve Division, captured the town of Bligny (southwest of Rheims), but lost it the same afternoon when the French counterattacked. The 86th Division had quite heavy losses. It was relieved on July 21 by the 50th Division and went to rest in the region northwest of Rheims.

4. On the 10th of August the division reenforced the front near Muizon (west of Rheims). It was relieved by the 10th Reserve Division on the 28th.

LAON.

5. During the night of September 18–19 it relieved the 50th Reserve Division near the Colombe farm south of Laon). It was relieved about the 23d of October.

6. The division came back into line on November 5 in the vicinity of Marle; on the 7th it was identified northeast of Vervins; and on the 9th at Hirson.

VALUE—1918 ESTIMATE.

The 86th was rated as a fourth-class division. It did not participate in any of the great offensives during 1918, but it did attack vigorously on two occasions and on the whole acquitted itself better than other divisions similarly rated.

87th Division.
COMPOSITION.

	1915		1916		1917		1918	
	Brigade.	Regiment.	Brigade.	Regiment.	Brigade.	Regiment.	Brigade.	Regiment.
Infantry	Griepenkerl. Normann.	Leimbach (345). Runge (346). Schwarz (347). 8 Landst.	173. 179.	345. 346. 347. 8 Landst.	173.	345. 347. 8 Landst.	179.	345. 347. 3d Res. Ers.
Cavalry	87 Cav. Rgt.		87 Cav. Rgt.		1 Sqn. 3 Horse. Gren. Rgt.		1 Sqn. 3 Jag. z. Pf.	
Artillery	87 F. A. Abt.		87 F. A. Rgt. 841 F. A. Btry.		Art. Command. 87 F. A. Regt.		3 Artillery Command: 38 Field Art. Rgt. 34 Ft. Art. Btn. 878 Light Mun. Col. 975 Light Mun. Col. 949 Light Mun. Col.	
Engineers and Liaisons.			4 Co. 26 Pions. 2 Ldw. Pion. Co. (Gd. C. Dist.). 87 T. M. Co.		Pion. Btn.: 4 Co. 26 Pions. 3 Ldw. Co. 6 Pions 87 T. M. Co. 264 Searchlight Section. 87 Tel. Detch.		87 Pion. Btn. 242 Pion. Co. 2 Ers. Pion. Btn. No. 26. 113 Searchlight Section. 87 Div. Signal Command. 87 Tel. Detch. 163 Div. Wireless. Detch.	
Medical and Veterinary.					69 Ambulance Co. 131 Field Hospital. 132 Field Hospital Vet. Hospital.		69 Ambulance Co. 131 and 132 Field Hospitals. 191 Vet. Hospital.	
Transport.					157 M. T. Col.			
Odd units.			156 Cyclist Co.		156 Cyclist Co.			
Attached.			10 Labor Btn. 75 Labor Btn.					

HISTORY.

(345th Regiment; 5th Corps District—Posen. 347th Regiment; 2d Corps District—
Pomerania. 3d Reserve Ersatz Regiment; 9th Corps District—Schleswig-Holstein.)

1915.

The 87th Division as well as the 89th Division came from the Thorn Corps, which
was engaged on the Eastern Front from the beginning of the war.

RUSSIA–POLAND.

1. Its battalions were made into a division at the beginning of June, 1915. Before
that time the Ersatz battalions, from which it was formed, belonged to the Griepenkerl
and Plantier detachments (Thorn Corps), and fought near the Polish frontier between
the Vistula and Prasnysz. These were the Leimbach–Zerener regiments which became the 345th, the Runge which became the 346th and the Schwarz which became the
347th, and to which latter unit the 8th Landsturm Regiment organized in June, 1915,
at the Elsenborn cantonment was joined,

2. Beginning in July the elements of the 87th Division took part in the offensive
against the Russians: Battles between Drobin and the Vistula, then to the west of
Pultusk; pursuit fighting up to lower Narew (July 18–22); siege of Novo–Georgiesvk
(Aug. 13–19); battles of Niemen (Aug. 31–Sept. 8) and of Vilna (Sept. 9–26).

3. After having fought between the Bogin and Drisviaty Lakes (Oct. 5–19), the
division took up a position in that region.

1916.

DRISVIATY LAKE.

1. The 87th Division occupied the Drisviaty-Vidzy line the entire year 1916 and
until the month of October, 1917.

1917.

COURLAND.

1. In October, 1917, the 87th Division relieved the 2d Division in the Illukst
sector. While there it received its first reenforcements from the 1919 class.

2. Relieved from that front at the end of December, the division was brought
together in the Kovno region. It got a great many men from the 23d Landwehr
Division, especially from the 26th and 66th Landwehr Regiments.

RECRUITING.

This division was one of the most heterogeneous of the Prussian Army. Not only
were its regiments recruited in three different Provinces, but the considerable amount
of replacements received since November, 1917, were from various different regions—
men from the class of 1919 from the 9th and 11th Corps Districts in November, 1917,
later from the 14th Corps District; Landwehr from the 4th and 6th Corps Districts at
the end of December; men from the 8th, 14th, and 18th Corps Districts (a small number)
during its stay in Champagne.

VALUE—1917 ESTIMATE.

The 87th Division coming from Russia at the end of March seemed to have but a
mediocre combat value (April, 1918).

1918.

I. The division held the quiet sector at St. Marie a Py until June 18, when it was
relieved by the extension of the flanking divisions. The division up to that time
had had slight losses and was available for active service.

SECOND BATTLE OF THE MARNE.

2. It entered line on June 22 on the Aisne front near Bouresches. During this period the division was engaged in harder fighting. In the American attack south of Torcy the division lost heavily in killed and wounded on June 25–26. Three hundred prisoners were taken on those days. It took part in the German retreat until July 26, when it was withdrawn near Charmel.

SCARPE–SOMME.

3. The division rested at Charleville until August 25. It entrained and moved to the Bapaume–Peronne area, where it was engaged on August 26–27, south of Longeuval. It was pushed back by Flers (29th), les Bouefs (Aug. 31), north of Morval (Sept. 1), Le Transloy (3d), east of Manancourt and northeast of Etricourt (4th), northeast of Fins (7th), northwest of Gonzencourt (9th). It was relieved on the night of September 11–12. During this period in line the losses of the division were severe. More than 1,000 prisoners were taken from this division.

4. In spite of heavy losses it was given only a short rest at Vaucelles (south of Cambrai), and again placed in line east of Villers Guislain on September 18 for the purpose of delivering a counterattack. It was held in line at this point until about September 28, when it retired to rest at Walincourt.

LORRAINE.

5. On October 12 the division came into line southwest of Chateau Salins. It rested on that quiet front until about November 1, when it was sent north, and on November 8 came in line at Haut Bugny. The last identification was northeast of Rocquigny on November 10.

VALUE—1918 ESTIMATE.

The division was rated as fourth class. As a sector holding unit it saw heavy service on the Marne and in Picardy.

88th Division.
COMPOSITION.

	1915 Brigade	1915 Regiment	1916 Brigade	1916 Regiment	1917 Brigade	1917 Regiment	1918 Brigade	1918 Regiment
Infantry	21 Ldw. 1 Ldw. Ers.	10 Ldw. 38 Ldw. 4 Ldw. Ers. 5 Ldw. Ers. 6 Ers. 8 Ers. 7 Ers. 9 Ers.	175 Ldw. 176. 177.	(349) Ldw. (350) Ldw. 351. 352. 353. (354).	176.	352. 353. 425.	176.	352. 353. 426.
Cavalry		6 C. Dist. Field Cav. Rgt. (2 Sqns. of 6 Hns. Rgt. and 2 Sqn. of 2 Uhlan Rgt.).	88 Cav. Rgt. (4 Sqns. ex-Field Cav. Rgt. 6 C. Dist.).		(?) Sqn. Horse Jag. Rgt. 2 Sqn. 88 Cav. Rgt.		1 Sq. 10 Jag. z. Pf.	
Artillery	1 Ers. Abt. 42 F. A. Rgt.		88 F. A. Rgt. 223 F. A. Rgt.			223 F. A. Rgt.	88th Field Art. Rgt. 123 Foot Art. Btn. 980, 982, and 1028 Light Mnn. Col.	
Engineers and Liaisons.	1 Ldw. Co. 6 Pions. 2 Ldw. Co. 6 Pions. 3 Ldw. Co. 6 Pions.		6 Ldw. Pion. Btn. 88 T. M. Co. 88 Pont. Engs. 88 Tel. Detch.		6 Ldw. Pion. Btn.: 1 Ldw. Co. 6 Pions. 2 Ldw. Co. 6 Pions. 88 T. M. Co. 249 Searchlight Section. Tel. Detch.		88 Pion. Btn. 249 Pion. Co. 3 Cq. Res. Pion. Btn. No. 33. 88 T. M. Co. 92 Div. Signal Command. 88 Div. Signal Command. 88 Tel. Detch. 102 B. Div. Wireless Detch.	
Medical and Veterinary.	....		....		277 Ambulance Co. 141 Field Hospital. 26 Ldw. Field Hospital. Vet. Hospital.		277 Ambulance Co. 54 and 141 Field Hospitals. 193 Vet. Hospital.	
Transport	....		....			M. T. Col.		
Attached	....		31 Landst. Inf. Rgt. 111 Labor Btn.		111 Labor Btn.			

HISTORY.

(352d and 353d Regiments; 6th Corps District—Silesia. 426th Regiments; 9th Corps District—Hanseatic cities.)

1915.

1. The 88th Division grew out of the war garrison of Breslau, which was made up of the 21st Brigade of Landwehr (10th and 38th Landwehr) and by Silesian and Saxon Ersatz battalions. This originally was the Breslau Corps, which after the brigade of Landwehr was taken from it, became the Menges Division. The Ersatz battalions being formed into regiments, the division then comprised three brigades—1st Landwehr Ersatz Brigade (later the Schmiedecker Brigade), Paczensky (later Buddenbrock) Brigade, and the Zenger Brigade. Its regiments bore the names 4th and 5th Landwehr Ersatz and 6th, 7th, 8th, and 9th Ersatz.

RUSSIA–POLAND.

2. In April–May, 1915, the Menges Division fought on the Pilica.

3. In July it was between the Vistula and Pilica taking part in the offensive against Russia.

4. It advanced in August through the region of Narew (to the south of Pultusk, Aug. 4; to the north of Bielsk, Aug. 19). At the end of August it reached the region of Vilna; to the west of Dvinsk in September.

DRISVIATY LAKE.

5. When the front became stationary it took a position near the Drisviaty Lake (September).

6. The Menges Division became the 88th Division. The Ersatz Battalion Brigades were regrouped and distributed between six regiments, numbered 349th and 350th Landwehr, 351st, 352d, 353d, 354th Regiments of Infantry, forming in turn the 175th, 176th, and 177th Brigades.

1916.

DRISVIATY LAKE.

1. The 88th Division occupied the Drisviaty Lake sector from September, 1915, until September, 1917.

2. In July, 1916, the division was reconstituted. The 354th Regiment went to the 216th Division. In August the 349th Landwehr and the 350th Landwehr Regiments were engaged on the Stokhod with the 150th Regiment of the 37th Division.

The 88th Division was now made up of the 351st, 352d, and 353d Regiments.

1917.

DRISVIATY LAKE.

1. In May, 1917, the 123d Division gave the 88th Division the 425th Regiment in exchange for the 351st Regiment of Infantry (Saxon). At this time all the Saxon elements were out of this division and it became entirely made up of Prussian personnel.

2. Thus constituted (352d, 353d, and 425th) the 88th Division was relieved from its position near Drisviaty Lake about September. It remained in the Dvinsk region.

3 The 425th Regiment was replaced by the 426th Regiment, the latter coming from the 3d Division.

RECRUITING.

The oldest regiments of the division, the 352d and the 353d, were primarily recruited in Silesia, and the 426th in the 9th Corps District.

Members of the 1919 class were identified with the division in April, 1918.

VALUE—1917 ESTIMATE.

Average.

1918.

ST. QUENTIN.

1. Early in January the division left Russia and, traveling via Kovno–Wirballen–Koenigsberg–Posen–Berlin–Trèves–Thionville, detrained at Sedan. After resting and training in the Cambrai region, it entered line in the Fresnoy sector (northwest of St. Quentin). It remained in line here, although it had two 10-day rest periods during which it was occupied only in field service training and in the usual practice marches, excepting two manœuvres with artillery. It attacked on the 21st, and although held up a day in front of Holnon wood it did very well, especially when it is considered that the division was considered unfit for combat upon its arrival from Russia.

2. Just before reaching Vermand on the 24th it stopped advancing, and the line continuing to go forward it remained in reserve. On the 27th it proceeded to the Moreuil area (southeast of Amiens), where it arrived when the German advance was already checked. It was withdrawn about the 2d of April, after having suffered very heavy losses.

CHAMPAGNE.

3. About the 12th of April it relieved the 11th Division south of Rouvroy in eastern Champagne. It was relieved about the 25th of June by the 33d Reserve Division and went to rest near Monthois, where it was trained.

4. About the 13th of July it came back into line in the Tahure sector just west of where it had previously been. The next day it attacked in the first line; it could make no progress (it will be remembered that thus the whole offensive was a failure) and suffered heavy losses, especially on account of gas. It was relieved early in September and was reported at rest south of Rethel on the 4th.

WOEVRE.

5. On September 12 the division moved up behind the front near Dampvitoux (north of Thiaucourt), but since it was soon seen that the American offensive had only a limited objective it did not enter line until the 23d. It was relieved by the 224th Division during the night of October 16–17.

MEUSE–ARGONNE.

6. The division arrived at Stenay during the night of the 19th–20th of October and on the 21st entered line near Cunel (north of Montfaucon). It remained in line until the armistice was signed.

VALUE—1918 ESTIMATE.

In March the British wrote: "From the bearing of prisoners of the 88th Division, recently captured, it appears that this formation, which from its composition might be expected to be indifferent is of a very fair quality and well-disciplined. Men and officers are mostly young and keen; many of the latter are active.

"As a fighting formation, the 88th Division thus appears to have been brought up to the standard of the majority of the German divisions in the western theater and in addition has a leader well acquainted with the conditions of warfare on this front."

Although its subsequent conduct was not such as to justify completely the above estimate, it did at least prove that its rating as a fourth-class unit was too low.

89th Division.

COMPOSITION.

	1915 Brigade	1915 Regiment	1916 Brigade	1916 Regiment	1917 Brigade	1917 Regiment	1918 Brigade	1918 Regiment
Infantry	21 Ldw. (In November the above passed to the 14 Ldw. Div.) Jonas (178).	10 Ldw. 38 Ldw. 333. 375. 8 Ldw.	178.	333. 375. 8 Ldw.	178.	333. 375. 8 Ldw.	178.	333. 375.
Cavalry	89 Cav. Rgt.		89 Cav. Rgt.		4 Sqn. 11 Drag. Rgt.		4 Sqn. 11th Drag. Rgt.	
Artillery	89 F. A. Abt.		89 F. A. Rgt. 911 F. A. Btry.		Art command: 89 F. A. Rgt.		89 Field Art. Rgt. (Rgt. Staff, 1 Abt. Staff Btries. 1 to 3).	
Engineers and Liaisons.			5 Co. 6 Pions. 2 Res. Co. 17 Pions. 89 T. M. Co. 89 Pont. Engs. 89 Tel. Detch.		Pion. Btn.: 5 Co. 26 Pions. 2 Res. Co. 17 Pions. 89 T. M. Co. Tel. Detch.		5 Co. 26th Pion. Btn. 89 Div. Signal Command. 89 Tel. Detch.	
Medical and Veterinary.					68 Ambulance Co. Field Hospital. Vet. Hospital.		68 Ambulance Co. 264 Field Hospital. 183 Vet. Hospital.	
Transport.			721 M. T. Col.		721 M. T. Col.		586 M. T. Col.	
Odd Units.							36 Bav. Mun. Col.	
Attached.			11 Labor Btn. 45 Labor Btn.					

HISTORY.

(333d Regiment: 5th and 6th Corps District—Silesia.   375th Regiment: 17th Corps District—Western Prussia.   8th Landwehr: 3d Corps District—Brandenburg.)

1915.

The 89th Division reached its present form of organization about October, 1915. With the 87th Division, it was used to form, while named Westernhagen Division, the Thorn Corps, and was engaged on the Eastern Front from the beginning of the war.   It at first was comprised of the 21st Landwehr Brigade, taken from the Breslau Corps and the Jonas Brigade (Keller Regiment and the 8th Landwehr) which became the 178th Brigade.   In November, 1915, this division having given up the 21st Landwehr Brigade to form the 14th Landwehr Division, it brought up its strength to three regiments by taking the 333d Regiment from the 84th Division.

RUSSIA.

1. During the middle of October, 1915, the 89th Division was identified in the Krevo sector, which it occupied until the end of August, 1916.

1916.

ROUMANIA.

1. About the 24th of August, 1916, the 89th Division was transported to the Transylvanian front (detraining near Maros-Ludas on Aug. 30).

2. It fought in the vicinity of St. Georges de Brasso (middle of October); near the Roumanian frontier in the valley of Buzeu (October-November); on the Buzeu-Rimnicu-Sarat highway (end of December); and near Plaginesci (Dec. 31).

1917.

ROUMANIA.

1. In the middle of January, 1917, the 89th Division was in line to the north of Rimnicu.

2. From the end of January to the middle of August it occupied a sector north of Focsani, east of Odobesci.   It took part in the attacks made, in August, north of Focsani and suffered very heavy losses.   After a few days' rest it took over the sector between Panciu and Marasesci.

RECRUITING.

The 89th Division took part in the entire campaign against Roumania.
It was kept on the Roumanian front until May, 1918.

VALUE—1917 ESTIMATE.

Its offensive value seemed mediocre.

1918.

ROUMANIA.

1. In January, 1918, the division furnished a great many replacements to the 76th Reserve Division which was destined to leave for the Western Front; men were also sent to the 115th Division.

2. Relieved southeast of Panciu early in January, the division remained for some time in reserve in the Focsani region, then came back into line northeast of that town.   It was identified there in March and April.   In June the 375th Regiment was identified by contact near Drenoud in Macedonia, but left soon after for the Panciu region where it was identified on the 28th of July.   The division was identified near Bucharest late in October.

VALUE—1918 ESTIMATE.

The Division was rated as fourth class.

91st Division.
COMPOSITION.

	1916 Brigade	1916 Regiment	1917 Brigade	1917 Regiment	1918 Brigade	1918 Regiment
Infantry	175 Ldw.	33 Ldw. 349 Ldw. 350 Ldw.	175 Ldw.	37 Ldw. 349 Ldw. 437.	175 Ldw.	37 Ldw. 349 Ldw. 437.
Cavalry	3 Sqn. 5 Cuirassier Rgt.			3 Sqn. 12 Mounted Jag. Rgt.	2 Sqn. 10 Drag. Rgt.	
Artillery			277 F. A. Rgt.		277 F. A. Rgt.	
Engineers and Liaisons	385 T. M. Co.		91 Pion. Btn.: 3 Co. 1 Pions. (?) 3 Ers. Co. 1 Pions. (91 T. M. Co.). Tel. Detch.		91 Pion. Btn. 3 Ers. Co. Pion. Btn. No. 1. 2 Ldst. Pion. Btn. 6 Army Corps. 219 Searchlight Section. 91 Div. Signal Command. 91 Tel. Detch.	
Medical and Veterinary			67 Ambulance Co. 27 Ldw. Field Hospital. Vet. Hospital.		67 Ambulance Co. 110 Field Hospital. 27 Ldw. Field Hospital. 241 Vet. Hospital.	
Transport			801 M. T. Col.			
Odd Units			Deuxponts Landst Inf. Btn. (2 C. Dist. Btn. No. 2).			

HISTORY.

(37th Landwehr; 5th Corps District—Posen. 349th Landwehr; 8th Corps District—
   Rhenish Province. 437th Regiment; 11th Corps District—Thuringe.)

1916.

The 91st Division (Clausius Division) was formed about August, 1916, from two Landwehr regiments—the 349th and the 350th, which constituted the 175th Brigade, taken from the 88th Division—and an active regiment, the 150th, temporarily transferred from the 37th Division. Later the organization of the 91st Division was modified.

VOLHYNIA.

1. As soon as it was organized the 91st Division was engaged on the Stokhod, north of the Kovel-Sarny railway and in the vicinity of Borovno (August, 1916). During these attacks the 150th suffered very big losses. This regiment rejoined its division (the 37th) shortly thereafter and was replaced by the 37th Landwehr, which had exercised a discreet surveillance over the Austrian troops (Russian information).

1917.

VOLHYNIA.

1. During the year 1917 the 91st Division was kept in Volhynia in the region of the Kovel-Sarny railway.

2. About the month of April it transferred the 350th Landwehr to the 45th Landwehr Division. It received the 437th Infantry, which had been organized in 1916 from Prussian elements taken from the 344th Infantry, the 349th Landwehr, and the 350th Landwehr, and which was with Austrian units.

In November the division seemed to have no particular sector and is "distributed among the little reliable troops of the Austrian Army," (Weekly Bulletin of Information of Russian Army, Dec. 16–23, 1917.

VALUE—1917 ESTIMATE.

Kept in Russia for the occupation of Ukrainia, the 91st Division had but a very small combat value (April, 1918).

1918.

1. The division was last identified in the Ukraine at the end of August. There is evidence that the division was brought to the Western Front in September. Reports and prisoners' statements pointed to the presence of the division in the Muelhausen area during October. However, it did not come into line on the Western Front. The division was not identified after the armistice among the retreating German units.

VALUE—1918 ESTIMATE.

The division was rated as fourth class.

92d Division.

COMPOSITION.

	1917		1918	
	Brigade.	Regiment.	Brigade.	Regiment.
Infantry...............	28 Ldw.	39 Ldw. 419. 432.	28 Ldw.	39 Ldw. 2 Ldw. 32 Ldw.
Cavalry................	(?)		1, 3, and 4 Sqns. 3 Cuirassier Rgt. 4 Sqn. Body Gd. Hus. Rgt.	
Artillery...............	Art. command: 2 F. A. Rgt 895 F. A. Btry.		12 Ldw. F. A. Rgt. (except Rgt. Staff, 1 Abt. Staff, 1 and 5 Btries., 2 Abt. Staff, 7 and 9 Btries.).	
Engineers and Liaisons.	Pion. Btn.: 346 Pion. Co. 92 T. M. Co. 92 Tel. Detch.		1 Ldw. Co. 14 C. Dist. Pions. 120 Searchlight Section. 92 Signal command: 92 Tel. Detch.	
Medical and Veterinary	276 Ambulance Co. 5 Ldw. Field Hospital. Vet. Hospital.		276 Ambulance Co. 5 Ldw. Field Hospital. 242 Vet. Hospital.	
Transport..............	M. T. Col.			

HISTORY.

(39th Landwehr; 7th Corps District—Westphalia. 32d Landwehr; 11th Corps District—Thuringen.)

1917.

The 92d Division (Rusche Division) was formed at about the end of November, 1916, on the Eastern Front.

VOLHYNIA.

1. At first as a part of the Bernhardi Army, the 92d Division occupied in Volhynia the Gorokhov–Kisselin sectors south of the Kovel–Rovno railway (February–August, 1917). It was then made up of the 419th, 432d, and the 133d Landwehr (Saxon), the latter being afterwards replaced by the 39th Landwehr.

GALICIA.

2. In August, 1917, the division was transferred toward the south and put into line in the Zalosce (Galicia) sector. The 419th Infantry left the division to join the 77th Division, with which it left for France.

VALUE—1917 ESTIMATE.

Having occupied from the time of its organization until April, 1918, but quiet Russian sectors, and, moreover, having given up its best men (those less than 35 years of age), who were transferred to other divisions on the Western Front, the 92d Division had but a mediocre combat value.

The 39th Landwehr, from the time of its formation in 1914, was noted in Belgium for its acts of insubordination (recruited from the mining population of Westphalia).

1918.

1. Relieved in the Zalosce sector in January, the division was in reserve in the vicinity of Zborow during February.

UKRAINE.

2. In April the division was in the Ukraine (39th Landwehr Regiment was identified near Kiev on the 23d; the 432d Regiment was in the vicinity of Klintsy on the 27th).   The third regiment was the 32d Landwehr, left behind by the 197th Division upon its departure for France in February.   The 432d Regiment sent to the Western Front was dissolved in May and was divided between the 22d Reserve and 82d Division.   The 2d Landwehr and the 32d Landwehr Regiment were identified in the Ukraine early in October.   Toward the end of the month elements of the division were reported along the Danube.

VALUE—1918 ESTIMATE.

The Division was rated as fourth class.

93d Division.

COMPOSITION.

	1916		1917		1918	
	Brigade.	Regiment.	Brigade.	Regiment.	Brigade.	Regiment.
Infantry	215.	342. 433. 434.	166.	342. 433. 434.	(?) (?)	433 (10 and 11 cos.). 434. (?)
Cavalry			5 Sqn. 16 Drag. Rgt. 4 Sqn. 85 Cav. Rgt.		5 Sqn. 16 Drag. Rgt. 4 Sqn. 4 Huss. Rgt. 85 Cav. (Heavy) Rgt.	
Artillery			Art. Command: 35 F. A. Rgt. 899 F. A. Btry. 900 F. A. Btry.		253 Ldw. F. A. Rgt. (except the Rgt. Staff, and 1 and 2 Abt. Staffs, and 4 and 6 Btries. of the 3 Abt.).	
Engineers and Liaisons	1 Res. Co. 26 Pions. 93 T. M. Co.		Pion. Btn.: 2 Ldw. Co. 1 Pions. 1 Ldw. Co. 17 C. Dist. Pions. 93 T. M. Co. 93 Tel. Detch.		81 Searchlight Section. 93 Signal Command: 93 Tel-Detch. (except 2 Sect.).	
Medical and Veterinary			233 Ambulance Co. Field Hospital. 243 Vet. Hospital.			
Transports			M. T. Col.			

HISTORY.

(433d Regiment: 18th and 20th Corps District—Hesse and Eastern Prussia. 434th Regiment: 4th Corps District—Prussian Saxony.)

1916.

The 93d Division (von Kramsta) was formed on the Eastern Front about the month of October, 1916 (region of Lida). One of its regiments, the 342d, had come from the 86th Division. The 433d and the 434th were newly created units.

RUSSIA.

1. In November, 1916, the 93d Division was in line to the southeast of Vichnev. At that time, with the 85th Landwehr Division, it formed the 17th Reserve Corps.

1917.

RUSSIA.

1. During the whole year 1917 the division stayed on the Little Berezina (Vichnev) front with the 12th Army.

VALUE—1917 ESTIMATE.

Mediocre combat value.

1918.

RUSSIA.

1. About the middle of December, 1917, the 93d Division left the Berezina and advanced toward the east.

2. It was in reserve near Minsk the 2d of March and in the Klintsy region the 27th of April. The 342d Regiment had entrained on April 10 at Lida for Belgium, where it was dissolved in May; its men being divided between the 22d Reserves and 119th Division.

UKRAINE.

3. About the middle of May the division was identified near Kiev, where it was also identified as late as the 9th of September.

RUMANIA.

4. Toward the end of October elements of the division were identified along the Danube.

VALUE—1918 ESTIMATE.

The Division was rated as fourth class.

94th Division.

COMPOSITION.

	1917		1918	
	Brigade.	Regiment.	Brigade.	Regiment.
Infantry	(?)	334. 423. 45 Landst.	(?)	365. 439. 24 Ldw.
Cavalry	1 Sqn. 84 Heavy Cav. Rgt.		1 Sqn. 7 Uhlan Rgt.	
Artillery	(?)		8 F. A. Rgt. (Staff, 1 Abt., 2 Abt., 4 and 5 Btries., 3 Abt.). 405 Ft. A. Btn. 1042 Light Am. Col. 1051 Light Am. Col.	
Engineers and Liaisons.	Pion. Btn.: T. M. Co. Tel. Detch.		411 Pion. Btn.: 2 Ldw. Co. 5 C. Dist. Pions. 2 Ldw. Co. 8 C. Dist. Pions. 85 Searchlight Section. 183 Signal Command: 183 Tel. Detch. 131 Wireless Detch.	
Medical and Veterinary	556 Ambulance Co. Field Hospital. Vet. Hospital.		551 Ambulance Co. 328 Field Hospital. 331 Field Hospital. 519 Vet. Hospital.	
Transport	1233 M. T. Col.			
Attached	Bitterfeld Landst. Inf. Btn. (4 C. Dist. Btn. No. 4). Cosel Landst. Inf. Btn. (6 C. Dist. No. 8).			

HISTORY.

(46th Landstrum: 2d Corps District—Pomerania; 5th Corps District—Silesia. 45th Landstrum: 6th Corps District—Silesia; 3d Corps District—Brandeberg; 21st Corps District—Lorraine.)

1917.

RUSSIA.

The 94th Division was formed on the Eastern Front about June, 1917. At that time it comprised the 334th and the 423d Regiments and the 45th Landwehr.

1. From June to December, 1917, the 94th Division occupied a sector in the region of Niemen (Negnevitchi).

2. In July, 1917, some elements of the division were transferred to the vicinity of Baranovitchi to oppose a possible attack in that sector.

In December the 423d Regiment was transferred to the 84th Division and went with the latter to France.

VALUE—1917 ESTIMATE.

Mediocre combat value.

1918.

1. When the 334th Regiment was transferred from Russia to the Western Front in May, 1918, and was disbanded, the 94th Division was considered as dissolved.

125651°—20——37

RIGA.

2. About September 21, the 94th Division was reformed at Riga out of the 439th Regiment and the 365th Regiment. The 439th Regiment was taken out of the 205th Division about the middle of September while stationed in Esthonia and sent to Riga. The 365th Regiment, which took part in the campaign of Osel Island, was sent to Riga in June. The 24th Landwehr Regiment joined the division at Metz.

3. The division left Riga about September 22 for Metz. (Route: Schawli-Kowno-Eydthkulnen-Bromberg-Posen-Leipsig-Erfurt-Frankfurt-Kreuzuach-Neunkirchen-Metz.) The trip lasted about six days.

METZ.

4. The division rested in the Metz area about one week. Then it was joined by the 7th Hussar Regiment and the 8th Field Artillery Regiment.

WOEVRE.

On October 11 the division relieved the 107th Division at Doncourt aux Templiers. It held that sector without event until the armistice.

VALUE—1918 ESTIMATE.

The division was fairly strong in effectives in October. The men had received little training and their morale was bad.

95th Division.

COMPOSITION.

	1917.		1918.	
	Brigade.	Regiment.	Brigade.	Regiment.
Infantry..............	(?)	271 Res. 422. 430 Ldw.	(?)	422 (2d Btn.). 52 Ldw. (?)
Cavalry..............	(?)		4 Sqn. 19 Drag. Rgt.	
Artillery..............	(?)		69 Res. F. A. Rgt. (except 1 and 5 Btries.). 1017 Light Am. Col. 1035 Light Am. Col.	
Engineers and Liaisons.	Pion. Btn.: 1 Landst. Pion. Co. 95 T. M. Co. 95 Tel. Detch.		1 Landst Co., 15 C. Dist. Pions. 148 Searchlight Section. 95 Signal Command: 95 Tel. Detch.	
Medical and Veterinary.	Ambulance Co. Field Hospital. 567 Vet. Hospital.		644 Ambulance Co. 117 Res. Field Hospital. 567 Vet. Hospital.	
Transport..............	1035 M. T. Col.			

HISTORY.

(422d Regiment: 4th Corps District—Prussian Saxony. 430th Landwehr: (?). 52d Landwehr: 3d Corps District—Brandenburg.)

1917.

RUSSIA.

1. The 95th Division was formed on the Eastern Front about the month of July, 1917. At that time it was made up of the 422d Regiment and 271st Reserve Regiment and of the 430th Landwehr, the 271st being temporarily transferred from the 82d Division.

PINSK.

2. Until the end of 1917 the 95th Division occupied a sector in the Pinsk region. In November it sent reenforcements to the 15th Division (Western Front).

3. In December it gave up its younger men to the 82d Reserve Division then sent to the Western Front, and received in exchange older men—men from Alsace and recruits from the class of 1919. At this time it is made up of the 422d Regiment, the 430th Landwehr and the 52d Landwehr, the 271st Reserve Regiment having been returned to the 82d Division.

VALUE—1917 ESTIMATE.

Composed of older men and recruits of the 1919 class, the 95th Division seemed to have but a mediocre combat value.

1918.

UKRAINE.

1. In January many men of the division were sent to the 14th Division, which was on the Western Front. In April the division was reported in the Ukraine. The 430th Landwehr Regiment was to the north of Gloukhov (east of Koursk) on April 27; the 52d Landwehr Regiment "400 kilometers from Pinsk" on the 9th of May, after a three-day railroad journey. The division was identified in the Gomel region toward the end of September. Soon afterwards it was reported as having come to the Western Front, but it was never identified there. It was rated as a fourth-class division.

96th Division.

COMPOSITION.

	1917		1918	
	Brigade.	Regiment.	Brigade.	Regiment.
Infantry...............	106 Res.	244 Res. 102 Ldw. 40 Ers.	(?)	244 Res. 102 Ldw. 40 Ers.
Cavalry................	4 Sqn. 18 Hus. Rgt.		4 Sqn. 18 Hus. Rgt.	
Artillery...............	Art. Command: 32 Res. F. A. Rgt.		53 Res. F. A. Rgt. 21 Ldw. Ft. A. Rgt. (1 and 6 Btries.). 876 Light Am. Col. 947 Light Am. Col. 1001 Light Am. Col.	
Engineers and Liaisons.	Pion. Btn.: 416 T. M. Co. Tel. Detch.		219 Pion. Btn.: 1 Co. 22 Pions. Ldw. Co. 19 C. Dist. Pions. 136 Searchlight Section. 96 Signal Command: 96 Tel. Detch.	
Medical and Veterinary.	278 Ambulance Co. 5 Res. Field Hospital. 6 Res. Field Hospital. Vet. Hospital.		278 Ambulance Co. 5 Res. Field Hospital. 6 Res. Field Hospital. 568 Vet. Hospital.	
Transport..............	608 M. t. Col.			

HISTORY.

(102d Landwehr: 12th Corps District—Saxony. 244th Reserve Regiment and 40th
Ersatz: 19th Corps District—Saxony.)

1917.

The 96th Division was a newly formed unit, being organized on the Galician front
in July, 1917.

One of its regiments, the 244th Reserve, was part of the 53d Reserve Division (until
the end of 1916) and later part of the 215th Division.

The 40th Ersatz, formerly of the 19th Ersatz Division, also came to this division
from the 215th Division. As to the 102d Landwehr, it was with the 82d Reserve Division in the vicinity of Pinsk.

GALICIA.

1. After the Russian offensive beginning in July the 96th Division was put into line
in the Zborow sector. At the end of July it took part in the German counteroffensive
and advanced up to the Russian–Galician frontier. It held the Husiatin sector until
February, 1918, sending important reenforcements in December, 1917, to the 241st
Division (Saxon).

RECRUITING.

Division is entirely Saxon.

VALUE—1917 ESTIMATE.

Coming from the Eastern Front at the beginning of April, 1918, the 96th Division
seemed to have only a mediocre combat value (April, 1918).

1918.

1. The division continued to hold the quiet sector south of Blamont until the armistice.

VALUE—1918 ESTIMATE.

The division was rated as fourth class. It had practically no losses on the Western Front. The companies averaged 115 men of an average age of 25 to 35 years.

101st Division.
COMPOSITION.

	1915		1916		1917		1918[1]	
	Brigade.	Regiment.	Brigade.	Regiment.	Brigade.	Regiment.	Brigade.	Regiment.
Infantry	201.	45. 59. 146.	201.	45. 59. 146. 15 Res. Jag. Btn.	201.	11 Gren. 146. 9 Jag. Rgt.	201.	45. 146. 21 Res.
Cavalry	1 Sqn. 10 Drag. Rgt.		11 Drag. Rgt. (2 Sqns.).		(?) Sqn. 10 Drag. Rgt.		3 Sqn. 10 Drag. Rgt.	
Artillery	201 F. A. Rgt.		201 F. A. Rgt. 1 Mountain A. Abt. Austro-Hung. Mountain Art. (3 Btries.).		(?) Art. Command: 209 F. A. Rgt. 201 F. A. Rgt. (elements). 3 Mountain A. Abt.		138 Art. Command: 201 F. A. Rgt.	
Engineers and Liaisons.	201 Pion. Co.		201 Pion. Co. 101 Mountain T. M. Co. 101 Pont. Engs. 101 Tel. Detch.		(101) Pion. Btn.: 101 (Mountain) Pion. Co. 201 Pion. Co. 205 Pion. Co. 2 Ldw. Co. 9 Pions. 101 Mountain T. M. Co. 171 Mountain T. M. Co. 201 Searchlight Section. 101 Tel. Detch.		101 Pion. Co. (Mountain). 201 Pion. Co. 201 Searchlight Section. 101 Mountain T. M. Co. 171 Mountain T. M. Co. 101 Tel. Detch. 101 Pion. Btn.	
Medical and Veterinary.					641 Ambulance Co. Field Hospital. Vet. Hospital.		101 Ambulance Co. 641 Ambulance Co. Field Hospital. Vet. Hospital.	
Transport.					M. T. Col.		590 M. T. Col. 4 Pack Trans. Col. (Wurtt.).	
Odd units.					101 Cyclist Co.		101 Cyclist Co.	

1 Composition at the time of dissolution, July, 1918.

HISTORY.

(146th Regiment: 20th Corps District—Eastern Prussia. 11th Grenadiers: 6th Corps District—Silesia.)

1915.

The 101st Division was formed in May, 1915, with the 45th Infantry (from the 2d Division), the 146th Regiment (from the 37th Division), and the 59th Regiment (from the 41st Division) all surplus regiments by reason of the reduction of divisions to three regiments. Later the 101st Division was subjected to a number of changes.

SERBIA.

1. After having been part of the Army of the South, on the Bug, the 101st Division was identified on the Serbian frontier at the end of May and the beginning of June.

GALICIA AND POLAND.

2. At the end of June it was brought back to Galicia by way of Budapest and Stry and took part in the German offensive in Galicia, in Poland. It was on the Dniester on June 30 and on the Zlota-Lipa on July 20.

It was in the neighborhood of Lublin on August 12, at Siedlce on the 29th and advanced up to a position near Brest-Litowsk.

SERBIA.

3. Chosen to participate in the offensive against Serbia, it was entrained at Warsaw and went into action on the Serbian front on October 7. It was at Nish on December 9.

1916.

SERBIA.

1. At the end of January, 1916, the 101st Division was still in Serbia and with the 103d Division formed the 4th Reserve Corps.

MACEDONIA.

2. In February it was in front of Monastir.

VARDAR.

3. In March, together with the 103d Division, it was near the Greek frontier in the Vardar Valley (Guevgueli) (March to November). In August it supported the 5th Bulgarian Division.

CERNA.

4. In November the 45th and the 146th Regiments occupied the bend of the Cerna, while the 59th Regiment continued to hold the left bank of the Vardar.

1917.

MACEDONIA.

1. The Division was materially changed in 1917. The 45th was replaced by the 11th Grenadiers, which had in November, 1916, left the 11th Division in France to join the Hippel Division in front of Monastir. In June the 59th Regiment was withdrawn from the division and sent to the Roumanian front. It was replaced by the 9th Jaeger Regiment.

2. The 101st Division was kept on the Macedonian front (Vardar Valley, Doiran, Monastir) to the end of 1917, seemingly after that it breaks up. The 146th Infantry was still in the vicinity of Monastir in December and was reported as being sent toward Constantinople and Palestine (March, 1918). In March, 1918, the 9th Regiment of Jaegers arrived in Alsace.

VALUE—1917 ESTIMATE.

The division is rated as third class.

1918.

The 101st Division is considered as consisting of a divisional staff only, administering Bulgarian units. The division is, therefore, no longer counted as a German infantry division. The 12th active and 12th and 13th Reserve Jaeger Battalions are considered independent units.

103d Division.

COMPOSITION.

	1915 Brigade	1915 Regiment	1916 Brigade	1916 Regiment	1917 Brigade	1917 Regiment	1918 Brigade	1918 Regiment
Infantry	205.	32. 71. 116 Res.	205.	32. 71. 116 Res.	205.	32. 71. 116 Res.	205.	32. 71. 144.
Cavalry	....		2 and 4 Sqn. Horse Gren. Rgt.		3 Sqn. 6 Drag. Rgt.		3 Sqn. 6 Drag. Rgt.	
Artillery	205 F.A. Rgt. 4 Mountain A. Abt.		205 F.A. Rgt. 4 Mountain A. Abt.		103 Art. Command: 205 F.A. Rgt. (9 Btries.).		103 Art. Command: 205 F.A. Rgt. 3 Abt. 11 Res. Ft. A. Rgt. 721 Light Am. Col. 919 Light Am. Col. 1228 Light Am. Col.	
Engineers and Liaisons.	205 Pion. Co.		205 Pion. Co. 9 Co. 28 Pions. 103 T.M. Co. 103 Pont. Engs. 103 Tel. Detch.		103 Pion. Btn.: 87 Res. Pion. Co. 9 Co. 28 Pions. 103 T.M. Co. (205) Searchlight Section. 103 Tel. Detch.		103 Pion. Btn. 87 Res. Pion. Co. 9 Co. 28 Pions. 103 M.Co. 208 Searchlight Section. 103 Signal Command: 103 Tel. Detch. 15 Wireless Detch.	
Medical and Veterinary.	....		....		103 Ambulance Co. 361 Field Hospital. 362 Field Hospital. 202 Vet. Hospital.		103 Ambulance Co. 361 Field Hospital. 362 Field Hospital. 202 Vet. Hospital.	
Transports	....		....		Divisional M. T. Col.		591 M. T. Col.	
Odd units	....		....		....			

Attached.......

M. G. Co. of the 4 Gd. Gren. Rgt.
12 T. M. Co.
24 Bomb Thrower.
14 M. G. Co.
75 M. G. S. S. Detch.
2 Bav. M. G. S. S. Detch.
1 Co. 629 Ambulance Co.
102 Gd. Pions.
2 Gd. Pion. Co.
1 Co. 29 Pions.
2 Co. 8 C. Dist. T. M. Btn.
1 Co. 8 C. Dist. T. M. Btn.
35 Flame-thrower Detch.
1 Btry. 107 F. A. Rgt.
22 Btries. 43 Res. F. Rgt.
1 Btry. 43 Res. F. A. Rgt.
2 Btries. 2 Gd. F. A. Rgt.
7 Ft. Art. Rgt.
4 Btries. 19 Ft. Art. Rgt.
2 Btries. 1 Res. Ft. Art. Rgt.
1 Btry. 16 Ft. Art. Rgt.
42 Art. Survey Section.
127 Giant Periscope Section.
306 Supply Train.
497 Ammunition Train.
117 Bav. Art. Ammunition Train.
42 Res. Art. Ammunition Train.
295 Ammunition Train.
28 Ammunition Train.
216 Ammunition Train.
31 Supply Depot.
13 Supply Depot.
81 Field Bakery.
10 Reconnaissance Flight.
265 Reconnaissance Flight.
111 Balloon Sqn.
107 Balloon Sqn.
37 Wireless Detch.
1135 Signal Detch.
289 Pigeon Loft.
92 Pigeon Loft.
2 Co. 87 Labor Btn.
3 Co. 87 Labor Btn.
100 Pris. of War Labor Btn.
Chemnitz Landst. Labor Btn.
2 Co. 11 Bav. Labor Btn.
1 and 4 Cos. 72 Road Building Btn.
(According to a captured document of Sept. 26, 1917.)

HISTORY.

(32d Regiment: 11th Corps District—Hesse-Electoral. 71st Regiment; 11th Corps District—Thuringen. 116th Reserve Regiment: 18th Corps District—Grand Duchy of Hesse.)

1915.

The 103d Division was formed at the Warthe cantonment in May, 1915, by taking the 32d Regiment from the 22d Division, the 71st Regiment from the 38th Division, and the 116th Reserve Regiment from the 25th Reserve Division.

SERBIA.

1. On May 10, 1915, the 103d Division was sent to a region near the Serbian frontier and stayed there, together with the 101st Division, until the end of June, between the Drave and the Save.

RUSSIA.

2. During the summer it appeared on the Russian front and participated in the offensive of the Linsingen Army—near Lemberg, July 29; near Sokal, August 16.

3. It was put at rest at the end of August.

SERBIA.

4. Transferred to southern Hungary (September), it took part in the Serbian campaign with the Gallwitz Army. It was at Kragujevac in November and at Nish at the beginning of December.

5. This expedition having been completed, it stayed at rest at Uskub, the 71st Infantry going to Veles.

1916.

MACEDONIA.

1. In January, 1916, the 116th Reserve Regiment advanced up to Macedonia and soon, at the end of February, the 103d Division was on the Greek frontier (Lake Doiran sector), to the left of the 101st Division, with which it formed the 4th Reserve Corps.

FRANCE.

2. Entrained for France about April 27.

CHAMPAGNE.

3. Detrained at Châtelet sur Retourne about May 6 and was reviewed at Avançon by the Emperor on the 9th and went into line on the 23d in the Prosnes-Prunay sector to the east of the 58th Division (these two divisions forming the 4th Reserve Corps).

VERDUN.

4. The 103d Division left Champagne on June 16 for the Verdun front. It was engaged on June 22 in the Vaux–Chapitre wood and took part in the big attack of June 23 on the Souville Fort and the attack of July 11. During this period (June–July) it suffered very heavy losses.

5. Relieved at the end of July, it went into line in a sector near Apremont Forest for a few days (until Aug. 2).

CÔTES DE MEUSE.

6. From the beginning of August to September 15 it occupied the front along the Côtes de Meuse (Bois des Chevaliers, Vaux les Palameix).

CHAMPAGNE.

7. Transferred to Champagne (Sept. 20), the division took over the Somme–Py sector, Tahure (until the beginning of October).

SOMME.

8. The 103d Division was next sent to the Somme (detrained at Bohain, Oct. 8). It was engaged between Bouchavesnes and the St. Pierre–Vaast wood (Oct. 15 to Nov. 10). The 116th Reserve Regiment was particularly put to the test.

CHAMPAGNE.

9. After a few days' rest the division came back to Champagne (Nov. 13). It occupied the Souain sector (Nov. 15 to Jan. 15, 1917). While there was engaged only in a few local raids. In December and January it received important reenforcements.

1917.

VERDUN.

1. The 103d Division in January, 1917, went to the Verdun front (Samogneux–Louvemont). It stayed there four months and was always on the defensive.

CHEMIN DES DAMES.

2. Relieved on May 23, the division was transferred to the Aisne. It held the Chemin des Dames sector (Malmaison, Les Bovettes, Panthéon, La Royère) from May 26 to October 11–12. It only participated in the attacks of June 6 and July 8 as supporting troops and as a result suffered but slight losses during that period.

3. Relieved from the Aisne front on October 11 the 103d Division was sent to rest in the region of Sissonne. It seems to have been transferred on October 24 toward the north of the Ailette as an attacking division.

ST. QUENTIN.

4. After a rest at the end of November and the first two weeks of December in the vicinity of Origny–Ste. Benoite, the division took over the sector of Itancourt (Dec. 27–28) near St. Quentin.

RECRUITING.

The 32d Regiment and the 71st Regiment, recruited in Thuringen and Hesse-Electoral, and the 116th Reserve Regiment in the Grand Duchy of Hesse. Although the 3d Batallion of the 85th Landwehr was transferred to the 116th as 3d Batallion of this unit, its recruiting was a great deal less from the 9th Corps District than from the 18th Corps District.

VALUE—1917 ESTIMATE.

The showing made by the 103d Division in the conflicts in which it was engaged warrants its being classed among the good units. Its losses in 1917 were comparatively small. Its strength was gradually made up of younger men by the transfer from it of the older soldiers. It was classed as an attack division by the German Command. A secret order of the 103d Division of September 20, 1917, contains the following: "Our division, which was specially trained for offensive work, and which is designated as an attack division (Angriffs division), is, in an offensive, very superior to the adversary * * *."

1918.

BATTLE OF PICARDY.

1. The division was in line south of St. Quentin on March 21 as the left division of Von Conta group. It advanced toward Vendeuil without meeting great resistance and reached there at midnight. The 22d it reached the Crozat Canal and crossed at Liezon the next day. Placed in reserve on the 23d, it followed the general advance by Villequier-Aumont (24th), Quesmy (25th), Lagny (27th). On the 28th the division captured the Dives-Lassigny road and relieved the 36th Division in that vicinity. It attacked Plemont on March 30, but was unable to maintain its position and fell back on April 1, after heavy losses. It was relieved about April 15.

AISNE.

2. About April 27 the division relieved the 108th Division at Corbeny. It was still in line when the attack of May 27 started and advanced to the Marne northwest of Chatillon via Romigny, Vandieres, Bois de Mareuil. It was relieved by the 22d Division between June 24 and 26.

BATTLE OF THE MARNE.

3. It rested near Fismes until it reentered line about July 14 in the sector Anthenay-Bois de Trottes. It was engaged until about August 1, when it was withdrawn from the battle front southwest of Rheims.

CHEMIN DES DAMES.

4. The division rested at Malmaison until August 22, when it was engaged north of St. Aubin. In that locality it remained in line until about September 5.

CHAMPAGNE.

5. On September 26 the division entered line in Champagne, relieving the 202d Division in the area south of Fontaine en Dormeois. It received the full weight of the French attack and in four days in line lost more than 2,000 prisoners, including 6 battalion commanders.

6. After three weeks of rest, elements of the division were reengaged southwest of Longwe on October 24. Other elements were identified in the sector of the 76th Reserve Division and the 2d Landwehr Division, near the junction of the American and French Armies. Elements continued to be identified in this general locality until the armistice. Most of the division appeared to have been opposed to the French Army. The last identification was at Sedan.

VALUE—1918 ESTIMATE.

The division was rated as third class. At the end its effectives were greatly reduced. Discontent over their prolonged service in line had lowered the morale of the division.

105th Division.

COMPOSITION.

	1915		1916		1917		1918	
	Brigade.	Regiment.	Brigade.	Regiment.	Brigade.	Regiment.	Brigade.	Regiment.
Infantry........	209.	21. 122 Fus. 129.	209.	21. 122 Fus. 129.	209.	21. 129. 400.	209.	21. 129. 400.
Cavalry........	4 Mounted Jag. Rgt. (2 Sqns.).		4 Mounted Jag. Rgt. (Sqns.).		5 Sqn. 4 Mounted Jag. Rgt.		5 Sqn. 4 Mounted Jag. Rgt.	
Artillery........	209 F. A. Rgt. (7 Btries.).		209 F. A. Rgt.		(?) Art. Command: 259 F. A. Rgt. (2 Abts.).		105 Art. Command: 259 F. A. Rgt. 1 Abt. 11 Ft. A. Rgt. 901 Light Am. Col. 1103 Light Am. Col. 1138 Light Am. Col.	
Engineers and Liaisons.	209 Pion. Co.		209 Pion. Co. 105 T. M. Co. 105 Pont. Engs. 105 Tel. Detch.		105 Pion. Btn.: 209 Pion. Co. 105 T. M. Co. 412 T. M. Co. 209 Searchlight Section. 105 Tel. Detch.		105 Pion. Btn.: 209 Pion. Co. 1 Co. 18 Pions. 105 T. M. Co. 22 Searchlight Section. 105 Signal Command: 105 Tel. Detch. 153 Wireless Detch.	
Medical and Veterinary.					105 Ambulance Co. 363 Field Hospital. 364 Field Hospital. 365 Field Hospital. Vet. Hospital.		105 Ambulance Co. 363 Field Hospital. 364 Field Hospital. 105 Vet. Hospital.	
Transports.....					M. T. Col.		592 M. T. Col.	

HISTORY.

(21st and 129th Regiments: 17th Corps District—Western Prussia.   400th Regiment:
8th Corps District—Rhine Province.)

1915.

The 105th Division was formed at Thorn in May, 1915.   At the outset it comprised
the 122d Regiment of Fusileers obtained from the 26th Division (13th Corps District),
the 21st Infantry from the 35th Division, and the 129th Infantry from the 36th Division (17th Corps District).

In 1917 the 400th replaced the 122d Regiment (Wurttemberg).

SERBIA.

1. In June, 1915, the 105th Division appeared on the Serbian front at the same time
as the 101st and 103d Divisions.

GALICIA.

2. At the end of June it was transferred to Galicia via Budapest and Stry.   It participated in the offensive against the Russians on the Gnila Lipa from June 24 to July
1, on the Zlota Lipa July 20.   From Galicia it went to Poland; fought at Krasnostaw
at the end of July and between Wieprz and the Jaselda until August 20.   At the end of
August it was on the Chtchertchev–Brest–Kobryn railway front.

SERBIA AND BULGARIA.

3. Chosen for the Serbian campaign, it again found itself in company with the 101st
and 103d Divisions and went into line on the Serbian front in October but did not stay
there long.   While the 122d fusileers pushed on in the south of this country, the 21st
and the 129th entrained in December for Eastern Bulgaria.

1916.

BULGARIA.

1. Assigned to watch the Roumanian frontier and the coast of the Black Sea, the 21st
went to Varna and the 129th from Choumla to the coast.   This mission did not end
until May, 1916.

MACEDONIA.

2. At this time the division was being re-formed in Macedonia, where the three
regiments were again together at the beginning of June.

GALICIA.

3. The June Russian offensive was responsible for its return to Galicia and at the
end of the month it was in Bukovina.   The 105th Division operated in the region of
Kolomea (end of June, beginning of July) and suffered heavy losses.   The 122d fusileers
reported 26 officers and 1,165 men out of action.   The division next fought in Galicia
to the east of Stanislau in July and August (east of Tlumacz–Tysmienica), to the east of
Halicz in September.

4. The division remained in the vicinity of Halicz until October.

COURLAND.

5. Relieved from Galicia, the division was sent to Courland, to the south of Kekkau
(October).

6. On October 20 it took over the sector to the west of Jakobstadt.

1917.

JACOBSTADT.

1. The 105th Division occupied the Jacobstadt front until November, 1917.   In
April the 400th Regiment replaced the 122d which was transferred to the 243d Division (old 8th Ersatz Division), a Wurttemberg unit.   The division took Jacobstadt
on September 21.

FRANCE.

2. On November 5 the 105th Division entrained at Mitau and was transported to France. (Itinerary: Kovno–Koenigsberg–Schneidemuehl–Berlin–Cassel–Coblenz–Treves–Thionville–Sedan–Mezieres.) It detrained at Juniville (south of Rethel) on November 11 and rested in this region.

RECRUITING.

The 21st and the 129th were classified as "troops from Western Prussia" in an official document. Although the 21st was called the 4th Pomeranian, it was actually recruited for the most part in the Province of Western Prussia, which was its station in peace time. The 400th was, by reason of its replacement depot, a Rhenish unit.

VALUE—1917 ESTIMATE.

The 105th Division was first put into line on the French front at the beginning of January, 1918. It suffered losses in Galicia during the Summer of 1916.

Its long stay in the Courland sector had not increased its combat value.

1918.

BATTLE OF PICARDY.

1. The division was engaged west of Noyon on April 15 and remained in that area until May 17, when it was relieved by the 223d Division. Losses were very considerable in the early part of the division's occupation of that sector.

NOYON.

2. It rested north of Noyon until May 31 when it reenforced the Aisne battle front at Nampcel, east of the Oise. Throughout June it was engaged in this sector. It attempted a local attack on Moulin sous Touvent on July 3 without success. In minor operations in June and July the division lost about 1,000 prisoners. In August it was heavily engaged and forced back on Noyon, where it was relieved by the 54th Division about September 1.

3. The division rested for about three weeks in the area south of Ferte Chevresis–Montigny sur Crecy. It was engaged at Septvaux about September 27. It fought in the retreat through Fourdrain as far as Mesbrecourt–Assis sur Serre. It held that sector until the capture of Mesbrecourt on October 22, after which it took up a position to the north. The division was in the neighborhood of Pargny wood until November 5. Thereafter it was identified at Vervins (6th), Voulpaix (7th), north of Wimy (9th).

VALUE—1918 ESTIMATE.

The division was rated as third class. As a sector holding division it saw almost constant service most of which was in the Noyon area. Its morale was greatly lowered in November.

107th Division.

COMPOSITION.

	1915		1916		1917		1918	
	Brigade.	Regiment.	Brigade.	Regiment.	Brigade.	Regiment.	Brigade.	Regiment.
Infantry	213.	52 Res. 227 Res. 232 Res.	213.	52 Res. 227 Res. 232 Res.	213.	52 Res. 227 Res. 232 Res.	....	52 Res. 232 Res. 448.
Cavalry		(?)		3 Sqn. 1 Uhlan Rgt.		3 Sqn. 1 Uhlan Rgt.		3 Sqn. 1 Uhlan Rgt.
Artillery	213 F. A. Rgt. (7 Btries.).		213 F. A. Rgt.		157 Art. command: 213 F. A. Rgt. (9 Btries.).		157 Art. command: 213 F. A. Rgt. 154 Ft. A. Btn. 713 Light Am. Col. 1283 Light Am. Col. 1353 Light Am. Col.	
Engineers and Liaisons.	213 Pion. Co.		213 Pion. Co. 4 Co. 21 Pions. 107 T. M. Co. 107 Pont. Engs. 107 Tel. Detch.		107 Pion. Btn.: 213 Pion. Co. 4 Co. 21 Pions. 91 T. M. Co. 107 T. M. Co. (213) Searchlight Section. 107 Tel. Detch.		107 Pion. Btn.: 4 Co. 21 Pions. 213 Pion. Co. 26 Searchlight Section. 107 Signal Command: 107 Tel. Detch. 128 Wireless Detch.	
Medical and Veterinary.					107 Ambulance Co. 366 Field Hospital (?). 166 Vet. Hospital.		107 Ambulance Co. 366 Field Hospital 97 Res. Field Hospital. 166 Vet. Hospital.	
Transport					593 M. T. Col.		593 M. T. Col.	

HISTORY.

(52d Reserve Regiment: 3d Corps District—Brandeberg. 227th Reserve Regiment: 4th Corps District—Prussian Saxony. 232d Reserve Division: 10th Corps District—Hanover.)

1915.

The 107th Division was formed at Glogau in May, 1915, with regiments transferred from the 49th Reserve Division (227th Reserve Regiment), from the 50th Reserve Division (232d Reserve Regiment), and from the 5th Reserve Regiment (52d Reserve Regiment).

GALICIA.

1. The division took part in the battles near Lemberg (June 17-22).

RUSSIA.

2. In July the division was engaged near the Bug, in the vicinity of Grubeszow (July 19-30).

3. On July 31 it fought to the northeast of Cholm. It was near Wlodawa from August 13 to 17.

4. On August 25 and 26 it participated in the taking of Brest-Litowsk. It entered Pinsk on September 16.

SERBIA.

5. From Pinsk it operated against Serbia, staying there from the beginning of October to the end of November, 1915.

1916.

COURLAND.

1. In January, 1916, the division was in reserve in the vicinity of Dvinsk, where it remained until March 15.

POSTAVY-SMORGONI.

2. On March 18 it took over the sector to the north of Postavy. From May to June 20 it was near Smorgoni. At the end of the month it was assigned to meet the Russian offensive in Volhynia.

VOLHYNIA.

3. It was engaged between the Styr and the Stokhod from June 21 until the middle of July.

4. In August and September it was still in Volhynia, near the Kovel-Rovno railway.

KOVEL.

5. The division stayed in this region and occupied the sector west of Kachovka until the beginning of November, 1917.

1917.

FRANCE.

1. Relieved about November 9, 1917, from the Kovel sector, the 107th Division entrained on the 13th at Poginski for the Western Front. (Itinerary: Kovel–Brest-Litovsk–Warsaw–Posen–Frankfort on the Oder–Berlin–Cassel–Coblenz–Treves–Thionville–Sedan–Charleville–Hirson.) It detrained east of Cambrai on the 18th.

CAMBRAI.

2. From November 21 on it was engaged to the southwest of Cambrai (Noyelles-Rumilly).

3. It was retired from the front about the end of December.

RECRUITING.

The 52d Reserve Regiment remained a Brandenburger regiment, as at time of its formation. The 227th Reserve Regiment, formed in the 5th Corps District at the end of 1915, had a majority of effectives from the 4th Corps District and still received replacements from Prussian Saxony.. On the other hand, the 232d Reserve Regiment, formed in the 4th Corps District, recruited principally in Hanover (10th Corps District). The 107th Division had hence a heterogeneous organization.

1918.

CAMBRAI.

1. The division remained in line in the Gonnelieu sector until about February 15, when it was relieved by the 18th Division from "B" Army and went into reserve. On March 1 it returned and relieved the 18th Division in its former sector at Gonnelieu.

BATTLE OF PICARDY.

2. It was still in line when the offensive of March 21 began and advanced via Mesnil to Avelny wood under the 39th Corps. It was relieved on April 16 by the 16th Reserve Division near Anthuille and went to rest near Cambrai.

3. On May 16 the division came into line at Morlancourt, relieving the 199th Division, and held that sector until the night of May 23-24. It rested in the Cambrai area until its return to line at Morlancourt on the night of June 20-21. It was withdrawn about August 1.

THIRD BATTLE OF THE SOMME.

4· When the British began the attack on August 8 the division hastily returned to line near Proyart. Until the 28th it was hotly engaged at Proyart, Mericourt, and Herleville. One thousand seven hundred prisoners were taken from the division in this fighting.

WOEVRE.

5. On September 3 the division started for Metz to rest. Its destination was changed and it detrained at Conflans on September 16, marched via Frianville-Brainville-Allamont-Moulotte to Harville, where it went into line. The sector was a quiet one, and the battalions were well rested.

MEUSE-ARGONNE.

6. The division left that sector on October 11 and went in trucks from Conflans to Stenay via Longuyon-Montmedy-Sedan. By way of Dun sur Meuse the division entered the line on October 14. One regiment had previously entered line on the 11th. Until the 20th the division was engaged in resisting without especial success the American attack. Two of the regiments of the division were out of the line from the 20th to November 1. The total losses of the division up to this time were estimated at 2,100, including 352 prisoners. Two regiments of the division were again engaged from November 1 to 10 in the Villers area, when the division was considered withdrawn following a failure to identify it by contact.

VALUE—1918 ESTIMATE.

The division was rated as third class. There was evidence that the morale of the men was low as a result of the heavy casualties that the division suffered throughout 1918.

108th Division.
COMPOSITION.

	1915		1916		1917		1918 [1]	
	Brigade.	Regiment.	Brigade.	Regiment.	Brigade.	Regiment.	Brigade.	Regiment.
Infantry	(?)	97. 137. 265 Res.	(?)	97. 137. 265 Res. 14 Jag. Btn.	(?)	97. 137. 265 Res. 14 Jag. Btn.	5.	97. 137. 265 Res.
Cavalry	(?)		1 Res. Drag. Rgt.		6 Sqn. 17 Hus. Rgt.		6 Sqn. 17 Hus. Rgt.	
Artillery	243 F. A. Rgt. (7 Btries.).		243 F. A. Rgt.		(?) Art. Command: 243 F. A. Rgt. (9 Btries.).		(?) Art. Command: 243 F. A. Rgt.	
Engineers and Liaisons.	(?)		1 Res. Co. 1 Pions. 108 Pont. Engs. 108 Tel. Detch.		(108) Pion. Btn.: 1 Res. Co. 1 Pions. 1 Co. 33 Res. Pion. Btn. 108 T. M. Co. 275 Searchlight Section. 108 Searchlight Section. 108 Tel. Detch.		108 Pion. Btn.: 1 Res. Co. 2 Pion. Btn. No. 1. 1 Co. 33 Res. Pions. 2 Landst. Co. 17 C. Dist. Pions. 275 Searchlight Section. 108 T. M. Co. 108 Tel. Detch. 108 Wireless Detch.	
Medical and Veterinary.					264 Ambulance Co. 94 Field Hospital. 258 Field Hospital. Vet. Hospital.		264 Ambulance Co. 94 Field Hospital. 334 Field Hospital. 197 Vet. Hospital.	
Transport.					M. T. Col.		M. T. Col.	
Attached.			885 F. A. Btry. 888 F. A. Bty.		2 Landst. Pion. Co. (17 C. Dist.).		Attached.	

[1] Composition at the time of dissolution, October, 1918.

HISTORY.

(97th and 137th Regiments: 21st Corps District—Lorraine. 265th Reserve Regiment:
9th Corps District—Mecklenburg.)

1915.

The 108th Division was formed during the summer of 1915 in the Niemen Army
(Scholtz Army) by taking the 137th Infantry from the 31st Division, the 97th Infantry
from the 42d Division, and the 265th Reserve Infantry from the 80th Reserve Division.
It was called the Beckmann Division in honor of its commanding general before it
received the number 108.

COURLAND.

1. About December 1 it went into line to the west of Sventen Lake (region
of Dvinsk).

1916.

VOLHYNIA.

1. In June, 1916, the division was transferred to Volhynia and opposed the Russian
offensive in the vicinity of Svinioukhi. Here it had heavy losses. On June 16 the
1st Battalion of the 137th Infantry reported 24 officers and 978 men out of action.
(Casualty List).

2. It was in this sector until its departure for the Western Front (middle of December, 1917.)

1917.

FRANCE.

1. Entrained on December 12 in the vicinity of Brest-Litowsk.

2. Detrained near Hirson about December 18 and stayed at rest for three weeks in
the vicinity of Aubenton.

RECRUITING.

The 97th and the 137th of the old 21st Corps were among those regiments which
did not find a sufficient source of recruits in their home stations and filled up their
ranks with soldiers from the Rhine Province and Westphalia.

The 265th Reserve Regiment, originally recruited from the Hanseatic cities, was
now principally recruited in Mecklenberg.

VALUE—1917 ESTIMATE.

The 108th Division, coming from Russia, only went in line on the Western Front on
January 1, 1918.

At the end of January, 1918, the 137th and 97th still had in its ranks many men from
Alsace and Lorraine, which must have been transferred shortly thereafter.

1918.

AISNE.

1. After having had some training in the Vervins area, the 108th Division relieved
the 5th Reserve Division near Corbeny (northeast of Craonne) during the night of January 22–23. It was relieved about the 21st of April by the 103d Division.

SOMME.

2. On the 30th it relieved the 9th Bavarian Reserve Division near Villers-Bretonneux (south of Corbie). During the night of May 19–20 it extended its front to the
south and relieved the jaeger division. It was relieved by the 41st Division on the
9th of July, and went to rest in the Cappy area, south of the Somme.

3. On the 7th of August it relieved the 43d Reserve Division astride the Somme
(west of Bray). The next day the British captured 1576 men from the division. It
was withdrawn from line about the 23d. It went to the Cambrai region, and was
there disbanded—the 137th Regiment was transferred to the 15th Division, the 97th
Regiment to the 202d Division, and the 265th Reserve Regiment was dissolved.

VALUE—1918 ESTIMATE.

The 108th was rated a third-class division, but considering that although it was trained in assault tactics (in January) it was not used in any of the German offensives, and that the only heavy fighting in which it participated was when it was caught by the British attack of the 8th of August, where it fought poorly, and also that the 15th and 202d Divisions—the units which received its regiments when it was disbanded—were second and third class, respectively, this rating seems to have been too high.

109th Division.
COMPOSITION.

	1915		1916		1917		1918¹	
	Brigade.	Regiment.	Brigade.	Regiment.	Brigade.	Regiment.	Brigade.	Regiment.
Infantry	174.	2 Gren. 26 Res. 376.	174.	2 Gren. 26 Res. 376. 4 Btn. (57 Ldw. Rgt.).	174.	2 Gren. 26 Res. 376.	174.	2 Gren. 26 Res. 376.
Cavalry			98 Cav. Rgt.		5 Sqn. 10 Drag. Rgt.		2 Sqn. 10 Drag. Rgt. 5 Sqn. 10 Drag. Rgt.	
Artillery	227 F. A. Rgt.		227 F. A. Rgt.		(?) Art. Command: 227 F. A. Rgt. (9 Btries.).		109 Art. Command: 227 F. A. Rgt. 2 Abt. 290 F. A. Rgt.	
Engineers and Liaisons			1 Ldw. Co. Gd. Pions. 109 Pont. Engs. 109 Tel. Detch.		(109) Pion. Btn.; 1 Ldw. Co. Gd. Pions. 2 Ldw. Co. 15 Pions. 109 T. M. Co 276 Searchlight Section. Tel. Detch.		218 Pion. Btn.; 338 Pion. Co. 2 Ldw. Co. 15 C. Dist. Pions. 276 Searchlight Section. 109 T. M. Co. 109 Tel. Detch.	
Medical and Veterinary					228 Ambulance Co. 98 Field Hospital. 277 Field Hospital. Vet. Hospital.		373 Ambulance Co. 98 Field Hospital. 27 Field Hospital. 109 Vet. Hospital.	
Transports					434 M. T. Col.		595 M. T. Col.	

¹Composition at the time of dissolution, September, 1918.

HISTORY.

(2d Grenadiers: 2d Corps District—Pomerania. 26th Reserve Regiment: 4th Corps District—Prussian Saxony. 376th Regiment: 1st Corps District—Eastern Prussia.

1915.

The 109th Division was formed in Courland in May, 1915. It obtained the 2d Grenadiers from the 3d Division, which has since then completely changed its organization. It obtained the 26th Reserve Infantry from the 6th Reserve Division (3d Reserve Corps), and the 2d Ersatz Infantry Regiment (Koenigsberg), which received the number 376.

PONIEVIEJ.

1. It was a part of the Niemen Army from the time that army was organized until its departure for the Roumanian front (November, 1916). In July it was in the vicinity of Ponieviej.

JAKOBSTADT.

2. At the end of October it took a position in front of Jakobstadt.

1916.

COURLAND.

1. In 1916 the 109th Division still occupied the same sector in the vicinity of Jakobstadt to the southwest of Lievenhof (Buschhof). It stayed there until November, 1916.

ROUMANIA.

2. Transferred to Roumania, it took part in the campaign, valley of Jiu (November), southeast of Rimnicu-Sarat (December). In the meanwhile it headed the troops which entered Bucharest on December 6 (2d Grenadiers).

1917.

ROUMANIA–NAMOLOASA.

With the stabilization of the Roumanian front, the division took a position near the junction of the Rimnicu in front of Namoloasa (southeast of Focsani). It held this sector during the entire year 1917.

RECRUITING.

A composite division. The 2d Grenadiers was Pomeranian; the 26th Reserve Regiment was originally from Prussian Saxony, and the 376th got its recruits from depots in Eastern Prussia. It first appeared on the Western Front at the end of March, 1918.

1918.

SOMME.

1. The division came into line on the night of April 27–28 and relieved the 19th Division west of Hangard. It continued to hold this sector until August 10. In the first two days of the British attack the division lost 1,544 prisoners. After its withdrawal the division was taken to the vicinity of Trelon and disbanded.

2. The 26th Reserve Regiment was drafted to the 36th Fusileer Regiment and the 66th Regiment to the 113th Division. The 2d Grenadier Regiment passed intact from the 109th Division to the 3d Reserve Division. The 376th Regiment was divided among the three regiments of the 1st Division.

VALUE—1918 ESTIMATE.

The division was rated as third class. After about four months in line on the Somme the losses in casualties and prisoners led to the dissolution of the division in September.

111th Division.

COMPOSITION.

	1915		1916		1917		1918	
	Brigade.	Regiment.	Brigade.	Regiment.	Brigade.	Regiment.	Brigade.	Regiment.
Infantry	221.	73 Fus. 76. 164.	221.	73 Fus. 76. 164.	221.	73 Fus. 76. 164.	221.	73. 76. 164.
Cavalry	3 and 4 Sqn. 22 Dragoon Rgt.		3 and 4 Sqn. 22 Dragoon Rgt.		4 Sqn. 22 Dragoon Rgt.		4 Sqn. 22 Drag. Rgt.	
Engineers and Liaisons.	221 Pion. Co.		221 Pion. Co. 262 Pion. Co. 111 T.M. Co. 111 Pont. Engrs. 111 Tel. Detch.		(111) Pion. Btn.: 221 Pion. Co. 262 Pion. Co. 111 T.M. Co. 221 Searchlight Section. 111 Tel. Detch.		111 Pion. Btn.: 221 Pion. Co. 262 Pion. Co. 111 T.M. Co. 199 Searchlight Section. 111 Signal Command: 111 Tel. Detch. 19 Wireless Detch.	
Artillery	221 F.A. Rgt. (7 Btries.).		221 F.A. Rgt.		111 Art. Command: 221 F.A. Rgt. (9 Btries.).		111 Art. Command: 94 F.A. Rgt. 2 Abt. 25 Ft. A. Rgt. (5 and 7 Btries.). 702 Light Am. Col. 758 Light Am. Col. 1341 Light Am. Col.	
Medical and Veterinary.	....		....		111 Ambulance Co. 370 Field Hospital. 371 Field Hospital. Vet. Hospital.		111 Ambulance Co. 370 Field Hospital. 371 Field Hospital. 111 Vet. Hospital.	
Transports	....		....		M. T. Col.			

HISTORY.

(73d Fusileers, 164th Regiment: 10th Corps District—Hanover.   76th Regiment: 9th Corps District—Hanseatic cities.)

1915.

The 111th Division was formed near Brussels on March 26, 1915, by obtaining the 73d Fusileers from the 19th Division, the 164th Infantry from the 20th Division, and the 76th Regiment from the 17th Division.

COTES DE MEUSE.

1. About the middle of April, 1915, the 111th Division was in line along the Cotes de Meuse (Calonne, Hattonchatel trench) after having detrained on April 11 at Mars la Tour.

ARTOIS.

2. In August it was transferred to Artois (Monchy au Bois sector).

1916.

1. The 111th Division stayed on the Artois front until August, 1916.

SOMME.

2. About August 21 it was relieved and sent to the north of the Somme.   Engaged near Guillemont and Guinchy, it suffered serious losses (Aug. 25–Sept. 6).

COTES DE MEUSE.

3. After a few days' rest in the Cambrai region it was put into line near Cotes de Meuse (Bois de Chevaliers, Sept. 15) and stayed there until October 26.   It was brought up to strength by the addition of 2,000 replacements.

SOMME.

4. At the end of October it was brought back to the Somme.   At first it was at rest in the region of Bohain and then took over a sector between Bouchavesnes and the St. Pierre-Vaast wood.

1917.

1. In January, 1917, it was south of the Somme near Barleux, from which position it was relieved a short time before it fell back on the Hindenberg Line.

HINDENBERG LINE.

2. It occupied the Bellicourt sector (north of St. Quentin) from May 10 to about June 24.   On May 7 and 15 it received 600 replacements (classes of 1917 and 1918) to make up the losses sustained on April 27 at Arleux en Gohelle.

3. The division was then put at rest for a month in the vicinity of Cambrai.

YPRES.

4. It entrained on July 25 and 26 and was transported to Flanders, where it was engaged on the 27th and 28th to the north of Ypres (Bœsinghe-Steenstraat).   It met the artillery preparation and the attack of July 31, which caused it considerable losses. It was relieved the very night of the attack and was temporarily reorganized at Bohain.

LORRAINE.

5. Sent to Lorraine, it took the Régniéville sector (west of Pont à Mousson) about August 20; rested and reorganized.

FLANDERS.

6. It left this sector on October 14 to return to Flanders (Poelcappelle).   It detrained on the 16th at Alost and was engaged from the 22d to the 26th and relieved November 4.

ARTOIS.

7. From the end of November to January 8, 1918, it held the Monchy le Preuxen-Vis en Artois sector (southeast of Arras).   The division received the remaining necessary

replacements; the 73d Fusileers received, on December 24, 400 men between the ages of 20 and 35, taken from the Russian front (especially from the 15th Landwehr Division).

RECRUITING.

The 76th Infantry was a Hanseatic unit while the 73d Fusileers was a Hanoverian organization. As men from the 9th Corps District quite frequently served in regiments from the 10th Corps District and reciprocally, in case of necessity, the regiments of a division drew without distinction from either source, it was to be expected that the 111th Division was termed as "regiments of Lower Saxony."

VALUE—1917 ESTIMATE.

The 111th Division, which was considered a good unit, was sorely tried in Flanders by the Franco-British attack of July 31, 1917. Many men left their formations either when going into line or under bombardment. The division stayed but four days in line and had to be relieved without having been able to counterattack. The 111th Division was composed of young men, part of whom had experience in very active sectors.

1918.

BATTLE OF PICARDY.

The division was relieved by the 234th Division at Arleux about the 1st of March. It remained in rear of the front until March 21 when it returned to its former sector to attack east of St. Leger. It had been resting at Auberchicourt, which place it left on the 17th and marched via Palluel to Villers lez Cagnicourt, arriving there on March 20.

The division was in the first wave of the attack and advanced via Ecoust, then south to Vaulx–Vraucourt on the 22d, Mory (24th). It passed into second line about this time and reentered line north of Hamelincourt on April 1 to relieve the 26th Division. After a week it side-slipped south and relieved the 239th Division northeast of Ayette, which sector it held until April 20. It was relieved by the 234th Division.

2. On May 6 the division relieved the 5th Bavarian Division north of Bucquoy. It continued to hold this sector until August 17, when it was relieved by the 4th Bavarian Division.

THIRD BATTLE OF THE SOMME.

The division taken from the comparatively quiet Bucquoy sector was used to reenforce the battle front at Favreuil on August 25. It was only engaged four days in this sector. Withdrawn on the 29th, it moved northward and on September 2 reenforced the front east of Hendecourt. It fought then for three days before it was withdrawn. In these two brief periods in line the division suffered very heavy casualties besides losing 500 prisoners.

LENS.

4. The division rested in the Tourcoing area until it reentered line south of Acheville on the night of September 24–25 in relief of the 207th Division. It was engaged here until October 11, when the 49th Reserve Division relieved it east of Lens.

5. The division rested in the Douchy–Haspres area in support until October 18, when it moved to Artres and came into line on the night of October 20–21 at Monchaux sur Ecaillon. Until November 7 the division was constantly in line. It was near Vendegies until October 24, and later at Arties (28th), Farmars (29th), Jenlain (Nov. 2), Sebourg (4th), west of Risin (5th), and near St. Amand (5th). It was out of line at the armistice.

VALUE—1918 ESTIMATE.

The division was rated as second class. It was used as an assault division on the Somme in March, but thereafter served as an intervention division in the Somme area. The division showed considerable power of resistance.

113th Division.

COMPOSITION.

	1915 Brigade.	1915 Regiment.	1916 Brigade.	1916 Regiment.	1917 Brigade.	1917 Regiment.	1918 Brigade.	1918 Regiment.
Infantry	225.	36 Fus. 48. 32 Res.	225.	36 Fus. 48. 32 Res.	225.	36 Fus. 66. 32 Res.	225.	36 Fus. 66. 27.
Cavalry	(?)		3 Sqn. 8 Cuirassier Rgt.		3 Sqn. 8 Cuirassier Rgt.		3 Sqn. 8 Cuirassier Rgt.	
Artillery	225 F. A. Rgt. (7 Btries.)		225 F. A. Rgt.		(?) Art Command: 225 F. A. Rgt.		225 F. A. Rgt. 407 Ft. A. Btn. 1089 Light Am. Col. 1172 Light Am. Col. 1200 Light Am. Col.	
Engineers and Liaisons.	225 Pion. Co.		225 Pion. Co. 251 Pion. Co. 252 Pion. Co. 113 T. M. Co. 113 Pont. Engrs. 113 Tel. Detch.		113 Pion. Btn.: 225 Pion. Co. 251 Pion. Co. 112 T. M. Co. 113 T. M. Co. (226) Searchlight Section. 113 Pont. Engs. 113 Tel. Detch.		113 Pion. Btn.: 225 Pion. Co. 251 Pion. Co. 113 T. M. Co. 67 Searchlight Section. 113 Signal Command: 113 Tel. Detch. 51 Wireless Detch.	
Medical and Veterinary.					212 Ambulance Co. 372 Field Hospital. 373 Field Hospital. 113 Vet. Hospital.		212 Ambulance Co. 372 Field Hospital. 373 Field Hospital. 113 Vet. Hospital.	
Transport.					597 M. T. Col.		597 M. T. Col.	
Attached.			114 Anti-Aircraft Section.					

HISTORY.

(4th Corps District—Prussian Saxony and part of Thuringe.)

1915.

The 113th division was organized near Sedan on March 26, 1915. Its three infantry regiments were taken from old divisions: the 48th from the. 5th Division (3d Corps District—Brandenburg), the 36th from the 8th Division (4th Corps District—Prussian Saxony), and the 32d Reserve from the 22d Reserve Division (11th Corps District—Thuringe).

In March, 1917, the 48th was replaced by the 66th Regiment (old 7th Division from Prussian Saxony) taken from the 52d Division.

1. Detraining at Conflans on April 8, the division spent a few days in the Woevre.

CÔTES DE MEUSE.

2. It appeared along the Côtes de Meuse (Calonne trench) on April 26, 1915.

3. From that date until January 14, 1916, it stayed around the Côtes de Meuse and in Woevre—Calonne trench, Ailly wood, St. Mihiel, Eparges, and Bois Bouchot.

1916.

1. January and February, 1916, rested at Brainville and Conflans.

VERDUN.

2. On February 24 the 113d Division was transferred to the Verdun front. It participated in the attacks of the 8th and 9th of March against the village of Douaumont and suffered considerable losses. In six weeks spent around Douaumont the losses are said to have been 30 officers and 2,000 men put out of action (letter).

OISE.

3. Relieved at the beginning of April it was put into line in a calm sector—region of Soissons, then in the region of the Oise (Tracy le Val, Puisaleine).

SOMME.

4. In July, at the beginning of the Franco-British offensive, it detached some of its elements in the Somme (Peronne, July 1, then at Frise, Assevillers, and Belloy). The three rest battalions of the division formed in an emergency an assembled regiment (notebook).

5. After a new stay in the Soissons region (August and September) the whole division was again engaged in the Somme between Rancourt and the St. Pierre—Vaast wood. It suffered very heavy losses near Bouchavesnes (Oct. 1–10).

6. At rest from October 14 to 21 in Woevre.

CÔTES DE MEUSE.

7. At the end of October, the 113th Division took over the Bonzee—Ronvaux sector (Côtes de Meuse).

1917.

1. The 113th Division stayed around the Côtes de Meuse until the end of January, 1917.

ALSACE.

2. At the beginning of February it went into Alsace and occupied a sector between the Thur and the Rhone-Rhine canal (March).

CHEMIN DES DAMES.

3. On April 21 it was hastily entrained at Mulhouse and transferred to the Aisne. It went into line on the 26th at Chemin des Dames and met the second French offensive in the Courtecon-Malval farm region (May 5).

ST. GOBAIN FOREST.

4. Relieved in the middle of May, it stayed at rest for six days in the vicinity of Assis sur Serre and thereafter in a sector in the St. Gobain forest (Deuillet-Fresnes).

5. On August 10 it was put at rest behind Laon.

CRAONNE.

6. It went back into line at the end of September in the Craonne sector. As a result of the French offensive it fell back to the east of Hurtebise where it was relieved about November 10.

7. It rested in the Laon region from the middle of November to January 20.

RECRUITING.

In 1917 the division took on a distinctly provincial aspect, its regiments receiving replacements from Prussian Saxony (the 36th Fusileers and the 66th Infantry) and in Thuringe (the 32d Reserve Regiment).

VALUE—1917 ESTIMATE.

The 113th Division was a good unit. It put up an energetic resistance on the Chemin des Dames on May 5, 1917. From that time up to the offensive of March, 1918, it had not been seriously engaged.

1918.

1. Having finished its training in the Sissonne region, the 113th Division relieved the 235th Division about the middle of January in the Juvincourt sector (east of Craonne), and was itself relieved by the 5th Reserve Division on the 21st of February. It trained for a week at Vervins, and then moved to Wassigny, where it underwent more training until the 16th of March, when it marched via Bohain and Fonsommes to Bellicourt.

ST. QUENTIN.

2. On the 21st it attacked in the first line near Maissemy (northwest of St. Quentin). Although suffering very heavy losses, the division had succeeded in pushing on as far as St. Christ-Briost and Pargny (on the Somme) on the 24th. It was withdrawn shortly after (probably on the 26th).

AISNE.

3. On the 27th of May the division reenforced the Aisne front near Craonne and attacked in the first line. It was withdrawn about the 14th of June and went to rest near Conde sur Aisne (east of Soissons).

4. The division reenforced the front near Troissy (east of Dormans) on the 15th of July. It was caught in the confusion caused by the Allied counteroffensive, and was forced to retire. It was not identified after the 22d, and so it seems as though it was not in line after that date until prisoners were again taken on the 29th near Villers-Agron (southeast of Fere en Tardenois), which is in a line almost due north of where it had previously been engaged. Here it took over the part of the line previously held by the 2d Guard Division. It was withdrawn early in August and went to rest in the region southeast of Maubeuge.

CAMBRAI.

5. On the 10th of September the division reenforced the front near Metz en Couture (southwest of Cambrai). It was withdrawn from line near Villers–Plouich (southwest of Cambrai) after having lost over 1,600 prisoners about the 2d of October, and went to rest east of Denain.

6. On the 22d it came back into line near Douchy (south of Denain). Two days later it side-slipped toward the south. It was identified in line to the north of Le Quesnoy in November, but was withdrawn a day or two later. It did not return to line.

VALUE—1918 ESTIMATE.

The 113th was rated as a second-class division. Although the division commander received Pour le Merite and the commander of the 36th Regiment was also decorated after the battle of the Somme, the division does not appear to have particularly distinguished itself there. On the whole, however, its conduct though not brilliant was dependable.

115th Division.

COMPOSITION.

	1915		1916		1917		1918	
	Brigade.	Regiment.	Brigade.	Regiment.	Brigade.	Regiment.	Brigade.	Regiment.
Infantry.......	229.	136. 171. 40 Res.	229.	136. 171. 40 Res.	229.	136. 171. 40 Res.	229.	136. 171. 173.
Cavalry.......	1 and 2 Sqn. 22 Dragoon Rgt. (one-half picked troops).		1 and 2 Sqn. 22 Dragoon Rgt.		2 Sqn. 22 Dragoon Rgt.		2 Sqn. 22 Dragoon Rgt.	
Artillery......	229 F. A. Rgt. (7 Btries.).		229 F. A. Rgt.		(?) Art. Command: 229 F. A. Rgt.		115 Art. Command: 229 Field Art. Rgt. 94 Foot Art. Btn. 1074, 1077, and 1078 Light Mun. Col.	
Engineers and Liaisons.	229 Pion. Co.		229 Pion. Co. 115 T. M. Co 115 Pont. Engrs. 115 Tel. Detch.		(115) Pion. Btn. 229 Pion. Co. 2 Co. 33 Res. Pion. 115 T. M. Co. 229 Searchlight Section. 115 Tel. Detch.		43 Pion. Btn. 229 Pion. Co. 2 Co. Res. Pion. Btn. No. 33. 115 T. M. Co. 74 Searchlight Section. 115 Div. Signal Command. 115 Tel. Detch. 89 Div. Wireless Detch.	
Medical and Veterinary.	....		....		115 Ambulance Co. 350 Filed Hospital. 376 Field Hospital. 377 Field Hospital. Vet. Hospital.		115 Ambulance Co. 376 and 377 Field Hospitals. 167 Vet. Hospital.	
Transport....	....		M. T. Col.		M. T. Col.		598 M. T. Col.	

HISTORY.

(136th and 171st Regiments: 15th Corps District—Alsace. 40th Reserve Regiment:
14th Corps District—Grand Duchy of Baden.)

1915.

Formed in April, 1915, near Tournai, the 115th Division received the 136th and
171st from the 30th and 39th Divisions (15th Corps), respectively, and the 40th Reserve
Regiment from the 28th Reserve Division (14th Reserve Corps).

1. In April, 1915, the 115th Division was in reserve in the Tournai–Courtrai region.

ARTOIS.

2. In May it was sent as a reenforcement to the north of Arras and fought at Notre
Dame de Lorette and Neuville St. Vaast and was sorely tried. The infantry losses
amounted to 128 officers and 5,208 men out of action (Casualty List), of which 47
officers and 2,258 men belonged to the 171st Regiment.

AISNE.

3. Relieved about June 15, the 115th Division took over the Missy sur Aisne sector
(east of Soissons), which it occupied until the last days of July.

RUSSIA.

4. At the end of July it was transferred to the Eastern Front, and for a time in
August operated on the Narew.

5. It took part in the summer offensive. It was before Kovno on August 19, in the
region of Vileiki at the end of September, and near Narotch Lake at the beginning of
October.

1916.

POSTAVY–NAROTCH LAKE.

1. The 115th Division occupied the Postavy–Narotch Lake sector until the beginning of August, 1916.

GALICIA.

2. About August 2 the division was transferred to Galicia. It was engaged to the
west of Zalosce (south of Brody), August to September.

VOLHYNIA.

3. In October it was in line in Volhynia to the west of Loutsk (Sviniouki). The
171st was kept to the southwest of Brody with the Melior detachment.

ROUMANIA.

4. In the middle of December the 115th Division was transferred from Volhynia
to Roumania, where, together with the 109th Division, it made up the 54th Corps,
which operated between Buzeu and the Danube.

1917.

ROUMANIA.

1. In January, 1917, the 115th Division took a position on the Roumanian front to
the south of ·Namoloasa and stayed in this sector until the middle of August.

2. It was then in line to the north of Focsani, in the Panciu–Marasesti region
(August–December).

RECRUITING.

The Grand Duchy of Baden and the Rhenish countries supplied the greater part
of the recruits.

1918.

1. The division was relieved on the Roumanian front on Fe bruary 1 by an Austrian
division and rested in the Braila area during February and March. On April 8 it
entrained and traveled via Budapest-Vienna-Prague-Dresden-Coblenz-Cologne-

Aachen–Liege–Brussels to Lille, when it detrained about April 18. About the 21st the division reentrained and was railed to Antwerp, where it went through a course of intensive training.

BATTLE OF THE MARNE.

The division left Antwerp on May 21 and traveled via Brussels–Mons–Maubeuge–Le Cateau–Bohain, detraining north of St. Quentin on May 22. Four days later it continued its journey by rail to Versigny, southeast of La Fere, and was billeted in the Crepy area until May 29. On the following day it left and marched via Chaille-voois–Vailly (May 31)–Ambrief (June 1)–Villers–Helon (2d) and relieved the 37th Division near Longpont on the Aisne battle front on the night of June 2–3. It withstood the Allied counterthrust at Corcy in July, suffering heavy losses. It was relieved on the night of July 19–20.

VERDUN.

2. The division was moved to Brieulles and in the first days of August relieved the 22d Reserve Division in the sector Malancourt–Forges. In this vicinity it remained until September 19, when it was relieved by the 7th Reserve Division.

MEUSE–ARGONNE.

3. On the second day of the American attack the division returned to bolster up the line in the Gesnes area. The division now included the 173d Regiment, which came from the 223d Division (dissolved) to supplant the 40th Reserve Regiment (disbanded). The division took part in the several captures and recaptures of Gesnes. It fought hard and suffered heavy losses before its relief on October 12 by the 3d. Guard Division. Two days later it came back to support the 3d Guard Division and was engaged in the fighting around Romagne until October 18. On November 1 the division again came into line near Remonville and fought until the armistice.

VALUE—1918 ESTIMATE.

The division was rated as third class. It was badly hit on July 18 by the French attack and later in the Argonne. It showed good qualities in the Meuse fighting and was mentioned in the official German communiqué.

117th Division.

COMPOSITION.

	1915		1916		1917		1918	
	Brigade.	Regiment.	Brigade.	Regiment.	Brigade.	Regiment.	Brigade.	Regiment.
Infantry	233.	157, 11 Res, 22 Res.	233.	157, 11 Res, 22 Res.	233.	157, 11 Res, 22 Res.	233.	11, 157, 450.
Cavalry	(?)		1 and 2 Sqn. 8 Cuirassier Rgt.		1 Sqn. 8 Cuirassier Rgt.		1 Sqn. 8 Cuirassier Rgt.	
Artillery	233 F. A. Rgt. (7 Btries.).		233 F. A. Rgt.		(?) Art. Command: 233 F. A. Rgt.		233 F. A. Rgt. 88 Foot Art. Btn. 1068, 1069, and 1070 Light Mun. Col.	
Engineers and Liaisons.	233 Pion. Co.		233 Pion. Co. 117 T. M. Co. 117 Pont. Engs. 117 Tel. Detch.		(117) Pion. Btn.: 233 Pion. Co. 263 Pion. Co. 117 T. M. Co. 233 Searchlight Section. 117 Tel. Detch.		117 Pion. Btn. 233 Pion. Co. 263 Pion. Co. 117 T. M. Co. 147 Searchlight Section. 117 Div. Signal Command. 117 Tel. Detch. 187 Div. Wireless Detch.	
Medical and Veterinary.					117 Ambulance Co. 379 Field Hospital. 380 Field Hospital. Vet. Hospital.		117 Ambulance Co. 378 and 379 Field Hospitals. 117 Vet. Hospital.	
Transport attached.					M. T. Col. 6 Mountain Art. Btry.			

HISTORY.

(6th Corps District—Silesia.)

1915.

The 117th Division was created by the 7th Army near Liart about April 7, 1915. Its three regiments were obtained from the 6th Corps and the 6th Reserve Corps—the 157th Infantry from the 12th Division, the 11th Reserve Regiment from the 11th Reserve Division, and the 22d Reserve Regiment from the 12th Reserve Division.

1. In April, 1915, the 117th Division was in Champagne (region of Châtelet).

ARTOIS–NOTRE DAME DE LORETTE.

2. Transferred to Artois, it was engaged to the north of Souchez and at Notre Dame de Lorette (May and June). In this fighting it was hard hit, 107 officers and 5,255 men out of action, of whom 44 officers and 2,161 men belong to the 11th Infantry. (Casualty List.)

3. The division was re-formed at the end of June in the region of Lille.

LENS.

4. Toward the middle of July it went back into line to the northwest of Lens (from Vermelles to the Grenay-Lens railway). It suffered very heavy losses in the attacks occurring at the end of September and the beginning of October (Loos)—109 officers and 6,463 men out of action. (Casualty List.)

5. Taken away from the Artois front in the middle of October, it was put at rest in the vicinity of Roubaix-Tourcoing.

FLANDERS.

6. At the end of October it took over the Messines sector.

1916.

1. The 117th Division occupied the Messines front until the beginning of March, 1916.

2. Rest at Courtrai; instruction and training at the Beverloo Camp (March–April and May).

YPRES.

3. At the beginning of June the division went into line to the east of Ypres (near the road from Ypres to Menin, and until July 20).

SOMME.

4. On July 23 it went to the Somme (Pozieres); it was engaged from the end of July to the middle of August.

5. On August 17 the division entrained for the Eastern Front.

BUKOVINE.

6. It was identified in the Carpathian Mountains as part of the 3d Austro-Hungarian Army (region of Jablonica, October).

1917.

CARPATHIAN MOUNTAINS.

1. The 117th Division remained here (Jablonica, Worochta, Koeroesmezoe, Jacobeni sectors) until the middle of May, 1917.

ROUMANIA.

2. At the end of May it was transferred via Maramaros-Sziget to the Roumanian front (Putna valley, region of Ocna, June–September). At rest in Transylvania in September and was there reequipped for mountain warfare.

ITALY.

3. Sent to Italy at the beginning of October, it was on the 24th behind Tolmino as an army reserve. In December it was on the left bank of the Piave.

Silesian division, with recruits coming especially from Upper Silesia (mining district and mountainous districts), it was used on several occasions as mountain troops (Carpathians, Italy).

On the Carpathian, Roumanian, and Italian fronts (August, 1916–March, 1918).

1918.

LORRAINE.

1. The division rested in the vicinity of Vahl-Ebersing until April 6, when it entrained at St. Avold and moved to Lille. It went into billets near there on the 7th and came into line near Neuve Eglise on April 13.

BATTLE OF THE LYS.

2. It was engaged in the Bailleul, Kemmel, and La Clyette area until the 1st of May. After a few days in support, the division reentered west of Dranoutre on May 4 and held that sector until mid-May.

3. The division rested near La Madeleine. Its units were very much weakened. The 11th Reserve Regiment was disbanded about May 16 and transferred its effectives to the other two regiments of the division. It was replaced by the 11th Grenadier Regiment, which was brought from the Macedonian front about May 21. The division remained at rest until about June 3, when it was again reported in line near Voormezeele.

BATTLE OF THE SOMME.

4. The division held that sector without event until June 25, when it was withdrawn and sent to rest near Ghent. On August 4 it was moved by rail to Peronne, where it went into the Vrely-Hangest wood sector until August 18. In the British attack south of the Somme on August 8 the division lost about 2,700 prisoners.

On August 27 it reenforced the battle front at Maricourt for a couple of days. It was withdrawn about September 1.

ARGONNE.

5. The division rested and was reconstituted in rear of the Argonne front in early September. The 22d Reserve Regiment suffered so heavily on the Somme that it was dissolved and its men divided between the other two regiments. The 450th Regiment from the dissolved 233d Division replaced the 22d Reserve Regiment in the division.

6. About September 12, the division relieved the 37th Division in line near Avocourt. It was swamped in the first drive of the American Army on September 26. Elements kept up the fight until September 29, when they were withdrawn after having been pressed back to about Cierges. Its defense was not particularly vigorous, but was better than that of the divisions on either side. Its total losses were estimated at 3,200, including 1,861 prisoners.

MEUSE.

7. On November 2 the division returned to line just west of the Meuse. While resting at Juvigny the division received replacements. In the retreat it crossed to the east bank of the Meuse and was in line on the day of the armistice.

VALUE—1918 ESTIMATE.

The division was rated as second-class. Up to the middle of June the division seems to have been a holding rather than an attacking one. After the Somme battle in August its effectives were feeble and morale low. It had many older men, returned wounded, and convalescents, and a large number of Poles and Alsatians.

119th Division.

COMPOSITION.

	1915 Brigade	1915 Regiment	1916 Brigade	1916 Regiment	1917 Brigade	1917 Regiment	1918 Brigade	1918 Regiment
Infantry	237.	46. 58. 46 Res.	237.	46. 58. 46 Res.	237.	46. 58. 46 Res.	237.	46. 58. 46 Res.
Cavalry			Wedel. Rgt. (1 and 3 Sqn. 1 Uhlan Rgt. and 4 Sqn. 1 Mounted Jag. Rgt.).		4 Sqn. 1 Mounted Jag. Rgt.		4 Sqn. 1 Jag. z. Pf.	
Artillery	237 F. A. Rgt. (7 Btries.).		237 F. A. Rgt.		119 Art. Command.; 237 F. A. Rgt. (9 Btries.).		119 Artillery Command. 237 Field Art. Rgt. 2 Abt. 27 Foot Art. Rgt. (Btries. 5 to 7). 1274, 1275, and 1338 Light Mun. Col.	
Engineers and Liaisons.	237 Pion. Co.		237 Pion. Co. 119 T. M. Co. 119 Pont. Engs. 119 Tel. Detch.		119 Pion. Btn.: 237 Pion. Co. 273 Pion. Co. 3 Res. Co. 32 Pion. Btn. 119 T. M. Co. 237 Searchlight Section. 119 Tel. Detch.		119 Pion. Btn. 273 Pion. Co. 91 Searchlight Section. 119 Div. Signal Command. 119 Tel. Detch. 65 Div. Wireless Detch.	
Medical and Veterinary.					119 Ambulance Co. 605 Ambulance Co. 381 Field Hospital. 382 Field Hospital. 383 Field Hospital. 168 Vet. Hospital.		119 Ambulance Co. 382 and 383 Field Hospitals. 168 Vet. Hospital.	
Transport					600 M. T. Col.		600 M. T. Col.	

Attached........

16, 17, 60, and 61 (?) Light Machine Gun Sections.
79 M. G. S. S. Detch.
1 Co. 3 T. M. Btn.
352 Pion. Mining Co.
Kortemarck Pion. Park.
Strovendorp Pion. Park.
57 Ft. Art. Btn.
157 Ft. Art. Btn.
5 Btry. 7 Res. Ft. A. Rgt.
404 Ft. Art. Btn.
5 Btry. 39 Ldw. Ft. A. Rgt.
6 Btry. 29 Ldw. Ft. A. Rgt.
8 Quick-firing Motar Co.
182 Ft. A. Btry.
187 Ft. A. Btry.
428 Ft. A. Btry.
478 and 642 Mountain Ft. Art. Btries.
2 and 4 Mountain Ft. Art. Btries. (18 C. Dist.)
1,000 Ft. Art. Btry.
9 Art. Survey Section.
819 Tel. Detch.
62 Div. Wireless Detch.
21 Pigeon Loft.
218 Messenger-dog Detch.
48 Reconnaissance Sqns.
26 Combat Sqn.
30 Balloon Sqn.
4 Co. 44 Labor Btn.
3 Co. 53 Labor Btn.
4 Co. 122 Labor Btn.
61 Supply Train.
19, 108, 121 Bav. and 835 M. T. Col.
491 Ammunition Train.
682, 711, and 758 Truck Trains.
587 Supply Train.
571 Depot Supply Col.
119 Supply Depot.

(According to a captured document dated Sept. 29, 1917.)

HISTORY.

(5th Corps District—Posen and Lower Silesia.)

1915.

GALICIA—POLAND.

1. Formed in April, 1915. Its three regiments were obtained from divisions belonging to the 5th Army—the 46th from the 10th Division, the 58th from the 9th Division, and the 46th Reserve from the 10th Reserve Division. Assembled in annexed Lorraine, it was sent to Galicia for the April German offensive. The division took part in the battle of Gorlice at the end of the month.

2. In July it was in Poland, west of the Wieprz, and at the end of October in the region of Baranovitchi.

1916.

BARANOVITCHI.

1. In January, 1916, the division held a sector to the east of Baranovitchi (Russia).

NAROTCH LAKE.

2. About March 28 it went to Narotch Lake and opposed the Russian offensive.

3. Sorely tried on March 30, it was relieved on April 7.

SMORGONI.

4. In May it was found at the west of Smorgoni.

GALICIA.

5. It was transferred to Galicia at the end of June at the time of the Russian offensive. Engaged on July 27, it suffered heavy losses. The 1st Battalion of the 58th was almost entirely captured and the division retired 15 km. (letter). On August 7 new losses at Tlumacz. The division was placed in reserve behind Stanislau until the beginning of September. On September 6 it reappeared on the front in the region of Haliez.

1917.

GALICIA.

1. The division stayed near Haliez until March 9, 1917. It was then sent to the vicinity of Brzezany, where it was almost immediately put in reserve.

2. At the beginning of May it was sent to the Western Front. (Itinerary: Brzezany (May 3)-Lemberg-Breslau-Liegnitz-Dresden-Leipzig-Cassel-Frankfort-Aix la Chapelle-Liége-Brussels-Roulers (May 8).

FLANDERS.

3. Ypres sector; went into line at the beginning of June and was relieved on July 18.

4. Bixschoote sector; went into line at the beginning of August. The division met the attack in Flanders, in which it suffered serious losses on August 16. The 9th Company of the 58th Infantry was reduced to 38 men (notebook). On the 9th and 10th of October there were new engagements.

5. Relieved from the front on October 15 the division rested in the vicinity of Gand.

CAMBRAI.

6. After a month's rest the 119th Division went into line on the Cambrai front to participate in the counterattacks which followed the surprise attack of November 20. It fought here from the 23d to the 27th, not without some losses.

7. Relieved after December 6, the division was reorganized in the vicinity of Solesmes.

RECRUITING.

This division recruited from the 5th Corps District. A document dated November 23, 1917, described the division as composed of "regiments of Lower Silesia and Posen." In order to overcome the majority of Poles, the division received recruits from the 3d and 6th Corps Districts (Brandenburg and Silesia), which were fruitful sources of recruiting.

Twenty-one per cent of the prisoners taken from the 119th Division in August, 1917, belonged to the 1917 class. The 1918 class was meagerly represented. The 46th Reserve Regiment had a large proportion of Poles. The soldiers from Alsace-Lorraine remained on the Eastern Front when the division left Galicia (May, 1917).

1918.

1. About the end of January the division was relieved near Pronville by the 20th Division. It replaced the 3d Guard Division astride the Bapaume–Cambrai road about February 12. The date of its relief in this sector is not known. A captured diary shows that the division was training in the Helesmes area (north of Denain) until the middle of March. On the 16th it marched to Noyelles sur Selle, and on the following day reached Cambrai, where it remained until March 20.

BATTLE OF PICARDY.

2. The division came into line near Inchy on the 21st and took part in the initial attack. It was withdrawn on the 23d and rested two days. It reappeared in line on the 25th and fought southeast of Hebuterne until relieved by the 5th Bavarian Reserve Division on April 7–8. The division lost heavily in this fighting.

BATTLE OF THE LYS.

3. Withdrawn from the Somme, the division reentered the Lys battle line on April 26 near Locon. It was engaged there until early in May (6th), when it was withdrawn near Hinges and rested in the area Lille–Tournai until June 11. On that date it marched to Orchies, was railed to Le Forest, and from there came into line via Noyelle, relieving the 12th Reserve Division on the night of June 13–14. While at rest the division received a number of drafts, mostly of the 1919 class.

4. The division held the Mericourt sector until the night of July 12-13, when it was relieved by the 52d Division and took over the billets of the 52d Division in the Orchies area.

5. The division rested until August 1, when it moved to Ham via Douai–Cambrai–Caudry–Bohain–St. Quentin. Then it rested until August 8, when it was alarmed and rushed up in busses to the Le Quesnel sector.

BATTLE OF THE SOMME.

6. On August 9 the division was engaged south of the Somme. In the fighting it lost about 900 prisoners before its relief on August 17. On August 27–28 it returned to line in the Misery–Licourt sector and remained in line until September 24, when it was withdrawn from west of Bellenglise. After a week's rest the division reentered line at Estrees; was engaged for 17 days in the Beaurevoir–Le Cateau area. Since August 8 it has lost nearly 3,000 prisoners.

YORES.

7. The division rested at Ghent until October 27, when it relieved the 3d Landwehr Division south of Machelen. It retreated via Olsene to Nazareth, in which area it was withdrawn about November 9.

VALUE—1918 ESTIMATE.

The division was rated as second class. It was used as an attack division in the March and April offensives. While on the defensive in August and September on the Somme it was decimated.

121st Division.

COMPOSITION.

	1915 Brigade	1915 Regiment	1916 Brigade	1916 Regiment	1917 Brigade	1917 Regiment	1918 Brigade	1918 Regiment
Infantry	241.	C). 7 Res. 56 Res.	241.	60. 7 Res. 56 Res.	241.	60. 7 Res. 56 Res.	241.	60. 7 Res. 56 Res.
Cavalry	2 and 3 Sqns. 12 Horse Jag. Rgt.		12 Horse Jag. Rgt. (? 2 Sqns.).		3 Sqn. 12 Horse Jag. Rgt. (?). 2 Sqn. 12 Horse Jag. Schuz. Rgt.		2 Sqn. 12 Jag. z. Pf.	
Artillery	211 F. A. Rgt.		241 F. A. Rgt.		(?) Art. Command: 241 F. A. Rgt.		121 Art. Command: 241 F. A. Rgt. 85 Foot Art. Btn. 1217, 1219, and 1223 Light Mun. Col.	
Engineers and Liaisons.	241 Pion. Co.		241 Pion. Co. 260 Pion. Co. 4 Co. 27 Pions. 121 T. M. Co. 121 Pont. Engs. 121 Tel. Detch.		(121 Pion. Btn.): 241 Pion. Co. 260 Pion. Co. 121 T. M. Co. 241 Searchlight Section. 121 Tel. Detch.		121 Pion. Btn. 241 Pion. Co. 260 Pion. Co. 104 Searchlight Section. 121 Div. Signal Command. 121 Tel. Detch. 59 Div. Wireless Detch.	
Medical and Veterinary.					229 Ambulance Co. 384 Field Hospital. 385 Field Hospital. Vet. Hospital.		229 Ambulance Co. 384 and 385 Field Hospitals. 206 Vet. Hospital.	
Transport.					M. T. Col.		601 M. T. Col.	
Attached.			Labor Btn. of the 121 Div.					

HISTORY.

(60th Regiment: 21st Corps District—Lower Alsace. 7th Reserve Regiment; 5th Corps District—Posen. 56 Reserve Regiment; 7th Corps District—Westphalia.)

1915.

The 121st Division was formed in the Falkenhausen Army in Lorraine in April, 1915. Its three regiments came from divisions which had been in existence for some time. The 60th came from the 31st Division (21st Corps), the 7th Reserve from the 9th Reserve Division (5th Reserve Corps), and the 56th Reserve from the 13th Reserve Division (7th Reserve Corps). These regiments were brought together in the region of St. Avold–Faulquemont at the beginning of April and on the 9th reached Thiaucourt, Euvezin, and the Mort Mare wood (notebooks).

HAYE.

1. The 121st Division next appeared in the Bois de Prêtre sector at the beginning of May, 1915.

2. It stayed there until the end of February, 1916.

1916.

1. The division left the Bois de Prêtre on March 1, 1916, and rested in the vicinity of Metz.

VERDUN.

2. On March 15 it came to the Verdun front (north of Vaux). On April 1 it attacked and took the village of Vaux; it again attacked on April 11 and made progress between Vaux and Douaumont, paying dearly for the advance.

3. Relieved from the Verdun front on April 20, it was put at rest near St. Avold until May 15. It had lost 58 per cent of its infantry strength in front of Verdun. From March 18 to May 30 the 6th Company of the 7th Reserve Regiment received no less than 192 replacements.

SOMME.

4. Transferred to Péronne by way of Sedan, Charleville, Hirson, and Bohain, the 121st Division went into line on the left bank of the Somme on May 18.

5. On July 1, while in this sector, it was surprised by the French offensive and suffered heavy losses (numerous prisoners).

6. Relieved on July 4, it was put at rest and reorganized.

RUSSIA.

7. On July 18 it entrained for the Eastern Front. (Itinerary: Aix la Chapelle–Cologne–Thorn, Warsaw, and Brest-Litowsk.)

KOVEL.

8. Taking over the Kovel sector on July 26, it launched counterattacks, in which it was sorely tried.

1917.

NAROTCH LAKE.

1. At the beginning of January, 1917, the 121st Division left the Kovel sector to go into the region of Narotch Lake and stayed in the latter place until May 17.

FRANCE.

2. On May 20 it entrained for France. (Itenerary: Vilna–Insterberg–Allenstein–Bromberg–Landsberg–Berlin–Stendal–Minden–Duesseldorf–Aix la Chapelle–Verviers–Liége–Brussels–Audenarde.) It detrained at Elsegem on May 25.

CAMBRÉSIS.

3. Transferred to Cambrai on June 10, it took over the Mœuvres–Avrincourt sector, which it occupied from June 12 to the beginning of August.

FLANDERS.

4. It was thereafter brought to the Ypres front to the south of the railway running from Ypres to Roulers (Aug. 19). Artillery fire caused it to lose heavily; the British attack of September 20, of which it bore the brunt, increased its losses. Before the battle of the 20th the 12th Company of the 56th Reserve Regiment was reduced to 65 men, of whom 40 were men of the class of 1918. The 9th Company was entirely destroyed or captured.

5. Relieved in the night of the 21st of September the division was sent to rest (region of Mars la Tour) and reorganized (more than 2,000 men coming from the 605th and 614th Landstrum, Batallion X 12, and the 109th Landwehr). These replacements were very heterogeneous—soldiers from Westphalia, Hanover, Baden, Magdeberg (men previously wounded and convalescents).

COTES DE MEUSE.

6. At the beginning of October the 121st Division took over a sector near Cotes de Meuse (les Éparges, Ravin de Malochis). It stayed there until about April 10, 1918.

RECRUITING.

The name "7th Brandeberger" for the 60th Infantry was only of historic interest. The regiment recruited almost entirely in Westphalia. The 56th Reserve Regiment was also recruited in Westphalia, and there were numerous soldiers from there in the 7th Reserve Regiment to counterbalance the numerous Poles in the 5th Corps District; hence the make-up of the division was for the most part Westphalian.

VALUE—1917 ESTIMATE.

The 121st Division fought very well in its last battle in Flanders (September, 1917) and was put to a good test.

In March, 1918, the number of men in the ranks who had taken part in these attacks was about 35 or 40 per cent, and the replacements used after the battle of Flanders were generally of inferior military value.

1918.

1. The division was relieved on the Woevre about April 11. It entrained on April 24 at Conflans and traveled via Sedan–Charleville–Hirson–Valenciennes to Pont a Marcq, where it detrained on April 26, after a journey of about 20 hours. It came into line in the Dranoutre sector on May 2 in relief of the 10th Erzsatz Division.

LOCRE.

2. It held the Locre sector until May 21, when it was relieved by the 16th Bavarian Division. On June 19 it returned to its former sector at Dranoutre and held it until July 7.

3. The division rested in the Tourcoing area until July 31, when it entrained and traveled via Courtrai–Valenciennes–St. Quentin to Laon, where it detrained on the following day. Here it rested until 5 p. m. on August 8, when it was alarmed and marched to the La Fere area (19 miles), arriving on the next day about 11 a. m. On the same day at 8 p. m. the division was again alarmed and was moved in motor busses via Chauny–Noyon–Roye to the Damery area, where it arrived on the 10th of August about 10 a. m. and was immediately engaged.

BATTLE OF THE SOMME.

4. The division fell back by Parvillers–Damery–Fresnoy–Cremery–Sept Fours–Nesle to the east bank of the Somme Canal. It was relieved on the night of September 1–2 by the 25th Reserve Division. The division lost 800 prisoners in this fighting.

5. It rested in early September in the Maretz area (southeast of Cambrai). On September 18 it was hurried to the line and counterattacked at Bonyon that evening.

Until October 1 it was engaged at Hargicourt, Villeret, and Le Catelet. After only four days of rest the division again came into line on October 5 in the Gouy area. It was withdrawn to be reorganized on October 9.

6. After resting near Maubeuge the division returned to line west of Catillon on the night of October 18–19. It fought for about seven days between that place and Ors. On November 6 it was engaged at Maroilles and was in line near Limont–Fontaine on the day of the armistice.

VALUE—1918 ESTIMATE.

The division was rated as third class. It was an average division. In the final campaign it showed no particular power of resistance and lost abnormally in prisoners.

123d Division.

COMPOSITION.

	1915 Brigade.	1915 Regiment.	1916 Brigade.	1916 Regiment.	1917 Brigade.	1917 Regiment.	1918 Brigade.	1918 Regiment.
Infantry	245.	178. 182. 106 Res.	245.	178. 182. 106 Res.	245.	178. 106 Res. 351.	245.	178. 106 Res. 351.
Cavalry			5 Sqn. 20 Hus. Rgt.		4 and 5 Sqn. 20 Hus. Rgt.		5 Sqn. 20 Hus. Rgt.	
Artillery	245 F. A. Rgt. 246 F. A. Rgt.		245 F. A. Rgt. 246 F. A. Rgt.		123 Art. Command: 245 F. A. Rgt.		123 Art. Command: 245 Field Hospital. 137 Ft. A. Btn. 816 Light Am. Col. 1148 Light Am. Col. 1149 Light Am. Col.	
Engineers and Liaisons.	245 Pion. Co.		245 Pion. Co. 264 Pion. Co. 1 Co. 2 Bav. Pions. 123 T. M. Co. 123 Pont. Engs. 123 Tel. Detch.		(123) Pion. Btn.: 245 Pion. Co. 264 Pion. Co. 123 T. M. Co. 245 Searchlight Section. 124 Tel. Detch.		123 Pion. Btn.: 245 (Saxon) Pion. Co. 264 (Saxon) Pion. Co. 123 T. M. Co. 128 Searchlight Section. 123 Signal Command: 123 Tel. Detch. 168 Wireless Detch.	
Medical and Veterinary.					123 Ambulance Co. 387 Field Hospital. Vet. Hospital.		123 Ambulance Co. 386 Field Hospital. 387 Field Hospital. 236 Vet. Hospital.	
Transports					M. T. Col.			
Attached			96 Antiaircraft Section.					

HISTORY.

(178th and 351st Regiments: 12th Corps District—Saxony. 106th Reserve Regiment: 19th Corps District—Saxony.)

1915.

The division was formed in April, 1915, by taking three regiments (178th, 182d, and 106th Reserve) from established divisions of the 12th Corps the 12th Reserve Corps (Saxons). In October, 1916, the 182d Regiment was transferred to the 216th Division and was replaced by the 425th Infantry, which was also transferred from this division in March, 1917, and replaced by the 351st Regiment (Saxon).

CHAMPAGNE.

1. In May, 1915, the 123d Division occupied the region northwest of Rheims.

2. At the end of May it was transported to Lille, where it seems to have been transferred as a reserve; in the middle of June it was in the vicinity of Arras.

ARTOIS.

3. It next occupied different sectors in Artois.

4. In September it held the Souchez front. On October 8 it took part in the attack on Loos and left Artois in the middle of that month.

FLANDERS.

5. After a rest at Lille the division went to Flanders (November), where it held a sector south of the canal from Ypres to Comines.

1916.
FLANDERS.

1. In the middle of March, 1916, the 123d Division was put at rest near Bruges.

2. It was temporarily in line about April 9 at St. Éloi; then remained as a reserve to the armies in the vicinity of Menin and Courtrai until July 5.

SOMME.

3. At this date it was transferred to the Somme and fought near Hardecourt and Maurepas until July 22, losing more than 6,000 men.

RUSSIA.

4. At the beginning of August, 1916, the 123d Division left the Western Front for the Russian front.

NAROTCH LAKE.

5. It went into line in the region of Narotch Lake about September.

1917.
NAROTCH LAKE-MITAU.

1. At the end of January, 1917, the 106th Reserve Regiment was detached as a reenforcement in the Mitau sector, which was menaced by a Russian attack.

In March the 425th Infantry (Prussian) was exchanged for the 351st Infantry, which had been grouped under this number since 1915, and was originally three battalions of the Saxon replacement depot of the old war garrison of Breslau.

SMORGONI.

2. In the middle of August the division, which up to that time had held the Narotch Lake sector, was engaged between Smorgoni and Krevo.

3. It again returned to the Narotch Lake vicinity in November.

FRANCE.

4. About November 8 it was transferred to France. (Itinerary: Chavli-Varsovie-Lodz-Kalich-Cottbus-Cassel-Frankfort on the Main-Sarrebrueck-Metz). It detrained at Piennes, Baroncourt, and was billeted in that district for eight days.

MEUSE.

5. About November 22 it took over a sector on the Verdun front (south of Bezon-vaux). It stayed there all winter. It was identified to the southeast of Damloup in February, 1918.

RECRUITING.

Since March, 1917, there have been but Saxons in the 123d Division.

VALUE—1917 ESTIMATE.

The 123d Division had but a mediocre combat value by reason of its long stay in calm sectors on the Russian front.

In Russia it fraternized on two occasions, the second one at the time of its last stay on the Russian front.

The losses of the division on the Russian front were almost nothing and it suffered no losses on the Verdun front until February, 1918.

1918.

VERDUN.

1. The division continued to hold the uneventful Bezonvaux sector until June 3, when it was relieved by the 7th Reserve Division.

RHEIMS.

2. On the night of June 18–19 it relieved the 232d Division north of the Bligny (southwest of Rheims). It participated in the attack of July 15 and made a slight advance. On the 20th it was relieved.

3. The division marched by Savigny–Trigny–Bourgogne–Houdicourt. It was railed to Asfeld and rested at Sery. On the 27th it marched to Novion–Porcien and was railed to Montmedy. From there it marched to Grand Failly, where it camped until the 31st.

VERDUN.

4. On August 8 the division relieved the 6th Bavarian Division near Samogneux and rested in that sector until September 3.

ST. MIHIEL.

5. After it rested in the St. Mihiel sector until September 12, it was put into line at Thiaucourt to check the American offensive. It remained there until the night of October 7–8, when it was withdrawn.

6. The division was moved by autotrucks to Dun via Spincourt–Billy–Damvillers–Haraumont–Fontaines, arriving there on the night of October 9–10. It marched into line near Cunel on October 11.

MEUSE-ARGONNE.

7. The division was engaged in almost continuous fighting without any major attack, until it was withdrawn on October 25. While it did not win special merit for its defense, it fought persistently and was quick to take every advantage of the terrain. The division lost 238 prisoners and 2,200 other casualties (estimated). The division was considered in reserve of the 5th Army at the time of the armistice.

VALUE—1918 ESTIMATE.

The division was rated as third class. Its conduct in the July offensive was medi-ocre and in the Argonne it did nothing to distinguish itself.

183d Division.

COMPOSITION.

	1915		1916		1917		1918[1]	
	Brigade.	Regiment.	Brigade.	Regiment.	Brigade.	Regiment.	Brigade.	Regiment.
Infantry	183.	183. 184. 122 Res.	183.	183. 184. 122 Res.	33 Res.	184. 418. 440 Res.	33 Res.	184. 418. (Saxon). 440 Res.
Cavalry					4 Sqn. 10 Hus. Rgt.		4 Sqn. 10 Hus. Rgt.	
Artillery	183 F. A. Abt. (3 Btries.).		183 F. A. Abt.		183 Art. Command:	183 F. A. Rgt. (9 Btries.).	183 Art. Command:	183 (Saxon) F. A. Rgt.
Engineers and Liaisons.	183 (Saxon) Pion. Co.		183 (Saxon) Pion. Co. 401 T. M. Co.		183 Pion. Btn.: 2 Res. Co. 16 Pions. 1 Res. Co. 20 Pions. 183 (Saxon) Pion. Co. 401 T. M. Co. 183 Searchlight Section. 183 (Saxon) Tel. Detch.		183 Pion. Btn.: 2 Res. Co. 2 Pion. Btn. No. 16 1 Res. Co. 20 Pions. 183 (Saxon) Pion. Co. 401 T. M. Co. 183 (Saxon) Tel. Detch.	
Medical and Veterinary.					575 Ambulance Co. 42 Field Hospital. 344 Field Hospital. 228 Vet. Hospital.		575 Ambulance Co. 42 Field Hospital. 344 Field Hospital. 228 Vet. Hospital.	
Transport					603 M. T. Col.		603 M. T. Col.	

[1] Composition at the time of dissolution October, 1918.

HISTORY.

(184th Regiment: 4th Corps District—Prussian Saxony. 418th Regiment: 18th Corps District—Grand Duchy of Hesse. 440th Reserve Regiment: 10th Corps District—Hanover and Grand Duchy of Oldenberg.)

1915.

The 183d Division (known as the 183d Brigade until June, 1916) was created at Cambrai in May, 1915. It comprised at that time the 183d Infantry (Saxon) and the 184th Infantry (Prussian), to which there was added in July, 1915, the 122d Reserve Regiment (Wurttemberg), three newly formed regiments, the 184th being organized out of companies taken from various regiments of the 7th and 8th Divisions. In November, 1916, the 183d Division was modified. Two of its original regiments (the 183d and the 122d Reserve) were respectively replaced by the newly formed 418th and 440th Reserve—the 418th Regiment being formed from companies of the 111th Division, the Ersatz Division of the Guard, the 8th Ersatz Division, and the 10th Ersatz Division, and the 440th Reserve Regiment being organized out of various elements, including the 3d Battalion of the 79th Reserve Regiment and the 4th Battalion of the 75th Landwehr.

AISNE.

1. In June, 1915, the 183d Brigade occupied the Missy sur Aisne sector (east of Soissons).

2. At the end of June it was engaged at Quenneviéres.

LORRAINE.

3. Transferred to Lorraine (end of July), it stayed there until the end of September (region of Benestroff).

CHAMPAGNE.

4. It was brought to the Champagne front (between Prunay and Souain) about September 23 and opposed the French offensive (September–October). The 184th Infantry was nearly wiped out on September 25, the 183d losing a very large number of prisoners.

5. Relieved from the front in November, the brigade was put at rest in the vicinity of Charleroi.

1916.

1. In January, 1916, the division was in reserve in the vicinity of Machault.

CHAMPAGNE.

2. From February to May it was on the Champagne front near the Souain-Somme Py road.

3. June; at rest (region of Tournai). At the end of June the 183d Brigade became the 183d Division by changing the 183d Field Artillery Detatchment into a regiment.

SOMME.

4. On July 2 it was brought to the north of the Somme and engaged in the vicinity of Pozières–Contalmaisou until July 24. It suffered very heavy losses here—from the 10th to the 15th the 184th Infantry lost about 2,000 men.

5. About July 25 it was withdrawn from the front and reorganized. (It received 2,000 replacements, mostly men from the 1916 and 1917 classes.)

ARTOIS.

6. From the end of July to September 21: Neuville–St. Vaast sector (north of Arras).

SOMME.

7. From the beginning of October to the 21st it went into its second engagement on the Somme (Belloy–Deniécourt sector) and was again sorely tried.

CÔTES DE MEUSE.

8. November 15 to February, 1917, Côtes de Meuse (Lamorville–Spada sector.) In November the 183d Division was reorganized and became entirely Prussian (present composition)

1917.

1. From the middle of February to the beginning of April, 1917, it was at rest in the region of Conflans, then in the vicinity of Anizy le Château.

CHEMIN DES DAMES.

2. At the beginning of April the 183d Division came to strengthen the Chavonne–Soupir–Braye en Laonnois sector. While opposing the French attack of April 16 it suffered very heavy losses (2,100 prisoners), and while fighting fell back to the Chemin des Dames (April 18–21). As a result of the losses on the 16th the companies of the 184th Regiment were reduced to 25 to 30 men.

3. The division was relieved on April 21. In May the 184th Regiment received 1,500 replacements from the 4th Corps District, half of which belong to the class of 1918.

ALSACE.

4. From May 11 to June 24 it held the Aspach–Rhone to Rhine Canal sector.

5. From the end of June to July 31 it was at rest, successively to the south of Colmar (15 days), near Friberg, and to the south of Longuyon (Pierrepont).

6. It entrained at Longuyon for Belgium (July 31) and detrained at Roulers the 1st and 2d of August.

FLANDERS.

7. On August 15 the division was engaged near St. Julien (southwest of Poelcappelle) until August 20.

CAMBRAI.

8. After a short rest in the region of Cambrai it took over the Vendhuile–Hargicourt sector, to the west of Catelet, on September 9. On November 20 part of the 440th Reserve Regiment was sent as a reenforcement to the south of Cambrai (Masnières); later the entire 183d Division was transferred to the northeast of Vendhuile to cover the flank of the German attack executed on November 30.

RECRUITING.

The 183d was more homogeneous than it seemed at first glance. The recruits of the 9th and 10th Corps District were often mixed and the 418th and 440th Regiments have many men from the same Provinces. Also the 184th received in the main men from that portion of the 4th Corps District which adjoined the 10th Corps District (Harz section).

VALUE—1917 ESTIMATE.

During the French attack of April 16, 1917, the division as a whole showed up well. The 418th and the 440th Reserve gave proof of vigor and courage and only gave way under continual pressure of the opposing troops.

It seemed that the German Command wished to reward the division for this resistance by giving Gen. von Schuessler, commanding the 183d Division, the Ordre pour le Mérite.

The 183d Division was sorely tried in the course of these attacks and had to be entirely reorganized.

1918.

BATTLE OF PICARDY.

1. The division held the Vendhülle sector until February 2, when it was relieved by the 79th Reserve Division. It returned to this part of the line on February 25, relieving the 79th Reserve Division. It took part in the attack of March 21, advancing by Epehy (21st), Manancourt (23d), to Bazentin (25th). It retired to rest at Contalmaison.

ALBERT.

2. The division received drafts in early April. On the 16th it came into line north of Albert and held there for four weeks. On the 13th of May it was relieved by the 243d Division.

3. On the 19th the division was engaged at Ville sur Ancre, but after four days in line it was relieved and sent to a quiet sector.

WOEVRE.

4. On June 22 the division took over the Regnieville sector, which it held until July 14 without event. It was relieved by the 77th Reserve Division on that date.

5. It entrained at Thiaucourt on July 16 and traveled via Montmedy–Sedan–Charleville–Charleroi–Mons–Valenciennes and detrained near Cambrai on the night of July 17–18. From there it marched to Ypres, rested there for six days, and on the 25th relieved the 26th Reserve Division in the Hebuterne sector.

BATTLE OF THE SOMME.

6. The division was struck by the British offensive in August, and before it was withdrawn near Irles on August 24 it had suffered heavy casualties, including the loss of 1,400 prisoners.

7. It marched to Cambrai, where it remained three days. On the 28th it was marched to Douai and entrained for Lille, from where it marched to Templemars. On the night of September 3–4 it relieved the 18th Reserve Division north of the La Bassee Canal.

8. The division was engaged in the La Bassee sector until September 10. Immediately after it was withdrawn from line the division was dissolved. The 440th Reserve Regiment was sent as a draft to the 11th Division. The other two regiments of the division were also disbanded and used as drafts.

VALUE—1918 ESTIMATE.

The division was rated as second class. It was used as an assault division in the March offensive but thereafter deteriorated. It was next seriously employed on the Somme in August, where its tremendous losses robbed it of further utility.

185th Division.

COMPOSITION.

	1915		1916		1917		1918	
	Brigade.	Regiment.	Brigade.	Regiment.	Brigade.	Regiment.	Brigade.	Regiment.
Infantry	185.	185, 186, 190.	185.	185, 186, 190.	29.	65, 161, 28.	29.	65, 161, 28 Res.
Cavalry					3 Sqn. 5 Mounted Jäg. Rgt. (?)		3 Sqn. 5 Mounted Jäg. Rgt.	
Artillery	185 F. A. Abt. (3 Btries.).		185 F. A. Abt.		(?)Art. Command: 185 F. A. Rgt. (9. Btries.).		185 F. A. Rgt. 2 Abt. 16 Res. Ft. A. Rgt. 838 Light Am. Col. 1281 Light Am. Col. 1348 Light Am. Col.	
Engineers and Liaisons.	185 Pion. Co.		185 Pion. Co. 186 Pion. Co. (dissolved in Aug.). 190 T. M. Co.		(185) Pion. Btn. 10 Co. 28 Pions. 185 Pion. Co. 402 T. M. Co. 185 Searchlight Section. 185 Tel. Detch.		185 Pion. Btn.: 10 Co. 28 Pions. 185 Pion. Co. 89 Searchlight Section. 185 Signal Command: 185 Tel. Detch. 134 Res. Wireless Detch.	
Medical and Veterinary.					576 Ambulance Co. 7 Field Hospital. 65 Field Hospital. 267 Field Hospital. Vet. Hospital.		576 Ambulance Co. 65 Field Hospital. 267 Field Hospital. 385 Vet. Hospital.	
Transport.					M. T. Col.			

HISTORY.

(65th and 161st Regiments: 8th Corps District—Rhenish Province. 28th Reserve Regiment: 8th Corps District—Rhenish Province.)

1915.

The division was created in May, 1915. Merely a brigade (the 185th) at the outset, it was composed of the 185th Infantry (from various Baden regiments), of the 186th Regiment (Hessian elements), and of the 190th Regiment (Westphalian elements). Later the 185th Brigade underwent changes which entirely changed its original composition.

HÉBUTERNE.

1. In June, 1915, the 185th and 186th Infantry Regiments were engaged in the vicinity of Hébuterne.

2. The three regiments of the 185th Brigade entrained at Douai at the end of July and were transferred to Alsace.

ALSACE.

3. At first it was in reserve in the region of Mulhouse; later it was put in line between Altkirch and the Swiss frontier, where it stayed until the end of September.

CHAMPAGNE.

4. At the beginning of October it was in Champagne holding the sector west of the Souain–Somme Py road.

1916.

1. The 185th Brigade stayed on the Champagne front (Tahure) until the middle of June, 1916.

SOMME.

2. At the beginning of July it opposed the Franco-British offensive in the Somme at the northeast of Fricourt, near Thiepval, Contalmaison, and Bazentin (beginning of July to the 18th). It suffered serious losses.

3. At the end of July it rested at St. Quentin, Vermand and Cateau. At this time the 185th Brigade became the 185th Division by the transformation of its field artillery detachment into a regiment.

OISE–AISNE.

4. In August it held a sector to the west of Soissons (from the Oise to Chevillecourt). The 185th Division was reorganized by the transfer of its three infantry regiments which were replaced by the 65th and the 161st Infantry from the 15th Division and by the 28th Reserve Regiment from the 16th Reserve Division—both Rhenish divisions.

SOMME.

5. The 185th, thus reorganized, was brought back to the Somme about September 7. It was engaged near Ginchy and Combles until the middle of October.

6. After a short stay north of Soissons (end of October to the beginning of November) it came back for a third time in the Somme district (Saillise, night of Nov. 10-11). Here it was again put to a test.

7. It left the Somme on December 9 and rested in Belgium (Alost).

1917.

1. At the beginning of January elements of the division were in line to the south of Grenier wood (region of Lille).

FLANDERS.

2. The division occupied a sector north of Ypres (Wieltje) from the beginning of February to April 15.

ARTOIS.

3. About April 20 it was engaged in front of Arras (to the north of the Scarpe until the beginning of May). Losses sustained obliged it to have recourse to a distant source for replacements: the Ersatz Truppe of Warsaw (class of 1918 and men put back of the 1917 class), which reenforcements arrived at top speed on May 5.

LA BASÉE.

4. The division held the La Basée sector (Hulluch–Vermelles) from the end of May to September 21.

5. In October it was at rest for three weeks in the vicinity of Carvin.

FLANDERS–CAMBRAI.

6. Transferred to Belgium (Oct. 28) it took over a sector to the west of Houthulst Forest (Nov. 6–7). In December it was on the Cambrai front (until about Jan. 10, 1918).

RECRUITING.

Since August, 1916, the division had been entirely composed of regiments coming from the Rhine Province (8th Corps District) and as such is entirely homogeneous.

VALUE—1917 ESTIMATE.

The 185th Division gave good account of itself in all the battles in which it took part.

1918.

1. The 185th Division was withdrawn from the Cambrai front near Gonnelieu, being relieved by the 9th Reserve Division during the night of January 11–12. It went to the Solesmes area, where it was trained with a view of being used in offensive operations.

ARRAS.

2. About the middle of February it relieved the 24th Division near Monchy le Preux (southeast of Arras). On the 28th of March it attacked with all three regiments, and suffered heavy losses from enfilade machine-gun fire; officer casualties for the division amounted to 90. It was withdrawn about the 27th of April.

3. It relieved the 26th Reserve Division near Mercatel (southeast of Arras) between the 13th and 16th of May. It was relieved by the 39th Division during the night of August 2–3.

SOMME.

4. On the 18th it reenforced the front near Herleville (south of Bray). It was withdrawn on September 5.

5. On the 18th it reenforced the front near Villeret (northwest of St. Quentin), and was withdrawn on the 1st of October. During these last two engagements the division lost heavily, more than 2,050 in prisoners alone.

6. A week later it reenforced the front near Ligny en Cambresis (west of Le Cateau). It was withdrawn on the 25th.

7. After a fortnight's rest it relieved the 6th Division southwest of Mons on the 8th of November.

VALUE—1918 ESTIMATE.

The 185th was rated as a second-class division. Although trained in open warfare, it was used in only one of the great German offensives, and there did nothing to indicate that it merited a better rating.

187th Division.
COMPOSITION.

	1915 Brigade.	1915 Regiment.	1916 Brigade.	1916 Regiment.	1917 Brigade.	1917 Regiment.	1918 Brigade.	1918 Regiment.
Infantry	187.	187. 188. 189.	187.	187. 188. 189.	187.	187. 188. 189.	187.	187. 188. 189.
Cavalry			5 and 6 Sqns. 16 Dragoon Rgt.		3 Sqn. 16 Dragoon Rgt.		5 Sqn. 16 Dragoon Rgt.	
Artillery	231 F. A. Abt.		231 F. A. Abt. 3 Mountain Art. Abt.		Art. Command: 231 Rgt. (9 Btries.).		6 Art. Command: 231 F. A. Rgt. 66 Ft. A. Btn. 720 Light Am. Col. 1267 Light Am. Col. 1320 Light Am. Col.	
Engineers and liaisons.	187 Pion. Co.		187 Pion. Co. 192 T. M. Co.		(187) Pion. Btn.: 187 Pion. Co. 1 Res. Co. 15 Pions. 187 T. M. Co. Tel. Detch.		187 Pion. Btn.: 1 Res. Co. 15 Pions. 187 Pion. Co. 187 T. M. Co. 60 Searchlight Section. 187 Signal Command: 187 Tel. Detch. 122 Wireless Detch.	
Medical and veterinary.					219 Ambulance Co. 28 Field Hospital. 33 Field Hospital. Vet. Hospital.		219 Ambulance Co. 28 Field Hospital. 33 Field Hospital. 255 Vet. Hospital.	
Transports					M. T. Col.		605 M. T. Col.	
Attached			417 Anti-Aircraft Section					

HISTORY.

(187th Regiment: 9th Corps District—Schleswig-Holstein. 188th Regiment: 4th Corps District—Prussian Saxony. 189th Regiment: 3d Corps District—Brandenburg.)

1915.

The 187th Division (the 187th Brigade until June, 1916) was created May 20, 1915. Its regiments were made up as follows: The 187th, from the 9th Corps District; the 188th, from the 4th Corps District; and the 189th, a Brandenburger unit.

ALSACE.

1. In June, 1915, the 187th Brigade was sent to Alsace and stayed in line in the Fecht valley and the vicinity (Metzeral–Sondernach–Hilsenfirst-Reichackerkopf) until the end of December.

2. It next went to rest in the vicinity of Colmar.

1916.

ALSACE.

1. At the end of January, 1916, it went back in line in the Fecht valley and the region of Guebwiller. It was kept there until the summer, participating in battles for the possession of the heights (Hartmannswillerkopf, Reichackerkopf).

2. At the beginning of July the 187th Brigade became the 187th Division by the transformation of its field artillery detachment into a regiment.

TRANSYLVANIA.

3. Relieved at the end of August from the Muenster, it rested eight days at Rouffach then entrained at Colmar for the Roumanian front. (Itinerary: Karlsruhe–Stuttgart–Ulm–Munich–Vienna–Budapest–Sieben–Buergen.)

ROUMANIA.

4. On September 13 it was engaged in Transylvania (region of Hermannstadt, Tour Rouge passes), then took part in the battle of Brasso (Kronstadt) at the beginning of October and in the operations in the vicinity of Slanic (December). It suffered heavy losses.

1917.

ROUMANIA—FRANCE.

1. On February 11, 1917, the 187th Division left Roumania for the Western Front. (Itinerary: Arad–Budapest–Oppeln–Breslau–Dresden–Wuerzberg–Strassberg.) It was at rest near Dieuze (about six weeks).

LORRAINE.

2. About April 20 it took over the Moncel–Arracourt sector.

AISNE.

3. Hastily relieved on April 28, it entrained at Morhange on May 2 and detrained in the vicinity of Amagne and was put into line on May 10 on the Rheims front (north of Bermericourt; southeast of Berry au Bac) until June 15.

4. At rest in the Aussonce-La Neuville area (end of June to July the 187th Division was held in reserve as a "Stossdivision" or "Eingriffsdivision."

CHAMPAGNE.

5. About July 14 it was engaged in the Cornillet, Mont Blond, Mont Haut sector, which it held until August 26. The 187th Infantry was particularly tried during the attack of July 26.

6. From August 26 to September 29 it was at rest in camps at La Neuville en Tourne à Fuii later in the region of Vervins.

FLANDERS.

7. Transferred to Belgium (Sept. 30), the division opposed the British attack near Poelcappelle. It was partially relieved after the attack and went into line and counter attacked on the 10th to the north of Langemarck. Its losses in this sector were heavy.

8. After a rest to the north of Bruges from the 12th of October to November, it went back to the front near Blankaart (south of Dixmude).

RECRUITING.

The three regiments of this division came from different Provinces—the 187th from Schleswig-Holstein, the 188th from Prussian-Saxony, and the 189th from Brandenburg. This was confirmed by a German communiqué which mentioned "the attack troops from Schleswig-Holstein and Brandenberg" at Mont Haut (July, 1917).

VALUE—1917 ESTIMATE.

The 187th Division was made up of young men who were well trained and who came from active divisions.

The 187th Division was a division equipped for mountain warfare.

1918.

ARMENTIERES.

1. The 187th Division was withdrawn from line south of Lake Blankaart about the 10th of January, and on the 16th relieved the 38th Landwehr Division near Bois Grenier (south of Armentieres). It was relieved by the 6th Bavarian Division about February 20 and went to the Lille area, where it most probably received training in open warfare, though the fact has not been definitely established.

ARRAS.

2. It left there and arrived at Douai on the 25th of March. It spent the night of the 27th–28th in Vitry. On the 28th it reenforced the front near Fampoux (east of Arras) on the 28th, when it attacked. A man of the 188th Regiment subsequently wrote: "We tried to break through on the 28/3/18, but only pushed Tommy back to his reserve line, and don't forget that it was with enormous losses to ourselves." It was relieved by the 2d Guard Reserve Division during the night of May 18–19, and went to rest in the region east of Douai.

3. During the night of June 18–19 it came back and relieved the 2d Guard Reserve Division. It was relieved by the 48th Reserve Division on the 7th of July.

ARMENTIERES.

4. After less than a week's rest, the division came to the Armentieres front and relieved the 39th Division between Neuf–Berquin and Vieux–Berquin (north of Merville). It was relieved early in September by the extension of fronts of the neighboring divisions.

CAMBRAI.

5. On the 7th it reenforced the front in the Inchy en Artois sector (west of Cambrai). After suffering exceedingly heavy losses, it was withdrawn about the 28th and went to rest in the Boushain region.

DOUAI.

6. October 3 it relieved the 15th Reserve Division in the Oppy sector (west of Douai), and was withdrawn about the 20th.

7. On the 27th it reenforced the front in the Chateau l'Abbaye sector (northeast of St. Amand), but was withdrawn a few days later.

VALENCIENNES.

9. It was identified in line near Quievrechain (northeast of Valenciennes) on November 5.

VALUE—1918 ESTIMATE.

The 187th was rated as a second-class division. The only offensive in which it participated was that of the Somme, where it did not distinguish itself. Subsequently it was used only to hold the front. Toward the end of the year it was very much reduced in strength.

192d Division.
COMPOSITION.

	1915 Brigade.	1915 Regiment.	1916 Brigade.	1916 Regiment.	1917 Brigade.	1917 Regiment.	1918 Brigade.	1918 Regiment.
Infantry	192.	192. 193. 25 Bav.	192.	192. 193. 25 Bav.	192.	183. 192. 245 Res.	192.	183. 192. 245 Res.
Cavalry			1 Ldw. Sqn. (12 C. Dist.).		(?. Sqn. 1 Res. Hus. Schutz. Rgt.		1 Sqn. 18 Res. Hus. Rgt.	
Artillery	192 F. A. Abt. (3 Btries.).		192 F. A. Abt.		(?) Art. Command: 192 F. A. Rgt. (9 Btries.).		192 Art. Command: 192 F. A. Rgt. 58 (Saxon) Ft. A. Btn. 830 Light Am. Col. 1150 Light Am. Col. 1162 Light Am. Col.	
Engineers and Liaisons.	192 Pion. Co.		192 Pion. Co. 404 T. M. Co.		(192) Pion Btn.; 4 Co. 22 Pions. 192 Pion. Co. 404 T. M. Co. 192 Searchlight Section. 192 Tel. Detch.		192 Pion. Btn. 4 Co. 22 Pions. 192 (Saxon) Pion. Co. 404 T. M. Co. 129 Searchlight Section. 192 Signal Command: 192 Tel. Detch. 173 Wireless Detch.	
Medical and Veterinary.					29 Ambulance Co. 5 Res. Field Hospital. 23 Ldw. Field Hospital. Vet. Hospital.		29 Ambulance Co. 2 Res. Field Hospital. 3 Res. Field Hospital. 292 Vet. Hospital.	
Transport					M. T. Col.			

HISTORY.

(12th and 19th Corps Districts—Saxony.)

1915.

The 192d Brigade (became the 192d Division in June, 1916) was formed out of regiments created by selection of men from various units. It was formed at the beginning of June, 1915, with the 192d Infantry (Saxon), formed out of elements taken from the 32d Division, the 193d (Westphalian, 7th Corps District), detached after its creation to the 13th Reserve Division, and with the 25th Bavarian Regiment, formerly belonging to the 4th Bavarian Division, the regiments of which had contributed to the formation of this last regiment.

1. Until the month of September, 1915, the three regiments of the brigade occupied different sectors on the Western Front—the 192d near Charency in August, the 193d on the Aisne (region of Chamouille), and the 25th Bavarian near Warneton (Flanders) in July.

CHAMPAGNE.

2. At the end of September the elements of the 192d Brigade were brought together in the rear of the Champagne front. Engaged as a reenforcement against the French offensive (Sept. 27 to the beginning of October) near the Souain–Somme Py road, it suffered heavy losses (50 officers and 3,594 men out of action, according to official lists). The brigade stayed in the Souain sector until the end of November.

3. In December it was at rest in the region of Bignicourt–Machault.

1916.

CHAMPAGNE.

1. At the beginning of January, 1916, the 192d Brigade again took a sector in Champagne (until Jan. 26).

2. From the end of January to the beginning of March it was at rest in the vicinity of Montcornet.

3. From the 4th to the 18th of March the regiments were engaged in making defensive works in the region of Laon.

VERDUN–BOIS D'AVOCOURT.

4. On March 18 the brigade was brought near Vouziers and Stenay, then assembled in the rear of the Verdun front on the left bank of the Meuse (Mar. 22). On the 23d it relieved the 11th Bavarian Division, sorely tried by the attacks on Malancourt and the Bois d'Avocourt. It took part itself in the battles which effected the capture of that wood and suffered heavy losses. From April 13 to May 10 the 11th Company of the 192d Infantry received at least 125 replacements and the 12th Company 116 replacements.

5. The 192d Brigade stayed in the Malancourt–Avocourt wood sector until the end of August, holding it alternately with the 11th Bavarian Division. During this period (May–August) it only took part in local engagements.

6. In June it was changed into a division, its composition remaining unchanged except for the expansion of its field artillery.

FLEURY–DOUAUMONT.

7. On August 22 the new division was relieved and transferred to the right bank of the Meuse (Charency–Longuyon). On the 28th it was engaged in the Fleury–Douaumont sector. Its regiments were sorely tried by the French attacks of September 3 and 9.

8. Relieved from the front at the end of September and beginning of October the division was entirely reorganized. The 193d Infantry went to the 222d Division (being organized) and was replaced by the 418th, newly formed; the 25th Bavarian went to the 14th Bavarian Division and was replaced by the 245th Reserve Regiment of the 54th Reserve Division.

CÔTES DE MEUSE.

9. About the end of October the 418th Regiment, which had been put in line in the Moranville sector (Côtes de Meuse), replaced the 183d Infantry in the 183d Division, the last-named regiment going to the 192d Division, which was now entirely Saxon.

BEZONVAUX.

The 192d Division, having thus acquired its present organization, took a position to the east of Bezonvaux in December.

1917.

VERDUN-BEZONVAUX.

1. It occupied this sector until December, 1917, and during this long period remained entirely passive.

HILL 344.

2. Relieved from this calm sector about December 10, 1917, it immediately went into line north of Hill 344, where it still was in January, 1918.

RECRUITING.

The division was entirely Saxon after the end of 1916.

VALUE—1917 ESTIMATE.

The 192d Division stayed more than a year in a very calm sector (east of Bezonvaux, December 1916, to December, 1917).

In January, 1918, the division might be considered as rested, but its combat value at that time seemed rather mediocre. In the various actions in which it took part on the Verdun front it did not distinguish itself.

1918.

OISE.

1. The division held the sector on the Verdun front until the middle of April, when it was relieved, and on May 19 it relieved the 200th Division southeast of Rouvrel. It was still in line when the Allies attacked on August 8. About August 11 the division was withdrawn.

ST. MIHIEL.

2. The division marched to Origny via Rosieres–Athies–St. Quentin. It left there August 25 and went by train to Chambley via Ribemont–Crecy–Mortiers–Marle–Charleville–Sedan–Montmedy–Longuyon–Metz, arriving on August 26. On the 20th the division entered line in the tip of the St. Mihiel salient.

3. The division extracted itself from the salient and was relieved about September 22, when the line had stabilized. It was moved west and again came into line at Bezonvaux.

MEUSE-ARGONNE.

4. From October 8 until about October 22 the division held the Bezonvaux sector. It was then shifted northward to the area south of Etrayes, where it remained until the armistice.

VALUE—1918 ESTIMATE.

The division was rated as third class. It did well at St. Mihiel, but in its other sectors its conduct was mediocre.

195th Division.

COMPOSITION.

	1916		1917		1918	
	Brigade.	Regiment.	Brigade.	Regiment.	Brigade.	Regiment.
Infantry	101 Res.	6 Jag. 8 Jag. 233 Res.	101 Res.	6 Jag. 8 Jag. 233 Res.	101 Res.	6 Jag. 8 Jag. 14 Jag.
Cavalry			(3 Sqn. 14 Uhlan Rgt.)		2 Sqn. 14 Uhlan Rgt.	
Artillery	260 F. A. Rgt.		Art. Command: 260 F. A. Rgt.		260 F. A. Rgt. 860 Light Am. Col. 873 Light Am. Col. 1282 Light Am. Col.	
Engineers and Liaisons			(195) Pion. Btn.: 1 Co. 32 Res. Pions. 55 Res. Pion. Co. 195 T. M. Co. 195 Tel. Detch.		195 Pion. Btn.: 1 Co. 32 Res. Pions. 55 Res. Pion. Co. 102 Searchlight Section. 195 Signal Command: 195 Tel. Detch. 66 Wireless Detch.	
Medical and Veterinary			207 Ambulance Co. 22 Field Hospital. 347 Field Hospital.		207 Ambulance Co. 22 Field Hospital. 347 Field Hospital. 231 Vet. Hospital.	
Transport			860 M. T. Col.		607 M. T. Col.	
Attached	64 (?) M. G. S. S. Detch.					

HISTORY.

(6th and 8th Jägers: Various sections of Prussia. 233d Reserve Regiment: 11th Corps District—Thuringen.)

1916.

1. The division was organized in July, 1916, in the Ruddervoorde region with the following elements: (1) 233d Reserve Regiment, obtained from the 51st Reserve Division; (2) the 6th Jägers (5th and 6th Battalions of Jägers, 14th Battalion of Jägers—the last after arriving on the Russian front was thereafter replaced by the 2d Reserve Battalion of Jägers); (3) 8th Jägers (4th, 16th, and 24th Battalions of Reserve Jägers).

GALICIA.

2. It was shortly thereafter transferred to Galicia.

3. The division took part in the open warfare of August, 1916.

4. It next went into line with Austrian troops in the Zloczow sector.

1917.

FRANCE.

1. It was transferred to the Western Front at the end of April, 1917. (Itinerary: Leniky–Cracovie–Oppeln–Breslau–Leipzig–Halle–Paderborn–Essen–Duesseldorf– Aix la Chapelle–Verviers–Liége–Louvain–Brussels–Cambrai.)

2. The division was successively in line in the Ypres sector (May), in the Wytschaete sector (June–July), and in the St. Quentin sector (August).

3. During the month of August it rested in the Walincourt region.

FLANDERS.

4. From October 3 to 12 it fought in the Passchendaele sector. It sustained heavy losses (more than 600 prisoners).

5. Relieved on October 12 the division was reorganized at Meulebecke from the 14th to the 18th and was transferred by rail to Gand. At the time it was relieved the 233d Reserve was reduced to 800 men (story of deserter).

6. On about the 21st it entrained at Heydinge and was brought via Brussels–Namur–Dinant–Givet–Charleville–Sedan–Montmedy and Conflans to Haye, where it detrained on the 23d.

HAYE.

7. On October 28 it took over a sector to the southwest of Thiaucourt (Flirey).

ITALY.

8. On November 11 the division was entrained at Metz for Italy. It detrained at Trente on November 14, where it rested until the 24th. It left Trente on December 3 without having participated in any engagement. (Itinerary: Trente–Innsbruck–Munich–Carlsruhe–Offenberg–Friberg–Mulhouse.)

ALSACE.

9. Arriving on December 6, it was billeted in the region of Sundgau, where it stayed until February, 1918.

RECRUITING.

The division was very heterogeneous. The 233d came from Thuringen (11th Corps District). The various jaeger regiments came from various depot jaeger battalions (2d, 4th, 5th, 6th, and 11th Corps Districts).

VALUE—1917 ESTIMATE.

The 195th Division was sorely tried in Flanders in October, 1917. In November, 1917, the greater part of its strength came from the classes called during the war. The average age was 25. It can be classed as a good division.

1918.

CAMBRAI.

1. The 195th Division left Alsace, where it had been resting since its return from Italy, the 5th and 6th of February, and proceeded to Valenciennes. On the 27th a prisoner was captured near Bullecourt (northeast of Bapaume), who stated that his battalion had relieved another battalion of the same regiment during the night of the 25th–26th. The 195th Division had probably relieved the 16th Bavarian Division some days before. It was relieved by the 16th Bavarian Division on the 2d of March. It was very probably trained in open warfare, but the fact has not been definitely established.

2. On the 21st it came back reenforcing the front near Noreuil (northeast of Bapaume). The heavy fighting on this front did not come in the first days of the offensive but a few days later the division was heavily engaged, especially on the 28th and 31st near Bucquoy. This represented an advance of only a few kilometers gained at the cost of heavy losses in many attacks. It was relieved by the 17th Division during the night of April 1–2.

3. On the 9th it relieved the 16th Bavarian Division in the Ayette sector (northwest of Bapaume). It remained here fighting hard until relieved by the 5th Bavarian Reserve Division about the 24th. In this fighting the losses were very heavy, especially in the 233d Reserve Regiment (the commander of which was awarded Pour le Merite) which was dissolved soon after; its place was taken by the 14th Jaeger Regiment. It was sent to the Cambrai region to rest and refit.

MARNE.

4. The first day of the battle of the Marne—July 15—it reenforced the front near Chatillon sur Marne (northwest of Epernay). It was withdrawn early in August and went to rest near Metz.

ST. MIHIEL.

5. On the 14th of September, after the line reached by the American First Army had stabilized, the division entered line in the Haumont sector (northeast of St. Mihiel). It was not heavily engaged and was withdrawn about the 28th.

MEUSE-ARGONNE.

6. The division then moved to the Champagne front, where it reenforced the front in the St. Etienne à Arnes sector (south of Machault) on the 6th of October. It was opposed by French troops until the 24th; after that it was opposite the Americans on account of a readjustment of sectors. It was withdrawn on the 29th.

7. On the 2d of November it was thrown back into line near Verrieres (northwest of Buzancy). Its losses were so heavy in this fighting, and the division was in such a state of exhaustion, that although the division was still in line on the 11th there were rumors that it was soon to be dissolved.

VALUE—1918 ESTIMATE.

The 195th was rated a second-class division. Its conduct whenever heavily engaged was such as to lead to the conclusion that it was one of the better divisions of that class.

197th Division.

COMPOSITION.

	1916		1917		1918	
	Brigade.	Regiment.	Brigade.	Regiment.	Brigade.	Regiment.
Infantry	210	273 Res. 7 Jag. (Saxon). 32 Ldw.	210	273 Res. 7 Jag. 32 Ldw.	210	273 Res. 7 Jag. (Saxon). 28 Ers.
Cavalry	2 Sqn. 14 Uhlan Rgt.		2 Sqn. 14 Uhlan Rgt.		2 Sqn. 14 Uhlan Rgt.	
Artillery		261 F. A. Rgt. .... 262 F. A. Abt. (Saxon).	(?) Art. Command: 261 F. A. Rgt.		(?) Art. Command: 261 F. A. Rgt.	
Engineers and Liaisons	170 T. M. Co.		197 Pion. Btn.: 90 Res. Pion. Co. 2 Co. 32 Res. Pions. 415 T. M. Co. 195 Tel. Detch.		197 Pion. Btn.: 90 Res. Pion. Co. 2 Co. 32 Res. Pions. 300 Searchlight Section. 426 T. M. Co. 197 Tel. Detch.	
Medical and Veterinary			208 Ambulance Co. 284 Field Hospital. 532 Field Hospital. Vet. Hospital.		208 Ambulance Co. 284 Field Hospital. 532 Field Hospital. Vet. Hospital.	
Transport			1053 M. T. Col.		M. T. Col.	

¹ Composition at the time of dissolution Nov. 1, 1918.

HISTORY.

(273 Reserve Regiment; 10th Corps District—Hanover and Brunswick. 7th Jaeger; 12th and 19th Corps Districts—Saxony. 28th Ersatz; 14th Corps District—Grand Duchy of Baden.)

1916.

The 197th Division was created in August, 1916, on the Eastern Front by the union of the following regiments: (1) 273d Reserve Regiment, formed out of four battallions taken from the 362d Infantry (4th Ersatz Division); the 368th Infantry (10th Ersatz Division); the 130th Reserve (33d Reserve) Division) which all came from France. (2) 7th Jaegers (13th Battalion of Jaegers, 25th and 26th Battalions of Reserve Jaegers, all Saxon, and also all coming from France. (3) The 32d Landwehr, which had been under orders of the 33d Division in the Argonne.

GALICIA.

1. As part of the 2d Austrian Army (Boehm-Ermoli), the 197th Division occupied in August 1916 the Zborow sector (northwest of Tarnopol) where it met the offensive carried on by Broussilov. On August 10 the 7th Regiment of Jaegers had 35 officers and 1,039 men out of action (letter).

2. In September it was in line to the northeast of Zalosce and to the north of Zborow and later in the vicinity of Zloczow.

1917.

GALICIA.

1. The 197th Division stayed in this same Zloczow sector until July, 1917. While there it met the Russian attack of July 1, which reduced the strength of the 1st Battalion of the 32d Landwehr to 160 men (letter).

2. The division participated in the German counteroffensive of July 19 and advanced by way of Zborow up to Husjatin (August), where it was relieved to go into reserve.

3. It went back into line at the beginning of September at Hlesczawa (region of Trembowla).

4. At the beginning of November the 32d Landwehr was replaced by the 28th Ersatz, taken from the Bavarian Ersatz Division, and originally from the 14th Corps District (Grand Duchy of Baden). This replacement of a mediocre regiment for a good one was the prelude of preparations for a transfer to the Western Front.

RECRUITING.

This division had a composite make-up. The 7th Jaegers was Saxon; the 28th Ersatz was from Baden; and the 273d was formed from battalions coming from the 7th, 9th, and 10th Corps District and got its replacements in theory from the 10th Corps District.

VALUE—1917 ESTIMATE.

The 197th Division, coming from Galicia, appeared for the first time on the Western Front in March, 1918. All th emaneuvers executed iu the rear and at rest in Galicia tended to accustom the units to defensive warfare methods (Verteidigungskrieg). (Interrogation of a prisoner of the 273d Reserve on Mar. 13, 1918.)

This was also true of its stay in the Marchais region (February 1918).

1918.

CHATEAU THIERRY.

The division held the quiet Chemin des Dames sector until the Aisne offensive of May 27. Attack divisions passed through the 197th Division, which followed up the attack in close reserve and was engaged on May 31 northwest of Chateau Thierry. It came in for some heavy local fighting while opposite the 2d United States Division near Veuilly before it was relieved on June 8.

Verdun.

2. It was moved to Eastern Champagne, and on June 23 relieved the 15th Bavarian Division in the Ornes sector. During July the division received drafts. It held this sector without loss until about the 1st of August.

St. Quentin-Oise.

3. On August 15 the division reenforced the front at Ribecourt. Until September 10 it was constantly engaged in the Noyon fighting. After resting nine days the division returned to line north of Gricourt, and until October 19 resisted every foot of the way to Seboncourt.

4. After the withdrawal from line the division was broken up. The 273d Reserve Regiment and the 28th Ersatz Regiment were disbanded, while the 7th Jaeger Regiment passed intact to the 241st Division.

VALUE—1918 ESTIMATE.

The division was rated as third class. It was heavily engaged on an active front for two months in 1918 during which fighting it suffered so heavily in casualties and morale that it was dissolved in late October.

125651°—20——41

199th Division.

COMPOSITION.

	1916		1917		1918	
	Brigade.	Regiment.	Brigade.	Regiment.	Brigade.	Regiment.
Infantry..........		237 Res. 4 Bav. Res. 9 Jäg.	59 Ldw.	114. 357. 237 Res.	59 Ldw.	114. 357. 237 Res.
Cavalry............	1 Sqn. 14 Uhlan Rgt.		1 Sqn. 14 Uhlan Rgt.		1 Sqn. 14 Uhlan Rgt.	
Artillery.........	263 F. A. Rgt.		Art. Command: 263 F. A. Rgt.		263 F. A. Rgt. 3 Abt. 2 Bav. Ft. A. Rgt. 927 Light Am. Col. 1240 Light Am. Col. 1241 Light Am. Col.	
Engineers and Liaisons...			(199) Pion. Btn.: 199 T. M. Co. 330 Searchlight Section. 199 Tel. Detch.		199 Pion. Btn.: 6 Co. 23 Pions. 286 Pion. Co. 199 T. M. Co. 38 Searchlight Section. 199 Signal Command: 199 Tel. Detch. 10 Wireless Detch.	
Medical and Veterinary...			209 Ambulance Co. Field Hospital. Vet. Hospital.		209 Ambulance Co. 68 Field Hospital. 339 Field Hospital. 244 Vet. Hospital.	
Transport.........			M. T. Col.		609 M. T. Col.	

HISTORY.

(114th Regiment: 14th Corps District—Southern part of the Grand Duchy of Baden. 357th Regiment: 2d Corps District—Pomerania. 237th Reserve Regiment: 8th Corps District—Rhine Province.)

1916.

The 199th Division was created in August, 1916, in the region of Stryj–Halicz (Galicia), with troops coming from the Western Front. Until the beginning of 1917 its infantry was made up as follows: The 237th Reserve Regiment (coming from the 52d Reserve Division), the 4th Bavarian Reserve Regiment (from the Bavarian Ersatz Division), and the 9th Jaegers (12th and 13th Battalions of Reserve Jaegers (Saxon) and the 8th Battalion of Jaegers).

GALICIA.

1. From the end of August to the beginning of November the 199th Division was engaged in Galicia (Brzezany, Halicz, Zlota-Lipa) and suffered heavy losses.

2. About November 1 the division was transferred to the Western Front. (Itinerary: Lemberg–Cracaw–Breslau–Dresden–Leipzig–Coblenz–Treves–Sedan.) It detrained at Dun and was billeted for three weeks in the vicinity of Spincourt.

SOMME.

3. Sent to the Champagne district at the end of November and then in the Bohain region, it went into line in the Rancourt–Saillizel sector (end of December).

1917.

1. At the beginning of 1917 the 114th and 357th replaced the 4th Reserve and the 9th Jaegers.

SOMME.

2. The 199th Division stayed on the Rancourt front until March, 1917.

HINDENBERG LINE.

3. On March 27 it was identified to the east of Longavesnes; then at Villers–Faucon, Lempire, in the new German positions (April).

ARTOIS.

4. Relieved about April 20, it was engaged to the southeast of Arras (Wancourt–Vis en Artois–Cherisy) and suffered heavy losses (April 27, May 3).

5. Coming back to the west of Catelet (Hargicourt–Bony) about the middle of May, it left this line on June 8 to go to rest in the vicinity of Ostend.

BELGIAN FLANDERS.

6. In the middle of July it took over the Nieuport–Lombartzyde sector, which it occupied until the beginning of August and was at rest near Ostend from August 10 to the middle of September.

7. It reappeared in the Lombartzyde sector until October 24. On November 10 after a short rest it was put in line to the north of Passchendaele, where it was found, with the exception of some brief withdrawals for rest, until February, 1918, when it went to rest near Courtrai.

RECRUITING.

Division with composite elements; a regiment from Baden (the 114th, active), a regiment from Pomerania (the 357th, growing out of brigade Ersatz Battalions), and a Rhenish regiment (the 237th).

VALUE—1917 ESTIMATE.

The 114th was considered the best in the division. The 237th Reserve did not seem to have a very good combat value. It did not hold its ground when opposed by the British at Chérisy (April, 1917). It is said that a company of this regiment refused to come out of the trenches in the month of July, 1917.

1918.

BATTLE OF PICARDY.

1. The division left Flanders at the end of February and trained in the Le Quesnoy area until the middle of March; left on the 17th for the battle front. It marched to Escaromain, and on the 18th to Quievy. On the day before the offensive the division marched via Caudry to Villers Outreaux. It was not identified in the fight until the 25th at Hardecourt. The next day it was at Maricourt wood, after which it appears to have been withdrawn. On April 4 it relieved the 243d Division south of Thennes.

2. After its relief the division marched by stages via Beaucourt en Santerre-Vauvillers-Peronne to Templeux, la Fosse, where it rested for a fortnight. The heavy losses incurred by the division during its last time in line south of the Somme were made good chiefly by drafts of the 1919 class from the depots at Warsaw and Bruges. The division contained a large proportion of this class and its fighting quality suffered in consequence. On the 26th of April the division moved to Maurepas and proceeded to Maricourt on the 28th; from there it marched into line in the Morlancourt sector.

3. The division held the Morlancourt sector from about May 1 to 16. It was relieved by the 107th Division and rested in the Valenciennes area in June.

CHAMPAGNE.

4. It was engaged at Le Teton on July 15 and held a sector in that area until the end of the month.

RHEIMS.

5. On August 3 it reenforced the battle front at Sapicourt west of Rheims. It was engaged in that area except for a week's rest until the end of September.

6. After October 1 the division was engaged in Champagne in the region of Orfeuil. It contested hotly the advance through Vaudy and Vouziers until its relief in late October. It rested but a few days out of line and after November 3 was engaged at St. Lambert, Roix-Terron, and Dom le Mesnil (Nov. 10).

VALUE—1918 ESTIMATE.

The division was rated as second-class. It was used as an attack division in March and did well. Thereafter it saw almost constant service in resisting allied pushes. In October's fighting it was frequently spoken of by the German official communique.

200th Division.
COMPOSITION.

	1916 Brigade	1916 Regiment	1917 Brigade	1917 Regiment	1918 Brigade	1918 Regiment
Infantry	2 Jag.	3 Jag. (4 Btns.)., 4 Jag., 5 Jag.	2 Jag.	3 Jag. (4 Btns.)., 4 Jag., 5 Jag.	2 Jag.	3 Jag., 4 Jag., 5 Jag.
Cavalry				1 Sqn. 1 Uhlan Rgt. (passed to 228 Div. in June, 1917). 2 Sqn. 2 Uhlan Rgt.	2 Sqn. 1 Uhlan Rgt.	
Artillery		257 F. A. Rgt. 2 Mountain Art. Abt. (Bavarian).	(?) Art. command: 257 F. A. Rgt. 7 Mountain Art. Abt.		22 F. A. Rgt. 1 Abt. 26 Ft. A. Rgt. (1 and 3 Btries.). 843 Light Am. Col. 1157 Light Am. Col. 1161 Light Am. Col.	
Engineers and Liaisons			(220) Pion. Btn.: 105 Pion. Co. 282 Pion. Co. 173 Mountain T. M. Co. 200 Tel. Detch.		42 Pion. Btn.: 105 Pion. Co. 282 Pion. Co. 173 T. M. Co. 99 Searchlight Section. 200 Signal Command: 200 Tel. Detch. 50 Wireless Detch.	
Medical and Veterinary			214 Ambulance Co. 44 Field Hospital. 370 Field Hospital. Vet. Hospital.		214 Ambulance Co. 44 Field Hospital. 19 Bav. Field Hospital. 300 Vet. Hospital.	
Transport				M. T. Col.		
Attached		35 Landst. Inf. Rgt. 37 Landst. Inf. Rgt.				

HISTORY.

1916.

CARPATHIAN MOUNTAINS.

1. The 200th Division, composed of three regiments of Jaegers, was formed in July, 1916, in Galicia with the 3rd Jaeger Regiment (4 batallions equipped with skiis) coming from the Alpine Corps, with the 4th Jaegers (11th Battalion of Jaegers, 5th and 6th Battalions of Reserve Jaegers, and with the 5th Jaegers (17th, 18th, and 23d Battalions of Reserve Jaegers).

BUKOVINA.

The 200th Division, together with the 1st Division, formed the Carpathian Corps. The division took part in the counteroffensive in the Carpathians against the Russians and beginning in September 1, 1916, occupied a sector to the north of Mont Tomnatik (Bukovina.)

1917.

BUKOVINA.

1. The 200th Division stayed in the same part of the Carpathians (south of Mt. Pnevié-Mt. Tomnatik) until July, 1917. At this time it took part in the offensive waged in Bukovina and took a position north of the Sereth. It was kept here until September.

2. At the end of September the 200th Division was entrained for Italy. Its itinerary to Vienna was Kolomea-Lemberg-Cracaw.

ITALY.

3. Detraining in the vicinity of Laibach, it went toward the Italian frontier, where it took about 15 days' rest. On October 22 it drew near the Italian frontier and on the 24th was engaged in the offensive on the Isonzo and advanced by way of Cividale and Udine, where it fought the Italian rear guards (Oct. 28-30). It reached Codroipo about November 3 and Quero on the Piave the 23d.

MONT TOMBA.

4. After a short period of rest it was again sent to the Mont Tomba region in December.

RECRUITING.

The 200th Division had recruits from the various mountainous districts of the empire—Upper Silesia, Harz, Black Forest, etc.—which gave it a certain character in spite of the different sources of its recruiting.

VALUE—1917 ESTIMATE.

Composed of young and vigorous men with high morale, the 200th was one of the best divisions in the German Army (1918).

1918.

FRANCE.

1. After having suffered heavy losses, the 200th Division was withdrawn about the 1st of January, and went to rest for about a month southeast of Bellune. Early in February, it entrained at Santa Lucia and traveled via Rosenheim-Munich-Ulm-Freiburg-Colmar. It detrained at Bening and went to rest and to be trained for about three weeks in the vicinity of St. Avold.

MONTDIDIER.

2. The division entrained near Marsal (southwest of Dieuze) on the 26th of March and, traveling via Thionville-Luxemburg-Namur, detrained at Cambrai two days later. It rested in the caserne here until the 31st, when it marched to Peronne, where it remained in the English barracks the 2d and 3d of April, when it marched via Guillaucourt to Moreuil (northwest of Montdidier). During the night of the 7th-8th it relieved the 14th Division west of Moreuil. It was relieved on May 14 by

the 192d Division. It was reported near Quesnoy the end of May and in the Le Cateau region early in June. Men of one of its regiments were reported as having been seen near Fere en Tardenois on the 3d of June. Again, parts of the division were reported near Caudry and Chateau Thierry during June.

MARNE.

3. On the 15th of July the division attacked west of Dormans. It crossed the Marne at Sailly, and was identified at Chapelle Monthod on the following day. In this fighting, the division suffered very heavy losses. The colonel and all the battalion commanders of the 3rd Jaeger Regiment were lost. It was withdrawn from line on the 21st.

4. During the night of the 26th–27th it came back into line near Roncheres (north of Dormans), its mission being to cover the retreat between Sergy and the Meuniere wood. It was withdrawn about the 3d of August and went to the Sedan area, where it rested for a fortnight.

5. During the night of the 22d–23d the division relieved the 22d Reserve Division northwest of Souain. In the heavy fighting that followed the division lost heavily. It was driven back to St. Etienne à Arnes, where it was relieved by the 195th Division on the 6th of October.

WASSIGNY.

6. The division then moved by easy stages, with frequent halts, via Rozoy-Montcornet–Origny–Escaupont–Le Nouvion–Beaurepaire–Barzy. During the night of October 22–23 it relieved the 5th Reserve Division near Oisy (east of Wassigny). It had not been withdrawn on the 11th of November. •

VALUE—1918 ESTIMATE.

The 200th was rated as a second-class division. Composed of Jaeger units, which are good fighters, it distinguished itself in the East and in Italy, and did well in the heavy fighting it was called upon to do on the Western Front, though not brilliantly. It was one of the best of the second-class divisions.

201st Division.
COMPOSITION.

	1916		1917		1918[1]	
	Brigade.	Regiment.	Brigade.	Regiment.	Brigade.	Regiment.
Infantry	401. 402.	401. 402. 403. 404.	402.	401. 402. 403.	402.	401. 402. 403.
Cavalry			4 Sqn. 4 Mounted Jag. Rgt. (?). 4 Sqn. 7 Drag. Rgt. (?).		4 Sqn. 7 Drag. Rgt.	
Artillery	401 F. A. Abt. 402 F. A. Rgt.		Art. Command: 401 F. A. Rgt.		156 Art. Command: 402 F. A. Rgt.	
Engineers and Liaisons	401 Pion. Co.		(201) Pion. Btn.: 385 Pion. Co. 401 Pion. Co. 181 T. M. Co. 50 Searchlight Section. 201 Tel. Detch.		201 Pion. Btn.: 385 Pion. Co. 401 Pion. Co. 358 Pion. Co. 2 Res. Co. 7 Pions. 50 Searchlight Section. 181 T. M. Co. 201 Tel. Detch.	
Medical and Veterinary			401 Ambulance Co. 401 Field Hospital. 402 Field Hospital. 66 Res. Field Hospital. Vet. Hospital.		401 Ambulance Co. 401 Field Hospital. 402 Field Hospital. 66 Res. Field Hospital. Vet. Hospital.	
Transport			863 M. T. Col.		611 M. T. Col.	
Odd Units			201 Cyclist Co.		201 Cyclist Co.	

[1] Composition at the time of dissolution, November, 1918.

HISTORY.

(401st Regiment; 20th Corps District. 402d Regiment; 17th Corps District. 403d Regiment, 5th Corps District.)

1916.

The 201st is one of a series of divisions (numbered 201–204) created at the beginning of July, 1916, at the time of the Russian offensive conducted by Broussilov.

The 201st Division was formed out of recruits obtained from depots in the 5th, 17th and 20th Corps Districts. The Allenstein (401st) Regiment and the Danzig (402d) Regiment came from the Arys cantonment. The Glogau (403d) Regiment and the Posen (404th) came from the Warthe cantonment. Men taken from the front, convalescents from depots and a majority of young men from the class of 1917 made up the initial strength, which was 230 to 240 men per company.

RUSSIA.

1. As soon as formed the division occupied a sector on the Russian front (north of Baranovitchi) and stayed there from the beginning of July, 1916, to the beginning of December, 1917. During this period it only took part in two local actions (November, 1916, and November, 1917).

1917.

1. The 404th Infantry was taken away from this division in the beginning of 1917 and was joined to the divisions in the neighborhood (the 18th Landwehr Division and later the 4th Landwehr Division).

RUSSIA–FRANCE.

2. At the end of November, 1917, the 201st Division was relieved, reassembled at Baranovitchi, and entrained for the Western Front. (Itinerary: Baranovitchi–Brest-Litowsk–Warsaw–Chemnitz–Nuerenberg–Heilbronn–Rastatt–Sarreguemines.

LORRAINE.

3. Beginning on December 15, elements of the 201st Division were put in line on the right bank of the Moselle opposite the Xon (northeast of Pont a Mousson).

RECRUITING.

The eastern Provinces of the Empire.

VALUE—1917 ESTIMATE.

The 201st Division was composed to the extent of at least one-half of young and vigorous men. It had not been exhausted physically and had in no way lost its morale. Fraternization did not lessen its morale, but rather raised it on account of their belief that war could be terminated on the Western Front by an easy victory after peace was concluded with Russia.

Since its return from Russia its regiments had undergone an intensive training in trench and open warfare (February, 1918).

1918.

WOEVRE.

1. The division held the Apremont sector (southeast of St. Mihiel) until the end of May, when it was withdrawn. It rested and trained in the Woevre (Sponville) until June 9. It entrained at Mars la Tour and moved to Laon via Sedan and Liart. From there it marched to the Marne front through Vailly–Lannoy–Brecy.

BATTLE OF THE MARNE.

2. It was in line on the Chateau Thierry–Vaux sector from June 15 to the end of July. In the attacks of late July the division was hit hard. It was thrown back on Bezu–St. Germain, Beuvardes, Pere en Tardenois and relieved about July 30.

3. The division was moved to the Argonne in early August and about the 10th entered the Vacquois sector, which it held until the end of the month.

BATTLE OF THE SOMME.

4. It returned to the Somme area and on the night of September 6–7 relieved the 6th Cavalry Division northeast of Fins. Until the 28th it was engaged at Fins, Hendicourt, Gouzeaucourt, Villers, and Guislan. Losses were very heavy, including 2,200 prisoners.

CAMBRESIS.

5. After a week's rest, the division reentered line south of Cambrai on October 5 and fought in this region until the 15th. Here it lost another 650 prisoners.

6. As a result of these extraordinary losses the division was dissolved at Maubeuge on October 22.

VALUE—1918 ESTIMATE.

The division was rated as third class. Its losses were unusually heavy in prisoners whenever it was engaged in an active front. When it was dissolved its effectives numbered less than 1,000 rifles.

202d Division.
COMPOSITION.

	1916		1917		1918	
	Brigade.	Regiment.	Brigade.	Regiment.	Brigade.	Regiment.
Infantry		405. 406. 407. 408.		408. 411. 412.	406.	97. 408. 411. 412.
Cavalry					3 Sqn. 2 Gd. Uhlan Rgt.	
Artillery	406 F. A. Rgt.		Art. Command: 406 F. A. Rgt.		66 Art. Command: 406 F. A. Rgt. 65 Ft. A. Btn. 867 Light Am. Col. 868 Light Am. Col. 1387 Light Am. Col.	
Engineers and Liaisons			(202) Pion. Btn.: 383 Pion. Co. 402 Pion. Co. 182 T. M. Co. 352 Searchlight Section. Tel. Detch.		202 Pion. Btn.: 383 Pion. Co. 402 Pion. Co. 98 Searchlight Section. 182 T. M. Co. 202 Signal Command: 202 Tel. Detch. 91 Wireless Detch.	
Medical and Veterinary			403 Ambulance Co. 403 Field Hospital. 404 Field Hospital. 302 Vet. Hospital.		403 Ambulance Co. 403 Field Hospital. 404 Field Hospital. 302 Vet. Hospital.	
Transport			867 M. T. Col. 983 M. T. Col. 1387 M. T. Col.		612 M. T. Col.	
Odd Units			203 Cyclist Co.			

HISTORY.

(408th Regiment: Guard.   411th and 412th Regiments: 10th Corps District—Hanover.)

1916.

The 202d Division was formed in October, 1916, in the Lockstedt cantonment (9th Corps District, Altona). The 405th and the 406th were organized at the Lockstedt cantonment, the 407th at the Altengrabow cantonment, and the 408th comes from Guard depots.

RUSSIA.

1. In the course of October, 1916, the 202d Division was sent to the Russian front. Its organization was changed; it gave up the 405th to the 203d Division, the 406th and the 407th to the 205th Division. It was at this time composed of the 408th and two regiments received from the 203d Division, the 411th and the 412th (Hanover), which were formed at the Munster cantonment as "coast-defense regiments."

COURLAND.

2. In December, 1916, the 202d Division was identified in the region of Riga.

1917.

1. In March, 1917, and until the end of August, 1917, the 202d Division occupied in Courland a sector in the vicinity of Toukkoum.

RIGA.

2. In the middle of September it was at the east of Riga. It was also identified at Riga on October 29.

3. In November the 202d Division was entrained for the Western Front. (Itinerary: Riga–Mitau–Insterburg–Koenigsberg–Thorn (408th)–Schneidemuehl–Posen–Leipzig–Halle–Frankfort on the Main–Sarrebrueck–Sarreguemines.) It detrained at Dieuze on November 20.

LORRAINE.

4. The division stayed in the rear of the front in the vicinity of Dieuze until the middle of January, 1918 (six weeks' training).

RECRUITING.

The 408th Regiment was built up out of depots of the Guard and was recruited from all sections of Prussia. The 411th and 412th were theoretically from Hanover, with some recruits furnished by the 9th Corps District.

1918.

1. The division held the Lorraine sector until May 19, when it was relieved by the 3d Guard Division. It entrained near Moyenvic on May 19 and traveled via Metz–Spincourt–Longuyon–Sedan–Charleville–Marle to Flavy le Martel, where it detrained on May 21.

OISE.

2. On the night of May 22–23 it relieved the 11th Division west of Noyon. It was in line when the attack of June was made and advanced by Orval as far as Bethencourt. Here it remained in sector until about July 10, when it exchanged sectors with the 105th Division at Autreches. In this area it was struck by the Allied attack in mid-August and forced back on Audignicourt. The losses were very heavy, including 2,000 prisoners. It was relieved on August 27.

3. The division was railed to the vicinity of Vouziers after its relief in line. While resting at Sugny (Sept. 2–12) it was re-formed. The 412th Regiment was dissolved and its effectives distributed between the 408th and 411th Regiments. The 97th

Regiment, from the dissolved 108th Division, replaced the 412th Regiment in the division.

4. It was engaged in Champagne near Maisons de Champagne from September 12 to 24. After that it was in close support of the 42d Division until the 27th, when it reentered line at Fontaine les Dormois. Until October 10 the division saw heavy fighting about Mause and Challerauge. It lost very heavily, including more than 800 prisoners.

5. The division rested from October 11 to 21. It was reengaged southeast of Vouziers (near Falaise) on the 21st, and after the 1st of November retreated by way of Longwe (2d), Boult aix Bois (34d) to the Meuse (8th).

When it appeared opposite the United States front on November 3, the division had been completely shattered. The 411th Regiment, for instance, had only three companies each with a rifle strength of 100 to 110 men.

VALUE—1918 ESTIMATE.

The division was rated as third class. After the battle in eastern Champagne in late September the division could be regarded as destroyed.

203d Division.
COMPOSITION.

	1916 Brigade	1916 Regiment	1917 Brigade	1917 Regiment	1918 Brigade	1918 Regiment
Infantry		405. 409. 410.	405.	405. 409. 410.	405.	406. 409. 410.
Cavalry					2 Sqn. Body Gd. Hus. Rgt.	
Artillery			203 Art. Command: 406 F. A. Rgt. (2 Abts.). 403 F. A. Rgt.		203 Art. Command: 403 F. A. Rgt. 2 Abt. 8 Res. Ft. A. Rgt. 778 Light Am. Col. 969 Light Am. Col. 977 Light Am. Col.	
Engineers and Liaisons	403 Pion. Co.		Pion. Btn.: 403 Pion. Co. 183 T. M. Co. Tel. Detch.		417 Pion. Btn.: 403 Pion. Co. 1 Ers. Co. 23 Pions. 20 Searchlight Section. 183 T. M. Co. 203 Signal Command: 203 Tel. Detch. 152 Wireless Detch.	
Medical and Veterinary			Ambulance Co. 405 Field Hospital. Vet. Hospital.		402 Ambulance Co. 405 Field Hospital. 406 Field Hospital. 303 Vet. Hospital.	
Transport			M. T. Col.			
Odd units			202 Cyclist Co.			

HISTORY.

(406th Regiment; 3d Corps District—Brandenburg. 409th and 410th Regiments; 9th Corps District—Schleswig-Holstein.)

1916.

The 203d Division was formed in Germany (September, 1916) and trained at the Lockstedt cantonment (a great many men from the class of 1917; also men previously wounded or sick and men taken from units at the front).

COURLAND.

1. On October 20 the 303d Division took over a sector on the Dvina (region north of Dvinsk.)

1917.

RIGA.

1. The division stayed on the Dvina until September, 1917. It participated in the offensive on the Riga and fought to the north of Friedrichstadt.

2. After the taking of the town the 203d Division occupied a sector at Grenyn. Favored by calm conditions, it gave up men to the 75th Reserve Division, which was preparing to go to France. On December 8 it was billeted in Riga. About December 18 the 405th Regiment left the Division and was replaced by the 406th, coming from the 205th Division. In the meanwhile the division had brought up its strength by obtaining men from the 332d Infantry, which did not intend to leave until March, 1918 (with the 77th Reserve Division).

FRANCE.

3. At the end of December the 203d Division entrained for the Western Front. The 410th left Riga on the 26th. (Itinerary: Eydtkuhnen–Koenigsberg–Schneide-muehl–Berlin–Giessen–Coblenz–Treves–Thionville–Charleville.) It detrained at Tournes in the night of January 1-2, 1918.

RECRUITING.

The 406th recruits in Brandenburg, Schleswig-Holstein, and, to a lesser extent, Hanover and the Hanseatic cities; furnished the recruits for the 409th and the 410th. The changes effected in the personnel during the last part of the stay on the Russian front left these units fairly heterogeneous

VALUE—1917 ESTIMATE.

The offensive value of the 203d Division in February, 1918, was only mediocre. Before leaving for the Western Front the 405th, which was to have remained in (hardly glorious) *Russia, changed all its young men for the older* men in the other two regiments. The 203d was said to have played a part in the Riga offensive. Gen. von Luettwitz commanding the division, was said to have been relieved of his command a short time thereafter.

1918.

BATTLE OF REIMS.

The division continued to hold the sector east of Reims (near Beine) until the German offensive of July 15. It attacked west of Prunay and penetrated as far as the Vesle. In front of Beaumont it lost very heavily. After the failure of the attack the division held the sector from Prunay to east of Les Marquises until August 30, when it was relieved by the 9th Division.

CHAMPAGNE.

2. It rested near Laon until October 1, when it was reengaged in Champagne between Orfeuil and Marvaux. In 8 days of evere fighting it lost very heavily and was obliged to retire from line.

3. The division was in army reserve until October 15, after which it was engaged southeast of Vouziers near Olizy and Falaise. On November 1 it was opposite the American front and took part in the final retreat of the Meuse at Mohon.

VALUE—1918 ESTIMATE.

The division was rated as second class. By the end of hostilities the division was decimated and completely exhausted.

204th Division.

COMPOSITION.

	1916 Brigade.	1916 Regiment.	1917 Brigade.	1917 Regiment.	1918 Brigade.	1918 Regiment.
Infantry	407. 408.	413. 414. 415. 416.	407.	413. 414. 120 Res.	407.	413. 414. 120 Res.
Cavalry			4 Sqn. 19 Uhlan Rgt.		4 Sqn. 19 Uhlan Rgt.	
Artillery	407 F. A. Abt. 408 F. A. Abt.		Art. command: 27 Res. F. A. Rgt.		204 Art. command: 27 Res. F. A. Rgt. 101 Ft. A. Btn. 1263 Light Am. Col. 1264 Light Am. Col. 1317 Light Am. Col.	
Engineers and Liaisons	404 Pion Co.		204 Pion Btn.: 3 Res. Co. 13 Pions. 116 Pion. Co. 184 T. M. Co. Tel. Detch.		204 Pion Btn.: 3 Res. Co. 13 Pions. 116 Pion Co. 204 Signal Command: 204 Tel. Detch. 75 Wireless Detch.	
Medical and Veterinary			563 Ambulance Co. 407 Field Hospital. 408 Field Hospital. Vet. Hospital.		563 Ambulance Co. 252 Field Hospital. 407 Field Hospital. 249 Vet. Hospital.	
Transport			M. T. Col.			
Odd units			204 Cyclist Co.			

HISTORY.

(13th Corps District—Wurttemberg.)

1916.

The 204th Division was formed in Germany in June and July, 1916. Its original composition was the 407th Brigade (413th and 414th Infantry, 13th Corps District, Wurttemberg) and the 408th Brigade (415th and 416th Infantry, 12th and 19th Corps Districts, Saxony).

1. The two brigades, which had respectively been trained at the Muensingen cantonment in Wurttemberg (the 407th) and at Neuhammer (the 408th), were brought together at the end of July, 1916. The division was then sent to Belgium. It detrained at Cortemarck on July 27.

FLANDERS.

2. Almost immediately put in line, the 204th occupied the Dixmude-Bixschoote sector until October 1 and then the Ypres salient (southeast). At the end of 1916 the 415th and the 146th Infantry were taken from the front and transferred to the 212th Division and replaced by the 120th Reserve Infantry (Wurttemberg), coming from the 58th Division.

1917.

1. After four weeks' rest in the region of Ghent in February, 1917, the division came back to the sector at the southeast of Ypres.

2. It was relieved on June 10, three days after the British attack against the heights of Wytschaete-Messines. The division was only partially subjected to this attack, but suffered some losses during the artillery preparation.

ALSACE.

3. After having been at rest at Gheluvelt on about June 20, the 204th Division was transferred to the vicinity of Sarreberg, then on July 8 to the west of Basle, where it remained until July 20. From July 20 until August 15 it held a sector in Upper Alsace (north of the Rhone-Rhine Canal).

FLANDERS.

4. Again sent to Belgium, it went into line to the north of St. Julien, southeast of Poelcappelle, at the end of August. No important engagement.

CAMBRÉSIS.

5. Relieved from the Ypres front on September 13, it took over a sector near Cambrai (Boursies-Demicourt; Sept. 24–Nov. 13).

FLANDERS.

6. Relieved about the middle of November, it went back to Flanders, where it alternated with the 58th Division to the north of Poelcappelle until the end of February.

RECRUITING.

The division has been entirely made up of Wurttemberg recruits since December, 1916.

VALUE—1917 ESTIMATE.

Fairly good division.

1918.

1. After its relief northeast of Poelcappelles on February 28, the division rested near Lille until March 21. Elements of the division were in line at Fromelles on March 9 and others participated in a raid (the 13th) in the Boutillerie sector.

2. The division left the Lille area on March 21 and marched in stages to Douai, arriving there on the 27th. It was in support northwest of Vitry en Artois on the 29th. On the 30th it marched toward the battle front south of the Somme via Inchy-Peronne (Apr. 1), Assevillers, Rosieres, south of Moreuil.

BATTLE OF PICARDY.

3. It was engaged in the Braches-Sauvillers sector from April 1 to May 11. It was relieved by an extension of the front of the neighboring divisions and retired to rest and train near Chaulnes until June 5.

BATTLE OF THE OISE.

4. The division left Chaulnes about June 5 and marched in three days to the Lassigny-Noyon front. It advanced in reserve on the 9th by Gury–Mareuil–Lamotte. It was engaged south of Ribecourt near Bethancourt until the 12th. From the 13th to the 18th the division was in reserve. It was reengaged on the night of the 18th–19th and held the sector of Vignemont–Antheuil until the 1st of August, when it was relieved by the 54th Division.

THIRD BATTLE OF THE SOMME.

5. It rested in the suburbs of Lassigny until August 8. It then marched to Damery, arriving there on the 10th and immediately entering line. In the next week the division was thrown back by Damery, Villery les Roye to Goyencourt. The division suffered heavy losses, including about 370 prisoners near Roye.

LORRAINE.

6. The division was railed to Lorraine and rested near Blamont during September. Drafts amounting to about 700 men were incorporated in the division in mid-September.

7. The division left Lorraine on October 5 and detrained at Bertry on the 7th. It was engaged on October 8 east of Catelet, and in the next 10 days fell back through Cremont, Maretz, Sains, Souplet, Catillon. Its heavy losses, including 1,200 prisoners, led to its withdrawal on October 18.

8. On October 22–23 the division was reengaged southeast of Le Cateau. It held there until the breakdown of the line on November 5. Thereafter it fell back on Maubeuge, through Favril, Limont, Fontaine.

VALUE—1918 ESTIMATE.

The division was rated as third class. Before the attack of August it had about 2,700 rifles. The losses in August had a depressing effect on the morale of the troops.

205th Division.

COMPOSITION.

	1916 Brigade	1916 Regiment	1917 Brigade	1917 Regiment	1918 Brigade	1918 Regiment	1918 Brigade	1918 Regiment
Infantry	403.	406. 407. 439.	403.	406. 407. 427. 439.	....	405. 407. 439.	403.	405. 407. 329.
Cavalry			(?)					2 Sqn. 13 Uhlan.
Artillery	405 F. A. Rgt.		Art. Command: 405 F. A. Rgt.		405 F. A. Rgt.		405 Field Art. Rgt. (Rgt. Staff, 1 and 2 Abt.).	
Engineers and Liaisons.	377 Pion. Co.		(205) Pion. Btn.: 377 Pion. Co. 408 T. M. Co. 205 Tel. Detch.				(?) Pions. 350 Searchlight Section. 71 Searchlight Section. 205 Div. Signal Command. 205 Tel. Detch.	
Medical and Veterinary.			255 Ambulance Co. Field Hospital. Vet. Hospital.				255 Ambulance Co. 215 and 216 Field Hospitals. 305 Vet. Hospital.	
Transport			615 M. T. Col.				615 M. T. Col.	
Attached			612 Landst. Inf. Rgt.		612 Landst. Inf. Rgt.			

HISTORY.

(405th, (?) 407th: 4th District—Prussian Saxony.)   (439th: 15th District—Alsace.)

1916.

The 205th Division was organized at the end of 1916, partly from new regiments formed in the interior, partly from regiments taken from the zone of the armies on the Eastern Front.

RUSSIA.

1. The end of November, 1916, the division was reported behind the front (region northeast of Vilna). At that time it comprised the 406th and 407th Infantry, taken from the 202d Division, and the 439th Infantry formed in the region of Vilna. With the 226th Division next to it, it belonged to the reenforced 3d Reserve Corps (10th Army).

1917.

COURLAND.

1. In January, 1917, the division was in line on the left bank of the Aa (Courland). The 407th Infantry lost heavily in January and February.

2. The division then occupied the front east of Kalzeen (region of Mitau) from April to September.

3. In October it was identified north of Lake Lobé. During the last three months of 1917 many men were taken from this division for the Western Front. In this manner it sent men to the 47th Reserve Division in April, to the 14th Division at the end of October, and to the 75th Reserve Division (before it left) in November.

RECRUITING.

The division from its origin was of a very mixed composition. This diversity increased following the many drafts taken from it in 1917 and the diversity of origin of the men sent in exchange.

VALUE—1917 ESTIMATE.

On the Russian front since its organization.
Fighting value mediocre.

1918.

COURLAND.

1. In February the 205th Division was to the southeast of Riga.

2. In April it was in Livonia near Walk. About this time the commanding general was decorated. Toward the beginning of June the division was identified in the Narva region, where it remained until the end of the war, with the exception of the 439th Regiment, which was transferred to the 94th Division about the middle of September.

VALUE—1918 ESTIMATE.

The division was rated third class.

206th Division.

COMPOSITION.

	1916		1917		1918	
	Brigade.	Regiment.	Brigade.	Regiment.	Brigade.	Regiment.
Infantry	2 Res. Ers.	359. 394. 4 Res. Ers.	2 Res. Ers.	359. 394. 4 Res. Ers.	2 Res. Ers.	359. 394. 4 Res. Ers.
Cavalry			2 Sqn. 2 Uhlan Rgt.		5 Sqn. 10 Drag.	
Artillery	265 F. A. Rgt.		206 Art. Command: 265 F. A. Rgt.		206 Art. Command: 265 Field Art. Rgt. 1 Abt. 27 Foot Art. Rgt. (Btries. 2 to 4). 781, 1215, and 1230 Light Mun. Cols.	
Engineers and Liaisons			(206) Pion. Btn.: 6 Co. 30 Pions. 2 Ldw. Co. 18 Pions. 167 T. M. Co. 206 Tel. Detch.		206 Pion. Btn.: 2 Res. Co. Pion. Btn. No. 27. 6 Co. 30 Pion. Btn. 204 Searchlight Section. 206 Div. Signal Command. 206 Tel. Detch. 142 Div. Wireless Detch.	
Medical and Veterinary			210 Ambulance Co. 157 Field Hospital. 158 Field Hospital. 306 Vet. Hospital.		210 Ambulance Co. 156 and 157 Field Hospitals. 306 Vet. Hospital.	
Transport			781 M. T. Col.		616 M. T. Col.	

HISTORY.

(359th Infantry: 3d District—Brandenberg. 394th Infantry: 9th District—Schleswig-Holstein. 4th Reserve Ersatz: 10th District—Hanover.)

1916.

The 206th Division was organized in Belgium at the beginning of 1916. It was composed of three infantry regiments—the 359th (9th, 10th, and 120th Brigade Ersatz Battalions), the 394th, composed of men taken from the 17th Reserve Division, and the 4th Reserve Ersatz (36th, 37th, and 38th Reserve Brigade Ersatz Battalions).

SOMME.

1. After holding for some time in September the sector of Dixmude (359th), the division was sent to the Somme in October, where it was engaged at four different times (region of Péronne, La Maisonnette, and vicinity of Marchelepot) and suffered heavy losses.

ALSACE.

2. Relieved November 25 and entrained near St. Quentin for Alsace. Took over the sector of Ban de Sapt until the beginning of January, 1917.

1917.

LORRAINE.

1. Sent to rest in the region of Chateau Salins and went into line about the middle of February, 1917, between the forest of Bezange and Leintrey. Remained there until April 20.

CHEMIN DES DAMES.

2. Sent to the Laonnois, where it was stationed near Mont Cornet from April 22 to 30, then at Laon from April 30 to May 4. Then went to the Chemin des Dames (Laffaux, west of the Oise–Aisne Canal). Relieved June 10, after suffering very heavy losses.

LORRAINE.

3. After a month's rest in Lorraine at Blamont=Sarrebourg, the division was in reserve about the middle of July in the region of Romagne–Montfaucon.

HILL 304.

4. At the end of July it took over the sector of Hill 304–Pommerieux, where its losses were very heavy during the French attack of August 20 (1,074 prisoners). Relieved in haste two days after this attack and sent to rest behind the Reims front until the middle of September, and received about 1,000 replacements taken from the Russian front.

REIMS.

5. The division then held the Berru–Cernay sector, where it did not take part in any important operations (middle of September to Nov. 24).

ST. QUENTIN.

6. About November 28 sent to the St. Quentin front (Pontruet sector).

RECRUITING.

"Regiments from Hanover, Schleswig-Holstein, and Brandenburg," according to a German communique which designated in this fashion the 4th Reserve Ersatz, the 394th Infantry, and the 359th Infantry.

VALUE—1917 ESTIMATE.

The division attacked energetically May 24, 1917, at the Panthéon, and June 6 at La Royere. Composed of men from the active army, the reserve and the Ersatz. It is a good division. Its three regiments gave proof of good fighting qualities during the many local attacks at the Chemin des Dames.

It should, however, be noted that in front of Verdun the division did not offer any resistance to the French attack of August 20, 1917. As early as August 14 two regiments of this division had already had 100 deserters.

The sanitary conditions of this division were bad at this period (many cases of dysentery).

1918.

1. The 206th Division was withdrawn from line in the sector northwest of St. Quentin early in February, and went to rest in the region of Fresnoy le Grand. After a short stay here it moved to the Fourmies area, where it received intensive training in open warfare.

PICARDY.

2. On March 16 the division began marching toward the front via Wassigny–Fresnoy le Grand–Fonsommes–Fontaine Uterte. On the 20th it rested in the Hindenburg Third Line. On the 22d it started out again via Lesdins–Fayet, crossed the old front lines northwest of St. Quentin, and spent the night in the former British lines in the Holnon wood. The following day it marched to Martigny, where it spent the night in tents. On the 24th it crossed the canal; the 4th Reserve Regiment encamped at Voyennes; the 394th Regiment marched to Bethencourt and attacked along the canal without suffering heavy losses. On the 26th, the 394th proceeded by Damery and Andechy without being engaged; the 359th was engaged at Guérbigny, and the 4th Ersatz reached the former German trenches near Roye. During the night of the 27th–28th the division entered Montdidier. The 28th, the 4th Ersatz was engaged at Mesnil–St. Georges, leaving many prisoners in the hands of the French. On the 30th the division attacked at Fontaine sous Montdidier. It was relieved during the night of the 12th–13th of April by the 6th Bavarian Reserve Division and went to rest in the region of Gruny, Sept-Fours and Languevoisin. Here it was reconstituted.

3. During the night of the 14th–15th it relieved the 45th Reserve Division near Assainvillers (southeast of Montdidier). It was relieved by the 222d Division on May 9, and was sent to the Nesles, where it was identified on the 26th. Three days later it received 700 replacements from its depot. It was also trained during the period spent here. Toward the end of May it came to the vicinity of Baboeuf (east of Noyon); eight days later it was near Bussy; then on June 8 in the Boulogne area.

.OISE.

4. On the 11th of June it came into line reenforcing the 19th Division near Belloy (southeast of Montdidier). It was still in line at the time of the attack of August 8, during the course of which it was forced back with heavy losses as far as Boulogne le Grasse. It was withdrawn near here on the 15th.

5. After a brief rest it came back into line on the 22d near Pontoise (southeast of Noyon). It was withdrawn on the 30th.

6. On the 6th of September it came back into line near Fresnes (south of Peronne). It was relieved by the 105th Division on the 20th.

CAMBRAI.

7. On the 3d of October it relieved the 3d Naval Division, north of Rumilly (south of Cambrai). From the 8th until the division was withdrawn (about the 11th) it was heavily engaged and severely punished, losing some 1,200 prisoners; it was forced back to Carnières (east of Cambrai).

8. The division rested and refitted for a fortnight and then reenforced the front on November 1 near Villers-Pol (southeast of Valenciennes). It continued in line but was made to fall back; prisoners were captured on the 11th at Hyon (south of Mons).

VALUE—1918 ESTIMATE.

The 206th was rated a second-class division. The division commander was decorated after the battle of the Somme. On the other hand, the brigade commander issued an order (Oct. 6) to remedy straggling in the division. On the whole, however, the division did well, though not brilliantly.

207th Division.

COMPOSITION.

	1916		1917		1918	
	Brigade.	Regiment.	Brigade.	Regiment.	Brigade.	Regiment.
Infantry	89 Res.	413. 209 Res. 213 Res.	89 Res.	98 Res. 209 Res. 213 Res.	89 Res	98 Res. 209 Res. 213. Res
Cavalry			(?) Sqn., 7 Uhlan Rgt.		4 Sqn., 7th Uhlan Rgt.	
Artillery	268 F. A. Rgt.		(?) Art. Commnad: 268 F. A. Rgt.		207 Art. Command: 75 Field Art. Rgt. 38 Ft. Art. Btn. 834, 1217, and 1330 Light Mun. Col.	
Engineers and Liaisons	236 Pion. Co.		(207) Pion. Btn.: 4 Co. 14 Pions. 336 Pion. Co. 169 T. M. Co. 207 Tel. Detch.		207 Pion. Btn. 3 Ers. Co. Pion. Btn. No. 24. 168 T. M. Co. 190 Searchlight Section. 207 Div. Signal Command. 207 Tel. Detch. 98 Div. Wireless Detch.	
Medical and Veterinary			211 Ambulance Co. 240 (?) Ambulance Co. 159 Field Hospital. 160 Field Hospital. 307 Vet. Hospital.		211 Ambulance Co. 159 and 160 Field Hospitals. 307 Vet. Hospital.	
Transport			M. T. Col.			

HISTORY.

(98th Reserve: 16th District—Lorraine. 209th Reserve: 2d District—Pomerania. 213th Reserve: 9th District—Schleswig-Holstein.)

1916.

1. The 207th Division was organized in Belgium toward the end of September, 1916. The 45th Reserve Division furnished the 209th Reserve and the 46th Reserve Division the 213th Reserve. Its third regiment, the 413th, which came from the 204th Division, was replaced by the 98th Reserve (from the 212th Division) at the beginning of 1917.

FLANDERS.

2. Assembled in October on the Belgium coast (Zeebrugge-Blankenberg) and went into line before Ypres toward the end of November (Zonnebeke-Ypres road to the Ypres-Comines Canal).

1917.

1. Held the Ypres front until the end of April, 1917.

ARTOIS.

2. At the beginning of May it fought in Artois (Bullecourt, south of Pronville).

MESSINES.

3. Relieved about June 3 and went back into line in the region of Ypres, east of Messines, June 12 to July 6. Did not have heavy losses in spite of serious fighting.

4. In July sent to rest in the vicinity of Roubaix.

YPRES.

5. Beginning on the night of August 1-2, it was again engaged east of Ypres in the vicinity of Hollebeke and Zandvoorde, and counterattacked to recapture Hollebeke. Remained in this sector until October 8.

LENS.

6. On October 20 took over the sector north of Lens, where it alternated with the 220th Division.

RECRUITING.

A composite division. The 98th Reserve got replacements principally from West-phalia; the 209th Reserve from Pomerania; the 213th Reserve from Schleswig-Holstein.

VALUE—1917 ESTIMATE.

This division has only a moderate fighting value.

1918.

LENS.

1. The division continued to hold the quiet Loos sector until April 13, when it was relieved by the 220th Division.

LA BASSE CANAL.

2. It was engaged north of the La Basse Canal on the night of April 13-14. The 98th Reserve Regiment attacked on the 18th on the canal. After the attack the three regiments held the line to the south of the canal until the end of April.

3. The division rested in early May. On the 18th it was engaged south of the La Basse Canal, near Hulluch and Anchy les La Basse. It held this sector without event until it was relieved on the night of July 1-2 by the 10th Erzsatz Division. The regiment marched to Wahagnies, entrained at Libercourt on the 3d and detrained near Bac St. Maur on the same day.

VIEUX BERGUIN–CAMBRAI.

4. It relieved the 44th Reserve Division during the nights of July 3–4 and 4–5 near Vieux Berguin. After a month it exchanged sectors (between Aug. 6 and 8) with the 52d Division which had been holding a sector south of Lens. The sector continued quiet in August and September. The division was relieved on the night of the 24th–25th by the 111th Division and reenforced the front northwest of Cambrai on September 28. After three days of severe fighting and heavy losses it was obliged to withdraw.

BELGIUM.

5. The division was taken to Deynze about October 8 and came into line on the 14th near Thielt between Pettem and Iseghem. It was pushed back toward Denterghem (18th–19th) and later toward the line Courtrai–Ghent (Deynze, Tulte, Waereghem, Oct. 21 to Nov. 1). The division withdrew to reserve on November 1 and thereafter was out of line.

VALUE—1918 ESTIMATE.

The division was rated as second class. Its morale was reported to be indifferent at the end of October.

208th Division.

COMPOSITION.

	1916		1917		1918	
	Brigade.	Regiment.	Brigade.	Regiment.	Brigade.	Regiment.
Infantry	185.	25. 185. 65 Res.	185.	25. 185. 65 Res.	185.	25. 185. 65 Res.
Cavalry			1 Sqn. 6 Res. Dragoon Rgt.		1 Sqn. 6 Res. Dragoon Rgt.	
Artillery	267 F. A. Rgt.		Art. Command: 267 F. A. Rgt.		267 Field Art. Rgt. 157 Foot Art. Btn. 819, 1284, and 1357 Light Mun. Col.	
Engineers and Liaisons			(208) Pion. Btn.: 252 Pion. Co. 338 Pion. Co. 16 T. M. Co. 291 Searchlight Section. 208 Tel. Detch.		208 Pion. Btn. 252 Pion. Co. 338 Pion. Co. 16 T. M. Co. 28 Searchlight Section. 208 Div. Signal Command. 208 Tel. Detch. 80 Div. Wireless Detch.	
Medical and Veterinary			113 Ambulance Co. 78 Field Hospital. 300 Field Hospital. 308 Vet. Hospital.		113 Ambulance Co. 78 and 300 Field Hospitals. 308 Vet. Hospital.	
Transport			618 M. T. Col.		618 M. T. Col.	

HISTORY.

(25th: 8th District—Rhine Province. 185th: 14th District—Grand Duchy of Baden. 65th Reserve: 8th District—Rhine Province.)

1916.

The 208th Division was organized in the region of Sissonne at the beginning of September, 1916. Its three infantry regiments came from older divisions—the 25th from the 15th Division, the 185th from the 185th Division, the 65th Reserve from the 16th Reserve Division.

Before being transferred to the 208th Division these regiments were engaged in the battle of the Somme, where the 18th Infantry especially was particularly tried (July 5–18).

GALICIA.

1. On September 3 the division was sent to the Eastern Front, via Luxemburg-Aix la Chapelle–Berlin–Leipzig–Cracow–Lemberg.

2. Fought at Brzezany and Halicz from the middle of September to the end of October.

FRANCE.

3. About the beginning of November it returned to the Western Front, via Lemberg-Budapest–Vienna–Salzburg–Rosenheim–Munich–Frankfurt–Cologne–Aix la Chapelle–Liege. Detrained November 13 at Caudry.

SOMME–ANCRE.

4. On November 18 it went into line north of the Ancre, where it was seriously engaged in a series of local attacks.

5. Relieved December 12 and went to rest northeast of Ghent.

1917.

FLANDERS.

1. At the beginning of February, 1917 the division took over the sector Ypres-Comines Canal, which it held until February 25.

2. After a month's rest in the region north of Ghent it returned to the front (sector Bixschoote–Langemarck) from March 28–29 to middle of April.

ARTOIS.

3. April 24 the division was engaged before Arras between Gavrelle and Roeux and was severely tried during the British offensive.

HINDENBURG LINE (OISE).

4. Withdrawn from the Artois front May 8 and went into line in a quiet sector south of St. Quentin, between Berthenicourt and Moy, where it remained for more than three months, May 14–15 to August 18. Received about 1,000 replacements, among others from the 616th Infantry dissolved, in May.

FLANDERS.

5. About August 23 went to Flanders, via Origny–Le Cateau–Mons–Ghent–Deynze–Lichtervelde. September 4–5 it went into the sector of Langemarck. Though already sorely tried by artillery fire, it was subjected to the British attack of September 20, which again caused it very heavy losses. The 1st and 3d Companys of the 185th Infantry were entirely destroyed or captured; the rest of the 1st Battalion was reduced to a handful of men (letter).

ST. MIHIEL.

6. Left the Flanders front September 29 and went to Lorraine where it took over the St. Mihiel sector.

CAMBRAI–ST. QUENTIN.

7. November 26 it entrained for the region of Cambrai where the 25th Infantry fought on the 30th in support of the 34th Division. The division then held the sector

southwest of Villers Guislain–north of Epehy until the beginning of February, 1918. Relieved at that time, and at the beginning of March took over the sector west of Bellenglise, northwest of St. Quentin.

RECRUITING.

The 185th Regiment is a Baden regiment (German communiqué of Nov. 26, 1916). The other two regiments are from the Rhineland, and thus the division may at times be designated under the general appellation of "Rhenish troops."

VALUE—1917 ESTIMATE.

The division took part in many battles on different fronts and generally did well. When it was put in line at Ypres in September, 1917, 25 per cent of its fighting forces belonged to the 1918 class, and these young elements seem at this time to have weakened the fighting spirit of the division. (Information from the British, October, 1917).

1918.
BATTLE OF PICARDY.

1. The division was in the Bellenglise line sector when the attack of March 21 began. By the evening of the 21st it had advanced as far as le Vergnier. The next day it advanced via Bernes and Catigny and entered Peronne on the following day, remaining there until the 25th, when it crossed the Somme near Biaches. On the 26th the division advanced 4 kilometers encountering slight opposition, and on the 27th advanced 12 kilometers without opposition. It reached Framerville on the 28th after some fighting and on the 29th was engaged against a British counterattack between Cayeux and Beaucourt. A day or so later it was retired from the front near Marcelcave. The casualties of the division in the offensive were estimated by the British as 70 per cent.

HANGARD.

2. It rested near Clery, in the vicinity of Peronne, from April 1 to 18. It came into line north of Hangard (night of Apr. 21–22) and was heavily engaged until May 4. Again the division suffered very heavy losses.

WOEVRE.

3. The division went to rest in the Valenciennes area on May 7. About June 4 it entrained and traveled via Mons–Namur–Charleville–Conflans to Chambley, where it detrained a day later. On the night of June 4–5 it entered line of the quiet St. Mihiel sector and stayed there until the end of July.

SECOND BATTLE OF PICARDY.

4. Relieved on July 28, at St. Mihiel, the division was transported to the Noyon area, and on August 12 was engaged near Belval (south of Lassigny). In the next two months the division was constantly being pressed back. The line of its retreat was through Beaurains–Genvry–Guiscard–Berlancourt–Ville Selves–Crigny–Flavy le Martel–Benay–Cerisy (south of St. Quentin). It was relieved by the 1st Reserve Division on September 30.

5. After hardly a week's rest, the division reentered lines near Cambrai (southwest of Merguies, later Haussy) about October 8. It held in that sector until the 23d. Few days later it was reengaged between Valenciennes and Le Quesnoy (Ruesnes), but after a few days in line retired from the front.

VALUE—1918 ESTIMATE.

The division was rated as second class. It took a prominent part in the March offensive and thereafter was a strong defensive division. Although its effectives were greatly diminished in the fall, its morale remained above the average.

211th Division.
COMPOSITION.

	1916 Brigade.	1916 Regiment.	1917 Brigade.	1917 Regiment.	1918 [1] Brigade.	1918 [1] Regiment.
Infantry		27. 75 Res. 103 Res.	211.	27. 75 Res. 390.	211.	27. 75 Res. 390.
Cavalry			1 Sqn. 2 Uhlan Rgt.		1 Sqn. 2 Uhlan Rgt.	
Artillery	269 F. A. Rgt.		Art. command: 269 F. A. Rgt.		(?) Art. command: 269 F. A. Rgt.	
Engineers and Liaisons			(211) Pion. Btn.: 1 Res. Co. 27 Pions. 268 Pion. Co. 421 T. M. Co. 211 Tel. Detch.		1 Res. Co. 2 Pion. Btn. No. 27. 421 T. M. Co. 211 Tel. Detch.	
Medical and Veterinary			222 Ambulance Co. 170 Field Hospital. 173 Field Hospital. Vet. Hospital.		222 Ambulance Co. 170 Field Hospital. 171 Field Hospital. 173 Field Hospital. Vet. Hospital.	
Transports			M. T. Col.		M. T. Col.	

[1] Composition at the time of dissolution, August, 1918.

HISTORY.

(27th; 4th District—Prussian Saxony. 75th Reserve; 9th District—Schleswig-Holstein and Hansa towns. 390th; 18th District—Hesse-Nassau.)

1916.

The 211th Division was organized September 15, 1916, at Tournai.

The 27th Infantry came from the 27th Division (4th Army Corps), the 75th Reserve from the 17th Reserve Division (9th Army Corps), the 103d Reserve (which was replaced by the 390th in January, 1917) came from the 23d Reserve Division (Saxon). These three regiments fought in July to August, 1916, in the battle of the Somme before being assigned to the 211th Division.

1. About September 20, its organization being completed, the division was sent north of the front of the Somme, to put up defensive works in the region of Nurlu-Manancourt.

SOMME.

2. October 14 it went into line at the St. Pierre-Vaast wood, from where it was relieved November 6.

SOISSONS.

3. It then took over the sector north and west of Soissons (Nov. 20).

1917.

1. In January, 1917, the 103d Reserve was transferred to the 58th Division (Saxon) and replaced by the 390th, recruited in the Rhineland and Hessa, coming from the 16th Reserve Division, which had been formed from drafted companies as well as from elements of the 21st and 25th Divisions and 25th Landwehr Brigade.

AISNE.

2. The division, thus composed, held the Soissons sector until about March 20. On this date it retired through Terny, Margival, to Vauxaillon, where it established its lines and opposed the French attack of April 16.

LAFFAUX.

3. Temporarily withdrawn from the front on April 20, the division went to the north of Laffaux, south of Vauxaillon, from May 10 to 25. During these two periods on the Aisne front the division suffered heavy losses (especially the 27th, which had already received men from the 1918 class, among other reenforcements, at the end of April). It was reorganized partly from the dissolution of the 625th Infantry (Hessian).

FOREST OF ST. GOBAIN.

4. June 25 the division held the forest of St. Gobain (sector of Bassoles-Aulers). At the end of July it took over the sector of Cerny-Malval Farm.

5. At the end of December it went to rest and train at Gizy (west of Liesse) and vicinity for four weeks.

RECRUITING.

The three infantry regiments came from three different Prussian Provinces—Prussian Saxony (27th Infantry), Schleswig-Holstein and Hanse towns (75th Reserve), Hesse-Nassau, 390th Infantry. The reenforcements from the Russian front in 1917 also gave a certain number of Hanoverians from the 411th Infantry.

VALUE—1917 ESTIMATE.

The division had many losses on the Aisne in April to May, 1917, and was completed by reenforcements containing a strong proportion of the 1918 class. These young soldiers, according to prisoners' statements, showed only mediocre military qualities (counterattacks at Laffaux).

During the four weeks which it spent in the vicinity of Liesse the division took part in several training exercises (breaking through maneuvers on an 8-kilometer front with simulated enemy tanks). (Interrogation of prisoners, Mar. 7, 1918.)

1918.

BATTLE OF PICARDY.

1. The division was relieved the 8th of March in the Chamouille area and went to rest and train near Laon until the 19th. It marched toward the jumping off point east of La Fere by Crepy en Laonnois, arriving there on the 20th. It followed up the attack at La Fere, crossing the Oise near Travecy, until the 22d, when it was engaged west of Travecy. It advanced through Farguiers–Quessy–Liez–Chauny–Quierzy–Varesnes, suffering heavy losses, until the line stabilized near the Aisne Canal at Manicamp and Champs. It held this sector until May 27.

OISE.

2. When the French retired on the front, following the German advance to the Marne, the division advanced as far as Moulin sous Touvent–Nampcel (May 27–31). It held that sector until the beginning of July. It withstood a French attack on July 3, lost 666 prisoners, and was at once relieved by the 15th Division.

SOISSONS.

3. The division rested until mid-July southeast of Soissons. It was brought back on the 20th at Mercin–Vauxbuin to oppose the Allied counterthrust and was in line until August 3.

4. After its withdrawal the division was taken to the neighborhood of Charleville and dissolved. The 390th Regiment and 75th Reserve Regiment were broken up and sent as drafts to the 42d Division and the 87th Division. The 27th Regiment replaced the dissolved 32d Reserve Regiment in the 113th Division.

VALUE—1918 ESTIMATE.

The division was rated as second class. It was in line almost without interruption from February to August, 1918. When the effective strength had reached a minimum the division was dissolved.

125651°—20——43

212th Division.
COMPOSITION.

	1916 Brigade.	1916 Regiment.	1917 Brigade.	1917 Regiment.	1918 Brigade.	1918 Infantry.
Infantry	57.	20. 114. 98 Res.	212.	415, 416, 182.	....	182.
Cavalry			2 Sqn. 18 Uhlan Rgt.		5 Sqn. 18 Hussars. Staff, 2 Bav. Uhlan Rgt. 1 to 4 Sqns. 2 Bav. Uhlan Rgt. M. G. Sqn. 2 Bav. Uhlan Rgt.	
Artillery	279 F. A. Rgt. (Saxon).		67 Art. Command: 279 F. A. Rgt.		67 Artillery Command: 279 Field Art. Rgt.	
Engineers and Liaisons	2 Ldw. Pion. Co. (14 C. Dist.).		(212) Pion. Btn.: 3 Res. Co. 22 Pions. 422 T. M. Co. 212 Tel. Detch.		212 Div. Signal Command: 212 Tel. Detch.	
Medical and Veterinary			225 Ambulance Co. 177 Field Hospital. Vet. Hospital.		177 Field Hospital. 312 Vet. Hospital.	
Transport			757 M. T. Col.			

HISTORY.

(12th and 19th Districts—Saxony.)

1916.

The 212th Division was organized between the 5th and 15th of September, 1916, in the region of St. Quentin. At that time it comprised the following three infantry regiments, taken from already existing divisions: The 20th from the 6th Division, the 114th from the 29th Division, and the 98th Reserve from the 10th Reserve Division. Later its infantry composition was completely changed until the division from being Prussian became entirely Saxon.

SOMME.

1. From September 15 to October 3–5 the division was engaged north of the Somme (sector of Cléry to Béthune–Péronne road).

2. Withdrawn from the front October 5 and sent to rest in the region of St. Quentin. Went back into line about the 25th, south of the Somme, between Genermont and Ablaincourt. Suffered heavy losses (the 3d Battallion of the 98th Reserves lost 297 prisoners).

CHAMPAGNE.

3. The division left the Somme November 23–25 and went to rest (end of November to beginning of December). Then went to the Champagne front (sector of Prosnes–south of Ste. Marie a Py).

1917.

1. In January, 1917, the division was reorganized. The 98th Reserve and the 20th went to the 207th Division and the 5th Guard Division, respectively, and were replaced by the 9th Jäger Regiment (from the 199th Division) and the 415th (from the 204th Division). These were Saxon regiments and they were joined a short time after by the 416th (also from the 204th Division and Saxon), in place of the 114th, assigned to the 199th Division.

CHAMPAGNE.

2. Thus composed the division continued to hold the Prosnes sector until the end of March, 1917.

ROUMANIA.

3. Relieved about March 25, before the attacks began and sent to Roumania.

At this time the 9th Regiment of Jägers left the division and went to the 101st Division, in Macedonia. The 415th and 416th were sent to the Russian–Roumanian front (region of Braila in July, then Focsani–Tecuciu). The division was brought up to three regiments by the assignment of the 182d (from the 216th Division), a Saxon regiment. The division suffered heavy losses, especially the 182d Infantry, on September 3.

4. In December the division was relieved from the sector west of Tecutiu. The 415th and 416th were identified southeast of Panciu December 14; the 182d, northwest of Namoloasa, on the 20th.

RECRUITING.

The division at the end of 1917 was entirely Saxon.

VALUE—1917 ESTIMATE.

Remained on the Roumanian front during a part of 1917 and the beginning of 1918. Moderate fighting value.

1918.

1. The division was still in Rumania on the 15th of April.

UKRAINE.

2. Toward the end of May the division was identified north of Kherson. All the younger men were sent to the Western Front, but the remainder of the division did not leave this region.

VALUE—1918 ESTIMATE.

The division was rated as fourth class.

213th Division.

COMPOSITION.

	1916		1917		1918	
	Brigade.	Regiment.	Brigade.	Regiment.	Brigade.	Regiment.
Infantry	37 Res.	149. 368. 74 Res.	37 Res.	149. 368. 74 Res.	37 Res.	149. 368. 74 Res.
Cavalry	2 Sqn. 5 Res. Hus. Rgt.		2 Sqn. 5 Res. Hus. Rgt.		2 Sqn. 5 Res. Hus.	
Artillery	272 F. A. Rgt.		213 Art. Command: 272 F. A. Rgt.		213 Art. Command: 272 Field Art. Rgt. 79th Foot Art. Btn. 733, 1104, and 1127 Light Mun. Col.	
Engineers and Liaisons	284 Pion. Co. 423 T. M. Co.		(213) Pion. Btn.: 2 Res. Co. 28 Pions. 284 Pion Co. 378 T. M. Co. 423 T. M. Co. Tel. Detch.		213 Pion Btn. 2 Res. Co. Pion Btn. No. 18. 284 Pion Co. 423 T. M. Co. 118 Searchlight Section. 234 Searchlight Section. 313 Div. Signal Command. 213 Tel. Detch. 26 Div. Wireless Detch.	
Medical and Veterinary			220 Ambulance Co. 68 (*) Field Hospital. 168 Field Hospital. 169 Field Hospital. Vet. Hospital.		220 Ambulance Co. 168 and 169 Field Hospitals. 313 Vet. Hospital.	
Transport			179 M. T. Col.		623 M. T. Col.	

HISTORY.

(149th: 2d District—Pomerania.   368th and 74th Reserves: 10th District—Hanover.)

1916.

The 213th Division was formed near Spincourt, northeast of Verdun, at the beginning of September, 1916.   Its three infantry regiments came from already existing divisions, the 149th from the 4th Division, the 74th Reserves from the 19th Reserve Division, and the 368th (former Brigade Ersatz Battalions 37 (Osnabrueck), 38 (Hanover), 39 (Hildesheim), from the 10th Ersatz Division.

SOMME.

1. Although apparently destined for the Roumanian front, the division was sent in all haste to the Somme on September 14.   It fought beginning the 18th east of Combles and suffered heavily.

AISNE.

2. Withdrawn from the front at the end of September and moved to Bohain by stages and from there was transported on October 1 to Coucy le Chateau.   On the same day it took over the Nouvron–Vingre sector north of Vic sur Aisne.   It remained there until the end of October, and after a short rest went back into line in the same region (Moulin sous Touvent-Autreches) at the beginning of November.

1917.

1. About January 4, 1917, the division was relieved from the Aisne front and sent for a rest and training to the camp at Sissonne (region of Lappion).   Maneuvers with a view to open warfare.)

OISE.

2. After three weeks training it entrained at St. Erme on January 22; detrained the same day at Apilly, near Chauny, and went into line between the Oise and Quennevieres (Bailly–Pracy le Val).

3. On March 17 it retired north of the Ailette in the direction of Chauny and went in reserve in the region of Laon.

AISNE.

4. An emergency call was sent for it at Sissonne April 16 and it was brought to St. Erme and engaged beginning April 16–17 east of Craonne (north of Ville aux Bois). Counterattacked violently in the region of Juvincourt, but suffered considerable losses, which necessitated its retreat, on April 21–22.

5. Sent to rest near Amifontaine and reorganized (replacements especially from the 617th Regiment (Stettin and vicinity), which was dissolved) April 26 it was reengaged south of Corbeny and again suffered heavily from the French attack of May 8 and from its counteroffensive of the 10th.

6. Left the Craonne front May 29 and went to rest by the Meuse (Spincourt).

HILL 304.

7. At the end of July, after two months' rest, went into line east of Hill 304.   Only the 149th was engaged during the French attack of August 20, and it suffered heavy losses.

CHAMPAGNE.

8. Relieved August 25 and sent to Champagne (5 weeks' rest near Asfeld), then went into line before Brimont on October 5.

RECRUITING.

Two of the regiments, the 74th Reserves and the 368th were from Hanover.   The 149th which as a rule was recruited in the second district (Pomerania), was as a matter of fact very mixed, like the other regiments of this district.

A good division. However, the 149th, in line east of Hill 304, offered no resistance to the French attack of August 20, 1917. The two other regiments gave no assistance. Relatively small proportion of 1918 class men in August, 1917.

During its stay in the rear (January, 1918) the division was trained for open warfare. (Examination of prisoners, March, 1918.)

1918.

BATTLE OF THE AISNE.

1. The division continued to hold the quiet Brimont Courcy sector until May 10, when it was relieved by the 242d Division. It rested near Asfeld until the 24th, when it returned to the Brimont sector on the night of the 24th–25th, and attacked on the 27th. It advanced through Loivre, Merfy, and Guex until the line stabilized west of Reims (Vrigny-Ormes-Champigny). It held that sector until September 27.

2. It was moved in motor trucks on the 27th to south of Arnes, and the next day was engaged near Ste. Marie a Py. The division was engaged without pause until the armistice. In the first week of October it was pushed back to Ste. Etienne a Arnes, losing 560 prisoners. From then it retreated to east of Machault, between Vouziers and Attigny and later to the region northeast of Attigny (Le Chesne-Louvergny). It was last identified at Louvergny on November 6.

The division was rated as third class. Its morale remained fairly high, and the division did well in the Ardennes in September–October.

214th Division.
COMPOSITION.

	1916 Brigade	1916 Regiment	1917 Brigade	1917 Regiment	1918 Brigade	1918 Regiment
Infantry		50. 358. 363.	214.	50. 358. 363.	214.	50. 358. 363.
Cavalry			(z)		1 Sqn., 16th Hus. Rgt.	
Artillery			(z) Art. Command: 44 F. A. Rgt.		214 Art. Command. 44 Field Art. Rgt. 1 Abt. 15 Foot Art. Rgt. (Btries. 1 to 3). 922, 1246, and 1300 Light Mun. Cols.	
Engineers and Liaisons			(214) Pion. Btn.: 2 Res. Co. 23 Pions. 341 Pion. Co. 424 T. M. Co. 214 Tel. Detch.		214 Pion. Btn. 2 Res. Co. Pion. Btn. No. 23. 341 Pion. Co. 47 Searchlight Section. 214 Div. Signal Command. 214 Tel. Detch. 112 Div. Wireless Detch.	
Medical and Veterinary			224 Ambulance Co. 25 Field Hospital. 274 Field Hospital. Vet. Hospital.		224 Ambulance Co. 25 and 274 Field Hospitals. 314 Vet. Hospital.	
Transport			M. T. Col.		624 M. T. Col.	
Attached					22, 59, and 20 M. G. Sec. Abt. 4 Btry 18 Foot Art. Regt. 150 Saxon Balloon Detch. 268 Aviation Detch. (Oct. 29, 1918.)	

HISTORY.

(50th: 5th District—Posen. 358th: 2d District—Pomerania. 363d: 8th District—Rhine Province.)

1916.

The 214th Division was formed in Lorraine in September, 1916. Two of its regiments came from the Ersatz Divisions—the 358th, former Brigade Ersatz Battalions Nos. 1, 2, 5, and 50; from the Ersatz Guard Division; the 363d, former Brigade Ersatz Battalions Nos. 29 (Aix la Chapelle), 30 (Coblentz), and 31 (Trèves), from the 8th Ersatz Division. These two regiments were for two years in the Haye. The 50th Infantry was taken from the 10th Division (Verdun front).

SOMME.

1. Started for the Eastern Front September 10, 1916, but was stopped at Frankfort on Main and brought back to France to oppose the offensive on the Somme. Hastily engaged at Rancourt September 19–20, but lost that village. Lost heavily (600 prisoners) and was relieved October 2.

BOIS LE PRETRE.

2. From October 15 to November 25 the division held the Bois le Pretre sector.

SOMME.

3. At the beginning of December it again went to the Somme in the region of Bapaume (Gueudecourt).

1917.

1. The division was withdrawn from the Somme about February 6, 1917, and went to rest; obtained replacements from the 609th Infantry (Rhineland).

CHAMPAGNE.

2. About February 20 the division was north of Nouroy–Moronvilliers. Its regiments were successively put in line beginning with the first part of March, then were placed all together in line April 15. April 17 and 18 the division opposed the French attacks on the Nauroy–Auberive front. Its losses were considerable (19 officers and 1046 unwounded prisoners). Losses of the 12th Company of the 50th Infantry, 129 men (document).

3. On the night of the 18th–19th the division was relieved and sent to rest southwest of Monthois and reorganized. The 5th Company of the 363d Infantry received at least 134 replacements, mostly from the 1918 class, some of them with only three months' training.

ARGONNE.

4. About May 4–5 the division went back into line south of Rouvroy (Cernay en Dormois) and stayed there until July 22 or 23. No important action during this period.

FLANDERS.

5. During the first days of August the division was sent to Flanders via Charleville, Namur, Brussels, and Ghent. It went to the Bixschoote–Langemarck sector, where it fought until August 17 (battle of Flanders, French attack of August 16).

CAMBRAI.

6. After a rest on the coast it went to Douai August 23 and took over the Oppy-Gavrelle sector (September to November). November 22 it went in all haste to oppose the advance of the British army southwest of Cambrai, and fought until December 4. At that date it was sent to rest near Valenciennes.

RECRUITING.

A composite division. The 50th (5th District) and the 358th (2d District) had a pretty large proportion of Poles, and some Brandenburgers to counterbalance them. The 363d was a Rhenish regiment, as well as the field artillery of the division.

The 214th Division must be considered as a good division. However, it should be noted that in Champagne during the attack of April 17, it was more or less demoralized by the losses suffered. A large number of men are said to have fled during the preparatory artillery fire.

At Ypres in August, 1917, the 358th and 363d opposed great resistance, particularly where there were enough officers to hold the men under the artillery fire.

Of the three regiments of the division, the 50th was the worst; many Poles.

1918.
BELGIUM.

1. The division held the Dixmude sector until April 5, when it was relieved by the 6th Bavarian Division. It was withdrawn to Couckelaere and Ichteghem, when it entrained on the 6th and 7th and traveled via Thourout–Lichtervelde–Roulers–Coutrai to Lauwe, from where they marched to Halluin

LYS.

2. It was engaged north of Armentieres from April 10 to 13 (Ploegsteert–Neuve Eglise). It was relieved on the 13th–14th and went to rest near Lille until May 19. On May 6 some elements of the division reenforced the Alpine Corps at Locre for a short time.

ARRAS.

3. On May 19–20 the division came in line east of Arras (Feuchy–Monchy le Preux) and held that quiet sector until the British attacked them on August 27. The division lost 1,171 prisoners and was relieved on the 28th.

PICARDY.

4. The division rested until September 24, when it entered line southwest of Douai (Sailly Ostrevent Biache, St. Vaast) and held there until October 8. It retreated between Douai and Valenciennes as far as east of St. Awand. It withdrew from line near Conde on the 24th. A day later it was reengaged south of Valenciennes (Famars) and in line until November 5. On the first 10 days of November the division lost 750 prisoners.

The division was rated as second class. In 1918 it played a rather colorless rôle. Its hardest fighting was in October in the Cambrai battle.

215th Division.

COMPOSITION.

	1916 Brigade.	1916 Regiment.	1917 Brigade.	1917 Regiment.	1918 Brigade.	1918 Regiment.
Infantry	61 Res. 61 Res.	60 Res. 2 Res. Ers. 40 Ers. (Saxon). 71 Ldw. 2 Res. Ers. 40 Ers. (Saxon). 244 Res. (Saxon).	61 Res.	71 Ldw. 224 Res. 2 Res. Ers.	61 Res.	224 Res. 2 Res. Ers.
Cavalry	3 Sqn. 8 Res. Hus. Rgt.		3 Sqn. 8 Res. Hus. Rgt.			
Artillery	274 F. A. Rgt.		274 F. A. Rgt.		274 Field Art. Rgt. 1413 Light Mun. Col.	
Engineers and Liaisons			(215) Pion. Btn.: 249 Pion. Co. 6 Co. 29 Pions. 425 T. M. Co. Tel. Detch.		6 Co. Pion. Btn. No. 29. 115 Searchlight Section. 215 Div. Signal Command. 215 Tel. Detch.	
Medical and Veterinary			221 Ambulance Co. 166 Field Hospital. 174 Field Hospital. Vet. Hospital.		221 Ambulance Co. 315 Vet. Hospital.	
Transport			M. T. Col.		625 M. T. Col.	
Attached				21 Res. Jäg. Btn. (Until fall of 1917.)		

HISTORY.

(224th Reserve Infantry Regiment: 18th Corps District—Hesse-Nassau. 2d Reserve
Ersatz and 71st Landwehr Regiments: 11th Corps District—Thuringia and Prussian
Saxony.)

1916.

CHAMPAGNE.

1. The 215th Division, formed about September, 1916, and comprising at this time
the 40th Ersatz Regiment, taken from the 19th Ersatz Division; the 2d Reserve
Ersatz, from the 1st Reserve Ersatz Brigade; the 60th Reserve, from the 13th Landwehr Division, was identified for the first time on September 29, 1916, on the Champagne front, east of Auberive. It occupied the sector of Prosnes, south of Ste.
Marie a Py, until the end of November.

2. Relieved in Champagne, the 215th Division was transferred to the Eastern Front,
leaving the 60th Reserve Regiment in France as a part of the 221st Division and taking
with it the 71st Landwehr Regiment from the 13th Landwehr Division.

RUSSIA.

3. Arriving in Russia at the beginning of December, the 215th Division formed a
part of the 22d Reserve Corps (Army of the Bug) and was reenforced by the addition
of the 244th Reserve Infantry Regiment from the 53d Reserve Division.

1917.

VOLHYNIA.

1. At the beginning of 1917 the composition of the 215th Division was again
changed—the 244th Reserve Infantry Regiment went over to the 119th Division and
was replaced by the 224th Reserve Infantry Regiment from the 48th Reserve Division.

2. During the year 1917 the 215th Division occupied, in Volhynia, the sector situated east of Gorokhov (northwest of Berestiecko).

3. Its composition was once more modified—the 40th Ersatz Regiment was transferred to a newly formed Saxon division, the 96th.

RECRUITING.

The 215th Division was fairly homogeneous. It was mostly recruited from the 11th
and to some extent from the 18th Corps Districts (Thuringia, the Electorate of Hesse,
and Hesse-Nassau).

VALUE—1917 ESTIMATE.

The division had been in Russia since December, 1916, and was only mediocre.

1918.

UKRAINE.

1. Early in the year the division was still in Russia. It was identified near Kiev
on the 12th of March and in the Kharkov region in April. Early in May the division
had advanced to the Sea of Azov. Early in September, all unmarried men less than
35 years of age (Alsace-Lorrainers included) were sent to the Western Front, which
probably explains the many reports of the division having been sent to France.
In all probability the division never left the Ukraine.

VALUE—1918 ESTIMATE.

The division was rated as fourth class.

216th Division.
COMPOSITION.

	1916		1917		1918	
	Brigade.	Regiment.	Brigade.	Regiment.	Brigade.	Regiment.
Infantry		182. 354. 21 Res.	177.	42. 354. 59.	(?)	42. 354. 59.
Cavalry					205 Cav. Sqn.	
Artillery	54 F. A. Rgt.		54 F. A. Rgt.		216 Art. Command: 54 F. A. Rgt. 3 Abt. 10 Ft. A. Rgt. (Staff, and 9 and 11 Btries.) 762 Light Am. Col.	
Engineers and Liaisons	2 Gd. Ldw. Pions.		(216) Pion. Btn.: 2 Ldw. Co. Gd. Pions. 216 Tel. Detch.		217 Pion. Btn.: 247 Pion. Co. 2 Ldw. Co. Gd. C. Dist. Pions. 78 Searchlight Section. 216 Signal Command: 216 Tel. Detch. 167 Wireless Detch.	
Medical and Veterinary			280 Ambulance Co. 53 Field Hospital. 324 Field Hospital. Vet. Hospital.		260 Ambulance Co. 324 Field Hospital. 332 Field Hospital. 257 Vet. Hospital.	
Transport			M. T. Col.			

HISTORY.

(42d Infantry Regiment; 2d Corps District—Pomerania. 59th Infantry Regiment; 20th Corps District—Eastern part of West Prussia. 354th Infantry Regiment; 6th Corps District—Silesia.)

1916.

The 216th Division was formed in Galicia in July, 1916, by drafts upon regiments of other divisions. At the time of formation it comprised the 182d Infantry Regiment, from the 123d Division (Saxon), the 354th Infantry Regiment from the 38th Division and the 21st Reserve Infantry Regiment from the 217th Division.

GALICIA–TRANSYLVANIA.

1. In Galicia (Brzezany) beginning of October, the 216th Division was transferred to the Transylvanian front (valley of the Olt) on November 8.

ROUMANIA.

2. It took part in the Roumanian campaign.

3. At the end of December it was south of Rimnicu-Sarat.

1917.

ROUMANIA.

1. In January, 1917, the 216th Division was in line east of Focsani, where it remained until August.

2. It took part in the attacks north of Focsani in August, where the 182d Infantry Regiment lost especially heavily.

3. At this time the 42d and 59th Infantry Regiments, filled up in June by men borrowed from the 76th Reserve Division, then in the rear of the Roumanian front replaced the 182d Infantry Regiment, transferred to the 212th Division and the 21st Infantry Regiment, sent to the Macedonian front.

4. With this composition the 216th Division occupied the line north of the mouth of the Buzeu. It was still there at the end of December. The 354th Infantry Regiment was identified on December 28 by fraternizing.

RECRUITING.

The 42d Infantry Regiment, Pomeranian, and the 59th Infantry Regiment, from Posen, also contained contingents from the 2d, 5th and 20th Corps Districts, and since 1915 have contained a large number of Alsace-Lorrainers. The 354 Infantry Regiment, formed from mobile depot battalions of the former Breslau Garrison, replaced its 3d Battalion (Saxon) by Prussians, and consisted almost entirely of drafts from Silesia.

VALUE—1917 ESTIMATE.

The 216th Division fought and held sectors almost entirely on the Roumanian front.

1918.

1. On the 1st of April the division started for the Western Front. It traveled via Bucharest – Budapest – Prague – Dresden – Leipsig – Erfurt – Frankfort – Thionville – Luxemburg – Namur – Mons – Valencennes, and detrained at Orchies and Sornain from April 12 to 20.

KEMME.

2. It entered line at Kemme on May 9 and with the exception of the first week in June held that sector until June 18.

3. The division rested and underwent training north of Courtrai (Ovstroosebeke-Marialoop) until July 23. It was then railed to Laon and marched toward the front south of Fismes through Urcel, Brenelle, Bozoches, Mont St. Martin. It was in reserve northeast of Cierges on July 28-29.

VESLE–AISNE.

4. It was engaged near Cierges and west of the Bois Meuniere on July 29 and 30. The next day it returned north of Cierges and later to the Vesle east of Fismes (Magneux). The division lost heavily in their retreat. It held the sector on the Vesle until September 5, when it fell back through Merval toward the line of the Aisne. It held on the line west of Revillon, south of Villers en Prayeres until October 10. Again it gave way before the Allied pressure and retired through Bouconville, north of Aubigny (11th–12th), Montaigu (13th) toward Liesse–Sissonne. In this area the division was withdrawn from line on October 23.

CHAMPAGNE.

5. Without having had an opportunity to rest, the division was returned to line northwest of Chateau Porcien on October 25 and fought until November 5.

6. At the time of the armistice the division was considered in reserve of 5th Army.

VALUE—1918 ESTIMATE.

The division was rated as third class. Its conduct during the retreat to the Vesle was good. The three months of constant service in line greatly fatigued the troops and lowered the morale of the division.

217th Division.

COMPOSITION.

	1916		1917		1918	
	Brigade.	Regiment.	Brigade.	Regiment.	Brigade.	Regiment.
Infantry		45. 9 Res. 22 Ldw. — Nov. to Jan. 1 — 9 Res. 22 Ldw. 21 Res.	18 Ldw.	9 Res. 22 Ldw. 29 Bav.	18 Ldw.	9 Res. 22 Ldw. 21 Res.
Cavalry			47 Res. Cav. Detch.		47 Res. Cav. Detch.	
Artillery			65 Res. F. A. Rgt.		274 F. A. Rgt. (2d Abt.), 65 Res. F. A. Rgt. (except 3d Btty. and 2 Abt. Staff and 4 and 6 Btries.). 1049, 1056, and 1073 Light. Am. Col.	
Engineers and Liaisons	2 Res. Co. 17 Pions.		(217) Pion. Btn.: 2 Res. Co. 17 Pions. 174 T. M. Co. 427 T. M. Co. 217 Tel. Detch.		2 Res. Co. 17 Pions. 130 Searchlight Section. 217 Signal Command: 217 Tel. Detch.	
Medical and Veterinary			Ambulance Co. 58 Field Hospital. 149 Field Hospital. 317 Vet. Hospital.		237 Ambulance Co. 149 Field Hospital. 317 Vet. Hospital.	
Transport			1044 M. T. Col. 1094 M. T. Col.			

HISTORY.

(9th Reserve Infantry Regiment: 2d. Corps District—Pomerania. 22d Landwehr Regiment: 6th Corps District—Upper Silesia. 29th Bavarian Infantry Regiment: Mixed—Prussia and Bavaria.)

1916.

The 217th Division was formed on the Eastern Front about August, 1916.

ROUMANIA.

1. Composed of the 9th Reserve Infantry Regiment from the 3d Reserve Division, the 45th Infantry Regiment from the 101st Division, and the 22d Landwehr Regiment from the 4th Landwehr Division, the 217th Division left the Brest-Litowsk area at the beginning of October, 1916, to take part in the Roumanian campaign.

2. It was in Dobroudja about the end of October; in the area south of Bucarest in November. At the beginning of November the 45th Infantry Regiment, which returned to Macedonia, was replaced by the 21st Infantry Regiment from the 36th Reserve Division.

3. At the end of December elements of the 9th Reserve Infantry Regiment occupied the front south of Isaccea (Dobroudja).

1917.

BRAILA.

1. In January, 1917, the 217th Division was in the Braila area; in February, at the mouth of the Buzeu.

ODOBESTI.

2. In the month of May the division left the Braila front and went into line northwest of Odobesti in the vicinity of Focsani. At this time it acquired its definite organization: 9th Reserve, 29th Bavarian, and 22d Landwehr Infantry Regiments.

PANCIU.

3. From July to December the 217th Division remained in line northwest of Panciu.

RECRUITING.

The 217th Division was one of the most heterogeneous.

VALUE—1917 ESTIMATE.

The division had been on the Roumanian front since October, 1916, and was mediocre.

1918.

ROUMANIA.

1. Early in April the division was still on the Roumanian front, but was leaving shortly for another theater.

UKRAINE.

2. At the beginning of May the division was in the Kherson region.

CRIMEA.

3. The middle of the month the division was near Sebastopol.

GEORGIA.

4. About the middle of July elements of the division were identified at Poti and Tiflis.

SERBIA.

5. Early in October the division having moved to the vicinity of Nish opposed the advance of the Serbian and allied troops.

VALUE—1918 ESTIMATE.

The division was rated as fourth class.

218th Division.

COMPOSITION.

	1916		1917		1918*	
	Brigade.	Regiment.	Brigade.	Regiment.	Brigade.	Regiment.
Infantry	....	204 Res. 256 Res. 5 Ldw.	62.	204 Res. 256 Res. 5 Ldw.	....	256 Res. 5 Ldw. (2d Btn.).
Cavalry	....		4 Sqn. 1 Gd. Drag. Rgt.		4 Sqn. 1 Drag. Rgt.	
Artillery	85 F. A. Rgt. 11 Mountain F. A. Btry.		85 F. A. Rgt.		85 F. A. Rgt. (except 2 Abt. Staff, 4 and 6 Btries.; 3d Abt. Staff, 7 and 9 Btries.).	
Engineers and Liaisons	....		(218) Pion. Btn.: 2 Res. Co. 26 Pions. 388 Pion. Co. 428 T. M. Co. 267 Searchlight Section. 218 Tel. Detch.		218 Signal Command: 218 Tel. Detch.	
Medical and Veterinary	....		121 Ambulance Co. 145 Field Hospital. 96 Field Hospital. 367 Field Hospital. Vet. Hospital.		121 Ambulance Co. 145 Field Hospital. 318 Vet. Hospital.	
Transport	....		628 M. T. Col.			

¹ The below comprises only the elements under 308th Postal Sector (Nov. 13, 1918). The 62d Infantry Brigade, and elements of the 5th Landwehr Regiment were in the 310th Postal Sector and are carried as attached to other divisions.

HISTORY.

(204th Infantry Regiment: Guard. 256th Reserve Infantry Regiment: 7th Corps District—Westphalia. 5th Landwehr Regiment: 17th Corps District—West Prussia.)

1916.

The division was formed on the Eastern Front about September, 1916.

GALICIA.

1. Concentrated, beginning of October, in the Brest-Litovsk area, the 218th Division was transferred to Galicia, in the Brody, sector in the middle of October.

ROUMANIA.

2. Beginning of December the 218th Division was sent to the Roumanian front. It was then composed of the 204th Infantry Regiment, taken from the 43d Reserve Division; the 256th Reserve Infantry Regiment, from the Mitau Group; and of the 5th Landwehr Regiment, taken from the 11th Landwehr Division. It occupied the sector of Oitoz (December).

1917.

ROUMANIA.

1. The 218th Division remained in line between the valleys of the Trotus and of the Putna (south of Ocna, northwest of Panciu) until July, 1917.

2. At the end of July it was engaged in its sector in front of Kezdi-Vasarhely and retired to the south bank of the Putna on July 29.

3. In August and until the end of the year 1917 the 218th Division remained in line in the vicinity of Soveja.

RECRUITING.

The 204th Reserve Infantry Regiment was recruited from the whole of Russia; the 256th Reserve Infantry Regiment from Westphalia and the Rhine Districts; the 5th Landwehr Regiment from West Prussia.

VALUE—1917 ESTIMATE.

The 218th Division had been on the Roumanian front since December, 1916, and was mediocre.

1918.

ROUMANIA.

In June the division was still in Roumania. Men under 35 years of age were sent to the Western Front, which gave rise to the report of the division's presence in the Lille-Armentières region early in June. The 256th Reserve Regiment was identified in Macedonia early in July, but the remainder of the division was still in Roumania the middle of October.

VALUE—1918 ESTIMATE.

The division was rated as fourth class.

219th Division.

COMPOSITION.

	1917		1918	
	Brigade.	Regiment.	Brigade.	Regiment.
Infantry...............	47 Ers.	101 Res. 391. 431. (100 Ldw.).	47 Ers.	101 Res. 391. 431.
Cavalry...............	(?)		4 Sqn. 19 Hus. Rgt.	
Artillery..............	(?)		45 Saxon Ers. F. A. Rgt. 767 Light Am. Col. 768 Light Am. Col. 785 Light Am. Col.	
Engineers and Liaisons.	(219) Pion. Btn: 254 Pion. Co. 54 Bav. Pion. Co. 416 T. M. Co. 219 Tel. Detch.		205 Pion. Btn. Rgt. 377 Pion. Co. 78 Res. Pion. Co. 222 Searchlight Section. 219 Signal Command: 219 Tel. Detch.	
Medical and Veterinary	444 Ambulance Co. 111 Field Hospital. 153 Field Hospital. Vet. Hospital.		404 Ambulance Co. 111 Field Hospital. 153 Field Hospital. 226 Vet. Hospital.	
Transports.............	M. T. Col.			

HISTORY.

(12th and 19th Corps Districts—Saxony.)

1917.

The 219th Division (Saxon) appeared to have been formed in January, 1917.

LORRAINE.

1. Concentrated in Lorraine and comprising the 431st Infantry Regiment, made up of drafts from various Saxon Regiments, the 101st Infantry Regiment, from the 23d Reserve Division, and the 100th Landwehr Regiment, a surplus regiment of the 19th Ersatz Division, the 219th Division occupied the sector of Blamont in February, 1917.

2. It remained on the Lorraine front in the vicinity of Leintrey-Badondiller until June 10.

ARTOIS.

*3. Sent to the north of France, it relieved the 79th Reserve Division north of La Bassée (Neuvechapelle–Fromelles) on July 8. With the 42d Landwehr Division, it exchanged the 100th Landwehr Regiment for the 391st Infantry Regiment, Saxon also.

RUSSIA.

4. About the end of September the 219th Division was withdrawn from the front and transferred to Russia at the beginning of October.

RIGA.

5. It was in the Riga area in October and November.

RECRUITING.

The division was entirely Saxon.

The 219th Division had been in Russia since October, 1917, and was a fairly good division.

1918.

LIVONIA.

1. The 219th Division took part in the occupation of Livonia; on the 17th of March it arrived at Dorpat.

SERBIA.

2. The 101st Reserve and the 431st Landwehr Regiments were identified at Nish on the 9th of October. The 391st Regiment was seen at Walk in Livonia at the beginning of October, when the men said they were leaving for the western theater (the regiment was never identified there). The whole of the 219th Division had thus left the Russian front and two regiments at least went to Serbia.

The division was rated as third class.

220th Division.

COMPOSITION.

	1916		1917		1918	
	Brigade.	Regiment.	Brigade.	Regiment.	Brigade.	Regiment.
Infantry	4 Gd.	55 Res. 99 Res. 207 Res.	4 Gd.	190. 55 Res. 99 Res.	4 Gd.	190. 55 Res. 99 Res.
Cavalry			4 Sqn. 14 Uhlan Rgt.		4 Sqn. 14 Uhlan Rgt.	
Artillery	51 F. A. Rgt.		220 Art. Command: 51 F. A. Rgt.		220 Art. Command: 51 F. A. Rgt. 87 Ft. A. Btn. 938 Light Am. Col. 1326 Light Am. Col. 1327 Light Am. Col.	
Engineers and Liaisons			220 Pion. Btn.: 2 Res. Co. Gd. Pions. 88 Bav. Pion. Co. 417 T. M. Co. 220 Tel. Detch.		220 Pion. Btn.: 2 Gd. Res. Pion. Co. 88 Res. Pion. Co. 417 T. M. Co. 149 Searchlight Section. 220 Signal Command: 220 Tel. Detch. 124 Wireless Detch.	
Medical and Veterinary			40 Ambulance Co. 55 Res. Field Hospital. 74 Res. Field Hospital. 276 Vet. Hospital.		40 Ambulance Co. 55 Res. Field Hospital. 74 Res. Field Hospital. 276 Vet. Hospital.	
Transport			630 M. T. Col.		630 M. T. Col.	

HISTORY.

(190th Infantry Regiment and 55th Reserve Infantry Regiment; 7th Corps District—
Westphalia. 99th Reserve Infantry Regiment; 15th Corps District—Alsace.)

1916.

The 220th Division was formed at the end of 1916 with regiments taken from divisions then in line on the Somme and south of Artois. The 207th Reserve Infantry Regiment coming from the 44th Reserve Division, the 55th Reserve Infantry Regiment and the 2d Reserve Guard Division and the 99th Reserve Infantry Regiment from the 26th Reserve Division.

1917.

ARTOIS.

1. Concentrated at Boyelles (west of Croisilles) on February 6, 1917, the 220th Division went into line at Ransart, south of Arras. About March 18 it took part in the retirement of the German forces and established its position at Hénin sur Cojeul, Ecoust St. Menin, Croisilles. It was engaged, in April, between Croisilles and Arras. In April the 190th Infantry Regiment replaced the 207th Reserve Infantry Regiment.

2. Withdrawn from the Arras front at the end of April, the 220th Division was sent to rest in the vicinity of Montagne du Nord, then to Belgium between May 6 and 15.

3. It came back to its old sector in Artois (Fontaine les Croisilles, Bullecourt) about May 29, and remained there until about July 6.

LENS.

4. After a rest in the rear of Douai, northwest of Lens, from the beginning of July to the middle of August, the division was engaged near Lens from August 16 to 22.

YPRES.

5. At the beginning of October it was sent to Belgium. On the 12th it went into line east of Zonnebeke.

CAMBRAI.

6. Sent to rest about October 15 in the vicinity of Bruges, it then fought on the Cambrai front, south of Crèvecoeur, at the end of November (German counterattack).

7. It was sent to rest in December.

RECRUITING.

The 220th Division may be considered as Westphalian since two of its regiments were normally filled up from the 7th Corps District, and since the 99th Reserve Infantry Regiment, like a number of regiments in Alsace, received most of its men from there.

VALUE—1917 ESTIMATE.

The regiments of the 220th Division did not appear to have any great offensive value.

The division lost quite heavily in the sector of Lens at the beginning of 1918.

1918.

LA BASSÉE.

1. During the night of December 31–January 1 it relieved the 1st Guard Reserve Division in the Hulluch–Loos sector (south of La Bassée). On the 27th it was relieved by the 1st Guard Reserve Division.

2. A day or two later it relieved the 207th Division in the sector to the right of the one it had just held. During the night of the 18th–19th of February it was relieved by the 207th Division.

3. It went back to the Lens sector then and relieved the 1st Guard Reserve Division on the 20th. It was not withdrawn until April 25, when it was relieved by the 42d Division. During these three months the division had about 1,600 casualties (mainly gas), and so now a week or so was spent refitting in the region north of Douai.

4. On May 6 it relieved the 44th Reserve Division southeast of Locon (west of La Bassée). This front had been stabilized by now, but still there was a great deal of artillery activity and constant raiding. The division was withdrawn about the 1st of August, the neighboring divisions extending their fronts.

BAPAUME.

5. After a fortnight's rest the division reenforced the front in the Biefvillers sector (northwest of Bapaume) about the 20th of August. It was withdrawn about the 3d of September after losing some 600 prisoners.

CAMBRAI.

6. It rested again for a fortnight, and then reenforced the front near Blécourt (north of Cambrai) about the 29th of the month. It was heavily engaged here and suffered severely; withdrawn on the 13th of October.

VALENCIENNES.

7. About the 21st it reenforced the front near Anzin (northwest of Valenciennes). It was withdrawn on November 4.

8. On the 7th it was put back into line near Elouges (southwest of Ghislain); it was not withdrawn before the armistice.

VALUE—1918 ESTIMATE.

The 220th Division was not used in any of the German offensives during 1918; on the contrary, its rôle seems to have been that of a holding division. The 55th Reserve Regiment was mentioned as having displayed "marked gallantry" in the German communiqué of October 2. It is rated as a second-class division.

221st Division.
COMPOSITION.

	1916		1917		1918	
	Brigade.	Regiment.	Brigade.	Regiment.	Brigade.	Regiment.
Infantry	1 Res. Ers.	41. 60 Res. 1 Res. Ers.	1 Res. Ers.	41. 60 Res. 1 Res. Ers.	1 Res. Ers.	41. 60 Res. 45.
Cavalry	1 Sqn. 2 Res. Uhlan Rgt.		1 Sqn. 2 Res. Uhlan Rgt.		5 Sqn. 8 Uhlan Rgt.	
Artillery	273 F. A. Rgt.		Art. Command: 273 F. A. Rgt.		221 Art. Command: 273 F. A. Rgt. 40 Ft. A. Btn. (Staff, and 1, 2, and 3 Btries.). 126 Light Am. Col. 1276 Light Am. Col. 1345 Light Am. Col.	
Engineers and Liaisons			(221) Pion. Btn.: 2 Res. Co. 21 Pions. 1 Res. Co. 25 Pions. 431 T. M. Co. 221 Tel. Detch.		(221) Pion. Btn.: 1 Res. Co. 25 Pions. 2 Res. Co. 21 Pions. 431 T. M. Co. 200 Searchlight Section. 221 Signal Command: 221 Tel. Detch. 71 Wireless Detch.	
Medical and Veterinary			223 Ambulance Co. 161 Field Hospital. Vet. Hospital.		223 Ambulance Co. 161 Field Hospital. 163 Field Hospital. 321 Vet. Hospital.	
Transport			M. T. Col.		631 M. T. Col.	
Attached					7 Art. Observation Section. 82 Carrier Pigeon Loft. 21 M. G. S. S. Detch. 1 Btry. 39 Ft. A. Rgt. 2 Btry. 39 Ft. A. Rgt. 119 Balloon Sqn. 238 Reconnaissance Flight. Elements attached Sept. 29, 1918.	

HISTORY.

(41st Infantry Regiment: 1st Corps District—East Prussia. 60th Reserve Infantry Regiment: 21st Corps District—Lorraine. 1st Reserve Ersatz Regiment: Guard Depots.)

1916.

The 221st Division was formed in the Ardennes (vicinity of Mouzon) in October, 1916, by taking the 41st Infantry Regiment from the 1st Division, the 60th Reserve Infantry Regiment (21st Corps District) from the 1st Bavarian Landwehr Division, and the 1st Reserve Ersatz Regiment (Guard Depots) from the 1st Reserve Ersatz Brigade.

SOMME.

1. A short time after its formation the 221st Division was transferred south of the Somme. On October 21–23 it went into line east of Berny; it remained there during the entire winter of 1916–17 and launched only a few local attacks.

1917.

HINDENBURG LINE.

1. At the end of March, 1917, the division withdrew with the German Army to the new positions on the Hindenburg Line, northwest of St. Quentin.

ARTOIS.

2. Relieved about April 8, it rested for 10 days near Tournai, and on April 27 went into line in the sector of Guemappe–Monchy le Preux (southeast of Arras). It was seriously engaged against the British offensive until May 8–9.

3. About May 28 it returned to the Hindenburg Line between Moevres and Havrincourt.

FLANDERS.

4. On July 12 it left this sector for Flanders, where it was sent into reserve near Winckel–St. Eloi. It did not take part as a whole in the British attack of July 31. On August 1 the entire division was engaged in the sector of Zonnebeke, where it launched a violent counterattack, in the course of which it lost heavily.

5. The 221st Division was relieved from the Ypres front during the night of August 3–4, but left some units in line until the 10th. Transferred to Champagne, it went into line east of Auberive on August 17, without having had any rest. It there filled up its effectives (with replacements comprising a large proportion of the 1918 class). Its activity was not manifested there except by a few raids.

CAMBRAI.

6. On November 7 the division left the Champagne front, was transferred to Belgium, and remained at rest at Deynze until November 23. On this date it was taken by railroad to the Cambrai front, attacked by the British troops. Sent into line between Bourlon and Fontaine–Notre Dame on the 27th, it took part in the German counterattack. Relieved on December 7, it rested for a month in the vicinity of Douai.

RECRUITING.

The division was very mixed. The 1st Reserve Ersatz Regiment, originating in the Guard depots, was recruited from the entire Province of Prussia; the 41st Infantry Regiment (from East Prussia) was one of the regiments of the Prussian Army which had received the most replacements because of losses; the 60th Reserve Infantry Regiment comprised a majority of Westphalians and men from the Rhine Province, but also a large number from other corps districts.

The 221st Division always gave a good account of itself in the battles in which it took part. The 1st Reserve Ersatz Regiment, especially, in the course of the attacks of November, 1916, showed great tenacity on the defensive and great vigor on the offensive.

The morale of the 221st Division was good in November, 1917. The general commanding the division and the major commanding the 41st Infantry Regiment both received the order "Pour le Merite."

1918.

BATTLE OF PICARDY.

1. The division continued to hold the sector near the Arras–Cambrai road until shortly before the March offensive. It was withdrawn, given a short rest, and attacked on the 21st at Queant. In two days it advanced as far as Ervillers (north of Bapaume). From the 25th of March to April 16 it rested in close support.

2. On April 16 the division was engaged the second time in the battle. It entered south of Arras in the Boyelles sector and remained there until May 25, when it was relieved by the 5th Bavarian Division.

3. The division rested and trained for almost two months in the locality east of Douai (Bruille, Somain, Aniches). The 45th Regiment, coming from the Macedonian front, replaced the 1st Reserve Ersatz Regiment, which was dissolved. Toward the end of July the division marched by stages to Noyon. It was held in reserve west of that place from July 30–August 8.

BATTLE OF THE SANTERRE AND SECOND BATTLE OF PICARDY.

4. On August 9 the division was engaged at Arvillers–Hengest. In two days it was thrown back on Andechy, west of Roye. It was re-formed to the north and then to the southwest of Nesle (Aug. 11–17). It was reengaged on the 18th, and between that and the 27th fought north and south of the Aore near Roye (St. Mard–Sancourt). Again it was pushed back on the Canal du Nord at Buverchy–Libermont (Aug. 26–27). Its retreat continued toward Ham (Sept. 3–4) and St. Quentin (5th–8th). After that the division was in line near Fontaine les Cleres and Dallon until September 28. About 1,000 prisoners were taken from the division in this last sector.

5. The division was reengaged almost immediately south of Joncourt, Levergies, and Sequehort (Sept. 30). By October 10 it had reached Fresnoy le Frand. It was withdrawn on the 10th and rested a week near Bergues sur Sambre.

6. On the 18th it was engaged in the sector of the forest d'Antigny (near Wassigny). It retreated across the Sambre Canal on the 19th and passed into reserve. On the 24th it was reengaged near the Serre River (west of La Ferte Chevresis). In the final retreat it fell back through La Herie la Vieville, Laigny, and east of Vervins. It was in line on November 11.

The division was rated as second class. It was used as an attack division in the March offensive and as a counterattack division in the last three months of the war. It was noted for its energetic higher command. When called in to oppose the French attack near Roye in August, the division had a rifle strength of 4,000. By the end of October this had been reduced to about 1,000. The 45th Regiment was reduced to four small companies by October 24. The 41st and 60th Reserve Regiments had but three companies to a battalion.

The division fought very well in spite of its losses and fatigue in the final months.

222d Division.
COMPOSITION.

	1916		1917		1918[1]	
	Brigade.	Regiment.	Brigade.	Regiment.	Brigade.	Regiment.
Infantry	7.	193. 81 Res. 397.	7.	193. 81 Res. 397.	7.	193. 397. 81 Res.
Cavalry			3 Sqn. 2 Res. Uhlan Rgt.			
Artillery	278 F. A. Rgt.		Art. Command: 278 F. A. Rgt.		222 (?) Art. Command: 278 F. A. Rgt.	
Engineers and Liaisons	2 Res. Co. 27 Pions.		Pion. Btn.: 2 Res. Co. 27 Pions. 345 Pion. Co. 432 T. M. Co. 222 Tel. Detch.		2 Res. Co. 2 Pion. Btn. No. 27. 345 Pion. Co. 432 T. M. Co. 222 Tel. Detch.	
Medical and Veterinary			231 Ambulance Co. 162 Field Hospital. 175 Field Hospital. 322 Vet. Hospital.		231 Ambulance Co. 162 Field Hospital. 175 Field Hospital. 322 Vet. Hospital.	
Transport			1071 M. T. Col.		M. T. Col.	

[1] Composition at the time of dissolution, October, 1918.

HISTORY.

(81st Reserve Regiment: 18th Corps District—Hesse-Nassau. 193d Reserve Regiment: 7th Corps District—Westphalia. 397th Reserve Regiment: 2d Corps District —Pomerania.)

1916.

Formed about September 11, 1916, behind the front north of Verdun, the 222d Division took two of its regiments from existing divisions—the 81st Reserve Regiment from the 21st Reserve Division, and the 193d Reserve Regiment from the 192d Division. Its third regiment, the 397th, was formed at Stenay from elements of the 16th and 53d Reserve Regiments (13th Reserve Division), of the 159th Regiment (14th Reserve Division), of the 118th Infantry Regiment (56th Division), and especially from the 140th Infantry Regiment (4th Division).

1. From September 15 to October 24, 1916, the 222d Division was at rest in Alsace in the vicinity of Rouffach.

SOMME.

2. Entrained on October 25, it was transferred to the vicinity of Cambrai by way of Sarrebruecken, Aix la Chapelle, Brussels, Tournai. About November 5 it went into action on the Somme front near Lesboeufs, Le Transloy, and remained in line until December 7-8.

3. After a few days of rest it was sent by railroad into the Laonnois. Detraining at St. Erme between December 15 and 29 it took over the sector of the Ville aux Bois (southeast of Craonne), which it occupied until February 15, 1917.

1917.

1. Upon its release the 222d Division was employed in defensive works behind the Aisne–Oise front (north of La Fère, St. Gobain, Laffaux, Chavignon).

AISNE.

2. About March 16, 1917, it was engaged east of Soissons (Vregny–Combe Plateau); counterattacked on March 21 north of Missy sur Aisne; retired in the direction of the Laffaux Mill–Jouy-Aizy (at the beginning of April) and fought on this front April 18 to 21.

The 193d Infantry Regiment, sent as reenforcement troops to Soupir, suffered serious losses there and retired by way of Ostel on April 20.

3. The 222d Division, having established its position between Laffaux Mill and Malmaison Farm, was again severely tried during the attacks of May 5 and 6.

4. Withdrawn from the Aisne front on May 13, it was sent to rest in the area Marle–Vervins and reorganized.

5. At the end of June the division took over its former sector (Laffaux), where the attack of July 8 was the only inportant action in which it took part during this time, which lasted until the beginning of August.

6. After a short rest in the vicinity of Montigny, it came back into line (Ailles-north of Hurtebise) about September 5 and remained in this sector until November 2. At this time it took part in the withdrawal and occupied new positions north of the Ailette.

7. On November 28, the 222d Division was relieved in the sector of Chermizy and sent to rest at Laon and in the vicinity of Marle (one month's training).

8. At the end of December it occupied the front Brancourt-Anizy.

RECRUITING.

The 81st Reserve Infantry Regiment and the 193d Infantry Regiment were recruited in the Rhine districts (Hesse-Nassau, Rhine Province, and Westphalia). Many elements from these same regions were in the 397th Infantry Regiment in addition to Pomeranians.

Although it had suffered only slight losses since the beginning of November, 1917, the 222d Division was exhausted by a stay of more than seven months in the different sectors of the Aisne. It is a mediocre division (January, 1918).

During its rest in December the division received continual but moderate training, like the maneuvers of peace times. (Interrogation of prisoner, Feb. 4, 1918.)

AILETTE.

1. This was a very quiet sector and the division remained here without incident until the Somme offensive was well under way. However, the division took part in the attacks of April 7 and 8, when the enemy endeavored to squeeze out the new salient of Coucy le Château, which was developed by the progress of the main advance toward Montdidier. It suffered heavily in several attacks but gained little ground.

MONTDIDIER.

2. About the 3d of May the division was withdrawn and sent to the front southeast of Montdidier, where the main battle line had stabilized, but where infantry was still continuing, and during the night of the 9th-10th relieved the 206th Division in the Assainvillers sector. However, the sector soon grew quiet. The division remained in line and took part in the battle of the Oise on June 9, advancing via Courcelles to Méry. The division made but little headway (it will be remembered that this whole offensive failed) and suffered heavy losses in several days of hard fighting. It was relieved by the 11th Division about the 8th of July and went to rest near Coucy le Château.

SOISSONS.

3. During the night of the 25th–26th the division reenforced the front near Nouvron (northwest of Soissons). Here it was subjected to the full weight of the attack of the 18th of August and was driven back to Audignicourt and the Ailette. After having suffered very heavy losses (1829 prisoners), it was withdrawn about the 27th and went to rest near Laon. About the middle of September it was disbanded, the 81st Reserve Regiment going to the 21st Reserve Division, the 193d Regiment going to the 14th Division, and the 397th Regiment going to the 45th Reserve Division.

The 222d was rated a second-class division. It took little part in offensive operations but was not incapable of putting up a tenacious defense. In June two of its regiments threatened to leave the trenches if they were not relieved, but the difficulty seems to have been smoothed over though there was no relief until July 8. It is interesting to note that the divisions receiving regiments when the 222d was disbanded were all second-class units.

223d Division.

COMPOSITION.

	1916 Brigade.	1916 Regiment.	1917 Brigade.	1917 Regiment.	1918[1] Brigade.	1918[1] Regiment.
Infantry	67.	144. 173. 29 Ers.	67.	144. 173. 29 Ers.	67.	144. 173. 29 Ers.
Cavalry	2 Sqn. 3 Res. Drag. Rgt.		(2 Sqn. 3 Res. Drag. Rgt.).		2 Sqn. 3 Res. Drag. Rgt.	
Artillery	280 F. A. Rgt.		Art. command: 280 F. A. Rgt.		(z) Art. command: 280 F. A. Rgt.	
Engineers and Liaisons	343 Pion. Co.		(223) Pion Btn.: 5 Co. 23 Pions. 343 Pion. Co. 433 T. M. Co. 223 Tel. Detch.		5 Co. 23 Pions. 343 Pion. Co. 433 T. M. Co. 223 Tel. Detch.	
Medical and Veterinary			232 Ambulance Co. 164 Field Hospital. 170 Field Hospital. 176 Field Hospital. Vet. Hospital.		232 Ambulance Co. 164 Field Hospital. 176 Field Hospital. Vet. Hospital.	
Transport			M. T. Col.		M. T. Col.	

[1] Composition at the time of dissolution, October, 1918.

HISTORY.

(144th Infantry Regiment: 16th Corps District—Lorraine.   173d Infantry Regiment: 16th Corps District—Lorraine.   29th Ersatz Regiment: 14th Corps District—Grand Duchy of Baden.)

1916.

The 223d Division was concentrated at Mulhousen at the beginning of October, 1916.   Its regiments formerly belonged to other divisions.   The 144th Infantry Regiment was taken from the 3d Division on the Verdun front; the 173d from the 34th Division, then at Thiaumont; the 29th Ersatz from the 39th Bavarian Reserve Division, on the Lorraine front.

1. Entraining at Mulhousen on October 26, 1916, the 223d Division was transferred to the north by way of Sarrelouis–Treves–Aix la Chapelle–Louvain–Brussels–Valenciennes, and detrained north of Cambrai on October 28.   During the night of November 11–12 it came to the Ancre front (Serre–Grancourt) and lost heavily there.

2. Relieved about November 25, it was sent to rest in the area east of Cambrai. Elements of the 173d Infantry Regiment were sent on detached service south of Bapaume (Ligny–Tilloy).

1917.

CHAMPAGNE.

1. At the end of January, 1917, the 223d Division left the Cambrai area for Champagne. It occupied the sector north of Rheims (Witry les Rheims, March and April).

2. About April 27 it was engaged south of Lauroy at Mont Cornillet and lost heavily between April 30 and May 8.

GALICIA.

3. Withdrawn from the Champagne front about May 18, the 223d Division was transferred to Galicia.   (Itinerary: Amagne (May 21)–Sedan–Thionville–Sarrebruecken–Frankfort–Leipzig–Breslau–Cracow–Lemberg.   It detrained at Zloczow, May 26.

4. At the beginning of July it opposed the Russian offensive in the vicinity of Brzezany; on July 18, it took part in the Austro-German counterattack and marched in the direction of Husiatyn, which it reached on the 30th and remained in line there until the middle of December.   It was sent in reserve on this date, and prepared to leave for the Western Front, borrowing men from the regiments of the 83d Division.

RECRUITING.

The 223d Division was recruited from Westphalia and the Rhine Province so far as concerns the 144th and 173d Infantry Regiments.   The 29th Ersatz Regiment came from the Grand Duchy of Baden.

VALUE—1917 ESTIMATE.

The 223d Division may be considered good.

1918.

BATTLE OF PICARDY.

1. The division rested in a camp at Sissonne until March 19, after which it was railed to La Fere, arriving there on March 21.

2. On the second day of the attack it was engaged near Tergnier–Chauny and advanced to the Guiscard region by the 24th.   Shortly after its withdrawal from Guiscard (25th) it took over the Morlincourt–Appilly sector on the Oise (east of Noyon) and held it until May 1.

EAST OF OISE.

3. It rested near Guiscard during the first half of May. On the 15th it was engaged in front of Noyon (Larbroye–Mont Renand–Pont l'Eveque) until the 30th. It took part in the Oise offensive of June, crossing the river and advancing in the Bois de Carlepont in the direction of Caisnes and Cuts. It established itself on the line Bailley–Tracy le Val–Oise and held that sector until the French attack of August 18.

OISE–AISNE.

4. The French attack of the 18th threw the division back on Salency. It was relieved on the 22d and railed to Anizy le Chateau the same day. From there it was taken to north of Soissons and reengaged on the 29th on the line Chauvigny–Juvigny. In these two engagements the division lost 688 prisoners.

5. The division had lost heavily in March and in the August fighting. Its morale was poor. The authority of the officers was low and desertions were frequent. As a result the division was dissolved in September. Its effectives were turned into the 52d, 103d, and 115th Divisions.

VALUE—1918 ESTIMATE.

The division was rated as third class. Prior to the March offensive it had been regarded a good division.

224th Division.
COMPOSITION.

	1916		1917		1918	
	Brigade.	Regiment.	Brigade.	Regiment.	Brigade.	Regiment.
Infantry		19 Ldw. 61 Ldw. 429 Ldw.	216.	19 Ldw. 61 Ldw. 429 Ldw.	216.	19 Ldw. 61 Ldw. 429 Ldw.
Cavalry			(?) Sqn. 10 Mounted Jäg. Rgt.		4 Sqn. 10 Mounted Jäg. Rgt.	
Artillery	284 F. A. Rgt.		224 Art. Command: 284 F. A. Rgt.		224 Art. Command: 284 F. A. Rgt. 795 Light Am. Col. 1015 Light Am. Col. 1029 Light Am. Col.	
Engineers and Liaisons			224 Pion. Btn.: 2 Co. 27 Pions. 434 T. M. Co. Tel.- Detch.		423 Pion. Btn.: 2 Co. 27 Pions. 3 Landst. Co. 9 C. Dist. Pions. 251 Searchlight Section. 224 Signal Command: 224 Tel. Detch.	
Medical and Veterinary			234 Ambulance Co. 181 Field Hospital. 330 Field Hospital. 324 Vet. Hospital.		234 Ambulance Co. 336 Field Hospital. 324 Field Hospital.	
Transport			794 M. T. Col. 795 M. T. Col.			
Attached				1 Landst. Pion. Co. (8 C. Dist.).		

HISTORY.

(429th Landwehr: 3d Corps District—Brandenburg. 19th Landwehr: 5th Corps District—Posen. 61st Landwehr: 17th Corps District—West Prussia.)

1916.

RUSSIA.

1. Upon its formation the 224th Division appeared on the Eastern Front about October, 1916.

2. At this time it was near the 31st Division, north of Lake Narotch.

1917.

VOLHYNIA–SVINIOUKI.

1. At the beginning of February, 1917, the composition of the 224th Division appeared to be as follows: 19th Landwehr Regiment taken from the 18th Landwehr Division; 61st Landwehr Regiment, from the 85th Landwehr Division, and the 429th Landwehr Regiment, a new formation (1916).

2. The 224th Division then occupied the sector of Sviniouki in Volhynia. It remained there during the entire year of 1917, during the latter months furnishing important replacements to the Western Front, to such a degree that in November the companies of the 429th Landwehr did not have more than 100 men left (Russian interrogation).

RECRUITING.

The 224th Division was recruited from Brandenburg and the eastern Provinces of the empire.

VALUE—1917 ESTIMATE.

The division was on the Russian front from its formation and was of mediocre combat value.

In December, 1917, in Volhynia, 50 men of the youngest classes were taken from each company of the 429th Landwehr Regiment to be sent to the Flanders front.

In January, 1918, the companies of the 61st Landwehr Regiment were composed of men of the Landsturm. (Prisoner's statement, Jan. 13.)

1918.

VOLHYNIA.

At the beginning of March the division left the Sviniouki region and went via Pinsk to Gomel.

UKRAINE.

2. Toward the end of April the division was identified in the Vorojva region (southwest of Koursk). On the 9th of September the division was identified a little farther to the north in the Delgorod region.

WOEVRE.

3. On September 29 the division was relieved (probably by the 45th Landwehr Division) and, entraining at Sadtowo, traveled via Kubiantz–Kharkov–Kiev–Kovel–Kattovitz–Dresden–Frankfort on the Main–Saarbrueken–Metz–Batilly, where it detrained on October 12. Resting here until the 16th, it marched via Bruville–Mars la Tour–Chambley and relieved the 88th Division during the night of the 16th–17th south of Dampvitoux. The division was identified by prisoners on November 7 here and does not seem to have been withdrawn before the armistice.

VALUE—1918 ESTIMATE.

The division was a very poor one. About the middle of the summer the best men were chosen to be sent to the Western Front. They were paraded before the commanding general and when they reached the place where he was standing they dropped their guns and went back to the casern. Later when the whole division was to come to the west, the men were far from satisfied, not being entirely consoled when they were informed that they were to enter a quiet sector.

225th Division.

COMPOSITION.

	1916		1917		1918 [1]	
	Brigade.	Regiment.	Brigade.	Regiment.	Brigade.	Regiment.
Infantry	5 Ers.	18 Res. 217 Res. 373.	5 Ers.	18 Res. 217 Res. 373.	5 Ers.	373. 18 Res. 217 Res.
Cavalry	3 Sqn. 13 Uhlan Rgt.		3 Sqn. 13 Uhlan Rgt.		3 Sqn. 13 Uhlan Rgt.	
Artillery			225 Art. Command: 47 F. A. Rgt.		225 Art. Command: 47 F. A. Rgt.	
Engineers and Liaisons			(225) Pion. Btn.: 259 Pion. Co. 344 Pion. Co. 413 T. M. Co. Tel. Detch.		259 Pion. Co. 413 T. M. Co. 225 Tel. Detch.	
Medical and Veterinary			259 Ambulance Co. 155 Field Hospital. 172 Field Hospital. 265 Vet. Hospital.		240 Ambulance Co. 259 Ambulance Co. 155 Field Hospital. Vet. Hospital.	
Transport					M. T. Col.	

[1] Composition at the time of the dissolution, September, 1918.

HISTORY.

(18th Reserve: 18th Corps Division—East Prussia. 217th Reserve: 7th Corps District—Westphalia. 373d Infantry Regiment: 1st Corps District—East Prussia.)

1916.

The 225th Division, including the 18th Reserve Infantry Regiment (from the 1st Reserve Division), the 217th Reserve Infantry Regiment (from the 47th Reserve Division), and the 373d Infantry Regiment (from the 10th Landwehr Division), was formed on the Eastern Front in the vicinity of Wladimir–Volynski about September, 1916.

ROUMANIA–TRANSYLVANIA.

1. In November, 1916, the 225th Division was transferred to the Roumanian Carpathians.. It was there in December in the valley of the Uz.

1917.

ROUMANIA.

1. During the first half of 1917 the 225th Division occupied the calm sectors in the vicinity of Uz (Hills 1031 and 1640).

2. In July the 373d Infantry Regiment was transferred to the valley of the Putna to withstand the Russo-Roumanian offensive. The division took part in the Austro-German counterattack and established its positions near Ocna in September and October.

FRANCE.

3. Relieved about November 11, it went to Bereczk, where it entrained on the 18th for the Western Front. (Itinerary: Kronstadt (Brasso)–Budapest–Vienna–Munich–Carlsruhe–Sarrebruecken.) It detrained on November 25 at Vallieres–Vantoux, near Metz, and from there was transferred to the vicinity of Vigneulles (Cote de Meuse).

COTE DE MEUSE.

4. On December 4–5, it took over the sector of Chevalierswood, south of Vaux les Palameix–Seuzey.

RECRUITING.

Two regiments were drawn from East Prussia (18th Reserve and 372d Infantry Regiment), the 217th Reserve from Westphalia.

VALUE—1917 ESTIMATE.

The 225th Division which comprised drafts from Baden, Alsace, Westphalia, East Prussia, and the Rhine was not homogeneous and was not considered as a fighting division.

The 18th Reserve Regiment had a bad reputation. On January 6, 1917, it refused to attack at Hill 1298 in Hungary. (Interrogation of prisoners Feb. 3 and Mar. 17, 1918.)

The division included a large number of Poles. However, men of the young classes gradually replaced the older men, who still made up a large part of the division in 1917; consequently, the combat value of the division may have improved.

1918.

1. The division held the Woevre sector until the beginning of May. It entrained at Jeandelize about May 15 and was railed by Sedan, Givet, Dmant, Namur, Charleroi, Mons, and Cambrai. It detrained near Peronne and marched toward the Avre front by Chaulnes, Rosieres en Santerre.

BATTLE OF THE SANTERRE.

2. It was engaged north of Moreuil (east of the Villers aux Erables–Thennes) on May 22. The Allied attack struck the division and threw it back on Beaufort, losing 2,358 prisoners. It was relieved on the 10th and rested 15 days. Reengaged on the 25th east of Albert (Contalmaison, Montauban) the division again lost heavily. It was withdrawn on the 30th.

3. After its withdrawal the division was dissolved to the profit of the 1st Reserve Division and 2d Division.

VALUE—1918 ESTIMATE.

The division was rated as third class. In the August fighting in Picardy it did not make a strong resistance. In the two engagements in August the division lost 3 593 prisoners.

226th Division.

COMPOSITION.

	1916		1917		1918¹	
	Brigade.	Regiment.	Brigade.	Regiment.	Brigade.	Regiment.
Infantry	5 Ldw.	2 Ldw. 9 Ldw. 439.	5 Ldw.	2 Ldw. 9 Ldw. 427.	5 Ldw.	2 Ldw. 9 Ldw. Rgt. 427.
Cavalry			1 Sqn. 4 Mounted Jag. Rgt.		1 Sqn. 4 Mounted Jag. Rgt.	
Artillery			64 Res. F. A. Rgt.		(?) Art. Command: 64 Res. F. A. Rgt.	
Engineers and Liaisons			(226) Pion Btn.: 2 Ers. Co. 18 Pions. (?) T. M. Co. 26 Searchlight Co. 226 Tel. Detch.		2 Ers. Co. 18 Pions. Searchlight Section. 430 T. M. Co. 226 Tel. Detch.	
Medical and Veterinary			257 Ambulance Co. Field Hospital. 262 Vet. Hospital.		257 Ambulance Co. Field Hospital. 262 Vet. Hospital.	
Transport			471 M. T. Col.		635 M. T. Col.	

¹ Composition at the time of dissolution, May, 1918.

HISTORY.

(2d Corps District—Pomerania.)

1916.

The 226th Division was formed about December, 1916.

RUSSIA.

1. At the end of December it was identified on the Eastern Front in the vicinity of Smorgoni, forming, with the 205th Division, the 3d (reenforced) Reserve Corps of the 10th Army.

1917.

1. The 226th Division included in 1917 the 2d and 9th Landwehr Regiments (5th Landwehr Brigade), taken from the 35th Reserve Division, and the 439th Infantry Regiment, formed in 1916.

SMORGONI.

2. The division occupied the sector of Smorgoni–Krevo from January until August, 1917. In this sector it received the Russian attacks of July 2 and 23, which caused it very heavy losses, in consequence of which Emperor William II called himself commander of the 2d Landwehr Regiment.

3. About the beginning of August the 226th Division was relieved south of Smorgoni and replaced the 123d Division south of Lake Svir. In November the 2d Landwehr Regiment sent men to reenforce the 121st Division and the 9th Landwehr to reenforce the 2d Guard Division.

LAKE NAROTCH.

4. In December the division was in line north of Lake Narotch, relieving the 31st Division, which was sent to the Western Front.

1918.

1. The division was still there in January, 1918. It was dissolved in June.

ROUMANIA.

2. The presence of the headquarters of the 226th Division at Targovistea was reported early in October. These headquarters apparently had under its order the 58th Reserve Field Artillery Regiment, of which the headquarters and three batteries are at Bucharest, the remaining batteries at Durnu Margurelf, Targovistea, and Cantulung.

VALUE—1918 ESTIMATE.

The division was rated as fourth class.

227th Division.

COMPOSITION.

	1917		1918	
	Brigade.	Regiment.	Brigade.	Regiment.
Infantry..............	49 Ldw.	417. 441. 477.	49 Ldw.	417 and 477.
Cavalry..............	(?)		1 Sqn. 10 Hus. Rgt.	
Artillery.............	92 F. A. Rgt.		227 Art. Command: 92 F. A. Rgt. 3 Abt. 20 Ft. A. Rgt. (9 and 11 Btries). 853 Light Am. Col. 1102 Light Am. Col. 113 Light Am. Col.	
Engineers and Liaisons.	227 Pion. Btn.: 339 Pion. Co. 347 Pion. Co. 162 T. M. Co. 227 Tel. Detch.		227 Pion. Btn.: 339 Pion. Co. 347 Pion. Co. 162 T. M. Co. 213 Searchlight Section. 227 Signal Command: 227 Tel. Detch. 155 Wireless Detch.	
Medical and Veterinary.	65 Ambulance Co. 278 Field Hospital. 285 Field Hospital. Vet. Hospital.		65 Ambulance Co. 278 Field Hospital. 285 Field Hospital. 208 Vet. Hospital.	
Transport..............	M. T. Col.		637 M. T. Col.	

HISTORY.

(417th Infantry Regiment; 14th Corps District—Grand Duchy of Baden. 441st Infantry Regiment; 18th Corps District—Hesse-Nassau. 477th Infantry Regiment; 8th Corps District—Rhine Province.)

1917.

The 227th Division, formed in March, 1917, was composed of three newly-formed regiments—the 417th (Baden), the 441st (18th District—Hesse), the 477th, formed by drafts upon the units of the 38th and 13th Divisions and upon the 16th Corps, then attached after its formation in the autumn of 1916 to the 33d Division of this corps.

ARGONNE.

1. The 227th Division was identified for the first time on March 27, 1917, on the Argonne front. It occupied the calm sector of the Fille-Morte until May 26.

AISNE.

2. About June 1 it went into line south of the Aisne (La Neuville–Godat) and extended its sector, at the beginning of July, to Hill 108 (Sapigneul).

3. Relieved about August 5, it was sent for rest and training to the Asfeld area. On August 20 it went into line north of Berry au Bac, between the Miette and Hill 108, from which it was withdrawn on August 2.

The division did not take part in any important engagement on the Aisne front. Its losses were very slight.

FLANDERS.

4. On October 5 and 6 the 227th Division entrained at Amagne (east of Rethel), and was transferred to Belgium by way of Hirson–Tournai–Courtrai–Thielt. Detraining at Pitthem on October 6 and 7, it reached the front north of Poepcappelle on the night of the 8th–9th, was in action for a week and suffered very heavy losses.

5. The division left the Ypres front about October 15 to go to Ghent (two days), then into the Champagne in the vicinity of Aussonce. It was filled up with three replacements, the most important of which was made up of 1,200 men taken from units on the Eastern Front, especially from the 12th Landwehr Division, from the same Provinces as the 227th Division (end of October).

CHAMPAGNE.

6. At the beginning of November the 227th Division went into line north of Cornillet.

RECRUITING.

The 227th Division was recruited from the Rhine Districts (Baden, Hesse–Nassau, the Rhine Province), which gives rise to a certain homogeneity.

VALUE—1917 ESTIMATE.

The 227th Division lost very heavily in Flanders and received as replacements a certain number of men coming from the Russian front whose combat value was mediocre (October, 1917).

The 227th Division was of only mediocre offensive value.

1918.

CHAMPAGNE.

1. About the middle of January the 227th Division was relieved by the 28th Division and went to the Juniville area, where it was intensively trained in open warfare with a view to its being used as an assault division.

2. On February 16 it relieved the 28th Division. It was withdrawn toward the end of March.

PICARDY.

3. About the 10th of April it relieved the 5th Guard Division near Canny sur Matz (west of Lassigny). The battle of the Somme had come to end by this time, and so, although there was still considerable artillery activity here, the division was not seriously engaged in infantry attacks, and remained in line until relieved by the 75th Reserve Division during the night of May 16–17, when it went to rest and be trained in the region of Ham.

OISE.

4. On June 7 it started to march to the front via Ognolles–Champien Wood–Beuvraignes–Crapeaumesnil. On the 9th it attacked through the line and succeeded in passing Ricquebourg, Ressons, and Marqueglise. This advance cost the divisions heavy losses, and it suffered still more heavily when the French counterattacked in force on the 12th; The following day it was relieved by the 17th Reserve Division and marched by stages to the region east of St. Quentin.

WOEVRE.

5. About the 20th it entrained at Origny and traveled via Charleville–Sedan–Longuyon–Conflans–Dampvitoux, where it detrained the 21st and 22d. It relieved the 8th Bavarian Reserve Division in the St. Baussant-Richecourt sector (south of Thiaucourt) on the 27th. It was relieved by the 10th Division on the 22d of August.

SOISSONS.

6. About the 30th it reenforced the front in the Terny–Sorny sector (north of Soissons). It was withdrawn about the 8th of September.

AISNE.

7. There was some talk of dissolving the division at this time, but it was not done, and it came back into line, relieving the 17th Division in the Pont-Arcy sector (east of Vailly) on the 17th. It remained in line, falling back via Monchâlons-Coucy les Eppes–Pierrepont–Montcornet–Ebouleau–Renneval–Jeantes la Ville. It had not been withdrawn on the 11th.

VALUE—1918 ESTIMATE.

The 227th was rated a third-class division. It was in no heavy fighting during 1918 until June, when it did not distinguish itself, neither advancing far nor holding its ground in counterattack. Its conduct, however, can not be characterized as poor. It is to be noted, moreover, that the division commander was awarded "Pour le Mérite" in July.

228th Division.

COMPOSITION.

	1917		1918	
	Brigade.	Regiment.	Brigade.	Regiment.
Infantry...............	104.	35 Fus. 48. 207 Res.	104.	35. 48. 207 Res.
Cavalry...............	1 Sqn. 1 Uhlan Rgt.		1 Sqn. 1 Uhlan Rgt.	
Artillery...............	228 Art. Command: 39 F. A. Rgt.		228 Art. Command: 39 F. A. Rgt. 92 Ft. A. Btn. (Staff, and 1, 2, and 3 Btries). 1143 Light Am. Col. 1144 Light Am. Col. 1145 Light Am. Col.	
Engineers and Liaisons.	(228) Pion. Btn.: 389 Pion. Co. 395 Pion. Co. 197 T. M. Co. Tel. Detch.		228 Pion. Btn.: 389 Pion. Co. 395 Pion. Co. 197 T. M. Co. 116 Searchlight Section. 228 Signal Command: 228 Tel. Detch. 56 Wireless Detch.	
Medical and Veterinary	567 Ambulance Co. 63 Field Hospital. 260 Field Hospital. Vet. Hospital.		567 Ambulance Co. 63 Field Hospital. 260 Field Hospital. 55 Vet. Hospital.	
Transport...............	M. T. Col.			

HISTORY.

(3d Corps District—Brandenburg.)

1917.

The 228th Division appears to have been formed in the Sedan area in May, 1917. Its three regiments belonged to the 3d Corps District—the 35th Fusileer Regiment was taken from the 56th Division, the 48th Infantry Regiment from the 113th Division, and the 207th Reserve Regiment from the 220th Division.

VERDUN.

1. On June 22, 1917, the 228th Division was identified on the Verdun front in the sector of Les Chambrettes (35th Fusileers). It was still in line on the right bank of the Meuse (Louvemont) when the French attacks of August 20–24 were launched. It lost heavily there. "Our regiment has only two companies left" (letter from a man of the 48th Infantry Regiment, Aug. 23).

CÔTES DE MEUSE.

2. Relieved about August 24, it was sent to rest for a few days, then into line again about September 6 on the Côtes de Meuse (between Moulainville and Damploup). It was reorganized in both men and material. At the end of September 900 men came as replacements from the 1st Corps District (returned wounded for the most part). The 35th Fusileer Regiment, decimated in August, remained in the rear for reorganization.

The division was purely Brandenburg (infantry and field artillery).

For its reorganization after the attacks of August 20–24, 1917, the 228th Division received replacements from the 1st Corps District. A replacement unit was formed from the 3d Corps District, but the men are said to have refused to leave for the Western Front. In default of men from Brandenburg, they called upon the 1st Corps District. (Interrogation of prisoner, Sept. 30, 1917.)

VALUE—1917 ESTIMATE.

This was a fairly good division.

1918.

1. The division was relieved northeast of Verdun in mid-February and went to rest and train southeast of Montmedy (near Marville) until March 17. It was then railed to Picardy via Montmedy, Sedan, Hirson, Aulnoye. From there it moved toward the front by Croix, Maurois, Beaurevoir, Bellicourt, Roisel, Maurepas, Bray, arriving there on the 27th.

BATTLE OF PICARDY.

2. It was engaged on the 29th–30th near Le Hamel, north of Marcelcave, and participated in heavy fighting about Hamel until April 13. All three regiments lost heavily in the attack. The 207th Reserve Regiment was too weak to hold more than 160 yards of front. The 35th Fusileer Regiment lost 700 men in killed and wounded. After resting from April 13 to 18 the division wass reengaged on the 18th. It attacked at Villers–Bretonneux on the 24th without success. After suffering very heavy losses the division was withdrawn on April 27–28.

CHAMPAGNE.

3. On the 28th it entrained east of Peronne and was railed to Valenciennes, where it rested until May 6–7. From rest the division proceeded to south of Vouziers (May 7) and entered line near Tahure on the 13th and held that quiet sector until July 15. It did not attack in the offensive in Champagne, but remained behind in reserve of the 88th Division. Later it was used by battalions in support of units in line until the end of the month.

4. From the end of July to September 12 the division held a quiet sector of the line near Maisons de Champagne.

5. On the 12th it was moved to Spincourt by Mezieres, Sedan, Montmedy, Longuyon. It rested and trained until the 28th, when it marched toward the front at Romagne sous Montfaucon (Sept. 28 to Oct. 2).

6. The division was engaged near Cunel on October 8. Four days later it shifted to the right bank of the Meuse (east of Sivry sur Meuse) and held there until November 5. It retreated toward Fontaine and Ecurey after that date. The division was still in line on the day of the armistice.

VALUE—1918 ESTIMATE.

The division was rated as third class. After its failure on the Somme in the spring it was used on unimportant sectors until October. It did not distinguish itself in the Meuse–Argonne battle.

231st Division.

COMPOSITION.

	1917		1918	
	Brigade.	Regiment.	Brigade.	Regiment.
Infantry.............	231.	442. 443. 444.	231.	442. 443. 444.
Cavalry.............	....		1 Sqn. 9 Drag. Rgt.	
Artillery.............	Art. Command: 3 Gd. Res. F. A. Rgt.		3 Gd. Res. F. A. Rgt. 90 Ft. A. Btn. 910 Light Am. Col. 912 Light Am. Col. 1135 Light Am. Col.	
Engineers and Liaisons.	(231) Pion. Btn.: 353 Pion. Co. 354 Pion. Co. 358 (?) T. M. Co. 418 T. M. Co. 231 Tel. Detch.		231 Pion. Btn.: 353 Pion. Co. 354 Pion. Co. 181 Searchlight Section. 231 Signal Command. 231 Tel. Detch. 57 Wireless Detch.	
Medical and Veterinary.	243 Ambulance Co. 183 Field Hospital. 184 Field Hospital. Vet. Hospital.		243 Ambulance Co. 184 Field Hospital. 217 Field Hospital. 227 Vet. Hospital.	
Transport.............	641 M. T. Col.		641 M. T. Col.	

HISTORY.

(Guard.)

1917.

The 231st Division was formed on January 15, 1917, at the Zossen Camp, near Berlin. Its infantry regiments (442d, 443d, and 444th) were formed from the depots of the Guard and the 43d Reserve Division, likewise a subsidiary of the Guard. Initial effectives: 235 to 240 men per company, one-half of the 1918 class, one-fourth of returned sick and wounded, one-fourth men withdrawn from the front. The composition is practically the same for the divisions Nos. 231 to 242, as regards infantry and pioneers.

HAYE.

1. The 231st Division left the Zossen Camp on March 30, 1917, detrained at Audun le Roman on April 3, and went into line on the 13th at Flirey (Haye). It did not show any activity there and left the front on May 12.

CHAMPAGNE.

2. Entraining at Jaulny on May 16, it was concentrated in the vicinity of Epoye, northeast of Rheims, and went into line on May 18–19 north of La Pompelle.

MONT HAUT.

3. In the middle of June it went into line in the Nauroy sector, between Cornillet and Mont Haut, and suffered the French attack of the 18th, which caused it heavy losses (especially in the 443d Infantry Regiment, where the 10th Company had only 1 officer and 10 men left). It was relieved about July 6.

4. After two weeks' rest in the vicinity of Rethel the division was sent into line at Berméricourt on July 21.

RECRUITING.

The 231st Division was recruited from the entire extent of Prussian territory, the same as the Guard from whose depots it was formed.

VALUE—1917 ESTIMATE.

At the time of the formation of the 231st Division 40 per cent of the men were of the 1918 class. In consequence of replacements, the proportion of the men of this class appeared to be 50 per cent in November, 1917.

The 231st Division opposed an honorable resistance to the French assault of June 18, 1917, at Le Cornillet.

However, taking into consideration that it has never given proof of offensive qualities, it seems impossible to class it among the good divisions.

1918.

CHAMPAGNE.

1. Early in February the 231st Division was relieved by the 213th Division and went to the Givet-Namur area for training in open warfare.

PICARDY.

2. On the 21st of March it was in support behind the 45th Reserve Division. Two days later it attacked southwest of Ham in the direction of Esmery-Hallon, suffering heavy losses. It was in reserve near Roye on the 28th. Early in April it was resting near Laon, and later in the month it moved to the Marle area, where it was reconstituted.

AISNE.

3. It then relieved the 3d Reserve Division in the Bouconville sector (southeast of Laon) early in May. On the 27th other divisions attacked through its sector, the 231st following up in reserve via Fismes and Fère en Tardenois. It became engaged on the 30th near Beuvardes and advanced through Verdilly to Château Thierry; relieved by the 201st Division about the 16th of June. It refitted in the Laon region, entrained at Sissonne, and traveled via Asfeld to Dun sur Meuse.

VERDUN.

4. About the 1st of July it relieved the Bavarian Ersatz Division in the Avocourt sector (northwest of Verdun). It was relieved by the 37th Division on the 7th of August.

PICARDY.

5. The division traveled via Sedan–Laon–Chauny and reenforced the front near Appilly (east of Noyon). In the fighting that followed the division was forced to withdraw through Lagny, Champagne, Villeselve, Artemps, Mont d'Origny, and Hauteville. It was withdrawn about the 20th of October.

6. After having rested about a week it came back into line west of Guise about the 28th. Again it fell back, being identified east of Guise and southeast of Etreux. It was still in line on the 11th of November.

VALUE—1918 ESTIMATE.

The division did not distinguish itself during the battle of the Somme, but, on the other hand, it did not do badly, for soon afterwards the division commander was granted "Pour le Mérite." After the Aisne offensive the brigade commander also received it. The division was mentioned in the German official communiqués of September 4 and October 31. Its losses necessitated the reduction of the battalions to three companies but did not lower the morale to any great extent. It should be considered as a good second-class division.

232d Division.

COMPOSITION.

	1917		1918	
	Brigade.	Regiment.	Brigade.	Regiment.
Infantry	232.	445. 446. 447.	232.	445. 446. 447.
Cavalry	4 Sqn. 1 Uhlan Rgt.		4 Sqn. 1 Uhlan Rgt.	
Artillery	37 F. A. Rgt.		232 Art. Command: 37 F. A. Rgt. 776 Light Am. Col. 981 Light Am. Col. 1093 Light Am. Col.	
Engineers and Liaisons.	(232) Pion Btn.: 355 Pion Co. 356 Pion. Co. 419 T. M. Co. 232 Tel. Detch.		232 Pion Btn.: 346 Pion. Co. 356 Pion. Co. 419 T. M. Co. 119 Searchlight Section. 232 Signal Command: 232 Tel. Detch. 162 Wireless Detch.	
Medical and Veterinary	244 Ambulance Co. 185 Field Hospital. 186 Field Hospital. Vet. Hospital.		244 Ambulance Co. 185 Field Hospital. 186 Field Hospital. 267 Vet. Hospital.	
Transport	642 M. T. Col.		642 M. T. Col.	

HISTORY.

(405th Infantry Regiment: 1st Corps District—East Prussia. 446th and 447th Infantry Regiments: 20th Corps District—Eastern section of West Prussia.)

1917.

The 232d Division belonged to the series of divisions 231 to 242, formed in January, 1917, by drafts upon the depots (1918 class) and upon the front. It was recruited principally from the 1st and 20th Corps Districts (East Prussia).

After its formation the division was sent for training to the Arys Camp and then, on April 3, 1917, to the Eastern Front.

COURLAND.

1. On April 6 the 232d Division went into line in the vicinity of Illukst; it remained there until July.

SMORGONI.

2. Relieved by the 2d Division, coming from Flanders on July 7, it entrained on the 9th, was transferred by railroad to Soly on July 11, and from there went to the sector of Smorgoni–Krevo, where it suffered the Russian attack of July 22.

GALICIA.

3. On July 31 the 232d Division left the Smorgoni front for Galicia. It went into line northeast of Tarnapol, west of Zbaraz. It was identified there on December 25 (fraternization with the Russians). It was during this rest period, in November and December, that the division received its first reenforcements of the 1919 class, which it later took to France.

The 232d Division was recruited from East and West Prussia, with a certain number of Alsace-Lorrainers.

VALUE—1917 ESTIMATE.

Having always occupied the Eastern Front from its formation (beginning of 1917) until March, 1918, the 232d Division was of mediocre combat value (April, 1918).

In the 445th Infantry Regiment the majority of men were very young; many belonged to the 1919 class (April, 1918). (Interrogation of prisoner.)

In the 2d Company of the 1st Battalion of the 447th Infantry Regiment, one-third belonged to the 1919 class (May, 1918). (Interrogation of prisoner.)

1918.

1. The division held the sector west of Vaudesincourt until about May 10, when it went to rest in the Juniville-Neuflize area. While there the division was trained for mobile warfare.

BATTLE OF THE AISNE.

2. On May 22 the division left the region of Juniville and moved in three marches to Lor and Le Thour (north of Asfeld). On May 26 the division left Lor and advanced toward the battle front, following the 86th Division. It passed the former French first line near Juvincourt, arrived near Treslon-Bouleuse on May 29, and on the 30th was engaged to the right of the 86th Division, near Sarey, where it relieved the troops of the 7th Reserve Division.

3. After that date the division was in the sector on the west bank of the Ardre near Chambrecy. The division losses were small during the first three days of the offensive, but later it suffered seriously, especially in its unsuccessful attack on Bligny on June 4. The division was relieved on the 18th by the 123d Division.

4. It marched by stages to Asfeld and was railed to Montmedy. On the night of June 28–29 it relieved the 19th Ersatz Division in the Beaumont sector. It held the quiet sector until August 18, when it was withdrawn. On the night of August 26–27 the division entrained and traveled via Montmedy-Sedan-Charleville-Revin-Charleroi-Mons-Valenciennes-Cambrai, detraining near Etricourt and Manancourt on August 28 after a journey of 28 hours.

BAPAUME.

5. The division was engaged in the Bapaume area (Le Forest, Bouchavesnes, Moislains) on August 29. It lost 1,500 prisoners before it was withdrawn on September 9.

6. It rested in the Le Cateau area until September 21, when it reenforced the battle front northwest of Hargicourt. After four days it was relieved by the 54th Division and rested near La Capelle. It had been there but 10 days when it was hurried to the Oise front by motor trucks.

7. On October 6 it was engaged at Lesdins, with the exception of the 447th Regiment, which remained at rest at Pont a Bucy and joined the division later. It continued in line until about the end of the month, when it retired from the Villers le Sec vicinity. It was considered in reserve of the German 18th Army at the time of the armistice.

VALUE—1918 ESTIMATE.

The division was rated as 4th class. By October its morale was very low and its combat value small. On October 25 the division had but 850 infantrymen, 300 machine gunners, and 120 trench mortar effectives. After August there were but three companies to a battalion and but two battalions to the 446th Regiment in October. Influenced by Bolshevists, elements of the division refused to go into action in October.

233d Division.

COMPOSITION.

	1917		1918 [1]	
	Brigade.	Regiment.	Brigade.	Regiment.
Infantry................	243.	448. 449. 450.	243.	448. 449. 450.
Cavalry................	....		3 Sqn. 9 Drag. Rgt.	
Artillery................	81 F. A. Rgt.		233 Art. Command: 81 F. A. Rgt.	
Engineers and Liaisons	(233) Pion. Btn.: 357 Pion. Co. 358 Pion. Co. 420 T. M. Co. 233 Tel. Detch.		233 Pion. Btn.: 357 Pion. Co. 358 Pion. Co. 420 T. M. Co. 233 Tel. Detch.	
Medical and Veterinary	245 Ambulance Co. 187 Field Hospital. 188 Field Hospital. Vet. Hospital.		245 Ambulance Co. 187 Field Hospital. 188 Field Hospital. 268 Vet. Hospital.	
Transport..............	880 M. T. Col.		643 M. T. Col.	

[1] Composition at the time of dissolution, September, 1918.

HISTORY.

(448th and 449th Infantry Regiments: 2d Corps District—Pomerania. 450th Infantry Regiment: 17th Corps District—West Prussia.)

1917.

The 233d Division, formed at the Hammerstein Camp in January, 1917, recruited its infantry (448th, 449th, 450th Regiments) from the 2d and 17th Corps Districts. It then contained 40 per cent of the 1918 class and 40 per cent returned wounded.

1. After six weeks in training at Hammerstein, the 233d Division was transferred to Beverloo, where it continued its training from the end of February to the beginning of April.

2. About April 10 it occupied a calm sector between La Fère and Alaincourt.

FLANDERS.

3. On May 16 it left the Oise front and went to Flanders. Sent into line at Ypres, on both sides of the Ypres–Roulers road (May 19–20), the division had very heavy losses in this sector toward the end of July, during the artillery preparation which preceded the British attack of the 31st. "In the course of the nine weeks passed in Flanders the 450th Infantry Regiment lost 900 men, more than half of whom were killed." (Letter of Aug. 6.)

4. Relieved on the eve of the attack, the 233d Division was brought back by railroad into the Guise area and sent to rest for two weeks.

5. From the middle of August until September 28 it occupied the sector of St. Quentin (Gauchy), after having pillaged the city the same as several other divisions.

FLANDERS.

6. On October 2 it entrained for Flanders and was sent by way of Origny, Le Cateau, Maubeuge, Mons, Ath, Ghent, Deynze. From October 5 to 12 it was engaged southeast of Sonnebeke and lost very heavily during the British attacks of October 6 and 9.

LORRAINE.

7. The division was withdrawn from the Ypres front on October 12, sent to rest for four days at Sotteghem, then sent to Lorraine by way of Brussels, Namur, Hirson, Charleville, Sedan, Metz. Detraining at Sarreburg, it rested from the 20th to the 29th, then went into line south of Blamont.

RECRUITING.

The 233d Division was recruited from Pomerania and West Prussia, with a certain admixture from the neighboring Provinces (3d and 5th Corps Districts).

VALUE—1917 ESTIMATE.

A German official document of June 12, 1917, gives the following appreciation of the troops of the 233d Division engaged at that moment in the Ypres sector: "These men are too young to be able to furnish prolonged resistance and to have great endurance in a critical situation. Nevertheless, their conduct is generally good. One cannot say that this organization is in a good condition; it is not suited for trench warfare." (Report from the 2d Battalion of the 450th Regiment.)

It is to be noticed, however, that the 233d Division was left in line northeast of Ypres until July 29.

Since that time the division took part in numerous battles and improved.

It contained a certain number of Poles and some Alsatians.

From January 20 to February 24, 1918, it received special training for the warfare of movement, in the vicinity of Zabern–Haguenau.

It was a fairly good division.

1918.

KEMMEL.

1. The division was railed to Flanders in the middle of April and detrained at Zarren (southwest of Thourout). It marched toward the front south of Ypres through Ardoye, Tourcoing. It was engaged on April 25 at Mount Kemmel and took part in the heavy fighting there until May 3. Its losses were heavy in this engagement.

2. The division rested near Sottegem in Belgium until May 19. It was then transferred to Peronne. During June a regiment of the division came into line southwest of Morlancourt for a short period and reenforced the 54th Division. The rest of the division rested at Caudry, Bretigny, Morcourt until July 6.

THIRD BATTLE OF THE SOMME.

3. It was engaged on that date north and south of Alvert, where it was still in line at the time of the British attack of August 22. It was thrown back on Fricourt, La Boisselle, Bazentin le Grand, Montauban, where it was relieved on August 30, after losing 1,422 prisoners.

4. Following the heavy losses in August the division was dissolved. The 448th Regiment was transferred to the 107th Division, replacing the 227th Reserve Regiment, dissolved. The 405th Regiment replaced the 22d Reserve Regiment, dissolved in the 117th Division; while the men of the 449th Regiment were allotted to the 448th and 450th Regiments.

VALUE—1918 ESTIMATE.

The division was rated as third class.

234th Division.

COMPOSITION.

	1917		1918	
	Brigade.	Regiment.	Brigade.	Regiment.
Infantry............	234.	451. 452. 453.	234.	451. 452. 453.
Cavalry.............	1 Sqn. 13 Dragoon Rgt.		1 Sqn. 13 Drag. Rgt.	
Artillery...........	Art. Command: 4 F. A. Rgt.		234 Art. Command: 4 F. A. Rgt. 3 Abt. 21 Ft. A. Rgt. (7 and 9 Btries.). 841 Light Am. Col. 847 Light Am. Col. 1340 Light Am. Col.	
Engineers and Liaisons.	(234) Pion. Btn.: 359 Pion. Co. 360 Pion. Co. 429 T. M. Co. 234 Tel. Detch.		234 Pion. Btn.: 359 Pion. Co. 360 Pion. Co. 201 Searchlight Section. 234 Signal Command: 234 Tel. Detch. 126 Wireless Detch.	
Medical and Veterinary	246 Ambulance Co. 189 Field Hospital. 190 Field Hospital. Vet. Hospital.		246 Ambulance Co. 189 Field Hospital. 190 Field Hospital. 269 Vet. Hospital.	
Transport.............	M. T. Col.............................		644 M. T. Col.	

HISTORY.

(451st and 452d Infantry Regiments: 3d Corps District—453d Infantry Regiment: 4th
Corps District—Prussian Saxony.)

1917.

The 234th Division was formed on January 6, 1917, at the camp of Altengrabow.
Its infantry regiments were recruited from the 3d and 4th Corps Districts (Berlin-
Magdeburg) and were composed of men of the 1918 class (50 per cent) and of returned
wounded and men withdrawn from the front (50 per cent).

St. Quentin.

1. After three months' training at Altengrabow, the 234th Division entrained, on
March 28, for the Western Front. Going by way of Magdeburg-Aix la Chapelle–Liége–
Brussels–Mons, it detrained on March 30–31 at Le Cateau, from which place it marched
to the sector of Fayet, northwest of St. Quentin (on the Hindenburg Line) on April 8.

On April 14 the division was attacked by British troops and lost heavily (451st
Infantry Regiment, 400 prisoners). This regiment again suffered seriously in the
course of violent battles with the French east of Fayet, August 9 to 11.

Ypres.

2. About September 1 the 234th Division was relieved northwest of St. Quentin
and sent to Roulers, by way of Bohain, Le Cateau, Denain, Lille, Courtrai, and Menin.
In reserve first near Hooglede, on the Ypres front at the time of the British attack, it
counterattacked on September 20, northeast of St. Julien. On September 23–24 it

again went into reserve and after the British attack of the 26th sent some of its elements into action southeast of Zonnebeke on September 27.

3. Exhausted by these battles the division left the Ypres front for the Lille area. It had lost about one-half of its effectives.

LA BASSÉE.

4. It went into line north of La Bassée Canal on October 7, remained there six weeks, and about November 24 went to the Cambrai area.

ARTOIS.

5. On December 7 it took over the sector north of Bullecourt.

RECRUITING.

The 234th Division was recruited from Brandenburg and Prussian Saxony.

VALUE—1917 ESTIMATE.

The 234th Division lost very heavily at Ypres in September, 1917; these losses had some effect upon its morale. At all events, it acquired a certain combat experience in the course of these engagements.

The 451st Infantry Regiment seemed to be considered the best one in the division by the German High Command.

In the 453d Infantry Regiment, September, 1917, many officers belonged to the Reserve and to the Landwehr; some of these, during the war, were retired for inefficiency (document).

1918.

PICARDY.

1. The 234th Division remained in the Bullecourt sector until relieved by the 111th Division on the 8th of February, when it went to rest in the Douai area.

2. About the end of the month it relieved the 111th Division. On the opening of the Somme offensive on the 21st of March, although not engaged in the initial attack, the division was severely engaged in the fighting around Croisilles, and on the 31st some of its elements carried out a costly and unsuccessful attack against Boisleux-St. Maré. It was relieved about the 7th of April by the 231st Division.

3. The division rested a fortnight and then relieved the 111th Division in the Ayette sector on the 20th. During the night of the 24th–25th of May it was relieved by the 17th Division.

4. About June 21 it relieved the 17th Division. When the British attacked on the 21st of August, the division was thrown back upon Hamelincourt with heavy losses (including 1,585 prisoners). It was withdrawn on the 24th to the Douai region.

5. On the 22d of September it reenforced the front in the Gavrelle sector, being withdrawn a few days later.

6. On the 30th it came into line north of Cambrai in the Tilloy sector. Withdrawn about the 15th of October.

7. On the 18th it reenforced the front near Raches (northeast of Douai). It was relieved by the 35th Division about the 10th of November.

VALUE—1918 ESTIMATE.

The 234th was rated a third-class division. In the fighting around Arras in the spring it acquitted itself fairly well, and its commanding general received the "Pour le Mérite." Its conduct during the rest of the year was mediocre.

235th Division.

COMPOSITION.

	1917		1918 [1]	
	Brigade.	Regiment.	Brigade.	Regiment.
Infantry.............	235.	454. 455. 456.	235.	454. 455. 456.
Cavalry...............	5 Sqn. 9 Dragoon Rgt.		5 Sqn. 9 Drag. Rgt.	
Artillery..............	235 Art. Command: 6 F. A. Rgt.		235 Art. Command: 6 F. A. Rgt.	
Engineers and Liaisons.	235 Pion. Btn.: 361 Pion. Co. 362 Pion. Co. 435 T. M. Co. 235 Tel. Detch.		235 Pion. Btn.: 361 Pion. Co. 362 Pion. Co. 435 T. M. Co. 235 Tel. Detch.	
Medical and Veterinary	247 Ambulance Co. 191 Field Hospital. 192 Field Hospital.		247 Ambulance Co. 191 Field Hospital. 192 Field Hospital. Vet. Hospital.	
Transport..............	961 M. T. Col.		645 M. T. Col.	

[1] Composition at the time of dissolution, August, 1918.

HISTORY.

(454th and 455th Infantry Regiments: 5th Corps District—Posen.   456th Infantry
Regiment: 6th Corps District—Silesia.)

1917.

The 235th Division was formed in January, 1917, in the camps of the Warta and of
Neuhammer, with elements from the 5th and 6th Corps District. Its regiments were
made up mostly of men from the 1918 class (50 per cent) and the remainder from
returned sick and wounded and men withdrawn from the front (initial strength, 230 to
235 men per company).

1. After six weeks of intensive training, the 235th Division was concentrated at
Posen and sent to the Western Front on February 20, by way of Dresden–Aschaffen
burg–Frankfort–Aix la Chappelle–Namur. It passed a new period of training in the
Sissonne Camp, and on March 15 was sent to the St. Quentin area.

St. Quentin.

2. At the beginning of April it went into line in the Itancourt sector. Its losses
were enormous, principally from the attack of April 13, which necessitated replace
ments of 2,216 men during the following weeks.

3. Relieved at the beginning of July, it was sent to rest east of St. Quentin (Fontaine
Notre Dame).

Ypres.

4. On July 25 it entrained at Guise for Belgium. Concentrated in the vicinity of
Iseghem–Roulers, it went to the Ypres front on July 28–31, east of Wieltje, received the
artillery preparation and the British attack of the 31st, which caused it very heavy
losses. The 454th Infantry Regiment had very heavy losses (4th Company was

reduced to 31 men) and was filled up hastily from the resources of the large depot at Beverloo (about 60 men per company).

5. The 235th Division was withdrawn from the front on August 1 and spent a week at rest in Flanders.

6. In the course of August it was transferred to Laonnois, in the vicinity of Mont-cornet.

AISNE.

7. About September 10 it took over the sector of Juvincourt-Corbeny, where the French attack of November 21 again occasioned it serious losses (400 prisoners). A prisoner of the 456th Infantry Regiment declared that in this company not more than one-fourth of the men were left who composed it in January.

RECRUITING.

The 235th Division was recruited from the Provinces of Posen and of Silesia; consequently, contained a large number of Poles.

VALUE—1917 ESTIMATE.

The 235th Division appeared to have only mediocre offense value.

Following the battle of November 21, 1917, in the Juvincourt sector, the commander of the 456th Infantry Regiment and the commander of the 2d Battalion of the same regiment were relieved in disgrace.

The division received training in the warfare of movement during January and February, 1918.

1918.

1. The division entrained at Sierentz (Alsace) April 4–5 and traveled via Mulhausen, Strasbourg, Treves, Cologne, Lille, Brussels, and Ghent. It detrained at St. Andre, north of Lille, on the 8th–9th and rested in that vicinity until the 22d.

FLANDERS.

2. It entered line east of Robecq on the night of April 22–23 and remained in that sector until May 11. During this engagement the division lost very heavily.

3. The division entrained at Lille on the 12th and was railed via Ghent, Brussels, Namur, Charleville, and Sedan. It detrained north of Briey on the 14th.

WOEVRE.

4. It was engaged on the heights of the Meuse (Vaux les Palameix–Bois des Chevaliers) from May 24–25 to August 8. It was withdrawn from north of St. Mihiel on the 8th and dissolved at Conflans.

5. The 545th Regiment was drafted to the 10th Division. The 11th Division and 82d Reserve Division received elements of the 456th Regiment.

VALUE—1918 ESTIMATE.

The division was rated as third class. Its only active service in 1918 was near Armentieres, for which the division was commended by the Kaiser in his order dissolving the division.

236th Division.

COMPOSITION.

	1917		1918	
	Brigade.	Regiment.	Brigade.	Regiment.
Infantry.................	236.	457. 458. 459.	236.	457. 458. 459.
Cavalry.................	4 Sqn. 13 Drag. Rgt.		4 Sqn. 13 Drag. Rgt.	
Artillery................	7 F. A. Rgt.		7 F. A. Rgt. 3 Abt. 16 Ft. A. Rgt. (11 and 13 Btries.) 956 Light Am. Col. 1337 Light Am. Col. 1343 Light Am. Col.	
Engineers and Liaisons.	363 Pion. Btn.: 363 Pion. Co. 364 Pion. Co. 436 T. M. Co. 236 Tel. Detch.		363 Pion. Btn.: 363 Pion. Co. 364 Pion. Co. 436 T. M. Co. 202 Searchlight Section. 236 Signal Command: 236 Tel. Detch. 125 Wireless Detch.	
Medical and Veterinary	248 Ambulance Co. 193 Field Hospital. 194 Field Hospital. Vet. Hospital.		248 Ambulance Co. 193 Field Hospital. 194 Field Hospital. 271 Vet. Hospital.	
Transport..............	M. T. Col.			

HISTORY.

(457th and 458th Infantry Regiments; 7th Corps District—Westphalia. 459th Infantry Regiment; 16th Corps District—Lorraine.)

1917.

The 236th Division was formed at the Senne Camp at the end of December, 1916 and the beginning of January, 1917. Recruited from the 7th and 16th Corps Districts its regiments were composed of men belonging to the 1918 class (40 per cent) and of returned wounded.

CAMBRESIS.

1. The 236th Division entrained at the Senne and Paderborn Camps on April 11 1917, and went to Cambrai by way of Dusseldorf-Aix la Chapelle-Liége-Namur-Charleroi-Valenciennes. Detraining at Caudry on April 13, it went into line southwest of Cambrai (Trestault-Gouzeaucourt) on the 18th. On April 24 it was attacked by British troops, lost the village of Villers Plouich, and suffered heavily (340 prisoners).

2. On May 9 it was sent to rest in the vicinity of Cambrai.

ARTOIS.

3. It then occupied the sector of Cherisy (southeast of Arras) from June 4 to September 2, and did not go into any serious action during this period.

FLANDERS.

4. The division left Artois at the beginning of September, was sent to rest at Courtrai until the 17th, went to Iseghem by railroad, then marched to Roulers. Until

September 20 it remained in reserve as a counterattacking division. Between the 20th and 26th, it was in a violent battle east of Ypres, toward the Polygon wood and between this wood and Zonnebeke to oppose the British advance. Before going into line, on September 20, the 2d Battalion of the 459th Infantry Regiment, had lost more than 200 men from artillery fire; on the 22d, the 8th Company had only 15 men left.

5. Withdrawn from the Flanders front, during the night of September 28–29, the 236th Division was sent to rest in the vicinity of Douai.

ARTOIS.

6. On October 6 it went into line north of the Scarpe, between the Roeux and the Gavrelle; it enlarged its sector toward the north at the beginning of November. It was filled up by replacements taken from the Russian front; 400 men coming from the 32d Landwehr Regiment (197th Division) arrived in November.

RECRUITING.

The 236th Division was recruited from Westphalia and the Rhine Province.

VALUE—1917 ESTIMATE.

The 236th Division had serious losses while fighting at Ypres and its morale was weakened in consequence. It may be considered a mediocre division (February, 1918).

According to a deserter's statement (Jan. 23, 1918), the 236th Division was a shock division in 1917.

1918.

1. The division was engaged from March 21 to April 3. On the March Somme offensive, first at Cherizy, later at Heninel. It was relieved south of Arras on the night of April 3–4 and moved to Passchendaele by way of Aubigny au Bac, Iseghem, and Meulebeke.

YPRES.

2. It entered line at Passchendaele on April 6 and held a sector in this vicinity until June 22, when it was relieved by the 31st Division. The division rested during July at Deynze. It again held the sector southwest of Ypres from August 10 to September 13.

LORRAINE.

3. The division moved from Flanders by way of Tourcoing–Brussels–Liége–Aachen–Cologne–Bonn–Bingen–Coblenz–Kreuznach to Strasburg. It did not detrain there, but was suddenly ordered to Metz, where it arrived on September 24 in the afternoon. It marched to Loringen, stayed one night and marched to Mars la Tour on September 26. The next morning it marched to Jarny and entrained there, going to Dun sur Meuse (via Longuyon and Montmedy). From Dun it marched through Doulcon to Villers, then to Cunel, and then forward into position.

4. The division was heavily engaged from September 29 to its retirement on October 17. It distinguished itself particularly, fighting stubbornly and successfully for many days in succession. It lost only 413 prisoners but its casualties were very heavy, estimated at 3,000. On November 4 the division was reengaged south of Beaumont and continued in line until the armistice.

VALUE—1918 ESTIMATE.

The division was rated as third class. Apart from the fighting on the Meuse, the division did not do anything notable.

237th Division.

COMPOSITION.

	1917		1918	
	Brigade.	Regiment.	Brigade.	Regiment.
Infantry	244.	460. 461. 462.	244.	460. 461. 462.
Cavalry	4 Sqn. 13 Uhlan Rgt.		4 Sqn. 13 Uhlan Rgt.	
Artillery	83 F. A. Rgt.		83 F. A. Rgt. 3 Abt. 23 Ft. A. Rgt. (7 and 9 Btries.). 783 Light Am. Col. 1013 Light Am. Col. 1057 Light Am. Col.	
Engineers and Liaisons.	(237) Pion. Btn.: 365 Pion. Co. 366 Pion. Co. (437) T. M. Co. 237 Tel. Detch.		237 Pion. Btn.: 365 Pion. Co. 366 Pion. Co. 124 Searchlight Section. 237 Signal Command: 237 Tel. Detch. 25 Wireless Detch.	
Medical and Veterinary.	249 Ambulance Co. 195 Field Hospital. 196 Field Hospital. 272 Vet. Hospital.		249 Ambulance Co. 195 Field Hospital. 196 Field Hospital. 198 Vet. Hospital.	
Transport	551 M. T. Col.			
Attached	4 Landst. Pion. Co. (10 C. Dist.).			

HISTORY.

(8th and 21st Corps Districts—Rhine Province and Lorraine.)

1917.

The 237th Division was formed in January, 1917, at the Elsenborn Camp (one-half men of the 1918 class; the rest, returned sick and wounded and men taken from the front).

RUSSIA.

1. Detraining in Russia in the vicinity of Baranovitchi in March, 1917, the 237th Division went into line south of Vichnev, on the Little Berezina, about the beginning of April.

GALICIA.

2. Relieved on June 25, it was transferred to Galicia by way of Brest-Litowsk. On July 7 it was sent into line in the vicinity of Konioukhi.

3. It was engaged on July 21 northwest of Zbrow, and pursued the Russians by way of Trembowla (July 26) as far as Husiatin, where the front became stabilized. The division continued to occupy various sectors in this area until the end of 1917. It was identified south of Husiatin on December 12 (fraternization).

RECRUITING.

The 237th Division was recruited principally from the Rhine District.

The 237th Division occupied the Russian front from its formation until the beginning of January, 1917.

Its combat value was mediocre.

1918.

1. On the 4th of January the division was relieved by Austrian troops and marched by easy stages to Buckas, in the direction of Lemberg. On March 4 it entrained between Brody and Lemberg and traveled via Lemberg–Brest-Litowsk–Warsaw–Kalisz–Goerlitz–Leipzig–Frankfort on the Main–Thionville–Sedan, detraining at St. Juvin on the 12th. It went into cantonments at St. Georges.

ARGONNE.

2. During the night of the 14th–15th it relieved the 80th Reserve Division west of Avocourt. While here it exchanged its Alsace-Lorrainers for more trustworthy men of the 9th Landwehr Division. It was withdrawn about the middle of May.

AISNE.

3. On the 26th and 27th the division entrained at Grandpré and St. Juvin, went through Sedan and Charleville and detrained at Bucy les Pierrepont (north of Sissonne) on the 27th and 28th. The division then marched via Sissonne–the Plateau de Californie–Fismes–Dravegny–Monthiers (northwest of Château Thierry). On the 1st of June it attacked in the Belleau wood, as a result of which it suffered heavy losses. It was withdrawn about the 22d.

ARGONNE.

4. The division entrained at Athies (east of Laon) and detrained near St. Juvin on the 30th. The division remained here a few days and then relieved the 240th Division in the Vauquois sector. While in line here the division received more than 2,000 replacements. It was withdrawn on August 14.

AILETTE.

5. It entrained at St. Juvin and went to St. Quentin and Ham; then it went by truck to the Coucy wood, and then to St. Paul aux Bois (south of Chauny). On the 21st it reenforced the 1st Bavarian and the 222d Divisions near St. Aubin. It was withdrawn early in September, after having fallen back upon Coucy le Château. It rested then for a fortnight in the St. Gobain forest.

SERRE-OISE.

6. On the 25th of September it relieved the 34th Division in the Servais sector (south of La Fère). The division remained in line until the end of the war, falling back through Deuillet–Anguilcourt–La Ferté–Chevresis–Villers le Sec to the La Capelle region, and suffering very heavy losses.

The 237th was rated a fourth-class division. While it was in line in the Argonne in the spring the men (encouraged by their officers) fraternized with the French troops opposing them. Its morale was influenced to a most surprising extent by the measure of success of the German forces. The result was that while it was high in the spring it became low as soon as the tide turned. On August 22, while the division was in line on the Ailette, 80 men, armed and with ammunition, surrendered to 4 French soldiers. In this engagement (about 10 days) more than 900 prisoners were lost. While the division was in line the last time it lost over 1,000 prisoners. At the end of October the division had only about 800 rifles.

238th Division.

COMPOSITION.

	1917		1918	
	Brigade.	Regiment.	Brigade.	Regiment.
Infantry...............	238.	463. 464. 465.	238.	463. 464. 465.
Cavalry...............	2 Sqn. 13 Drag. Rgt.		2 Sqn. 13 Drag. Rgt.	
Artillery...............	238 Art. Command: 62 F. A. Rgt.		238 Art. Command: 62 F. A. Rgt. 53 Ft. A. Rgt. (Staff and 1, 2, and 4 Btries.). 944 Light Am. Col. 1211 Light Am. Col. 1233 Light Am. Col.	
Engineers and Liaisons.	238 Pion. Btn.: 367 Pion. Co. 438 T. M. Co. 238 Tel. Detch. 368 Pion. Co.		238 Pion. Btn.: 367 Pion. Co. 368 Pion. Co. 205 Searchlight Section. 238 Signal Command: 238 Tel. Detch. 30 Wireless Detch.	
Medical and Veterinary.	250 Ambulance Co. 197 Field Hospital. 198 Field Hospital. Vet. Hospital.		250 Ambulance Co. 197 Field Hospital. 198 Field Hospital. 273 Vet. Hospital.	
Transport...............	648 M. T. Col.		648 M. T. Col.	

HISTORY.

(463d Infantry Regiment: 9th Corps District—Hanseatic cities. 464th Infantry Regiment: 9th Corps District—Schleswig-Holstein and Meklemburg. 465th Infantry Regiment: 10th Corps District—Hanover.)

1917.

The 238th Division was formed at the beginning of January, 1917, at the Lockstedt Camp, near Hamburg. Its infantry regiments were recruited from the 9th Corps District (Schleswig-Holstein, Hanseatic cities, and Mecklemburg) and from the 10th Corps District (Hanover), and were composed in part (50 per cent) of men of the 1918 class.

1. After a training of almost three months, the 238th Division entrained at Lockstedt, on April 13, 1917, by way of Hamburg, Trèves, Sedan, Namur, Cambrai; it went to Caudry and Bertry (north), where it detrained on the 16th.

HINDENBURG LINE.

2. On April 20 it went into line in the sector of Vendhuille–Bellicourt, which it left on May 20 to go to rest in the vicinity of Douai (until May 28).

ARTOIS.

3. At the end of May it took over the sector of Roeux–Gavrelle, north of the Scarpe. It remained on this part of the front until September 27 and was not in any serious engagement. On June 6, however, the 463d Infantry Regiment suffered heavy losses in its 3d Battalion, which the two others hastily filled up (letter of June 10), and left 170 prisoners.

FLANDERS.

4. Sent to Flanders, the division remained at rest for a few days at Roulers, then in reserve in the vicinity of West–Roosebeke. On October 13 it went into line southwest of Passchendaele. Having suffered heavily from the British attack of October 30, it was hastily relieved on the 31st.

ST. QUENTIN.

5. It entrained on November 6 at Ledeghem. Detraining at Geise, it went to Macquigny, and after a few days of rest occupied the sector south of St. Quentin–Itancourt (Nov. 11–12).

RECRUITING.

The 238th Division was recruited the same as the 111th Division, from Schleswig-Holstein, Mecklemburg, the Hanseatic cities, and Hanover.

VALUE—1917 ESTIMATE.

The 238th Division was of mediocre value, but better than the majority of the divisions of this series.

The large proportion of young recruits in the ranks of the 238th Division gave rise to the nickname "The Division of the First Communicants."

1918.

1. The division rested and underwent training in the vicinity of Origny–St. Benoite from the 1st of February to March 19. It was brought up to the front south of St. Quentin during the night of March 19–20.

BATTLE OF PICARDY.

2. On the 21st the division attacked at Grugies and in two days advanced by Grand-Serancourt and across the canal near St. Simon. From the 23d to the 29th it advanced in reserve by Libermont–Beaulieu les Fontaines–Beuvraignes. It was reengaged on the 29th at Rollot and Boulogne la Grasse until mid-April. The division suffered heavy casualties in the Somme battle.

RHEIMS.

3. The division was engaged southeast of Rheims (Cernay les Rheims, northeast of St. Leonard) from April 18 to July 20. It carried out a local attack on Rheims on May 30 and June 1. The division did not take part in the offensive of July 15 except by artillery activity.

4. The division rested at Boult sur Suippe from July 20 to 28. From the end of July to August 20 it held its former sector at Cernay les Rheims. Relieved in that sector, it marched by stages toward Brancourt–Coucy le Chateau via Neufchatel sur Aisne, Marchais, Bruyeres (Aug. 21–28).

AISNE.

5. On August 31 the division was engaged at Leuilly–Terny. After September 10 it fought in the vicinity of Quincy–Basse–Aulers until October 12. On that date it retired toward Crepy and withdrew from line. The division started for Marle to rest but was alerted on the 14th and taken in trucks to east of Mart d'Origny. On the 15th it was again in the first line. Two of the regiments had but two battalions and the infantry effectives totaled 1,800. The period between the 18th and 24th of October was relatively quiet on the divisional sector. Following French attacks of October 25 and 26, the division fell back on a prepared position in front of Guise. Here it held until November 5, when it began a retreat by Audigny in the direction of La Capelle.

The last identification was at Buironfosse on November 6.

VALUE—1918 ESTIMATE.

The division was rated as third class. Its morale was mediocre, and its effectives few during the latter half of 1918.

239th Division.

COMPOSITION.

	1917		1918	
	Brigade.	Regiment.	Brigade.	Regiment.
Infantry................	239.	466. 467. 468.	239.	466. 467. 468.
Cavalry................	4 Sqn. 9 Drag. Rgt.		4 Sqn. 9 Drag. Rgt.	
Artillery................	Art. Command: 55 F. A. Rgt.		55 F. A. Rgt. 78 Ft. A. Btn. 909 Light Am. Col. 1239 Light Am. Col. 1293 Light Am. Col.	

Engineers and Liaisons.	(239) Pion. Btn.:
	    369 Pion. Co.
	    370 Pion. Co.
	    439 T. M. Co.
	    239 Tel. Detch.
			239 Pion. Btn.:
			    369 Pion. Co.
			    370 Pion. Co.
			    439 T. M. Co.
			    88 Searchlight Section.
			    237 Searchlight Section.
			239 Signal Command:
			    239 Tel. Detch.
			    11 Wireless Detch.	

Medical and Veterinary	251 Ambulance Co. 199 Field Hospital. 200 Field Hospital. Vet. Hospital.		251 Ambulance Co. 199 Field Hospital. 200 Field Hospital. 239 Vet. Hospital.	
Transport..............	M. T. Col.		649 M. T. Col.	

HISTORY.

(466th Infantry Regiment: 11th Corps District—Electorate of Hesse.   467th Infantry Regiment: 11th Corps District—Thuringia.   468th Infantry Regiment: 18th Corps District—Hesse-Nassau.)

1917.

The 239th Division belonged to the series of 12 divisions (231st to 242d) formed in Germany at the beginning of 1917, a strong proportion (50 per cent) of the 1918 class. It includes the 466th, 467th, and 468th Infantry Regiments recruited from the 11th and 18th Corps Districts (Electorate of Hesse, Thuringia, and Hesse-Nassua, and the Grand Duchy of Hesse).

I. From the beginning of January, 1917, to the middle of February, the 239th Division was in the training camps Ohrdruf and of Darmstadt.   It entrained on February 17 and went to Rethel.   It continued its training for some time behind the Champagne front.

CHAMPAGNE.

2. The entire division went into line north of Souain (Somme Py) on March 27. It remained there until May 15 without any important engagement.   One battalion of the 467th Infantry Regiment was sent to Auberive as a reenforcement at the time of the French attack on April 16.

3. The division was at rest in the vicinity of Machault and at Asfeld from the end of May to the beginning of June.

4. About June 10 it went into line northeast of Reims (Cernay sector), then at the beginning of August northeast of Courcy.   It occupied this sector until October 6 without having any important battle.

FLANDERS.

5. Transferred to Flanders by way of Hirson and Courtrai, the 239th Division went into line northeast of Poelcappelle on October 23. It lost heavily during the British attack of November 26 and continued to hold this sector, alternating with the 3d Naval Division.

6. Relieved about November 24, the 239th Division was sent to rest northeast of Ghent, then to the vicinity of Lille, at the beginning of September.

RECRUITING.

The 466th Infantry Regiment came from the Electorate of Hesse; the 467th Regiment was called Thuringian in an official document; the 468th Regiment came from Hesse-Nassau.

VALUE—1917 ESTIMATE.

The 239th was a fairly good division.

Considering the missions which have been assigned to it by the German High Command, it seems that the 239th Division is better than most of the divisions of this series.

1918.

1. The division trained in the Bourghelles area until March 17. On that date the division marched toward the front via Bersee–Douai–Estrees–Soudemont–Villers les Cagnicourt–Noreuil–Mory.

BATTLE OF PICARDY.

2. It came into line on the 26th north of Courcelles, attacking Ayette on the 27th. It lost heavily, including numerous prisoners on April 2. The division was relieved on April 6 and rested a week at Aubigny au Bac. It entrained on the 11th and moved to Libercourt.

HANDES.

3. The division was engaged from April 15 to 23 east of Robecq. Elements took part in the attack of the 18th, in which the losses were very heavy.

LORRAINE.

4. After its relief on the 23d the division was railed to Lorraine by Mons–Namur–Sedan–Montmedy–Metz. It rested and was reconstituted near Dieuze from the end of April to May 13. At this time the division was reenforced by a draft coming from the 233d Reserve Regiment of the dissolved 195th Division.

AVRICOURT.

5. The division held the quiet Avricourt sector from May 13 to June 20. It was relieved by the 7th Cavalry Division and railed to Champagne.

CHAMPAGNE.

6. It rested and trained in the vicinity of Rethel-Attigny. About the 10th of July it marched toward the front and on the 15th was engaged in the Champagne offensive at Vaudesincourt. After the attack it held the sector until the beginning of October.

7. The division was attacked at Mont sans Nom on September 26, and on October 4 fell back on the line Betheniville–Hauvine, and later in the direction of Rethel (Oct. 12). The division was in reserve during the middle of October. Toward the end of the month the division was reengaged near Rethel Its line of retreat in the last weeks was through Le Quesnoy, Jolimetz, Bermeries, south of Bavai, where it was identified on November 8.

VALUE—1918 ESTIMATE.

The division was rated as third class. In October the division was very tired and its morale was low. Numerous infractions of discipline occurred. Its battalions were reduced to three companies at the beginning of August.

240th Division.
COMPOSITION.

	1917		1918	
	Brigade.	Regiment.	Brigade.	Regiment.
Infantry...............	240.	469. 470. 471.	240.	469. 470. 471.
Cavalry...............	8 Sqn. 13 Drag. Rgt.		3 Sqn. 13 Drag. Rgt.	
Artillery...............	Art. command: 271 F. A. Rgt.		240 Art. Command: 271 F. A. Rgt. 3 Abt. 6 Res. Ft. A. Rgt. 1092 Light Am. Col. 1336 Light Am. Col. 1342 Light Am. Col.	
Engineers and Liaisons.	(240) Pion Btn.: 371 Pion Co. 372 Pion Co. 440 T. M. Co. 240 Tel. Detch.		240 Pion Btn.: 371 Pion. Co. 372 Pion Co. 440 T. M. Co. 203 Searchlight Section. 240 Signal Command: 240 Tel. Detch. 127 Wireless Detch.	
Medical and Veterinary.	252 Ambulance Co. 204 Field Hospital 205 Field Hospital Vet. Hospital.		252 Ambulance Co. 204 Field Hospital. 205 Field Hospital. 240 Vet. Hospital.	
Transport..............	1092 M. T. Col.		650 M. T. Col.	

HISTORY.

(469th and 470th Infantry Regiments: 14th Corps District—Grand Duchy of Baden. 471st Infantry Regiment: 15th Corps District—Alsace.)

1917.

The 240th Division was recruited in the depots of the 14th Corps District (Baden). Like all the divisions of this series, the 240th Division received a large contingent from the 1918 class at the time of its formation.

ALSACE.

1. After a period of intensive training (Feb. 4, to Mar. 28) in the training camps of Oberhofen and of Heuberg, the 240th Division was sent to Mulhousen about the end of March and went into line between the Rhone-Rhine Canal and Hirzbach (south of Altkirch) until August 20.

WOEVRE.

2. About August 25 it was sent to the Woevre in the sector of Calonne trench, in September.

YPRES.

3. Entraining at Conflans (Oct. 5–6) it appeared in Flanders on the 9th. It went into action between the Ypres–Staden railroad and Poelcappelle and suffered heavy losses in the course of the British attacks of October 9 and 12.

CAMBRAI.

4. Relieved during the night of October 13–14, it was sent to Artois. On October 23 it took over the sector of Bullecourt (southeast of Arras). On November 20, it lost heavily from the British attack launched north of Bullecourt at the same time as on the Cambrai front (700 prisoners).

5. About the middle of December it was withdrawn from the front and sent to rest in the vicinity of Douai.

RECRUITING.

The 240th Division was recruited principally from Baden, some elements from the Rhine Districts.

VALUE—1917 ESTIMATE.

The 240th Division appeared to be of mediocre combat value.

1918.

LENS.

1. The division was in line in the sector Fresnoy–Oppy at the beginning of the Somme offensive. It took no part in the attack on Vimy Ridge of March 28, but remained in support. It was relieved in this sector on April 8.

BATTLE OF THE LYS.

2. It moved northward and was engaged north of Bethune (Hinges-Robecq on April 14.) In two weeks' fighting in this sector the division lost very heavily including many prisoners.

ARGONNE.

3. Withdrawn on April 27, the division rested at Lille a week. It entrained about May 8 for the Argonne and detrained at St. Juvin. Engaged at Boureuilles–Vauqunois on May 13 the division held that quiet sector until July 10.

CHAMPAGNE.

4. The division was taken to Semide and held in reserve during the offensive of the 15th to be used as an exploiting division. When the attack failed the division was directed west of Reims via Machault, Warmeriville, Brimont. It camped at Jonchery from July 21 to 23.

REIMS.

5. On the 23d the division was engaged in the Bois de Reims. After the 27th it retreated on the Montagnes de Bligny, and later toward Aubilly-Bouleuse. On August 5 it passed into second line, and was relieved 10 days later. It rested 5 days west of Chateau Porcien and returned to line in the Prunay sector on August 13. There it held firm until October 10.

6. After its relief it waited near Rethel until the 14th, when it was railed to Stenay via Sedan. On October 17 it was engaged north of St. Juvin, Champigneulle, east of the Argonne forest. It continued in line until the end, retreating toward Mouzon.

VALUE—1918 ESTIMATE.

The division was rated as third class. Its effectives were greatly reduced and its morale low in October.

241st Division.

COMPOSITION.

	1917		1918	
	Brigade.	Regiment.	Brigade.	Regiment.
Infantry...............	246.	472. 473. 474.	246.	472. 473. 474.
Cavalry...............	(?) 5 Sqn. 18 Hus. Rgt.		2 Sqn. 18 Hus. Rgt.	
Artillery...............	48 F. A. Rgt.		241 Art. Command: 48 F. A. Rgt. 102 Ft. A. Btn. (Staff, 1, 2, and 3 Btries.). 1055, 1061, and 1062 Light Am. Col.	
Engineers and Liaisons.	(241) Pion. Btn.: 373 Pion Co. 374 Pion. Co. (441) T. M. Co. 241 Tel. Detch.		241 Pion. Btn. 373 Pion. Co. 374 Pion. Co. 441 T. M. Co. 5 Searchlight Section. 241 Signal Command: 241 Tel. Detch. 27 Wireless Detch.	
Medical and Veterinary	253 Ambulance Co. 206 Field Hospital. 207 Field Hospital. Vet. Hospital.		253 Ambulance Co. 206 Field Hospital. 207 Field Hospital. 274 Vet. Hospital.	
Transport.............	M. T. Col.		651 M. T. Col.	

HISTORY.

(12th and 19th Corps Districts—Saxony.)

1917.

The 241st Division was formed at the beginning of 1917 and composed of new regiments (type of divisions 231 and following).

The 473d and 574th Infantry Regiments were formed in the camp at Zeithain in January, 1917, by drafts from the 1918 class and the depots and regiments of the 19th Corps District (Saxony). The 472d Infantry Regiment was originally in the 12th Corps District (Dresden) formed in the same way.

RUSSIA.

1. On March 1, 1917, the 241st Division went to Brest-Litowsk. In April it took over the sector of Postavy in the vicinity of Lake Narotch, where it remained until the middle of June.

GALICIA.

2. Relieved by the 21st Division, it entrained on June 17 at Sventsiany, northwest of Lake Narotch, and went to Galicia, southwest of Brzezany, detraining on June 22. At the beginning of July, it went into line in this region and took part in the German counteroffensive at the end of July advancing south of Skala at the beginning of August. It took up a position on the Zbrucz.

3. After this time the 241st Division occupied various sectors of the Galician front (Koroskow, Husiatin).

125651°—20——47

The 241st Division was entirely Saxon.

It was on the Eastern Front from the time of its formation until February, 1918. "Our new regiment is a gang of headstrong kids." (Letter from a man of the 473d Infantry Regiment, Apr. 2, 1917.)

1918.

1. The division rested in the vicinity of Signy l'Abbaye until March 15. It then proceeded by steps toward the St. Gobain forest (Fressancourt, Mar. 24).

BATTLE OF PICARDY.

2. It was engaged south of the Oise (Amigny-Septvaux) from March 25–26 to April 5. Between the 6th and 9th it advanced from Septvaux and Fresnes toward Coucy, encountering heavy losses. The division received the thanks of the King of Saxony for its conduct in this fighting.

BATTLE OF THE AISNE.

3. The division held the sector of Coucy le Chateau until May 29. On the 29th it attacked and advanced as far as Crecy au Mont. It halted on the line Nouvron–Vingre and held there until relieved at the end of June. In the attack of June 5–6 toward Vic sur Aisne the division lost heavily. On the 23d of June it received a draft of 1,500 men.

SECOND BATTLE OF THE MARNE.

It rested near Coucy le Chateau for about a week, and on July 10 was engaged south of the Aisne between Ambleny and Pernaut. Then it was struck by the Allied attack on the 18th and thrown back on Mercin. The division lost 42 officers and 2,074 men as prisoners alone. It was relieved at a date between July 22 and 26.

SECOND BATTLE OF PICARDY.

5. The division rested and was reconstituted at Vouplaix, Sains Richaumont near Vervins until August 20. It was moved to La Fere (22d) and on the 25th engaged east of Noyon (Baboeuf-Appilly) and September 4. After that date it fell back gradually by Chauny, Fravecy, on Vendeuil, where it was relieved about September 20.

CAMBRAI–ST. QUENTIN.

6. After 10 days' rest the division was reengaged north of St. Quentin (Romicourt–Montbrehain) from October 1 to 10. It lost about 1,900 prisoners in this engagement.

MEUSE–ARGONNE.

7. The division rested nearly a month at Audun la Roman after October 22. The 7th Saxon Jaeger Regiment from the dissolved 197th Division had replaced the dissolved 472d Regiment when it appeared in line on November 5 east of the Meuse. The last identification was at Murvaux on November 7.

The division was rated as fourth class. Its heavy losses of prisoners indicate its poor quality.

242d Division.

COMPOSITION.

	1917		1918	
	Brigade.	Regiment.	Brigade.	Regiment.
Infantry...............	242.	127. 475. 476.	242.	127. 475. 476.
Cavalry...............	2 Sqn. Wurtt. Res. Drag. Rgt.		2 Sqn. Wurtt. Res. Drag. Rgt.	
Artillery...............	Art. Command: 281 F. A. Regt.		242 Art. Command: 281 F. A. Regt. 3 Abt. 13 Ft. A. Rgt. (9 and 10 Btries.). 751 Light Am. Col. 1091 Light Am. Col. 1105 Light Am. Col.	
Engineers and Liaisons.	39 Pion. Btn.: 375 Pion. Co. 376 Pion. Co. 442 T. M. Co. 242 Tel. Detch.		242 Pion. Btn.: 375 Pion. Co. 376 Pion. Co. 442 T. M. Co. 242 Signal Command: 76 Wireless Detch.	
Medical and Veterinary	32 Ambulance Co. 208 Field Hospital. 503 Field Hospital. 275 Vet. Hospital.		32 Ambulance Co. 208 Field Hospital. 503 Field Hospital. 275 Vet. Hospital.	
Transport.............	M. T. Col.		652 M. T. Col.	
Attached.............			78 M. G. S. S. Detch. 14 Art. Observation Section. 221 Reconnaissance Flight. 17 Balloon Sqn. 243 Carrier Pigeon Loft. Elements attached, June 7, 1918. (German document.)	

HISTORY.

(13th Corps District—Wurttemberg.)

1917.

The 242d Division was formed at the end of 1916. Like all of the divisions of the same series, the 1918 class entered largely into the composition of the regiments (475th and 476th). These two were recruited from the 13th Corps District (Wurttemberg). Initial effectiveness, 235 to 240 men per company.

The 127th Infantry Regiment is an active peace-time regiment taken from the 27th Division.

1. On March 11, 1917, the 475th and 476th Infantry Regiments left the camp of Muensingen, where they had received training since January, and went to Lorraine They were joined there by the 127th Infantry Regiment.

LORRAINE.

2. From March 29 to April 30 the 242d Division was in line between Abaucourt and Bezange wood.

3. From May 4 to 15 it was employed upon defensive works north of the Suippe.

CHAMPAGNE–CORNILLET.

4. During the night of May 15–16 it went into line south of Nauroy (Grille-Cornillet wood), where the French attack of May 20 caused it heavy losses (3 officers and 194 men prisoners). Several companies of the 476th Infantry Regiment remained in the Cornillet tunnel.

5. The 242d Division was relieved during the night of May 31–June 1, and after a few days' rest northeast of Lavannes went into line in a calm sector near Betheny from June 3–4 until August 6.

6. The 242d Division was at rest in the Charleville area from August 7 to 20.

MEUSE.

7. On August 20 it was transferred to the right bank of the Meuse (Beaumont sector). It received the French attack of August 26 (7 officers and 390 men prisoners, mostly from the 475th Infantry Regiment). It counterattacked to relieve Beaumont and remained in line until September 10.

AISNE.

8. From the beginning of October until December 16 it held the sector of Berry au Bac, where its only activity consisted in one raid on November 12.

RECRUITING.

The 242d Division was recruited entirely from Wurttemberg.

VALUE—1917 ESTIMATE.

In Champagne the 242d Division showed itself energetic and tenacious (May, 1917). It was a good division, with a high morale, and the prisoners talked very little (December, 1917).

The 242d Division was listed as an assault division and received the training for divisions of that category (February–March, 1918).

The 475th and 476th Infantry Regiments, however, were considered only mediocre.

1918.

1. The division marched to its entraining point at Bergnicourt (west of Junville) on March 22–24 and entrained for Guise. From there it marched by night toward the Montdidier–Noyan front via Ly Fontaine, Guiscard, Margny aux Cerises.

BATTLE OF PICARDY.

2. It was engaged near Conchy les Pots, Orvillers, Sorel from March 29 to April 8, then near Boulogne la Grasse, Mortemer, from April 10 to 26. The division's losses were heavy.

BATTLE OF THE AISNE.

3. After its relief it was transported to Champagne, detraining near Le Chatelet sur Retourne. There it rested three weeks. It entered in line between Brimont and Vitry les Reims after May 20. It attacked on the 27th and advanced by Merfy (29th), Tinquex (31st), as far as the line Betheny, Courcelles, St. Brice (June 2). It held that sector until the 1st of August, when it retreated on La Neuvillette and held the front Betheny–Vitry road. It was relieved about September 26.

4. The division was engaged northeast of St. Pierre a Arnes from October 5 to 11. It then fell back on Rethel. On the 20th it was moved to the area east of Vouziers and put in reserve. On October 23 it was engaged near Chestres, and later near Ballay, Quatre–Champs until November 4. Beginning on the 4th it retired in the direction of Sedan by Rancourt (Nov. 8).

VALUE—1918 ESTIMATE.

The division was rated as third class. It was a fair division, although the discipline was relaxed after September.

243d Division (formerly 8th Ersatz Division).

COMPOSITION.

	1914-15 Brigade.	1914-15 Regiment.	1916 Brigade.	1916 Regiment.	1917 Brigade.	1917 Regiment.	1918 Brigade.	1918 Regiment.
Infantry	29 Mixed Ers.	29, 30, and 31 Brig. Ers. Btns. 32, 80, and 86 Brig. Ers. Btns.	29 Mixed Ers.	363. 364. 365.	247.	122 Fns. 478. 479.	247.	122. 478. 479.
	41 Mixed Ers.	41, 42, 49, and (50), Brig. Ers. Btns.	51 Mixed Ers.	51 Ers. 52 Ers. (Composition in October.) 51 Ers. 52 Ers. 365. 400.				
	51 Mixed Ers.	51 and 52 Brig. Ers. Btns. 53 and 54 Brig. Ers. Btns.						
Cavalry	Cav. Detchs. of the 29, 41, and 51 Ers. Brigs.		8 Cav. Sqn.		3 Sqn. 19 Uhlan Rgt. 13 C. Dist. Ers. Cav. Detch.		3 Sqn. 19 Uhlan Rgt.	
Artillery	Ers. Abtls. of the 23, 27, 44, 29, and 65 F. A. Rgts.		8 Ers. Brig.: 92 F. A. Rgt. 65 Ers. F. A. Rgt		238 F. A. Rgt. (formerly 65 Ers. F. A. Rgt.).		238 F. A. Rgt. 36 Ft. A. Btn. 1151 Light Am. Col. 1152 Light Am. Col. 1163 Light Am. Col.	
Engineers and Liaisons.	1 Ers. Co. 16 Pions. 1 Ers. Co. 21 Pions.		1 Ers. Co. 3 Pion. Btn. No. 16. 1 Ers. Co. 21 Pions. 253 Pion. Co. 306 Pion. Co. 162 T. M. Co.		(243) Pion. Btn. Co. 253 Pion. Co. 306 Pion. Co. 100 T. M. Co. 162 T. M. Co. 443 T. M. Co. 248 Searchlight Section. Tel. Detch.		243 Pion. Btn.: 1 Res. Co. 13 Pions. 2 Res. Co. 13 Pions. 16 Searchlight Section. 243 Signal Command: 243 Tel. Detch. 8 Wireless Detch.	
Medical and Veterinary.					420 Ambulance Co. 137 Field Hospital. 138 Field Hospital. Vet. Hospital.		420 Ambulance Co. 93 Res. Field Hospital. 94 Res. Field Hospital. 277 Vet. Hospital.	
Transport					M. T. Col.		653 M. T. Col.	
Attached	117 Labor Btn. 44 Ldw. Brig. (98 Ldw. and 382 Ldw. Rgts.).							

HISTORY.

(243d Division (former 8th Ersatz Division): 18th Corps District—Wurttemberg.)

1914-15.

The 243d Division is the former 8th Ersatz Division. The latter was formed in August, 1914, with the help of the surplus trained men in the depots (Reserve and Landwehr 1st Ban.) in the proportion of 1 battalion per active brigade. In this way it comprised 13 brigade Ersatz battalions grouped into 3 mixed brigades (29th, 41st, and 51st).

LORRAINE.

1. Detraining on August 17, 1914, at Sarrebruecken, in the rear of the 6th Army, elements of the 8th Ersatz Division went into action on the 20th. It fought at Hoeville and Serres, north of Luneville, on the 25th and took part in the attacks upon Nancy the first part of September. Sent to the rear of the front in the vicinity of Morhange, it was transferred to Haye at the end of September to relieve the 14th Corps. It stayed there for two years between Limey on the west and Le Pretre wood on the east.

2. In August, 1915, the brigade Ersatz battalions were grouped into regiments. The 8th Ersatz Division was then composed of the 363d, 364th, and 365th Infantry Regiments (Prussian) and of the 51st and 52d Ersatz Regiments (Wurttemberg). It continued to hold the lines in Haye, south of Thiaucourt.

1916.

LE PRETRE WOOD.

1. Until the beginning of October, 1916, the 8th Ersatz Division occupied the sector of the Pretre wood, north of Fey en Haye. In August it lost the 364th Infantry Regiment, assigned to the 33d Reserve Division, and on September 20 the 363d, which entered into the composition of the 214th Division. It received a new regiment, the 400th Infantry Regiment, formed in September by drafts upon its infantry units.

SOMME.

2. Leaving the 400th Infantry Regiment in Haye, and composed of three regiments (365th Infantry Regiment, 51st and 52d Ersatz Regiments), the 8th Ersatz Division went to the Somme on October 3. After a rest in the vicinity of Le Catelet until the 10th it went into the sector east of south of Bouchavesnes, where it did not take part in any important action.

LORRAINE.

3. Relieved on November 18, it returned to Lorraine at Fey en Haye. It went into line southeast of Thiaucourt November 25, where the 400th Infantry Regiment was again assigned to the division.

1917.

1. The 8th Ersatz Division remained on the Lorraine front, southeast of Thiaucourt, until about May 10, 1917. In February the 400th Infantry Regiment was sent to Russia.

At the beginning of May the division underwent several changes—it gave the 365th Infantry Regiment to the 5th Landwehr Division and received the 122d Fusileer Regiment (Wurttemberg) from the 105th Division. The 51st and 52d Ersatz Regiments received the 478th and 479th. The 8th Ersatz Division, already called Wurttemberg, then became the 243d Division.

AISNE.

2. The reserve, first (behind the Rheims front), behind Brimont and Neufchâtel, the 243d Division then occupied the front between Miette and the Aisne (north of Berry au Bac) from May 29 to August 20.

MEUSE HILL 344.

3. Transferred to Verdun, the division went into action at Hill 344 on September 9. The 479th Infantry Regiment lost heavily during the attack of the 9th. The 122d Infantry Regiment took part in the attack of October 2 and also had losses.

MEUSE (LEFT BANK).

4. About October 6 the 243d Division was relieved and sent to rest near Stenay. On October 17 it took up its position on the left bank of the Meuse (Béthincourt sector), where it still remained in December.

RECRUITING.

The division had became purely Wurttemberg.

VALUE—1917 ESTIMATE.

The elements of the 243d Division appeared good. They were never engaged in very active sectors, except at Hill 344 in September, 1917. At Verdun they showed only mediocre combat value.

1918.

1. The division was relieved in the sector northwest of Verdun at the end of January and traveled by rail to the Stenay area north of Montfaucon, where it rested and trained until March 20. On that day it entrained at Stenay and traveled via Sedan–Charleville–Hirson–Ors to Bazeul. On the 22d the division marched by night via Le Cateau and Montbrehain to Raisel, crossed the Somme at St. Christ-Briost and came into line reenforcing the front on the night of March 25–26.

BATTLE OF PICARDY.

2. It advanced in the first line of the attack through Guillancourt, Villers aux Erables, and attacked Moreuil on the 30th. It suffered very heavy losses, amounting to 50 per cent between March 26–30 at Estrees and Ignancourt, and in the attack on Moreuil. Two companies of the 122d Fusileer Regiment lost more than 207 of their fighting strength. The division was withdrawn about April 4. On April 2 the division received a draft of 350 to 400 men.

PICARDY.

3. The division was reengaged north and east of Villers Bretonneux, relieving the 228th Division. On the 24th it made an unsuccessful attack on Villers Bretonneux. On the 27th it was withdrawn to close reserve and rested until May 13.

THIRD BATTLE OF THE SOMME.

4. Between May 13 and July 7 the division was in line near Albert. It rested until August 10, when it was engaged east of Morlancourt, north of the Somme. It was forced back by Chuignolles, Proyart, Fouconcourt, Fay, Dompierre until its relief on August 29. Four hundred prisoners were lost in that engagement. It was again in line between September 2 and 9 east of Bouchavesnes.

5. The division rested in upper Alsace during September. It returned to Coutrai on October 6 and was engaged south and east of Le Cateau (St. Benin, Bazeul, Catillon and later east of Landrecies), mid-October to 1st of November. On November 6 it was again engaged south of Aulnoye and retreated east of Maubeuge, where it was last identified on November 9.

VALUE—1918 ESTIMATE.

The division was rated as third class. It was largely used on active fronts and did creditably.

255th Division.

COMPOSITION.

	1915 Brigade.	1915 Regiment.	1916 Brigade.	1916 Regiment.	1917 Brigade.	1917 Regiment.	1918 Brigade.	1918 Regiment.
Infantry	31 Ldw.	30 Ldw. 68 Ldw. 1 Ers. Ldw. 2 Ers. Ldw. 3 Ers. Ldw.	31 Ldw. (?)	30 Ldw. 68 Ldw. 2 Ers. Ldw. 3 Ers. Ldw.	31 Ldw. 32 Ldw. 31 Ldw.	30 Ldw. 86 Ldw. 68 Ldw. 94 Ldw. 153 Ldw. (Composition after August, 1917.) 68 Ldw. 94 Ldw. 153 Ldw.	82 Ldw.	68 Ldw. 94 Ldw. 153 Ldw.
Cavalry	Hus. Detch.				4 Sqn. 7 Hus. Rgt. 1 Sqn. 15 C. Dist. Landst. Cav. Detch.		4 Sqn. 7 Hus. Rgt.	
Artillery					Art. Command: 301 F. A. Rgt.		301 F. A. Rgt.	
Engineers and Liaisons.			2 Ldw. Co. 11 C. Dist. Pions. 1 Ldw. Co. 16 C. Dist. Pions.		(255) Pion. Btn.: 1 Ldw. Co. 8 C. Dist. Pions. Metz Landst. Pion. Co. 455 T. M. Co. 15 Searchlight Section. 255 Tel. Detch.		255 Pion. Btn.: 1 Ldw. Co. 8 C. Dist. Pions. Landst. Ers. Co. 11 C. Dist. Pions 209 Searchlight Section. 255 Signal Command: 255 Tel. Detch.	
Medical and Veterinary.					623 (?) Ambulance Co. Field Hospital. 566 Vet. Hospital.		627 Ambulance Co. 192 Field Hospital.	
Transport					M. T. Col.			

HISTORY.

(Former Metz Detachment. 68th Landwehr: 16th Corps District—Lorraine and the Rhine Province. 94th Landwehr: 11th Corps District—Electorate of Hesse and Thuringia. 153d Landwehr: 4th Corps District—Prussian Saxony.)

1915–16.

LORRAINE.

1. The 255th Division is the former Metz Detachment, the composition of which was remodeled and which was changed into a division in May, 1917.

2. The Metz Detachment, composed of the 31st Landwehr Brigade (30th and 68th Landwehr Regiments) and of the 1st, 2d, and 3d Ersatz Landwehr Regiments, occupied the same sector of Lorraine between the Moselle and Abaucourt (north of Pont à Mousson) from the end of October, 1914, to 1917.

1917.

1. About May, 1917, the Metz Detachment became the 255th Division. It then comprised the 31st Landwehr Brigade (30th and 68th Landwehr Regiments) and three regiments of recent organization, the 86th, 94th, and 153d Landwehr, formed by grouping the battalions of the old dissolved Ersatz regiments.

2. With this composition, the 255th Division continued to hold the front along the Moselle (right bank) until the month of October.

3. In July and August the 30th and 86th Landwehr Regiments left the 255th Division to form the new 31st Independent Landwehr Brigade. The latter remained in line on the right bank of the Moselle. The 255th Division, reduced to three regiments (68th, 94th, and 153d Landwehr), went to the left bank (Le Prêtre wood) about October 13.

VALUE—1917 ESTIMATE.

Mediocre.

1918.

1. The division continued to hold its sector in the Bois le Pretre until the American attack on September 12. At that time the company strength was 180 to 200, with an effective rifle strength of 100. The men were mostly between 37 and 45 years of age.

2. The attack of the 12th of September threw the division back on Vandieres and Preny, where it was still in line at the time of the armistice.

VALUE—1918 ESTIMATE.

The division was rated as fourth class.

301st Division.

COMPOSITION.

	1917		1918	
	Brigade.	Regiment.	Brigade.	Regiment.
Infantry............	....	....	....	48 Landst.
Cavalry...........		....	1 Sqn. 9 Res. Hus. Rgt. 3 Sqn. 9 Res. Hus. Rgt. 4 Sqn. 9 Res. Hus. Rgt.	
Artillery		....	217 F. A. Rgt.	
Engineers and Liaisons.	....		342 Pion. Co. 410 T. M. Co. 310 Tel. Detch.	
Medical and Veterinary	....		Ambulance Co. Field Hospital. Vet. Hospital.	
Transport...........	....		M. T. Col.	

Attached..............	84 Brig.:
	  70 Res. Inf. Rgt.
	  9 Res. Hus. Rgt.
	  252 F. A. Rgt.
	  342 Pion. Co.
	  410 T. M. Co. Landst. Inf. Btns.
	  3 Bav. C. Dist. No. 13 (2 Nurnberg).
	  16 C. D. No. 7 (2 Sarre–Louis).
	  14 C. D. No. 5 (Rastatt).
			1 Rastatt Landst. Inf. Btn. (XIV/5).
			10 Ldw. Rgt.
			56 Ldw. Rgt.
			3 Btn. 2 Bav. Ers. Rgt. Landst. Inf. Btns.
			2 Koeln (8 C. Dist. Btn. No. 14).
			8 C. D. No. 7 (Bonn).
			14 C. D. No. 1 (Mosbach).
			18 C. D. No. 10 (Friedberg).
			1 Bav. C. D. No. 15 (Dillingen).
			1 Bav. C. D. No. 9 (Augsburg).
			7 C. D. No. 49 (Elberfeld).
			(According to order of battle, Aug. 12, 1918.)	

HISTORY.

(10th Landwehr Regiment: 6th Corps District—Silesia. 56th Landwehr Regiment: 7th Corps District—Westphalia.)

1917.

VOSGES.

1. The 301st Division, apparently formed about the middle of 1917, was simply a military unit without permanent elements.

2. To this division were attached the 70th Reserve (84th Landwehr Brigade) from April, 1917, until the beginning of June, 1918 (Vosges front west of Senones and in the vicinity of Ban de Sapt), the 2d Bavarian Ersatz Regiment (an organic part of the 39th Bavarian Reserve Division) from June, 1917, and several Landsturm Battalions.

3. The sector of the 301st Division extends on the Vosges front from La Plaine as far as Provenchères. The headquarters of the division was at Saulxures.

VALUE—1917 ESTIMATE.

The division was mostly made up of elderly men. The troops assigned to the 301st Division were supposed to occupy calm sectors.

The 10th Landwehr Regiment was made up for the most part (three-quarters) of Silesians and Prussians from the Province of Posen.   There were some Alsatians (4 in the 6th Company).

1918.

1. The division remained in its sector in Army Detachment A without event throughout 1918.   Its losses were negligible.   The companies had an average ration strength of 170 men; an average trench strength of 105.

VALUE—1918 ESTIMATE.

The division was rated as fourth class.   It was one of the lowest of that class in value.   The morale was low and desertions frequent.

302d Division.

COMPOSITION.

	1917		1918	
	Brigade.	Regiments.	Brigade.	Regiments.
Infantry...............	(?). 22.	42. 45. 10 Jag. (After June, 1917.) 45. 21 Res. 10 Jag.	22.	11 Gren. 9 Jag. 10 Jag.
Artillery...............	Art. Command: 10 F. A. Rgt. (elements).			
Engineers and Liasions.	Pion. Btn.: 19 Pion. Btn. (elements). 205 Pion. Co. 172 Mountain T. M. Co. Tel. Detch.		Pion. Btn. No, 19 (elements). 205 Pion. Co. 172 Mountain T. M. Co. 302 Tel. Detch.	
Medical and Veterinary.	202 Ambulance Co. Field Hospital. Vet. H˙spital.		Ambulance Co. Field Hospital. Vet. Hospital.	
Transport..............	672 (?) M. T. Col.		(?) 672 M. T. Col.	

HISTORY.

1917.

MACEDONIA.

1. The 302d Division (former Hippel Division) was organized on the Macedonian front toward the end of 1916. At the beginning it included elements of various nationalities. It appears to have become entirely German during the first part of 1917. At this time its composition was as follows: The staff of the 22d Infantry Brigade (coming from the 11th Division); the 42d Infantry Regiment from the 3d Division; the 45th Infantry Regiment from the 101st Division and the 10th Jäger Regiment (the latter formed by grouping the Jäger and Fusileer Battalions of the Guard and the 9th and 12th Jäger Battalions). In January, 1917, the 45th Infantry Regiment had replaced the 11th Grenadier Regiment, transferred to the 101st Division and which had come to the Hippel Division in November.

2. The elements of the 302d Division occupied the Macedonian front (Monastir-Boucle de la Cerna) in 1917 and until the end of February, 1918.

3. In June, 1917, the 42d Infantry Regiment, the same as the 59th Regiment of the 101st Division, left the Macedonian front for Roumania (vicinity of Rimnicu–Sarat). It was definitely detached from the 302d Division and replaced by the 21st Reserve Infantry Regiment from the 216th Division.

1918.

1. The divisional staff operated in Macedonia until it surrendered as a complete unit, divisional commander, staff, and troops, numbering 7,000, about the 1st of October.

VALUE—1918 ESTIMATE.

The division was rated as third class at the time of its retirement from the Western Front.

CPSIA information can be obtained
at www.ICGtesting.com
Printed in the USA
LVHW100204130522
718702LV00004B/66

9 789353 860899